Foundations of Environmental Philosophy

A Text with Readings

FREDERIK A. KAUFMAN
Ithaca College

Boston Burr Ridge, IL Dubuque, IA Madison, WI New York San Francisco St. Louis
Bangkok Bogotá Caracas Kuala Lumpur Lisbon London Madrid Mexico City
Milan Montreal New Delhi Santiago Seoul Singapore Sydney Taipei Toronto

McGraw-Hill Higher Education

A Division of The ***McGraw-Hill*** *Companies*

FOUNDATIONS OF ENVIRONMENTAL PHILOSOPHY: A TEXT WITH READINGS
Published by McGraw-Hill, a business unit of The McGraw-Hill Companies, Inc., 1221 Avenue of the Americas, New York, NY, 10020.

This book is printed on acid-free paper.

1 2 3 4 5 6 7 8 9 0 FGR/FGR 0 9 8 7 6 5 4 3 2

ISBN 0-7674-1980-4

Publisher: *Kenneth King*
Associate editor: *Jon-David Hague*
Marketing manager: *Gregory Brueck*
Project manager: *Christina Thornton-Villagomez*
Production supervisor: *Carol Bielski*
Coordinator of freelance design: *Mary E. Kazak*
Cover design: *Srdjan Savanovic*
Cover photo: *David Hague*
Typeface: *9.5/12 New Baskerville*
Compositor: *Carlisle Communications, Ltd.,*
Printer: *Quebecor World Fairfield Inc.*

Library of Congress Cataloging-in-Publication Data

Kaufman, Frederik A.
Foundations of environmental philosophy: a text with readings/Frederik A. Kaufman.
p. cm.
Includes index.
ISBN 0-7674-1980-4 (softcover: alk. paper)
1. Environmental ethics. 2. Environmental sciences—Philosophy. I. Title.
GE42 .K38 2003
179'.1—dc21

2002021906

www.mhhe.com

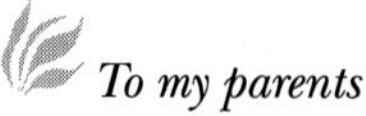

To my parents

About the Author

Frederik A. Kaufman is associate professor in the Department of Philosophy and Religion at Ithaca College in Ithaca, New York. In addition to teaching courses in environmental philosophy, medical ethics, and moral philosophy, he helped develop and coordinate Ithaca College's environmental studies program.

Preface

Different textbooks have different strengths. This text is written with the student firmly in mind. It seeks to introduce the fundamental questions and concepts of environmental philosophy in a lively, nontechnical manner, without sacrificing intellectual rigor. It is thus appropriate for students who are new to philosophy. Moreover, as a reader/text, this book seeks to combine the strengths of both an anthology and a secondary source into a single text. With a few exceptions, the reprinted articles are classics in environmental philosophy.

The central question in environmental ethics is this: Which things count morally? Attempts to answer this question provide an intuitive basis for structuring the material. We start with the narrowest position that only people count morally, expanding to broader and broader conceptions of the moral community. What about animals, plants, species, mountains, forests, or even entire ecosystems? The chapters thus consider, more or less progressively, differing attempts to incorporate into our moral outlook organisms and things that are increasingly different from ourselves. Each conception of what constitutes the moral community is critically examined with the aim of coming to appreciate the strengths and weaknesses of competing answers to the central question in environmental ethics.

The text is organized in the following manner: Chapter 1 begins with a case study about the banana industry—the environmental impact of growing them and how they are distributed—that serves as a springboard into moral philosophy and the relevance of utilitarianism, Kantianism, natural law, and virtue ethics to the environment. Chapter 2 is devoted to moral reasoning and argument identification and analysis. It includes examples and exercises connected to environmental matters. Chapters 3 through 10 are devoted to differing conceptions of our relation to the nonhuman world.

They are each structured as follows:

A. Informative introductory discussion about an important aspect of contemporary life relevant to the chapter topic (e.g., gasoline, the broiler industry, global warming, biotechnology, the Environmental Protection Agency, Thoreau and ways of life). Explicit connection is made between practical issues and environmental philosophy.

B. Exploration and consideration of the philosophical issues raised by the informative discussions, especially as they pertain to the readings.

C. A brief biography and introduction for each reading, including preliminary questions to aid comprehension. Follow-up questions for discussion and review for each reading.

D. You Decide! case studies. Topics include: litter, suburban hunting, ecoterrorism, urban ecology, lawn care, arsenic and drinking water, whaling and indigenous people, DDT, snowmobiles in Yellowstone National Park, patterns of consumption.

This book is intended as a pedagogical tool. I have done my best to make accessible material that is often intimidating to newcomers. This is not to say that I have made it easy. I cannot do that. I have instead sought to equip students to participate in discussions that are worthy of their time, effort, and reflection, for much is at stake.

ACKNOWLEDGMENTS

I wish to thank my philosophical colleagues Carol Kates, Robert Klee, and Stephen Schwartz, as well as my colleagues-at-large, John Confer in biology and Kevin Murphy in English, for their assistance in thinking through the issues discussed in this text. I wish also to thank the Ithaca College Summer Grants Committee for financial support, and Ken King and Jon-David Hague at McGraw-Hill for their excellent guidance and advice. I appreciate, too, the many valuable suggestions for improvement from reviewers: Philip Scheider, Coastal Carolina University; Hamner Hill, Southeast Missouri State University; Bob Snyder, Humbolt State University; Charles List, SUNY–Plattsburgh; Peter List, Oregon State University; Chris Crittenden, University of Tennessee–Knoxville; Jordan Lindberg, Central Michigan University. Finally, I wish to acknowledge the love and calm sound judgment of my wife, Donna Fleming.

Contents

CHAPTER 1

Moral Philosophy and the Natural World

The natural world has been an object of reflection for ages. How could it not be, given its inescapable presence and overwhelming importance? It sustains and nurtures us, fascinates and engages us, terrifies and humbles us. It is both a reality and an abstraction; a reality because we can see it and must deal with it; an abstraction because we find in it much of what we want to see—a dark side of ourselves or, alternatively, goodness and purity. For some, the natural world is merely the context in which we "strut and fret our hour upon the stage" before moving on. Others see us as part of nature rather than an alien sojourner, a thinking, sensitive, self-aware part but part of it all the same.

Nature is many things to many people, and thinking about nature involves us in some of the most fascinating questions we can ask, for such thought engages us at a fundamental level. We have to ask questions about our origins, our position among other beings, our future; we have to ask scientific questions and also questions of a very different sort. Thinking about nature leads us into philosophy, for we have to ask not only who and what we are but also how we ought to be. Philosophy is that area of inquiry that is conceptually most basic; it is in philosophy that we ask questions about fundamental principles concerning the world and our place in it.

MORAL DELIBERATION

This book will engage us in philosophical questions about the natural world. Much of it will focus on issues that arise in a particular area of philosophy called ethics, or moral philosophy (I shall not distinguish between the terms *ethics* and *morality*). In moral philosophy we investigate questions about how we ought to act and what sorts of lives we ought to lead. The key notion here is "ought." Much of moral philosophy is an attempt to understand what this crucial little word means in different situations.

Perhaps it seems that ethics is basically a private, personal matter so raising large questions of how we ought to act or live is pointless. Each person has his or her "own ethics," and aside from noting our differences on certain issues there is little more to say. If ethics is fundamentally a private matter, though, it is hard to see how "ought" can even play a role in moral deliberation because that word suggests some sort of ideal or standard against which we compare our behavior. To say, for example, that you ought to consider others implies that there is some basis or standard for assessing your treatment of others, that it is not simply up to you how you should treat others, as one might prefer chocolate ice cream over vanilla. What that standard of assessment could possibly be and how it is grounded are matters of deep controversy—is it just the expected norms of society or is there more to it than that? Different accounts of ethics that we shall study answer this question differently, but they agree on the fundamental point that moral judgments cannot be mere expressions of private, personal preference because moral judgments require reasons to back them up. This is because moral judgments employ in some form or other the idea of what one ought or ought not to do and 'ought' requires reasons. This is how the word 'ought' functions—its logic. It makes no sense to say that something ought (or ought not) to be done but there are no reasons why. And the reasons used to back up a moral judgment can be evaluated. Are they good reasons?

I can hear the complaints now: "But whose ethics?" "Who is to say what we ought to do?" "What makes a reason a good one?" To ask these excellent questions takes us into the complexities of moral philosophy. Ethical questions are among the most fascinating that we can ponder and they are thrust upon us by life. Like it or not, we have to wrestle with questions of what we ought to do. Consider, for example, the front page of any newspaper. There you will find questions of morality—abortion, war, suicide, crime, aid to the needy, justice, rights, and on and on. We can't avoid dealing with them; to function as individuals and as a society we have to make decisions and formulate policy. Also, questions of this sort require us to think at a very abstract level. We are called upon to articulate general principles about rights, harms, justice, value, and human life.

What does moral philosophy have to do with the environment? I can't give a straightforward answer, but the question goes to the heart of the subject of this book. I can begin with an example that will connect environmental issues and moral philosophy and will identify many of the kinds of questions for us to consider.

MODERN TIMES: BEHOLD THE BANANA

Bananas are the most popular fruit in the world. In the United States, we consume approximately 28 pounds of bananas per person each year. With roughly 3 bananas to the pound, that means we eat some 84 bananas yearly. And no wonder; they are a tasty, nutritious, healthy food. When the fruit made its debut to the public at the 1876 Centennial Exhibition in Philadelphia, few Americans had ever tasted a banana. Today they are purchased by more than 96 percent of households in the country. Bananas are the most profitable item in the produce section of the grocery store. This is remarkable, because they are cheap, sometimes even 20 cents a pound, much less expensive than other kinds of fruit grown regionally. They are also a highly perishable tropical fruit and available all year. This suggests an exquisitely developed and extraordinarily efficient system of production and distribution. It also suggests a hidden story.

There are some 500 varieties of bananas in the world, though in the United States we consume mostly a single variety called the Cavendish. The great Swedish botanist and taxonomist Carolus Linnaeus (1707–1778) dubbed the banana plant *Musa sapientum,* or "fruit of the wise men," because the Roman scientist Pliny (A.D. 23–79) reported that sages in India lived on bananas. The banana plant is not a tree, but basically a large herb that grows from roots, or rhizomes, with new shoots emerging from buds similar to the way shoots emerge from the "eyes" of a potato; and though it is hard to believe, botanists classify bananas as a kind of berry! The word *banana* comes from the arabic word *banan,* which means finger. Bananas are thought to have originated in Southeast Asia, but today they can be found worldwide within approximately 15 degrees north or south of the equator. Bananas were introduced to the Western Hemisphere from the Canary Islands by Friar Tomas de Berlanga in 1516. Most of the bananas consumed in the United States are produced in the lowlands of Central and South America. Ecuador, Colombia, Guatemala, and Costa Rica supply two-thirds of the almost 11 million tons on the international market. Three U.S. companies—Chiquita (formerly United Fruit), Dole, and Del Monte—dominate banana production in those countries.

You might have images of lush banana plants interspersed throughout a steamy tropical rain forest, heavy with ripe fruit, as workers forage for the abundance provided by nature amid the exotic jungle sounds of startled arboreal creatures. Like so many of the images we have about how our food is produced, this one is false. Banana production and distribution is a marvel of technological sophistication and control of nature.

Most of the bananas we consume are produced on vast single-crop plantations. Land that was once rain forest is cleared, and banana plants are grown under carefully monitored conditions. The large stems upon which the bananas grow are cut while the bananas are green and rock hard, then transported in special refrigerator ships to climate-controlled distribution centers where they are scientifically coaxed to a stage of being almost ripe before being sent to the retailer. There is a veritable conveyor belt of ships transporting green bananas from Central and South America to the United States. Chiquita, the largest of the three U.S. firms, owns 15 ships and charters up to 15 others. Chiquita's banana boats are known as the "Great White Fleet" because their ships are painted white to reflect the sun's heat.

Banana plants are routinely sprayed with pesticides, fungicides, herbicides, nematocides, and other chemicals. There is continual controversy about the health effects of these chemicals on plantation workers. In 1995, for example, several thousand banana workers filed a class action suit against Chiquita, Dole, and Del Monte, alleging reproductive injuries from exposure to dibromochloropropane (DBCP), a pesticide used to control worms. Also named in the suit were producers of the chemical, Dow Chemical, Shell Oil, and others. The case was settled out of court for $41 million. (An Associated Press article notes that Medardo Varela, a leader of the banana workers in Honduras who filed the suit, was murdered in 1998.) DBCP is no longer used, but controversy remains about other chemicals used in banana production. A class of pesticides known as Organochlorines, which are mostly banned in the United States, are still produced by U.S. chemical companies and extensively used in banana production. These compounds affect normal endocrine functioning and have other adverse effects, which are still being studied. Alarmingly high concentrations of these chemicals have been found in human tissue samples taken from Costa Rican hospitals.

The heavy use of agricultural chemicals in banana production affects fish and wildlife. Not only do the chemicals have a direct effect on those nontarget creatures unlucky enough to be on the banana plantation, but it also is hard to keep the chemicals confined to the plantation. Since airplanes are often used to spray the chemicals, especially fungicides, clouds of noxious mist can drift from the intended target, settling on nearby areas; rains wash agricultural chemicals into irrigation ditches and ultimately into rivers where fish and other aquatic creatures are harmed; and many of the chemicals "bioaccumulate"—a bug will eat a leaf that has been sprayed and a bird will then eat the bug, thus incorporating the chemical into its body, and so on throughout the food chain. The long-term ecological effects of the potent agricultural chemicals used in raising bananas is largely unknown.

Major producers, notably Chiquita, have made some efforts to raise bananas without such heavy reliance on chemicals. The Rainforest Alliance, a conservation and advocacy group based in New York City, initiated a "Better Banana" certification program in partnership with Chiquita in 1991. The "ECO-OK" program is designed to inform consumers that the certified bananas have been produced in a manner that is, if not wholly sustainable, at least better than it was (current methods of banana production, which involve rain forest destruction, are not sustainable). Chiquita has apparently made some changes in its production methods and it promotes its corporate environmental awareness heavily on its website (www.Chiquita.com), though a cloud of controversy still surrounds the company. An exposé of Chiquita's business and production practices was published by the *Cincinnati Enquirer* in 1998 (Chiquita is based in Cincinnati). However, the investigative reporter was found to have stolen crucial internal information from Chiquita, and, under threat of a huge lawsuit, the newspaper retracted the story, published an apology, and payed Chiquita $10 million. Unfortunately, the issue turned into one of journalistic ethics rather than focusing on the detailed charges aired in the series of articles, one of which was that Chiquita's actual environmental practices do not match its soothing public rhetoric. It is virtually impossible for the consumer to find out the truth regarding Chiquita's production and environmental practices. So far, neither Dole nor Del Monte have become partners in the Rainforest Alliance's ECO-OK certification program.

Recently the World Trade Organization ruled in favor of a complaint lodged by the United States (on behalf of the major banana producers based in the United States) concerning access to the European banana market. Several European countries were giving economic protection to their former colonial islands in the Caribbean, thus closing portions of the European banana market to major U.S. producers (Chiquita, Dole, Del Monte, and their subsidiaries). Europeans had to buy more expensive bananas from their former colonies, rather than cheaper bananas from the major U.S.-based producers. The United States objected that this protectionist practice violates free trade agreements. With the World Trade Organization ruling in favor of the United States, the economies of many Caribbean islands will suffer, since the smaller island producers cannot compete economically with the less expensive bananas produced by the major multinational corporations. Bananas are a major export crop for such islands as Jamaica, Surinam, Dominica, St. Lucia, and St. Vincent, among other Caribbean countries. Those bananas are more expensive because few large-scale monoculture banana plantations exist (there simply isn't enough room on some of the smaller islands), ships must make frequent stops among the widely dispersed islands to collect relatively small quantities of harvested bananas, producers rely less on agricultural chemicals, and banana workers in the Caribbean have higher wages and, generally, better working conditions than banana workers in Latin America. (Apparently, the major producers in Latin America achieve lower costs not only by economies of scale but by engaging in questionable labor relations.)

FROM BANANAS TO MORAL PHILOSOPHY

The banana industry is a window into many ethical issues. It is not unique in that respect; any industry involves a complicated web of interconnections, avenues along which people may relate to one another, thus allowing for assessments of what is fair or unfair, just or unjust, right or wrong; that is, moral assessments. But the banana industry is also intimately connected to the natural world. It is a sophisticated system of agricultural production and distribution that makes a delicate, perishable tropical fruit available year-round in every state, at a lower cost than other fruits grown regionally.

What ethical questions emerge from our brief consideration of the banana industry? We have to raise questions about the treatment of banana workers, their exposure to potentially harmful chemicals and the shady labor practices of the major producers (the term *banana republic,* originally used to describe Latin American countries where United Fruit's economic and political power was paramount, is not wholly a thing of the past). Also, current methods of banana production take a heavy toll on the environment; rain forests are cleared and various tropical pests are kept at bay with a mix of powerful agricultural chemicals, and these chemicals are finding their way into the surrounding areas, with unknown consequences. Though talk of "unknown consequences" puts a somewhat bland spin on the issue; what is the likelihood that the environmental consequences are good or even neutral? Odds are that the environmental consequences are bad; what is unknown is how bad, not whether they are bad. Is this a moral issue? Unless people are harmed by the environmental consequences of raising bananas, perhaps no moral issues are raised. This is an important question we shall consider closely later. I mention it now only to point out that it embodies a theory about morality, namely, that moral considerations apply only to people. To be sure, irresponsible use of chemicals and clearing forests will affect people, but it might be claimed that it is only because of the effects our activities in the natural world have on people that moral questions arise at all. As we shall see, the assumption that moral issues arise only because our actions in the environment affect people has been challenged by environmental philosophers.

The World Trade Organization's ruling in favor of the United States means that many of the smaller Caribbean producers will be unable to compete economically, and the pace of banana production among the major producers will be accelerated, which means bringing more land into production and spreading even more chemicals throughout the region. This is likely to make less expensive bananas available to more people in Europe, but at the expense of the environment in Latin America. Is that something we should care about? Is the basis of our concern merely the fact that people in Latin America are likely to suffer the brunt of the environmental impact of increased banana production?

It is easy to sit back and criticize. One thing we haven't discussed yet is the demand for bananas. The demand comes from us, a demand encouraged by the banana producers, to be sure, but a demand over which we have control. We are not forced to eat bananas; they are not addictive, and we can have healthy, interesting lives eating regionally produced fruits. Bananas have become a normal part of everyday life. Like so many other things, we simply don't bother to think about them. Thinking about our way of life—a way of life that makes bananas cheap and readily available—can cause moral discomfort because after we gain insight into the banana industry, it is hard just to ignore the moral questions that arise from it. Not only do we have to contemplate the effects of banana production on the people most closely connected to it, but we also have to wonder about how we are affecting the environment and whether this even counts as a moral issue. In short, we have to engage in moral philosophy.

BUT ISN'T ETHICS RELATIVE?

It is easy to throw up your hands at this point and say that moral philosophy is of no help in sorting through complicated environmental issues because people disagree about ethical matters. Different people just have different beliefs about what's right and what's wrong, with no one's opinion better or worse than another; there are simply no objectively correct moral principles to which we can appeal in a moral disagreement. You might think it is wrong to clear rain forests for banana production and I might be in favor of it. Other than noting our disagreement, there is no rational method for us to settle our disagreement, since there is no objectively correct answer to the question of right and wrong; or so it seems. The idea that there are no objectively correct standards for moral assessment is known as **moral relativism.** At best, perhaps, we can make moral judgments relative to a particular society's moral standards, but those society-wide standards themselves have no objective status—just as individuals may differ among themselves about moral issues, so may societies, with no individual or society being correct in an objective sense, since, according to moral relativism, there is no such thing as objective moral correctness.

Without argument, however, we should not just assume there are no objective standards for moral evaluation, that ethics, like beauty, is in the eye of the beholder. A perennially popular argument for thinking that ethics is devoid of objective standards goes like this: Because people disagree about moral matters, there must not be any objectively correct moral answers. But upon reflection we see that this cannot be right, because in other contexts the mere fact that people disagree about a claim is not taken to show that there are no correct positions. Science, for example, has disagreements, but we don't throw up our hands and say it is all opinion and no one's opinion is better than anyone else's. But, someone might object, science is different from ethics—in science we can prove things, in ethics we cannot. But can't we prove things in ethics? If you were called upon to prove that what Hitler did to the Jews was wrong, would you be able to do it, or is Hitler's view just as good as yours, only different? That the Nazis will disagree with you is irrelevant, isn't it? Don't you think it is possible to make mistakes about moral matters, and that the Nazis got things terribly wrong? If morality is relative, then it would be impossible to make moral mistakes—no one could be wrong (or right, for that matter), there would just be a variety of differing views. Or, to put a different spin on the point, if inconsistent views can both be correct, then it makes little sense to talk of correct and incorrect.

Still (one wants to say), ethics doesn't prove things conclusively; there always seems to be room to argue one side or the other, and who is to say what is correct? OK, ethics doesn't prove things in that sense. But if the only standard for rational assent is incontrovertible proof, then outside of mathematics nothing can be proved. In many areas of human inquiry, we function perfectly well with standards of demonstration that are rationally convincing even though they may fall short of rigorous proof. A jury is asked to decide guilt or innocence on the basis of evidence that, though perhaps overwhelming, cannot possibly be absolutely conclusive. A novel may be open to several plausible interpretations, but not any old interpretation is as worthy as any other; you are not free to think that *Charlotte's Web* is a story about space travel. Historians may disagree on subtle points, but has it been demonstrated beyond reasonable doubt that Hitler's mad vision of a world ruled by his conception of a superior people caused World War II? In the areas of law, literature, history, and many others, we make plausible decisions and judgments even though the conclusions we reach fall far short of certainty. There is no reason to hold ethics to standards of demonstration that are higher than what we accept in other areas of inquiry.

Rather than fixate on the idea of whether we can generate incontrovertible proofs in ethics, consider instead the notion of giving good reasons for claims. This is something we do all the time: if a store's lights are out and a sign in the window says "Sorry, We're Closed," these are good reasons to think the store is closed. The store might be open nonetheless, so these reasons don't *prove* that the store is closed, but that doesn't matter. We can do the same thing in ethics: Suppose I stole your car and upon being apprehended I offered no explanation for my actions. I did not have to get an injured person to the hospital, need your car to run an important errand, or anything of the sort. I simply wanted your car. That I displayed such indifference to your property is a good reason to think me a bad person. Moreover, if I have displayed a similar pattern of indifference to others, if I am generally inconsiderate and quick to take advantage of others for personal gain, then your confidence in your judgment of me will be increased. My actions don't conclusively prove that I am a bad person, but they are nevertheless excellent reasons for thinking I am, and unless some other explanation is forthcoming, what better reasons could you want for thinking me evil? Would you be comfortable making the moral judgment that I ought not to have stolen your car? Your assessment of me is not relative in the sense that someone could acknowledge those same facts but draw a different conclusion about me. Anyone who acknowledges those facts will have to draw a similar conclusion about my actions and character.

If we keep the "good reasons" approach to ethics in mind, we can avoid a mindless sort of relativism that stops us from even attempting ethical inquiry. We routinely make moral judgments, frequently defending them with emotion and action. Yet when called upon to reflect philosophically about the nature of morality, we quickly embrace a simplistic relativism, a theory that seems at odds with the seriousness we otherwise accord our moral judgments, since relativism entails that all moral judgments are equally worthy. If I may indulge in a bit of armchair psychoanalysis: I think we are inclined to embrace moral relativism because we regard tolerance as a virtue; we are reluctant to impose our moral beliefs on others, in part because we don't want it done to us. At root, our motivation to accept relativism is laudable, but we should not confuse worthy motivation with a questionable theory. We don't want to be preachy or sanctimonious, but wanting to avoid these undesirable character traits shouldn't drive us to the opposite extreme of thinking that it is impossible ever to make moral assessments, assessments that can be backed up by good reasons.

MORAL REASONS AND THE MORAL POINT OF VIEW

The **moral point of view** means being prepared to regulate our behavior by moral reasons, not merely prudential or other nonmoral kinds of reasons. When we deliberate about an action, various considerations can be brought to bear: economic, prudential, aesthetic, and so on. When we adopt an "economic point of view," for example, we would consider monetary costs and likely profits. For a range of activities, the economic point of view is perfectly appropriate and indispensable, as are any of the other points of view we could hold.

From the moral point of view, we consider moral reasons for or against a contemplated activity. Moral reasons are reasons that refer in some way to what is morally correct or incorrect. Reasons that involve talk of rights, fairness, justice, well-being, and the like are moral considerations, and to appeal to them is to adduce moral considerations. We aren't always clear about what is the morally correct thing to do, but considering moral reasons, rather than just nonmoral, is to operate from the moral point of view.

The moral point of view is not simply another view among any of the other points of view we could adopt. For example, I might do something for aesthetic reasons that makes no economic sense. My action might be criticized as a foolish waste of money, but I might still think it is worth it for the aesthetic experience, and my good standing as a member of society is not questioned.

The moral point of view, however, is different. It cannot be similarly overridden by other considerations. Think how peculiar it would be to admit that a contemplated action is clearly and deeply immoral, but we should still do it because it makes good economic sense or it would be aesthetically pleasing. People do things all the time that they think are morally wrong for other kinds of reasons, but they do not think their actions are morally justified, and they often come to regret them. Moral reasons trump other sorts of reasons, not the other way around, at least in normal cases. Whether moral reasons always trump nonmoral reasons is a hotly contested issue in moral philosophy, something we do not have to settle here. All we have to note is that moral reasons normally override nonmoral reasons; they stand above other kinds of considerations and overrule them when a conflict arises.

MORAL PHILOSOPHY AND THE ENVIRONMENT

Socrates (469–399 B.C.), one of the most famous philosophers of all time, proclaimed that the unexamined life is not worth living, thus putting questions of how we ought to live squarely before our minds. In the *Apology* (a dialogue written by Plato in which Socrates defends his practice of doing philosophy, i.e., questioning and examining our lives) Socrates admonishes us as follows: "O my friend, why do you . . . care so much about laying up the greatest amount of money and honor and reputation, and so little about wisdom and truth and the greatest improvement of the soul, which you never regard or heed at all? Are you not ashamed of this?" For Socrates, morality is constitutive of the good life. Is Socrates right? How are we to think about morality? It seems so vast, and so far we have been speaking unhelpfully in the most general ways about moral questions, moral inquiry, and the like. Since the time of Socrates, philosophers have developed various moral theories that purport to show us how to think about morality and, ultimately, what we ought to do. These theories are not lists of dos and don'ts; rather, they are attempts to systematize moral deliberation, give it a coherent structure and rational basis. What they each do, in their own way, is provide a kind of reason that backs up a moral judgment. We might all agree that banana production ought to be done in a manner that is environmentally friendly because . . . and here each theory will have something to say about why.

I shall give brief sketches of four major moral theories: utilitarianism, Kant's ethics, natural law ethics, and virtue ethics. These theories have had enormous influence on our thinking about morality, and each expresses a deep ethical insight. In considering these theories, our aim is not only to gain an understanding of the rudiments of philosophical ethics, but also to see whether these theories can form the basis for ethical reflections about the environment. Each theory has something to say about the natural world and our relation to it.

UTILITARIANISM

Utilitarianism is the name of a moral theory that judges actions according to their consequences. The theory was systematically expounded by Jeremy Bentham (1748–1832) and John Stuart Mill (1806–1873), both English philosophers and social reformers. Utilitarians begin with an account of what is good—pleasure (or happiness) according to the classical utilitarians—and then define as right those actions that produce as much good as possible in a particular situation. In other words, we are to judge the *utility* of various actions in producing certain consequences. According to the utilitarians, we ought to bring about the greatest happiness for the greatest number. So stated, utilitarianism seems utterly straightforward; it tells us that we should aim to produce as much good as we can. What could be more obvious? Problems emerge, however, when we think a bit more carefully about what utilitarianism requires. What if we can produce a lot of good but at the expense of a few individuals? Suppose, for example, more overall happiness could be produced if we had a slave society? The slaves would be unhappy, true, but their unhappiness might be outweighed by the greater happiness of the rest of society. According to utilitarianism, if that were to happen, then a slave society would be not only morally acceptable but also required, since our obligation is to maximize happiness.

Can utilitarianism be refuted by such an obvious objection? The theory is vast and has many resources for dealing with objections (as do all of the major moral theories), and whatever its flaws, consequentialist thinking is a deep feature of moral deliberation. Utilitarians might respond to the slave society objection by denying it could happen or by arguing that in the long run we would be happier in a society that accorded all citizens individual liberties. Nevertheless, the thought that maximizing happiness could require us to do dreadful things remains a source of deep discomfort about utilitarianism.

How is utilitarianism relevant to environmental thinking? An emphasis on the consequences of our actions is in keeping with environmental awareness. Too often in our dealings with nature we have been unaware of, or indifferent to, the consequences of our actions. When utilitarians say that we should assess the morality of our actions by their consequences, we should ask, "Consequences for whom?" Do we mean consequences just for those people around us—our families, neighbors, fellow citizens—or are we talking about all of humanity? As a grand moral theory, utilitarianism is understood to apply to all of humanity—this is implied by the "greatest good for the greatest number" principle. So according to utilitarianism, the morality of our current method of banana production, for example, can be determined by seeing whether it produces more happiness than unhappiness for all persons affected by it. This is a daunting task to be sure, but not impossible in principle and, in some broad respects, actually calculable. The utilitarian will approach any environmental question in a similar fashion: Which action will have the best consequences for all those affected by it?

Utilitarianism is not limited to assessing the consequences of actions only for people. If the fundamental category of good is pleasure (or absence of pain)—as it is understood by the classical utilitarians—then we have to consider the consequences of our actions for all people who will be affected by them and for all beings who can experience pleasure or pain. Hence, the pleasures and pains of nonhuman **sentient** animals will have to be considered in a utilitarian calculation of best overall consequences. Peter Singer, a contemporary utilitarian, objects to many of our current dealings with animals on these grounds. For utilitarians, however, the boundary of feeling will be the boundary of moral concern. Because they cannot feel any pleasure or pain, things like trees or rivers or ecosystems cannot be of direct moral concern to the utilitarian. What we do to trees or rivers can cause other beings to experience pleasure or pain, and so we have to worry about those consequences of our actions, but the trees and rivers are only intermediaries linking us to those other beings. For utilitarians, the ability to experience pleasure or pain is necessary for an entity to figure directly in our moral deliberations.

Here is a brief statement of utilitarianism from John Stuart Mill, one of the foremost proponents of the view.

> The creed which accepts as the foundation of morals, Utility, or the Greatest Happiness Principle, holds that actions are right in proportion as they tend to promote happiness, wrong as they tend to produce the reverse of happiness. By happiness is intended pleasure, and the absence of pain; by unhappiness, pain, and the privation of pleasure. To give a clear view of the moral standard set up by the theory, much more requires to be said; in particular, what things it includes in the ideas of pain and pleasure; and to what extent this is left an open question. But these supplementary explanations do not affect the theory of life on which this theory of morality is grounded—namely, that pleasure, and freedom from pain, are the only things desirable as ends; and that all desirable things (which are as numerous in the utilitarian as in any other scheme) are desirable either for the pleasure inherent in themselves, or as means to the promotion of pleasure and the prevention of pain.
>
> —J. S. Mill *Utilitarianism* 1861 Chapter 2

Utilitarianism is crisp and straightforward, at least at the outset. Since pleasure and pain are "the only things desirable as ends," that is, the only things that matter, right and wrong will be defined with respect to the only things that matter. So "right" means "productive of happiness" and "wrong" means "productive of pain." For the utilitarian, morality is a matter of calculation. We just figure out (as best we can!) which action will produce the greatest balance of pleasure over pain, and that is the right thing to do. People sometimes object to utilitarianism on grounds that it appears to advocate wallowing in sensuality—lots of partying, games, rich food, and so on. But this is to misconstrue Mill. Not only is a life of fun and games unlikely to produce a lot of happiness in the long run, but because we are complex creatures, we also require a different kind of happiness to be satisfied. Mill thinks (in a different passage) that some pleasures—the ones resulting from employment of our "higher faculties"—are better. As Mill observes, "Few human creatures would consent to be changed into any of the lower animals for a promise of the fullest allowance of a beast's pleasures . . . It is better to be a human being dissatisfied than a pig satisfied; better to be Socrates dissatisfied than a fool satisfied." Thus, if Mill is right, even a little bit of the higher pleasure is worth more than a lot of the lower pleasure.

As mentioned earlier in discussing utilitarianism, the theory explicitly includes anything that can feel pleasure or pain within the moral sphere. If pleasure or pain are the only things "desirable as ends," then nonhuman pleasure and pain must figure into the overall calculation as well. Notice how, in the following passage, another prominent utilitarian, Jeremy Bentham, refers to the irrelevance of the "number of legs, the villosity of the skin, or the termination of the *os sacrum*" [tail bone] to whether or not a creature "counts" morally. According to Bentham, "the insuperable line," that is, the basis for moral concern, is the ability to suffer.

> The day *may come,* when the rest of the animal creation may acquire those rights which never could have been withholden from them but by the hand of tyranny. The French have already discovered that the blackness of the skin is no reason why a human being should be abandoned without redress to the caprice of a tormentor. It may come one day to be recognized, that the number of the legs, the villosity of the skin, or the termination of the *os sacrum,* are reasons equally insufficient for abandoning a sensitive being to the same fate. What else is it that should trace the insuperable line? Is it the faculty of reason, or, perhaps, the faculty of discourse? But a full-grown horse or dog is beyond comparison a more rational, as well as a more conversable animal, than an infant of a day, or a week, or even a month, old. But suppose the case were otherwise, what would it avail? the question is not, Can they *reason?* nor, Can they *talk?* but, Can they *suffer?*
>
> —From Jeremy Bentham, *The Principles of Morals and Legislation* (1789) Chapter XVII, Section 1

This is relevant to environmental matters, since in many of our activities and interaction with nature we are indifferent to the animal suffering we cause. A utilitarian assessment of banana production, for example, will have to assess not only the total balance of human happiness, but the effects of banana production on animals as well. This is interesting because suddenly morality involves us in a wider circle of beings than we are normally inclined to consider.

KANTIANISM

The great German philosopher Immanuel Kant (1724–1804) cautioned against the "serpent windings of utilitarianism." According to Kant, morality is a matter of acting on principle rather than looking to the consequences of our actions. It is the character of the actions themselves, not something "external" to them (such as their consequences), that determine their morality. Kant's view is thus deeply at odds with the utilitarian conception of morality; whereas theirs is consequentialist, Kant's is nonconsequentialist. According to **Kantianism,** a conscientious **moral agent** is not someone who simply acts, but someone who acts for the sake of a principle. Compare my driving the speed limit of 65 mph because I cannot make my old car go any faster to my driving the speed limit because I regard it as my duty not to drive faster. In each case, I am going 65 mph, but for different reasons. If I am driving 65 mph because I think I ought not to go any faster, then, and only then, does my action have moral content, for it is an act of my will. I choose to obey the law. Morality, for Kant, is a matter of acting for the sake of principle, not a matter of personal preference.

Kant's central principle (known as the "categorical imperative"), has several formulations. One formulation of particular importance is the notion of treating persons with respect. Kant defines persons as rational autonomous beings, that is, beings who can act for the sake of moral principles they have freely imposed upon themselves. This ability is possessed only by persons (by definition) and is the source of our duty to respect them. For Kant, the categories of **person** and **thing** exhaust the contents of the universe; everything is either a person or a thing. You are a person because you are a rational being; a mountain or a tree or a cat is a thing. Kant's idea of respecting persons means not viewing them merely as things to be manipulated in accordance with our wills. Think of how we view things—a table, for instance. We do with it what we want, place it where we want, sell it or destroy it if we want. It has no will of its own for us to consider. In our dealings with persons, Kant insists that we not adopt the attitude we have toward things.

What about Kant and the natural world? Persons, as Kant has defined them, have paramount importance. The environment, trees, rivers, species, ecosystems, animals—all nonpersons—are relegated to thinghood, unworthy of respect in their own right. Because they do not have autonomous wills, there is nothing for us to respect about them. I saw a bumper sticker recently that pictured the earth and said, "Respect Your Mother." The suppressed claim is that the earth is our mother, implying that we are to respect the earth. For Kant, the earth is a clear example of something that cannot be respected (unless the earth can be somehow turned into a person, which, as we will see, some have tried). Since persons are the only entities that are valuable in themselves, nonpersons—things—have derivative value only and are supposed to be manipulated in accordance with the wills of persons and used for their good. It is precisely this attitude that some regard as leading to environmental problems. Placing people at the center of the moral universe, thereby supposing that the value of everything else is dependent upon us, displays a breathtaking hubris. But we should not be terribly surprised at Kant's view. He has put in secular terms the traditional Christian conception of the relation between humanity and nature; namely, that we have a divine spark that sets us above the things around us, things that are here for our use. However, as uncompromising as Kant's position seems, it does not portend the destruction of the natural world, as some fear, for nature's preservation can be construed as a way of respecting persons. If I am indifferent to how my polluting the river adversely affects those who live downstream, then I can hardly be said to show those people respect. And respect for persons can be stretched to cover future generations as well. So stern as Kant's morality seems, it does not portend the destruction of nature. It is true, however, that on Kant's moral theory, the only entities of moral significance are persons. Nonpersons, including all animals, are "mere things," subject to the wills of persons.

The first selection is from Kant's great work in ethics, the *Foundations of the Metaphysics of Morals.* Even this brief passage will give you a sense of its profundity and majesty, as well as its difficulty! Here Kant lays out the essential difference between *persons* and *things* and argues that only persons have "unconditioned worth," that is, value that is independent of use.

> Now I say: man and generally any rational being *exists* as an end in himself, *not merely as a means* to be arbitrarily used by this or that will, but in all his actions, whether they concern himself or other rational beings, must be always regarded at the same time as an end. All objects of the inclinations have only a conditional worth; for if the inclinations and the wants founded on them did not exist, then their object would be without value. But the inclinations themselves, being sources of want, are so far from having an absolute worth for which they should be desired that, on the contrary, it must be the universal wish of every rational being to be wholly free from them. Thus the worth of any object which is *to be acquired* by our action is always conditional. Beings whose existence depends not on our will but on nature's, have nevertheless, if they are nonrational beings, only a relative value as means, and are therefore called *things;* rational beings, on the contrary, are called *persons,* because their very nature points them out as ends in themselves, that is, as something which must not be used merely as means, and so far therefore restricts freedom of action (and is an object of respect).
>
> —Immanuel Kant *Foundations of the Metaphysic of Morals* 1785 second section

Kant proclaims *persons,* in his sense of the word (read: rational beings), to be distinct from *things.* Persons are ends, meaning they are the entities for which things have value. Not all value can be instrumental, because there must be something for the sake of which **instrumental value** is instrumental, an end that its instrumentality serves. For Kant, that end is persons. What does it mean to be valuable as an end rather than as a means? Consider a 10-dollar bill. Its value resides in its usefulness—you want it because of what you can do with it; its value is purely instrumental. The value of *things* (any nonrational entity), according to Kant, lies in their instrumentality. And this is true not only of things we make but also of "beings whose existence depends not on our will but on nature's." All of nature, then, is relegated to "thinghood" and is of instrumental value only. But persons are different. Their rationality separates them from things, making them ends; that is, entities with **intrinsic value,** not just instrumental value. Kant is saying that because people are rational beings (by definition) their value is not conditioned by their usefulness. As such, then, we ought never to treat persons merely as things, that is, as objects to be manipulated or used. This is what Kant means by **respect for persons.**

For Kant, persons ought never to be used solely as instruments, even if doing so will have good consequences. This means that persons have an inviolable right to be treated with respect, a right that cannot legitimately be overridden by utility. If utilitarianism accords individuals rights at all (the utilitarian Jeremy Bentham called rights "nonsense upon stilts") rights will always be dependent on utility. That is, for utilitarians we are accorded rights because that makes us happy. By contrast, for Kant the idea of a right is fundamental. The right to be treated with respect does not depend upon our being made happier if we are respected, it is instead an absolute requirement that follows from our nature as persons, beings with intrinsic value. The thought that rights can block utility calculations is important. In social policy deliberations, for instance, we do not think that individuals may simply be sacrificed for the greater good, by, say, performing dangerous medical experiments on people against their will. We will talk more about rights in Chapter 5, but for now we should note that a rights-based ethic is different from one based on utility. Kant's moral philosophy can serve as plausible foundation for such an ethic, for it defines the boundary of legitimate treatment of persons.

Like many other thinkers, Kant places persons in the center of the moral universe. The entire natural world, including all animals (since according to Kant they are nonrational), occupy the realm of things, and may, indeed *ought,* be used solely for the well-being of persons. Since the highest moral failing is to treat persons as mere things, Kant would probably regard treating mere things with respect to be the highest moral perversion, for it would display not only a deep misunderstanding of things, but also of persons. So for Kant, respecting nature is impossible, since there is nothing about nature worthy of respect. Does this mean we can do anything we want to natural entities, including animals, since they are things? Well, in one sense, the answer is yes, but only if it doesn't affect persons. In our next selection from Kant, notice how he argues that our obligations to animals are indirect only.

> Animals are not self-conscious and are there merely as a means to an end. That end is man. We can ask, "Why do animals exist?" But to ask, "Why does man exist?" is a meaningless question. Our duties towards animals are merely indirect duties towards humanity. Animal nature has analogies to human nature, and by doing our duties to animals in respect of manifestations of human nature, we indirectly do our duty towards humanity. Thus, if a dog has served his master long and faithfully, his service, on the analogy of human service, deserves reward, and when the dog has grown too old to serve, his master ought to keep him until he dies. Such action helps to support us in our duties towards human beings, where they are bounden duties. If then any acts of animals are analogous to human acts and spring from the same principles, we have duties towards the animals because thus we cultivate the corresponding duties towards human beings. If a man shoots his dog because the animal is no longer capable of service, he does not fail in his duty to the dog, for the dog cannot judge, but his act is inhuman and damages in himself that humanity which it is his duty to show towards mankind. If he is not to stifle his human feelings, he must practice kindness towards animals, for he who is cruel to animals becomes hard also in his dealing with men. We can judge the heart of a man by his treatment of animals. Hogarth depicts this in his engravings. He shows how cruelty grows and develops. He shows the child's cruelty to animals, pinch the tail of a dog or a cat; he then depicts the grown man in his cart running over a child; and lastly, the culmination of cruelty in murder. He thus brings home to us in a terrible fashion the rewards of cruelty, and this should be an impressive lesson to children. The more we come in contact with animals and observe their behavior, the more we love them, for we see how great is their care for their young. It is then difficult for us to be cruel in thought even to a wolf. Leibnitz used a tiny worm for purposes of observation, and then carefully replaced it with its leaf on the tree so that it should not come to harm through any act of his. He would have been sorry—a natural feeling for a humane man—to destroy such a creature for no reason. Tender feelings towards dumb animals develop humane feelings towards mankind. In England butchers and doctors do not sit on a jury because they are accustomed to the sight of death and hardened. Vivisectionists, who use living animals for their experiments, certainly act cruelly, although their aim is praiseworthy, and they can justify their cruelty, since animals must be regarded as man's instruments; but any such cruelty for sport cannot be justified. A master who turns out his ass or his dog because the animal can no longer earn its keep manifests a small mind. The Greeks' ideas in this respect were highminded, as can be seen from the fable of the ass and the bell of ingratitude. Our duties towards animals, then, are indirect duties towards mankind.
>
> —Immanuel Kant, "Duties to Animals and Spirits," in *Lectures on Ethics,* Trans. Louis Infield

We can have only **indirect** duties to animals; the duties are indirect because our only **direct** duties are to persons and animals are not persons. So we ought not to mistreat animals, not because of anything about them, but because "he who is cruel to animals becomes hard also in his dealing with men." Given the strong similarities between people and animals, there is an armchair psychological plausibility to Kant's claim about the effects cruelty toward animals is likely to have on us, though whether this is the only reason to oppose cruelty to animals is a question we shall consider shortly. Kant's view would presumably extend beyond animals to cover other living things and even natural objects. If behaving ruthlessly toward trees, for example, tended to make people insensitive to others, then Kant would be against that as well. His view could be extended to natural objects such as rivers or mountains too. Anything we do that lessens our respect for persons, Kant is against. So to return to our banana story, for Kant the only morally relevant considerations are the effects of banana production on persons. That animals suffer and rain forests are destroyed is, in itself, not a moral consideration. Here we can see a disagreement between Kant and utilitarianism; utilitarians were at least willing to make animal suffering a matter of direct moral concern. But in each view, rivers, mountains, trees, and other nonsentient natural objects remain "things," in the sense that they do not directly count in moral deliberation.

NATURAL LAW ETHICS

The basic idea of **natural law ethics** is that within our nature is a guide for how we ought to act. This insight has undergone multiple interpretations over many centuries, but there is something remarkably persistent in the notion that how we ought to act is a function of how we are, that because we have a certain nature, there are certain things that contribute to our good, our happiness and flourishing as human beings, and the right thing to do is that which will contribute to realizing our ends, as established by our nature. Natural law ethics, therefore, will seek to show that there are fundamental moral principles binding on all people, irrespective of the laws and conventions imposed by governments or cultures, and that these fundamental principles are to be found within human nature itself. Natural law thinking has been enormously influential in grounding basic human rights, since in discussing such rights one necessarily appeals to moral standards outside the laws and conventions of society. The natural law theorist claims there are principles of conduct and decency that transcend governments that we apprehend intuitively. The Declaration of Independence, for example, appeals to various "self-evident" truths, namely that we have rights to freedom and to pursue happiness. Such 'self-evident' truths allegedly reflect moral principles embedded within us.

The idea that human nature contains principles for conduct raises the inevitable questions of what they are and how they got there. Since these principles are held to be authoritative, an especially powerful reason is needed to warrant following them. The mere fact that we are inclined to behave in a certain way does not show that we ought to behave the way we are inclined. The foremost natural law theorist, the 13th century philosopher and theologian St. Thomas Aquinas, gave a decidely religious answer to those questions. On the assumption that God is the omnipotent, omniscient, and supremely good creator of all that exists, creation itself must reflect the intentions of the divine maker. God made the world to suit his purposes and things function according to his plan. The laws of nature—natural laws—are the instantiation of God's divine plan for how the world, and all within it, is supposed to function. Since God is good (by definition) and the world functions according to his intentions, the natural order is also the moral order. In other words, all of nature is imbued with moral significance because it was created by God to function a certain way. So going against nature is actually going against God, a serious charge for the believer. Aquinas' view is the official moral philosophy of the Roman Catholic Church, and even our brief sketch of natural law allows us to see why the church has been traditionally opposed to birth control, abortion, masturbation, homosexuality, and other practices that allegedly thwart the "natural" function of sex, namely, reproduction. (Though how reproduction is determined to be *the* natural function of sex is unclear.)

Here is a brief passage from Aquinas' *Summa Theologica* in which he discusses natural law:

> Now rational creatures are also subject to God's provident direction, but in a way that makes them more like God than all other creatures. For God directs rational creatures by instilling in them certain natural inclinations and capacities that enable them to direct themselves as well as other creatures. Thus human beings also are subject to the eternal law and they too derive from that law certain natural inclinations to seek their proper end and proper activity. These inclinations of our nature constitute what we call the natural law; they are the effects of the eternal law imprinted "in" our nature.
>
> —Saint Thomas Aquinas *Summa Theologica*
> Treatise on Law, Article 2

But what are the principles put there by God? According to Aquinas, certain basic human goods are evident to reason, such as preservation of life, community, family, and knowledge, among others. These are recognized by all as fundamental to our well-being, and God has given us natural inclinations toward these desiderata, it making no sense for a good God to incline us otherwise. So those things toward which we have natural inclinations must be the things that constitute our good. Working out precisely which of our inclinations are natural, rather than cultural or idiosyncratic, is a major challenge for natural law ethics. The worry is that we are dressing up our preconceptions, biases, and intuitions as lofty principles allegedly found within human nature.

Natural law ethics has obvious connections to the environment. Shades of it are surely to be found in the often expressed connection between what is natural and what is good, a connection relentlessly exploited by advertising. "Natural" is supposed to be pure, unaltered, desirable. But do we want to say that whatever is natural is invariably good? Is cancer natural? What about earthquakes? Even if we don't want to admit that everything natural is good, Aquinas' thought that there is some overarching purpose or grand scheme to nature is irresistible. We infuse the natural world with intentionality, direction, and purpose, and our task is to conform to the principles "imprinted in our nature" according to the way we have been designed. It seems so obvious that living things in particular have been designed—as obvious as the "fact" that the sun moves, something we can each see every day with our own eyes. After all, birds have wings so that they can fly, trees have leaves to capture sunlight, we have hands in order to grasp, and rains fall to water the plants; or so it seems.

That nature manifests a scheme or plan is challenged by evolutionary theory. Irresistible appearances not withstanding, in evolutionary theory, creatures have not been designed. No guiding purpose shapes them; organisms are the way they are because of blind chance operating over millions and millions of years. It very much *appears* as if birds were designed to fly, but wings are the accumulated results of many small changes. The small changes came about by chance (mutation) and most had no survival value. But some did, and they were passed from generation to generation. On this view, there is no intentionality, no plan; the evolution of life is a directionless, purposeless, utterly unconscious mechanical process. That evolutionary theory can explain away what seems so apparent, namely, that there is design and purpose in the world, undercuts the idea that we have within our natures immutable principles placed there by our creator as guides for how our behavior should conform to some grand scheme for all of nature.

Natural law ethics is widely criticized for trying to determine what we ought to do from the way we are. The two ideas, **are** and **ought,** are logically distinct; we cannot simply conclude that we ought to do something because we are disposed to do it. This complaint goes right to the heart of natural law ethics since the way we are, suitably understood, is absolutely crucial for determining what we ought to do. Yet despite criticism, natural law theorists persist in holding that our happiness is ultimately a matter of properly fitting ourselves into the world, that we have a particular kind of constitution, a human nature, against which our practices and behavior should be compared. This fundamental insight is not so easy to abandon, though it may be difficult to give it precise content.

Recall our discussion of bananas at the beginning of the chapter. What kinds of concerns might a natural law ethic raise about that activity? The banana industry would likely be seen within a broader context of our relation to nature. Just as certain ways of treating people violate an innate sense of what is right, so domination and ruthless exploitation of the natural world would appear to an enlightened environmental awareness as similarly wrong. Among the principles "imprinted in our nature," there could easily be norms for how we ought to act toward nature as well as toward our fellow human beings. Natural law, in other words, might cover more than how we treat each other. Moreover, as we shall see, the basic idea of natural law ethics that there is value in the unmolested functioning of nature is developed by several environmental thinkers. Just as we have our own nature, our good, toward which we aim, so other living things, perhaps even entire ecosystems, have their own goals and conditions that contribute to their flourishing. Banana plantations, among other activities that are deeply invasive of natural processes, might represent a kind of intrusion and mastery over those natural processes that goes against natural law. Moreover, such meddling with the good of natural entities can raise vexing moral questions. Why, for example, should our needs and goals automatically be assumed to take precedence over the needs and goals of other living things?

VIRTUE ETHICS

Our discussion of ethical theories so far has focused on the question of how one ought to act. Utilitarianism says one ought to maximize happiness, Kant tells us we ought to conform to duty, and natural law ethics says we ought to follow innate principles found in our natures. But what about the person who acts? None of the theories has addressed the question of what we should be like as people; they have told us what we ought to do, but is that all there is to ethics? Suppose your friend helps you move. You thank him for his assistance, but he says he is only doing what he ought. Suppose that as the conversation proceeds you discover that he really means it. He is a utilitarian and he was only trying to maximize happiness, or he is a Kantian and helping you is a way to respect persons, or he wanted to act compatibly with natural law. None of these reasons for helping you move seems appropriate for a friendship. You would expect that he helped you move because he cares about you, not because he has a theoretical commitment to an abstract principle about the right thing to do. **Virtue ethics** focuses on how we ought to be as people; it attempts to articulate what it means to be a good person, thereby broadening the domain of moral analysis to cover more than just how people act.

Aristotle begins his great work, the *Nicomachean Ethics,* with the thought that the good is "that at which all things aim." For people, this means happiness. If you ask people what they want out of life invariably they say they want to be happy. Human happiness, for Aristotle, is not a mere sensation of pleasure or feeling of contentment; he is speaking of fulfillment or flourishing as a human being. So what is human happiness? For Aristotle, flourishing or happiness is being a good instance of its kind. A flourishing or "happy" oak tree, for example, is one that displays the proper oak tree properties, the oak tree virtues, as it were. Human beings too have a way of being that constitutes their flourishing or fulfillment, namely, to display the various human virtues. The word *virtue* is not one we often use; it has an antique sound to our ear. But it refers to something vitally important: the character traits it is good for us to have.

Good character traits start with the traditional cardinal virtues, courage, justice, temperance, and wisdom ("cardinal" because the other virtues can be allegedly derived from these four). Other positive character traits quickly come to mind: generosity, compassion, loyalty, industriousness, honesty, self-control, self-reliance, aesthetic sensitivity, tactfulness, cooperativeness, friendliness, civility, reasonableness, dependability, benevolence, inquisitiveness, magnanimity, and on and on. According to Aristotle, it is good for us to display these and other character traits because they constitute what it means for us to flourish as human beings.

How do we acquire the virtues? For Aristotle it is simple: practice. We become virtuous by habituation. The virtues are not just innate capacities that some of us have and others not, nor are they feelings. They are dispositions that can be cultivated by practice. We can become good people very much the way in which we can acquire any other skill, such as learning to play a musical instrument or to cook. A virtuous person displays what Aristotle calls a kind of practical wisdom, that is, he or she responds properly in a variety of situations because of a seasoned character. Consider, by way of analogy, the experienced cook who can prepare a tasty meal from the ingredients on hand, who adjusts the cooking temperature and spices appropriately, and who operates with a calm natural confidence in the kitchen. Compare this person to the nervous cook who slavishly and mechanically follows a recipe, measuring each ingredient as if it all were a chemistry experiment, and who is incapable of adjusting to unforeseen developments as the meal is being prepared. The first person knows how to cook, the second does not. The same holds for living one's life. The virtuous person knows how to live. Rather than mechanically following rules such as one might find in self-help books on how to make friends or avoid debt or be happy and healthy, the virtuous person displays a practical wisdom in life by adjusting appropriately to the infinite variety of situations that confront us. But how does the virtuous person do that? According to Aristotle, such a person is practiced in discovering the mean between extremes, since virtue lies between "too much" and "too little." So, for example, courage is the mean between being rash and timid; generosity is the mean between being stingy and flamboyant. In the following passage from Aristotle, notice how virtue is defined as "a sort of middle state."

> If then we are right in saying that good craftsmen when at work keep their eyes fixed on a middle point, and if virtue, no less than nature herself, surpasses all the arts and crafts in accuracy and excellence, it follows that excellence will be the faculty of hitting a middle point. I refer to moral excellence or virtue; and this is concerned with emotions and actions, in which it is possible to have excess, or deficiency, or a medium amount. For instance you can feel either more or less than a moderate amount of fear and boldness, and of desire and anger and pity, and of pleasant or painful emotions generally; and in both cases the feelings will be wrong. But to feel these emotions at the right time and on the right occasion and towards the right people and for the right motives and in the right manner is a middle course, and the best course; and this is the mark of goodness. And similarly there is excess and deficiency or a middle amount in the case of actions. Now it is with emotions and actions that virtue is concerned; excess and deficiency in them are wrong, and a middle amount receives praise and achieves success, both of which are marks of virtue. It follows that virtue is a sort of middle state, in the sense that it aims at the middle.
>
> —Aristotle, *Nicomachaen Ethics Book I,* Chapter 2

Virtue ethics has important implications for our relation to the natural world. The virtuous person, in having the practical wisdom to live well, will also have the proper attitude toward nature. He or she will display a sensitivity to natural beauty and an appropriate sense of humility before the wonders of the natural world. People who know a lot about nature seem wise. They sense our position among other living things and how the cycles of life apply to us. The characters of these people have been instructed by paying close attention to nature and it seems as if they have achieved a high level of self-acceptance from contemplating the intricate workings of the natural world.

A recently developed version of virtue ethics emphasizes the virtue of care. Although **care ethics** is associated with feminist moral theory, there is no necessary connection between the two, for care would be an important virtue for anyone to have. An ethics of caring has its foundations in the writings of Carol Gilligan in the early 1980s. In her view, women have a different sort of moral experience than men (she is speaking in broad generalities; not all women fit the mold and some men do). Gilligan claims that men focus on moral rules, adjudication of disputes, balancing competing claims, protecting interests, and the like, whereas women in their moral thinking emphasize relationships, interpersonal commitments, and bonds of affection. For women, according to Gilligan, "the moral problem arises from conflicting responsibilities rather than from competing rights and requires for its resolution a mode of thinking that is contextual and narrative rather than formal and abstract."

This means the moral experience of women is not well represented by moral theories that emphasize moral "winners" and "losers" at the expense of maintaining caring relationships. The behavior of children on a school playground, claims Gilligan, gives insight into the moral orientation of men and women. Boys frequently play competitive games, handling disputes by appeal to rules, thereby developing skills at manipulating abstract rules, whereas girls typically play noncompetitive "turn-taking" games where disputes are less likely to erupt, and when they do, "rather than elaborating a system of rules for resolving disputes, girls subordinated the continuation of the game to the continuation of relationships."

Gilligan observes that differences in moral orientation between men and women have been portrayed by traditional moral psychologists, such as Lawrence Kohlberg and Sigmund Freud, as a lack of moral development among women (hence the title of her celebrated book, *In a Different Voice*). If there are the differences in moral thinking between men and women that Gilligan cites, is the most plausible explanation that women are morally undeveloped or that they are attuned to different moral concerns? Gilligan's work forces us to consider whether a male gender bias pervades moral theory. Think, for example, of the sort of ethical relations appropriate for a family. Here we are expected to operate with principles of love, affection, and, in the fullest sense of the term, care for others. Talk of rights and protection of individual interests at the expense of others seems inappropriate.

But can care be the foundation of an entirely "different" moral scheme, or can care be accommodated by expanded versions of the moral theories with which we are already familiar? For example, in so far as care will maximize happiness, utilitarians will approve; Kantians can accept care as a duty; and natural law theorists might see it as an aspect of our nature. Since men and women inhabit the same moral universe—that is, the moral concerns of men and women are mutually comprehensible—odds are that expanded and refined moral theories can accommodate care as an important moral trait, rather than trying to construct a completely different ethical system based on care.

Be that as it may, care is surely important for environmentalism. People often talk of our need to cultivate a harmonious relation with nature. If this is put forward as a moral claim about how we ought to relate to nature, then it is an obvious extension of care ethics. Our relation to the natural world, they claim, should not be one of conflict, domination, or mastery. Care ethics would call attention to our abilities to nurture and to respect the potentialities of other forms of life. It would emphasize the importance of maintaining a healthy relationship with not only other people but our surroundings as well, the key word being *relationship*. The ruthlessness we often display toward nature—the cultivation of bananas, for example—would likely be condemned by an ethics of care. In Chapter 10, we shall see how virtue ethics and care ethics have been developed by environmental thinkers in very insightful ways.

WHAT TO MAKE OF THE MORAL THEORIES?

The theories we considered, utilitarianism, Kantianism, natural law, and virtue ethics, all contribute to our understanding of morality. Apparently, morality is a complex and multifaceted domain of inquiry and each theory illuminates a dimension of that domain. Moral theories each offer a perspective, a kind of consideration we can use in our own deliberations. This is an important point to keep in mind. The theories give us broad avenues for reflection, but they are no substitute for sensitive, mature, independent moral deliberation. The worst way for us to proceed is simply to grab a theory and apply it in an unreflective "top-down" fashion to environmental questions. At best, such an approach will yield a perspective as limited as the theory we choose. Moreover, why choose one theory over another? Moral deliberation requires sensitivity to the range of considerations that can be brought forward, and we impoverish our understanding of moral questions by failing to entertain different dimensions of those questions articulated by each of the theories.

Questions for discussion

1. People sometimes say that each person has his or her "own morality." What might that mean? Is it true? How can you tell?
2. Why are moral issues thought to be important? Give some examples of what you take to be moral issues and explain what it is about them that makes them moral issues.
3. Do you think that morality and religion are essentially connected so that it is impossible to have one without the other?
4. Is it morally wrong to drive a species to extinction? Why, why not? What considerations do you think are relevant in answering this question? How might the moral theories (utilitarianism, Kantianism, natural law, virtue ethics) answer this question? What would either substantial agreement or disagreement among the moral theories show?
5. "Since morality is made by people to promote group living, it makes no sense to apply it to nonhumans. Thus the whole idea of environmental ethics is fundamentally misguided." Explain, consider, discuss.

References for Bananas

1. "Avian Exposure to Pesticides in Costa Rican Banana Plantations," S. R. Mortensen, et al. *Bulletin of Environmental Contamination and Toxicology* (1998) 60: 562–568.
2. "Agrichemical Use on Banana Plantations in Latin America: Perspectives on Echological Risk," William Henriques, et al. *Environmental Taxicology and Chemisty,* vol 16, no. 1. 1997, pp. 91–99.
3. "Environmental Aspects of Pesticide Use on Banana Plantations," Thomas Lacher, et al, *Pesticides Outlook,* December 1997, pp. 24–28.
4. "Tropical Ecotoxicology: Status and Needs," Thomas Lacher, et al, *Environmental Toxicology and Chemistry* vol 16, no. 1, pp. 100–111, 1997.
5. *Biodiversity in Agroecosystems,* by Wanda Collina and Calvin Qualset. CRC Press, Boca Raton, FL, 1999.

CHAPTER 2

Moral Reasoning

RATIONAL INQUIRY AND THE CONCEPT OF AN ARGUMENT

As we get further into the complexities of moral thinking and the environment, we should pay particular attention to a core feature of philosophy: rational inquiry. When we inquire rationally we accept or reject claims based solely on the strength of the reasons for or against those claims. Nothing else is relevant; not what we would like, not what our friends think, not what our culture or tradition holds, nor how much money we could make from adopting a different view. This is an austere intellectual posture, but ultimately one of supreme dignity, for we are then moved only by what we accept as legitimate reasons, rather than being manipulated by forces external to our rational wills. Compare someone who accepts the Pythagorean Theorem because it was taught in school to someone who worked through its derivation and now accepts it on that basis; or someone who has examined reasons for and against the existence of God and accepts (or rejects) God's existence on that basis rather than accepting God's existence (or nonexistence) simply because that is how one was raised.

If the dignity of rational inquiry sounds vaguely Kantian, it is. Presenting reasons is yet another way to respect a person, including oneself. Intellectual manipulation by, say, brainwashing, inducements, deception, coercion, and the like, is incompatible with the dignity of a rational and autonomous being, a being that is moved on the basis of reason. Rational agency is certainly part of what Socrates was talking about when he famously claimed that the unexamined life is not worth living.

In his essay "What is Enlightenment?" Kant has some important observations about being an independent rational thinker. He writes,

> Enlightenment is man's release from his self-incurred tutelage. Tutelage is man's inability to make use of his understanding without direction from another. Self-incurred is this tutelage when its cause lies not in lack of reason but in lack of resolution and courage to use it without direction from another. *Sapre aude!* [dare to know!]—that is the motto of enlightenment. . . . If I have a book which understands for me, a pastor who has a conscience for me, a physician who decides my diet, and so forth, I need not trouble myself. I need not think, if I can only pay—others will readily undertake the irksome work for me.

Central to rational inquiry is the concept of an argument. In philosophy, the term **argument** does not mean an acrimonious exchange, though philosophical discussions sometimes do disintegrate into acrimonious exchanges. *Argument* refers instead to the giving of reasons in support of a claim. An argument consists of a conclusion, that is, the point one is trying to establish, supported by premises, or the reasons that are intended to show the conclusion is true. The relation between the premises and the conclusion is crucial, for the whole idea of an argument is that the truth of the premises is supposed to show us that the conclusion is true as well. This is what it means to say that the conclusion "follows from" the premises.

Consider a time-honored textbook example of an argument:

All men are mortal.

Socrates is a man.

Socrates is mortal.

The underline indicates an inference. You conclude that Socrates is mortal based on the premises All men are mortal and Socrates is a man. Notice the relation between the premises and the conclusion. *If* it is true that Socrates is a man and *if* it is true that all men are mortal, then it *must* be the case that Socrates is mortal. This is the essential idea of an argument, namely, the logical relation between the premises and conclusion. In logic (a branch of philosophy that investigates that relation) this particular relation between premises and conclusion is called validity. The term *valid* is being used in a technical sense. In everyday conversation, an independently standing remark can be said to be valid, as when someone says that my point is a valid one. Not in logic. Validity refers to a specific relation between premises and conclusion. As we saw in the example above, if the premises are true, then the conclusion must be true as well; so the argument is valid.

Another technical term is *soundness*. An argument is sound if it is valid *and* the premises are actually true. A sound argument is one that actually works, and by that I mean not only would the conclusion have to be true if the premises are true but also the premises really are true. The conclusion of a sound argument must be accepted, on pain of irrationality. The simple argument above is valid; is it also sound? That depends on whether the premises are true. On any ordinary understanding of the terms they are, although because of his extraordinary intellectual powers, some thought Socrates no mere man and, interestingly, Socrates argued for immortality.

DEDUCTIVE AND INDUCTIVE ARGUMENTS

We can distinguish two kinds of argument, deductive and inductive. In deductively valid arguments, as just discussed, the truth of the premises is sufficient for the truth of the conclusion. Inductive arguments, on the other hand, fall short of deductive validity. In inductive arguments, the truth of the premises does not guarantee the truth of the conclusion, rather, the truth of the premises makes the conclusion likely or probable. The majority of arguments encountered in ordinary discourse are inductive, so they will be the focus of our discussion in this chapter. However, with the addition of appropriate premises, inductive arguments can always be turned into deductively valid arguments. But this procedure will merely transform whatever uncertainty there is regarding the inference of the inductive argument into a premise problem in the deductive argument, since a premise that is not clearly true will have to be added to turn an inductive argument into one that is deductively valid.

Inductive arguments are often more useful than deductive arguments because the conclusion contains more information than is contained in the premises. In deductive reasoning, for the truth of the premises to guarantee the truth of the conclusion, they cannot jointly say more than the conclusion, otherwise the conclusion could fail to be true if the premises are true. So the guarantee offered by deductive arguments comes at a stiff price. Deductive arguments do not tell us anything we did not already know once we have accepted the premises. The conclusion of an inductive argument, however, contains more information than is contained in the premises. But this too comes at a price: The truth of the premises is not sufficient for the truth of the conclusion. In an inductive argument, even a good one, it is possible for the premises to be true and the conclusion to be false. A good inductive argument is one in which the truth of the premises makes the conclusion probable or likely. How likely? The minimum is more likely than not. We shall then say the argument is cogent or that the conclusion is warranted, given the supporting reasons.

MORAL ARGUMENTS

Moral arguments are arguments that contain moral concepts. They purport to show us what we ought or ought not to do, what is fair or right or just in a particular situation. Such arguments can be either deductive or inductive. In moral arguments, it is important to pay particular attention to how the premises and the conclusion are expressed. It is a fallacy to try to infer what ought to be done merely from what is the case. For example, someone might point out that dumping used motor oil in a stream will pollute it, concluding that we ought not to dump used motor oil in the stream. But this conclusion follows provided we ought not to pollute the stream. Within the context, however, we can assume that "we ought not to pollute the stream" is an unstated premise. Since there is an "ought" in the premises, the "ought" in the conclusion did not just come out of thin air. Analysis of moral arguments frequently involves making clear such hidden assumptions.

Suppose we agree that dumping used motor oil in the stream will pollute it. This is a scientific fact about how streams react to having used motor oil dumped in them. What about the previously hidden assumption that we ought not to pollute the stream? Is it true that we ought not to pollute the stream? Statements about what we ought to do are not shown to be true or false in the same way statements about the effects of oil on the stream are shown to be either true or false. This is where the moral theories we discussed in Chapter 1 come in. Each theory supplies its own kind of reason for thinking that we ought not to pollute the stream. In utilitarianism, polluting the stream will not maximize happiness for all concerned; for Kant, pollution can be a failure to respect persons; natural law might see pollution as ultimately self-destructive, making it incompatible with a natural inclination to preserve our lives; and virtue ethics would not condone the character of a person who would do such a thing. The moral theories provide very abstract considerations that serve to justify moral claims that appear in moral arguments.

RECOGNIZING ARGUMENTS

As Aristotle told us in Chapter 1, the virtues are acquired by practice (I suppose the vices are too). Good reasoning is a virtue, one many of us already have to one degree or another, but we can always develop this virtue further. The first step in developing our skills as moral reasoners is to learn to extract arguments from passages, since not everything you read or hear involves argumentation. Much of it is expository, or entertainment, or serves some function other than argument presentation. It may just be rhetoric, that is, material designed to persuade without supplying reasons. Rational persuasion is our main concern in moral philosophy; we want to hold those moral beliefs that have the best reasons in support of them. For then and only then can we have confidence in our moral positions. If they are backed up by good reasons and rational anaylsis, then we are not merely expressing our opinions—which may be biased and ill-informed—but presenting views that can withstand critical scrutiny.

In everyday discourse, certain words are typically used to indicate the presence of argumentation. *Therefore* almost always indicates that a conclusion is being drawn. Ordinary language uses other conclusion indicators, including *hence, thus, so, consequently, it follows that, which shows that.* Sometimes there is no conclusion indicator. Sensitivity to the dialectical structure of a passage can indicate the conclusion when there is no explicitly stated conclusion indicator. Identifying the conclusion is the most important part of argument analysis because you can then see what reasons are offered in support of it, and until you know what the argument is, you cannot properly evaluate it.

Premises are frequently indicated by everyday words too. If someone says, "A because B" (though outside of a reasoning discussion no one would ever actually say such a thing!) B is offered as the reason for A. The same point could be put like this: "Because B, A." Other common words also frequently indicate premises, such as *since, for, as shown by, for the reason that.* Like conclusion indicators, premise indicators are not always explicitly stated. You will have to use your best judgment in determining what is offered as a reason for what. This is the practical wisdom of argument evaluation that comes with practice, since you cannot mechanically apply conclusion and premise indicators; sometimes they do not indicate argumentation and sometimes argumentation occurs without them. Again, practice and sensitivity to context are your best guides to argument recognition.

EXERCISES

Which of the following passages contain arguments? For those that do, state the conclusion and the reason(s) offered in support of it.

1. Sometimes there are flash floods in the desert.
2. Overprescription of antibiotics is causing infectious bacteria to develop resistance.
3. The Earth is over 4.5 billion years old. Human beings have existed for just a fraction of that time. It is therefore incorrect to think that the earth was made for us.
4. Since people are part of nature, all that they do is natural; so gasoline is natural and so is plastic.
5. Since 1980 the use of wind to produce electricity has been growing rapidly. At the end of 1995, there were more than 25,000 wind turbines worldwide.

6. There would be more food to feed a hungry world if we did not consume so much meat.
7. It is wrong to use animals to test products for human consumption. They feel pain just like we do.
8. Because organisms produce more offspring than can possibly survive, there is a competition among them for the resources needed to live.
9. Living things were put here for some purpose, so we should respect their lives.
10. "What goes around comes around," is one of the basic laws of ecology. For reasons of self-interests, if no other, we should be careful about what we do to the environment.

ARGUMENT RECOGNITION IN PASSAGES

Except in chapters on reasoning, arguments rarely come neatly packaged. They are imbedded in text and it can take considerable work to recognize them and then to extract and analyze them. In this section, we will consider passages that contain arguments. I will identify and interpret the arguments. Sometimes it is not clear what the argument is supposed to be, though some interpretations will be more plausible than others. The rule here is the principle of charity: Construe the argument in the most favorable way possible. That's how you would want your arguments to be taken by others. We will begin with a fairly straightforward example and move on to increasingly difficult passages.

1. "Because most people around the world now live, or will live, in urban areas, improving the quality of urban life is an urgent priority. Increased urbanization and urban density are better than spreading people out over the countryside, which would destroy more of the planet's biodiversity."

—Tyler Miller, *Living in the Environment,* 1998

The first step is to read the passage through carefully and identify the main point. This passage is arguing that improving the quality of urban life is an urgent priority. One way to make the structure of the reasoning clear is to number the relevant points as follows:

> Because most ① people around the world now live, or will live, in urban areas, improving the quality of urban life is an ② urgent priority. Increased urbanization and urban ③ density are better than spreading people out over the countryside, which would destroy ④ more of the planet's biodiversity.

Once the conclusion has been identified you can ask youself what reasons the author gives for thinking it is so. The claim is that 'improving the quality of urban life is an urgent priority.' Why should we think that? The author supplies two lines of support for that claim: Most people live in cities, and increased urbanization is better than spreading people out over the countryside. We can diagram the argumentative structure as follows:

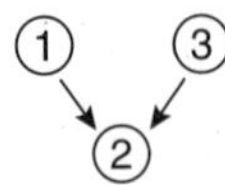

Notice too that the author supplies a reason for thinking that it is better to pack people into cities than to have them spread out over the countryside; it will lessen humanity's impact on nature:

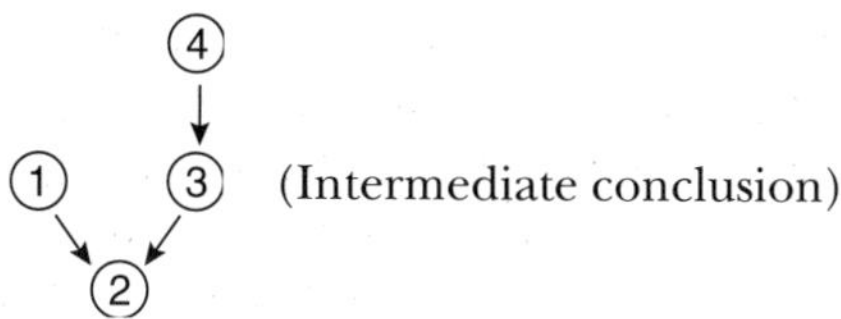

Now that we have the structure of the argument, we can evaluate it. Are the reasons good ones for thinking that improving the quality of urban life is an urgent priority? The fact that most people live in cities is surely a relevant consideration because it would be bad for most of us to lead lower-quality lives than we otherwise could. (Think about the moral theories.) Also, if life in cities is awful, then people won't want to live there. They will spread "out over the countryside" and from an ecological point of view that is worse than having them packed tightly together. When spread out on large lots, people need individual septic systems and wells, more roads and infrastructure, and so on. This all has a greater impact on the environment than if they lived more closely together. It looks like making urban environments attractive and livable is an important issue, an "urgent priority." I would say the author gives good grounds for thinking the conclusion is warranted.

We could carry the analysis further if we wanted. We could inquire into the truth of the premises (maybe most people don't live in cities, maybe spreading people out over the countryside need not tax the environment, maybe there is no reason to keep from destroying more of the planet's biodiversity, etc.). Further, we could turn the inductive inferences into deductively valid ones by supplying suppressed premises that we can then assess. For example, to conclude that we should work to make cities livable from the fact that most people live in cities, we need to add a step that says we should do what will improve the lives of most people, thus:

> Most people live in cities.
>
> Improving the quality of urban life will improve the lives of most people (assumed).
>
> We should do what will improve the lives of most people (assumed).
>
> *Therefore,* we should improve the quality of urban life.

As you can see, we can carry on the analysis to considerable depth, if we choose. But you do not have to do this for every argument in every passage that you read. However, you should realize when argumentation is present and have a sense of how to assess it.

2. Let's try a more difficult passage. This one is from Darwin's immortal book, *On the Origin of Species.*

> With respect to the belief that organic beings have been created beautiful for the delight of man,—a belief which it has been pronounced is subversive of my whole theory,—I may first remark that the sense of beauty obviously depends on the nature of the mind, irrespective of any real quality in the admired object; and that the idea of what is beautiful, is not innate or unalterable. We see this, for instance, in the men

> of different races admiring an entirely different standard of beauty in their women. If beautiful objects had been created solely for man's gratification, it ought to be shown that before man appeared, there was less beauty on the face of the earth than since he came on the stage. Were the beautiful volute and cone shells of the Eocene epoch, and the gracefully sculptured ammonites of the Secondary period, created that man might ages afterwards admire them in his cabinet? Few objects are more beautiful than the minute siliceous cases of the diatomaceæ: were these created that they might be examined and admired under the higher powers of the microscope?
>
> —Charles Darwin, *On the Origin of Species.* Chapter 6, 1898

What is the passage about? Darwin is apparently responding to an argument against his theory. If we imaginatively reconstruct the opponent's argument, it might go something like this: *Since* it would be pointless for there to be beauty without anyone around to appreciate it, "organic beings" were made beautiful for us to admire. In other words, the fact that there is beauty in nature shows intentional creation, not pointless and blind evolution, as Darwin's theory of evolution would have it. How does Darwin respond? His contention is that nature was *not* created beautiful for us. We can now work back through the passage to see how Darwin supports this claim. Here is how the structure of the argument appears to me:

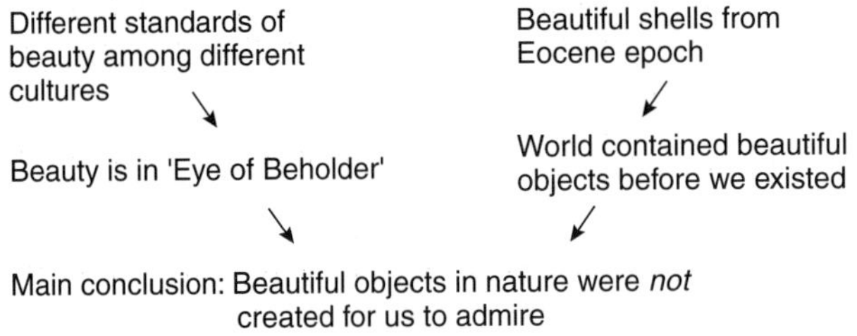

Different standards of beauty among different cultures ↘

Beauty is in 'Eye of Beholder' ↘

Beautiful shells from Eocene epoch ↙

World contained beautiful objects before we existed ↙

Main conclusion: Beautiful objects in nature were *not* created for us to admire

There is a lot to discuss. First, notice what seems to be an inconsistency between the two lines of support Darwin offers. If beauty is in the "eye of the beholder," as allegedly demonstrated by the fact that different men find different women beautiful, then how does this square with the claim that certain organic beings—the volute and cone shells—really are beautiful? Darwin appeals to the *objective* beauty of organisms that existed before we existed to argue that beautiful things were not created for us to admire. He cannot argue both that beauty depends solely on our perceptions and that there are beautiful things independent of our perceptions, which his appeal to the objective beauty of the shells implies. Second, is the "fact" that different men find different women beautiful enough to show that beauty "depends on the nature of the mind"? Might some things be objectively beautiful (such as the shells to which Darwin refers) even if standards of beauty among women differ? And how likely is it that there are entirely different standards of beauty among women? On good evolutionary grounds, it seems more probable that men will tend to find roughly similar standards for beauty among women, minor variations notwithstanding. So the line of support based on standards of beauty among women seems dubious at best as a way to show that beauty in nature was not created for us. The other line of support is much more convincing; namely, *because* beautiful things were around before there were people, they were not created beautiful for us.

This claim, however, depends on there being objectively beautiful things in nature, and those things being around before people. Someone in Darwin's time who thought that the natural world was created all at once would deny that people came into existence millions of years after other forms of life.

3. This fairly complicated passage is from *Biology, Ethics, and Animals,* by Rosemary Rodd.

> Some opponents of animal rights may genuinely believe that the consequences of ending animals' exploitation would be an actual increase in *net* suffering. The most extreme version of this would be the belief that all products of animal suffering, including such apparent trivia as furs, cosmetics, and hunting for sport, are actually essential to the happiness and welfare of human beings, whose refined sensibilities would suffer a degree of anguish unknown to mere animals if deprived. Were this view factually correct, I think it would have to give consequentialist supporters of animal rights some concern. However, the existence of humans who willingly choose to experience such deprivation tends to disprove the view that all products of animal exploitation are of overwhelming importance. Thus, in these cases, if our treatment of animals ought to depend upon balancing the competing interests involved, it seems that we must either do without products which involve significant harms to animals, or reform the systems of production to a point where these harms are eliminated.
>
> —Rosemary Rodd, *Biology, Ethics and Animals.* Clarendon Paperbooks, Oxford University Press, 1992, p. 177. Reprinted by permission of Oxford University Press.

As always, the first step is to read carefully to see what is going on. Rodd is responding to an argument put forward by "some opponents of animal rights." According to Rodd, their claim is that ending exploitation of animals would increase suffering, not reduce it. The reason to think this is because the anguish caused humans by not using animals in various ways would be more significant (because of our refined sensibilities) than the happiness produced by our using animals in those ways. We can structure their argument as follows:

"Their" argument: All products of animal suffering are essential to human happiness (which is worth more than animal happiness)

↓

Conclusion: Ending even trivial use of animals would produce a net increase in suffering

This is a straightforward utilitarian argument. The claim is that not exploiting animals in the ways indicated will produce more unhappiness than happiness for all concerned, the animals too. Their suffering, so the claim goes, is offset by much higher-quality pleasures experienced by human beings. The human pleasure of wearing fur, for example, is much more significant than whatever pain is caused to the animal. This is a direct appeal to the quantity/quality distinction among pleasures articulated by J. S. Mill (see Chapter 1). Since, on utilitarian grounds, the right thing to do is to maximize happiness, we should continue to exploit animals.

Rodd responds to this argument by denying that all exploitation of animals is essential to human happiness, as shown by the fact that some people willingly forgo products that rely on animal exploitation. Although Rodd doesn't explicitly say so, we can assume from the context that those people are still happy. We can structure her argument as follows:

	Some people willingly forgo such trivial products (and they are still happy)
	↓
Intermediate Conclusion:	Not all products of animal suffering are essential to human happiness
	↓
Main Conclusion:	(If our treatment of animals ought to balance interests) we should either do without products that involve animal suffering or reform their production

Note her main conclusion. It is stated hypothetically; *if* our treatment of animals ought to balance their interests against ours, *then* their significant interests come before our trivial interests. She is considering in this argument only "such apparent trivia" as furs, cosmetics, hunting, and so on.

Does Rodd present a good argument? What counts as trivial and important will be hotly contested, even among the uses she mentioned. Is hunting a trivial use of animals? Why? What about cosmetic testing? But suppose we can agree that certain uses of animals count as trivial. Does the fact that some people choose to "experience such deprivation" by not using trivial products involving animal exploitation (she could have put it better—do those people experience deprivation?) provide a good reason to think the rest of humanity can? There is a jump from what some people do to what everyone could do. This needs more support. Further, why should we balance competing interests, so that significant animal interests win over trivial human interests? To consider this will immerse us in questions about the moral status of animals, something we shall consider in Chapter 5. Finally, who puts forward the extreme argument to which Rodd is responding? Who thinks that "all products of animal suffering . . . are actually essential to the happiness and welfare of human beings"? The worry is that Rodd has refuted an argument no one holds. This is a certain kind of fallacy called the straw person (formerly straw man) because one beats up on a dummy position, one not held by anyone. It seems to me that Rodd's argument opens numerous areas of inquiry for us, rather than establishing her point. Perhaps the case can be made, but more support is required. In fairness to Rodd, much of her book is intended to provide the additional support.

FALLACIES

One of the most important critical thinking skills for you to develop is a sensitivity for fallacies, or ways in which premises can fail to support the conclusion. Premises can fail to support the conclusion in a bewildering variety of ways, so we always have to be alert, but there are also characteristic ways in which this happens. Many fallacies are psychologically compelling, and unless we are careful, we may unwittingly accept an argument that we should reject. Common fallacies have been given names, such as straw person mentioned before, but the name is only a place-holder, really just a promisory note. The real work comes in explaining why an argument suffers from a particular fallacy. But don't go overboard with the fallacies. Resist the temptation to see them everywhere; after all, many arguments are fine. The trick is to be able to separate the good ones from the fallacious ones.

Here are some typical fallacies.

1. **Straw person:** distorting a position to make it easy to criticize. Be on the look out for straw people whenever someone characterizes a position that is then criticized; "they think X, but if we look at their position we will see that . . ." Ask yourself whether the opponent would accept the description.

Example: I'm in favor of wise use of the national forests. The environmentalists think a fence should be put around them to keep out loggers and anyone else who wants to use our natural resources.

Are environmentalists against using our natural resources?

2. **False alternatives:** a distortion by illegitimately reducing the alternatives. Is there an alternative that is being ignored or do we have to choose just from the alternatives offered?

Example: Farmer: "I don't know what all the big fuss is over the pesticides we use. After all, if people want to eat we have to kill the bugs that would otherwise destroy the crops."

Are the choices just between not eating and using dangerous pesticides?

3. **Appeal to tradition:** arguing that because something has been done a certain way, we should continue to do it that way. We want to know is why it has been done, not merely that it has been done (or thought, believed, etc.). No independent reason is offered other than tradition.

Example: Humanity has been affecting the environment for a long time. I read somewhere that aboriginal peoples hunted many species to extinction. So the current hysteria about species extinction is misplaced.

The mere fact that we have driven species into extinction doesn't show that we shouldn't be concerned now. What about the rates of species extirpation?

4. **Appeal to popularity:** arguing that merely because a practice (policy, belief, etc.) is popular or widespread it is therefore correct. No reason is offered for being believed by many. Why do so many people accept it? Do they have good reasons?

Example: Father to young child who expresses reservations about eating meat because animals are our friends: "Most people use animals for food."

Does it follow that it is therefore ok? At one time a similar remark could have been made about slavery.

5. **Appeal to authority:** expert opinion can be used to support a claim. A statement is alleged to be true because Expert Jones says it is true. This is acceptable provided the authority is appropriate and represents prevailing opinion among the relevant authorities. If the expert is not relevant, then his or her opinion is no more valuable than anyone else's. The issue can become tricky if the authority is relevant but holds a minority opinion among the relevant experts. As nonexperts, we have no basis for believing the minority opinion over prevailing expert opinion. A minority of paleontologists, for example, think

dinosaurs were warm blooded. Is this a good reason for thinking they were warm blooded? Another concern is over moral issues. Do the opinions of some people count for more than others on moral matters? Are there moral experts?

Example: My dentist said that human activity is the cause of global warming.

Is the dentist an expert of the relevant sort? We'd like to hear from meteorologists and geologists.

6. Hasty generalization: as the name implies, a conclusion is drawn too quickly from limited evidence. Recall the example from Rodd discussed above; she concluded that humanity can change its ways because a few people can change their ways. Stereotypical thinking often uses a hasty generalization.

Example: Construction boss: "Look at that, somebody monkey-wrenched the bulldozer by putting sugar in the gas tank. Those damn environmentalists will do anything to stop development."

Are environmentalists against development? Note too that several fallacies can sometimes be applied. This might also count as a straw person or false alternatives—either development as usual or none at all.

7. Ad hominem: literally "against the person," or attacking a person (corporation, viewholder) rather than the position held. Sometimes it is legitimate to criticize a view by pointing out something about the person holding the view, other times not, so ad hominem reasoning is not always fallacious. You need to be very clear about what is at issue to see whether qualities of the viewholder are relevant to the view held.

Example: Those animal rights people get so upset about our treatment of animals. They say it violates their rights, as if animals could have rights. I'll bet they wouldn't hesitate to eat a cow if they were starving.

So? How does this show that animals cannot have rights?

8. Begging the question: every argument has to start somewhere with unargued assumptions as premises. But there is one thing that cannot be assumed—the conclusion! Sometimes arguments do precisely that. They assume either the conclusion itself or some close variation of it. Circular reasoning is one way to beg the question. The phrase *begging the question* is widely misused to refer to a particular context or situation giving rise to a question. This is incorrect. To beg the question means to assume precisely what one is trying to show. It can be a very subtle fallacy, since the idea expressed by the conclusion can appear reworded as a premise.

Example: It is wrong to exploit the environment just for our benefit because it is not right to treat the nonhuman world merely as a means.

Saying that it is "wrong because it is not right" is not to give a reason; the original claim is simply repackaged. We want an independent reason to think that it is wrong.

9. Causal fallacies: mistakes made when we engage in reasoning about causes. One prominent version is called (in Latin) *post hoc, ergo propter hoc,* or "after this, therefore because of this." It is tempting to think that just because one event comes after another that the first was the cause. This is a very hasty conclusion to draw. The first *may* be the cause of the second, but much more is needed to establish a causal relation than temporal succession.

Example: Scientists note an increase in average temperature worldwide which tracks industrialization. So industrialization causes global warming.

Maybe. But what if there are naturally occurring warm spells over geologic time and we just happen to be entering one?

10. Fallacies of division and composition: mistakes made in reasoning about parts and wholes. It does not follow that because the whole has a certain property that its parts will too (division), nor does it follow that because the parts have a property, the whole will (composition).

Example: (Composition) Because individual animals and plants seek to maintain their bodily integrity, so the ecosystem which is made out of those individuals also seeks to maintain a kind of internal homeostatic balance. (Division) Since an organism is alive, its components must be alive.

11. Slippery slope: arguing that if we start with a certain policy, belief, or mode of behavior, it will inevitably lead to another, which will lead to another, and so on down the "slope" to something bad, so we should not even take the first step. Slippery slope is not itself a fallacy but a style of argumentation. If we will indeed slide all the way to the bottom of the slope and if the thing at the bottom is bad, then what better reason could you want not to take that first step? The problem occurs, however, when either we will not slide all the way down or the bottom is not (so) bad.

Example: Once we start restricting access to the national forests, then you can bet other rights will be under attack as well. Next we will have to register all our guns and before you know it we will be living in a police state.

12. Naturalistic fallacy: arguing from *is* to *ought*. There can be more or less subtle versions of this inference, but in general just because something is the case is not a reason to suppose it ought to be the case.

Example: In nature it is survival of the fittest. So we ought not help those who are less fortunate than ourselves, since they are obviously not fit.

The best way to avoid the naturalistic fallacy is to make sure there is an *ought* statement among the premises.

EXERCISES

Here are some passages for you to analyze. For each passage you should do the following: determine whether there is an argument and structure the argument; that is, diagram what is offered as a reason for what. The best way to proceed is to ask yourself, What is the point? and then work backward to see what is offered to support the claim. Remember that sometimes argument structure can be complex; intermediate conclusions function as premises for the main conclusion:

Next, determine whether the reasons provided are good ones; that is, first, are they true, and second, if true, does their truth make the conclusion more likely to be true than not? If not, why not? Does the argument contain fallacious reasoning?

1. "Farmers recognize more than anyone that healthy growing environments define their future. Thus, they always seek better ways to control weeds with the least toxic herbicides available that do not damage food crops." (From International Food Information Council, *Food Biotechnology and the Environment,* March 1998)
2. "All things that accord with nature are good. But what can be more in accordance with nature than for old men to die?" (Cicero, *On Growing Old.* See if you can put this one in deductive form.)
3. "We can no longer afford to be careless about what we kill—whether it be coyotes and other alleged varmints trapped by professionals, or does shot by sport hunters in order to trim overpopulated herds of suburban whitetail—for every such death may bring with it consequences we are only now learning to comprehend." (T. H. Watkins, *Audobon,* March–April 1997, p. 128)
4. "The battery-powered car confronts several severe challenges today. Its range, the distance it can travel on a fully charged battery before the battery must be recharged, is currently less than 150 km (roughly 100 miles), far below the range of today's gasoline-powered cars on the road. The time required for battery recharging considerably exceeds the time required for filling a gasoline tank. And the production cost appears to be considerably greater than the production cost of the gasoline-powered vehicle. Principally for these reasons, the battery-powered car is expected to be competitive only in niche markets." (From Robert Socolow and Valerie Thomas, Center for Energy and Environmental Studies, Princeton University, in *Journal of Industrial Ecology,* 1997)
5. "Some claim that for moral reasons, whales, even if very abundant, should not be killed. We recognize that there are diverse food cultures in the world, and that some people only accept the eating of pigs, cattle, or poultry as appropriate, while others regard eating wild animals as normal. Whales have been on our diet for thousands of years, and we do not subscribe to the recent paradigm created by the anti-whaling lobby that enshrines the whale as a sacrosanct creature that should not be taken as food." (Joji Morishita, Deputy Director of the Far Seas Fisheries Division of Japan's Fisheries Agency, quoted in *The Ecologist* 31, no. 6 [July/August 2001], p. 18)
6. "As environments deteriorate, so does the physical and mental health of the people who live in them. There is a connection, for example, between the fact that the urban sprawl we live with daily makes no room for sidewalks or bike paths and the fact that we are an overweight, heart-disease-ridden society." (Richard Jackson, in a CDC report; quoted in *National Wildlife,* February/March 2002)
7. "Wilderness is a resource which can shrink but not grow. Invasion can be arrested or modified in a manner to keep an area usable either for recreation, or for science, or for wildlife, but the creation of new wilderness in the full sense of the word is impossible. It follows, then, that any wilderness program is a rear-guard action through which retreats are reduced to a minimum." (Aldo Leopold, *A Sand County Almanac,* p. 200)
8. "The states offer a far more productive stage for the development and institution of environmental policy. Those closest to a problem are the most likely to invest the greatest energy in its solution. The EPA is a centralized and distant bureaucracy and

thus cannot match the flexibility of state and local government. The 'laboratory of the states' is far more likely to yield productive results than cloistered bureaucracies more concerned with environmental rules than environmental results." (Fred Smith, president of Competitive Enterprise Institute, in "The Future of Environmental Policy," *Environment News,* May 1998)

9. "Today, it's snowmobiling and tomorrow it will be motorhomes, campers, hikers, mountain bikers and equestrians, who will no longer be welcome in our national parks. It's important that anyone who enjoys the right to use our nation's parks realize what's happening. The Clinton Administration wants the people out of the parks. It has authorized an enormous land grab that will turn our parks into cloistered preserves where the public is not invited." (Ed Kim, president of the International Snowmobile Manufacturers Association, commenting on a National Park Service proposal to ban snowmobiles from national parks)

Remember:

Rational inquiry is central to philosophy. This is a book about environmental philosophy. Therfore . . .

CHAPTER 3

The Human–Nature Relation

"The Congress finds and declares that:

(1) various species of fish, wildlife, and plants in the United States have been rendered extinct as a consequence of economic growth and development untempered by adequate concern and conservation;

(2) other species of fish, wildlife, and plants have been so depleted in numbers that they are in danger or threatened with extinction;

(3) these species of fish, wildlife, and plants are of aesthetic, ecological, educational, historical, recreational, and scientific value to the Nation and its people . . ."

The Endangered Species Act

MODERN TIMES: ENDANGERED SPECIES ACT

So begins the Endangered Species Act of 1973, a federal regulation intended "to provide a means whereby ecosystems upon which endangered species and threatened species depend may be conserved, [and] to provide a program for the conservation of such endangered species and threatened species." Upon signing the Endangered Species Act (ESA) in 1973, President Nixon said, "Nothing is more priceless and worthy of preservation than the rich array of animal life with which our country has been blessed. It is a many-faceted treasure, of value to scholars, scientists, and nature lovers alike, and it forms a vital part of the heritage we all share as Americans."

The act is the most comprehensive legislation for the preservation of endangered species ever enacted by any nation; it passed Congress by a nearly unanimous vote in 1973. Today, however, its support is much less certain. Some are calling for major revisions, even its elimination. Why would anyone be against a federal program designed to save endangered species? As with most things, the devil dwells in the details.

Species covered by the ESA are designated by the Secretary of the Interior as either "endangered" or "threatened" (i.e., soon to be endangered) "solely on the basis of the best scientific" data available. Political, economic, and other nonscientific considerations may play a role later in the administration of the ESA, but scientific integrity of the initial designation is paramount. Classifying a species as endangered or threatened can have enormous consequences, for it sets in motion the power of the federal government. This is where the controversy begins.

The ESA prohibits "taking" species so designated. What does that mean? According to the ESA "The term 'take' means to harass, harm, pursue, hunt, shoot, wound, kill, trap, capture, or collect, or to attempt to engage in any such conduct." This covers a lot of activities, not just direct injury to individuals of a listed species, but also indirect effects such as habitat alteration that might harass or harm species protected by the act. Land development and land use, such as construction, mining, logging, highway and bridge construction, farming, and so on, can harass or harm endangered species and so can be prohibited. It doesn't matter if the land on which it occurs is public or private. Business interests are affected, as are the activities of municipalities, state governments, private citizens, and the federal government itself.

Also, since the ESA is committed to protecting "any" endangered or threatened species "without regard to taxonomic classification," very obscure species of plants, mollusks, or worms, known to only a few biologists, can alter or even halt expensive development projects. Perhaps the most notorious case is the snail darter, a three-inch endangered fish that blocked completion of a $165 million dam being built by the Tennessee Valley Authority in 1978. The case went all the way to the U.S. Supreme Court, which sided with the fish, not because the Supreme Court is full of environmentalists, but because that is how the ESA was drafted by Congress. In response to public outcry surrounding the snail darter case, Congress amended the ESA to allow for a so-called "God Committee" to grant exemptions in special cases. The snail darter lost and the dam was built. Later, populations of snail darters were discovered elsewhere. Rather than endangered the species was quickly reclassified as threatened, a category below endangered. For the snail darter this is still not great, but better than extinct, as had been anticipated by the God Committee.

There are success stories. The American bald eagle was recently declared recovered; peregrine falcon, sea otter, and brown pelican may soon be removed from the list; increases in the American alligator population have been attributed to the ESA; and other species have been brought back from the brink of extinction. However, very few species have been taken off the list, while new ones continue to be added. Critics argue that this shows the ESA doesn't save species, though this seems an unfair charge, since protecting habitat and rebuilding populations takes time. Currently some 1,177 species are covered by the act. But as more and more species are added to the list (especially obscure and/or aesthetically unappealing ones), objections concerning the expense and limitation of human activity that results from species protection are bound to increase, and what political support the ESA currently has could weaken even further. Apparently, we like the idea of saving species, at least in the abstract, provided it costs nothing. If we have to make sacrifices—even relatively minimal ones—or forgo economic opportunities for a little-known and seemingly inconsequential species of grass or rodent or bug, many of us will be unwilling to do so. Recently, several species of salmon were declared endangered, affecting the entire Seattle metropolitan area—the first time such a heavily populated region will be called upon to alter its activities for the sake of an endangered species.

The future success of the ESA appears to lie in walking a fine line between protecting species (at least the most visible "poster child" species that attract public attention) and developing what is known as "habitat conservation plans" (HCP). Under such a plan, land use and development can go forward even if it "takes" from an endangered species, provided compensating preservation measures are implemented in exchange. It's a trade; a portion of an endangered species is allowed to be harmed in exchange for protection elsewhere. The hope is that this kind of negotiation will maintain political support for the ESA while protecting endangered species and the ecosystems upon which they depend. The worry is that HCPs will be poorly designed and ineffectively administered, thus greatly weakening preservation efforts.

Cast by its critics as the iron fist of federal bureaucracy running roughshod over the rights of individuals, the ESA is at least an attempt to temper and guide our interaction with nature. Whether it can succeed in its grand mission and whether we are willing to impose economic restrictions on ourselves for the sake of endangered species, only time will tell. Whatever its faults, the ESA is surely the noble legislative expression of a democratic society's commitment to the preservation of nature.

OUR RELATION TO THE NATURAL WORLD

What is our relation to the natural world and what ought it to be? The Endangered Species Act embodies a conception of what our relation ought to be, driven by the unfortunate necessity of how things are. Were we not in danger of forcing so many species into extinction, there would be no need for such legislation. For people living just several generations ago, such an act by Congress would have been virtually unthinkable, akin perhaps to legislation for use of the moon. How did we get to this point?

Our relation to the natural world is shaped by our attitudes and our attitudes are shaped by our beliefs, beliefs about what we are like and what the natural world is like. These are very large issues, but not impossibly large. The questions are eternal; every culture strives to deal with them in a way that provides insight and meaning to life. Such questions have long been the preoccupation of religion and philosophy, and though the answers vary, one question looms large: Are we made of the same stuff as the rest of nature, governed by the same principles that guide the rest of the world, or are we ultimately and essentially distinct from it? How we answer this question will have an enormous impact on our conception of ourselves and on our views regarding our relation to the world.

A powerful, well-developed tradition in Western thought holds we are fundamentally distinct from the natural world. The view stretches back at least as far as Plato some 500 years B.C., and probably goes back even further. The natural world, conceived as a world of matter, is regarded as a prison for the soul, which is the nonphysical essence of a person. In this view, we are essentially different from nature and superior to it. This thought comes to fruition in the Christian notion that we are made in the image of God. Since we are something like God, to understand our relation to the world we have first to understand God's relation to the world. Traditional Christian theology has it that God created the world. He is not identical to the world but stands apart from it; creator and created are distinct. Also, God is held to be superior to his creation. By definition, God is perfect. Since God transcends the world and we are something like God, then we too must transcend the world and, like God, are superior to it. For whatever inscrutable reason, God chose to put us here for a while, but this is not our real home. Our real home is with "our heavenly Father," with whom we one day hope to be united. Or so goes a familiar version of the story.

This "other-worldy account" of humanity is not just an article of religious faith. It has been defended on philosophical grounds. No one has done more to ground this conception of humanity than René Descartes (1596–1650). In one of the most brilliant works in all of philosophy, *Meditations on First Philosophy,* Descartes argues that you are not the very same thing as your body. You, according to Descartes, are essentially a mind, a consciousness, and that is not the same thing as a lump of matter. Descartes undertakes to show this by arguing that you could conceivably exist without your body. If this is possible (not actual, but merely possible), then you cannot be the very same thing as your body because if it is possible to have one thing without another, then they cannot be identical. How can Descartes argue this? Think about circumstances under which you might have the experiences you are currently having even if you are massively mistaken about them. What if, for example, you are dreaming right now? Is that possible? It might be a very realistic dream, but is there anything to which you can point that shows you that you could not be dreaming? If you *could* be dreaming at this very moment, then what you experience is not veridical. It sure seems like you are reading a book, but there is no book in front of you; you are asleep in bed.

By considering such unlikely but still conceivable possibilities, Descartes concludes, in his most famous line, "I think therefore I am." He means that the mere fact that I think—which for Descartes is any state of awareness—shows that I exist, for if I did not exist then I could not think. And this is true no matter what may be the case regarding my body. Even if I am dreaming right now and my body is asleep in bed so that none of what I see or touch is really there, the fact that I experience anything at all shows that I must exist. Perhaps I am hallucinating; it still follows that I exist. As long as things *seem* to me to be a certain way, irrespective of how they really are, I exist. And what if—and this is the big one—what if I am mistaken about the existence of my body? Just as amputees have phantom limb experiences, might I be having a phantom body experience? Even in this most extreme case, I exist nonetheless. According to Descartes, this means that it is at least *possible* for me to exist as a thinking self-aware consciousness without my body; if so, then I cannot be the same thing as my body. For if it is possible to have one thing without another, then they cannot be the same. This is an astonishing conclusion because if Descartes is right, then people are not material beings. And if the natural world is material, as Descartes thought, then we are distinct from it. The view that minds are fundamentally distinct from matter is called **dualism.**

But is the natural world entirely material, that is, made of atoms? Even if Descartes is right about a fundamental distinction between mind and matter (and this is by no means clear), we can still wonder about the extent of mind or consciousness throughout nature. Descartes was convinced that only people are conscious and nothing else is because only people use language. For him, linguistic ability is the only sure sign of mentality. That consciousness should be so restricted is implausible on evolutionary grounds since the properties of one species blend seamlessly with those to which it is related. This is true for wings and feet, and it should also be true for consciousness. Writing in the 17th century, Descartes did not have the insights of Darwin. But his view is hard to believe given the evidence of which he was fully aware. Many animals have bodily and behavioral similarities to human beings. Dogs, for example, seem to be fully conscious. We have the same grounds for thinking a dog is conscious as we do for thinking a nonlinguistic human being, such as a baby, is conscious.

So even if Descartes is right about a fundamental division between mind and matter, it is implausible to think that mind is restricted to human beings. The possibility of other centers of consciousness existing in nature beyond humanity has important moral implications. For if there are other conscious beings who are similar to us in certain respects, then we can ask how we ought to relate to them. We might even be dealing with other persons! As we shall see, there is a great temptation to turn nature into a person, or at least something person-like, as a way of envisioning moral obligations to nature.

The thought that there might be mentality in nature, hence no sharp division between us and nature, can be turned around. Perhaps there are no minds in nature, nor in us either, hence no sharp division between us and nature! In this view, we are made of matter through and through, just like the rest of the physical world. We do not have minds, in Descartes' sense of a non-physical center of conscious awareness, and neither does anything else. We would thus be part of the world, not somehow distinct from it, as Descartes and most of Western religion and philosophy have it. This view is very much a minority opinion in the history of thought because it must explain our mentality and all that comes with it—our freedom and rationality—in physical terms alone. This means that consciousness must somehow *be* (not caused by, but be) a neurochemical state of brains. If we are made of matter just like everything else that exists, then this is what it would have to come to.

The possibility that we are simply a complex form of life, in principle no different from any other natural entity, makes us uncomfortable. Apparently, our commitment to a scientific understanding of the natural world is fine, as long as we stick just to the natural world; people resist being understood in precisely the same terms as the rest of nature, governed by the same laws and subject to the same constraints. Think for a moment what such a view implies. If you are ultimately nothing but a material being, a being made of atoms just like everything else in nature, then your behavior is really just a result of atoms bumping into one another in accordance with causal laws that govern the rest of the world. You would not act because you freely chose to do so but because you were caused by prior physical conditions in your brain. Gone from such an account is human freedom in the sense that you could have done other than you did on any particular occasion. Our continuity with the rest of nature seems to threaten what is most distinctive about us, namely, our ability to rise above the physical world by acting freely. It is no wonder that the other-worldly account of humanity has had such appeal. Descartes' view—dualism—has been called "humanity's official view of itself," which, of course, is not at all the same as saying it's true.

Our relation to the natural world thus turns on how we conceive ourselves and how we conceive nature. We might see ourselves as utterly separate and distinct from our surroundings—made of a different stuff entirely. This is Descartes' view, one which is very much alive today. Alternatively, we might see ourselves as made of the same physical substance as the rest of nature and situated in the material world just as any other thing that exists. And we might try to split the difference, basically agreeing with Descartes that we are not wholly physical beings, but finding mentality in nature nonetheless. Which parts of nature contain minds is a separate issue, one for which there can be considerable controversy. It is easy enough to suppose the so-called higher mammals have minds, if we do. But does consciousness extend beyond that? On some views, the entire natural world is inspirited, that is, consists of minds associated with bodies just as we are minds associated with bodies. In such a view, our relation with nature would essentially be an extension of our relation with other persons, just a vastly expanded concept of who the persons are. Variations on this view have been held not only by ancient animists but, as we shall see, by some contemporary environmental thinkers as well.

THE READINGS

The readings for this section are organized around our relation to the natural world, which, as we have seen, involves us in questions about who we are and what the natural world is like. In addition to a short introductory paragraph at the beginning of each selection, I have asked questions that you should consider as you work through the material. These questions will alert you to significant concepts and arguments that appear in the essays and can serve as a guide to your reading. I have marked up the first essay to demonstrate how these questions will aid your comprehension. Questions for further discussion appear at the end of each selection. Comprehending the argument of a particular author is just the first step. We have to ask ourselves whether the arguments are good ones and what might be said by way of response, and, ultimately, whether we agree. As you progress through the material in this book, my hope is that you will become skilled in reading critically essays on environmental philosophy that are worthy of your close attention.

At the end of this chapter, and all subsequent chapters, is a set of exercises called *You Decide!* These are brief case studies about a range of environmental issues that call upon you to render an opinion—a reasoned opinion. *You Decide!* is an opportunity for you to employ some of the ideas in each chapter in practical decision making.

LYNN WHITE, JR.

The Historical Roots of Our Ecologic Crisis

Lynn White (1907–1987) was a prominent medieval historian. In this widely celebrated article, White argues that the mid-19th century marriage between science and technology—a union that has given us the power to affect nature in profound ways—has its roots in medieval ideas of our place in the cosmos. Christianity taught that we are special, made in the image of God, and since God transcends nature, we too transcend the natural world. Natural objects, though made by God, are not themselves inhabited by God and thus cannot be sacred. This is in sharp contrast to **animism,** the belief that God or the gods are actually *in* the natural world, not apart from it. As White claims, "By destroying pagan animism, Christianity made it possible to exploit nature in a mood of indifference to the feelings of natural objects."

CRITICAL READING QUESTIONS

1. What does White see as the basic difference in attitude between science and technology?
2. What evidence does White offer to show that technology is basically Western?
3. How did our attitude to nature become one of exploitation, according to White?
4. Why does White think the "ecological backlash" is not to be solved by more science and technology?
5. Why, according to White, were St. Francis' views heretical, and why does White propose St. Francis as a new patron saint for environmentalists?

As a beginning we should try to clarify our thinking by looking, in some historical depth, at the presuppositions that underlie modern technology and science. Science was traditionally aristocratic, speculative, intellectual in intent; technology was lower-class, empirical, action-oriented. The quite sudden fusion of these two, towards the middle of the 19th century, is surely related to the slightly prior and contemporary democratic revolutions which, by reducing social barriers, tended to assert a functional unity of brain and hand. Our ecologic crisis is the product of an emerging, entirely novel, democratic culture. The issue is whether a democratized world can survive its own implications. Presumably we cannot unless we rethink our axioms.

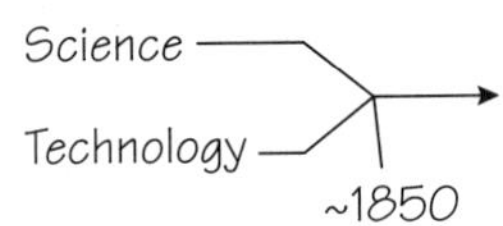

THE WESTERN TRADITIONS OF TECHNOLOGY AND SCIENCE

Basic difference between historical attitudes of science and technology. Science: Aristocratic intellectual Technology: Working class, empirical

One thing is so certain that it seems stupid to verbalize it: both modern technology and modern science are distinctively *occidental* [Western]. Our technology has absorbed elements from all over the world, notably from China, yet everywhere today, whether in Japan or in Nigeria, successful technology is Western. Our science is the heir to all the sciences of the past, especially perhaps to the work of the great Islamic scientists of the Middle Ages, who so often outdid the ancient Greeks in skill and perspicacity: al-Razin medicine, for example; or ibn-al-Haytham in optics; or Omar Khayyám in mathematics. Indeed, not a few works of such geniuses seem to have vanished in the original Arabic and to survive only in medieval Latin translations that helped to lay the foundations for later Western developments. Today, around the globe, all significant science is Western in style and method, whatever the pigmentation or language of the scientists.

Reasons for thinking technology is largely Western

A second pair of facts is less well recognized because they result from quite recent historical scholarship. The leadership of the West, both in technology and in science, is far older than the so-called scientific revolution of the seventeenth century or the so-called industrial revolution of the eighteenth century. These terms are in fact outmoded and obscure the true nature of what they try to describe—significant stages in two long and separate developments. By A.D. 1000 at the latest—and perhaps, feebly, as much as 200 years earlier—the West began to apply water power to industrial processes other than milling grain. This was followed in the late twelfth century by the harnessing of wind power. From simple beginnings, but with remarkable consistency of style, the West rapidly expanded its skills in the development of power machinery, laborsaving devices, and automation. Those who doubt should contemplate that most monumental achievement in the history of automation: the weight-driven mechanical clock, which appeared in two forms in the early fourteenth century. Not in craftsmanship but in basic technological capacity, the Latin West of the later Middle Ages far outstripped its elaborate, sophisticated, and esthetically magnificent sister cultures, Byzantium and Islam. In 1444 a great Greek ecclesiastic, Bessarion, who had gone to Italy, wrote a letter to a prince in Greece. He is amazed by the superiority of Western ships, arms, textiles, glass. But above all he is astonished by the spectacle of waterwheels sawing timbers and pumping the bellows of blast furnaces. Clearly, he had seen nothing of the sort in the Near East.

Reprinted Lynn White, "The Historical Roots of Our Ecological Crisis," *Science,* vol. 155, no. 3767, March 10, 1967, pp. 1203–7 with permission from American Association for the Advancement of Science.

By the end of the fifteenth century the technological superiority of Europe was such that its small, mutually hostile nations could spill out over all the rest of the world, conquering, looting, and colonizing. The symbol of this technological superiority is the fact that Portugal, one of the weakest states of the Occident, was able to become, and to remain for a century, mistress of the East Indies. And we must remember that the technology of Vasco da Gama and Albuquerque was built by pure empiricism, drawing remarkably little support or inspiration from science.

In the present-day vernacular understanding, modern science is supposed to have begun in 1543, when both Copernicus and Vesalius published their great works. It is no derogation of their accomplishments, however, to point out that such structures as the *Fabrica* and the *De revolutionibus* do not appear overnight. The distinctive Western tradition of science, in fact, began in the late eleventh century with a massive movement of translation of Arabic and Greek scientific works into Latin. A few notable books—Theophrastus', for example—escaped the West's avid new appetite for science, but within less than 200 years effectively the entire corpus of Greek and Muslim science was available in Latin, and was being eagerly read and criticized in the new European universities. Out of criticism arose new observation, speculation, and increasing distrust of ancient authorities. By the late thirteenth century Europe had seized global scientific leadership from the faltering hands of Islam. It would be as absurd to deny the profound originality of Newton, Galileo, or Copernicus as to deny that of the fourteenth-century scholastic scientists like Buridan or Oresme on whose work they built. Before the eleventh century, science scarcely existed in the Latin West, even in Roman times. From the eleventh century onward, the scientific sector of occidental culture has increased in a steady crescendo.

Since both our technological and our scientific movements got their start, acquired their character, and achieved world dominance in the Middle Ages, it would seem that we cannot understand their nature or their present impact upon ecology without examining fundamental medieval assumptions and developments.

Argument indicator!

MEDIEVAL VIEW OF MAN AND NATURE

Until recently, agriculture has been the chief occupation even in "advanced" societies; hence, any change in methods of tillage has much importance. Early plows, drawn by two oxen, did not normally turn the sod but merely scratched it. Thus, cross-plowing was needed and fields tended to be squarish. In the fairly light soils and semi-arid climates of the Near East and Mediterranean, this worked well. But such a plow was inappropriate to the wet climate and often sticky soils of northern Europe. By the latter part of the seventh century after Christ, however, following obscure beginnings, certain northern peasants were using an entirely new kind of plow, equipped with a vertical knife to cut the line of the furrow, a horizontal share to slice under the sod, and a moldboard to turn it over. The friction of this plow with the soil was so great that it normally required not two but eight oxen. It attacked the land with such violence that cross-plowing was not needed, and fields tended to be shaped in long strips.

In the days of the scratch-plow, fields were distributed generally in units capable of supporting a single family. Subsistence farming was the presupposition. But no peasant owned eight oxen: to use the new and more efficient plow, peasants pooled their oxen

Plow changed our relation to land—now have power to exploit

to form large plow-teams, originally receiving (it would appear) plowed strips in proportion to their contribution. Thus, distribution of land was based no longer on the needs of a family but, rather, on the capacity of a power machine to till the earth. Man's relation to the soil was profoundly changed. Formerly man had been part of nature; now he was the exploiter of nature. Nowhere else in the world did farmers develop any analogous agricultural implement. Is it coincidence that modern technology, with its ruthlessness toward nature, has so largely been produced by descendants of these peasants of northern Europe?

Link between Philosophy, Religion and Ecology

This same exploitive attitude appears slightly before A.D. 830 in Western illustrated calendars. In older calendars the months were shown as passive personifications. The new Frankish calendars, which set the style for the Middle Ages, are very different: they show men coercing the world around them—plowing, harvesting, chopping trees, butchering pigs. Man and nature are two things, and man is master.

These novelties seem to be in harmony with larger intellectual patterns. What people do about their ecology depends on what they think about themselves in relation to things around them. Human ecology is deeply conditioned by beliefs about our nature and destiny—that is, by religion. To Western eyes this is very evident in, say, India or Ceylon. It is equally true of ourselves and of our medieval ancestors.

Major claim →

[The victory of Christianity over paganism was the greatest psychic revolution in the history of our culture.] It has become fashionable today to say that, for better or worse, we live in "the post-Christian age." Certainly the forms of our thinking and language have largely ceased to be Christian, but to my eye the substance often remains amazingly akin to that of the past. Our daily habits of action, for example, are dominated by an implicit faith in perpetual progress which was unknown either to Greco-Roman antiquity or to the Orient. It is rooted in, and is indefensible apart from, Judeo-Christian teleology. The fact that communists share it merely helps to show what can be demonstrated on many other grounds: that Marxism, like Islam, is a Judeo-Christian heresy. We continue today to live, as we have lived for about 1,700 years, very largely in a context of Christian axioms.

Christian worldview infused throughout Western culture

What did Christianity tell people about their relations with the environment?

While many of the world's mythologies provide stories of creation, Greco-Roman mythology was singularly incoherent in this respect. Like Aristotle, the intellectuals of the ancient West denied that the visible world had had a beginning. Indeed, the idea of a beginning was impossible in the framework of their cyclical notion of time. In sharp contrast, Christianity intended from Judaism not only a concept of time as nonrepetitive and linear but also a striking story of creation. By gradual stages a loving and all-powerful God had created light and darkness, the heavenly bodies, the earth and all its plants, animals, birds, and fishes. Finally, God had created Adam and, as an afterthought, Eve, to keep man from being lonely. Man named all the animals, thus establishing his dominance over them. God planned all of this explicitly for man's benefit and rule: No item in the physical creation had any purpose save to serve man's purposes. And, although man's body is made of clay, he is not simply part of nature: He is made in God's image.

Image of God

Especially in its Western form, Christianity is the most anthropocentric religion the world has seen. As early as the second century both Tertullian and Saint Irenaeus of Lyons were insisting that when God shaped Adam he was foreshadowing the image of the Incarnate Christ, the Second Adam. Man shares, in great measure, God's transcendence of nature. Christianity, in absolute contrast to ancient paganism and Asia's reli-

We transcend nature

gions (except, perhaps, Zoroastrianism), not only established a dualism of man and nature but also insisted that it is God's will that man exploit nature for his proper ends.

Key idea: For Christian, nature not sacred—the gods not in the world

At the level of the common people this worked out in an interesting way. In antiquity every tree, every spring, every stream, every hill had its own *genius loci*, its guardian spirit. These spirits were accessible to men, but were very unlike men; centaurs, fauns, and mermaids show their ambivalence. Before one cut a tree, mined a mountain, or dammed a brook, it was important to placate the spirit in charge of that particular situation, and to keep it placated. By destroying pagan animism, Christianity made it possible to exploit nature in a mood of indifference to the feelings of natural objects.

It is often said that for animism the Church substituted the cult of saints. True; but the cult of saints is functionally quite different from animism. The saint is not *in* natural objects; he may have special shrines, but his citizenship is in heaven. Moreover, a saint is entirely a man; he can be approached in human terms. In addition to saints, Christianity of course also had angels and demons inherited from Judaism and perhaps, at one remove, from Zoroastrianism. But these were all as mobile as the saints themselves. The spirits *in* natural objects, which formerly had protected nature from man, evaporated. Man's effective monopoly on spirit in this world was confirmed, and the old inhibitions to the exploitation of nature crumbled.

When one speaks in such sweeping terms, a note of caution is in order. Christianity is a complex faith, and its consequences differ in differing contexts. What I have said may well apply to the medieval West, where in fact technology made spectacular advances. But the Greek East, a highly civilized realm of equal Christian devotion, seems to have produced no marked technological innovation after the late seventh century, when Greek fire was invented. The key to the contrast may perhaps be found in a difference in the tonality of piety and thought which students of comparative theology find between the Greek and the Latin churches. The Greeks believed that sin was intellectual blindness, and that salvation was found in illumination, orthodoxy—that is, clear thinking. The Latins, on the other hand, felt that sin was moral evil, and that salvation was to be found in right conduct. Eastern theology has been intellectualist. Western theology has been voluntarist. The Greek saint contemplates; the Western saint acts. The implications of Christianity for the conquest of nature would change more easily in the Western atmosphere.

The Christian dogma of creation, which is found in the first clause of all the Creeds, has another meaning for our comprehension of today's ecologic crisis. By revelation, God had given man the Bible, the Book of Scripture. But since God had made nature, nature also must reveal the divine mentality. The religious study of nature for the better understanding of God was known as natural theology. In the early church, and always in the Greek East, nature was conceived primarily as a symbolic system through which God speaks to men: the ant is a sermon to sluggards; rising flames are the symbol of the soul's aspiration. This view of nature was essentially artistic rather than scientific. While Byzantium preserved and copied great numbers of ancient Greek scientific texts, science as we conceive it could scarcely flourish in such an ambience.

Basic idea behind natural law ethics

However, in the Latin West by the early thirteenth century natural theology was following a very different bent. It was ceasing to be the decoding of the physical symbols of God's communication with man and was becoming the effort to understand God's mind by discovering how his creation operates. The rainbow was no longer simply a symbol of hope first sent to Noah after the Deluge: Robert Grosseteste, Friar Roger Bacon, and Theodoric of Freiberg produced startingly sophisticated work on the optics of the rainbow, but they did

Scientists study God by studying nature

it as a venture in religious understanding. From the thirteenth century onward, up to and including Leibnitz and Newton, every major scientist, in effect, explained his motivations in religious terms. Indeed, if Galileo had not been so expert an amateur theologian he would have got into far less trouble: the professionals resented his intrusion. And Newton seems to have regarded himself more as a theologian than as a scientist. It was not until the late eighteenth century that the hypothesis of God became unnecessary to many scientists.

It is often hard for the historian to judge, when men explain why they are doing what they want to do, whether they are offering real reasons or merely culturally acceptable reasons. The consistency with which scientists during the long formative centuries of Western science said that the task and the reward of the scientist was "to think God's thoughts after him" leads one to believe that this was their real motivation. If so, then modern Western science was cast in a matrix of Christian theology. The dynamism of religious devotion, shaped by the Judeo-Christian dogma of creation, gave it impetus.

AN ALTERNATIVE CHRISTIAN VIEW

We would seem to be headed toward conclusions unpalatable to many Christians. Since both *science* and *technology* are blessed words in our contemporary vocabulary, some may be happy at the notions, first, that, viewed historically, modern science is an extrapolation of natural theology and, second, that modern technology is at least partly to be explained as an occidental, voluntarist realization of the Christian dogma of man's transcendence of, and rightful mastery over, nature. But, as we now recognize, somewhat over a century ago, science and technology—hitherto quite separate activities—joined to give mankind powers which, to judge by many of the ecologic effects, are out of control. If so, Christianity bears a huge burden of guilt.

No technological fix B/C cause is religion

I personally doubt that disastrous ecologic backlash can be avoided simply by applying to our problems more science and more technology. Our science and technology have grown out of Christian attitudes toward man's relation to nature which are almost universally held not only by Christians and neo-Christians but also by those who fondly regard themselves as post-Christians. Despite Copernicus, all the cosmos rotates around our little globe. Despite Darwin, we are *not,* in our hearts, part of the natural process. We are superior to nature, contemptuous of it, willing to use it for our slightest whim. The newly elected governor of California, like myself a churchman, but less troubled than I, spoke for the Christian tradition when he said (as is alleged), "When you've seen one redwood tree, you've seen them all." To a Christian a tree can be no more than a physical fact. The whole concept of the sacred grove is alien to Christianity and to the ethos of the West. For nearly two millennia Christian missionaries have been chopping down sacred groves, which are idolatrous because they assume spirit in nature.

Right—we have not appreciated impact of Copernicus and Darwin

President Regan, then Governor of California

Nature not sacred—sacred is in heaven, not here on earth

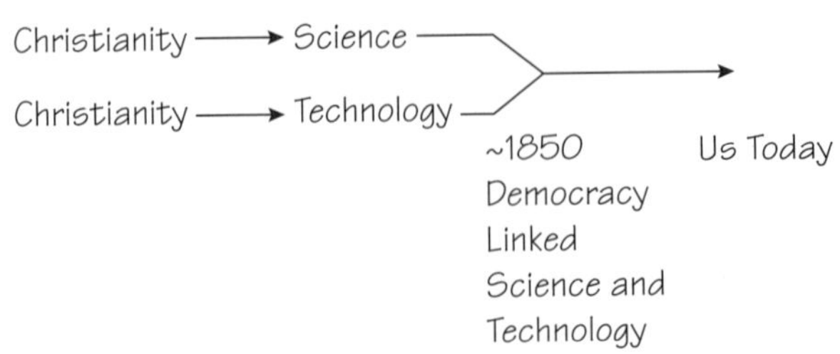

What we do about ecology depends on our ideas of the man–nature relationship. More science and more technology are not going to get us out of the present ecologic crisis until we find a new religion, or rethink our old one. The beatniks, who are the basic revolutionaries of our time, show a sound instinct in their affinity for Zen Buddhism, which conceives of the man–nature relationship as very nearly the mirror image of the Christian view. Zen, however, is as deeply conditioned by Asian history as Christianity is by the experience of the West, and I am dubious of its viability among us.

Again, no technology solution

Possibly we should ponder the greatest radical in Christian history since Christ: Saint Francis of Assisi. The prime miracle of Saint Francis is the fact that he did not end at the stake, as many of his left-wing followers did. He was so clearly heretical that a general of the Franciscan Order, Saint Bonaventura, a great and perceptive Christian, tried to suppress the early accounts of Franciscanism. The key to an understanding of Francis is his belief in the virtue of humility—not merely for the individual but for man as a species. Francis tried to depose man from his monarchy over creation and set up a democracy of all God's creatures. With him the ant is no longer simply a homily for the lazy, flames a sign of the thrust of the soul toward union with God; now they are Brother Ant and Sister Fire, praising the Creator in their own ways as Brother Man does in his.

Attempt to rethink old religion

Democracy of creation—no being higher or lower

Later commentators have said that Francis preached to the birds as a rebuke to men who would not listen. The records do not read so: He urged the little birds to praise God, and in spiritual ecstasy they flapped their wings and chirped rejoicing. Legends of saints, especially the Irish saints, had long told of their dealings with animals but always, I believe, to show their human dominance over creatures. With Francis it is different. The land around Gubbio in the Apennines was being ravaged by a fierce wolf. Saint Francis, says the legend, talked to the wolf and persuaded him of the error of his ways. The wolf repented, died in the odor of sanctity, and was buried in consecrated ground.

Old view:
God
|
Humanity
|
Nature

What Sir Steven Ruciman calls "the Franciscan doctrine of the animal soul" was quickly stamped out. Quite possibly it was in part inspired, consciously or unconsciously, by the belief in reincarnation held by the Cathar heretics who at that time teemed in Italy and southern France, and who presumably had got it originally from India. It is significant that at just the same moment, about 1200, traces of metempsychosis are found also in western Judaism, in the Provençal *Cabala*. But Francis held neither to transmigration of souls nor to pantheism. His view of nature and of man rested on a unique sort of panpsychism of all things animate and inanimate, designed for the glorification of their transcendent Creator, who, in the ultimate gesture of cosmic humility, assumed flesh, lay helpless in a manger, and hung dying on a scaffold.

I am not suggesting that many contemporary Americans who are concerned about our ecologic crisis will be either able or willing to counsel with wolves or exhort birds. However, the present increasing disruption of the global environment is the product of a dynamic technology and science which were originating in the Western medieval world against which Saint Francis was rebelling in so original a way. Their growth cannot be understood historically apart from distinctive attitudes toward nature which are deeply grounded in Christian dogma. The fact that most people do not think of these attitudes as Christian is irrelevant. No new set of basic values has been accepted in our society to displace those of Christianity. Hence we shall continue to have a worsening ecologic crisis until we reject the Christian axiom that nature has no reason for existence save to serve man.

Fundamental claim—growth of science & technology cannot be understood apart from Christianity

Conclusion indicator!

The greatest spiritual revolutionary in Western history, Saint Francis, proposed what he thought was an alternative Christian view of nature and man's relation to it: He tried to substitute the idea of the equality of all creatures, including man, for the idea of man's limitless rule of creation. He failed. Both our present science and our present technology are so tinctured with orthodox Christian arrogance toward nature that no solution for our ecologic crisis can be expected from them alone. Since the roots of our trouble are so largely religious, the remedy must also be essentially religious, whether we call it that or not. We must rethink and refeel our nature and destiny. The profoundly religious, but heretical, sense of primitive Franciscans for the spiritual autonomy of all parts of nature may point a direction. I propose Francis as a patron saint for ecologists.

'Since . . .' premise indicator

Key argument—we need to supply suppressed premise:

1. Cause of problem is religious
2. ____?____
3. Solution must be religious

Suppressed premise: Solution must be like cause.

Question: Should we accept the suppressed premise?

DISCUSSION QUESTIONS

1. Do you agree with White that "The victory of Christianity over paganism was the greatest psychic revolution in the history of our culture"?
2. In your view, is White correct to link our current environmental crisis to medieval, and specifically Christian, views of the human–nature relation?
3. White claims, "Since the roots of our trouble are so largely religious, the remedy must also be essentially religious, whether we call it that or not." What does he mean? Is he right?
4. What is the worldview of St. Francis of Assisi, as outlined by White? What sort of an environmental attitude would that entail? Is it possible for us to adopt such a view? Should we? Why, why not?
5. By castigating Christianity as the source of environmental despoliation, White has irritated many believers who respond by pointing out that God's giving us dominion over the earth doesn't mean that we can trash the place. Do you think that Christianity itself is the source of our current attitudes or how Christianity is interpreted?
6. Might there be other forces at work in the development of our environmental attitudes besides religion? Has White unfairly singled out just one of a number of possible influences, or is he correct to lay the majority of the blame on Christianity?

WALTER H. O'BRIANT

Man, Nature, and the History of Philosophy

Walter O'Briant was professor of philosophy at the University of Georgia. In "Man, Nature, and the History of Philosophy," O'Briant briefly sketches the history of philosophical thinking about nature, which, not surprisingly, has certain broad affinity to the religious traditions to which White drew attention. Most notably, according to O'Briant, the history of philosophy has vacillated uneasily between two conceptions of humanity: We are part of nature, and we are not part of nature. The view that we are part of nature is broadly scientific—we are of the same stuff as the rest of the world. The view that we are not essentially of the natural world is broadly religious—we are somehow special. According to O'Briant, our vacillation between these two views is the fundamental cause of our failure to deal adequately with the environment. Like White, O'Briant calls for the construction of a "new ethic," one which is more holistic in dealing with our legacy of Descartes'dualism between mind and body.

CRITICAL READING QUESTIONS

1. What are the two views of humanity, according to O'Briant, and how do they affect our conception of the human–nature relation?
2. How, according to O'Briant, is our status as beings ambiguous?
3. How is the "crisis of the environment" related to our conception of ourselves in O'Briant's view?
4. What remedy does O'Briant propose to our predicament?

My study of the history of Western philosophy indicates that there have been two quite different ways of viewing the relation between man and nature. These views have not always been explicitly formulated or even clearly distinguished from one another. Indeed, over the history of Western thought it has been usual for these two views to be so intertwined with one another that it becomes quite difficult for the interpreter of the thought of a given man or movement to delineate these views and determine their importance in relation to other views.

In this essay I propose to define these two views with particular attention to our Western tradition and the role which they have played in shaping our current notions about man and his relation to nature. I intend to show that a part of our inability to deal conceptually with what has come to be called "the crisis of the environment" is due to a failure to be clear and consistent about what we believe to be the nature of man and to understand fully the implications of these beliefs.

TWO VIEWS OF MAN AND NATURE

I propose to designate these two views as "man apart from nature" and "man a part of nature." The view that man is apart from nature is a corollary of the belief that man is a unique creature. Historically, those who hold this belief have maintained that man possesses a faculty which sets him apart from all other creatures. Man alone has a soul—or, more precisely,

Walter O'Briant, "Man, Nature and the History of Philosophy," reprinted with permission from Mrs. Blackstone.

a rational soul. Thus, man is different *in kind* from everything else in creation. It is noteworthy here that this characterization has been made in relation to the notions of creature, Creator, and creation, for in our religious tradition particularly the basis for man's uniqueness has been found in his relation to his Creator. The most important feature of this relation is that man was made in the image of God.

Now whatever specific interpretation we put upon this notion of *imago Dei,* it seems clear that it is an attempt to assert a degree of similarity between whatever it is which makes man man and his Creator. "We were made in His likeness." For some interpreters this has been a matter even of physical resemblance such as we find in Michelangelo's depiction of God giving life to Adam. For others, man is godlike in his ability to reason. But in any case man occupies a very special place. He belongs, as it were, to two worlds. He is a creature, and so is a natural man. Yet he is also made in the image of his Creator, and so is a supernatural man, one who in some way transcends the bounds of nature.

This special relation to his Creator means also that man has a special relation to the other creatures. He has dominion over them, signified in our tradition by the claim that Adam gave the names to all the other creatures. According to this view the other creatures were put here by the Creator for man's use and enjoyment.

This ambiguous status of man has been most often expressed in our tradition by the claim that, when a man dies, his body returns to the earth from whence it came and his soul—or some part of it—returns to the Creator. Thus the natural man, corruptible man, is mortal, but supernatural man, incorruptible man, is immortal. Such a view constitutes a rather explicit dualism: a man consists of two elements, a body and a soul, neither of which is reducible to or derivative from the other. The body is material; the soul, immaterial. And this dualistic view involves an additional ambiguity by leaving unsettled the answer to the question, What is man?

On the one hand, it has been maintained that man is composed of both a soul and a body, each having characteristics which fit it to be a *human* soul or a *human* body, as the case may be. But neither a body alone nor a soul alone can constitute a human being on this view. A man cannot be a disembodied spirit or an unensouled body. In the dance of life, on this view it "takes two to tango." Anything less must be either superhuman or subhuman. Man then is a natural being.

In contrast, there has been at least an equally strong tendency in our tradition to hold that man is essentially a soul, his body being an unnecessary and even obstructing adjunct. What makes us what we are is our soul. Our body is at best an earthen vessel which the soul occupies during its brief sojourn in this world; at worst the body is a tomb for the soul, preventing it from achieving its highest potentialities by weighing it down with the bodily appetites for the things of this world. Only when it is freed from bondage can the soul soar to the heights of which it is capable. Our life so far as this world is concerned must be one of constant vigilance lest we succumb to the demands of the body and thereby condemn our soul. Man then is a supernatural being who finds himself for the moment in a natural world—a world which cannot be his home.

Consequently, the question What is man? is open to two quite different answers. The proponents of the first view would say that man is composed of a soul and a body somehow constituting a unity, while the proponents of the second view would hold that man is a soul and his body plays no significant role in making him what he is. Strange as it might seem in view of our quite pronounced tendency to establish personal identity on the basis of bodily characteristics such as one's height, manner of speaking, or fingerprints, the latter view—that the body is nonessential—seems to have been the dominant one in our tradition.

This brings us to the second view—the view that man is a part of nature. For the advocates of this view, man is not unique—at least not in the sense that he possesses some special faculty which no other living thing possesses. Rather man is seen as one animal among many other animals from whom he differs, not in kind, but only in degree. His distinctiveness is not a matter of possessing a soul or some special kind of a soul which no other animal possesses; it is a matter of his possessing certain abilities to a higher—or lower—degree. Thus, for example, man is distinguished from the other animals, not by mere rationality, but by the degree to which he is capable of exercising this reason.

On this view, it is no "slap in the face" to say of a man that he behaves like an animal; he *is* an animal, and it would be paradoxical were he to behave in some other way. Man is an animal among his fellow animals. He has not been given "dominion" over them except in the sense in which any living thing possessing some relatively high-order function has "dominion" over other living things which possess that function to a lesser degree. Moreover, like all the other animals, man is mortal. He has his day—"three score years and ten"—and then perishes just as they do; though perhaps generally not so violently or miserably. "Ashes to ashes; dust to dust." His mortality is mitigated only to the extent that he may be remembered by his fellows or may have played some significant role in shaping the welfare of his society or species.

This view is quite clearly monistic. Man consists fundamentally of one sort of stuff, body, and this is the stuff out of which everything else in the universe is made. The world of nature is all there is. There is no supernatural realm, no soul which survives the death of the body, no spiritual Creator presiding over the natural world. Man is his own last, best hope. What is man? The proponents of this view would answer: one of the animals, distinctive in certain respects, but not unique. We find this view quite explicitly in the zoologist Desmond Morris's contention that were we to compare man with the so-called apes the only truly distinctive human feature would be the relative absence of body hair. Hence the title of Morris's book *The Naked Ape.* Quite literally, we and the apes are brothers under the skin, and in Morris's view it is our failure to recognize fully our animality which has cost us so dearly both individually and socially.

RELIGION AND SCIENCE

Despite the relatively clear distinctions between these two views of man and nature which have been outlined above and the quite different sets of corollary views which belong to each, we have tried in our tradition to hold on rather firmly to both of them without making the major revisions which would be requisite for resolving conflicts between these views. Moreover, each of these views has become so firmly embedded in a major element of our tradition that for many an attempt at revision would require either a major recasting of that element or its total rejection—perhaps without being able to find a suitable substitute. The two elements involved here are religion and science.

Our religious tradition—the Judeo-Christian tradition—has been dominated by the first view, the view that man is apart from nature. It has rather consistently held that this world is not our home, that our primary business—indeed our only business—is the salvation of our immortal souls, and that our animal nature is vile and contemptible. There is then a distinctively "otherworldly" character to this element of our tradition.

Our scientific tradition, in contrast, has—at least in more recent times—embraced the view that man is a part of nature and that comprehending the character and function of man is not fundamentally different from that of the proverbial white rat, the amoeba, or the rings of Saturn. Man's makeup may be a bit more complicated and his behavior relatively sophisticated, but he is at bottom explicable in the same terms as everything else in nature. The exclusion from the scientific element of such notions as soul and Creator has been reinforced by the scientist's insistence that all legitimate claims must be open to empirical investigation; it must be possible to see or taste or in some other way sense them. The consequence of this view has been to give a decidedly "this worldly" emphasis to the scientific element. The claims for a supernatural realm are either regarded as not legitimate concerns of the scientist or, more likely, dismissed as without foundation in fact.

We should not then be amiss to call our first view the religious view and our second the scientific view.

CARTESIANISM

These tendencies are clearly reflected in the thought of René Descartes whose philosophical views so dominated the early modern period that they became the commonsense views of succeeding centuries and have persisted relatively unchanged into our own time. With a brashness and optimism typical of the early modern period Descartes took upon himself the task of reconstituting philosophy so as to ensure a firm foundation upon which to erect a sound superstructure. A metaphysics firmly rooted in its method would yield as its fruit a sound mechanics, medicine, and morals. And the method which Descartes pursued was that of doubt—the refusal to give his assent to any proposition which seemed open to the least questioning.

The initial result of this method in Descartes's hands was to lay open the possibility of doubting the existence of the external world and even that of a benevolent God. The only thing of which Descartes could be initially assured was his own existence. His certainty of this lay in the dictum *cogito, ergo sum.* Consequently, in attempting to answer the question Who am I? Descartes characterized himself solely as "a thing which thinks."

Thus this phase of his thought embodies two of the most fundamental aspects of the religious view: (1) I am essentially a soul (since only a soul can think), and (2) the external world—which is material—is less real than my self—which is spiritual. There is also a third element, a radical subjectivism, which, though not prominent in our religious tradition until modern times, has come to assume an increasingly conspicuous role, particularly in the development of what is usually called "Protestantism"—a view which now ranges far beyond its original religious context.

But Descartes was not content to stop at this point, and the second phase of his thought resulted in a radically different position. Descartes was also convinced that what was so persistently and strongly impressed upon his senses, namely, the corporeal world, could not be ultimately unreal or illusory even though he might be misled in a particular instance about the character of some detail of that world. The influence of atomism and his own investigations in analytics and physics disposed him to believe that the method for understanding this world must be essentially mathematical.

In this second phase of his thought Descartes is much more the scientific man. He is committed to (1) the reality of an independent external world (corporeal substance in particular) and (2) its comprehension by quantization. The opposing commitments which shaped Descartes's philosophy have continued to pull at us. In particular this vacillation has prevented us from adopting a consistent, adequate attitude toward ourselves and our world.

To the extent that we are religious men we have been willing to divide the furniture of the universe into two kinds: the furniture of earth, which is material, inert, and corruptible, and the furniture of heaven, which is spiritual, living, and incorruptible. Man as a creature little lower than the angels has a foot in both worlds; he is lord of the earth, and it is intended for his use as he makes his journey through this land of cares and temptations on his way to his true home.

This careless attitude toward his environment has been reinforced by what we may call a frontier attitude—the notion that whenever our surroundings are depleted of the elements needed for our mode of life there will always be virgin territory open for our expropriation and exploitation. Just as we tend to see ourselves as exempt from the fate which has befallen other creatures in the course of natural history, so we also regard our present and future as free from the consequences of our past misbehavior. Our God shall save us from our sins, and we shall ultimately be transported to glory to live forever in comfort and ease.

To the extent that we are scientific men we have come to view everything as ultimately reducible to atoms in motion, the interactions of which are describable in terms of physical laws which hold with absolute certainty. Any uncertainty is due to our observational or experimental limitations, not to some indeterminacy about behavior at the atomic and subatomic level. Man like everything else is explicable in terms of collocations of atoms following inexorable laws. There is no place here for such notions as "soul." Witness how psychology—literally, the study of the *psyche*—has turned increasingly toward the view that its proper sphere of study is overt human and animal behavior. The treatment of mental illness is now seen largely as a matter of manipulating the processes of a physical organ, the brain, and its associated systems by drugs or surgery, not the attempt to treat some nonphysical entity called "the mind." One of the most basic assumptions of contemporary science is that results obtained from experiments with the so-called lower animals are applicable to man also with the only changes in applicability being those of degree, not of kind.

As religious men, we have thought of the universe as embodying certain moral and aesthetic values and as being ultimately friendly and supportive toward man because we live under the watchful and loving care of a fatherly Creator. But as scientific men, we see the universe as morally and aesthetically neutral. Whatever morality and beauty we see is solely in the eye of the beholder. Likewise, the universe is neither supportive nor hostile as far as man is concerned; it is simply neutral. Whatever Creator there might once have been has now retired from the scene, and the universe is left to operate according to its laws. Miracles simply do not happen.

Thus we find ourselves with two world views which involve quite different sorts of beliefs and commitments. The religious man is ill at ease with the scientific man, and the result is that most of us suffer from a split personality. We have attempted to reduce the conflict between these different views by compartmentalizing them. For some six days of the week we are scientific men, accepting with little misgiving the presuppositions and ramifications of the atomic theory and indeed rejoicing in the devices which the resulting technology has made available for our comfort and amusement. On perhaps one day of the week we are religious again, reaffirming our belief in the existence of a spiritual realm where we find forgiveness for our iniquity and healing for our diseases. But of course the compartmentalization does not work. The rationale for some of our actions is based upon one view; the rationale for others upon the second view. And the disconsonance of these actions soon becomes obvious.

The crisis of the environment is just one aspect of the vastly more pervasive crisis of our culture—our failure to deal promptly, efficiently, and effectively with this dichotomy. Our religious views allowed us to be comfortable in raping and pillaging this earthly abode because we saw ourselves as not ultimately a part of this world and we failed to recognize that having dominion over the earth involved exercising responsible stewardship over it, while our scientific theories again and again proclaimed that we were part of nature and that whatever affected any aspect of nature would ultimately have its effect upon us. We are beginning to see—though only dimly—the terrible price which we shall have to pay for our past negligence. The injury inflicted upon our fellow creatures, especially those yet unborn, is beyond estimation. But we have not yet begun to deal constructively with the more fundamental problem of developing a consistent, adequate, and unambiguous view of man's relation to nature. Until we have done so, our attempts at resolution will be like the shuffling of the pieces of a puzzle which do not fit.

PHILOSOPHY, RELIGION, AND ECOLOGY

Our understanding of our world and of ourselves has been perverted by a faulty religion and philosophy which we have used as instruments to pay homage to our ego, and in tragic terms we are paying the price for our sin of pride. But a healthy religious and philosophical outlook can do much to help us remove the critical state in which we find ourselves and our environment. We need a Weltanschauung—a view of the whole—to guide us in establishing our priorities for action. Science and technology can give us the means, but religion and philosophy must delineate the ends.

The abandonment of atomistic individualism and the adoption of a holistic approach must be a task not only for the ecologist, but also for the philosopher, the theologian, indeed for everyman. This will not be accomplished easily or quickly, for the concepts which we need to overhaul are among the most fundamental of our culture. They are embedded in our laws and customs, our traditions and our institutions. We shall have to write a new ethic and reorient ourselves to a quite different world. A difficult task? Yes, and an imperative one. We really have no choice if man and nature are to thrive.

DISCUSSION QUESTIONS

1. Can you identify elements of the two views (humanity in nature, humanity apart from nature) in your own thinking? In what way are you *in* nature; in what way are you *apart* from nature?
2. What does it mean to be "made in the image of God"? Is it even true? Is this relevant to environmental matters?
3. Can you think of any arguments in support of Descartes' dualism? Can you think of any arguments against it? Is dualism true, in your view? Why, why not? Is dualism connected to environmental matters in the way O'Briant thinks?
4. In calling for a new vision, O'Briant claims, "Science and technology can give us the means, but religion and philosophy must delineate the ends." What does that mean? Do you agree? Are our environmental problems amenable to technological solutions? Explain. Recall from the earlier reading that White too claimed that more technology would not correct our relation to the natural world. Whether we acknowledge it or not, White thinks the change must be primarily religious. Do you agree?

JOHN PASSMORE

Attitudes to Nature

Australian philosopher John Passmore brings together some of the ideas developed at length in his influential book, *Man's Responsibility for Nature* in our reading "Attitudes to Nature." He begins by noting the "strangeness" of nature—strange in the sense that we cannot relate to it in the way we relate to a person. This may seem obvious, but Passmore reminds us that throughout much of history, nature was regarded as person-like; it could be moved by prayer, appeal, and entreaty. Nature-as-person was rejected by Western religion and science, and because (according to tradition) moral considerations apply only to persons and nature isn't a person, morality doesn't apply to it. Whereas White and O'Briant both called for a new ethical relation with nature, Passmore is less certain such a thing is possible and surely not for the reason that a different ethical outlook might alter our behavior. What we need, according to Passmore, is a satisfactory philosophy of nature, one which naturalizes us rather than spiritualizes nature.

CRITICAL READING QUESTIONS

1. What does Passmore mean by saying that nature is "strange"?
2. Why does Passmore think it is a mistake to trace our attitudes to nature to the Old Testament?
3. On Passmore's view, why is the issue of animal cruelty so significant for the human–nature relation?

---

4. What are the two leading intellectual traditions Passmore identifies for our relation to nature?
5. Why, according to Passmore, is a new ethical relation to nature not warranted?
6. What does Passmore mean by a "satisfactory philosophy of nature"?
7. How, according to Passmore, is the "last man" supposed to act? Why?
8. What objection does Passmore have to the "primitivist wing" of the environmental movement?

The question I am raising, then, is what our attitudes have been, and ought to be, to nature in this narrow sense of the word, in which it excludes both the human and the artificial. And more narrowly still, I shall be devoting most of my attention to our attitudes towards that part of nature which it lies within man's power to modify and, in particular, towards what Karl Barth calls 'the strange life of beasts and plants which lies around us', a life we can by our actions destroy.

In what respect is animal and plant life 'strange'? The attitudes of human beings to other human beings are themselves variable and complicated; our fellow human beings often act in ways which are, in our eyes, strange. But there are ways of dealing with human beings which fail us when we confront nature. We can argue with human beings, expostulate with them, try to alter their courses by remonstration or by entreaty. No doubt there are human beings of whom this is not true: the hopelessly insane. And just for that reason there has been a tendency to exclude them from humanity, in some societies as supernatural beings, in others as mere animals: old Bedlam was, indeed, a kind of zoo. The psychopath, immune to argument or entreaty, arouses in us a quite peculiar fear and horror. As for artefacts, these admittedly we cannot modify in the ways in which we modify human beings; it is pointless to entreat a building to move out of the way of our car. But we understand them as playing a designed part in a form of human behaviour which we might, in principle, attempt to modify; we look through them to their human makers. When this is not so, when we encounter what clearly seems to be an artefact but cannot guess in what way of life it played a part, we find it, like Stonehenge, 'uncanny'.

'Strange', as Karl Barth uses the word, connotes not only unfamiliar but foreign, alien. (The uneducated find any foreigner 'uncanny' because they cannot communicate with him—to get him to act they have to *push* him like a natural object rather than speak to him.) That nature is thus alien, men have, of course, by no means always recognized. During most of their history they have thought of natural processes as having intentions and as capable of being influenced exactly in the manner of human beings, by prayer and entreaty—not by way of an anthropomorphically conceived God but directly, immediately.

For the last two thousand years, however, the Graeco-Christian Western world has entirely rejected this conception of nature. At least, it has done so in its *official* science, technology, and philosophy: the ordinary countryman was harder to convince that natural processes cannot have intentions, even when they are not so much as animal. As late as the nineteenth century German foresters thought it only prudent to explain to a tree they were about to fell exactly why it had to be cut down. In Ibsen's *Wild Duck,* Old Ekdal is convinced that the forest will 'seek revenge' for having been too ruthlessly thinned; in Büchner's *Woyzeck* a countryman explains the drowning of a man in a river by telling his companion the river had been seeking a victim for a long time past. (Recall the familiar newspaper metaphor: a dangerous stretch of coast 'claims another victim'.)

Such attitudes, I believe, still exert an influence; in some of the recent ecological literature, the view that nature 'will have its revenge' on mankind for their misdeeds operates as something more than a metaphor, just as old ideas of pollution, sacrilege, hubris, are still, in such writings, potent concepts.

The fact remains that the Stoic-Christian tradition has insisted on the absolute uniqueness of man, a uniqueness particularly manifest, according to Christianity, in the fact that he alone, in Karl Barth's words, has been 'addressed by God' and can therefore be saved or damned but also, in the Stoic-Christian tradition as a whole, apparent in his capacity for rational communication. If nature, on that view, is not wholly strange, this is only because it has been created by God for men to use. Animals and plants can for that reason be assimilated, at least in certain respects, to the class of tools, dumb beasts but none the less obedient to men's will. Peter Lombard summed up the traditional Christian view in his *Sentences:* 'As man is made for the sake of God, namely that he may serve him, so is the world made for the sake of man, that it may serve him.' So although nature is 'alien' in so far as it is not rational, it is for orthodoxy neither hostile nor indifferent, appearances to the contrary notwithstanding. Every natural process exists either as an aid to men materially or as a spiritual guide, recalling, as flood or volcano or tempest, their corrupt state.

In this doctrine, which they trace back to the Old Testament, the ecologically-minded critics of Western culture discern the roots of its destructiveness. This is a mistake on two accounts. First, that everything exists to serve man is certainly not the regular teaching of the Old Testament, which constantly insists that, in the words of the Book of Job, God 'causes it to rain on the earth, where no man is; on the wilderness, wherein there is no man; to satisfy the desolate and the waste ground; and to cause the bud of the tender herb to spring forth'. To Paul's rhetorical question: 'Doth God care for oxen?' an Old Testament Jew would have answered 'Yes, of course.' It was the Stoics who took the contrary view. And it is they, under the pretence that it was the Old Testament, who were followed by such influential Christian intellectuals as Origen. Secondly, the doctrine that 'everything is made for man' does not at once entail that man should go forth and transform the world. On the contrary, it was for centuries interpreted in a conservative fashion: God knows best what we need. To attempt to reshape what God has created is a form of presumption, of hubris. Sinful corrupt men ought not to attempt to reshape the world in their own image.

Yet there is this much truth in the ecological diagnosis: the view that everything exists to serve man encouraged the development of a particular way of looking at nature, not as something to respect, but rather as something to utilize. Nature is in no sense sacred; this was a point on which Christian theology and Greek cosmology agreed. God, no doubt, could make particular places or objects sacred by choosing to take up residence in them, as in Roman Christianity he made sacred the sacrificial bread and wine. But no natural object was sacred in itself; there was no risk of sacrilege in felling a tree, or killing an animal. When Bacon set up as his ideal the transformation of nature—or, more accurately, the re-creation of the Garden of Eden—he had to fight the view that man was too corrupt to undertake any such task but not the view that nature was too sacred to be touched. It was man, he pointed out, whom God made in his own image, not nature.

Associated with the Christian concept of nature was a particular ethical thesis: that no moral considerations bear upon man's relationship to natural objects, except where they happen to be someone else's property or except where to treat them cruelly or destructively might encourage corresponding attitudes towards other human beings. This thesis the Stoics had strongly maintained and it was no less warmly advocated by Augustine. Jesus, Augustine argues, drove the devils into swine—innocent though the swine were of any crime—instead of destroying them, as a lesson to men that they may do as they like with animals. Not even cruelty to animals, so Aquinas tells us, is wrong in itself. 'If any passage in Holy Scripture seems to forbid us to be cruel to brute animals that is either . . . lest through being cruel to animals one becomes cruel to human beings or because injury to animals leads to the temporal hurt of man.' In other words, cruelty to animals is wrong only in virtue of its effects on human beings, as Kant, in this same tradition, still maintained in the final decades of the eighteenth century. And what is true of cruelty to animals applies, on this view, even more obviously to our dealings with other members of the non-human world. Only in Jewish, or Jewish-inspired, speculation, was the opposite view at all widespread. The Talmud in several places advocates a more considerate attitude to nature and when Kant reaffirms the traditional position it is in opposition to Baumgarten, who had on this question followed the Talmud.

The question whether it is intrinsically wrong to be cruel to animals has an importance much greater than at first sight appears: it is precisely for that reason that philosophers like Kant, humane though they certainly were, insist that cruelty to animals is wrong only on the—in fact very dubious—empirical hypothesis that it encourages cruelty to human beings. For if cruelty to animals is intrinsically wrong, then it is *not* morally indifferent how men behave towards nature; in at least one case—and then perhaps in others—man's relationship with nature ought to be governed by moral considerations which are not reducible to a concern for purely human interests, to a duty either to others or, as Kant thought, to oneself.

There is one simple and decisive way of denying that it is wrong unnecessarily to cause suffering to animals, namely by denying that animals can in fact suffer. This is the step Descartes took. The philosophy of Descartes represents, in certain respects, the culmination of the tendency of Graeco-Christian thought to differentiate man from his fellow-animals. For Descartes denies that animals can so much as feel, let alone exercise intelligence. (One is forcibly reminded at this point of the Ciceronian dictum, to which he subscribes, that there is no doctrine so absurd but that some philosopher has held it.) All suffering, so his follower Malebranche tells us, is the result of Adam's sin: animals, as not implicated in that sin, cannot suffer. As a result of our actions animals do not *really* suffer, they only behave exactly as if they suffered—a doctrine that some of the Stoics had also managed to believe. So it is not only wrong to suppose that we can reason with animals but wrong to suppose, even, that we can sympathize with them. It is true that this conclusion was reached at the cost of placing the human body itself within nature, as something not sacred; what was left outside nature was only consciousness. Yet at the same time the human body was for Descartes unique in being in some way 'united' with consciousness; the human person, conjoining mind and body, could thus be set in total opposition to the non-human world it encounters.

So the Cartesian dualism could be used, and was used, to justify the view that, in his relationships with nature, man was not subject to any moral curbs. Yet at the same time Descartes broke this doctrine loose from its historical association with the view that everything is made for man's use—a view he characterized as 'childish and absurd'. It was, he thought, *obvious* that 'an infinitude of things exist, or did exist, which have never been beheld or comprehended by any man and which have never been of any use to him'. No doubt, man could in fact make use of what he found in nature, and he ought indeed to do so, but nature did not exist as something ready-made for him. Effectively to use it, he had first to transform it. One is not surprised, then, to find Descartes proclaiming that it is man's task 'to make himself master and possessor of nature': the proper attitude to the world, in his eyes, is exploitative. The paradigmatic case of a material substance is, for Descartes, a piece of wax, the traditional symbol of malleability.

Of course, this attitude to nature has always had its critics. Poets like Blake protested against it; painting, before painters, too, were beguiled into pure geometry, drew attention, sensually, to the forms and colours in the world around us. Biologists like John Ray emphasized against Descartes the importance of the multiplicity and diversity of forms of life. But the mainstream of science has been Cartesian–Platonic.

Philosophers, however, were generally unhappy with Cartesian dualism, for reasons which practising scientists found, and still find, it difficult to understand. Descartes, so philosophers argued, had separated consciousness from nature so absolutely that the two could no longer be brought into any relationship with one another. In general, if in very different ways, they reacted against Descartes by trying to maintain that nature was a great deal more human-like than Descartes had been prepared to admit. But they did so, in many cases, at the cost of denying to nature a wholly independent existence, or, at best, by treating independent nature as a sort of 'thing in itself', not as the nature we encounter and try to deal with in our everyday life.

Associated with this attitude to nature is a depreciation of natural beauty as vastly inferior to works of art: the feeling one finds in classical literature and which is still enunciated by Hegel that nature deserves appreciation only when it has been transformed into a farm, a garden, and so has lost its wildness, its strangeness. It was a common theme in Christian thought that the world had been created a perfect globe; nature as we now see it with its mountains and its valleys is a dismal ruin, a melancholy reminder of Adam's sin. Malebranche regretted that nature contains shapes other than the regular solids; the seventeenth-century formal gardener, in the most Augustinian of centuries, did his best to convert nature into such shapes with his pyramidal trees and cubic hedges. The less geometrically-minded Hegelians were no less confident that nature was as it ought to be only when man had transformed it, converting wildernesses into tamed landscapes. Herbert Spencer saw the human task as the conversion of the world into one vast garden.

The two leading traditions in modern Western thought, then, can be put thus: the first, Cartesian in inspiration, that matter is inert, passive, that man's relationship to it is that of an absolute despot, reshaping, reforming, what has in it no inherent powers of resistance, any sort of agency; the second, Hegelian, that nature exists only *in potentia,* as something which it is man's task to help to actualize through art, science, philosophy, technology, converting it into something human, something in which he can feel thoroughly 'at home', in no sense strange or alien to him, a mirror in which he can see his own face. Man, on this second view, *completes* the universe not simply by living in it, as the Genesis myth suggests, but by actually helping to make it.

It is easy to see from this brief historical excursus why the ecological critics of Western civilization are now pleading for a new religion, a new ethics, a new aesthetics, a new metaphysics. One could readily imagine a sardonic history of Western philosophy which would depict it as a long attempt to allay men's fears, their insecurities, by persuading them that natural processes do not represent any real threat, either because they are completely malleable to human pressures, or because men are ultimately safe in a universe designed to secure their interests—an enterprise which issued in wilder and wilder absurdities in a desperate attempt to deny the obvious facts. This would not be a wholly accurate history of philosophy; even phenomenalism has its merits as the *reductio ad absurdum* of the plausible-looking theory of perception. Philosophy, as we have already suggested, had good reasons for rejecting the Cartesian dualism even if its reasons are less good for replacing it with a new version of anthropocentrism. At the same time, to think of philosophy thus is not an entirely monstrous interpretation; it is quite understandable that philosophy should look like an apologia for anthropocentrism to those who now so urgently emphasize man's responsibility for nature. Western metaphysics and Western ethics have certainly done nothing to discourage, have gone a great deal to encourage, the ruthless exploitation of nature, whether they have seen in that exploitation the rightful manipulation of a nature which is wax in man's hands or the humanizing of it in a manner which somehow accords with nature's real interests.

As philosophers, of course, we cannot merely acquiesce in the demand for a new metaphysics or a new ethics on the simple ground that the widespread acceptance of the older metaphysics, the older ethics, has encouraged the exploitation of nature—any more than a biologist would acquiesce in the demand for a new biology if that demand were grounded merely on the fact, or alleged fact, that men would be less inclined to act in ecologically destructive ways if they were persuaded that all living things possessed a developed brain. The philosopher is unlikely to be at all satisfied, in particular, with the demand of the primitivist wing of the ecological movement that he should encourage man to revert to the belief that nature is sacred. We are in fact *right* in condemning as superstitious the belief that trees, rivers, volcanoes, can be swayed by arguments; we are *right* in believing that we have found in science ways of understanding their behaviour; we are *right* in regarding civilization as important and thus far in attempting to transform nature. It is not by abandoning our hard-won tradition of rationality that we shall save ourselves.

We can, however, properly ask ourselves what general conditions any philosophy of nature must fulfil if it is to do justice to the scientific themes of the ecological movement, as distinct from its reactionary, mystical overtones. Any satisfactory philosophy of nature, we can then say, must recognize:

1. That natural processes go on in their own way, in a manner indifferent to human interests and by no means incompatible with man's total disappearance from the face of the earth.

2. When men act on nature, they do not simply modify a particular quality of a particular substance. What they do, rather, is to interact with a system of interactions, setting in process new interactions. Just for that reason, there is always a risk that their actions will have consequences which they did not predict.

3. In our attempt to understand nature the discovery of physics-type general laws is often of very limited importance. The complaint that biology and sociology are inferior because they know no such laws can be reversed, formulated as an argument against an undue emphasis on a Platonic-Cartesian analysis of 'understanding'. When it comes to understanding either biological or social structures, we can then say, what is important is a detailed understanding of very specific circumstances rather than a knowledge of high-level functional relationships. The 'laws' involved are often trite and ill-formulated, serving only as boundaries to what is possible. Whales, to revert to my previous example, must, like every other animal, eat and breed; we can describe it, if we like, as a 'biological law' that every animal must ingest food and must have a way of reproducing itself. But these 'laws' leave almost everything of interest about whales still to be discovered.

One could put the general conditions I have laid down by saying that in an important sense the philosopher has to learn to live with the 'strangeness' of nature, with the fact that natural processes are entirely indifferent to our existence and welfare—not *positively* indifferent, of course, but *incapable* of caring about us—and are complex in a way that rules out the possibility of our wholly mastering and transforming them. So expressed, these conclusions sound so trite and obvious that one is almost ashamed to set them out. But, from what has already been said, it will be obvious that they have not been satisfied in most of the traditional philosophies of nature. To that degree it is true, I think, that we do need a 'new metaphysics' which is genuinely not anthropocentric and which takes change and complexity with the seriousness they deserve. It must certainly not think of natural processes either as being dependent upon man for their existence, as infinitely malleable, or as being so constructed as to guarantee the continued survival of human beings and their civilization.

Such a philosophy of nature, of course, would be by no means entirely new. Its foundations have been laid in the various forms of naturalism. Naturalistic philosophies, however, like the Darwinian biology which lends them support, often attempt to reduce the 'strangeness' of nature—even if they do this by naturalizing man rather than by spiritualizing nature. That way of using the word 'nature' which I have so far employed is, so many naturalistic philosophers would say, wholly misleading; we should think of 'nature' only as something of which man forms part, not alien to him because he is a full member of it.

What of the contention that the West now needs a new ethics, with responsibility for nature lying at its centre? This, too, is often carried further than I am prepared to follow it. Men need to recognize, it is then suggested, that they 'form a community' with plants, animals, the biosphere, and that every member of that community has rights—including the right to live and the right to be treated with respect. In opposition to any such doctrine, the Stoics long ago argued that civilization would be quite impossible, that indeed human beings could not even survive, if men were bound to act justly in relation to nature. Primitivists would reverse this argument; since civilization depends upon men acting unjustly towards nature, civilization ought, they would argue, to be abandoned. Men, so Porphyry for one maintained, ought to reduce their claims to the barest minimum, surviving, under these minimal circumstances, on nothing but the fruits which plants do not need for *their* survival.

To a not inconsiderable degree, it can be added, very familiar ethical principles are quite strong enough to justify action against ecological despoilers. We do not need the help of a 'new ethics' in order to justify our blaming those who make our rivers into sewers and our air unbreathable, who give birth to children in an over-populated world or—this is a little more disputable—who waste resources which posterity will need. Only where specifically human interests are not so obviously involved does the question of a 'new ethics' so much as arise. Even the preservation of wild species and of wildernesses can largely be defended in a familiar utilitarian fashion.

What has certainly to be dropped, nevertheless, is the Augustinian doctrine that in his dealings with nature man is simply not subject to moral censure, except where specifically human interests arise. Few moral philosophers would now accept that view in its original unrestricted form. It is, indeed, very striking with what unanimity they condemn the older doctrine that cruelty to animals is morally wrong only when it does direct harm to human beings. Their predecessors, they say, were guilty of moral blindness, a blindness with theological origins, in not seeing that it was wrong to cause animals unnecessarily to suffer. The question remains, however, whether moral philosophers are not still to some extent 'morally blind' in their attitudes to nature and especially to those parts of nature which are not sentient and therefore do not suffer.

Certainly, they—and we—have a tendency to restrict such condemnatory moral epithets as vandalism and philistinism to the destruction of property and indifference to works of art. On the face of it, however, the condemnation of vandalism is as applicable to those who, damage or destroy the natural as it is to those who damage or destroy artefacts. When, for example, Baumgarten condemns what he calls 'the spirit of destruction' this has as much application to the wilful destruction of natural objects as it does to the wilful destruction of property, or of things likely to be useful to our fellow human beings. The last man on earth would for that reason be blameable were he to end his days in an orgy of destruction, even though his actions could not adversely affect any other human being.

Similarly, a failure to appreciate the natural scene is as serious a human weakness as a failure to appreciate works of art. Once we fully free ourselves from the Augustinian doctrine that nature exists only as something to be used, not enjoyed, the extension of such moral notions as vandalism and philistinism to man's relationship with trees and landscapes will seem as obvious as the extension of the idea of cruelty of man's relationships with animals. It is the great importance of Romanticism that it partly saw this and encouraged us to *look* at nature, to see it otherwise than as a mere instrument. But we do not need to accept the Romantic identification of God with nature in order to accept this way of looking at the world. Indeed, the divinization of nature, even apart from the philosophical problems it raises, dangerously underestimates the *fragility* of so many natural processes and relationships, a fragility to which the ecological movement has drawn such forcible attention.

In general, if we can bring ourselves fully to admit the independence of nature, the fact that things go on in their own complex ways, we are likely to feel more respect for the ways in which they go on. We are prepared to contemplate them with admiration, to enjoy them sensuously, to study them in their complexity as distinct from looking for simple methods of manipulating them. The suggestion that we *cannot* do this, that, inevitably, so long as we think of nature as 'strange' we cannot, as Hegel thought, take any interest in it or feel any concern for it underestimates the degree to which we can overcome egoism and achieve disinterestedness. The emergence of new moral attitudes to nature is bound up, then, with the emergence of a more realistic philosophy of nature. That is the only adequate foundation for effective ecological concern.

DISCUSSION QUESTIONS

1. On what grounds does Passmore object to the sort of ethical reform suggested by White and O'Briant? Is he correct? What might ethical reform toward nature involve?
2. In what ways might accepting Passmore's three-point philosophy of nature alter our behavior toward the natural world? Should we accept his view? Why or why not?
3. Is Passmore right to reject the primitivist wing of the environmental movement? Is White a primitivist of the sort Passmore criticizes?
4. Explain the Cartesian and Hegelian strains of thought regarding the human–nature relation, according to Passmore. Can you detect elements of each in your own thinking about nature?

J. BAIRD CALLICOTT

Traditional American Indian and Western European Attitudes Toward Nature: An Overview

J. Baird Callicott, professor of philosophy at the University of South Texas and a prolific and influential writer in environmental philosophy, seeks to compare the two traditions mentioned in the title. He finds the wellspring of our attitudes toward nature in the very beginnings of Western science, in the ancient Greek concept of the atom. Atoms, by definition, are very tiny indivisible bits of matter (*a*—not, *tomos*—to cut). Since physicists today "cut" atoms, what we call atoms are obviously not what the ancient Greeks meant by the term—for them atoms are the ultimate constituents of matter. According to ancient Greek cosmologists, the world is made up of unimaginable zillions of these little inert pieces of stuff in various complex arrangements. This is our view! Science has filled in the details, but this is basically how we see it.

Pythagoras (ca. 550–500 B.C.) introduced into Western thought the idea that the soul is trapped in the body. The soul is pure, ethereal, other worldly; the body is base, convulsed by emotion, swept by desire, lust, and subject to decay and corruption. Plato, seemingly influenced by Pythagoras, held a similar revulsion to the world of atoms, though it was up to Descartes to give the "entrapped soul" view its most rigorous philosophical formulation. Our antipathy toward nature has a long and venerable legacy.

As explicated by Callicott, and to the extent that it is even possible to make such generalizations, many traditional Native Americans view nature as inspirited. This means, "Most American Indians lived in a world which was peopled not only by human persons, but by persons and personalities associated with all natural phenomena." If so, then dealing with nature is not just rearranging inert objects to suit our interests, for we are enmeshed in a wider community of kindred spirits.

CRITICAL READING QUESTIONS

1. How does Callicott describe ancient Greek cosmology and what relation does it have to contemporary scientific views?
2. Note the reference to Lynn White.
3. According to Callicottt, what does John Fire Lame Deer mean when he says stones are alive?
4. How does Callicott characterize the basic difference between a Western and a Native American attitude toward nature?

J Baird Callicott, "Traditional American Indian and Western European Attitudes Toward Nature: An Overview," *Environmental Ethics*, 4, 1982, pp. 293–318. Reprinted with permission from J. Baird Callicott.

In this paper I sketch (in broadest outline) the picture of nature endemic to two very different intellectual traditions: the familiar, globally dominant Western European civilization, on the one hand, and the presently beleaguered tribal cultures of the American Indians, on the other. I argue that the world view typical of American Indian peoples has included and supported an environmental ethic, while that of Europeans has encouraged human alienation from the natural environment and an exploitative practical relationship with it. I thus represent a romantic point of view; I argue that the North American "savages" were indeed more noble than "civilized" Europeans, at least in their outlook toward nature.

As the European style of thought was set by the Greeks of classical antiquity, I begin with them. I treat modern science, that is, modern European natural philosophy, as a continuation and extrapolation of certain concepts originating with the fifth and fourth century B.C. Greeks. Greek ideas about nature were remarkably rich and varied, but only some of these ideas, for historical reasons which cannot be explored in this discussion, inspired and informed modern natural philosophy. They became institutionalized in the modern Western world view. It is upon them, accordingly, that I especially focus.

Mythopoeic Greek cosmology had curious affinities with some of the central cosmological concepts of the American Indians. Sky and Earth (Uranus and Gaia) are represented by Hesiod in the *Theogony* as male and female parents (Father and Mother) of the first generation of gods and either directly or indirectly of all natural beings. Some Ionian Greeks in the city of Miletus apparently became disenchanted with traditional Greek mythology and embarked upon speculations of their own. Everything, they said, is water or air. Things change because of the struggle of the Hot with the Cold and the Wet with the Dry. The implicit question—what is the nature of that out of which all things come and into which all things are resolved?—proved to be both fascinating and fruitful. After about one hundred and fifty years of uninterrupted controversy, Leucippus and Democritus, with characteristic Ionian simplicity and force, brought this line of thought to a brilliant culmination in the atomic theory of matter. The atom was conceived by them to be an indestructible and internally changeless particle, "so small as to escape sensation." There are infinitely many of these. They have substance, that is they are solid or "full," and possess shape and relative size. All other qualities of things normally disclosed by perception exist, according to Democritus, only by "convention," not by "nature." In the terms of later philosophical jargon, characteristics of things such as flavor, odor, color, and sound were regarded as *secondary* qualities, the subjective effects of the primary qualities on the sensory patient. Complementary to the concept of the atom is the concept of the void—free, homogeneous, isotropic space. The atoms move haphazardly about in this space. Macroscopic objects are assemblages of atoms; they are wholes exactly equal to the sum of their parts. These undergo generation and destruction, which were conceived as the association and dissociation of the atomic parts. The atomists claimed to reduce all the phenomena of nature to this simple dichotomy: the "full" and the "empty," "thing" and "no-thing," the atom and space.

Thomas Kuhn succinctly comments that "early in the seventeenth century atomism experienced an immense revival . . . Atomism was firmly merged with Copernicanism as a fundamental tenet of the 'new philosophy' which directed the scientific imagination." The consolidated Newtonian world view included as one of its cornerstones the atomists' concept of free space, thinly occupied by moving particles or "corpuscles," as the early moderns called them. It was one of Newton's greatest achievements to supply a quantitative model of the regular motion of the putative material particles. These famous "laws of motion" made it possible to represent phenomena not only materially, but also mechanically.

That the *order* of nature can be successfully disclosed only by means of a quantitative description, a rational account in the most literal sense of that word, is itself, of course, an ideal which originated in sixth-century-B.C. Greece with Pythagoras. Pythagoras's insight had such tremendous scientific potential that it led Plato to eulogize it as Promethean, a veritable theft from the gods of the key to the secrets of the cosmos. It was cultivated and developed by the subsequent Pythagorean school and by Plato himself in the *Timaeus,* a work which enjoyed enormous popularity during the Renaissance. Modern philosophy of nature might be oversimply, but nonetheless not incorrectly, portrayed as a merger of the Pythagorean intuition that the structure of the world order is determined according to ratio, to quantitative proportions, and the Democritean ontology of void space (so very amenable to geometrical analysis) and material particles. The intellectual elegance and predictive power of the Newtonian natural philosophy resulted, as Kuhn suggests, in it becoming virtually institutionalized in the nascent European scientific community. Its actual and potential application to practical matters, to problems of engineering and tinkering, also made it a popular, working picture of nature, gladly and roundly embraced by all Europeans participating in enlightenment.

Paul Santmire characterized the modern European attitude toward nature as it took root in the American soil in the nineteenth century as follows:

> Nature is analogous to a machine; or in the more popular version nature is a machine. Nature is composed of hard, irreducible particles which have neither color nor smell nor taste . . . . Beauty and value in nature are in the eye of the beholder. Nature is the dead *res extensa,* perceived by the mind, which observes nature from a position of objective detachment. Nature in itself is basically a self-sufficient, self-enclosed complex of merely physical forces acting on colorless, tasteless, and odorless particles of hard, dead matter. That is the mechanical view of nature as it was popularly accepted in the circles of the educated [white Americans] in the nineteenth century.

Santmire's comments bring to our attention a complementary feature of the European world view of particular interest to our overall discussion. If no qualms were felt about picturing rivers and mountains, trees, and (among the legions of Cartesians) even animals as inert, material, mechanical "objects," the line was drawn at the human mind. Democritus and later Hobbes had attempted a thoroughgoing and self-consistent materialism, but this intrusion of matter into the very soul of man did not catch on—everything else, maybe, but not the human ego.

The conception of the soul as not only separate and distinct from the body, but as essentially alien to it (i.e., of an entirely different, antagonistic nature) was also first introduced into Western thought by Pythagoras. Pythagoras conceived the soul to be a fallen divinity, incarcerated in the physical world as retribution for some unspecified sin. The goal in life for the Pythagoreans was to earn the release of the soul from the physical world upon death and to reunite the soul with its proper (divine) companions. The Pythagoreans accomplished this by several methods: asceticism, ritual purification, and intellectual exercise, particularly in mathematics. This led Plato, who was more than passingly influenced by Pythagoras, to (half-) joke in the *Phaedo* that philosophy is the study of death, an exercise in the disentanglement of the soul from the body. The Pythagoreans and Plato indeed inverted the concepts of life and death. In the *Cratylus,* for example, Plato alleges that the word *body (sôma)* was derived from *tomb (sêma).* The body is thus the tomb of the soul as well as its place of imprisonment.

The Pythagorean–Platonic concept of the soul as immortal and otherworldly, essentially foreign to the hostile physical world, has profoundly influenced the European attitude toward nature. It was not only revived in a particularly extreme form by Descartes in the seventeenth century, it became popularized much earlier in Pauline Christianity. The essential self, the part of a person by means of which he or she perceives and thinks, and in which resides virtue or vice, is not of this world and has more in common with god(s) than with nature. If the natural world is the place of trial and temptation for the soul, if the body is the prison and the tomb of the soul, then nature must be despised as the source of all misery and corruption, a place of fear and loathing: "a joyless place where murder and vengeance dwell, and swarms of other fates—wasting diseases, putrefactions, and fluxes—roam in darkness over the meadow of doom."

So what attitude to nature does modern classical European natural philosophy convey? In sum, nature is an inert, material, and mechanical continuum exhaustively described by means of the arid formulae of pure mathematics. In relation to nature the human person is a lonely exile sojourning in a strange and hostile world, alien not only to his physical environment, but to his own body, both of which he is encouraged to fear and attempt to conquer. Add to this Cartesian picture the Judaic themes forthrightly set out in Genesis (which Lynn White, Jr., Ian McHarg, and others have so thoroughly criticized—themes of dominion of man over nature, of its subjugation and domestication, of the *imago Dei,* and so on) and we have a very volatile mixture of ingredients set to explode in an all-out war on nature, a war which in the twentieth century has very nearly been won. To victors, of course, belong the spoils!

The late John Fire Lame Deer, a reflective Sioux Indian, comments, straight to the point, in his biographical and philosophical narrative, *Lame Deer: Seeker of Visions,* that although the whites (i.e., members of the European cultural tradition) imagine earth, rocks, water, and wind to be dead, they nevertheless "are very much alive." In the previous section I tried to explain in what sense nature, as the *res extensa,* is conceived as "dead" in the mainstream of European natural thought. To say that rocks and rivers are dead is perhaps misleading since what is now dead once was alive. Rather in the usual European view of things such objects are considered inert. But what does Lame Deer mean when he says that they are "very much alive"?

He doesn't explain this provocative assertion as discursively as one might wish, but he provides examples, dozens of examples, of what he calls the "power" in various natural entities. According to Lame Deer, "Every man needs a stone. . . . You ask stones for aid to find things which are lost or missing. Stones can give warning of an enemy, of approaching misfortune." Butterflies, coyotes, grasshoppers, eagles, owls, deer, especially elk and bear all talk and possess and convey power. "You have to listen to all these creatures, listen with your mind. They have secrets to tell."

It would seem that for Lame Deer the "aliveness" of natural entities (including stones which to most Europeans are merely "material objects" and epitomize lifelessness) means that they have a share in the same consciousness that we human beings enjoy. Granted, animals and plants (if not stones and rivers) are recognized to be "alive" by conventional European conceptualization, but they lack awareness in a mode and degree comparable to human awareness. Among the Cartesians, as I mentioned earlier, even animal behavior was regarded as altogether automatic, resembling in every way the behavior of a machine. A somewhat more liberal and enlightened view allows that animals have a dim sort of consciousness, but get around largely by "instinct," a concept altogether lacking a clear definition and one very nearly as obscure as the notorious occult qualities (the "soporific virtues," and so on) of the Schoolmen. Of course, plants are regarded as, although alive, totally lacking in **sentience.** In any case, we hear that only human beings possess *self*-consciousness, that is, are aware that they are aware and can thus distinguish between themselves and everything else!

Every sophomore student of philosophy has learned, or should have, that solipsism is an impregnable philosophical position, and corollary to that, that every characterization of other minds—human as well as nonhuman—is a matter of conjecture. The Indian attitude, as represented by Lame Deer, apparently was based upon the consideration that since human beings have a physical body *and* an associated consciousness (conceptually hypostatized or reified as "spirit"), all other bodily things, animals, plants, and, yes, even stones, were also similar in this respect. Indeed, this strikes me as an eminently reasonable assumption. I can no more directly perceive another human being's consciousness than I can that of an animal or plant. I *assume* that another human being is conscious since he or she is perceptibly very like me (in other respects) and I am conscious. To anyone not hopelessly prejudiced by the metaphysical apartheid policy of Christianity and Western thought generally, human beings closely resemble in anatomy, physiology, and behavior other forms of life. The variety of organic forms themselves are clearly closely related, and the organic world, in turn, is continuous with the whole of nature. Virtually all things might be supposed, without the least strain upon credence, like ourselves, to be "alive," that is, conscious, aware, or possessed of spirit.

Lame Deer offers a brief, but most revealing and suggestive, metaphysical explanation:

> Nothing is so small and unimportant but it has a spirit given it by Wakan Tanka. Tunkan is what you might call a stone god, but he is also a part of the Great Spirit. The gods are separate beings, but they are all united in Wakan Tanka. It is hard to understand—something like the Holy Trinity. You can't explain it except by going back to the "circles within circles" idea, the spirit splitting itself up into stones, trees, tiny insects even, making them all *wakan* by his ever-presence. And in turn all these myriad of things which makes up the universe flowing back to their source, united in one Grandfather Spirit.

This Lakota panentheism presents a conception of the world which is, to be sure, dualistic, but it is important to emphasize that, unlike the Pythagorean-Platonic-Cartesian tradition, it is not an *antagonistic* dualism in which body and spirit are conceived in contrary terms and pitted against one another in a moral struggle. Further, and most importantly for my subsequent remarks, the pervasiveness of spirit in nature, a spirit *in everything* which is a splinter of the Great Spirit, facilitates a perception of the human and natural realms as unified and akin.

Consider, complementary to this pan-psychism, the basics of Siouan cosmogony. Black Elk rhetorically asks, "Is not the sky a father and the earth a mother, and are not all living things with feet or wings or roots their children?" Accordingly, Black Elk prays, "Give me the strength to walk the soft earth, a relative to all that is!" He speaks of the great natural kingdom as, simply, "green things," "the wings of the air," "the four-leggeds," and "the two-legged." Not only does everything have a spirit, in the last analysis all things are related together as members of one universal family, born of one father, the sky, the Great Spirit, and one mother, the Earth herself.

More is popularly known about the Sioux metaphysical vision than about those of most other American Indian peoples. The concept of the Great Spirit and of the Earth Mother and the family-like relatedness of all creatures seems, however, to have been very nearly a universal American Indian idea, and likewise the concept of a spiritual dimension or aspect to all natural things. N. Scott Momaday remarked, " 'The earth is our mother. The sky is our father.' This concept of nature, which is at the center of the Native American world view, is familiar to us all. But it may well be that we do not understand entirely what the concept is in its ethical and philosophical implications." And Ruth Underhill has written that "for the old time Indian, the world did not consist of inanimate materials. . . . It was alive, and everything in it could help or harm him."

The French fur traders and missionaries of the seventeenth century in the Great Lakes region were singularly impressed by the devotion to dreams of the savages with whom they lived. In 1648, Ragueneau speaking of the Huron, according to Kinietz, first suggested that dreams were "the language of the souls." This expression lacks precision, but I think it goes very much to the core of the phenomenon. Through dreams, and most dramatically through visions, one came into direct contact with the spirits of both human and nonhuman persons, as it were, naked of bodily vestments. In words somewhat reminiscent of Ragueneau's, Hallowell comments, "It is in dreams that the individual comes into direct communication with the *ati-so'kanak,* the powerful 'persons' of the other-than-human class." Given the animistic or pan-spiritualistic world view of the Indians, acute sensitivity and pragmatic response to dreaming makes perfectly good sense.

Dreams and waking experiences are sharply discriminated, but the theater of action disclosed in dreams and visions is continuous with and often the same as the ordinary world. In contrast to the psychologized contemporary Western view in which dreams are images of sorts (like afterimages) existing only "in the mind," the American Indian while dreaming experiences reality, often the same reality as in waking experience, in another form of consciousness, as it were, by means of another sensory modality.

As one lies asleep and experiences people and other animals, places, and so on, it is natural to suppose that one's spirit becomes temporarily dissociated from the body and moves about encountering other spirits. Or, as Hallowell says, "when a human being is asleep and dreaming his *otcatcakwin* (vital part, soul), which is the core of the self, may become detached from the body *(miyo).* Viewed by another human being, a person's body may be easily located and observed in space. But his vital part may be somewhere else." Dreaming indeed may be one element in the art of American Indian sorcery ("bear walking" among the Ojibwa). If the state of consciousness in dreams may be seized and controlled, and the phenomenal content of dreams volitionally directed, then the sorcerer may go where he wishes to spy upon his enemies or perhaps affect them in some malevolent way. It follows that dreams should have a higher degree of "truth" than ordinary waking experiences, since in the dream experience the person and everyone he meets is present in spirit, in essential self. This, notice, is precisely contrary to the European assumption that dreams are "false" or illusory and altogether private or subjective. For instance, in the Second Meditation, Descartes, casting around for an example of the highest absurdity, says that it is "as though I were to say 'I am awake now, and discern some truth; but I do not see it clearly enough; so I will set about going to sleep, so that my dreams may give me a truer and clearer picture of the fact.'" Yet this, in all seriousness, is precisely what the Indian does. The following episode from Hallowell's discussion may serve as illustration. A boy claimed that during a thunderstorm he saw a thunderbird. His elders were skeptical, since to see a thunderbird in such fashion, that is, with the waking eye, was almost unheard of. He was believed, however, when a man who had dreamed of the thunderbird was consulted and the boy's description was "*verified!*"

The Ojibwa, the Sioux, and, if we may safely generalize, most American Indians lived in a world which was peopled not only by human persons, but by persons and personalities associated with all natural phenomena. In one's practical dealings in such a world it is necessary to one's well-being and that of one's family and tribe to maintain good social relations not only with proximate human persons, one's immediate tribal neighbors, but also with the nonhuman persons abounding in the immediate environment. For example, Hallowell reports that among the Ojibwa "when bears were sought out in their dens in the spring they were addressed, asked to come out so that they could be killed, and an apology was offered to them."

In characterizing the American Indian attitude toward nature with an eye to its eventual comparison with ecological attitudes and conservation values and precepts I have tried to limit the discussion to concepts so fundamental and pervasive as to be capable of generalization. In sum, I have claimed that the typical traditional American Indian attitude was to regard all features of the environment as enspirited. These entities possessed a consciousness, reason, and volition no less intense and complete than a human being's. The Earth itself, the sky, the winds, rocks, streams, trees, insects, birds, and all other animals therefore had personalities and were thus as fully persons as other human beings. In dreams and visions the spirits of things were directly encountered and could become powerful allies to the dreamer or visionary. We may therefore say that the Indian's social circle, his community, included all the nonhuman natural entities in his locale as well as his fellow clansmen and tribesmen.

Now a most significant conceptual connection obtains in all cultures between the concept of a person, on the one hand, and certain behavioral restraints, on the other. Toward persons it is necessary, whether for genuinely ethical or purely prudential reasons, to act in a careful and circumspect manner. Among the Ojibwa, for example, according to Hallowell, "a moral distinction is drawn between the kind of conduct demanded by the primary necessities of securing a livelihood, or defending oneself against aggression, and unnecessary acts of cruelty. The moral values implied document the consistency of the principle of *mutual obligations* which is inherent in all interactions with 'persons' throughout the Ojibwa world."

The implicit overall metaphysic of American Indian cultures locates human beings in a larger *social,* as well as physical, environment. People belong not only to a human community, but to a community of all nature as well. Existence in this larger society, just as existence in a family and tribal context, places people in an environment in which reciprocal responsibilities and mutual obligations are taken for granted and assumed without question or reflection. Moreover, a person's basic cosmological representations in moments of meditation or cosmic reflection place him or her in a world all parts of which are united through ties of kinship. All creatures, be they elemental, green, finned, winged, or legged, are children of one father and one mother. One blood flows through all; one spirit has divided itself and enlivened all things with a consciousness that is essentially the same. The world around, though immense and overwhelmingly diversified and complex, is bound together through bonds of kinship, mutuality, and reciprocity. It is a world in which a person might feel at home, a relative to all that is, comfortable and secure, as one feels as a child in the midst of a large family.

DISCUSSION QUESTIONS

1. As presented by Callicott, do you think a Native American attitude toward nature is the kind of reformed view White was considering? Is such a Native American attitude toward nature true? Can worldviews be either true or false? How are Passmore's views relevant to Callicott's discussion?
2. In light of the fact that people can be ruthless toward one another, do you think personifying nature, as the Native Americans apparently did (according to Callicott), will alter environmental attitudes?
3. If the Native Americans feared the spirits with whom they dealt, would that constitute an ethical outlook, in your opinion? How might similar thoughts apply to a Western ethic? What does it mean to have an ethic at all?
4. Callicott thinks the attitude of the Native Americans is a genuine environmental ethic; is he right? Or is it merely anthropocentrism, since, according to Callicott, Native Americans conceived of nature as enspirited and hence just like themselves?

HOLMES ROLSTON

Duties to Endangered Species

Holmes Rolston is professor of philosophy at Colorado State University. In addition to contributing significantly to environmental philosophy, he is an accomplished naturalist. In "Duties to Endangered Species," Rolston examines our relationship to nature by considering what our attitude toward endangered species should be. He argues that over and above the usual anthropocentric reasons for species protection, such as those set out in the Endangered Species Act, we have a moral obligation to the form of life represented by a species, claiming that "the appropriate survival unit is the appropriate level of moral concern."

CRITICAL READING QUESTIONS

1. How does Rolston answer the charge that there cannot be direct duties to endangered species?
2. What concerns does Rolston express about the very concept of a species and how does he answer them?
3. What is it about species that human beings ought ultimately to respect, according to Rolston?

4. What does Rolston mean by "superkill" and how is that relevant to moral concern for species?
5. What examples does Rolston give to show that harm to individual members of a species can be beneficial to the species as a whole? What are these cases supposed to demonstrate about species?
6. Which process does Rolston identify as "near to ultimacy" as we can come in our relationship to the natural world?
7. Which ethic does Rolston claim to be endangered?

The usual way to approach a concern for species is to say that there are no duties directly to endangered species, only duties to other persons concerning species. From a utilitarian standpoint, summarized by Hampshire, the protection of nature and "the preservation of species are to be aimed at and commended only in so far as human beings are, or will be, emotionally and sentimentally interested." In an account based on rights, Feinberg reaches a similar conclusion. "We do have duties to protect threatened species, not duties to the species themselves as such, but rather duties to future human beings." Using traditional ethics to confront the novel threat of extinctions, we can reapply familiar duties to persons and see whether this is convincing. This line of argument can be impressive but seems to leave deeper obligations untouched.

Persons have a strong duty not to harm others and a weaker, though important, duty to help others. Arguing the threat of harm, the Ehrlichs maintain, in a blunt metaphor, that species are rivets in the Earthship in which humans are flying. Extinctions are maleficent rivet-popping. In this model, nonrivet species, if there are any, would have no value; humans desire only the diversity that prevents a crash. The care is not for particular species but, in a variant metaphor, for the sinking ark. To worry about a sinking ark seems a strange twist on the Noah story. Noah built the ark to preserve each species. In the Ehrlich/Myers account, the species-rivets are preserved to keep the ark from sinking! The reversed justification is revealing.

On the benefits side, species that are not rivets may prove resources. Thomas Eisner testified to Congress that only two percent of the flowering plants have been tested for alkaloids, which often have medical value. A National Science Foundation report advocated saving the Devil's Hole Pupfish, *Cyprinodon diabolis,* because it thrives in extremes and "can serve as useful biological models for future research on the human kidney—and on survival in a seemingly hostile environment." Myers further urges "conserving our global stock." At first this advice seems wise, yet later somewhat demeaning for humans to regard all other species as *stock.*

Destroying species is like tearing pages out of an unread book, written in a language humans hardly know how to read, about the place where they live. No sensible person would destroy the Rosetta Stone, and no self-respecting persons will destroy the mouse lemur, endangered in Madagascar and thought to be the nearest modern animal to the relatively unspecialized primates from which the human line evolved. Still, following this logic, humans do not have duties to the book, the stone, or the species, but to ourselves, duties of prudence and education. Humans need insight into the full text of ecosystem evolution. It is not endangered species but an endangered human future that is of concern. Such reasons are pragmatic and impressive. They are also moral, since persons are benefited or hurt. But are they exhaustive?

Let's be frank. A substantial number of endangered species have no resource value. Beggar's ticks, *Bidens* spp., with their stick-tight seeds, are a common nuisance through much of the U.S. One species, tidal shore beggar's tick, *B. bidentoides,*

---

which differs little in appearance from the others, is endangered. It seems unlikely to be a potential resource. As far as humans are concerned, its extinction might be good riddance.

We might say that humans ought to preserve for themselves an environment adequate to match their capacity to wonder. But this is to value the *experience* of wonder, rather than the *objects* of wonder. Valuing merely the experience seems to commit a fallacy of misplaced wonder, for speciation is itself among the wonderful things on Earth. Valuing speciation directly, however, seems to attach value to the evolutionary process, not merely to subjective experiences that arise when humans reflect over it.

We might say that humans of decent character will refrain from needless destruction of all kinds, including destruction of species. Vandals destroying art objects do not so much hurt statues as cheapen their own character. But is the American shame at destroying the passenger pigeon only a matter of self-respect? Or is it shame at our ignorant insensitivity to a form of life that (unlike a statue) had an intrinsic value that placed some claim on us?

The deeper problem with the anthropocentric rationale, beyond overstatement, is that its justifications are submoral and fundamentally exploitative even if subtly. This is not true, intraspecifically, among humans, when out of a sense of duty an individual defers to the values of fellows. But it is true interspecifically, since *Homo sapiens* treats all other species as rivets, resources, study materials, or entertainments. Ethics has always been about partners with entwined destinies. But it has never been very convincing when pleaded as enlightened self-interest (that one ought always to do what is one's intelligent self-interest), including class self-interest, even though in practice genuinely altruistic ethics often needs to be reinforced by self-interest. To value all other species only for human interest is like a nation's arguing all its foreign policy in terms of national interest. Neither seems fully moral.

SPECIFIC FORMS OF LIFE

There are many barriers to thinking of duties to species, however, and scientific ones precede ethical ones. It is difficult enough to argue from the fact that a species exists to the value judgment that a species ought to exist—what philosophers call an argument from *is* to *ought.* Matters grow worse if the concept of species is rotten to begin with. Perhaps the concept is arbitrary and conventional, a mapping device that is only theoretical. Perhaps it is unsatisfactory theoretically in an evolutionary ecosystem. Perhaps species do not exist. Duties to them would be as imaginary as duties to contour lines or to lines of latitude and longitude. Is there enough factual reality in species to base duty there?

Betula lenta uber, round-leaf birch, is known from only two locations on nearby Virginia creeks and differs from the common *B. lenta* only in having rounded leaf tips. For thirty years it was described as a subspecies or merely a mutation. But M. L. Fernald pronounced it a species, *B. uber,* and for forty years it has been considered one. High fences have been built around all known specimens. If a greater botanist were to redesignate it a subspecies, would this change in alleged facts affect our alleged duties? Ornithologists recently reassessed an endangered species, the Mexican duck, *Anas diazi,* and lumped it with the common mallard, *A. platyrhynchos,* as subspecies *diazi.* U.S. Fish and Wildlife authorities took if off the endangered species list partly as a result. Did a duty cease? Was there never one at all?

It is admittedly difficult to pinpoint precisely what a species is, and there may be no single, quintessential way to define species; a polythetic or polytypic gestalt of features may be required. All we need for this discussion, however, is that species be objectively there as living processes in the evolutionary ecosystem; the varied criteria for defining them (descent, reproductive isolation, morphology, gene pool) come together at least in providing evidence that species are really there. In this sense, species are dynamic natural kinds, if not corporate individuals. A species is a coherent, ongoing form of life expressed in organisms, encoded in gene flow, and shaped by the environment.

The claim that there are specific forms of life historically maintained in their environments over time does not seem arbitrary or fictitious at all but, rather, as certain as anything else we believe about the empirical world, even though at times scientists revise the theories and taxa with which they map these forms. Species are not so much like lines of latitude and longitude as like mountains and rivers, phenomena objectively there to be mapped. The edges of all these natural kinds will sometimes be fuzzy, to some extent discretionary. We can expect that one species will slide into another over evolutionary time. But it does not follow from the fact that speciation is sometimes in progress that species are merely made up, instead of found as evolutionary lines articulated into diverse forms, each with its more or less distinct integrity, breeding population, gene pool, and role in its ecosystem.

At this point, we can anticipate how there can be duties to species. What humans ought to respect are dynamic life forms preserved in historical lines, vital informational processes that persist genetically over millions of years, overleaping short-lived individuals. It is not *form* (species) as mere morphology, but the *formative* (speciating) process that humans ought to preserve, although the process cannot be preserved without its products. Nor should humans want to protect the labels they use, but the living process in the environment. Endangered "species" is a convenient and realistic way of tagging this process, but protection can be interpreted (as the Endangered Species Act permits) in terms of subspecies, variety, or other taxa or categories that point out the diverse forms of life.

Here the question about species, beyond individuals, is both revealing and challenging because it offers a biologically based counterexample to the focus on individuals—typically sentient and usually persons—so characteristic in Western ethics. In an evolutionary ecosystem, it is not mere individuality that counts, but the species is also significant because it is a dynamic life form maintained over time by an informed genetic flow. The individual represents (re-presents) a species in each new generation. It is a token of a type, and the type is more important than the token.

It is as logical to say that the individual is the species' way of propagating itself as to say that the embryo or egg is the individual's way of propagating itself. We can think of the cognitive processing as taking place not merely in the individual but in the gene pool. Genetically, though not neurally, a species over generations "learns" (discovers) pathways previously unknown. A form of life reforms itself, tracks its environment, and sometimes passes over to a new species. There is a specific grouping for a valued *ought*-to-be beyond what now *is* in any individual. Though species are not moral agents, a biological identity—a kind of value—is here defended. The dignity resides in the dynamic form; the individual inherits this, instantiates it, and passes it on. To borrow a metaphor from physics, life is both a particle (the individual) and a wave (the specific form).

A species lacks moral agency, reflective self-awareness, sentience, or organic individuality. So we may be tempted to say that specific-level processes cannot count morally. But each ongoing species defends a form of life, and these are on the whole good things, arising in a process out of which humans have evolved. All ethicists say that in *Homo sapiens* one species has appeared that not only exists but ought to exist. But why say this exclusively of a late-coming, highly developed form? Why not extend this duty more broadly to the other species (though perhaps not with equal intensity over them all, in view of varied levels of development)? These kinds defend their forms of life too. Only the human species contains moral agents, but perhaps conscience *ought not* be used to exempt every other form of life from consideration, with the resulting paradox that the single moral species acts only in its collective self-interest toward all the rest.

Extinction shuts down the generative processes. The wrong that humans are doing, or allowing to happen through carelessness, is stopping the historical flow in which the vitality of life is laid. Every extinction is an incremental decay in stopping life processes—no small thing. Every extinction is a kind of superkilling. It kills forms (*species*), beyond individuals. It kills "essences" beyond "existences," the "soul" as well as the "body." It kills collectively, not just distributively. It is not merely the loss of potential human information that is tragic, but the loss of biological information, present independently of instrumental human uses for it.

"Ought species *x* to exist?" is a single increment in the collective question, "Ought life on Earth to exist?" The answer to the question about one species is not always the same as the answer to the bigger question, but since life on Earth is an aggregate of many species, the two are sufficiently related that the burden of proof lies with those who wish deliberately to extinguish a species and simultaneously to care for life on Earth. To kill a species is to shut down a unique story; and, although all specific stories must eventually end, we seldom want unnatural ends. Humans ought not to play the role of murderers. The duty to species can be overriden, for example with pests or disease organisms. But a prima facie duty stands nevertheless.

One form of life has never endangered so many others. Never before has this level of question—superkilling by a superkiller—been faced. Humans have more understanding than ever of the speciating processes, more predictive power to foresee the intended and unintended results of their actions, and more power to reverse the undesirable consequences. The duties that such power and vision generate no longer attach simply to individuals or persons but are emerging duties to specific forms of life. If, in this world of uncertain moral convictions, it makes any sense to claim that one ought not to kill individuals without justification, it makes more sense to claim that one ought not to superkill the species, without superjustification.

INDIVIDUALS AND SPECIES

Many will be uncomfortable with this claim because their ethical theory does not allow duty to a collection. Feinberg writes, "A whole collection, as such, cannot have beliefs, expectations, wants, or desires . . . Individual elephants can have interests, but the species elephant cannot." Singer asserts, "Species as such are not conscious entities and so do not have interests above and beyond the interests of the individual animals that are members of the species." Regan maintains, "The rights view is a view about the moral rights of individuals. Species are not individuals, and the rights view does not recognize the moral rights of species to anything, including survival." Rescher says, "Moral obligation is thus always interest-oriented. But only individuals can be said to have interests; one only has moral obligations to particular individuals or particular groups thereof. Accordingly, the duty to save a species is not a matter of moral duty toward it, because moral duties are only oriented to individuals. A species as such is the wrong sort of target for a moral obligation."

Even those who recognize that organisms, nonsentient as well as sentient, can be benefited or harmed may see the good of a species as the sum of and reducible to the goods of individuals. The species is well off when and because its members are; species well-being is just aggregated individual well-being. The "interests of a species" constitute only a convenient device, something like a center of gravity in physics, for speaking of an aggregated focus of many contributing individual member units.

But duties to a species are not duties to a class or category, not to an aggregation of sentient interests, but to a lifeline. An ethic about species needs to see how the species *is* a bigger event than individual interests or sentience. Making this clearer can support the conviction that a species *ought* to continue.

Events can be good for the well-being of the species, considered collectively, although they are harmful if considered as distributed to individuals. This is one way to interpret what is often called a genetic "load," genes that somewhat reduce health, efficiency, or fertility in most individuals but introduce enough variation to permit improving the specific form. Less variation and better repetition in reproduction would, on average, benefit more individuals in any one next generation, since individuals would have less "load." But on a longer view, variation can confer stability in a changing world. A greater experimenting with individuals, although this typically makes individuals less fit and is a disadvantage from that perspective, benefits rare, lucky individuals selected in each generation with a resulting improvement in the species. Most individuals in any particular generation carry some (usually slightly) detrimental genes, but the variation is good for the species. Note that this does not imply species selection; selection perhaps operates only on individuals. But it does mean that we can distinguish between the goods of individuals and the larger good of the species.

Predation on individual elk conserves and improves the species *Cervus canadensis.* A forest fire harms individual aspen trees, but it helps *Populus tremuloides* because fire restarts forest succession without which the species would go extinct. Even the individuals that escape demise from external sources die of old age; their deaths, always to the disadvantage of those individuals, are a necessity for the species. A finite lifespan makes room for those replacements that enable development to occur, allowing the population to improve in fitness or adapt to a shifting environment. Without the "flawed" reproduction that permits variation, without a surplus of young, or predation and death, which all harm individuals, the species would soon go extinct in a changing environment, as all environments eventually are. The individual is a receptacle of the form, and the receptacles are broken while the form survives; but the form cannot otherwise survive.

When a biologist remarks that a breeding population of a rare species is dangerously low, what is the danger to? Individual members? Rather, the remark seems to imply a specific-level, point-of-no-return threat to the continuing of that form of life. No individual crosses the extinction threshold; the species does.

Reproduction is typically assumed to be a need of individuals, but since any particular individual can flourish somatically without reproducing at all, indeed may be put through duress and risk or spend much energy reproducing, by another logic we can interpret reproduction as the species keeping up its own kind by reenacting itself again and again, individual after individual. In this sense a female grizzly does not bear cubs to be healthy herself, any more than a woman needs children to be healthy. Rather, her cubs are *Ursus arctos,* threatened by nonbeing, re-creating itself by continuous performance. A species in reproduction defends its own kind from other species, and this seems to be some form of "caring."

Biologists have often and understandably focused on individuals, and some recent trends interpret biological processes from the perspective of genes. A consideration of species reminds us that many events can be interpreted at this level too. An organism runs a directed course through the environment, taking in materials, using them resourcefully discharging wastes. But this single, directed course is part of a bigger picture in which a species via individuals maintains its course over longer spans of time. Thinking this way, the life the individual has is something passing through the individual as much as something it intrinsically possesses. The individual is subordinate to the species, not the other way round. The genetic set, in which is coded the *telos,* is as evidently a "property" of the species as of the individual.

Biologists and linguists have learned to accept the concept of information in the genetic set without any subject who speaks or understands. Can ethicists learn to accept value in, and duty to, an informed process in which centered individuality or sentience is absent? Here events can be significant at the specific level, an additional consideration to whether they are beneficial to individuals. The species-in-environment is an interactive complex, a selective system where individuals are pawns on a chessboard. When human conduct endangers these specific games of life, duties may appear.

A species has no self. It is not a bounded singular. Each organism has its own centeredness, but there is no specific analogue to the nervous hookups or circulatory flows that characterize the organism. But, like the market in economics, an organized system does not have to have a controlling center to have identity. Having a biological identity reasserted genetically over time is as true of the species as of the individual. Individuals come and go; the marks of the species collectively remain much longer.

A consideration of species strains any ethic focused on individuals, much less on sentience or persons. But the result can be a biologically sounder ethic, though it revises what was formerly thought logically permissible or ethically binding. The species line is quite fundamental. It is more important to protect this integrity than to protect individuals. Defending a form of life, resisting death, regeneration that maintains a normative identity over time—all this is as true of species as of individuals. So what prevents duties arising at that level? The appropriate survival unit is the appropriate level of moral concern. . . .

What is valuable about species is not to be isolated in them for what they are in themselves. Rather, the dynamic account evaluates species as process, product, and instrument in the larger drama toward which humans have duties, reflected in duties in species. Whittaker finds that on continental scales and for most groups, "increase of species diversity . . . is a self-augmenting process without any evident limit." There is a tendency toward "species packing." Nature seems to produce as many species as it can, not merely enough to stabilize an ecosystem or only species that can directly or indirectly serve human needs. Humans ought not to inhibit this exuberant lust for kinds. That process, along with its product, is about as near to ultimacy as humans can come in their relationship with the natural world.

Several billion years worth of creative toil, several million species of teeming life, have been handed over to the care of this late-coming species in which mind has flowered and morals have emerged. Ought not those of this sole moral species do something less self-interested than to count all the produce of an evolutionary ecosystem as rivets in their spaceship, resources in their larder, laboratory materials, recreation for their ride? Such an attitude hardly seems biologically informed, much less ethically adequate. Its logic is too provincial for moral humanity. Or, in a biologist's term, it is ridiculously territorial. If true to their specific epithet, ought not *Homo sapiens* value this host of species as something with a claim to care in its own right?

AN ENDANGERED ETHIC?

The contemporary ethical systems seem misfits in the role most recently demanded of them. There is something overspecialized about an ethic, held by the dominant class of *Homo sapiens,* that regards the welfare of only one of several million species as an object of duty. If this requires a paradigm change about the sorts of things to which duty can attach, so much the worse for those ethics no longer functioning in, nor suited to, their changing environment. The anthropocentrism associated with them was fiction anyway. There is something Newtonian, not yet Einsteinian, besides something morally naive, about living in a reference frame where one species takes itself as absolute and values everything else relative to its utility.

DISCUSSION QUESTIONS

1. Do you agree with Rolston's rejection of anthropocentric rationale for species protection?
2. What does Rolston mean when he claims that ethics "has never been very convincing when pleaded as enlightened self-interest." Is he right? How is this relevant to the issue of species protection?
3. Do species actually exist? Is Rolston's answer to this question satisfactory?
4. On what basis should we respect "dynamic life forms"? Is Rolston ultimately committed to a version of natural law ethics?
5. What does the fact that we can allegedly help species by harming individuals show, according to Rolston? Do you agree?
6. Assess Rolston's pronouncement that "the appropriate survival unit is the appropriate level of moral concern." (Supply a suppressed premise needed to conclude that species are the appropriate objects of moral concern.) If Rolston is right, are individuals not at the appropriate level for moral concern?
7. Which process is "about as near to ultimacy as humans can become in their relationship with the natural world"? Does Rolston give any reasons why that process ought to be respected?

You Decide!

1. CAMPSITE LITTER

"Whew!" said Steve as he and Rick trudged with their heavy packs through the underbrush, "the campsite should be just ahead."

"Yeah, I'll bet we'll have the place to ourselves—no one else is going to go through all this effort," sputtered Rick through heavy breathing.

As they emerged into the clearing they noticed that the trail they had argued about earlier had indeed swung to the north and apparently led right to the campsite. They could have cut at least 45 minutes off their hike had they taken the trail; this meant the site was more accessible than they thought, but no one else was there. They would have the campsite to themselves.

As they surveyed the setting—and it really was an ideal site, on a nice bluff overlooking the lake, surrounded by tall trees—they quickly realized the campsite was a popular one. There were burned cans and melted plastic in the stone fire pit, cigarette butts and candy wrappers here and there, some broken glass, pieces of string scattered about, and a bent fork stuck into a log. "What jerks," exclaimed Steve. "All right, let's clean this place up."

"But what are we going to do with the stuff?" Rick asked.

"We're going to pack it out, of course," came Steve's response.

"No way—we didn't trash the place. Let's just toss it in the weeds over there. We won't see it."

"Nope," replied Steve, "we've got an obligation to bring at least some of this trash out."

Rick couldn't believe it. "Look," he continued, "you mean we are going to put extra weight in our packs and schlepp this crap out of here? And even if we do that, some jerks will come along right behind us and trash the place all over again."

"Hey, it's your conscience," retorted Steve sharply. "I'm taking some out, OK?"

"OK," said Rick glumly, "but I'm just going to hide what I pick up in the underbrush over there."

Discussion Questions

1. Do you think it is OK just to hide the litter or should it be packed out of the campsite?
2. What might be the basis of the obligation claimed by Steve to pack out at least some trash?
3. Is "out of sight, out of mind" an acceptable approach to trash in any situation?
4. Should we leave our surroundings better than we find them or just no worse?
5. Is campsite litter different from other kinds of litter?

2. URBAN SPRAWL

"Oh no," exclaimed Mary as she looked up from the local paper at her husband, Bill. "Listen to this. You know that parcel of land down by the inlet to the lake? Well, there are plans to develop it. Some 'big box' retail outlets are thinking of moving in and the city government is going along with it."

"So?" said Bill.

"So! So! Is that all you can say?" asked Mary. "I'm tired of the development going on around here. We have a nice community, but now all these big retail stores and corporations want to move in and that will change the character of the town. More land being turned into parking lots, more cars, more sprawl. Don't you care about those things?"

Mary could feel her anger rising. Bill didn't intend to irritate Mary, but when he responded by pointing out that having some big retailers within the city limits would contribute a lot of taxes she got even madder.

"Look, that's just the problem. People want more and more stuff. We don't need more Wal-Marts and Kmarts and Home Depots and whatever else is planning to come here. It's our demand for all the stuff that brings these companies to town."

"Right," said Bill, "and until we curb our consumer desires our town and places like it all across the nation will be attractive to big retail outlets. As I see it, the big outlets come because of us—we buy the stuff they sell. We can chase them out of the urban core with all kinds of ordinances, but then they just locate in nearby areas that are still pretty rural, and that's worse. There will be more roads built and satellite communities begin to form around these new economic centers. Housing, restaurants, small malls, fast-food places, bowling alleys, and all kinds of stuff will start to spring up. And those places all require water and sewer lines, gas and electric, and on and on. Now that's real urban sprawl. I say that the best thing is to concentrate the development in one area. It's coming one way or another, so we might as well try to manage it wisely. Rather than just opposing development within the town, let's cut our losses. Have the big outlets all bunched together on that piece of land near the inlet."

"Mmm," said Mary.

Discussion Questions

1. Are our consumer desires out of hand, as Mary seems to think?
2. Is Bill right to hold that large-scale retail development is inevitable?
3. What is the best way to manage development? Should we seek to pack businesses tightly together instead of allowing them to settle in less-expensive areas outside the urban core? Why?
4. Are you willing to pay higher retail costs for installing "big box" outlets in the urban core?

3. EXOTIC SPECIES—ZEBRA MUSSELS

As Tom winched his boat out of the water and onto the trailer he happened to run his hand along the hull. It felt oddly rough, like sandpaper. He knew this meant zebra mussel larvae. Zebra mussels arrived in the United States in the mid-1980s from the Black Sea and have become a nuisance in Midwestern rivers and lakes. They are an exotic species of mussel—a species not native to the area—having been introduced by ships discharging ballast water in the Great Lakes. Ships take on ballast to maintain trim as they load or unload cargo. Some 21 billion gallons of ballast water are released into U.S. harbors each year, water that often comes from foreign ports and can contain stowaway organisms. Concern about such biological hitchhiking has even prompted legislation requiring ships to exchange ballast water at sea which will much reduce the incidence of organisms from one region being introduced to another. How the U.S. Coast Guard could enforce such a requirement is a bureaucratic headache yet to be solved.

Tom was planning to drive to a nearby lake and launch his boat in a body of water that has not yet been invaded by zebra mussels. He knew that in all probability some of the larvae adhering to his boat hull would survive the journey and he would be responsible for spreading zebra mussels further. In reporting the emerging zebra mussel problem, the press had used inflammatory words such as *invasion* and *infestation* to describe the rapid spread of these highly prolific mussels. To Tom this all sounded a bit xenophobic, like the hysteria surrounding immigrant people who, because of purported reproductive fecundity, will soon "take over," marginalizing the native population.

Even though zebra mussels clog industrial water-intake valves and cause other damage (to the tune of an estimated $5 billion), and they annoy bathers with their sharp little shells, Tom read somewhere that as filter feeders, zebra mussels clear turgid water of excess nutrients that contribute to eutrophication. They have even been credited with "saving" several lakes that were nearly dead because of the high amounts of nutrients in the water from agricultural runoff, sewage treatment plant discharge, and the like. Moreover, excess nutrients gathered by the mussels are deposited into particles that collect on the bottom, affording excellent habitat for organisms upon which small fish feed. And the little fish feed bigger fish. Whether the zebra mussel is a good thing or a bad thing is evidently a debate among the experts. But if they can't decide, ruminated Tom as he lashed down his boat, then why should he worry?

Discussion Questions

1. Is Tom acting irresponsibly in planning to launch his boat in a lake that does not yet have zebra mussels?
2. Are native species to be preferred over exotic species? Why? Why not? Which species in your area are native? (This will likely require a bit of research.) What does *native* mean?
3. Is there, to your mind, a prejudice against exotic species?
4. How are we to assess the harms and benefits of either native or exotic species?
5. What should our position as nonexperts be with regard to disputes among experts?

4. NATURALLY

Craig was delighted to land his first real job out of college. With a degree in art he never thought he would wind up employed, but here he was in the graphic arts section of the marketing division of a major food manufacturer. His job was to design the wrapper for a candy bar currently under development. Well, it wasn't actually a candy bar. The new product had some ingredients such as soy flour and oats and honey that were supposed to make it competitive in the burgeoning natural food market, though it was hard to say what was natural about the new product since it also contained corn syrup, preservatives, and food coloring. According to a market tracking service, so-called natural energy bars have recently shown a 65 percent jump in annual sales. The large food manufacturers have taken note, and Craig's company wants some of the almost $100 million energy bar market.

Always resourceful, Craig went to the Internet to research packaging design for natural products. He came across an article titled, "Packaging Challenges Multiply for 'Natural' Food Marketers." It said: "Brand product identity and taste appeal are as important in this niche as in other foods, but they have to be augmented with the 'natural' message. To consumers, 'natural' products may evoke a simpler lifestyle and a no-brainer diet based on healthful foods. But to food marketers, there's nothing simple about designing a natural-foods package—it's anything but a no-brainer. Like any other successful package design, a natural-foods package must convey at least three messages: brand identity, product or product line identity, taste and visual appeal. The relative weight of each criterion may differ from product to product, line to line, or even company to company. But successful packaging of these brands has to encompass a fourth message: the 'natural' or, increasingly, organic message. In short, designing a natural-food package is not easier than designing any other package. But it's worth the trouble: The market for natural foods is expanding—and will continue on that course for the foreseeable future. Retail sales of health and natural foods stores grew 21 percent annually from 1993 to 1997, according to the market research firm Packaged Facts, a division of Kalorama Information. In its January 1998 report, the U.S. Health and Natural Food Store Market, the company predicts that sales will increase from $11.23 billion in 1997 to $26.43 billion in 2002—an annual growth rate of 18.7 percent. A caveat on the data. The broad category of 'natural' foods is not clearly defined. Indeed, the U.S. Food and Drug Administration has issued no labeling regulations governing the use of the term 'natural' on a food package."

Discussion Questions

1. If you were in Craig's position, how might you design the wrapper to take advantage of the natural food market?
2. Is it objectionable for advertisers to market their products as natural? What, in your estimation, counts as a natural product?
3. How many different senses of *natural* can you identify? Is natural good?
4. Why do you think there is such a strong market for natural foods?
5. Should the FDA issue guidelines for using the term *natural* on food labels? If yes, what might the regulation look like? If no, why not?

FOR FURTHER READING

The entire Endangered Species Act of 1973 is available online. Go to the U.S. Fish and Wildlife Service home page at www.fws.gov.

Frayed Safety Nets: Conservation Planning Under the Endangered Species Act. Defenders of Wildlife, Washington, DC, 1998.: See also, *Saving America's Wildlife: Renewing the Endangered Species Act.* Defenders of Wildlife, Washington, DC, 1995.

The Endangered Species Act: A Train Wreck Ahead, Thomas Lambert. Publication of the Center for the Study of American Business, Policy Study 126, 1995. Washington University, St. Louis, MO. See also *The Endangered Species Act: Time for a Change,* by Robert Smith and Thomas Lambert, Center for the Study of American Business, Policy Study 119, Washington University, St. Louis, MO, 1994.

Lexis-Nexis Academic Universe (or any other good database), for a listing of the numerous articles from newspapers and magazines dealing with the Endangered Species Act.

CHAPTER 4

An Environmental Ethic?

MODERN TIMES: VITAL FLUIDS—GASOLINE

Next to water and blood, gasoline is undoubtedly the most precious liquid known. It underpins our entire economy and makes possible a way of life that was unimaginable just several generations ago. Wars are fought for it, vast fortunes are made producing and selling it, every aspect of it is steeped in intense political debate, and its environmental consequences are staggering. It is hard to think of another substance that has had such an enormous effect on the environment. How did we get here?

It all started in 1859. Edwin Drake drilled the world's first commercially successful oil well in Titusville, Pennsylvania. At the time, gasoline was a waste product of petroleum (petro: rock; oleum: oil) refining. Crude oil was first distilled to extract kerosene for lighting, eventually displacing the need for whale oil by the late 1800s. But demand for kerosene was itself being displaced by electricity as a light source. With demand down for kerosene and gasoline a worthless by-product of kerosene production, things did not look promising for the oil industry. However, the emergence of internal combustion engines in the early 1900s ensured a market for gasoline as an important fuel. "Straight-run" gasoline from primitive distillation techniques initially used in petroleum refining is a far cry from the highly evolved fluid sucked up today by our minivans and SUVs. Modern gasoline is a sophisticated blend of straight-run gasoline, numerous other petroleum distillates, additives, stabilizers, oxygenators, inhibitators, octane boosters—the list goes on and on.

The story of gasoline is a fascinating one, every bit as complex as the crude oil from which it is refined. As it comes from the ground crude oil is a soup of many thousands of hydrocarbon compounds ranging from the very volatile, such as butane, to semisolids, such as bitumen (asphalt used to make roads). Each component has a specific boiling point: for example, straight-run naphtha–the forerunner of finished gasoline–boils between 100 and 220 degrees Fahrenheit; heavier naphthas boil between 220 and 320 degrees; kerosene 300–475. After naphtha naturally present in crude oil is removed by distillation, modern refineries use a process known as "catalytic cracking" in which the remaining heavier components are subjected to heat and pressure in the presence of a catalyst (a substance that promotes a chemical reaction but is not consumed by it), thereby "cracking" them into lighter products to be blended with other fractions of the refining process to produce gasoline. Catalytic cracking allows a greater volume of gasoline to be produced from a given quantity of crude oil. Modern gasoline is thus not a single component of crude oil but a blend of refining products.

One of the most important features of gasoline is its octane rating. Octane is an arbitrary measure of the extent to which a gasoline will prevent "knocking." Sometimes when you accelerate up a hill or otherwise put a strain on your car's engine, you will hear a funny rattling sound—sort of like marbles rolling around in a can. That's knocking. It is caused by improper ignition of gasoline in the engine's cylinders. Cylinders are, as the name implies, tubes inside of which pistons move up and down. Most cars have four-stroke piston engines.

Since the four-stroke internal combustion engine is emblematic of our entire way of life and for many of us what goes on under the hood of our cars is a complete mystery, it might be interesting briefly to review how they work. On what is known as the intake stroke, as the piston goes down inside the cylinder, a valve at the top opens and a gas/air mixture is sucked into the cylinder. The valve at the top of the cylinder closes and the piston now comes back up, compressing the mixture. This is the compression stroke. At the very top of the compression stroke, when the gas/air mixture is compressed as far as it can be, the spark plug fires. The resulting explosion forces the piston back down the cylinder, hence the power stroke. Since the piston is tied by a connecting rod to a crankshaft, vertical motion of the piston is transferred into rotary motion, which is relayed via the transmission to the wheels. (When you pedal a bike, your legs go up and down, like pistons; that motion is translated into rotary motion by the crankshaft.) At the bottom of the power stroke, when the piston is driven as far down the cylinder as it can go because of the explosion, an exhaust valve at the top of the cylinder opens. The piston glides back up, pushing hot exhaust gases out of the cylinder. When it is all the way back to the top, the exhaust valve closes and the intake valve opens, and the cycle is repeated. Car engines typically have four, six, or eight cylinders in various configurations, with a 'V' arrangement more or less standard.

The timing of the explosive gas/air mixture detonation is crucial. Knocking occurs when the mixture ignites at the wrong time or burns improperly once ignited. It reduces efficiency and, over time, can damage the engine. Gasoline has to be designed to resist igniting from residual heat in the cylinder or heat from compression, and once ignited, it must explode smoothly. Octane ratings for gasoline are derived from the knocking properties of two petroleum distillates, isooctane and heptane. Using a standard test engine, isooctane, which produces no knocking, is assigned an octane rating of 100. Heptane, which is all knock (as it were), is assigned an octane rating of 0. Gasoline octane numbers are thus a relative measure of the extent to which knocking is prevented compared to these two substances. So 87 octane means that particular gasoline is functionally equivalent to a mixture of 87 percent isooctane and 13 percent heptane in the standard test engine. A particular batch of 87 octane gasoline might not have any isooctane in it, but it functions as if it did in the standard test engine. Refiners blend low-octane components with high-octane distillates to achieve a final product with a specified octane rating.

It is thus a mistake to think that a higher-octane gasoline has "more power" or is "hotter." In fact, a higher-octane gas is designed to resist premature ignition, so in that sense is less hot. You can get 'more power' from higher-octane gasoline, but not because the gasoline is more powerful. The extra power comes because your engine won't knock. If your car engine doesn't knock with lower-octane gasoline, there is no reason to buy more expensive higher-octane gasoline. Often at the gas pump you will see a note that octane ratings for the gas were determined by the "R + M/2 method." This refers to the average between the knock resistance of the gasoline in a lower rpm standard engine (*Re*search octane number) and a higher rpm standard engine (*M*otor octane number).

Various substances affect octane rating, the most notorious being tetraethyl lead—the lead of leaded gasoline, now banned in the United States but still widely used throughout the world. How lead, a known toxin, got in gasoline is a case study in corporate interests trumping public safety. In 1921, the car market was dominated by Ford's Model T. GM, a distant second, planned to compete against Ford through increased engine performance. This meant higher-compression engines—more compression means bigger bang, which means more power. The trouble was that higher compression also meant engine knocking because gasoline would ignite prematurely due to the heat caused by higher compression. So GM sought an additive that would retard ignition until just the right instant when the spark plug could detonate the air/gas mixture in the cylinder. Various substances were tried, but a chemical developed by Germany for possible use in gas warfare during World War I, tetraethyl lead, was found to reduce engine knock when even minute quantities were added to gasoline.

The first "ethyl gasoline" went on sale in Ohio in 1923—the word *lead* was deliberately omitted—and when, that same year, the winners of the Indianapolis 500 were cars powered by ethyl, sale of ethyl gasoline boomed nationwide. As production of tetraethyl lead increased, warnings about its toxicity surfaced; some workers became delirious, others died violently crazed. Ethyl Corporation (the main producer of tetraethyl lead) explained away the deaths and psychotic incidents but quietly sought to have toxicity studies done under the auspices of the U.S. Bureau of Mines, suspecting that the public would not accept the results of any studies it did itself. The U.S. Bureau of Mines agreed (despite the misgivings of some within the bureau) to undertake a toxicity study funded by Ethyl Corporation, which inappropriately retained control over dissemination of the results, clearly compromising the neutrality and regulatory authority of a government agency. On May 24, 1925, the U.S. Surgeon General convened a special meeting to consider the toxicity of tetraethyl lead in gasoline. Although public health experts were present, their arguments were speculative and relied on animal studies. Industry representatives claimed that nothing less than industrial civilization was at stake. One even claimed that tetraethyl lead was an "apparent gift of God" because it allowed gasoline to be used so much more effectively. A special panel subsequently appointed by the Surgeon General found no evidence that leaded gasoline posed a public health risk. How that decision was reached is beyond comprehension because the toxic properties of lead were well known at the time. It was not until 1975 that the Environmental Protection Agency (EPA) banned leaded gasoline for use in automobiles.

Today a similar battle over the composition of gasoline is raging. In 1970, Congress passed the Clean Air Act (CAA) authorizing the EPA to establish air quality standards (this act was also responsible for phasing out leaded gasoline). In 1990, the act was amended to address certain parts of the country that were not in compliance with air quality standards by requiring that gasoline used in those areas contain a certain amount of chemically bound oxygen, which promotes more complete combustion, thereby releasing fewer hydrocarbons into the atmosphere. Petroleum refiners were able not only to meet the oxygen requirements but also to boost octane ratings by adding a substance called methyl tertiary butyl ether (MTBE) to gasoline. However, MTBE is extremely soluble in water, and leaks from underground storage tanks have contaminated thousands of wells and aquifers throughout New England and California. The health risks of MTBE, a suspected carcinogen, are under debate. Apparently, only a minute amount—some 10 parts per *billion*—makes water extremely unpalatable. And to make matters worse, the effects of MTBE on underground water will be with us for years even if the additive is banned, which the EPA sought to do.

Ethanol, a kind of alcohol, is a possible replacement for MTBE, since it too contains chemically bound oxygen. "Gasohol" could contain as much as 10 percent ethanol. Since ethanol is fermented from biomass, primarily corn, it is backed by agricultural interests. As a clean-burning and renewable energy source, it also has the backing of many environmental groups. But ethanol has drawbacks. It lowers octane, unlike MTBE which raises it; so other octane-boosting substances will have to be added to gasohol. Also, there is a geographical mismatch between the current location of most ethanol production facilities—the corn-growing areas of the country—and areas where gasohol is needed, mainly the coasts. So transportation costs will raise the price of gasoline, and current ethanol production capacity might not be adequate to meet the demand. Further, unlike MTBE, ethanol evaporates readily. So storage and transfer of gasoline, especially during summer, will release smog-causing hydrocarbons into the atmosphere. Thus, air quality in those areas not in compliance with EPA standards will remain largely unaffected by requiring gasohol, which was the reason for requiring oxygenated fuels in the first place.

Congress is considering yet another amendment to the CAA to drop the oxygenated fuel requirement and substitute instead a "renewable fuel" requirement. Seen largely as a political gesture to agricultural interests that support ethanol production, gasohol would be initially used primarily in the Midwest rather than on the coasts where air quality is lower. So in the short run, eliminating an oxygenated fuel requirement from the CAA will mean that air quality will not improve in those areas that currently fail to meet EPA standards. But in the long run, encouraging an ethanol industry is, perhaps, a small step in the right direction especially if gasohol becomes used nationwide.

AN ETHIC FOR THE ENVIRONMENT VERSUS AN ENVIRONMENTAL ETHIC

Reflecting on gasoline and our way of life leads us to philosophical issues. When all is said and done, what is the point of wrangling over the formulation of gasoline? How gasoline is formulated has enormous effects on the environment, which in turn has enormous effects on us. So, the formulation of gasoline affects our well being. Putting lead in gasoline does not promote our well-being and apparently neither does adding MTBE. It is, therefore, a matter of rational self-interest that we pay close attention to the effects of gasoline on the environment. But is that the end of the story? According to **anthropocentrism,** the view that only people count morally, it is. In this view, there are no moral aspects to environmental management over and above how our actions affect people. So if we knowingly risk harm to others by, say, putting lead in gasoline, then we can be held morally accountable in the same way that any action that subjects people to harm can be appraised. The fact that the harm is mediated through the environment presents little theoretical interest. The only morally relevant consideration is that people are harmed by the actions of others. (And it is only the actions of people that are subject to moral assessment. People are harmed by hurricanes, but we do not morally condemn hurricanes. They are bad because of the harm they cause us, not wrong.) But is harm to persons the only morally relevant consideration in our relation to the environment? This is one of the foundational questions raised by environmental ethics.

Consider viewing the world solely in terms of what promotes or hinders your interests. Suppose that the only reasons you regard as proper for action are ones that somehow engage your interests. If your interests are advanced, then that is the only reason to do it; if your interests are not advanced, that is the only reason against it. Nothing else counts in your deliberations. How will you act? Because you live in a social setting where your good is inextricably bound to the good of others, rational self-interest shows that your well-being is best promoted by treating others with respect, not taking advantage of them, treating them as you wish to be treated, and so forth. You will realize that the best way to get your back scratched is to scratch the backs of others. So even though your behavior will be impeccable, your motivation is thoroughly self-centered.

The view that only one's own interests *ought* to count in moral deliberation is called ethical **egoism.** As a moral theory, ethical egoism presents a rather stubborn challenge since it goes against almost everything we think about morality. Morality says you ought to consider others; ethical egoism says you ought to consider only yourself. But is there any reason I ought to consider interests other than my own when I deliberate about what I ought to do? Is it irrational to be an ethical egoist?

Perhaps the first thing that comes to mind about ethical egoism is that it is selfish. But without an analysis of selfishness, this observation is not very illuminating. What is wrong with being selfish? The selfish person is not simply one who acts in his or her own interest, but one who acts in his or her own interest when the interests of others *ought* to be considered. That is, the selfish person fails to acknowledge the moral importance of the interests of other people. But is the egoist making an intellectual error? Can the egoist rationally defend promoting his or her own interests to the exclusion of other interests that are at stake? Unless that point can be established, the ethical egoist will be acting arbitrarily in preferring his or her own interests when there are other interests to consider. And how could it possibly be shown that one's own interests are more important than anyone else's? Since one person's interests are relevantly similar to another's, the egoist has no basis for concluding that his and his alone are more deserving or more worthy of recognition. This means the egoist would be unjustified in promoting his interests to the exclusion of the interests of anyone else. In short, ethical egoism is arbitrary.

What does our analysis of ethical egoism have to do with the environment? The worry is that anthropocentrism is like ethical egoism. Just as the ethical egoist fails to acknowledge the importance of interests other than one's own (if interests other than one's own are even acknowledged to exist), so the anthropocentrist holds that nonhuman interests either don't exist or, if they do, they pale by comparison to human interests. And just as ethical egoism was found to be selfish, might anthropocentrism also suffer from a kind of selfishness? For if there are other interests, albeit nonhuman interests, then we would be selfish (i.e., unjustified) in pursuing human interests to the exclusion of the other interests that are at stake.

Are there nonhuman interests that we ought to consider in our interaction with the natural world? We need to ask questions about interests—what are they and why think that only people have them? Very broadly, your interests are connected to your good. So, for example, it is in your interest to eat properly. This means that eating properly contributes to your good. Whether being aware of your good is necessary for having interests (and hence a good at all) is a deeply contested point. When a lawyer seeks to protect the interests of a dead person in court, is this just a legal fiction or do the dead person's interests somehow outlive the individual? We do not have to settle the question of whether awareness is necessary for interests, however, to see the theoretical importance of interests for a nonanthropocentric ethic. If we can make sense of interests in various natural entities in virtue of their having a good of their own, then their interests cannot justifiably be ignored, no more than the interests of other people can be justifiably ignored by the egoist.

Which natural entities have **interests?** The controversy surrounding this question turns on how we shall conceive interests. Other things being equal, it is not in your interest to suffer. But if so, then the very same point holds for any being capable of suffering. Certain animals—the ones that can suffer—have an interest in not doing so, and the challenge to an anthropocentric ethic will be to explain why an animal's interest in not suffering is not also worthy of moral consideration. Further, if an entity can have interests simply in virtue of having a good of its own, irrespective of whether or not it is aware of its good, then the range of entities with interests expands dramatically. Plants, for example, seem to have a good of their own, a sake for which we can act, even though they are not aware of anything, and this might ground interests. It appears perfectly intelligible to say that sunlight and fertilizer promote the plant's interests. But if having interests forms the core of being an appropriate subject of moral concern, does this mean the interests of plants merit moral consideration? And if it makes sense to talk about plants this way, what about other natural objects? Perhaps species or even entire ecosystems can have interests in virtue of having a good of their own. These are all questions for careful exploration as we delve deeper into environmental philosophy. In subsequent chapters, we shall encounter sophisticated defenses of the idea that plants and other living things, even ecosystems, have interests, and that for us to ignore those interests in the promotion of our own good is for us to act something like the egoist we considered above.

The search for interests in nature as the basis of an environmental (nonanthropocentric) ethic can be called **extensionism.** A feature of ordinary human-centered morality—having interests—might extend further than we initially thought. In this respect a nonanthropocentric ethic need not be a "new" ethic. An environmental ethic might just be a rigorously consistent application of principles and ideas that were previously (and unjustifiably) limited only to human beings. Various "liberation" movements in our society present a good analogy, since extending constitutional protections to blacks, women, and homosexuals does not involve a reformulation of first principles, just their consistent application. Similarly, extending morally significant interests to nonhuman entities need not involve theoretical revisions, though it will require a new attitude on our part even to comprehend such a vastly expanded moral domain. But whether interests can be so extended is a disputed question in environmental philosophy, one that we shall consider in our readings.

INTRINSIC VALUE IN NATURE?

Another way to think about a moral dimension to the natural world is via the concept of **inherent value.** Inherent (or intrinsic) value contrasts with instrumental (or extrinsic) value. Something has instrumental value if its value resides in its usefulness. A shovel, for instance, has instrumental value—you value it for what you can get using it. As Kant would put it, a *thing* has instrumental value only, by definition. But not all value is instrumental; there must be intrinsic value, since things are instrumentally valuable only because they are instrumental in getting what is valuable in itself; that is, intrinsically valuable. Recall from our discussion in Chapter 1 where Kant claims that only people are intrinsically valuable; everything else may be viewed as instruments for the well-being of people. This is why, for Kant, all nonpersons, including the entire natural world, are relegated to thinghood. As we shall see, however, restricting intrinsic value only to people can be questioned. If the concept of intrinsic value has application to entities besides people, then those entities ought not to be viewed merely as instruments. So if nature, or aspects of it, have that sort of value, then we cannot legitimately regard those natural objects just as resources, for they would merit our reverence and protection in virtue of their intrinsic value. It would be wrong, in other words, to treat that which is intrinsically valuable merely as a means to our ends. But can we make sense of intrinsic value in nonhumans?

Attributions of intrinsic value are hard to understand. We understand what it means for something to be instrumentally valuable and that kind of value can be very important, but it has no moral content. My car is instrumentally valuable to me and I take good care of it for that reason, not because I think the car counts for anything in its own right. Because the value of my car is exhausted by its instrumentality, it has no direct moral significance; its value is derivative, contingent upon my ends. However, if something is intrinsically valuable, then its value is not derivative. Something intrinsically valuable would be valuable in itself and worthy of our respect for that reason. The natural world is clearly instrumentally valuable. Might it, or aspects of it, also be intrinsically valuable?

It is easy to assert that a river or a forest or an ecosystem has intrinsic value; it sounds so high-minded to say so. But how could assertions of intrinsic value possibly be defended to someone who disagrees? Intrinsic value seems utterly mysterious, like an occult feature that some of us just don't see. Is there really an ineffable something in the river or forest?

If intrinsic value is understood as an objective feature of objects themselves, then it is hard to comprehend, for things would then be valuable independent of valuers. We (or at least those who are sensitive to such things) would then regard, say, the forest as intrinsically valuable because it really is intrinsically valuable. An explanation of how something could be valuable prior to our valuing it will take us into some very murky areas of philosophy. But intrinsic value does not have to be construed as an objective feature of the world. It might be better understood as a sophisticated projection on our part, a way of looking, rather than a structural component of reality. In this sense, even though all value depends upon valuers—conscious beings who can value things—the value attributed still need not be instrumental. This understanding of intrinsic value is less baffling and, in fact, plays an important role in our conception of ourselves.

Think about the importance you attach to your own concerns, choices, and aspirations; is your conception of yourself and your worth as a person exhausted by your usefulness to others or society? Do you think that your dignity and self-worth are independent of all that? No doubt usefulness plays a big role in our in our sense of self-worth—the mother feels important because her children depend on her—but it would be hard, if not impossible, to conceive of oneself in instrumental terms alone. To see yourself in purely instrumental terms, you would have to extinguish your personhood, turn yourself into a thing. You would have to conceive of yourself as the slave of another, completely devoid of your own intentions, desires, and goals; you would have no will of your own. As we saw in Chapter 1, Kant captured this sense that we each have about our own value by claiming that all persons (and for Kant, only persons) are intrinsically valuable. The intrinsic value of persons resides in the rational autonomy of their wills, so to respect a person is to acknowledge the choices and intentions emanating from that will.

Kant's point about the intrinsic value we each attach to ourselves in virtue of our rational autonomy—our wills—can be generalized. The value we each see in ourselves can explain our tendency to see intrinsic value beyond our selves. For example, many people consider great art intrinsically valuable. They are willing to protect great art they may never actually see and they regard its destruction as a desecration. Art's intrinsic value is not just a function of its appearance, otherwise forgeries would be as valuable as an original. Great art is an expression of genius, a powerful, perceptive, and exquisitely sensitive mind at work, so by revering great art we actually revere the creative powers of the person who produced it. A similar account can be given for the intrinsic value many people see in cultural artifacts. Museums store the daily implements of aboriginal and ancient cultures and many people find these items to be immensely valuable, not just because we can learn from these distant cultures but because their artifacts represent an entire way of life, the sum total of their creative powers to forge a life in harsh or unusual circumstances, thereby expressing a view of their world and themselves. We see acts of will, wills very much like our own, behind their artifacts. Our tendency to see such cultural artifacts as intrinsically valuable is similar to our tendency to see great art as intrinsically valuable. Both rely on our appreciating and in some sense identifying with the creative powers at work.

Generalizing the kind of value we each assign to ourselves can explain why we are so willing to see intrinsic value in great art, literature, music, cultural artifacts, and the like. It is not as if a great work of art *really* is intrinsically valuable. Rather, seeing it as intrinsically valuable is an irresistible response on our part to the manifestations of inspiring and ingenious creative power. We recognize the intrinsic value we necessarily attach to the operation of our own minds expressed in the creations of others.

Understanding intrinsic value this way can also explain why so many see intrinsic value in nature, since we are inclined to see the natural world in human terms. It is almost impossible for us not to read intentionality into the world, despite all the efforts of science to give us a purely mechanistic view of the workings of nature. We like to think that things happen for a reason, not just that they are caused. This has been our attitude toward the natural world for a long time. There are many variations on the theme of a world infused with intentionality, but in its simplest form, the world was created by a benevolent God. All of nature would thus be a manifestation of divine will—a stupendous work of art from an infinitely powerful, sublime, and wise creative force.

Inscribed on the rotunda ceiling of the Toronto Museum of Natural History are these words: "That all men may know His work." Archaic language aside, the message is inescapable: This is God's art museum where you can see the amazing things he made. Just as we ascribe intrinsic value to the great artistic and cultural products of human creativity, all the more reason to see intrinsic value in manifestations of the largest conceivable creative will of all.

Such an unrefined theological account of intrinsic value in nature is doubtless of limited appeal. Perhaps it seems naive, a view of the world we have outgrown. However, attenuated versions of that view are likely at work in those who see intrinsic value in nature. In our unguarded moments, for example, we speak about the *products* of nature or of the various *experiments designed* by the evolutionary *struggle;* we infuse rivers with intention as they *carve* canyons in their *rush* to the sea, or we lament a previously *majestic* and *free* river transformed into a *placid* reservoir by a dam; storms *howl* and *rage;* mountains *thrust* to the sky; and plants *seek* light. Nature is seen not as an accidental arrangement of inert stuff operating by blind causal mechanisms, but as manifestations of will. A purely scientific account of the world, one without intentionality, purpose, or direction to events, is difficult to accept, even if true. We irresistibly fill the nonintentional void with the contents of our own minds and see instead a more recognizable world. Because we invariably romanticize and personify nature, it is hardly surprising that we should suffuse it with something of ourselves—the most important part, namely, our intrinsic value. So is there intrinsic value in nature? Well, not exactly, but no more than there is intrinsic value "in" us. In so far as our own sense of intrinsic value is connected to the creative power of our wills, our propensity to see similar creative powers at work in nature makes it easy to posit intrinsic value there as well.

IMPLICATIONS OF A NONANTHROPOCENTRIC ETHIC

We have been considering foundational questions of moral philosophy and their implications for a nonanthropocentric ethic. The intellectual resources are available at least to make sense of interests or intrinsic value beyond the realm of humanity. Modest though that point may seem, it is actually an amazing realization. For it means that if beings with interests or intrinsic value define the moral realm, the moral realm is potentially much larger than we thought. How much larger is, of course, subject to debate. Different theories of environmental philosophy disagree about the range of entities that merit direct **moral standing** and why, and in subsequent chapters we shall examine those theories. However, all nonanthropocentric moral theories agree that an anthropocentric ethic—the dominant form of moral theory—is deficient. Theoretically, much is at stake. The emergence and widespread acceptance of a nonanthropocentric ethic would be a psychic revolution of staggering proportions. Our worldview would shift dramatically and, presumably, so would our behavior, in so far as ethical concerns modify behavior.

There is, however, a nagging question to keep in mind before we run off intoxicated by the theoretical possibilities now available to us. It is one thing to argue that entities other than human beings have moral standing and another to assess the extent or significance of that moral standing. Surely we want to be able to make discriminations among the entities—whatever they are—that would now inhabit a much-expanded nonanthropocentric moral universe. If not, then a nonanthropocentric ethic is not very interesting, for it would have turned whatever is covered by it into a person. Arguing that, say, plants have moral standing because they have interests is the easy part. But how morally significant is a plant? Is a plant as morally significant as a person? And if people are more morally significant than various nonhuman entities, why isn't their welfare always more important whenever there is a conflict and isn't this right back where we started? In other words, we need a method to adjudicate conflicts among the members of the new world order created by a nonanthropocentric ethic. An anthropocentric ethic at least has a rough framework for handling such difficulties: all persons (and there could be disagreement about who is a person) count the same—anthropocentrism is a great moral democracy where competing claims are hashed out among moral equals. This is not to say that it is easy to assess conflicting claims among persons, but we know that we start with moral equals. Is the nonanthropocentrist making a similar proposal, just that we start with a much larger moral democracy; or are some members of the nonanthropocentrist's **moral community** "more equal" than others?

THE READINGS

The readings for this chapter are organized around the question of what an environmental ethic might be like. An alternate conception of ethics is, from a theoretical point of view, a large undertaking. In addition to explaining the limitations of anthropocentrism, "conceptual space" has to be made for a nonanthropocentric ethic. It must be shown that a moral position of that sort is even a theoretical possibility. Consider, as an absurd analogy, a "numerical ethic." Because it does not even make sense to speak of a moral relation to numbers, such an ethic is doomed from the start—it is conceptually incoherent. Is an environmental ethic similarly incoherent? A first task in considering what an environmental ethic would be like involves defending it against charges of incoherence.

TOM REGAN

The Nature and Possibility of an Environmental Ethic

Tom Regan is emeritus professor of philosophy at North Carolina State University in Raleigh. He has a long and distinguished publication record in environmental philosophy and animal rights, including his influential book, *The Case for Animal Rights.* In our selection, "The Nature and Possibility of an Environmental Ethic," Regan examines, and rejects, three arguments that purport to show that an environmental ethic is impossible. He claims, "An environmental ethic must recognize that the class of beings having moral standing is larger than the class of conscious beings," and, "the basis on which an environmental ethic must pin this enlargement is the idea that nonconscious beings can have a good or value in their own right." For Regan, then, the possibility of an environmental ethic rides on making sense of intrinsic value (he calls it "intrinsic goodness") in nonconscious entities.

CRITICAL READING QUESTIONS

1. Identify the three arguments Regan rejects that purport to show an environmental ethic is impossible. On what basis does Regan reject the arguments?
2. How does Regan construe intrinsic value?
3. What does Regan mean when he claims, "Certain regions of the Colorado River, for example, are free, not subjectively, but objectively"? How is this claim relevant to his theory of intrinsic value in nature?

I. INTRODUCTION

Is an environmental ethic possible? Answers to this question presuppose that we have an agreed upon understanding of the nature of an environmental ethic. Evidently we do not, and one fundamental problem for this burgeoning area of ethics is to say what such an ethic must be like. In the present essay, I characterize and defend, although incompletely, a particular conception of an environmental ethic. My modest objective is to show that there is something worth thinking about completing.

II. TWO CONDITIONS OF AN ENVIRONMENTAL ETHIC

The conception I favor accepts the following two conditions:

1. An environmental ethic must hold that there are nonhuman beings which have moral standing.
2. An environmental ethic must hold that the class of those beings which have moral standing includes but is larger than the class of conscious beings—that is, all conscious beings and some nonconscious beings must be held to have moral standing.

If both conditions are accepted, then a theory that satisfies neither of them is not a false environmental ethic; it is not an environmental ethic at all. Any theory that satisfies (1), but does not satisfy (2) might be regarded as a theory "on the way to becoming" such an ethic, in that it satisfies a necessary condition, but, since it fails to satisfy condition (2), it fails to qualify as a genuine environmental ethic. Only theories that satisfy (2), on the conception advanced here, can properly be regarded as environmental ethics, whether true, reasonable, or otherwise.

Though only a necessary condition, (1) assists us in distinguishing between (a) an ethic *of* the environment, and (b) an ethic *for the use* of the environment. Suppose we think that only the interests of human beings matter morally. Then it certainly would be possible to develop a homocentric ethic for the use of the environment. Roughly speaking, such an ethic would declare that the environment ought to be used so that the quality of human life, including possibly that of future generations, ought to be enhanced. I do not say developing such an ethic (what I shall call "a management ethic") would be simple or unimportant, but a management ethic falls short of an ethic of the environment, given the conditions stated earlier. It restricts the loci of value to the lives and interests of *human* beings, whereas an environmental ethic requires that we recognize the moral standing of nonhumans . . .

I do not wish to minimize the difficulties that attend the development of an environmental ethic which is consequentialist in nature (e.g., some form of utilitarianism). There are difficulties of comparison, perhaps themselves great enough to foreclose the possibility of developing a consequentialist environmental ethic. I shall have more to say on this matter as we proceed. First, though, a more fundamental problem requires our atten-

---

Tom Regan, "The Nature and Possibility of an Environmental Ethic," *Environmental Ethics,* vol 3, no. 1, 1981, pp. 19–34. Reprinted by permission from Tom Regan.

tion. Is it even logically possible for a theory to meet both the conditions I have recommended for an environmental ethic? The answer clearly is no if compelling reasons can be given for limiting moral standing *only* to conscious beings. In the following section I reject three arguments that attempt to establish this restriction.

III. ARGUMENTS AGAINST THE POSSIBILITY OF AN ENVIRONMENTAL ETHIC

The first argument to be considered I call the "interest argument":

1. The only beings which can have moral standing are those beings which can have interests.
2. The only beings which can have interests are those which have the capacity for consciousness.
3. Therefore, the only beings which can have moral standing are beings having the capacity for consciousness.

Now, this argument, as I have argued elsewhere against a similar argument, has apparent plausibility because it exploits an ambiguity in the concept of something having interests. To speak of *A*'s interests in *X* might mean either (a) that *A* is interested in (wants, desires, hopes for, cares about, etc.) *X*, or (b) that *X* is in *A*'s interest (that *X* will contribute to *A*'s good, or well-being, or welfare). Clearly *if* the only beings which can have moral standing are those which can be interested in things (have desires, wants, etc.), then only conscious beings can have moral standing. The idea of nonconscious beings having desires, wants, etc., at least in any literal sense, seems plainly unintelligible. If, on the other hand, we mean beings which can be benefited or harmed by what is given or denied them, then it is an open question whether the class of beings which can have moral standing is coextensive with the class of beings having the capacity for consciousness. Perhaps other beings can have a good or value that can be advanced or retarded depending on what is done to them. The interest argument provides us with no resolution of this question, and so fails to demonstrate the impossibility of an environmental ethic.

A second argument, which I shall call the "sentience argument," closely resembles the interest argument and is vulnerable to the same type of objection:

1. The only beings which can have moral standing are those which are sentient.
2. The only beings which are sentient are those which have the capacity for consciousness.
3. Therefore, the only beings which can have moral standing are those which have the capacity for consciousness.

I shall limit my critical remarks to step (1). How might it be supported? First, one might argue that only sentient beings have interests; that is, one might seek to support the sentience argument by invoking the interest argument, but since we have shown this latter argument is incomplete, at best, this defense of the sentience argument must bear the same diagnosis. A second defense consists in claiming that it is "meaningless" to think that nonconscious beings possibly have moral standing. This is unconvincing. *If* it is meaningless, there ought to be some way of illuminating why this is so, and this illumination is not provided by the mere charge of meaninglessness itself. Such a defense has more the aura of rhetoric than of philosophy.

A third defense consists in arguing that the only beings having moral standing are those having value in their own right, *and* that only sentient beings have value of this kind. This defense, as I argue in a moment, is a token of the argument type I call the "goodness argument." Its major liability is that by itself it provides no justification for its two central claims—namely, (a) that only beings which can have value in their own right can have moral standing and (b) that only sentient beings have value in their own right. For reasons to which I come below, I believe (b) is false while (a) is true. Meanwhile, neither is self-evident and so each stands in need of rational defense, something not provided by the sentience argument itself.

The final argument to be considered is the goodness argument:

1. The only beings which can have moral standing are those which can have a good of their own.
2. The only beings which can have a good of their own are those capable of consciousness.
3. Therefore, the only beings which can have moral standing are those capable of consciousness.

Premise (1) of the goodness argument seems to identify a fundamental presupposition of an environmental ethic. The importance of this premise is brought out when we ask for the grounds on which we might rest the obligation to preserve any existing *X*. Fundamentally, two types of answer are possible. First, preserving *X* is necessary to bring about future good or prevent future evil for beings other than *X;* on this account *X's* existence has instrumental value. Second, the obligation we have might be to *X* itself, independently of *X's* instrumental value, because *X* has a good or value in its own right. Given our condition for an environmental ethic, not all of the values recognized in nonconscious nature can be instrumental. Only if we agree with premise (1) of the goodness argument, therefore, can we have a necessary presupposition of an environmental ethic. How inherent goodness or value can be intelligibly ascribed to nonconscious beings is a difficult question, one we shall return to later (section 5). At present, we must consider the remainder of the goodness argument, since if sound, it rules out the logical possibility of nonconscious beings having a good or value of their own.

"The only beings which have a good of their own," premise (2) states, "are those capable of consciousness." What arguments can be given to support this view? I have examined suggested answers elsewhere at length. What these arguments come to in the end, if I am right, is the thesis that consciousness is a logically necessary condition of having only *a certain kind* of good of one's own, happiness. Thus, though we may speak, metaphorically, of a "happy azalea" or a "contented broccoli," the only sorts of beings which literally can have happiness are conscious beings. There is no disputing this. What is disputable is the tacit assumption that this is the *only* kind of good or value a given *X* can have in its own right. Unless or until a compelling supporting argument is supplied, for limiting inherent goodness to happiness, the goodness argument falls short of limiting moral standing to just those beings capable of consciousness.

Four truths result if the argument of the present section is sound. First, an environmental ethic must recognize that the class of beings having moral standing is larger than the class of conscious beings. Second, the basis on which an environmental ethic must pin this enlargement is the idea that nonconscious beings can have a good or value in their own right. Third, though it remains to be ascertained what this goodness or value is, it is not happiness; and fourth, efforts to show that nonconscious beings cannot have moral standing fail to show this. The conclusion we guardedly reach, then, is that the impossibility of an environmental ethic has not been shown. . . .

IV. INHERENT GOODNESS?

In this final section, I offer some tentative remarks about the nature of inherent goodness, emphasizing their tentativeness and incompleteness. I comment first on five different but related ideas.

(1) The presence of inherent value in a natural object is independent of any awareness, interest, or appreciation of it by any conscious being. This does not tell us what objects are inherently good or why, only that *if* an object is inherently good its value must *inhere in (be in)* the object itself. Inherent value is not conferred upon objects in the manner of an honorary degree. Like other properties in nature, it must be discovered. Contrary to the *Tractatus,* there *is* value *in* the world, if natural objects are inherently valuable.

(2) The presence of inherent value in a natural object is a consequence of its possessing those other properties which it happens to posses. This follows from (1), given the further assumption that inherent goodness is a consequential or supervenient property. By insisting that inherent goodness depends on an

object's *own* properties, the point made in (1) that inherent goodness is a value possessed by the object independently of any awareness is reemphasized. *Its* goodness depends on *its* properties.

(3) The inherent value of a natural object is an objective property of that object. This differs from but is related to Sagoff's objectivity of the freedom and majesty of natural objects. Certain stretches of the Colorado River, for example, are free, not subjectively, but objectively. The freedom expressed by (or in) the river is an objective fact. But this goes beyond Sagoff's position by insisting that *the value of the river's being free* also is an objective property of the river. If the river is inherently good, in the sense explained in (1), then it is *a fact about the river* that it is good inherently.

(4) The inherent value of a natural object is such that toward it the fitting attitude is one of admiring respect. This brings out the appropriateness of regarding what is inherently valuable in a certain way and this provides a way of connecting what is inherently valuable in the environment with an ideal of human nature. In part, the ideal in question bids us be appreciative of the values nature holds, not merely as a resource to be used in the name of human interests, but inherently. The ideal bids us, further, to regard what is inherently valuable with both admiration and respect. Admiration is fitting because not everything in nature is inherently valuable (what is is to be admired both because of its value *and* because of its comparative uniqueness). Respect is appropriate because this is a fitting attitude to have toward that which has value in its own right. One must realize that its being valuable is not contingent on one's happening to value it, so that to treat it *merely* as a means to human ends it to mistreat it. Such treatment shows a lack of respect for its being something which has value independently of these ends. Thus, I fall short of the ideal if I gratuitously destroy what has inherent value, or even if I regard it merely as having value only relative to human desires. But half the story about ideals of human nature remains untold if we leave out the part about the value inherent in those things toward which we can act in the ideal way. So it is vital to insist that our having ideals is neither to deny nor diminish the further point that this ideal requires postulating inherent value in nature, independently of these ideals.

(5) The admiring respect of what is inherently valuable in nature gives rise to the preservation principle. By the "preservation principle" I mean a principle of nondestruction, noninterference, and, generally, nonmeddling. By characterizing this in terms of a principle, moreover, I am emphasizing that preservation (letting be) be regarded as a moral imperative. Thus, if I regard wild stretches of the Colorado River as inherently valuable and regard these sections with admiring respect, I also think it wrong to destroy these sections of the river, I think one ought not to meddle in the river's affairs, as it were.

A difficult question to answer is whether the preservation principle gives us a principle of *absolute or* of prima facie duty. It is unclear how it can be absolute, for it appears conceivable that in some cases letting be what is at present inherently good in nature may lead to value diminution or loss in the future. For example, because of various sedimentary changes, a river which is now wild and free might in time be transformed into a small, muddly creek; thus, it might be necessary to override the preservation principle in order to preserve or increase what is inherently valuable in nature. However, even if the preservation principle is regarded as being only prima facie, it is still possible to agree on at least one point with those who regard it as absolute, i.e., the common rejection of the "human interests principle," which says:

> Whenever human beings can benefit more from overriding the preservation principle than if they observe it, the preservation principle ought to be overridden.

This principle *must* be rejected by anyone who accepts the preservation principle because it distorts the very conception of goodness underlying that principle. If the sort of value natural objects possess is inherent, then one fails to show a proper respect for these objects if one is willing to destroy them *merely* on the grounds that this would benefit human beings. Since such destruction is precisely what the human interests principle commits one to, one cannot *both* accept the preservation principle, absolute or prima facie, *and* also accept the human interests principle. The common enemy of all preservationists are those who accept the human interests principle.

This brief discussion of the preservation principle may also cast some light on the problem of making intelligible cross species value comparisons, e.g., in the case of the survival of caribou versus the economic development of wilderness. The point preservationists must keep in mind is that to ask how many caribou lives equals in value the disvalue of how much economic loss is unanswerable because it is an improper question. It confounds two incommensurable kinds of good, the inherent good of the caribou with the noninherent good of economic benefits. Indeed, because these kinds of good are incommensurable, a utilitarian or consequentialist environmental ethic, which endeavors to accommodate both kinds of goodness, is doomed to fail. The inherent value of the caribou cannot be cashed in in terms of human economic benefit, and such a theory ends up providing us with no clear moral direction. For the preservationist, the proper philosophical response to those who would uproot the environment in the name of human benefit is to say that they fail to understand the very notion of something being inherently good.

Two questions which I have not endeavored to answer are: (a) what, if anything in general, makes something inherently good, and (b) how can we know, if we can, what things are inherently good? The two questions are not unrelated. If we could establish that there is something (*X*) such that, whenever any object (*Y*) has *X* it is inherently good, we could then go on to try to establish how we can know that any object has X. Unfortunately, I now have very little to say about these questions, and what little I do have to say concern only how not to answer them.

Two possible answers to question (a) merit mention. The first is that an object (*X*) is inherently good if it is good of its kind. This is a view I have assumed and argued for elsewhere, but it now appears to me to be completely muddled. The concept of inherent goodness cannot be reduced to the notion of something being good of its kind, for though I believe that we can conceive of the goodness any *X* has, if *X* is good of its kind, as a value it has in its own right, there is no reason to believe that we ought to have the attitude of admiring respect toward what is (merely) good of its kind. A good murderer is good-of-his-kind, but is not thereby a proper object of admiring respect, and similarly in the case of natural objects. The type of inherent goodness required by an environmental ethic is conceptually distinct from being good of its kind.

The second possible answer to (a) is that life makes something inherently good. To what extent this view is connected with Schweitzer's famous ethic of reverence for life, or with Kenneth Goodpaster's recent argument for considering life as a necessary and sufficient condition of something being "morally considerable," I do not know, and I cannot here explore these matters in detail. But limiting the class of beings which have inherent value to the class of living beings seems to be an arbitrary decision and one that does not serve well as a basis for an environmental ethic. That it appears arbitrary is perhaps best seen by considering the case of beauty, since in nature, as in art, it is not essential to the beauty of an object to insist that something living be involved.

As for question (b), I have even less to say and that is negative also. My one point is that we cannot find out what is inherently good merely by finding out what those things are toward which we have admiring respect. All that this tells us is facts about the people who have this attitude. It does not tell us whether it is the fitting attitude to have. To put the point differently, we can be as mistaken in our judgment that something is inherently good as we can be in our judgment about how old or how heavy it is. Our feeling one way or another does not settle matters one way or the other.

How, then, are we to settle these matters? I wish I knew. I am not even certain that they can be settled in a rationally coherent way, and hence the tentativeness of my closing remarks. But more fundamentally, there is the earlier question about the very possibility of an environmental ethic. If I am right, the development of what can properly be called an environmental ethic requires that we postulate inherent value in nature. I have tried to say something about this variety of goodness as well as something about its role in an ethic of the environment. If my remarks have been intelligible and my arguments persuasive, then, though the project is far from complete, we at least know the direction in which we must move to make headway in environmental ethics, and that is no small advantage.

DISCUSSION QUESTIONS

1. If Regan is right that the three arguments he rejects fail to show that an environmental ethic is impossible, can we conclude that an environmental ethic is possible? How can we determine whether an environmental ethic is possible?
2. Assess Regan's account of intrinsic goodness. What problems do you see with it?
3. Is Regan attempting to find person-like properties in nature (think of his claim about the Colorado River) to support claims of intrinsic value in nature? Is the river free in anything like the same sense in which you are free? Are you free? How could the sense in which you are free apply to the river and could it ground intrinsic value for the river?

RICHARD SYLVAN

Is There a Need for a New, an Environmental, Ethic?

Richard Sylvan was a fellow with the Research School of Social Sciences at the Australian National University in Canberra. Published in 1973, "Is There a Need for a New, an Environmental, Ethic?" considers the possibility of an environmental ethic as a "new" sort of ethical view. As Sylvan explains, what counts as a new, opposed to a modified or extended "old," ethic is itself a controversial issue, since moral perspectives are not tidy theoretical structures. Sylvan identifies individual freedom as a core principle of our "old" Western moral outlook. He calls this principle "human chauvinism," and produces a series of counterexamples intended to show that this core principle is flawed. Most famous is his "last man" story. Does the last man to exist do anything wrong if he sets out to destroy the natural world?

CRITICAL READING QUESTIONS

1. In what way is the dominant Western moral view inconsistent with an environmental ethic, according to Sylvan?
2. What does Sylvan mean when he claims such an environmental ethic would not be primitive, mystical, or romantic?
3. How does Sylvan define the central principle of human chauvinism?

Richard Sylvan, "Is There a Need for a New, An Environmental, Ethic?" *Proceedings of the XV World Congress of Philosophy* No. 1, Varna, Bulgaria, 1973, pp. 205–210. Reprinted by permission.

4. What are the "last man" stories supposed to show and how are they supposed to show it?
5. What kinds of changes would an environmental ethic force in our moral deliberations, according to Sylvan? (Hint: See his discussion of natural rights and species bias.)
6. What does Sylvan mean by an expansion of the "base class"?

1

It is increasingly said that civilization, Western civilization at least, stands in need of a new ethic (and derivatively of a new economics) setting out people's relations to the natural environment, in Leopold's words "an ethic dealing with man's relation to land and to the animals and plants which grow upon it."[1] It is not of course that old and prevailing ethics do not deal with man's relation to nature; they do, and on the prevailing view man is free to deal with nature as he pleases, i.e., his relations with nature, insofar at least as they do not affect others, are not subject to moral censure. Thus assertions such as "Crusoe ought not to be mutilating those trees" are significant and morally determinate but, inasmuch at least as Crusoe's actions do not interfere with others, they are false or do not hold—and trees are not, in a good sense, moral objects.[2] It is to this, to the values and evaluations of the prevailing ethics, that Leopold and others in fact take exception. Leopold regards as subject to moral criticism, as wrong, behavior that on prevailing views is morally permissible. But it is not, as Leopold seems to think, that such behavior is beyond the scope of the prevailing ethics and that an *extension* of traditional morality is required to cover such cases, to fill a moral void. If Leopold is right in his criticism of prevailing conduct what is required is a *change* in the ethics, in attitudes, values and evaluations. For as matters stand, as he himself explains, men do not feel morally ashamed if they interfere with a wilderness, if they maltreat the land, extract from it whatever it will yield, and then move on; and such conduct is not taken to interfere with and does not rouse the moral indignation of others. "A farmer who clears the woods off a 75 percent slope, turns his cows into the clearing, and dumps its rainfall, rocks, and soil into the community creek, is still (if otherwise decent) a respected member of society."[3] Under what we shall call *an environmental ethic* such traditionally permissible conduct would be accounted morally wrong, and the farmer subject to proper moral criticism.

Let us grant such evaluations for the purpose of the argument. What is not so clear is that a *new* ethic is required even for such radical judgments. For one thing it is none too clear what is going to count as a new ethic, much as it is often unclear whether a new development in physics counts as a new physics or just as a modification or extension of the old. For, notoriously, ethics are not clearly articulated or at all well worked out, so that the application of identity criteria for ethics may remain obscure.[4] Furthermore we tend to cluster a family of ethical systems which do not differ on core or fundamental principles together as one ethic; e.g. the Christian ethic, which is an umbrella notion covering a cluster of differing and even competing systems. In fact then there are two other possibilities, apart from a new environmental ethic, which might cater for the evaluations, namely that of an extension or modification of the prevailing ethics or that of the development of principles that are already encompassed or latent within the prevailing ethic. The second possibility, that environmental evaluations can be incorporated within (and ecological problems solved within) the framework of prevailing Western ethics, is open because there isn't a single ethical system uniquely assumed in Western civilization: on many issues, and especially on controversial issues such as infanticide, women's rights, and drugs, there are competing sets of principles. Talk of a new ethic and prevailing ethics tends to suggest a sort of monolithic structure, a uniformity, that prevailing ethics, and even a single ethic, need not have.

Indeed Passmore has mapped out three important traditions in Western ethical views concerning man's relation to nature; a dominant tradition, the despotic position, with man as despot (or tyrant), and two lesser traditions, the stewardship position, with man as custodian, and the co-operative position with man as perfecter.[5] Nor are these the only traditions; primitivism is another, and both romanticism and mysticism have influenced Western views.

The dominant Western view is simply inconsistent with an environmental ethic; for according to it nature is the dominion of man and he is free to deal with it as he pleases (since—at least on the mainstream Stoic-Augustine view—it exists only for his sake), whereas on an environmental ethic man is not so free to do as he pleases. But it is not quite so obvious that an environmental ethic cannot be coupled with one of the lesser traditions. Part of the problem is that the lesser traditions are by no means adequately characterized anywhere, especially when the religious backdrop is removed, e.g. *who* is man steward for and responsible to? However both traditions are inconsistent with an environmental ethic because they imply policies of complete interference, whereas on an environmental ethic some worthwhile parts of the earth's surface should be preserved from substantial human interference, whether of the "improving" sort or not. Both traditions would in fact prefer to see the earth's land surfaces reshaped along the lines of the tame and comfortable north-European small farm and village landscape. According to the co-operative position man's proper role is to develop, cultivate and perfect nature—all nature eventually—by bringing out its potentialities, the test of perfection being primarily usefulness for human purposes; while on the stewardship view man's role, like that of a farm manager, is to make nature productive by his efforts though not by means that will deliberately degrade its resources. Although these positions both depart from the dominant position in a way which enables the incorporation of some evaluations of an environmental ethic, e.g. some of those concerning the irresponsible farmer, they do not go far enough: for in the present situation of expanding populations confined to finite natural areas, they will lead to, and enjoin, the perfecting, farming and utilizing of all natural areas. Indeed these lesser traditions lead to, what a thoroughgoing environmental ethic would reject, a principle of total use, implying that every natural area should be cultivated or otherwise used for human ends, "humanized."[6]

As the important Western traditions exclude an environmental ethic, it would appear that such an ethic, not primitive, mystical or romantic, would be new all right. The matter is not so straightforward; for the dominant ethic has been substantially qualified by the rider that one is not always entitled to do as one pleases where this physically interferes with others. Maybe some such proviso was implicit all along (despite evidence to the contrary), and it was simply assumed that doing what one pleased with natural items would not affect others (the non-interference assumption). Be this as it may, the *modified* dominant position appears, at least for many thinkers, to have supplanted the dominant position; and the modified position can undoubtedly go much further towards an environmental ethic. For example, the farmer's polluting of a community stream may be ruled immoral on the grounds that it physically interferes with others who use or would use the streams. Likewise business enterprises which destroy the natural environment for no satisfactory returns or which cause pollution deleterious to the health of future humans, can be criticized on the sort of welfare basis (e.g. that of Barkley and Seckler) that blends with the modified position; and so on.[7] The position may even serve to restrict the sort of family size one is entitled to have since in a finite situation excessive population levels will interfere with future people. Nonetheless neither the modified dominant position nor its Western variants, obtained by combining it with the lesser traditions, is adequate as an environmental ethic, as I shall try to show. A new ethic *is* wanted.

2

As we noticed (an) *ethic* is ambiguous, as between a specific ethical system, a *specific* ethic, and a more generic notion, a super ethic, under which specific ethics cluster.[8] An ethical system S is, near enough, a propositional system (i.e. a structured set of propositions) or theory which includes (like individuals of a theory) a set of values and (like postulates of a theory) a set of general evaluative judgments concerning conduct, typically of what is obligatory, permissible and wrong, of what are rights, what is valued, and so forth. A general or lawlike proposition of a system is a principle; and certainly if system S_1 and S_2 contain different principles, then they are different systems. It follows that any environmental ethic differs from the important traditional ethics outlined. Moreover if environmental ethics differ from Western ethical systems on some *core* principle embedded in Western systems, then these systems differ from the Western super ethic (assuming, what seems to be so, that it can be uniquely characterized)—in which case if an environmental ethic *is* needed then a new ethic is wanted. It suffices then to locate a core principle and to provide environmental counter examples to it.

It is commonly assumed that there are what amount to core principles of Western ethical systems, principles that will accordingly belong to the super ethic. The fairness principle inscribed in the Golden Rule provides one example. Directly relevant here, as a good stab at a core principle, is the commonly formulated liberal principle of the modified dominance position. A recent formulation runs as follows: "The liberal philosophy of the Western world holds that one should be able to do what he wishes, providing (1) that he does not harm others and (2) that he is not likely to harm himself irreparably."[9]

Let us call this principle *basic (human) chauvinism*—because under it humans, or people, come first and everything else a bad last—though sometimes the principle is hailed as a *freedom* principle because it gives permission to perform a wide range of actions (including actions which mess up the environment and natural things) providing they do not harm others. In fact it tends to cunningly shift the onus of proof to others. It is worth remarking that *harming others* in the restriction is narrower than a restriction to the (usual) interests of others; it is not enough that it is in my interests, because I detest you, that you stop breathing; you are free to breathe, for the time being anyway, because it does not harm me. There remains a problem however as to exactly what counts as harm or interference. Moreover the width of the principle is so far obscure because "other" may be filled out in significantly different ways: it makes a difference to the extent, and privilege, of the chauvinism whether "other" expands to "other human"—which is too restrictive—or to "other person" or to "other sentient being"; and it makes a difference to the adequacy of the principle, and inversely to its economic applicability, to which class of others it is intended to apply, whether to future as well as to present others, whether to remote future others or only to nondiscountable future others and whether to possible others. The latter would make the principle completely unworkable, and it is generally assumed that it applies at most to present and future others.

It is taken for granted in designing counterexamples to basic chauvinist principles, that a semantical analysis of permissibility and obligation statements stretches out over ideal situations (which may be incomplete or even inconsistent), so that what is permissible holds in some ideal situation, what is obligatory in every ideal situation, and what is wrong is excluded in every ideal situation. But the main point to grasp for the counterexamples that follow, is that ethical principles if correct are universal and are assessed over the class of ideal situations.

(i) The *last man* example. The last man (or person) surviving the collapse of the world system lays about him, eliminating, as far as he can, every living thing, animal or plant (but painlessly if you like, as at the best abattoirs). What he does is quite permissible according to basic chauvinism, but on environmental grounds what he does is wrong. Moreover one does not have to be committed to esoteric values to regard Mr. Last Man as behaving badly (the reason being perhaps that radical thinking and values have shifted in an environmental direction in advance of corresponding shifts in the formulation of fundamental evaluative principles).

(ii) The *last people* example. The last man example can be broadened to the last people example. We can assume that they know they are the last people, e.g. because they are aware that radiation effects have blocked any chance of reproduction. One considers the last people in order to rule out the possibility that what these people do harms or somehow physically interferes with later people. Otherwise one could as well consider science fiction cases where people arrive at a new planet and destroy its ecosystems, whether with good intentions such as perfecting the planet for their ends and making it more fruitful or, forgetting the lesser traditions, just for the hell of it.

Let us assume that the last people are very numerous. They humanely exterminate every wild animal and they eliminate the fish of the seas, they put all arable land under intensive cultivation, and all remaining forests disappear in favor of quarries or plantations, and so on. They may give various familiar reasons for this, e.g. they believe it is the way to salvation or to perfection, or they are simply satisfying reasonable needs, or even that it is needed to keep the last people employed or occupied so that they do not worry too much about their impending extinction. On an environmental ethic the last people have behaved badly; they have simplified and largely destroyed all the natural ecosystems, and with their demise the world will soon be an ugly and largely wrecked place. But this conduct may conform with the basic chauvinist principle, and as well with the principles enjoined by the lesser traditions. Indeed the main point of elaborating this example is because, as the last man example reveals, basic chauvinism may conflict with stewardship or co-operation principles. The conflict may be removed it seems by conjoining a further proviso to the basic principle, the effect (3) that he does not willfully destroy natural resources. But as the last people do not destroy resources willfully, but perhaps "for the best of reasons," the variant is still environmentally inadequate.

(iii) The *great entrepreneur* example. The last man example can be adjusted so as to not fall foul of clause (3). The last man is an industrialist; he runs a giant complex of automated factories and farms which he proceeds to extend. He produces automobiles among other things, from renewable and recyclable resources of course, only he dumps and recycles these shortly after manufacture and sale to a dummy buyer instead of putting them on the road for a short time as we do. Of course he has the best of reasons for his activity, e.g. he is increasing gross world product, or he is improving output to fulfill some plan, and he will be increasing his own and general welfare since he much prefers increased output and productivity. The entrepreneur's behavior is on the Western ethic quite permissible; indeed his conduct is commonly thought to be quite fine and may even meet Pareto optimality requirements given prevailing notions of being "better off."

Just as we can extend the last man example to a class of last people, so we can extend this example to the *industrial society* example: the society looks rather like ours.

(iv) The *vanishing species* example. Consider the blue whale, a mixed good on the economic picture. The blue whale is on the verge of extinction because of his qualities as a private good, as a source of valuable oil and meat. The catching and marketing of blue whales does not harm the whalers; it does not harm or physically interfere with others in any good sense, though it may upset them and they may be prepared to compensate the whalers if they desist; nor need whale hunting be willful destruction. (Slightly different examples which eliminate the hunting aspect of the blue whale example are provided by cases where a species is eliminated or threatened through destruction of its habitat by man's activity or the activities of animals he has introduced e.g. many plains-dwelling Australian marsupials and the Arabian oryx.) The behavior of the whalers in eliminating this magnificent species of whale is accordingly quite permissible—at least according to basic chauvinism. But on an environmental ethic it is not. However, the free-market mechanism will not cease allocating whales to commercial uses, as a satisfactory environmental economics would; instead the market model will grind inexorably along the private demand curve until the blue whale population is no longer viable—if that point has not already been passed.[10]

In sum, the class of permissible actions that rebound on the environment is more narrowly circumscribed on an environmental ethic than it is in the Western super ethic. But aren't environmentalists going too far in claiming that these people, those of the examples and respected industrialists, fishermen and farmers are behaving, when engaging in environmentally degrading activities of the sort described, in a morally impermissible way? No, what these people do is to a greater or lesser extent evil, and hence in serious cases morally impermissible. For example, insofar as the killing or forced displacement of primitive peoples who stand in the way of an industrial development is morally indefensible and impermissible, so also is the slaughter of the last remaining blue whales for private profit. But how to reformulate basic chauvinism as a satisfactory freedom principle is a more difficult matter. A tentative, but none too adequate beginning might be made by extending (2) to include harm to or interference with others who would be so affected by the action in question were they placed in the environment and (3) to exclude speciecide. It may be preferable, in view of the way the freedom principle sets the onus of proof, simply to scrap it altogether, and instead to specify classes of rights and permissible conduct, as in a bill of rights.

3

A radical change in a theory sometimes forces changes in the meta-theory; e.g. a logic which rejects the Reference Theory in a thoroughgoing way requires a modification of the usual meta-theory which also accepts the Reference Theory and indeed which is tailored to cater only for logics which do conform. A somewhat similar phenomenon seems to occur in the case of a meta-ethic adequate for an environmental ethic. Quite apart from introducing several environmentally important notions, such as *conservation, pollution, growth,* and *preservation,* for meta-ethical analysis, an environmental ethic compels re-examination and modified analysis of such characteristic actions as *natural right, ground* of right, and of the relations of obligation and permissibility to rights; it may well require reassessment of traditional analyses of such notions as *value* and *right,* especially where these are based on chauvinist assumptions; and it forces the rejection of many of the more prominent meta-ethical positions. These points are illustrated by a very brief examination of accounts of *natural right* and then by a sketch of the species bias of some major positions.[11]

Hart accepts, subject to defeating conditions which are here irrelevant, the classical doctrine of natural rights according to which, among other things, "any adult human . . . capable of choice is at liberty to do (i.e. is under no obligation to abstain from) any action which is not one coercing or restraining or designed to injure other persons."[12] But this sufficient condition for a human natural right depends on accepting the very human chauvinist principle an environmental ethic rejects, since if a person has a natural right he has a right; so too the *definition* of a natural right adopted by classical theorists and accepted with minor qualifications by Hart presupposes the same defective principle. Accordingly an environmental ethic would have to amend the classical notion of a natural right, a far from straightforward matter now that human rights with respect to animals and the natural environment are, like those with respect to slaves not all that long ago, undergoing major re-evaluation.

An environmental ethic does not commit one to the view that natural objects such as trees have rights (though such a view is occasionally held, e.g. by pantheists. But pantheism is false since artifacts are not alive). For moral prohibitions forbidding certain actions with respect to an object do not award that object a correlative right. That it would be wrong to mutilate a given tree or piece of property does not entail that the tree or piece of property has a correlative right not to be mutilated (without seriously stretching the notion of a right). Environmental views can stick with mainstream theses according to which rights are coupled with corresponding responsibilities and so with bearing obligations, and with corresponding interests and concern; i.e. at least, whatever has a right also has responsibilities and therefore obligations, and whatever has a right has interests. Thus although any person may have a right by no means every living thing can (significantly) have rights, and arguably most sentient objects other than persons cannot have rights. But persons can relate morally, through obligations, prohibitions and so forth, to practically anything at all.

The species bias of certain ethical and economic positions which aim to make principles of conduct or reasonable economic behavior calculable is easily brought out. These positions typically employ a single criterion p, such as preference or happiness, as a *summum bonum;* characteristically each individual of some *base* class, almost always humans, but perhaps including future humans, is supposed to have an ordinal p ranking of the states in question (e.g. of affairs, of the economy); then some principle is supplied to determine a collective p ranking of these states in terms of individual p rankings, and what is best or ought to be done is determined either directly, as in act-utilitarianism under the Greatest Happiness principle, or indirectly, as in rule-utilitarianism, in terms of some optimization principle applied to the collective ranking. The species bias is transparent from the selection of the base class. And even if the base class is extended to embrace persons, or even some animals (at the cost, like that of including remotely future humans, of losing testability), the positions are open to familiar criticism, namely that the whole of the base class may be prejudiced in a way which leads to unjust principles. For example if every member of the base class detests dingoes, on the basis of mistaken data as to dingoes' behavior, then by the Pareto ranking test the collective ranking will rank states where dingoes are exterminated very highly, from which it will generally be concluded that dingoes ought to be exterminated (the evaluation of most Australian farmers anyway). Likewise it would just be a happy accident, it seems, if collective demand (horizontally summed from individual demand) for a state of the economy with blue whales as a mixed good, were to succeed in outweighing private whaling demands; for if no one in the base class happened to know that blue whales exist or cared a jot that they do then "rational" economic decision making would do nothing to prevent their extinction. Whether the blue whale survives should not have to depend on what humans know or what they see on television. Human interests and preferences are far too parochial to provide a satisfactory basis for deciding on what is environmentally desirable.

These ethical and economic theories are not alone in their species chauvinism; much the same applies to most going meta-ethical theories which, unlike intuitionistic theories, try to offer some rationale for their basic principles. For instance, on social contract positions obligations are a matter of mutual agreements between individuals of the base class; on a social justice picture rights and obligations spring from the application of symmetrical fairness principles to members of the base class, usually a rather special class of persons, while on a Kantian position which has some vague obligations somehow arise from respect for members of the base class persons. In each case if members of the base class happen to be ill-disposed to items outside the base class then that is too bad for them: that is (rough) justice.

NOTES

1. Aldo Leopold, *A Sand County Almanac with Essays on Conservation from Round River* (New York: Ballantine, 1966), p. 238.
2. A view occasionally tempered by the idea that trees house spirits.
3. Leopold, *Sand County,* p. 245.
4. To the consternation no doubt of Quineans. But the fact is that we can talk perfectly well about inchoate and fragmentary systems the identity of which may be indeterminate.
5. John Passmore, *Man's Responsibility for Nature: Ecological Problems and Western Traditions* (New York: Scribner's, 1974).
6. If "use" is extended, somewhat illicitly, to include use for preservation, this total use principle is rendered innocuous at least as regards its actual effects. Note that the total use principle is tied to the resource view of nature.
7. P. W. Barkley and D. W. Seckler, *Economic Growth and Environmental Decay: The Solution Becomes the Problem* (New York: Harcourt, Brace, Jovanovich, 1972).
8. A *meta-ethic* is, as usual, a theory about ethics, super ethics, their features and fundamental notions.
9. Barkley and Seckler, *Economic Growth and Environmental Decay,* p. 58. A related principle is that (modified) free enterprise can operate within similar limits.
10. The tragedy of the commons type reasons are well explained in Barkley and Seckler, *Economic Growth and Environmental Decay.*
11. Some of these points are developed by those protesting about human maltreatment of animals; see especially the essays collected in S.

and R. Godlovitch and J. Harris, eds., *Animals, Men and Morals: An Enquiry into the Maltreatment of Non-humans* (New York: Grove Press, 1971).

12. H. L. A. Hart, "Are There any Natural Rights?" reprinted in A. Quinton, ed., *Political Philosophy* (London: Oxford University Press, 1967).

DISCUSSION QUESTIONS

1. Why, according to Sylvan, is a "new" ethic of the environment necessary? What is wrong with simply trying to extend or modify our "old" ethics to cover environmental matters? Is he right? (Recall Passmore's discussion here about a new environmental ethic.)
2. Do you think it is possible to construct an environmental ethic that is not primitive, mystical, or romantic? What would such an ethic even be like?
3. How are the "last man" stories supposed to be counterexamples against the principle of human chauvinism? Might the last man do wrong for a different reason, such as how his behavior reflects on his own character?
4. Sylvan claims, "An environmental ethic does not commit one to the view that natural objects such as trees have rights." Why not? Could trees have rights?
5. Why are human interests and preferences "far too parochial to provide a satisfactory basis for deciding on what is environmentally desirable"? Is Sylvan correct?
6. Why ought the "base class" to be expanded? Are some members of the base class more morally significant than others? What effect will this have on an environmental ethic of the sort Sylvan is calling for?

MARY MIDGLEY

Duties Concerning Islands

Mary Midgley is senior lecturer in philosophy, emeritus, University of Newcastle. She has written very influential books and articles in environmental philosophy, including *The Beastly Mirror.* In her famous article "Duties Concerning Islands," Midgley asks, in a variation on the last man stories in Passmore and Sylvan, whether Robinson Crusoe had any obligations toward his island. The central target for her discussion is a contract account of morality. Contract accounts of morality begin with a hypothetical "state of nature," people living outside of society and any moral restraints whatsoever. There is no rule of law, no society, no custom, no morality, no property (since property entails rightful ownership); just people in their "natural state," shorn of all that social living confers. Life in the state of nature is allegedly dreadful—"solitary, poor, nasty, brutish, and short," as Thomas Hobbes (1588–1679) memorably described it. In desperation we are driven to contract with each other; I agree not to kill you, if you agree not to kill me; I agree not to steal from you, if you agree not to steal from me. And so on for all the rules that make for harmonious social living. So ethics consists of those principles that rational agents would agree to in order to live together, thereby promoting their individual well-being.

Mary Midgley, "Duties Concerning Islands," from *Environmental Philosophy,* R. Elliot and A. Gare, eds., 1983, pp., 166–81. Reprinted by permission from University of Queensland Press.

Contract accounts of morality are elegant and explanatorily powerful. But are they correct? Mary Midgley, thinks not. As she puts it, "All the terms which express that an obligation is serious or binding—duty, right, law, morality, obligation, justice—have been deliberately narrowed in their use so as to apply only in the framework of contract." This means, of course, there can be no duties to natural objects, plants, animals, species, ecosystems, or, indeed, to anything other than rational agents because we can enter into contracts only with rational agents.

CRITICAL READING QUESTIONS

1. What contrast does Midgley set up between moral theory and everyday moral consciousness?
2. What is Midgley's criticism of Grice's position and how is that relevant to her overall criticism of contract ethics?
3. In what way is social contract ethics like 17th century physics, according to Midgley?
4. What is the list of beings cited by Midgley supposed to show and how is it supposed to show it?
5. According to Midgley, which moral term best captures our relationship to the members on the list she provides?
6. What, according to Midgley, is the basis for duties to the animate and inanimate beings on her list?

Had Robinson Crusoe any duties?

When I was a philosophy student, this used to be a familiar conundrum, which was supposed to pose a very simple question: namely, can you have duties to yourself? Mill, they correctly told us, said no. "The term *duty to oneself,* when it means anything more than prudence, means self-respect or self-development, and for none of these is anyone accountable to his fellow-creatures."[1] Kant, on the other hand, said yes. "Duties to ourselves are of primary importance and should have pride of place . . . nothing can be expected of a man who dishonors his own person."[2] There is a serious disagreement here, not to be sneezed away just by saying, "it depends on what you mean by duty." Much bigger issues are involved—quite how big has, I think, not yet been fully realized. To grasp this, I suggest that we rewrite a part of Crusoe's story, in order to bring in sight a different range of concerns.

> 19 Sept. 1685. This day I set aside to devastate my island. My pinnace being now ready on the shore, and all things prepared for my departure. Friday's people also expecting me, and the wind blowing fresh away from my little harbour. I had a mind to see how all would burn. So then, setting sparks and powder craftily among certain dry spinneys which I had chosen. I soon had it ablaze, nor was there left, by the next dawn, any green stick among the ruins . . .

Now, work on the style how you will, you cannot make that into a convincing paragraph. Crusoe was not the most scrupulous of men, but he would have felt an invincible objection to this senseless destruction. So would the rest of us. Yet the language of our moral tradition has tended strongly, ever since the Enlightenment, to make that objection unstateable. All the terms which express that an obligation is serious or binding—duty, right, law, morality, obligation, justice—have been deliberately narrowed in their use so as to apply only in the framework of contract, to describe only relations holding between free and rational agents. Since it has been decided a priori that rationality admits of no degrees and that cetaceans are not rational, it follows that, unless you take either religion or science fiction seriously, we can only have duties to humans, and sane, adult, responsible humans at that. Now the morality we live by certainly does not accept this restriction. In common life we recognize many other duties as serious and binding, though of course not necessarily overriding. If philosophers want to call these something else instead of duties, they must justify their move.

We have here one of those clashes between the language of common morality (which is of course always to some extent confused and inarticulate) and an intellectual scheme which arose in the first place from a part of that morality, but has now taken off on its own claims of authority to correct other parts of its source. There are always real difficulties here. As ordinary citizens, we have to guard against dismissing such intellectual schemes too casually; we have to do justice to the point of them. But, as philosophers, we have to resist the opposite temptation of taking the intellectual schemes as decisive, just because it is elegant and satisfying, or because the moral insight which is its starting-point is specially familiar to us. Today, this intellectualist bias is often expressed by calling the insights of common morality mere "intuitions." This is quite misleading, since it gives the impression that they have been reached without thought, and that there is, by contrast, a scientific solution somewhere else to which they ought to bow—as there might be if we were contrasting commonsense "intuitions" about the physical world with physics or astronomy. Even without that word, philosophers often manage to give the impression that whenever our moral views clash with any simple, convenient scheme, it is our *duty* to abandon them. Thus, Grice states:

> It is an inescapable consequence of the thesis presented in these pages that certain classes cannot have natural rights: animals, the human embryo, future generations, lunatics and children under the age of, say, 10. In the case of young children at least, my experience is that this consequence is found hard to accept. But it is a consequence of the theory; it is, I believe, true; and I think we should be willing to accept it. At first sight it seems a harsh conclusion, but it is not nearly so harsh as it appears.[3]

But it is in fact extremely harsh, since what he is saying is that the treatment of children ought not to be determined by their interests but by the interests of the surrounding adults capable of contract, which, of course, can easily conflict with them. In our society, he explains, this does not actually make much difference, because parents here are so benevolent that they positively want to benefit their children, and accordingly here "the interests of children are reflected in the interests of their parents." But this, he adds, is just a contingent fact about us. "It is easy to imagine a society where this is not so," where, that is, parents are entirely exploitative. "In this circumstance, the morally correct treatment of children would no doubt be harsher than it is in our society. But the conclusion has to be accepted." Grice demands that we withdraw our objections to harshness, in deference to theoretical consistency. But "harsh" here does not mean just "brisk and bracing," like cold baths and a plain diet. (There might well be more of those where parents do feel bound to consider their children's interests.) It means "unjust." Our objection to unbridled parental selfishness is not a mere matter of tone or taste; it is a moral one. It therefore requires a moral answer, an explanation of the contrary *value* which the contrary theory expresses. Grice, and those who argue like him, take the ascetic, disapproving tone of those who have already displayed such a value, and who are met by a slovenly reluctance to rise to it. But they have not displayed that value. The ascetic tone cannot be justified merely by an appeal to consistency. An ethical theory which, when consistently followed through, has iniquitous consequences, is a bad theory and must be changed. Certainly we can ask whether these consequences really are iniquitous, but this question must be handled seriously. We cannot directly conclude that the consequences cease to stink the moment they are seen to follow from our theory.

The theoretical model which has spread blight in this area is, of course, that of social contract, and, to suit it, that whole cluster of essential moral terms—right, duty, justice and the rest—has been progressively narrowed. This model shows human society as a spread of standard social atoms, originally distinct and independent, each of which combines with others only at its own choice and in its own private interest. This model is drawn from physics, and from 17th-century physics, at that, where the ultimate particles of matter were conceived as hard, impenetrable, homogeneous little billiard-balls, with no hooks or internal structure. To see how such atoms could combine at all was very hard. Physics, accordingly, moved on from this notion to one which treats atoms and other particles as complex items, describable mainly in terms of forces, and those the same kind of forces which operate outside them. It has abandoned the notion of ultimate, solitary, independent individuals. Social-contract theory, however, retains it . . .

Writers who treat morality as primarily contractual tend to discuss noncontractual cases briefly, casually, and parenthetically, as though they were rather rare. Rawls's comments on the problem of mental defectives are entirely typical here. We have succeeded, they say, in laying most of the carpet; why are you making this fuss about those little wrinkles behind the sofa? This treatment confirms a view, already suggested by certain aspects of current politics in the United States, that those who fail to clock in as normal rational agents and make their contracts are just occasional exceptions, constituting one more "minority" group—worrying, no doubt, to the scrupulous, but not a central concern of any society. Let us, then, glance briefly at their scope, by roughly listing some cases which seem to involve us in noncontractual duties. (The order is purely provisional and the numbers are added just for convenience.)

Human sector	1. The dead
	2. Posterity
	3. Children
	4. The senile
	5. The temporarily insane
	6. The permanently insane
	7. Defectives, ranging down to "human vegetables"
	8. Embryos, human and otherwise
Animal sector	9. Sentient animals
	10. Nonsentient animals
Inanimate sector	11. Plants of all kinds
	12. Artifacts, including works of art
	13. Inanimate but structured objects—crystals, rivers, rocks, etc.
Comprehensive	14. Unchosen groups of all kinds, including families and species
	15. Ecosystems, landscapes, villages, warrens, cities, etc.
	16. Countries
	17. The biosphere
Miscellaneous	18. Oneself
	19. God

No doubt I have missed a few, but that will do to go on with. The point is this; if we look only at a few of these groupings, and without giving them full attention, it is easy to think that we can include one or two as honorary contracting members by a slight stretch of our conceptual scheme, and find arguments for excluding the others from serious concern entirely. But if we keep our eye on the size of the range, this stops being plausible. As far as sheer numbers go, this is no minority of the beings with whom we have to deal. We are a small minority of them. As far as importance goes, it is certainly possible to argue that some of these sorts of beings should concern us more and others less: we need a priority system. But, to build it, *moral* arguments are required. The various kinds of claims have to be understood and compared, not written off in advance. We cannot rule that those who in our own and other cultures, suppose that there is a direct objection to injuring or destroying some of them, are always just confused, and mean only, in fact, that this item will be needed for rational human consumption.[4]

The blank antithesis which Kant made between rational persons (having value) and mere things (having none) will not serve us to map out this vast continuum. And the idea that, starting at some given point on this list, we have a general license for destruction, is itself a moral view which would have to be justified. Western culture differs from most others in the breadth of destructive license which it allows itself, and, since the 17th century, that license has been greatly extended. Scruples about rapine have been continually dismissed as irrational, but it is not always clear with what rational principles they are supposed to conflict. Western destructiveness has not in fact developed in response to a new set of disinterested intellectual principles demonstrating the need for more people and less redwoods, but mainly as a by-product of greed and increasing commercial confidence. Humanistic hostility to superstition has played some part in the process, because respect for the non-human items on our list is often taken to be religious. It does not have to be. Many scientists who are card-carrying atheists can still see the point of preserving the biosphere. So can the rest of us, religious or otherwise. It is the whole of which we are parts, and its other parts concern us for that reason . . .

What, then, about duties? I believe that this term can properly be used over the whole range. We have quite simply got many kinds of duties to animals,[5] to plants, and to the biosphere. But to speak in this way we must free the term once and for all from its restrictive contractual use, or irrelevant doubts will still haunt us. If we cannot do this, we shall have to exclude the word "duty," along with "rights" from all detailed discussion, using wider words like "wrong," "right," and "ought" instead. This gymnastic would be possible but inconvenient. The issue about duty becomes clear as soon as we look at the controversy from which I started, between Kant's and Mill's views on duties to oneself. What do we think about this? Are there duties of integrity, autonomy, self-knowledge, self-respect? It seems that there are. Mill is right, of course, to point out that they are not duties *to* someone in the ordinary sense. The divided self is a metaphor. It is as natural and necessary a metaphor here as it is over, say, self-deception or self-control, but it certainly is not literal truth. The form of the requirement is different. Rights, for instance, certainly do not seem to come in here as they often would with duties to other persons; we would scarcely say, "I have a right to my own respect." And the *kind* of things which we can owe ourselves are distinctive. It is not just chance who they are owed to. You cannot owe it to somebody else, as you can to yourself, to force him to act freely or with integrity. He owes that to himself, the rest of us can only remove outside difficulties. As Kant justly said, our business is to promote our own perfection and the happiness of others; the perfection of others is an aim which belongs to them.[6] Respect, indeed, we owe both to ourselves and to others, but Kant may well be right to say that self-respect is really a different and deeper requirement, something without which all outward duties would become meaningless. (This may explain the paralyzing effect of depression.)

Duties to oneself, in fact, are duties with a different *form*. They are far less close than outward duties to the literal model of debt, especially monetary debt. Money is a thing which can be owed in principle to anybody, it is the same whoever you owe it to, and if by chance you come to owe it to yourself, the debt vanishes. Not many of our duties are really of this impersonal kind; the attempt to commute other sorts of duties into money is a notorious form of evasion. Utilitarianism, however, wants to make all duties as homogeneous as possible. And that is the point of Mill's position. He views all our self-concerning motives as parts of the desire for happiness. Therefore he places all duty, indeed all morality, on the outside world, as socially required restriction of that desire—an expression, that is, of other people's desire for happiness.

> We do not call anything wrong, unless we mean that a person ought to be punished in some way or another for doing it; if not by law, by the opinion of his fellow-creatures; if not by opinion, by the reproaches of his own conscience. This seems the real turning point of the distinction between morality and simple expediency. It is a part of the notion of Duty in every one of its forms, that a person may rightly be compelled to fulfil it. Duty is a thing which may be *exacted* from a person, as one exacts a debt.[7]

To make the notion of wrongness depend on punishment and public opinion in this way instead of the other way round is a bold step. Mill did not mind falling flat on his face from time to time in trying out a new notion for the public good. He did it for us, and we should, I think, take proper advantage of his generosity, and accept the impossibility which he demonstrates. The concepts cannot be connected this way round. Unless you think of certain acts as wrong, it makes no sense to talk of punishment. "Punishing" alcoholics with aversion therapy or experimental rats with electric shocks is not really punishing at all; it is just deterrence. This "punishment" will not make their previous actions wrong, nor has it anything to do with morality. The real point of morality returns to Mill's scheme in the Trojan horse of 'the reproaches of his own conscience'. Why do *they* matter? Unless the conscience is talking sense—that is, on Utilitarian principles, unless it is delivering the judgment of society—it should surely be silenced. Mill, himself a man of enormous integrity, deeply concerned about autonomy, would never have agreed to silence it. But, unless we do so, we shall have to complicate his scheme. It may well be true that, in the last resort and at the deepest level, conscience and the desire for happiness converge. But in ordinary life and at the everyday level they can diverge amazingly. We do want to be honest but we do not want to be put out. What we know we ought to do is often most unwelcome to us, which is why we call it duty. And whole sections of that duty do not concern other people directly at all. A good example is the situation in Huxley's *Brave New World,* where a few dissident citizens have grasped the possibility of a fuller and freer life. Nobody else wants this. Happiness is already assured. The primary duty of change here seems to be that of each to himself. True, they may feel bound also to help others to change, but hardly in a way which those others would *exact.* In fact, we may do better here by dropping the awkward second party altogether and saying that they have a duty *of* living differently—one which will affect both themselves and others, but which does not require, as a debt does, a named person or people *to* whom it must be paid. Wider models like "the whole duty of man" may be more relevant.

This one example from my list will, I hope, be enough to explain the point. I cannot go through all of them, nor ought it to be necessary. Duties need *not* be quasi-contractual relations between symmetrical pairs of rational human agents. There are all kinds of other obligations holding between asymmetrical pairs, or involving, as in this case, no outside beings at all. To speak of duties *to* things in the inanimate and comprehensive sectors of my list is not necessarily to personify them superstitiously, or to indulge in chatter about the "secret life of plants."[8] It expresses merely that there are suitable and unsuitable ways of behaving in given situations. People have duties *as* farmers, parents, consumers, forest dwellers, colonists, species members, shipwrecked mariners, tourists, potential ancestors, and actual descendants, etc. As such, it is the business of each not to forget his transitory and dependent position, the rich gifts which he has received, and the tiny part he plays in a vast, irreplaceable and fragile whole.

It is remarkable that we now have to state this obvious truth as if it were new, and invent the word "ecological" to describe a whole vast class of duties. Most peoples are used to the idea. In stating it, and getting back into the centre of our moral stage, we meet various difficulties, of which the most insidious is possibly the temptation to feed this issue as fuel to long-standing controversies about religion. Is concern for the nonhuman aspects of our biosphere necessarily superstitious and therefore to be resisted tooth and nail? I have pointed out that it need not be religious. Certified rejectors of all known religions can share it. No doubt, however, there is a wider sense in which any deep and impersonal concern can be called religious—one in which Marxism is a religion. No doubt, too, all such deep concerns have their dangers, but certainly the complete absence of them has worse dangers. Moreover, anyone wishing above all to avoid the religious dimension should consider that the intense individualism which has focused our attention exclusively on the social-contract model is itself thoroughly mystical. It has glorified the individual human soul as an object having infinite and transcendent value; has hailed it as the only real creator; and bestowed on it much of the panoply of God. Nietzsche, who was responsible for much of this new theology,[9] took over from the old theology (which he plundered extensively) the assumption that all the rest of creation mattered only as a frame for humankind. This is not an impression which any disinterested observer would get from looking round at it, nor do we need it in order to take our destiny sufficiently seriously.

Crusoe then, I conclude, did have duties concerning his island, and with the caution just given we can reasonably call them duties *to* it. They were not very exacting, and were mostly negative. They differed, of course, from those which a long-standing inhabitant of a country has. Here the language of *fatherland* and *motherland,* which is so widely employed, indicates rightly a duty of care and responsibility which can go very deep, and which long-settled people commonly feel strongly. To insist that it is really only a duty to the exploiting human beings is not consistent with the emphasis often given to reverence for the actual trees, mountains, lakes, rivers and the like which are found there. A decision to inhibit all this rich area of human love is a special manœuvre for which reasons would need to be given, not a dispassionate analysis of existing duties and feelings. What happens, however, when you are shipwrecked on an entirely strange island? As the history of colonization shows, there is a tendency for people so placed to drop any reverence and become more exploitative. But it is not irresistible. Raiders who settle down can quite soon begin to feel at home, as the Vikings did in East Anglia, and can, after a while, become as possessive, proud, and protective towards their new land as the old inhabitants. Crusoe himself does, from time to time, show this pride rather touchingly, and it would, I think, certainly have inhibited any moderate temptation, such as that which I mentioned, to have a good bonfire. What keeps him sane through his stay is in fact his duty to God. If that had been absent. I should rather suppose that sanity would depend on a stronger and more positive attachment to the island itself and its creatures. It is interesting, however, that Crusoe's story played its part in developing that same icy individualism which has gone so far towards making both sorts of attachment seem corrupt or impossible. Rousseau delighted in *Robinson Crusoe,* and praised it as the only book fit to be given to a child, *not* because it showed a man in his true relation to animal and vegetable life, but because it was the bible of individualism. "The surest way to raise him [the child] above prejudice and to base his judgements on the true relations of things, is to put him in the place of a solitary man, and to judge all things as they would be judged by such a man in relation to their own utility . . . So long as only bodily needs are recognized, man is self-sufficing . . . the child knows no other happiness but food and freedom."[10] That false atomic notion of human psychology—a prejudice above which nobody ever raised Rousseau—is the flaw in all social-contract thinking. If he were right, every member of the human race would need a separate island—and what, then, would our ecological problems be? Perhaps, after all, we had better count our blessings.

NOTES

1. John Stuart Mill, *Essay on Liberty* (London: Dent, Everyman's Library, 1910), p. 135.
2. Immanuel Kant, "Duties to Oneself," in *Lectures on Ethics,* tr. Louis Infield (London: Methuen, 1930), p. 118.
3. G. R. Grice, *Grounds for Moral Sentiments* (Cambridge: Cambridge University Press, 1967), 147–9.
4. For details, see John Rodman, "Animal Justice: The Counter-Revolution in Natural Right and Law," *Inquiry,* 22/1–2 (Summer 1979).
5. A case first made by Jeremy Bentham. *An Introduction to the Principles of Morals and Legislation* (1784) chap. 17, and well worked out by Peter Singer. *Animal Liberation* (New York: Avon, 1975), chap. 1, 5, and 6.
6. Immanuel Kant, *Preface to the Metaphysical Elements of Ethics.* "Introduction to Ethics," 4 and 5, tr. Thomas K. Abbot.
7. John Stuart Mill, *Utilitarianism* (London: Dent, Everyman's Library, 1910), chap. 5, 45; first published 1863.
8. P. Tompkins and C. Bird, *The Secret Life of Plants* (New York: Harper and Row, 1973), claimed to show, by various experiments involving electrical apparatus, that plants can feel. Attempts to duplicate their experiments have, however, totally failed to produce any similar results. (See A. W. Galston and C. L. Slayman, "The Secret Life of Plants," *American Scientist,* 67 (1973), p. 337.) It seems possible that the original results were due to a fault in the electrical apparatus. The attempt shows, I think, one of the confusions which continually arise from insisting that all duties must be of the same form. We do not need to prove that plants are animals in order to have reason to spare them. The point is well discussed by Marian Dawkins in her book *Animal Suffering* (London: Chapman and Hall, 1981), pp. 117–19.
9. See particularly, Friedrich Nietzsche, *Thus Spake Zarathustra,* 3, s. "Of Old and New Tables" and *The Joyful Wisdom* (otherwise called *The Gay Science*), 125 (the Madman's Speech). I have discussed this rather mysterious appointment of man to succeed God in a paper called "Creation and Originality," to be published in a volume of my essays forthcoming from the Harvester Press.
10. Barbara Foxley, tr., *Emile* (London: Dent, Everyman's Library, 1966), pp. 147–48.

DISCUSSION QUESTIONS

1. How might a social contractarian handle questions about our obligations to children and nonrational human beings?
2. Assess the list of beings to whom Midgley claims we have noncontractual duties. Is her claim plausible?
3. The key move in Midgley's argument occurs in the following passage: "To speak of duties *to* things in the inanimate and comprehensive sectors of my list is not necessarily to personify them superstitiously, or to indulge in chatter about the 'secret life of plants.' It expresses merely that there are suitable and unsuitable ways of behaving in given situations." What does she mean? How are we to identify "suitable" and "unsuitable" ways of behaving in given situations and how is this relevant to environmental ethics?

CHRISTOPHER D. STONE

Should Trees Have Standing?

TOWARD LEGAL RIGHTS FOR NATURAL OBJECTS

Christopher Stone is professor of law at the University of Southern California, Los Angeles. In his influential book, *Should Trees Have Standing,* from which our selection is taken, Stone argues for the "unthinkable," namely, that natural objects should be granted legal rights. Stone points out that the lawyer's world is already populated with inanimate rights-holders, such as corporations, trusts, municipalities, and so forth, so why not include natural objects as well?

CRITICAL READING QUESTIONS

1. Why, according to Stone, is the extension of legal rights always unthinkable, at least at first?
2. For Stone, what does it mean to have legal rights?
3. How does Stone deal with the objection that natural objects cannot have legal rights because they cannot speak?
4. How might a natural object function in the legal system, according to Stone?
5. Why does Stone think that we should give rights to various natural objects? What effect would doing so have on us, in his view?
6. What is Stone's attitude about the relation between the law and our personal development?

INTRODUCTION: THE UNTHINKABLE

In *Descent of Man,* Darwin observes that the history of man's moral development has been a continual extension in the objects of his "social instincts and sympathies." Originally each man had regard only for himself and those of a very narrow circle about him; later, he came to regard more and more "not only the welfare, but the happiness of all his fellow-men"; then "his sympathies became more tender and widely diffused, extending to men of all races, to the imbecile, maimed, and other useless members of society, and finally to the lower animals . . ."[1]

The history of the *law* suggests a parallel development. Perhaps there never was a pure Hobbesian state of nature, in which no "rights" existed except in the vacant sense of each man's "right to self-defense." But it is not unlikely that so far as the earliest "families" (including extended kinship groups and clans) were concerned, everyone outside the family was suspect, alien, rightless.[2] And even within the family, persons we presently regard as the natural holders of at least some rights had none. Take, for example, children. We know something of the early rights-status of children from the widespread practice of infanticide—especially of the deformed and female.[3] (Senicide,[4] as among the North American Indians, was the corresponding rightlessness of the aged.)[5] Maine tells us that as late as the Patria Potestas of the Romans, the father had *jus vitae necisque*—the power of life and death—over his children. A fortiori, Maine writes, he had power of "uncontrolled corporal chastisement; he can modify their personal condition at pleasure; he can give a wife to his son; he can give his daughter in marriage; he can divorce his children of either sex; he can transfer them to another family by adoption; and he can sell them." The child was less than a person: an object, a thing.[6]

The legal rights of children have long since been recognized in principle, and are still expanding in practice. Witness, just within recent time, *In re Gault,*[7] guaranteeing basic constitutional protections to juvenile defendants, and the Voting Rights Act of 1970.[8] We have been *making persons* of children although they were not, in law, always so. And we have done the same, albeit imperfectly some would say, with prisoners,[9] aliens, women (especially of the married variety), the insane,[10] Blacks, fetuses,[11] and Indians.

Nor is it only matter in human form that has come to be recognized as the possessor of rights. The world of the lawyer is peopled with inanimate right-holders: trusts, corporations, joint ventures, municipalities, Subchapter R partnerships,[12] and nation-states, to mention just a few. Ships, still referred to by courts in the feminine gender, have long had an independent jural life, often with striking consequences.[13] We have become so accustomed to the idea of a corporation having "its" own rights, and being a "person" and "citizen" for so many statutory and constitutional purposes, that we forget how jarring the notion was to early jurists. "That invisible, intangible and artificial being, that mere legal entity" Chief Justice Marshall wrote of the corporation in *Bank of the United States v. Deveaux*[14]—could a suit be brought in *its* name? Ten years later, in the *Dartmouth College* case,[15] he was still refusing to let pass unnoticed the wonder of an entity "existing only in contemplation of law."[16] Yet, long before Marshall worried over the personifying of the modern corporation, the best medieval legal scholars had spent hundreds of years struggling with the notion of the legal nature of those great public "corporate bodies," the Church and the State. How could they exist in law, as entities transcending the living Pope and King? It was clear how a king could bind *himself*—on his honor—by a treaty. But when the king died, what was it that was burdened with the obligations of, and claimed the rights under, the treaty *his* tangible hand had signed? The medieval mind saw (what we have lost our capacity to see)[17] how *unthinkable* it was, and worked out the most elaborate conceits and fallacies to serve as anthropomorphic flesh for the Universal Church and the Universal Empire.[18]

It is this note of the *unthinkable* that I want to dwell upon for a moment. Throughout legal history, each successive extension of rights to some new entity has been, theretofore, a bit unthinkable. We are inclined to suppose the rightlessness of rightless "things" to be a decree of nature, not a legal convention acting in support of some status quo. It is thus that we defer considering the choices involved in all their moral, social, and economic dimensions. And so the United States Supreme Court could straight-facedly tell us in

Dred Scott that *blacks* had been denied the rights of citizenship "as a subordinate and inferior class of beings, who had been subjugated by the dominant race . . ."[19] In the 19th century, the highest court in California explained that *Chinese* had not the right to testify against white men in criminal matters because they were "a race of people whom nature has marked as inferior, and who are incapable of progress or intellectual development beyond a certain point . . . between whom and ourselves nature has placed an impassable difference."[20] The popular conception of the *Jew* in the 13th century contributed to a law which treated them as "men *ferae naturae,* protected by a quasi-forest law. Like the roe and the deer, they form an order apart."[21] Recall, too, that it was not so long ago that the *fetus* was "like the roe and the deer." In an early suit attempting to establish a wrongful death action on behalf of a negligently killed fetus (now widely accepted practice), Holmes, then on the Massachusetts Supreme Court, seems to have thought it simply inconceivable "that a man might owe a civil duty and incur a conditional prospective liability in tort to one not yet in being."[22] The first *woman* in Wisconsin who thought she might have a right to practice law was told that she did not, in the following terms:

> The law of nature destines and qualifies the female sex for the bearing and nurture of the children of our race and for the custody of the homes of the world . . . [A]ll life-long callings of women, inconsistent with these radical and sacred duties of their sex, as is the profession of the law, are departures from the order of nature; and when voluntary, treason against it . . . The peculiar qualities of womanhood, its gentle graces, its quick sensibility, its tender susceptibility, its purity, its delicacy, its emotional impulses, its subordination of hard reason to sympathetic feeling, are surely not qualifications for forensic strife. Nature has tempered woman as little for the juridical conflicts of the court room, as for the physical conflicts of the battle field . . .[23]

The fact is, that each time there is a movement to confer rights onto some new "entity," the proposal is bound to sound odd or frightening or laughable. This is partly because until the rightless thing receives its rights, we cannot see it as anything but a *thing* for the use of "us"—those who are holding rights at the time.[24] In this vein, what is striking about the Wisconsin case above is that the court, for all its talk about women, so clearly was never able to see women as they are (and might become). All it could see was the popular "idealized" version of *an object it needed.* Such is the way the slave South looked upon the black.[25] [There is something of a seamless web involved: There will be resistance to giving the thing "rights" until it can be seen and valued for itself; yet, it is hard to see it and value it for itself until we can bring ourselves to give it "rights"—which is almost inevitably going to sound inconceivable to a large group of people.

The reason for this little discourse on the unthinkable, the reader must know by now, if only from the title of the paper. I am quite seriously proposing that we give legal rights to forests, oceans, rivers, and other so-called "natural objects" in the environment—indeed, to the natural environment as a whole.

As strange as such a notion may sound, it is neither fanciful nor devoid of operational content. In fact, I do not think it would be a misdescription of recent developments in the law to say that we are already on the verge of assigning some such rights, although we have not faced up to what we are doing in those particular terms.[26] We should do so now, and begin to explore the implications such a notion would hold.

TOWARD RIGHTS FOR THE ENVIRONMENT

Now, to say that the natural environment should have rights is not to say anything as silly as that no one should be allowed to cut down a tree. We say human beings have rights, but—at least as of the time of this writing—they can be executed. Corporations have rights, but they cannot plead the fifth amendment; *In re Gault* gave 15-year-olds certain rights in juvenile proceedings, but it did not give them the right to vote. Thus, to say that the environment should have rights is not to say that it should have every right we can imagine, or even the same body of rights as human beings have. Nor is it to say that everything in the environment should have the same rights as every other thing in the environment.

What the granting of rights does involve has two sides to it. The first involves what might be called the legal-operational aspects; the second, the psychic and socio-psychic aspects. I shall deal with these aspects in turn.

THE LEGAL-OPERATIONAL ASPECTS

What It Means to be a Holder of Legal Rights

There is, so far as I know, no generally accepted standard for how one ought to use the term "legal rights." Let me indicate how I shall be using it in this piece.

First and most obviously, if the term is to have any content at all, an entity cannot be said to hold a legal right unless and until *some public authoritative body* is prepared to give *some amount of review* to actions that are colorably inconsistent with that "right." For example, if a student can be expelled from a university and cannot get any public official, even a judge or administrative agent at the lowest level, either (i) to require the university to justify its actions (if only to the extent of filling out an affidavit alleging that the expulsion "was not wholly arbitrary and capricious") or (ii) to compel the university to accord the student some procedural safeguards (a hearing, right to counsel, right to have notice of charges), then the minimum requirements for saying that the student has a legal right to his education do not exist.[27]

But for a thing to be *a holder of legal rights,* something more is needed than that some authoritative body will review the actions and processes of those who threaten it. As I shall use the term, "holder of legal rights," each of three additional criteria must be satisfied. All three, one will observe, go towards making a thing *count jurally*—to have a legally recognized worth and dignity in its own right, and not merely to serve as a means to benefit "us" (whoever the contemporary group of rights-holders may be). They are, *first,* that the thing can institute legal actions *at its behest; second,* that in determining the granting of legal relief, the court must take *injury to it* into account; and *third,* that relief must run to the *benefit of it.* . . .

The Rightlessness of Natural Objects at Common Law

Consider, for example, the common law's posture toward the pollution of a stream. True, courts have always been able, in some circumstances, to issue orders that will stop the pollution . . . But the stream itself is fundamentally rightless, with implications that deserve careful reconsideration.

The first sense in which the stream is not a rights-holder has to do with standing. The stream itself has none. So far as the common law is concerned, there is in general no way to challenge the polluter's actions save at the behest of a lower riparian—another human being—able to show an invasion of *his* rights. This conception of the riparian as the holder of the right to bring suit has more than theoretical interest. The lower riparians may simply not care about the pollution. They themselves may be polluting, and not wish to stir up legal waters. They may be economically dependent on their polluting neighbor. And, of course, when they discount the value of winning by the costs of bringing suit and the chances of success, the action may not seem worth undertaking. Consider, for example, that while the polluter might be injuring 100 downstream riparians $10,000 a year *in the aggregate,* each riparian separately might be suffering injury only to the extent of $100—possibly not enough for any one of them to want to press suit by himself, or even to go to the trouble and cost of securing co-plaintiffs to make it worth everyone's while. This hesitance will be especially likely when the potential plaintiffs consider the burdens the law puts in their way:[28] proving, *e.g.,* specific damages, the "unreasonableness" of defendant's use of the water, the fact that practicable means of abatement exist, and overcoming difficulties raised by issues such as joint causality, right to pollute by prescription, and so forth. Even in states which, like California, sought to overcome these difficulties by empowering the attorney-general to sue for abatement of pollution in limited instances, the power has been sparingly invoked and, when invoked, narrowly construed by the courts.[29]

The second sense in which the common law denies "rights" to natural objects has to do with the way in which the merits are decided in those cases in which someone is competent and willing to establish standing. At its more primitive levels, the system protected the "rights" of the property owning human with minimal weighing of any values: "*Cujus'est solum, ejus est usque ad coelum et ad infernos.*"[30] Today we have come more and more to make balances—but only such as will adjust the economic best interests of identifiable humans. For example, continuing with the case of streams, there are commentators who speak of a "general rule" that "a riparian owner is legally entitled to have the stream flow by his land with its quality unimpaired" and observe that "an upper owner has prima facie, no right to pollute the water."[31] Such a doctrine, if strictly invoked, would protect the stream absolutely whenever a suit was brought; but obviously, to look around us, the law does not work that way. Almost everywhere there are doctrinal qualifications on riparian "rights" to an unpolluted stream.[32] Although these rules vary from jurisdiction to jurisdiction, and upon whether one is suing for an equitable injunction or for damages, what they all have in common is some sort of balancing. Whether under language of "reasonable use," "reasonable methods of use," "balance of convenience" or "the public interest doctrine," what the courts are balancing, with varying degrees of directness, are the economic hardships or the upper riparian (or dependent community) of abating the pollution vis-à-vis the economic hardships of continued pollution on the lower riparians. What does not weigh in the balance is the damage to the stream, its fish and turtles and "lower" life. So long as the natural environment itself is rightless, these are not matters for judicial cognizance. Thus, we find the highest court of Pennsylvania refusing to stop a coal company from discharging polluted mine water into a tributary of the Lackawana River because a plaintiff's "grievance is for a mere personal inconvenience; and . . . mere private personal inconveniences . . . must yield to the necessities of a great public industry, which although in the hands of a private corporation, subserves a great public interest."[33] The stream itself is lost sight of in "a quantitative compromise between *two* conflicting interests."[34]

The third way in which the common law makes natural objects rightless has to do with who is regarded as the beneficiary of a favorable judgment. Here, too, it makes a considerable difference that it is not the natural object that counts in its own right. To illustrate this point, let me begin by observing that it makes perfectly good sense to speak of, and ascertain, the legal damage to a natural object, if only in the sense of "making it whole" with respect to the most obvious factors. The costs of making a forest whole, for example, would include the costs of reseeding, repairing watersheds, restocking wildlife—the sorts of costs the Forest Service undergoes after a fire. Making a polluted stream whole would include the costs of restocking with fish, water-fowl, and other animal and vegetable life, dredging, washing out impurities, establishing natural and/or artificial aerating agents, and so forth. Now, what is important to note is that, under our present system, even if a plaintiff riparian wins a water pollution suit for damages, no money goes to the benefit of the stream itself to repair *its* damages. This omission has the further effect that, at most, the law confronts a polluter with what it takes to make the plaintiff riparians whole; this may be far less than the damages to the stream, but not so much as to force the polluter to desist. For example, it is easy to imagine a polluter whose activities damage a stream to the extent of $10,000 annually, although the aggregate damage to all the riparian plaintiffs who come into the suit is only $3,000. If $3,000 is less than the cost to the polluter of shutting down, or making the requisite technological changes, he might prefer to pay off the damages (*i.e.,* the legally cognizable damages) and continue to pollute the stream. Similarly, even if the jurisdiction issues an injunction at the plaintiffs' behest (rather than to order payment of damages), there is nothing to stop the plaintiffs from "selling out" the stream, *i.e.,* agreeing to dissolve or not enforce the injunction at some price (in the example above, somewhere between plaintiffs' damages—$3,000—and defendant's next best economic alternative). Indeed, I take it this is exactly what Learned Hand had in mind in an opinion in which, after issuing an anti-pollution injunction, he suggests that the defendant "make its peace with the plaintiff as best it can."[35] What is meant is a peace between *them,* and not amongst them and the river.

I ought to make clear at this point that the common law as it affects streams and rivers, which I have been using as an example so far, is not exactly the same as the law affecting other environmental objects. Indeed, one would be hard pressed to say that there was a "typical" environmental object, so far as its treatment at the hands of the law is concerned. There are some differences in the law applicable to all the various resources that are held in common: rivers, lakes, oceans, dunes, air, streams (surface and subterranean), beaches, and so forth. And there is an even greater difference as between these traditional communal resources on the one hand, and natural objects on traditionally private land, *e.g.*, the pond on the farmer's field, or the stand of trees on the suburbanite's lawn.

On the other hand, although there be these differences which would make it fatuous to generalize about a law of the natural environment, most of these differences simply underscore the points made in the instance of rivers and streams. None of the natural objects, whether held in common or situated on private land, has any of the three criteria of a rights-holder. They have no standing in their own right; their unique damages do not count in determining outcome; and they are not the beneficiaries of awards. In such fashion, these objects have traditionally been regarded by the common law, and even by all but the most recent legislation, as objects for man to conquer and master and use—in such a way as the law once looked upon "man's" relationships to African Negroes. Even where special measures have been taken to conserve them, as by seasons on game and limits on timber cutting, the dominant motive has been to conserve them *for us*—for the greatest good of the greatest number of human beings. Conservationists, so far as I am aware, are generally reluctant to maintain otherwise.[36] As the name implies, they want to conserve and guarantee *our* consumption and *our* enjoyment of these other living things. In their own right, natural objects have counted for little in law as in popular movements.

As I mentioned at the outset, however, the rightlessness of the natural environment can and should change; it already shows some signs of doing so.

Toward Having Standing in Its Own Right

It is not inevitable, nor is it wise, that natural objects should have no rights to seek redress in their own behalf. It is no answer to say that streams and forests cannot have standing because streams and forest cannot speak. Corporations cannot speak either; nor can states, estates; infants, incompetents, municipalities or universities. Lawyers speak for them, as they customarily do for the ordinary citizen with legal problems. One ought, I think, to handle the legal problems of natural objects as one does the problems of legal incompetents—human beings who have become vegetable. If a human being shows signs of becoming senile and has affairs that he is de jure incompetent to manage, those concerned with his well being make such a showing to the court, and someone is designated by the court with the authority to manage the incompetent's affairs. The guardian (or "conservator" or "committee"—the terminology varies) then represents the incompetent in his legal affairs. Courts make similar appointments when a corporation has become "incompetent"—they appoint a trustee in bankruptcy or reorganization to oversee its affairs and speak for it in court when that becomes necessary.

On a parity of reasoning, we should have a system in which, when a *friend of a natural* object perceives it to be endangered, he can apply to a court for the creation of a guardianship. Perhaps we already have the machinery to do so. California law, for example, defines an incompetent as "any person, whether insane or not, who by reason of old age, disease, weakness of mind, or other cause, is unable, unassisted, properly to manage and take care of himself or his property, and by reason thereof is likely to be deceived or imposed upon by artful or designing persons."[37] Of course, to urge a court that an endangered river is "a person" under this provision will call for lawyers as bold and imaginative as those who convinced the Supreme Court that a railroad corporation was a "person" under the fourteenth amendment, a constitutional provision theretofore generally thought of as designed to secure the rights of freedmen . . .[38]

The guardianship approach, however, is apt to raise . . . [the following objection]: a committee or guardian could not judge the needs of the river or forest in its charge; indeed, the very concept of "needs," it might be said, could be used here only in the most metaphorical way . . .

Natural objects *can* communicate their wants (needs) to us, and in ways that are not terribly ambiguous. I am sure I can judge with more certainty and meaningfulness whether and when my lawn wants (needs) water, than the Attorney General can judge whether and when the United States wants (needs) to take an appeal from an adverse judgment by a lower court. The lawn tells me that it wants water by a certain dryness of the blades and soil—immediately obvious to the touch—the appearance of bald spots, yellowing, and a lack of springiness after being walked on; how does "the United States" communicate to the Attorney General? For similar reasons, the guardian-attorney for a smog-endangered stand of pines could venture with more confidence that his client wants the smog stopped, than the directors of a corporation can assert that "the corporation" wants dividends declared. We make decisions on behalf of, and in the purported interests of, others every day; these "others" are often creatures whose wants are far less verifiable, and even far more metaphysical in conception, than the wants of rivers, trees, and land . . .

The argument for "personifying" the environment, from the point of damage calculations, can best be demonstrated from the welfare economics position. Every well-working legal-economic system should be so structured as to confront each of us with the full costs that our activities are imposing on society. Ideally, a paper-mill, in deciding what to produce—and where, and by what methods—ought to be forced to take into account not only the lumber, acid and labor that its production "takes" from other uses in the society, but also what costs alternative production plans will impose on society through pollution. The legal system, through the law of contracts and the criminal law, for example, makes the mill confront the costs of the first group of demands. When, for example, the company's purchasing agent orders 1000 drums of acid from the Z Company, the Z Company can bind the mill to pay for them, and thereby reimburse the society for what the mill is removing from alternative uses.

Unfortunately, so far as the pollution costs are concerned, the allocative ideal begins to break down, because the traditional legal institutions have a more difficult time "catching" and confronting us with the full social costs of our activities. In the lakeside mill example, major riparian interests might bring an action, forcing a court to weigh *their* aggregate losses against the costs to the mill of installing the anti-pollution device. But many other interests—and I am speaking for the moment of recognized homocentric interests—are too fragmented and perhaps "too remote" causally to warrant securing representation and pressing for recovery: the people who own summer homes and motels, the man who sells fishing tackle and bait, the man who rents rowboats. There is no reason not to allow the lake to prove damages to them as the prima facie measure of damages to it. *By doing so, we in effect make the natural object, through its guardian, a jural entity competent to gather up these fragmented and otherwise unrepresented damage claims, and press them before the court even where, for legal or practical reasons, they are not going to be pressed by traditional class action plaintiffs.* Indeed, one way—the homocentric way—to view what I am proposing so far, is to view the guardian of the natural object as the guardian of unborn generations, as well as of the otherwise unrepresented but distantly injured contemporary humans.[39] By making the lake itself the focus of these damages, and incorporating it so to speak, the legal system can effectively take proof upon, and confront the mill with a larger and more representative measure of the damages its pollution causes.

So far, I do not suppose that my economist friends (unremittent human chauvinists every one of them) will have any large quarrel in principle with the concept. Many will view it as a *trompe l'oeil* that comes down, at best, to effectuate the goals of the paragon class action, or the paragon water pollution control district. Where we are apt to part company is here—I propose going beyond gathering up the loose ends of what most people would presently recognize as economically valid damages. The guardian would urge before the court injuries not presently cognizable—the death of eagles and inedible crabs, the suffering of sea lions the loss from the face of the earth of species of commercially valueless birds, the disappearance of a wilderness area. One might, of course, speak of the damages involved as "damages" to us humans and indeed the widespread growth of environmental groups shows that human beings do feel these losses. But they are not, at present, economically measurable losses: how can they have a monetary value for the guardian to prove in court?

The answer for me is simple. Wherever it carves out "property" rights, the legal system as engaged in the process of *creating* monetary worth. One's literary works would have minimal monetary value if anyone could copy them at will. Their economic value to the author is a product of the law of copyright; the person who copies a copyrighted book has to bear a cost to the copyright-holder because the law says he must. Similarly, it is through the law of torts that we have made a "right" of—and guaranteed an economically meaningful value to—privacy. (The value we place on gold—a yellow inanimate dirt—is not simply a function of supply and demand—wilderness areas are scarce and pretty to—but results from the actions of the legal systems of the world, which have institutionalized that value; they have even done a remarkable job of stabilizing the price.) I am proposing we do the same with eagles and wilderness areas as we do with copyrighted works, patented inventions, and privacy: *make* the violation of rights in them to be a cost by declaring the "pirating" of them to be the invasion of a property interest.[40] If we do so, the net social costs the polluter would be confronted with would include not only the extended homocentric costs of his pollution (explained above) but also costs to the environment *per se.*

How, though, would these costs be calculated? When we protect an invention, we can at least speak of a fair market value for it, by reference to which damages can be computed. But the lost environmental "values" of which we are now speaking are by definition over and above those that the market is prepared to bid for they are priceless.

One possible measure of damages suggested earlier, would be the *cost of making the environment whole,* just as, when a man is injured in an automobile accident, we impose upon the responsible party the injured man's medical expenses. Comparable expenses to a polluted river would be the costs of dredging, restocking with fish, and so forth. It is on the basis of such costs as these, I assume, that we get the figure of $1 billion as the cost of saving Lake Erie.[41] As an ideal, I think this is a good guide applicable in many environmental situations. It is by no means free from difficulties, however.

THE PSYCHIC AND SOCIO-PSYCHIC ASPECTS

The strongest case can be made from the perspective of human advantage for conferring rights on the environment. Scientists have been warning of the crises the earth and all humans on it face if we do not change our ways—radically—and these crises make the lost "recreational use" of rivers seem absolutely trivial. The earth's very atmosphere is threatened with frightening possibilities: absorption of sunlight, upon which the entire life cycle depends, may be diminished; the oceans may warm (increasing the "greenhouse effect" of the atmosphere), melting the polar ice caps, and destroying our great coastal cities; the portion of the atmosphere that shields us from dangerous radiation may be destroyed. Testifying before Congress, sea explorer Jacques Cousteau predicted that the oceans (to which we dreamily look to feed our booming populations) are headed toward their own death: "The cycle of life is intricately tied up with the cycle of water . . . the water system has to remain alive if we are to remain alive on earth."[48] We are depleting our energy and our food sources at a rate that takes little account of the needs even of humans now living.

These problems will not be solved easily; they very likely can be solved, if at all, only through a willingness to suspend the rate of increase in the standard of living (by present values) of the earth's "advanced" nations, and by stabilizing the total human population. For some of us this will involve forfeiting material comforts; for others it will involve abandoning the hope someday to obtain comforts long envied. For all of us it will involve giving up the right to have as many offspring as we might wish. Such a program is not impossible of realization, however. Many of our so-called "material comforts" are not only in excess of, but are probably in opposition to, basic biological needs. Further, the "costs" to the advanced nations is not as large as would appear from Gross National Product figures. GNP reflects social gain (of a sort) without discounting for the social *cost* of that gain, *e.g.,* the losses through depletion of resources, pollution, and so forth. As has well been shown, as societies become more and more "advanced," their real marginal gains become less and less for each additional dollar of GNP.[49] Thus, to give up "human progress" would not be as costly as might appear on first blush.

Nonetheless, such far-reaching social changes are going to involve us in a serious reconsideration of our consciousness towards the environment . . .

A radical new conception of man's relationship to the rest of nature would not only be a step towards solving the material planetary problems; there are strong reasons for such a changed consciousness from the point of making us far better humans. If we only stop for a moment and look at the underlying human qualities that our present attitudes toward property and nature draw upon and reinforce, we have to be struck by how stultifying of our own personal growth and satisfaction they can become when they take rein of us. Hegel, in "justifying" private property, unwittingly reflects the tone and quality of some of the needs that are played upon:

> A person has as his substantive end the right of putting his will into any and every thing and thereby making it his, because it has no such end in itself and derives its destiny and soul from his will. This is the absolute right of appropriation which man has over all "things."[50]

What is it within us that gives us this need not just to satisfy basic biological wants, but to extend our wills over things, to object-ify them, to make them ours, to manipulate them, to keep them at a psychic distance? Can it all be explained on "rational" bases? Should we not be suspect of such needs within us, cautious as to why we wish to gratify them? When I first read that passage of Hegel, I immediately thought not only of the emotional contrast with Spinoza, but of the passage in Carson McCullers' *A Tree, A Rock, A Cloud,* in which an old derelict has collared a twelve year old boy in a streetcar cafe. The old man asks whether the boy knows "how love should be begun?"

The old man leaned closer and whispered:

> "A tree. A rock. A cloud."
>
> . . .
>
> "The weather was like this in Portland," he said. "At the time my science was begun. I meditated and I started very cautious. I would pick up something from the street and take it home with me. I bought a goldfish and I concentrated on the goldfish and I loved it. I graduated from one thing to another. Day by day I was getting this technique . . .
>
> "For six years now I have gone around by myself and built up my science. And now I am a master. Son. I can love anything. No longer do I have to think about it even. I see a street full of people and a beautiful light comes in me. I watch a bird in the sky. Or I meet a traveler on the road. Everything, Son. And anybody. All stranger and all loved! Do you realize what a science like mine can mean?"[51]

To be able to get away from the view that nature is a collection of useful senseless objects is, as McCullers' "madman" suggests, deeply involved in the development of our abilities to love—or, if that is putting it too strongly, to be able to reach a heightened awareness of our own, and others' capacities in their mutual interplay. To do so, we have to give up some psychic investment in our sense of separateness and specialness in the universe. And this, in turn, is hard giving indeed, because it involves us in a flight backwards, into earlier stages of civilization and childhood in which we had to trust (and perhaps fear) our environment, for we had not then the power to master it. Yet, in doing so, we—as persons—gradually free ourselves of needs for supportive illusions. Is not this one of the triumphs for "us" of our giving legal rights to (or acknowledging the legal rights of) the Blacks and women?. . .

A few years ago the pollution of streams was thought of only as a problem of smelly, unsightly, unpotable water, *i.e.,* to us. Now we are beginning to discover that pollution is a process that destroys wondrously subtle balances of life within the water, and as between the water and its banks. This heightened awareness enlarges our sense of the dangers to us. But it also enlarges our empathy. We are not only developing the scientific capacity, but we are cultivating the personal capacities *within us* to recognize more and more the ways in which nature—like the woman, the black, the Indian, and the alien—is like us, (and we will also become more able realistically to define, confront, live with and admire the ways in which we are all different).

The time may be on hand when these sentiments, and the early stirrings of the law, can be coalesced into a radical new theory or myth—felt as well as intellectualized—of man's relationships to the rest of nature. I do not mean "myth" in a demeaning sense of the term, but in the sense in which, at different times in history, our social "facts" and relationships have been comprehended and integrated by reference to the "myths" that we are co-signers of a social contract, that the Pope is God's agent, and that all men are created equal. Pantheism, Shinto, and Tao all have myths to offer. But they are all, each in its own fashion, quaint, primitive and archaic. What is needed is a myth that can fit our growing body of knowledge of geophysics, biology, and the cosmos. In this vein, I do not think it too remote that we may come to regard the earth, as some have suggested, as one organism, of which mankind is a functional part—the mind, perhaps: different from the rest of nature, but different as a man's brain is from his lungs . . .

> As I see it, the Earth is only one organized "field" of activities—and so is the *human person*—but these activities take place at various levels, in different "spheres" of being and realms of consciousness. The lithosphere is not the biosphere, and the latter not the . . . ionosphere. The Earth is not *only* a material mass. Consciousness is not only "human"; it exists at animal and vegetable levels, and most likely must be latent, or operating in some form, in the molecule and the atom; and all these diverse and in a sense hierarchical modes of activity and consciousness should be seen integrated in and perhaps transcended by an all-encompassing and "eonic" planetary Consciousness.
>
> . . .
>
> Mankind's function within the Earth-organism is to extract from the activities of all other operative systems within this organism the type of consciousness which we call "reflective" or "self"-consciousness—or, we may also say to *mentalize* and give meaning, value, and "name" to all that takes place anywhere within the Earth-field . . .[52]

As radical as such a consciousness may sound today, all the dominant changes we see about us point in its direction. Consider just the impact of space travel, of worldwide mass media, of increasing scientific discoveries about the interrelatedness of all life processes. Is it any wonder that the term "spaceship earth" has so captured the popular imagination? The problems we have to confront are increasingly the world-wide crises of a global organism: not pollution of a stream, but pollution of the atmosphere and of the ocean. Increasingly, the death that occupies each human's imagination is not his own, but that of the entire life cycle of the planet earth, to which each of us is as but a cell to a body.

To shift from such a lofty fancy as the planetarization of consciousness to the operation of our municipal legal system is to come down to earth hard. Before the forces that are at work, our highest court is but a frail and feeble—a distinctly human—institution. Yet, the court may be at its best not in its work of handing down decrees, but at the very task that is called for: of summoning up from the human spirit the kindest and most generous and worthy ideas that abound there, giving them shape and reality and legitimacy. Witness the school desegregation cases which, more importantly than to integrate the schools (assuming they did), awakened us to *moral* needs which, when made visible, could not be denied. And so here, too, in the case of the environment, the Supreme Court may find itself in a position to award "rights" in a way that will contribute to a change in popular consciousness. It would be a modest move, to be sure, but one in furtherance of a large goal: the future of the planet as we know it.

How far we are from such a state of affairs, where the law treats "environmental objects" as holders of legal rights, I cannot say. But there is certainly intriguing language in one of Justice Black's last dissents, regarding the Texas Highway Department's plan to run a six-lane expressway through a San Antonio Park.[53] Complaining of the court's refusal to stay the plan, Black observed that "after today's decision, the people of San Antonio and the birds and animals that make their home in the park will share their quiet retreat with an ugly, smelly stream of traffic . . . Trees, shrubs, and flowers will be mowed down."[54] Elsewhere he speaks of the "burial of public parks," of segments of a highway which "devour parkland," and of the park's heartland.[55] Was he, at the end of his great career, on the verge of saying—just saying—that "nature has 'rights' on its own account"? Would it be so hard to do?

NOTES

1. C. Darwin, *Descent of Man,* pp. 119, 120–21 (2nd ed. 1874). *See also* R. Waelder, *Progress and Revolution,* p. 39 *et seq.* (1967).
2. See Darwin, *supra* note 1, at pp. 113–14.
3. See Darwin, *supra* note 1, at p. 113. *See also* E. Westermarck 1 *The Origin and Development of the Moral Ideas* pp. 406–12 (1912).
4. There does not appear to be a word *gericide* or *geronticide* to designate the killing of the aged. *Senicide* is as close as the Oxford English Dictionary comes, although, as it indicates, the word is rare. 9 Oxford English Dictionary, p. 454 (1933).
5. See Darwin, *supra* note 1, at pp. 386–93. Westermarck, *supra* note 3, at pp. 387–89, observes that where the killing of the aged and infirm is practiced, it is often supported by humanitarian justification; this, however, is a far cry from saying that the killing is *requested* by the victim as his right.
6. H. Maine, *Ancient Law* p. 153 (Pollock, ed. 1930).
7. 387 U.S. 1 (1967).
8. 42 U.S.C. §§ 1973 *et seq.* (1970).
9. See *Landman v. Royster,* 40 U.S.L.W. 2256 (E.D. Va., Oct. 30, 1971).
10. *But* see T. Szasz, *Law, Liberty and Psychiatry* (1963).
11. See note 22. The trend toward liberalized abortion can be seen either as a legislative tendency back in the direction of rightlessness for the fetus—or toward increasing rights of women. This inconsistency is not unique in the law of course; it is simply support for Hohfeld's scheme that the "jural opposite" of someone's right is someone elses "no-right." W. Hohfeld, *Fundamental Legal Conceptions* (1923).
12. Int. Rev. Code of 1954, § 1361 (repealed by Pub. L. No. 89–389, effective Jan. 1, 1969).
13. For example, See *United States v. Cargo of the Brig Melek Adhel,* 43 U.S. (2 How.) 210 (1844). There, a ship had been seized and used by pirates. All this was done without the knowledge or consent of the owners of the ship. After the ship had been captured, the United States condemned and sold the "offending vessel." The owners objected. In denying release to the owners, Justice Story cited Chief Justice Marshall from an earlier case: "This is not a proceeding against the owner; it is a proceeding against the vessel for an offense committed by the vessel; which is not the less an offense . . . because it was committed without the authority and against the will of the owner." 43 U.S. at 234, quoting from *United States v. Schooner Little Charles,* 26 F. Cas. 979 (No. 15,612) (C.C.D. Va. 1818).
14. 9 U.S. (5 Cranch) 61, 86 (1809).
15. *Trustees of Darmouth College v. Woodward,* 17 U.S. (4 Wheat.) 518 (1819).
16. *Ibid,* at 636.
17. Consider, for example, that the claim of the United States to the naval station at Guantanamo Bay, at $2000-a-year rental, is based upon a treaty signed in 1903 by José Montes for the President of Cuba and a minister representing Theodore Roosevelt; it was subsequently ratified by two-thirds of a Senate no member of which is living today. Lease [from Cuba] of Certain Areas for Naval or Coaling Stations, July 2, 1903, T.S. No. 426; C. Bevans, 6 Treaties and Other International Agreements of the United States 1776–1949, at 1120 (U.S. Dep't of State Pub. 8549, 1971).
18. O. Gierke, Political Theories of the Middle Age (Maitland transl. 1927), especially at 22–30. . . .
19. *Dred Scott v. Sandford,* 60 U.S. (19 How.) 396, 404–05 (1856). . . .
20. *People v. Hall,* 4 Cal. 399, 405 (1854). . . .
21. Schechter, *The Rightlessness of Mediaval English Jewry,* 45 Jewish Q. Rev. 121. 135 (1954) quoting from M. Bateson, *Medieval England* 139 (1904). . . .
22. *Dietrich v. Inhabitants of Northampton,* 138 Mass. 14, 16 (1884).
23. *In re* Goddell, 39 Wisc. 232, 245 (1875). The court continued with the following "clincher":

    And when counsel was arguing for this lady that the word, person, in sec. 32, ch. 119 [respecting those qualified to practice law], necessarily includes females, her presence made it impossible to suggest to him as *reductio ad absurdum* of his position, that the same construction of the same word . . . would subject woman to prosecution for the paterinty of a bastard, and . . . prosecution for rape.

    Id. at 246.

    The relationship between our attitude toward woman, on the one hand, and on the other, the more central concern of this article—land—is captured in an unguarded aside of our colleague, Curt Berger: ". . . after all, land, like woman, was meant to be possessed. . . ." Land Ownershp and Use 139 (1986).

24. Thus it was that the Founding Fathers could speak of the inalienable rights of all men, and yet maintain a society that was, by modern standards, without the most basic rights for Blacks, Indains, children and women. There was no hypocrisy; emotionally, no one *felt* that these other things were men.

25. The second thought streaming from . . . the older South [is] the sincere and passionate belief that somewhere between men and cattle, God created a tertium quid, and called it a Negro—a clownish, simple creature, at times even lovable within its limitations, but straitly foreordained to walk within the Veil. W. E. B. DuBois, The Souls of Black Folk 89 (1924).

26. The statement in text is not quite true; *cf.* Murphy, *Has Nature Any Right to Life?*, 22 Hast. L. J. 467 (1971). An Irish court, passing upon the validity of a testamentary trust to the benefit of someone's dogs, observed in dictum that "lives means lives of human beings, not of animals or trees in California." *Kelly v. Dillon,* 1932 Ir. R. 255, 261. (The intended gift over on the death of the last surviving dog was held void for remoteness, the court refusing "to enter into the question of a dog's expectation of life," although prepared to observe that "in point of fact neighbor's [sic] dogs and cats are unpleasantly long-lived. . . ." *Id.* at 260–61).

27. *See Dixon v. Alabama State Bd. of Educ.,* 294 F.2d 150 (5th Cir.), *cert. denied,* 368 U.S. 930 (1961).

28. The law in a suit for injunctive relief is commonly easier on the plantiff than in a suit for damages. See J. Gould, Lay of Waters § 206 (1883).

29. However, in 1970 California amended its Water Quality Act to make it easier for the Attorney General to obtain relief, e.g., one must no longer allege irreparable injury in a suit for an injuction. Cal. Water Code § 13350(b) (West 1971).

30. To whomsoever the soil belongs, he owns also to the sky and to the depths. See W. Blackstone, 2 Comentaries *18.

31. *See* Note, *Statutory Treatment of Industrial Stream Pollution,* 24 Geo. Wash. L. Rev. 302, 306 (1655); H. Farnham, 2 Law of Waters and Water Rights § 461 (1904); Gould, *supra* note 32, at § 204.

32. For example, courts have upheld a right to pollute by prescription, *Mississippi Mills Co. v. Smith,* 69 Miss. 299, 11 So. 26 (1882), and by easement, *Luama v. Bunker Hill & Sullivan Mining & Concentrating Co.,* 41 F.2d 358 (9th Cir. 1930).

33. *Pennsylvania Coal Co. v. Sanderson,* 113 Pa. 126, 149, 6 A. 453, 459 (1886).

34. Hand, J. in *Smith v. Staso Milling Co.,* 18 F2d 736, 738 (2d Cir. 1927) (emphasis added). *See also Harrisonville v. Dickey Clay Co.,* 289 U. S. 334 (1933) (Brandeis, J.).

35. *Smith v. Stato,* 18 F.2d 736, 738 (2d Cir. 1927).

36. By contrast, for example, with humane societies.

37. Cal. Prob. Code § 1460 (West Supp. 1971). . . .

38. *Santa Clara County v. Southern Pac. R.R.,* 118 U.S. 394 (1886). . . .

39. *Cf.* Golding, *Ethical Issues in Biological Engineering,* 15 U.C.L.A L. Rev. 443, 451–63 (1986).

40. Of course, in the instance of copyright and patent protection, the creation of the "property right" can be more directly justified on homocentric gounds.

41. *See* Schrag, *Life on a Dying Lake,* in The Politics of Neglect 167, at 173 (R. Meek & J. Strayyer eds. 1971).

42. On November 2, 1971, the Senate, by a vote of 86–0, passed and sent to the House the proposed Federal Water Pollution Control Act Amendments of 1971, 117 Cong. Rec. S17464 (daily ed. Nov. 2, 1971). Sections 101(a) and (a)(1) of the bill declare it to be "national policy that, consistent with the provisions of this Act—(1) the discharge of pollutants into the navigable waters be eliminated by 1985." S.2770, 92d Cong.,1st Sess., 117 Cong. Rec. S17464 (daily ed. Nov. 2, 1971).

43. 334 F.2d 608, 624 (2d Cir. 1965).

44. Again, there is a problem involving what we conceive to be the injured entitiy.

45. *N.Y. Times,* Jan 14, 1971, § 1, col. 2, and at 74, col. 7.

46. Courts have not been reluctant to award damages for the destruction of heirlooms, literary manuscripts or other property having no ascertainable market value. In *Willard v. Valley Gas Fuel Co.,* 171 Cal. 9, 151 Pac. 286 (1915), it was held that the measure of damages for the negligent destruction of a rare old book written by one of

plantiff's ancestors was the amount which would compensate the owner for all detriment including sentimental loss proximately caused by such destruction. . . .

47. It is not easy to dismiss the idea of "lower" life having consciousness and feeling pain, especially since it is so difficult to know what these terms mean even as applied to humans. *See* Austin, *Other Minds, in Logic and Language* 342 (S. Flew ed. 1965); Schopenhauer, *On the Will of Nature,* in Two Essays by Arthur Schopenhauer 193, 281–304 (1889). Some degrees of extravangance in their claims—including Lawrence, *Plants Have Feelings, Too. . . ,* Organic Gardening & Farming 64 (April 1971); Woodlief, Royster & Huang, *Effect of Random Noise on Plant Growth,* 46 J. Acoustical Soc. Am. 481 (1969); Backster, *Evidence of a Primary Perception in Plant Life,* 10 Int'l J. Parapsychology 250 (1968).
48. Cousteau, The Oceans: No Time to Lose, *L.A. Times,* Oct. 24, 1971, § (opinion), at 1, col. 4.
49. *See* J. Harte & R. Socolow, *Patient Earth* (1971).
50. G. Hegel, Hegel's *Philosophy of Rigtht* 41 (T. Knox transl. 1945).
51. C. McCullers, *The Ballad of the Sad Cafe and Other Stories* 150–51 (1958).
52. D. Rudhyar, *Directives for New Life* 21–23 (1971).
53. 136. *San Antonio Conservation Soc'y v. Texas Highway Dep't. cert. denied,* 400 U.S. 968 (1970) (Black, J. dissenting to denial of certiorari).
54. *Id.* at 969.
55. *Id.* at 971.

DISCUSSION QUESTIONS

1. If natural objects can have legal rights, can they also have legal responsibilities? What if, instead of the chemical company polluting the lake, the lake floods the chemical company? How might this scenario play out legally on Stone's view?
2. If inanimate objects such as ships and municipalities can have legal rights, why is it so "unthinkable" for natural objects?
3. Presumably we could extend legal right to cars, in Stone's view. What reasons does Stone give for extending legal rights to natural objects but not to cars?
4. Is Stone, in the end, personifying nature, since he claims granting natural objects legal rights will "enlarge our empathy" and cultivate "the personal capacities *within us* to recognize more and more the ways in which nature—like the woman, the black, the Indian, and the alien—is like us"? Is nature "like us" in a morally significant way?

JOHN RODMAN

The Liberation of Nature?

John Rodman's trenchant essay "The Liberation of Nature?" is a review of Stone's *"Should Trees Have Standing?"* and should therefore be read in conjunction with the previous selection. (Rodman also discusses Peter Singer, a philosopher whose work we will

John Rodman, "The Liberation of Nature?" *Inquiry,* vol 20, 1977, pp. 83–131. Reprinted by permission.

consider in Chapter 5. I have edited out most of the references to Singer, but they occasionally arise in the text nonetheless.) Not only does Rodman have acute criticisms of Stone, but he also offers a diagnosis of what drives the need to construct an environmental ethic. He observes that the "logical gymnastics" of its proponents suggest "they want to say something less moralistic, less reasonable, more expressive of their total sensibility, but are afraid of seeming subjective, sentimental, or something that's somehow not quite respectable." This more basic motivation, claims Rodman, is a concern over monoculture.

CRITICAL READING QUESTIONS

1. What problems does Rodman find in Stone's conception of the human–nature relation?
2. Rodman claims that Stone has failed to grasp the full implication of his own view for the institution of law and the very concept of property. How?
3. If we are going to experiment with the "unthinkable," what does Rodman propose for us to consider?
4. What connection does Rodman draw between Hitler and current attitudes toward nature?
5. Why does Rodman propose J. S. Mill as an example of ecological resistance?
6. What, in the end, motivates ecological resistance, according to Rodman?

Domestic races of animals and cultivated races of plants often exhibit an abnormal character as compared with natural species; for they have been modified not for their own benefit, but for that of man. Darwin.

ACTS AND EXPLANATIONS

Every reviewer brings to a book some personal solicitude, and I shall make mine explicit at the outset. I have wondered what it meant (as if it were possibly some symbolic turning point in history) when John Lilly opened the tank and freed the dolphins to return to the sea. And I have sometimes wondered why I spent a year out of my life struggling to save a 100-acre stretch of rather unremarkable southern California coastal sage and chaparral from being turned into a golf course. It is not the particular idiosyncratic motivations that interest me, but the principles implicit in the actions and what their implications are.

Christopher Stone has shrewdly remarked that people who justify their efforts to save wilderness or protect endangered species in the homocentric language of Resource Conservation or Survival Ecology often sound as if they are rationalizing, as if they 'want to say something less egoistic and more emphatic but the prevailing and sanctioned modes of explanation in our society—our rhetorics of motive—are not quite ready for it'. I confess that I sometimes have a similar impression of the logical gymnastics of moral and legal philosophers, who sound as if they want to say something less moralistic, less reasonable, more expressive of their total sensibility, but are afraid of seeming subjective, sentimental, or something that's somehow not quite respectable . . .

Stone's *Should Trees Have Standing?* contains, if not the first, then at least the most sweeping statement that I have seen of the increasingly popular view that Nature (not just animals) has, or should be given, rights. Stone's brief for "extending legal rights to natural objects" proceeds by indirection, suggestion, and the double-negative technique, so as gradually to build up a presumption that it is "not unthinkable" that the doctrine of judicial standing could be broadened so as to allow the Sierra Club and similar organizations or environmentally concerned individuals to bring suit for injunctions and damages on behalf of the rights of "natural objects" themselves (rather than having to establish a presumption of injury to the interests of their human members). The charm of Stone's essay lies in its stimulating blend of an almost Humean skepticism about commonsense certitudes, a perceptive awareness of the extent to which legal systems already operate with metaphors and fictions, an audacious willingness to risk trying to influence a case under adjudication, and a venturesome interest in "trying to imagine what a future consciousness might look like." Its effect is to leave the reader wondering, not whether some different conception of the human/nature relationship than the conventional modern one is needed, but which of the alternative models implicit in Stone's own essay, or what other model not contained in his essay, would be the most appropriate. The weakness lies in the author's unwillingness to take responsibility for the suggestions he makes and to risk trying to persuade us that what is "not unthinkable" should actually be thought, in his failure to confront the implicit tension between a rights model and an ecological model of nature, and in his apparent failure to see that *his ultimate vision of the human/nature relationship is probably* incompatible with a legal system that operates in terms of objects, interests property rights, compensable damages, and national forests . . .

EXTENDING RIGHTS TO 'NATURAL OBJECTS'

How does Stone cross the boundary established by the humane movement's extension (and delimitation) of rights to sentient animals? Partly by arguments from a developmental view of law: "each successive extension of rights to some new entity [e.g. slaves, women, children, aliens, human fetuses] has been, theretofore, a bit unthinkable." Partly by the use of legal analogy: the Anglo-American legal system already grants rights of one sort or another to corporations, municipalities, ships, and some animals. If we point out that slaves, women, *children,* and aliens *are all human beings,* that human fetuses are potential human beings, and that corporations and municipalities are associations of human beings, we are left with ships and (some) animals. Stone chooses not to make much of animals—perhaps because he does not want to get trapped within the traditional limitations of the humane movement. But ships (human artifacts) do not seem a very promising base from which to extend rights to natural entities. Stone uses all these examples merely to point out that legal systems already accord rights to entities that are not wholly reducible to individual human beings, so that it would not be much more "unthinkable" for the law to "personify" trees and streams than for it to "personify" corporations and ships. Stone is a kind of legal existentialist/pragmatist with no fixed ontology: legal systems *create* persons, property, and rights, and can do pretty much what they please—hence the language of "giving," "granting," and "extending" rights predominates over the language of "recognizing" or "acknowledging" rights.

Stone's underlying skepticism is reflected in his inconsistent use of the term "natural object." At times he speaks of extending legal rights to natural objects as if there were nothing strange in the notion of an object having a right. At other times he puts "natural objects" in quotation marks or even speaks of "so-called natural objects," so as to indicate that there may be more possibilities than ordinary language and the vocabulary of the law have considered. Indeed, Stone claims in effect that natural objects are really subjects in that they have "needs (wants)" and "interests" and can communicate these to human beings pretty clearly. For example, Stone says it is safe to assume that the smog-endangered stand of pines "wants" the smog stopped. Moreover, Stone raises the possibility that subjectivity in the sense of sentience and/or consciousness may be present in all natural entities, vegetable as well as animal, and even "latent" in molecules and atoms. Aside from citing several reports of experiments in plant perception, Stone presents no evidence or arguments for the universality of subjectivity. It appears as an alternative way of looking at the world, an ontology that would be appropriate if we were to extend rights to all natural entities. A reader (like Mr. Justice Douglas) passionately concerned to defend wilderness, or (like Professor Garrett Hardin) deeply worried about impending ecocatastrophe, can applaud Stone's proposal to extend rights to natural entities as a useful weapon in the warfare of environmental litigation or a catchy idea in the campaign for consciousness raising, without paying much attention to Stone's metaphysics. Indeed, Stone has made it easy for them by introducing the postulate of universal subjectivity so indirectly and diffidently that he does not commit himself to its defense: it is an idea "not easy to dismiss," a view that we "may" come to hold. And the concession of legal rights to ships, corporations, and states does not seem to presuppose that they are conscious or sentient entities. Yet without some such postulate it is unclear what entitles an entity to rights. Either natural "objects" are really subjects with their own natures and needs, or else Stone's whole essay is an exercise in arbitrary legal "creation," a forced attempt to graft a new ethics and legal theory onto the stock of the old Cartesian/ Kantian ontology that dichotomizes (human) subjects from (nonhuman) objects. Some such postulate as universal consciousness is therefore necessary if the notion of rights for trees is not to seem a rootless fancy. But it is suspicious when a new ontology suddenly appears upon the scene to support a moral/legal theory that is presented as desirable for practical reasons. Stone seems to assume a commitment to Saving Nature which he neither justifies nor really explores. Perhaps it is as obvious to him that we should save nature as it is to Singer that we should minimize suffering . . .

THE DOUBLE MESSAGE

I have suggested that the process of "extending" rights to nonhumans conveys a double message. *On the one hand,* nonhumans are elevated to the human level by virtue of their sentience and/or consciousness; they now have (some) rights. On the other hand, nonhumans are by the same process degraded to the status of inferior human beings, species-anomalies: imbeciles, the senile, "human vegetables"—moral half-breeds having rights without obligations (Singer), "legal incompetents" needing humans to interpret and represent their interests in a perpetual guardian/ward relationship (Stone).

Is this, then, the new enlightenment—to see nonhuman animals as imbeciles, wilderness as a human vegetable? As a general characterization of nonhuman nature it seems patronizing and perverse. It is not so much that natural entities are degraded by being represented in human legal actions, or by not having us attribute to them moral obligations. They are degraded rather by our failure to respect them for having their own existence, their own character and potentialities, their own forms of excellence, their own integrity, their own grandeur—and by our tendency to relate to them either by reducing them to the status of instruments for our own ends or by 'giving' them rights by assimilating them to the status of inferior human beings. It is perhaps analogous to regarding women as defective men who lack penises, or humans as defective *sea mammals who lack sonar capability and have to be rescued* by dolphins . . .

ETHICS AND INTERSPECIES IMPERIALISM

Why do our "new ethics" seem so old, and our exercises in exploring the "unthinkable" so tame? Because the attempt to produce a "new ethics" by the process of "extension" perpetuates the basic presuppositions of the conventional modern paradigm, however much it fiddles with the boundaries.

The call for a "new ethics" to guide the human–nature relationship has grown increasingly insistent in the last decade, stemming from such varied sources as "the ecological crisis," the changing impression that ethology has wrought in our conceptions of "man" and "beast," and the widespread yearning revealed in the popular reception of studies of plant perception and interspecies animal communication.

But what would a "new ethics" involve, and how might it be arrived at? Many writers on "the environmental crisis," including some who seem to think they are propounding a new ethics, simply reaffirm the conventional homocentric goals of human survival, human civilization, the quality of [human] life, etc. while advocating more ecologically sophisticated means for securing those goals. Others see homocentrism itself as at least one root of the crisis, and, whether it is or not, it certainly appears to be an increasingly arbitrary perspective in an age when the ecological imagination can shift reference points within the system and imagine the world to some extent from the standpoint of "the muskrat and its environment." Efforts to purge our traditions of the homocentric perspective by reinterpreting the Judeo-Christian mandate of "man's dominion" in terms of enlightened "stewardship" rather than a license to dominate and exploit are doubtless therapeutic, but they reshuffle the elements of a tradition in accordance with criteria of ecologically "better" and "worse" that have been brought to the task. And so we come to Hans Jonas's sober statement:

> Only an ethic which is grounded in the breadth of being, not merely in the singularity or oddness of man, can have significance in the scheme of things . . . an ethics no longer founded on divine authority must be founded on a principle discoverable in the nature of things.

For all the classical overtones of "the nature of things," this is a radical statement by virtue of its discarding two of the major props of traditional moral philosophy—the reliance upon divine authority, and the even more basic reliance upon human *areté* (the assumed coincidence of species-specific peculiarity with goodness). From Plato and Aristotle through Augustine and Aquinas to Mill, Marx, and Sartre, it has been assumed that human beings ought to maximize their species-specific differentia (formulated variously in terms of rationality, spirituality, self-consciousness, freedom, speech, symbolic activity, creativity, etc.) rather than the capacities shared with other species. This axiom is now reduced to absurdity by the fact that it seems equally plausible to say (on the basis of comparative ethology) that man's uniqueness (if there is any) lies in his tendency to interspecies imperialism or in his lack of effective inhibition against intraspecific aggression. So the question of Aristotle's *Ethics*—"what is the good for man?"—appears to presuppose a more fundamental question: what is the good for that larger whole (life? nature?) of which humanity is a part, and which is a part of humanity?

But between a felt need to transcend a homocentric ethics and an ability to discover an ontologically grounded moral order in "the phenomenon of life" or "the nature of things" there lie three serious obstacles. First, there is the powerful prohibition of modern culture against confusing "is" and "ought," "fact" and "value," the "natural" with the "moral"—in short, the taboo against committing "the naturalistic fallacy." Thanks to this, the quest for an ethics is reduced to prattle about "values" taken in abstraction from the "facts" of experience; the notion of an ethics as an organic ethos, a way of life, remains lost to us. Second, we have become self-conscious about the apparent circularity involved in projecting models upon nature and then selectively applying them back again to society, lest we find that we have done with ecology what the Social Darwinists did with natural selection. In our very notion of "projection" we implicitly reaffirm the dogma of two unrelated realms, nature and society, that are and must be kept distinct. Finally, we are uneasily aware that there is some truth to the contention that we cannot "return to nature" or even invoke "nature" as an absolute standard by which to criticize social practices, since nature itself is now seen to be historical, meaning that (a) nature is not static but in process, (b) the process of becoming is not obviously teleological, (c) we encounter nature as it has already been transformed by human impact, and (d) we tend to perceive nature through cultural lenses. It is, I suspect, partly in order to avoid these formidable obstacles (and partly for lack of an obvious alternative starting point) that we try to transcend homocentrism by *building up* a larger moral order through the *extension* of "basic moral principles which we [humans] all accept."

From the amnesiac perspective of modern culture, we then presume to be able to envisage the course of human evolution in terms of an ever-progressive widening of the sphere of moral concern from the individual ego to the family, to the clan, to the village, to the city, to the nation, to humanity ("regardless of race, creed, color, sex, or national origin"), and thence to "the lower animals," perhaps now to "the land" and all its inhabitants, culminating in "the rights of rocks." The fact that this model is abstractly unhistorical, leaving out of account the historical priority of animistic and totemic societies, the tradition of Pythagoras and Empedocles, the Roman and Thomistic conception of the *jus naturae* as "that which nature has taught all animals," and the historical modernity of individualism, does not seem to lessen its appeal. That appeal lies, I suggest, in the model's accidental association with the notion of evolution (accidental in that while Darwin held it, it is in no way entailed by the theory that species evolve by natural selection, sexual selection, etc.), in its bold simplicity and optimism, in its apparent avoidance of the various modern "fallacies" that we fear to commit because we have not thought our way through or around them, and, above all, in the fact that the progressive extension model of ethics, while holding out the promise of transcending the homocentric perspective of modern culture, subtly fulfills and legitimizes the basic project of modernity—the total conquest of nature by man. Instead of discovering a larger normative order within which we and our species-specific moral and legal systems have a niche, limits, and responsibilities, we construct a transhuman moral/legal order by extending selected principles of modern human morality (individuals have rights, pain is bad, all interests should be equally considered, etc.) to encompass all or part of nonhuman nature.

BEYOND PROPERTY?

Stone is somewhat more willing than Singer to develop the theme that doing right by nonhuman nature is not only to "human advantage" in an extrinsic sense but will make us intrinsically "far better humans," and not simply "better" in the sense of more just. Extending rights to nonhuman entities would not only emancipate them from objecthood, in effect, but would also liberate us from the stultifying notion that we can actualize ourselves by acting out our felt "need" to "extend our wills over things, to objectify them, to make them ours, to manipulate them, and to keep them at a psychic distance." In contrast to this image of man as dominator/appropriator, Stone poses an alternative vision of the person of 'heightened awareness' and enlarged "empathy" who, like the "madman" in McCullers's *A Tree, a Rock, a Cloud,* has developed the "science" of loving to the point where he can "love anything . . . Everything . . . And anybody." The emancipation of nonhuman nature from objecthood is also seen, in effect, as involving the liberation of humanity from the constrictions of conventional scientific/technological/economic "objectivity," which imposes the subject/object dichotomy upon the world, imposes upon human beings the role of dominator and manipulator, and obstructs the development of the potentiality for empathy and love.

This vision, invoked in three pages of Stone's essay, raises many unanswered questions. The superiority of one type of human character over another is simply assumed to be self-evident. And the person who loves everything and everybody (Hitler? water pollution? Walt Disney Enterprises, Inc.?) may well be in some sense "mad." At least we need some discussion of different modes of love, including the love that expressed itself in the wrath of Jesus towards the merchants and money-changers defiling the temple, or the wrath of John Muir at resource "conservationists" who would desecrate a holy place by damming Hetch Hetchy valley to make a reservoir for the city of San Francisco. (I have the same kind of problem with Zen masters who talk of "accepting" all things, including smog.)

I also suspect there is a deeper meaning implicit in the neo-Fichtean notion that object-ivity is projected upon the nonhuman world by humans. If the project of redeeming nature from objecthood is also a project for humanity, it must mean that underneath all the conventional rhetoric about human rights and human dignity we have come to suspect that *we* are really objects or things—at worst, simply manipulated and molded by alien powers; at best, capable of acquiring worth by doing something that achieves market value or moral merit. In this context, to affirm that "natural objects" have ('rights') is symbolically to affirm that all natural entities (including humans) have intrinsic worth simply by virtue of being, and being what they are; and, by implication, that human "power trips" and other nasty forms of behavior are understandable as efforts to compensate for an underlying lack of a sense of worth.

I miss in these suggestive pages of Stone's any exploration of the roots of that especially (although not exclusively) modern "need" to dominate and appropriate, which, although not one of man's "basic biological wants" seems powerful and unlikely to be exorcised by quoting a passage from Carson McCullers.

I also miss any awareness on Stone's part of how deeply the ethos of domination-and-appropriation has penetrated our culture so that it infects even our countercultural vision. Thus, when Stone operationalizes his slogan of "legal rights for natural objects" he absorbs natural entities into a legal system founded on property rights and economic cost-accounting:

> Wherever it carves out "property" rights, the legal system is engaged in the process of *creating* monetary worth . . . I am proposing that we do the same with eagles and wilderness areas as we do with copyrighted works, patented inventions, and privacy: *make* the violation of rights in them to be a cost by declaring the "pirating" of them to be the invasion of a property interest.

At this point (as at some others) I believe we are justified in asking whether Stone has grasped the full implications of his own vision of an alternative human–nature relationship—which I should think would be incompatible with the institution of property. Socialists appear to have recognized that the reduction of the varied potentialities of human experience to the one dimension of "having" has impoverished humanity; but they formulated the indictment so as to apply only to *private* property. Now, as the human–nature relationship comes more into view, we begin to suspect that property *per se* (at least as conventionally understood), whether private or public, may be an outer and visible sign of an alienated mode of existence. Yet we still tend to formulate the future in terms of the old alternatives: e.g., "ocean resources: the private property of nation-states or the common property of all mankind?" (*From the standpoint* of a sperm whale, what does, it matter whether it is chased, killed, and butchered by a private or by a public enterprise, by Japanese or by a mixed crew working for the United Nations?) It is hard to break out of the Lockean universe which begins with everything (including human beings) as the property of the creator and evolves as the gigantic commons of nonhuman nature is transformed by labor into private property, after which people seizing political power and invoking the authority of Marx "expropriate the expropriators" and convert private property into state property, after which every state having a seacoast proceeds to carve out of the ocean a property right of up to 200 miles (for a beginning) and tries to exclude all other nation-states from the use of its "resources."

There is an older view that property is not part of the law of nature but a human "addition" to it, and that what has been added can be subtracted (St. Thomas Aquinas). It may be that the human institution of property is in some sense an outgrowth of a wider animal propensity to "territoriality," but ethological studies have now reached the point where we must acknowledge a vast range of forms, including some so amorphous that they lend no support whatever to the notion that "property" as we know it is a part of a larger *jus animalium*. Moreover, we look in vain for anything clearly species-specific and species-universal to humanity in this regard: human societies are almost as varied as animal species, and there have clearly been human societies which, if not lacking altogether some minimal notion of personal property, at least lacked the presumption that the land, the animals, the waters, the skies, etc. could be human property. Hence the tragic misunderstanding between European settlers, for whom all land was potential property, and Native Americans (Indians), who thought land ownership as unnatural a notion as owning one's mother. "We" won, but we now worry where the logic of our property obsession is taking us, as we hold endless international conferences on "the law of the seas," to be followed by conferences on solar access rights and the law of outer space.

If we are going to experiment with thinking the "unthinkable," we might as well see if we can liberate our imaginations from the property paradigm and envision a society not based on the principle of property but on the principle of propriety, i.e. the principle that action should be appropriate to the nature of all parties involved in the transaction, accompanied by the corollary recognition that nonhuman species exist "in their own right" (have their own origin, structure, tendencies, etc.) and not simply "for us." In doing this, we might critically explore the potential of some notions already present, such as Stone's legalistic version of Biblical "trusteeship," the kind of rights that are not "strongly preclusive," and the sense in which, early in this review, I spoke of a particular coastal sage landscape as "my" area.

On the basis of the text we can only speculate about Stone's ultimate position. Possibly he does not believe that attributing rights to 'natural objects' negates the property relationship. (After all, slaves had certain rights under the Roman law and were still the property of their owners.) Or perhaps he is aware of the incompatibility between his ultimate vision and the basic presuppositions of the existing legal system but prudently refrains from declaring it, preferring the Hegelian/Fabian strategy of representing his vision as if its basic principles were already accepted and as if institutions were already developing in accordance with the unfolding of those principles. But history betrayed Hegel, and the Fabians have had to settle for a National Coal Board and call it "socialism." The risk is great that the wild vision will be only too easily domesticated by the established system. Perhaps Stone's secret intent is that a property-oriented legal system that swallows the notion of the rights and liabilities of natural entities will experience such inner contradictions that it will self-destruct. This is, in its way, an appealing prospect if we are ready for it. But domestication of the radical potential of his vision seems to me the more likely outcome, unless that vision can be rendered more vivid and can be more firmly grounded in an analysis of the dialectic of liberation and "the nature of things."

ECOLOGICAL RESISTANCE

Why did John Lilly let the dolphins go? Why has the Greenpeace Foundation obstructed the Soviet whaling fleet? Why did I make a crusade out of saving some local coastal sage and chaparral from becoming another golf course? Why did Stone choose to devise a way of defending Mineral King in order to demonstrate "what a future consciousness might look like"? Why does Singer advocate, in effect, the abolition of domesticated farm and lab animals? It would be foolhardy to try to answer with a simple formula. We are, as Stone suggests, at a curious point in time when actions tend to be rationalized in obsolete or otherwise inappropriate terms. Unlike the Pythagoreans, we lack a suitable myth that comprehends and integrates our feelings and perceptions, articulates our intuitions, allows our actions ritual status, and makes us intelligible to ourselves in terms of an alignment with a larger order of things. Camus's portrait of Sisyphus, continually pushing the rock up the mountain only to have it roll down again, is a *tour de force* that we can admire but not imitate for long. "Absurdity," after all, may characterize the relationship between human effort and the universe only in cases where man has chosen to work against rather than with the course of nature (symbolized here by the force of gravity).

Instead of trying to fabricate a mythology out of the materials of contemporary biology, let us instead pay attention to the patterns of metaphor already present in the language of those who protest the exploitation and liquidation of nonhuman nature. Lilly, Singer, and others are prone to invoke analogies with Nazi concentration camps, the Nürnberg trials, etc., as if our treatment of nonhuman nature involved acts that were crimes whether they violated established human law or not. The function of the Nazi analogy, I assume, is that it associates the extermination of a species with the attempted "liquidation" of a people, experimentation on "subhuman" animals in the name of science with experimentation on humans classified as "subhuman" in the name of science, crimes against humanity with crimes against nature, one group of "war crimes" with another, while carrying connotations of that which is unqualifiedly evil, wrong, atrocious, abominable, and absolutely forbidden. It is comforting to think of the Nazi experience as a pathological deviation from the course of modern history, but I suggest that it is rather a caricature of the ethos of modernity, that it takes to their logical conclusion two powerful themes in modern society—the ontological and moral dualism and the crusade to replace diversity with monoculture. It is not always realized that Hitler's conceptualization of Jews as subhuman animals went hand-in-hand with his vision of man's relation to nonhuman nature as a war of conquest culminating in the enslavement or liquidation of all competing forms of life down to the level of micro-organisms.

> The struggle against the great beasts is ended, but it is being inexorably carried on against the tiny creatures—against bacteria and bacilli. There is no . . . reconciliation on this score: it is either you or I, life or death, either extermination or servitude.

Hitler's view is merely an extreme version of the modern but pre-ecological "germ theory of disease," and it is closely related to the widespread tendency to classify nonhuman animals into "good" ones and "bad" ones and to demand policies of "predator control"—a euphemism for the liquidation of wolves, coyotes, etc. In this kind of mentality there is no appreciation of diversity, no perception of "others" as having a right to exist, a niche to fill, a role to play. The insane vision of an Aryan Europe purged of Jewish influence is intimately bound up with the equally insane vision of a humanized planet on which all other species have been either enslaved or liquidated.

The key to the myth that I see emerging is the principle of metaphoric mirroring in accordance with which certain archetypal patterns—such as the struggle to defend diversity against the juggernaut of monoculture—are seen to be operative in several spheres, e.g. on a biological, a social, and a psychological level. Within this frame of reference, acts of ecological resistance do not stem so much from calculations of enlightened self-interest (whether of the individual, the group, or the species), or from a conscientious sense of moral or legal obligation to see that justice is done to others, as from a felt need to resist the repression, censorship, or liquidation of potentialities that lie within both human and nonhuman nature, and to liberate suppressed potentialities from the yoke of domestication and threatened extinction. From this perspective it matters little whether the primary victims are cooperatively organizing their own resistance. That pattern is carried over from the analogy of human liberation movements; it seems inapplicable in the case of most nonhuman animals and totally irrelevant in the case of, say, a wild river that is being dammed by the Bureau of Reclamation. The point is that the natural flow of the river is interrupted, diverted, distorted by the dam; the river struggles against the dam like an instinct struggles against an inhibition or a social movement struggles against a restrictive institution. The threat perceived by the human "Friends of the River" who try to prevent the dam's being built in the first place (or by "the monkey wrench gang" who blow up the dam after it has been constructed) is the threat of *wildness* being tamed, of a natural process interrupted and distorted, of the 'individuality' of a natural being made to conform to an artificial pattern imposed upon it, of repression in the most general sense. The threat to the river is no less a threat to the river for being also a threat to social and psychic diversity. In its broadest signification, the proposed dam is a threat to the very nature of things. The resistance of a single person to that threat has thus a multidimensional depth of meaning impossible to translate into the language of mere self-interest or mere justice.

Let me offer for contemplation an exemplary character from the ecological resistance movement. My choice may seem surprising at first, for John Stuart Mill may seem anachronistic or irrelevant. But my Mill is not so much the encyclopedic philosopher whose *Logic* and *Political Economy* became standard Victorian textbooks, or even the Utilitarian who remained true to Bentham's inclusion of sentient animals within the sphere of morals and legislation, but the lesser-known mountain climber, "botanizer," and "lover of nature" who indignantly protested the Royal Horticultural Society's contest for the two best herbaria collected in each county in England as an event that would make 1864 the last year that many already-rare species of wild flora would exist. It was this same Mill who, as political/social theorist, so eloquently defended human "individuality" and "diversity" against the growing social pressures for conformity in belief and conduct, the same Mill who authored the classic feminist tract of the 19th century, not only championing women's right to participate in public life but diagnosing the patriarchal family as the major agency of sexual stereotyping. Finally, it was this same Mill who, as autobiographer, recorded for posterity the classic case study of a sensitive person trained to operate as an analytic thinking-machine who "died" and was "reborn" through rediscovering the capacity for feeling, intuition, imagination, the enjoyment of poetry and natural beauty, the ability to cry and to contemplate—without losing the capacity for rational analysis or practical action.

It would not, I think, violate the spirit of the term to speak of Mill as having displayed an "ecological" sensibility. His views of psyche, polity, and cosmos all have a common structure. Diversity and richness of potentiality are natural conditions endangered by oppressive monoculture on all levels, and each level is a metaphor of the others. Thus Mill's feminism expressed itself both in the liberation of his own "feminine" side and in his attack upon the subjection of women as a social group. His defense of human individuality was expressed in the contrast between 'a machine to be built after a model, and set to do exactly the work prescribed for it' and a 'tree, which requires to grow and develop itself on all sides, according to the tendency of the inward forces which make it a living thing.'

Mill's prophetic vision of a steady-state society, limited in population and devoting itself more to cultural than to economic growth, emerged out of his nightmare anticipation of what could occur if "the unlimited increase of wealth and population" should continue to the point where we would be left to inhabit "a world from which solitude has been extirpated," a world:

> with nothing left to the spontaneous activity of nature; with every rood of land brought into cultivation, which is capable of growing food for human beings; every flowery waste or natural pasture ploughed up, all quadrupeds or birds which are not domesticated for man's use exterminated as his rivals for food, every hedgerow or superfluous tree rooted out, and scarcely a place left where a wild shrub or flower could grow without being eradicated as a weed in the name of improved agriculture.

Such a world, Mill suggests, is "not good for man" (not to mention for the flora and the other fauna). But what does it mean to say that a totally humanized world would diminish us as human beings, to imply that we need nonhuman nature, that we draw sustenance from it, commune with it, find inspiration in its example? Does it not indirectly affirm the intrinsic value of the nonhuman realm, or at least suggest that common principles, common values, animate both it and us and that their loss in either realm is a loss of value?

Exactly what is so frightening about the prospective death of nature? Three possible answers occur. *One* is suggested by Mill's metaphoric representation of human beings as trees: what happens when trees become uprooted? In René Dubos's version:

> Man is still of the earth, earthy, notwithstanding all the technological and medical advances that superficially seem to dissociate him from his evolutionary past. As happened to Anteus of the Greek legend, his strength will probably wane if he loses contact with the biological ground from which he emerged and which still feeds him, physically and emotionally.

The *second* possibility is that external nature, for all its historicity in the perspective of geologic and evolutionary time, provides a "regulative idea" of an ultimate and eternal reality against which we measure the ephemeral, the superficial, and the false. Thus political societies have always tended to articulate their structure as reflecting that of the cosmic order: this is as true for modern Newtonian constitutions as for archaic theocracies. On the level of exceptional individuals, we see throughout recorded history the ritual pattern of a withdrawal from society to the solitude of wilderness in order to "get into another space" and make contact with a different order of time, to transcend the demands of workaday and family life, the time clock, expectations of respectability, and even the moral/legal consciousness, in order to "take one's bearings" and discover who one really is and what one really needs to do, and then to return to society. In this respect nature lies "beyond good and evil," which is why the attempt to bring it within the framework of the moral/legal consciousness is ultimately so perverse.

The *third* possibility is simply that the very otherness of nature, together with the diversity characteristic of natural ecosystems, provides for us an objective model of alternative possibilities and potentialities within the human psyche and human society, and that the loss or suppression of natural diversity "out there" tends to provoke in us an anxiety as if we felt increasingly trapped in a particular condition and could envision no alternatives.

These three possibilities connect in the notion of human nature as grounded in an order of biological diversity that is increasingly threatened by monoculture, so that every potentiality seems an endangered species, and every extinction of a species seems an impoverishment of human life. The struggle for the liberation of nature, both human and nonhuman, from the threat of totalitarian monoculture or one-dimensionality goes on at all levels.

To depict an action in terms of "liberation," to depict it in terms of resisting oppression, and to depict it in terms of preserving integrity express different aspects (and sometimes stages) of the same phenomenon. The nonhuman world is full of what Mill called "inward forces," potentialities striving to actualize themselves; we can ally ourselves with those tendencies and resist the efforts of other human beings to obstruct them. In doing so we can speak (with Leopold) of the integrity of natural ecosystems, more familiarly of the *integrity of the personality, and without* any violence or mystery of the alignment of these two dimensions of experience as also involving a kind of integrity.

"Nature, too, awaits the revolution!" writes Marcuse, stressing the "receptive" capacity to "see things *in their own right,*" as having their own character and direction independent of us. Given the history of homocentric imperialism the emphasis is a valid one. Yet a fully ecological sensibility knows with Carl Sandburg that:

> There is an eagle in me and a mockingbird . . .
> and the eagle flies among the Rocky Mountains of
> my dreams and fights among the Sierra crags of
> what I want . . . and the mockingbird warbles in
> the underbrush of my Chattanoogas of hope,
> gushes over the blue Ozark foothills of my
> wishes—And I got the eagle and the mockingbird
> from the wilderness.

The "receptive" capacity by itself does not lead to action. Action is made possible by the recognition that, beyond the perception of otherness lies the perception of psyche, polity, and cosmos as metaphors of one another, and that the ancient dictum to "live according to nature" now translates into Thoreau's maxim, "Let your life be a counter friction to stop the machine."

DISCUSSION QUESTIONS

1. Assess Rodman's Propriety Principle that "action should be appropriate to the nature of all parties involved." What does this mean? How are we to determine what is appropriate? Compare Rodman's Propriety Principle with Midgley's notion of suitable and unsuitable behavior mentioned in her article above. Are these helpful guides for environmental thought or mere platitudes?
2. Assess Rodman's complaint that granting natural objects rights amounts to a subtle fulfillment of our dream to conquer nature. What does Rodman propose instead?
3. Evaluate Rodman's claim about the struggle to defend diversity in the face of monoculture and the various levels that this struggle can assume. According to Rodman, what is at stake in this struggle? Do you think he is right? How do you understand *monoculture* and what is wrong with it, if anything? How is Thoreau's quote at the end of the article relevant? (We will study Thoreau in Chapter 10, but his ideas are clearly invoked by Rodman's analysis of those who seek to erect an environmental ethic. One of Thoreau's main points is about the importance of *wildness* in our lives.)

JANNA THOMPSON

A Refutation of Environmental Ethics

Our next reading by Janna Thompson, professor of philosophy at La Trobe University in Australia, indicates some problems that arise in attempting to construct an environmental ethic. As she argues in "A Refutation of Environmental Ethics," proposals to ground intrinsic value in natural objects quickly get out of hand, for there does not seem to be any nonarbitrary way to stop everything from becoming intrinsically valuable. Environmental philosophers have been concerned to establish that some natural objects have intrinsic value; according to Thompson they have not given sufficient thought how to keep the idea from spreading absurdly once established.

CRITICAL READING QUESTIONS

1. What, according to Thompson, must an environmental ethic hold?
2. What formal principles must any ethic hold, according to Thompson?
3. Note that Thompson assesses a representative argument from Paul Taylor, a philosopher we shall read in Chapter 6. But Thompson mentions Taylor as just a typical example of the sort of thing that can "go wrong" with environmental ethics. What is it?
4. What two ways have environmental philosophers used to try to show that there are intrinsic values in nature?
5. According to Thompson, why do machines have intrinsic value, if natural objects do?
6. What sort of an ethic is Thompson willing to endorse?

An environmental ethic, as I understand it, is an ethic which holds that natural entities and/or states of affairs are intrinsically valuable, and thus deserve to be the object of our moral concern. What exactly it means to say that something is intrinsically valuable depends on the account given of what values are and where they come from. At a minimum, however, those who find intrinsic value in nature are claiming two things: first, that things and states which are of value are valuable for what they are in themselves and not because of their relations to us (and in particular, not because they provide us with pleasure and satisfaction). Second, the intrinsic value which these states of nature have is objective in the sense that its existence is not a matter of individual taste or personal preference. Any rational, morally sensitive person ought to be able to recognize that it is there. This means, of course, that those who claim that intrinsic value exists in nature must provide some criteria for identifying what is of value and some reasons for believing that the things and states in question are valuable.

In general, an ethic is supposed to tell us two things: (1) what states of affairs, things, and properties are intrinsically desirable or valuable (as opposed to what is valuable as a means to an end); and (2) what we should do or not do in order to promote, protect, or bring into existence that which is of intrinsic value. Given that an ethic is supposed to tell us these things, it must satisfy the following formal requirements in order to count as an ethic at all:

Janna Thompson, "A Refutation of Environmental Ethics," *Environmental Ethics*, vol 12, 1990, pp. 147–160. Reprinted by permission.

(1) *The Requirement of Consistency.* If a thing or state of affairs is thought to be intrinsically valuable, then all things that are like it in relevant respects must also be judged to have intrinsic value. On the other hand, if something is thought not to have intrinsic value, then all things that are like that thing in relevant respects must be regarded as not having intrinsic value. Supporters of animal liberation and environmental ethics have made heavy use of the consistency requirement in their condemnations of "human chauvinism." They argue, for example, that if human beings are regarded as being intrinsically valuable, and if some animals are like human beings in all respects that seem relevant, then a consistent ethic must regard these animals as valuable. If animals are not regarded as being valuable, then those human beings that are like animals in relevant respects (babies, children, the mentally retarded) must be judged by a consistent ethic not to have intrinsic value.

The requirement of consistency presupposes that the ethic in question has provided us with an account of what differences and similarities are relevant and why. If that ethic is to have any claim to being objective, then that account must not seem arbitrary. In other words, if something is thought to be of value and another thing is not, then there must be reason for believing that the differences between them justify making that judgment, and if two things are regarded to be of equal value then the similarities they have must be such so that this judgment can reasonably be made.

(2) *The Requirement of Nonvacuity.* The criteria for determining what things or states of affairs are intrinsically valuable must not be such so that it turns out that every thing and every state of affairs counts as equally valuable. The reason why this requirement must be satisfied should be clear. An ethic is supposed to tell us what we ought or ought not to do; however, it cannot do so if it turns out that all things and states of affairs are equally valuable, for if they are, then there is no reason to do one thing rather than another, to bring about one state of affairs rather than another.

(3) *The Decidability Requirement.* The criteria of value which an ethic offers must be such that in most cases it is possible to determine what counts as valuable and what does not. Probably all ethical systems will have problems with borderline cases. For example, an ethic which regards sentient creatures as objects of moral concern and their well-being as something that we should promote may have difficulties determining what counts as a sentient creature and that the well-being of a particular creature consists of. Nevertheless, in general is usually clear what satisfies the criteria and what does not. A more serious difficulty arises if the criteria leave us in doubt in most cases. If this happens, then we do not simply have a problem within an ethic, but a problem regarding something as an ethic in the first place. The reason for having a decidability requirement is much the same as the reason for requiring nonvacuity. If an ethic is to make prescriptions, then we have to have a good idea of what we are supposed to be promoting and avoiding. If an ethic can't tell us this, if it leaves us uncertain in too many cases about what things or states of affairs are valuable and which are more valuable than others, then its claim to be an ethic is brought into question.

My claim is that proposals for an environmental ethic either fail to satisfy one or more of these formal criteria or fail to give us reason to suppose that the values they promote are intrinsic values. It should be noted that my objection to environmental ethics is not that its ideas about what is valuable are implausible, or that rational, morally sensitive people should not value what environmental ethicists tell them to value. Rather, if my arguments are correct, what is called environmental ethics is not properly ethics at all.

What can go wrong with environmental ethics is illustrated by an argument presented by Paul Taylor in *Respect for Nature.* The argument is meant to establish that there is no good reason for thinking that sentient creatures alone have intrinsic value *(inherent worth),* indeed, that there is no reason to deny that nonsentient creatures—plants, lower animals—have less intrinsic value than sentient creatures. Human beings, Taylor admits, have properties that many living things do not have—e.g., intelligence—and some philosophers, most notoriously Descartes, have believed that human beings are distinguished from all other creatures by the possession of mind. Apart from the question of whether other creatures do not have minds, however, there is no reason in nature why we should regard the qualities that human beings happen to have as making them more valuable than living creatures that do not have these qualities—no reason why creatures who can think or feel should be regarded as more valuable than plants and other nonsentient creatures.

A natural response to this argument is to ask, "Why stop here?" Why should we regard rocks, rivers, volcanoes, molecules as being of less value simply because they happen to lack the properties associated with life? Why indeed should we say that anything is more valuable than any other thing? The argument Taylor uses to overthrow human chauvinism seems to undermine the very possibility of an ethic. We might conclude that if we leave it up to nature to tell us what we should or should not value, that we get no answer—that we can only find nature to be valuable insofar as natural states of affairs are related to us; to our interests and concerns, or more generally the interests and concerns of sentient creatures. This is in fact the position I hold, but to establish it requires much more argument, for environmental ethicists do think that they can give us criteria for discovering objective value in nature, criteria which do not set us on the slipperly slope into inconsistency, vacuity, or undecidability.

There are two ways in which environmental ethicists have tried to establish their thesis that there are intrinsic values in nature. The first is to argue by analogy. Let us assume that human individuals are intrinsically valuable and that it is desirable that their well-being be promoted. The reason we think that this is so (the argument goes) is that human individuals have interests, preferences, purposes—a good that can be frustrated or furthered. But if this is our criterion for having value, then in all consistency we must recognize that since some animals also have interests, preferences, and purposes, they too should count as having intrinsic value. Plants, nonsentient creatures, may not have interests in a true sense, but they do have a good (unlike a rock). "Once we come to understand the life cycle of a butterfly," Taylor says, "and know the environmental conditions it needs to survive in a healthy state, we have no difficulty speaking about what is beneficial to it and what might be harmful to it." The same can be said about bacteria or plants. Furthermore, the good that a butterfly and a blue gum have is a good of their own. Unlike machines, the good of which is determined by human purposes, we can say what is good for a natural organism without reference to any other entity. Thus, we can understand how nonsentient organisms can be candidates for having intrinsic value, and once we come to appreciate their nature and the role that they play in environmental systems, we will be inclined to say that they do have intrinsic value.

The second approach to environmental ethics is not to argue by analogy but simply to try to persuade us as valuers that there are certain things or states of affairs in nature that we as rational, morally sensitive people ought to regard as having a value independent of our needs and interests and that there are other states of affairs (like defoliated jungles or exotic pine plantations) that we ought to regard as having a disvalue. We simply have to come to recognize that these values or disvalues are there, and the job of the proponent of environmental ethics is to encourage us to do this by persuading us to appreciate certain aspects of nature and by trying to show us that an ethic which does not acknowledge these values cannot satisfy our intuitive understanding of what is bad or good, right or wrong . . .

Because both approaches claim to be laying the foundations of an environmental ethic, it is presupposed that they can satisfy the formal requirements of an ethic. Indeed, it seems that they do satisfy these requirements. Each claims to have the virtue of consistency—unlike ethics which are described as being "human chauvinist." Each tells us that some things or states of affairs are valuable and some are not; and each presents criteria that we are supposed to be able to use to decide what is valuable and to what extent.

But what exactly is valuable? On this matter environmental ethicists do not speak with one voice.

Taylor insists that it is individual organisms that have intrinsic value and not environmental systems or species. The Routleys regard environmental systems as holders of value. Rolston thinks that individual organisms, species, and ecosystems all have value, though perhaps to different degrees. Is this disagreement about what in nature has value a little problem that environmental ethicists should be able to solve among themselves, or is it a symptom of a larger difficulty? To answer this question let us look more closely at each of the two approaches.

Once again I take Taylor's argument as illustrating what goes wrong with the analogical approach. Taylor argues that if a thing has a good of its own, then it is a candidate for having intrinsic value. He assumes that it is individual living organisms and only individual living organisms that can have this value but there is nothing in the criterion, or the mode of argument used to support it that requires this limitation. It is not difficult to use Taylor's way of determining what is of value to insist that other kinds of things must also have the same intrinsic value if we are to be true to the consistency requirement.

Why can't we say, for example, that hearts, lungs, livers, and kidneys have intrinsic value and thus deserve in themselves to be objects of our moral concern. Once we come to appreciate how a kidney or some other internal organ develops within the embryo, how it functions and maintains itself, what makes it flourish and what harms it, then surely as in the case of the butterfly or the bacteria we have to recognize that it has a good of its own.

But isn't the good of a kidney defined in terms of the good of the organism that has the kidney? It is true that my own good and the good of my kidneys are intimately related. We depend upon each other (though modern technology has made it possible for me to get on without my kidneys and my kidneys to continue to exist without me). But my purposes and goals do not define what is good for a kidney. This can be determined independently to the same extent that the good of a wood-boring insect can be determined independently of the good of the tree it feeds on or that the good of intestinal bacteria can be defined independently of the good of the intestine or the good of the creature who has the intestine. Kidneys, like insects and bacteria, need certain kinds of nourishment; they are healthy under some conditions and are caused harm by others. These conditions can be specified without mentioning the organism in which the organs reside.

So using the same kind of argument which Taylor uses to persuade us that organisms have a good of their own, we have to conclude that internal organs have such a good too. For the same reason, it seems that we also ought to say that individual leaves, buds, and bits of bark have a good of their own and are equally candidates for having intrinsic value. And what will stop us from saying that a piece of skin, a bodily cell, or a DNA molecule has a good of its own?

Why discriminate against rocks? Once we appreciate how crystals form according to a pattern determined by molecular structure, what conditions make it possible for this pattern to form in a characteristic way, what maintains its structural integrity, and what conditions cause it to be deformed or to break up, then surely we will want to say that in an extended sense of the phrase a crystal has a "good of its own." It is true that it sounds odd to say this. But why should we be any more impressed by the fact that crystals, strictly speaking, do not have a good of their own than Taylor is impressed by the fact that nonsentient creatures, strictly speaking, do not have interests? Surely it is the relevant similarities between bacteria, cells, and crystals that should be crucial for our ethical reasoning, just as it is the relevant similarities between sentient creatures and nonsentient creatures that are crucial for Taylor. The same thing that is said about crystals can be said about any natural entity, whether a rock, a molecule, an atom, or a solar system. Each has an integrity of its own which it can maintain under certain conditions, but which will be destroyed under others.

It is time to reassess the status of machines. Although it is true that we think that the purpose of a machine is to serve a human need, the matter is really not so simple, for machines, because of their structure, have a potential, a way of doing things of their own, and in order to accomplish their purposes people often have to conform to the ways of the machine. In fact, it is frequently the case that people have to redefine their goals or are caused to discover new ones as a consequence of realizing the potential of a machine or in the course of adapting themselves to it. It seems as if the good of a machine is best defined in terms of the structures and capacities it has and what operations will realize its potential and which ones will tend to destroy it or not allow it to fulfill its potential. Moreover, if a machine has a good of its own, then so do the parts of a machine for the same reason that a liver or a heart have a good of its own.

What can be said about a machine might also be said about other constructed entities like social institutions and societies, for these also have a structure, a potential, a way of operating which the individuals in them don't necessarily appreciate. The same can be said of ecological systems. Taylor objects to regarding systems as being objects of respect, probably because he assumes that the good of a system is reducible to the goods of the individual animal and plant populations that make it up; however, ecological systems, like social systems, have a potential for change and development and a dynamic which may be compatible with the destruction of particular populations—as when a forest develops toward a climax state. So why not admit that ecological systems have a good of their own and are thus in themselves candidates for our moral concern? If ecological systems are entities with a good of their own, then why not parts of ecological systems—e.g., the relation between a predator population and a prey population? Why not a whole wilderness? Why not the relations between plants and animals on a continent? Why not nature as a whole?

One of the problems which this vigourous use of analogy brings out in the open is the problem of determining what should count as an individual for the purposes of environmental ethics. It is perhaps natural to think that particular plants and animals are the individuals that we need to be concerned with. But why shouldn't we count the parts of an animal or plant as individuals, their cells, organs, or molecules? Why not the complex consisting of an animal or a plant and its various parasites and bacteria? Why not the plant and the soil that nourishes it? Why not an interrelated system of animals and plants? There doesn't seem to be any good reason why one thing should be counted as an individual and others not. How we divide up the world depends upon context and convenience. But surely an environmental ethic which claims to discover intrinsic value in nature shouldn't depend upon the way we happen to look at things.

Once we do (somehow) pick out the individuals we are concerned with it is still a problem to decide what is good for them. So far, like Taylor, I have assumed that this is generally obvious. However, there is another way of viewing the matter. An individual plant or animal has a genetic potential to manifest a range of properties, but what properties it realizes depends on its environment. Why should we regard it to be for the good of a plant if it realizes one aspect of its potential rather than another? Once again it is natural to think that it is for the good of a plant to be raised in conditions which encourage it to be vigourous and healthy and that disease and poor nutrition are bad for a plant. Nevertheless, a diseased plant displays properties, realizes a potential, which it would not have manifested if it had been healthy. Why should we regard it as a worse thing for it if it has these properties? The answer might be that if the ability of a plant to survive and reproduce is threatened, then this is not to its good. However, if this is our criterion of what is bad for natural things, why should we say that it is bad for the plant's sake that it dies of disease rather than that this is bad for its genes or bad for the species? Moreover, why should it be bad for the plant's sake to live a short time rather than a longer time? One reason why we find it so natural to suppose that it is better for an organism's sake that it be healthy and have a long productive life is because this is what we want for ourselves and what we want for the plants we grow. Nevertheless, plants don't want anything. Thus, as this discussion shows, determining what a nonsentient organism's own good is, is not as straightforward as it sometimes appears and this difficulty throws into question the analogy between sentient creatures and nonsentient organisms upon which Taylor's approach to environmental ethics depends.

Of course, the fact that a few proponents of environmental ethics have failed to establish that there can be such an ethic is not conclusive. Is there a way of improving the argument from analogy and/or sharpening up the criteria of value so that they satisfy the requirements? It might be suggested that environmental ethicists should simply declare that what is of intrinsic value are living creatures, or wilderness, or ecological systems. The obvious problem with this idea, however, is that in making this declaration they would be committing the same sin of arbitrariness which they accuse human chauvinists of committing. If they claim to be uncovering intrinsic values in nature, then we are entitled to get an answer to the question "What is it about living creatures or wilderness that is valuable?" and when the answer is given, in attempting to satisfy the consistency requirement for the ethic, they are likely once again to encounter the problems I have already discussed above.

Although I cannot rule out the possibility that someone might someday state a criterion of value which would include in its scope all and only those things and states that environmental ethicists want included and which would satisfy the formal requirements of ethics, it seems to me to be unlikely. The problem, as I have suggested, is that how we view the world, how we divide it up into individuals and systems, what we regard as good or bad for an individual or a system is too arbitrary—i.e., too dependent on point of view, interest, and convenience—to support an ethic that purports to be based on value in nature independent of our interests and concerns. Every criterion of environmental value seems to depend for its application on our taking a particular point of view, upon using a particular set of concepts, and there does not seem to be any nonarbitrary reason (as far as ethics is concerned) for taking up one point of view or using one set of concepts rather than another. As a result, the attempt to be objective and to avoid assuming an interest or a point of view risks vacuity or at the very least producing something too indeterminate in scope to be useful as an ethic.

If there is something so fundamentally wrong with environmental ethics, then two questions are critical. First, is any ethic possible at all? If environmental ethics is flawed, then what reason do we have for supposing that a nonenvironmental ethic is any less arbitrary or any more likely to satisfy formal requirements? Second, if environmental ethics is impossible, what we are going to say about those practices—our destruction of wilderness, species, environmental systems, creatures—which environmental ethicists believe that they need an environmental ethics to condemn?

To establish the possibility of ethics it is enough to give an example of a system of ethics which satisfies the formal criteria for an ethic and includes reference to intrinsic values. I believe that an ethic which takes individuals who have a point of view (i.e., that are centers of consciousness) as having intrinsic value—an ethic which supports the satisfaction of the interests, needs, and preferences of those individuals—is such an ethic. The fact that individuals have a point of view, and can therefore be caused anguish, frustration, pleasure, or joy as the result of what we do, is one good reason for valuing such individuals and requiring that their interests and preferences be a matter of moral concern to all rational, morally sensitive agents. Equally important, in satisfying the formal requirements of an ethic, is the fact that individuals with a point of view—with consciousness, desires, feelings, goals, etc.—are self-defining. What in the framework of the ethic counts as an individual is not an arbitrary matter, not a question of the valuer's point of view. That they have a point of view decides the matter. It is also not an arbitrary matter, not a question of the valuer's point of view, what counts as the good of such individuals. They themselves define their good by how they feel, what they say, by how they behave. Because we are able to use the value criteria of this ethic consistently, nonvacuously, and without any overwhelming problems of undecidability, it is clear that a nonarbitrary ethic is possible, though, of course, much more discussion is needed to determine what an ethic which values sentient beings requires of us.

If environmental ethics is nonviable, if we are stuck with a sentient-being-centered ethic, then what about the needs of the environment? What do we say about the intuitions and attitudes of those people who think that we ought to preserve wilderness, species, and nonsentient organisms even when these things have no instrumental value for human beings or other sentient creatures? Do we really need an environmental ethic in order to do justice to the standpoint of the environmentalist who abhors a defoliated jungle or a strip-mined hillside?

Perhaps the reason why so many people think we do is because they are operating within an unnecessarily narrow conception of what is instrumentally valuable. They think that within the framework of a human-centered or sentient-being-centered ethic we can only value natural things if they satisfy a well-defined need which we (or some other sentient creatures) have. Dissatisfied with this ethic, they mistakenly want to argue for the preservation of something that is not valuable in this sense and thus feel obliged to embark on the project of constructing an environmental ethic. Fortunately, there is another possibility. We might be able to argue that something is valuable and therefore ought to be preserved because our lives and our conception of ourselves will be enhanced—in a spiritual sense—if we learn to appreciate it for what it is and we learn how to live with it in harmony. Although such an approach does not pretend to go beyond the human point of view, beyond our concerns and interests, it is not confined to a concern with obvious and traditional material and psychological needs, for it permits us to define a new conception of what we are as individuals and what a good life is. My view is that those who want to develop a deep approach to environmental concerns have everything to gain and nothing to lose by following this approach. Environmental ethics is not only a dead end, but also an unnecessary diversion.

DISCUSSION QUESTIONS

1. Why is the division between sentient beings and nonsentient natural objects important, according to Thompson? Is she right?
2. How might a proponent of environmental ethics respond to Thompson's criticisms?
3. Assess Thompson's claim about the moral status of machines. Is the fact that machines do not have their *own* goals relevant to distinguishing them from nonsentient living organisms, such as plants?

You Decide!

1. AMERICA THE BEAUTIFUL

What one agricultural product covers more square *miles* in the United States (some 50,000) than any other single crop? Corn? Wheat? Rice? Another hint. A $39.3 billion industry surrounds this agricultural undertaking, though nothing that you can eat or wear or otherwise consume is produced by it. Give up? Lawns. Growing grass is a major preoccupation for homeowners, golf courses, municipalities, corporations, universities—almost anyone with a building and a piece of land. Tremendous amounts of time, energy, water, fertilizers, chemicals, and money (not to mention anxiety and self-esteem) are expended seeking that most elusive suburban dream: the velvety green carpet of a yard. As a symbol of American culture, the manicured lawn is so common as to make residential life without it nearly unthinkable. A springy, uniformly green, well-kept lawn with sharp clean edges says the homeowner cares about appearances. It reflects the values of orderliness, attention to detail, a willingness to do what's expected, and, in general, good citizenship. Neglecting one's lawn quickly makes one the object of ridicule and contempt; most local governments have ordinances regarding their care. Lawns are serious business.

Modern lawns descended from our fascination with European aristocracy. The ideal English manor consisted of a grand mansion surrounded by fields on which deer grazed, representing an abundance of food for the taking by the lord. It is not uncommon even today to find ceramic deer or other animals decorating American lawns. Influenced by European standards of good taste, Thomas Jefferson is credited with bringing the lawn to Monticello, his home in Virginia. Since only the wealthy could afford such an extravagance, the lawn quickly became a status symbol. It was only after World War II, however, with the boom of suburban homes, that the lawn became the ubiquitous feature of the American landscape that it is today.

Growing and maintaining a lawn is not simple. Virtually none of the grasses (with the exception of the detested crabgrass) are native to this continent, having been developed by plant scientists from seed stocks from around the world. Most major land-grant universities have "turf science" departments housed somewhere within the horticultural sciences. Turf scientists are constantly looking for ways to breed drought-resistant, insect-resistant, temperature-resistant strains of grass; some people even grow lawns in the desert, lavishing water and attention on a horticultural undertaking that makes about as much sense as maintaining a tropical garden in the Arctic.

Walk into your local lawn and garden center and gaze upon the bewildering variety of implements and magic potions devoted to lawn care, each with its own special promise. Here the war between humanity and nature is most evident as numerous pesticides and herbicides are advertised with unmistakable military imagery—how to eliminate dandelions forever, your struggle against crabgrass, insect invasions, and so on. Contemporary lawns bespeak, perhaps more than any other aspect of the natural world with which we have routine contact, of our desire to subject and control nature. Our attitudes are reflected back to us unambiguously in the name of the nation's largest lawn care company: TruGreen ChemLawn.

Discussion Questions

1. TruGreen ChemLawn claims on its website (www.trugreenchemlawn.com) that, "Your lawn is your welcome mat. A healthy landscape, including perfectly pruned trees and shrubs, says a lot about you and your home or business." What do you think it "says" about you? Explore the multiple messages implicit in a "perfect" yard. Consider, too, the messages implicit in the name "TruGreen ChemLawn."
2. TruGreen ChemLawn also lists the environmental benefits of a lawn: reduce runoff and erosion, reduce temperature, absorb glare, absorb pollutants from vehicles and help combat global warming, provide oxygen, trap dust and pollen, reduce noise. Assess these claims. Are any environmental negatives associated with lawns?
3. Suppose your neighbor is indifferent to lawn care. What, if anything, do you think should be done about it? Suppose your neighbor has eccentric tastes in yard care, such as planting odd vegetation, should that also be subject to control? The City of Ithaca Code says the following about lawns: "It shall be the duty and responsibility of all owners in the City of Ithaca to ensure that grass, weeds or other vegetation on grounds and exterior property are maintained so that the height of vegetation is limited to nine inches, except for trees, bushes and other vegetation planted, maintained or kept for some ornamental or other useful purpose." The code further specifies, "No grass, weeds or vegetation whatsoever shall be permitted to grow or remain on the side, front and/or rear yards of any property . . . to such an extent as to produce an unsightly, disagreeable appearance objectionable to the neighborhood and not consistent with neighborhood standards of yard upkeep . . . Any vegetation planted for some useful or ornamental purpose shall not be governed by this requirement."

4. Is it OK to water your lawn during a summer drought? Suppose you are willing to pay whatever higher water costs are involved?
5. Check out the Lawn Institute website (www.lawninstitute.com), an organization for the lawn care industry, with links to the Professional Lawncare Association of America. The PLAA has a statement of ethics for lawn care professionals worth seeing.

2. WOOD WISE

"Wow, look at these lumber prices," fumed Chris as he and Geoff made their way down the aisle of their local home improvement center. "How are we ever going to build that shed for what we estimated?"

"Looks tough," Geoff responded. "But you know," the prices reflect the reality of the lumber market. Fewer trees to cut down, higher labor and transportation costs, and all that."

"Well, if liberal democrats in the government quit keeping loggers out of the national forests, then we wouldn't have to pay so much. I mean, it's just stupid not to make use of the wood. The U.S. Forest Service is supposed to ensure that the nation's forests are used for the good of the people; they're not to be set aside for environmentalists to cavort in," said Chris, who heard something the other day on the radio about President Clinton in 1999 seeking to protect 40 million acres of wilderness from logging. The U.S. Forest Service (a branch of the Department of Agriculture) manages 191 million acres of national forests, an area the size of Texas. Long perceived as an ally of the logging industry, the Forest Service has traditionally sold timber off federal lands at low prices as it oversaw the construction of a system of logging roads throughout the national forests an astonishing eight times longer than the entire interstate highway system. But the agency is undergoing a subtle shift in orientation as the guiding concept of "multiple use" for the national forests becomes more than a license for the timber industry to acquire inexpensive lumber. According to the Forest Service's 1905 charter, while "the prime object of the forest reserves is use," they were "to be devoted to its most productive use for the permanent good of the whole people, and not for the temporary benefit of individuals or companies." Currently, controversy rages over where the permanent good of the whole people lies.

"Your picture isn't very subtle," Geoff said. "I mean, the alternatives aren't between letting the logging companies clear-cut the national forests or preserving them for nature freaks. Everyone agrees that the national forests should be used for the good of the people."

"Yeah, well I guess the good of some people doesn't count as much as the good of others," mused Chris. "What about my good? How is my good advanced by having to pay so much for lumber?"

Discussion Questions

1. Gifford Pinchot, first director of the U.S. Forest Service, articulated the concept of "wise use" for the national forests. What constitues wise use, in your view? Remember, the Forest Service is not the same as the U.S. Park Service; much of the land it manages is inaccessible and of interest to only a very small minority of people.
2. The U.S. Forest Service website states, "Multiple use means managing resources under the best combination of uses to benefit the American people while ensuring the productivity of the land and protecting the quality of the environment." Reflect on this statement. What

role does *and* play? Is protecting the environment a separate component of "multiple use"? Is the idea of nature having intrinsic value compatible with the mission of the Forest Service?
3. Can we have obligations to future generations? What is the basis of those obligations? What sorts of burdens should we impose on ourselves for the well-being of people who will live after us?

3. GESTURES

Beth was furious. She knew that Brian knew how she felt about plastic utensils and he deliberately bought plastic utensils for the party. It was a slap in the face. "So, Brian," she began, "why did you buy plastic knives and forks and spoons and cups and plates?"

"Uh," said Brain playing dumb, "I thought it would be easier."

"You know," but before Beth could finish the sentence Brian interrupted, "I know you have a problem with these things, but I wish you would get off it. It really doesn't matter all that much."

"What do you mean 'it really doesn't matter'?" shot back Beth.

"What I mean," continued Brian, "is that using plastic utensils for a party really won't have that big an effect on the environment."

"Oh, I see," continued Beth, "a bunch of individual decisions don't add up to a big problem? You probably don't vote either for the same reason—my one little vote won't make a difference. Don't you realize that if everyone thought the way you did, our problems would be even worse?"

"Well, it depends," responded Brian. "Look, deciding not to use plastic forks is small potatoes compared to our general way of life and the effect that has on the environment. Sure, you recycle, you avoid plastic plates, you take your own bags to the grocery store, you've even got nature bumper stickers on your car, but so what? This is all just a way for you to feel as if you are doing something while continuing to live basically like the rest of us. It has no real effect. You even have some do-gooder nature credit card that gives a zillionth of a percent or something to preserve the world, or however it was they sold you on it. Your 'holier than thou environmentalism' is pretty thin."

"Yeah, well, your cynicism is despicable. Go ahead and make fun of me," began Beth in very measured tone of voice. "Sure, my efforts probably don't add up to much, though I doubt it, but even if they are largely symbolic, that is at least something—more than what you do, which is nothing. If there were more people like me, and fewer like you, then things would be a lot better."

Discussion Questions

1. Are Beth's actions largely symbolic? Does this matter?
2. Would things be appreciably different if there were more people like either Beth or Brian?
3. Which of our routine activities do you think have the biggest impact on the environment? Can this be determined objectively?
4. Is the fact that not everyone can live like us relevant to determining whether or not it is OK for us to live as we do? Why, why not?

Further Reading on Gasoline

1. "Clamped in a Straightjacket: The Insertion of Lead into Gasoline," by Herbert Needleman. *Environmental Research* 74, 1997, pp. 95–103.

2. "Gasoline Additive's Going, but Far from Gone," Janet Raloff, *Science News,* Vol 157, No. 15, 2000.
3. Hearing before the Subcommittee on Oversight and Investigations of the Committee on Energy and Commerce House of Representatives; "Reformulated Gasoline" June 22, 1994, Serial No. 103–155.
4. *Profile of the Petroleum Refining Industry,* Office of Enforcement and Compliance Assurance, U.S. Environmental Projection Agency; Washington, DC, 1995.
5. "Understanding Gasoline Additives," Lewis Gibbs, *Automotive Engineering,* Jan. 1990 vol 98, pp. 43–49.

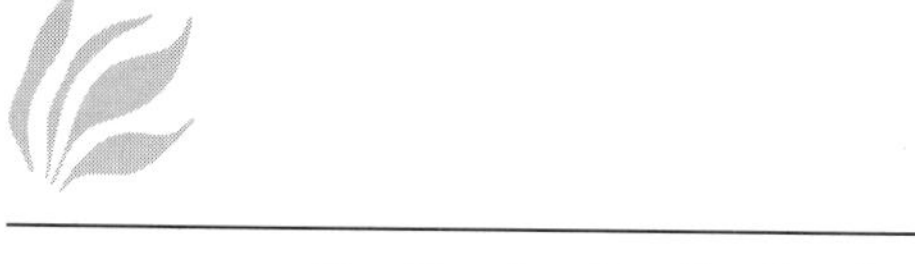

CHAPTER 5

The Moral Status of Animals

MODERN TIMES: FOWL DEEDS—BROILERS

The chicken industry distinguishes between broilers and layers. Broilers are chickens raised directly for food and layers produce eggs first, but are then slaughtered for food after their egg productivity drops. According to the trade journal *Poultry USA,* 9 out of 10 U.S. households consume chicken at least once a week, making chicken the most widely consumed meat (some 81 pounds per capita, compared to beef at 69 and pork at 52). The number of chickens slaughtered in this country is truly staggering—some 8.7 *billion* a year—and the survey conducted by *Poultry USA* anticipates the market to expand, since chicken is affordable, convenient, and tasty. Almost one-third of the broilers produced are sold through fast-food outlets such as KFC and McDonald's.

Broilers are reared intensively in long, low windowless sheds containing many thousands of birds, reaching 20,000 birds per shed at some of the largest producers. The effects of such crowding are minimized by keeping the lights low to reduce aggression and by debeaking the chickens so they will not injure or eat each other. More space would ameliorate some of the problems, but it would also make chicken more expensive. It takes just seven weeks to go from a chick to slaughter with every aspect of the bird's short life managed to promote the swiftest possible growth. With strains selectively bred to develop massive breast muscles (white meat), the birds are pumped with high-protein, high-energy feed, antibiotics, and growth hormones. Growth is so rapid and disproportionate that many birds are unable to walk, developing sores and infections from having to squat on the fetid, manure-encrusted floor. Because rearing is done on an all-in/all-out policy—chickens in a particular shed are all started and slaughtered together—the sheds are cleaned only between batches. Disposal of manure and dead chickens culled from the sheds is a major environmental problem.

You have probably seen large trucks on the highway transporting thousands of chickens in crates to the slaughterhouse. Getting chickens from rearing sheds into the shipping crates is a nasty task, often performed in the early morning by teams of catchers who chase the panic-stricken birds, grabbing four at a time by the legs. Mechanical methods of crating chickens have been developed in an attempt to increase efficiency and reduce injury and death from rough handling, though the industry remains skeptical of their effectiveness. One system resembles a kind of street sweeper. It has long, rotating rubber fingers on the front of a covered conveyor belt that can be swept from side to side as the machine is driven through the shed. The "Techno-Catch" system promises to crate 8,000 birds an hour (compared to 7,000 to 10,000 birds per hour for crews of catchers), with "less bird damage."

According to a spokesperson for the National Broiler Council's Processing Committee, once at the slaughterhouse, chickens

> are hung in an inverted position on shackles, suspended from an overhead conveyor in a darkened area which helps keep the birds calm. As the birds move on the conveyor to the stunner, their breasts gently rub against a plate which also has a calming effect. The birds are then conveyed through a brine water bath charged with an electric current where each bird is rendered unconscious. The unconscious birds then go through a machine where a rotary knife blade cuts the carotid artery and the jugular vein. This immediately cuts off all blood supply to the brain and the birds die from loss of blood. An establishment employee is also stationed by this machine to hand cut any birds that may have been missed by the machine. The electrical stun procedure used by the U.S. broiler industry is very similar to the procedure approved as humane by the U.S. Department of Agriculture for the slaughter of swine, sheep, calves, cattle, and goats.

Once stunned and bled, the birds are immersed in scalding water to facilitate removal of their feathers. The National Broiler Council official gave this testimony before a congressional subcommittee on methods of chicken slaughter in 1994.

In 1958, Congress passed the Humane Methods of Slaughter Act, finding that, "the use of humane methods in the slaughter of livestock prevents needless suffering. . . It is therefore declared to be the policy of the United States that the slaughtering of livestock and the handling of livestock in connection with slaughter shall be carried out only by humane methods." However, the Humane Methods of Slaughter Act does not apply to poultry. The poultry industry claims its method of slaughter is humane ("very similar to the procedure approved as humane by the U.S. Department of Agriculture"), so it says legislation governing chicken slaughter is not necessary.

But under dispute is whether the amount of current used to stun the birds does render them unconscious. According to expert testimony at the congressional hearing, "a stunning current of not less than 105 milliamperes should be used" to provide insensibility. However, in the United States only 15 milliamperes are used, since higher amounts of electricity would allegedly affect the quality of the carcass. The concern is that chickens have not been rendered insensible to pain and have their throats cut while conscious or, as apparently sometimes happens, make it to the scalding tank alive if the rotary blade or employee miss a bird. There is reason to think that chicken slaughter is not as humane as it could be.

The United States is the only developed country in the world that fails to cover poultry by humane methods of slaughter legislation. In the words of Ian Duncan, professor of poultry ethology at the University of Guelph, "All poultry species are sentient vertebrates and all the available evidence shows that they have a very similar range of feelings as have the mammalian species already included in this legislation. By this I mean that poultry can suffer by feeling pain, by feeling frightened and by feeling stressed as can cattle or sheep or swine. If the reason for having humane slaughter legislation is to reduce the suffering of the mammalian species (as surely it is), then, logically, this legislation should also cover poultry." The act under consideration to extend humane slaughter methods to chickens never made it out of the congressional subcommittee.

It is interesting that there is a humane methods of slaughter act at all. Why should the suffering of animals slaughtered for food even be an issue? And it is curious that in the United States, chickens are not covered by the humane slaughter act. Why is that? Perhaps chickens are not as psychologically compelling as other animals we eat. But however dim-witted, chickens nevertheless are sentient beings capable of suffering. (Recall the Broiler Council official describing how lowering the lights and rubbing their breasts calms them; why do they need to be calmed? Answer: they are terrified. Question: Why should chicken terror matter? Answer:. . .)

Perhaps, too, the sheer numbers of chickens slaughtered inures us to their plight. Just as dealing with masses of humanity can desensitize, so contemplating the billions of chickens slaughtered becomes another abstraction. Probably most significant is the fact that many of us have little contact with the chickens and other animals we routinely consume. They come cut up in little plastic trays in the supermarket. We do not have a good sense of what they are like as creatures. Modern methods of food production sever the link between the piece of meat on our plate and the animal we are consuming.

WHAT ARE ANIMALS LIKE?

It is worth contemplating the nature of animals. For biologists, the category "animal" is broad, including creatures as diverse as sponges and insects to birds and mammals—basically anything that is not a plant. We can begin by thinking about the (live) animals with which we are most likely to have everyday contact such as dogs and cats. What are these animals like? We have a propensity to **anthropomorphize** our pets (that is, to make human); we fill their heads with our own thoughts and concerns, turning them into furry four-legged people. When asked, we deny that our pets are like us, but our behavior suggests we think otherwise; we continue to treat our pets as something akin to a person. Is this silly on our part or is there something to it?

Think of the range of mental and emotional states you are comfortable ascribing to dogs and cats: consciousness, curiosity, happiness, fear, contentment, jealousy, memory, love, intentionality, anxiety, hate, playfulness, generosity, kindness, depression, joy, courage, loyalty, determination, sensitivity, excitement, cunning, and on and on. None of this seems remarkable until we remind ourselves that we are talking about nonhuman animals. We are talking about creatures that, in broad respects, are apparently very much like ourselves. The various mental attributes may not be as sophisticated as they are in normal human beings, but that dogs and cats possess these traits to one degree or another is beyond doubt. Also, you ascribe these emotional and mental states to dogs and cats easily and without the sense of absurdity you would have in trying to talk about a tree or a table that way. It is, we might say, "natural" to see dogs and cats and a range of other animals as having a complex mental and emotional life. In the *Descent of Man,* Darwin claims, "There is no fundamental difference between man and the higher mammals in their mental faculties."

I said that mentality in at least certain animals is beyond doubt. This is not quite correct, for Descartes (see Chapter 3) denied what seems so obvious, arguing that animals were devoid of mind. "It seems reasonable," he wrote, "since art copies nature, and men can make various automata which move without thought, that nature should produce its own automata, much more splendid than artificial ones. These natural automata are the animals." Only people, Descartes held, are conscious, as our use of language shows. One wonders, though, why linguistic ability is enough to establish consciousness and why its absence is enough to show lack of consciousness. The neurophysiological similarities between human beings and other animals suggests, on the contrary, that if our mentality is a function of the structures of our brains and nervous systems, then other animals with those neural structures would also be conscious.

One suspects Descartes' insistence that only people are conscious was driven by a theory, as indeed it was. He wrote, "If they [animals] thought as we do, they would have an immortal soul like us. This is unlikely, because there is no reason to believe it of some animals without believing it of all, and many of them such as oysters and sponges are too imperfect for this to be credible." The theological absurdity of immortal animal souls forces Descartes to restrict mentality to humanity. Moreover, from a theological point of view, animal sensitivity raises serious questions. For suppose animals can feel pain and suffer, just as we do. Now ask yourself why a loving, all-powerful God would make creatures who suffer pointlessly. This is the traditional problem of evil, namely, how to reconcile God with suffering in the world. Human suffering can perhaps be explained in a way that is compatible with God; suffering may improve our characters or result from our own free choices. But animal suffering seems to make no sense since animals are not subject to moral improvement nor do they freely choose. Surely a loving, all-powerful God could make creatures that behave merely in accordance with the "disposition of their organs," as Descartes put it, but who did not actually experience anything—natural automata. So animal suffering presents problems for the theist because it seems to introduce pointless suffering into the world. Descartes' astonishing response is to deny that animals suffer, thereby removing a problem for the theist to explain.

If, irrespective of Descartes, attributions of mentality to animals like dogs and cats (for example) are perfectly sensible, and if we are dealing with creatures that are broadly similar to ourselves, then the moral question is inescapable: We cannot admit that another creature is similar to ourselves but deny that its interests ought to figure into our moral deliberations. To do so would violate a fundamental principle of rationality, namely, the idea that we are to treat similar cases similarly. Consider, as an example of the requirement to treat like cases alike, the grade you receive in a course. Suppose you and your friend got the same grades on the exams, participated in class, and performed equally well throughout the semester. You naturally expect the same grade as your friend. Now suppose she received an A in the course and you got a D. This outcome makes no sense. The requirement to treat likes alike means that the burden of proof is now on the professor to show that the two cases are *not* relevantly similar, for if they are relevantly similar then the discrepancy in grade is inexplicable.

Suppose you pursue the matter with your professor, who agrees that like cases should be treated alike, but denies that your performance in the class was similar to your friend's. You show your professor all the work graded in his hand, which corresponds exactly to the grades entered in his grade book. "Ah," he says, "you are forgetting the most important thing. You are a woman" (black, gay, have long hair/short hair). This is a new development. Your professor is trying to argue that your case is not similar to your friend's and that he is justified in treating them differently. The appropriate response is: How is being a woman (black, Latino, gay, straight, short, tall, etc.) relevant to the grade in the course? It is not, of course, and your professor has discriminated against you in the crudest possible fashion. Discrimination is not just a matter of treating different people differently, but treating different people differently without a good reason for doing so; in other words, not treating like cases alike. So when we talk about relevantly similar cases, we have to figure out what counts as a relevant or an irrelevant difference in the case under consideration. Some differences are relevant in a particular instance, others not. Skin color, gender, sexual orientation, national origin, height, and weight are irrelevant considerations for the assignment of course grades. They are surely differences among people, but when it comes to grades, they do not count.

A big question to consider is whether certain animals are relevantly similar to us so that their interests merit equal consideration to our own according to the "treat likes alike" principle. Consider an interest we share with animals, an interest in not suffering. Since (some) animals can feel pain, and thereby suffer, they too have an interest in not suffering for the same reason you have an interest in not suffering. If we focus simply on the pain, we can ask whether human pain, *because* it is human pain, is morally different from, say, dog pain. If we think it is, then we have to explain why species membership in itself is a morally relevant difference. With respect to the interest in not suffering, the worry is that species membership is irrelevant, much as skin color and gender are irrelevant to the assignment of grades in a course. And unless we can show that species membership in itself is a morally significant difference between human pain and dog pain, we will run afoul of the requirement to treat likes alike.

The claim that human suffering, simply because it is human suffering, is morally more significant than nonhuman suffering has been called "speciesism," on analogy with racism or sexism. If there is no good reason to hold human suffering to be morally significant in a way that nonhuman suffering is not, then the preference for human over nonhuman suffering would reflect an irrational bias, for we would not be treating likes alike. But are cases of, say, dog suffering comparable to your suffering? Suppose that sticking the dog with the pin hurts it as much as it hurts you. Might there still be good reasons to prefer causing the dog to experience that amount of pain rather than you? We might consider the impact on your life compared to the dog's life, your dread of anticipation, humiliation that you would experience over and above just the pain from the pin prick, and so on. Since the negative effects of the pain and the total experience under which you experienced it arguably would have a greater impact on your life than on the dog's, it might be better to inflict the pain on the dog rather than you.

The problem with this line of argument, however, is what do we say in a case where the human being and the dog are mentally and emotionally equivalent? Sadly, some brain-damaged human beings function only at the cognitive and emotional level of a normal dog. Their condition will never change. Now consider sticking each with the pin; is there a basis on which to insist that the human suffering is morally more important, that if we have to choose between the beings in question is it morally better to cause the dog to experience the pain than the human being? We might say that the brain-damaged human being's loved ones will be upset, but we can always reform the example so that there are people who care more about the dog than the human being. Such examples present a significant challenge to speciesism. Perhaps it seems that this example is unrealistic; we would never have to make such a choice. But painful medical experiments are routinely performed on dogs; we would never even consider using brain-damaged human beings for those same experiments. Is that choice justified?

ANIMAL RIGHTS

When considering the moral status of animals, the issue of animal rights inevitably arises. In my experience, mentioning animal rights almost always throws the discussion into a tailspin. The topic of animal rights is as emotion-laden as abortion, making calm, reasonable philosophical exploration all the more difficult. Talk of rights can get out of hand pretty fast—people are quick to assert or deny rights in heated moral disputes—so we need to be clear about the nature of the rights at issue. Let's begin by noting the difference between legal (or conventional) rights and moral rights. You have all sorts of legal (or conventional) rights—these are the rights that the law or some authoritative body recognizes. For example, if you are a student at a university, you have the right to check books out of the library or the right to swim in the pool (provided you meet whatever other conditions are imposed by the university). This is a right that not everyone has; you have it solely by virtue of your association with your university. Your legal rights are similarly contingent on your citizenship in this country. We can go to the county courthouse and inspect the law books to see what legal rights you actually have. But, it is alleged, not all rights rest upon institutions or conventions.

Some rights stand apart from convention, legal systems, and institutions. These are **moral rights,** rights that *ought* to be recognized, whether or not they appear in a legal code. Moral rights are best conceived as legitimate claims that can be supported by moral theory independent of the institutions with which you are associated, the legal system, or the conventions of your society. Your legal and conventional rights are most plausibly seen as resting upon your moral rights; at least that would be the order of explanation. That is, you have this or that legal right *because* of some underlying moral right that we could articulate if the inquiry were pushed far enough.

Talking about rights can become confusing because we sometimes think of rights as a special sort of "thing" that an entity either has or does not have. But that is to misconstrue the issue. Careful inspection of a person will not allow us to detect whether he or she really has rights; rather, attributing rights is a way of conceiving what our moral obligations are toward one another. Rights are not just arbitrarily bestowed; it will make sense to attribute rights only where there is some interest that the rights serve to protect. You have a right to liberty, for instance, because you have an interest in functioning autonomously, and you have a right to life because you have an interest in living.

Appealing to rights is thus a dimension of our moral discourse; it is yet another way for us to conceive of what we ought or ought not to be doing. Conceiving of our duties in terms of rights does, however, have a logic of its own. If you have a right to something, then that claim has moral force, for it will impose on others an obligation to respect that right. In other words, your having a particular right implies that others ought either to do or forbear from doing something with regard to your right. So if you have a right to peaceful enjoyment of your property, for example, then that imposes a moral obligation on me not to play loud music. Think of it this way: Rights can be understood with respect to the obligations that they imply; part of what we mean by asserting a right is that there are attendant obligations that correspond to the right. No wonder people are quick to cast moral controversies in terms of rights! Rights are very powerful "moral currency," when properly used.

It is common to divide rights into two sorts based upon the nature of the obligations that are involved: liberty rights and claim rights (sometimes called "negative" and "positive" rights, respectively). Liberty rights are basically rights of noninterference. I respect your liberty rights by not interfering with your activities, within certain limits, of course. These are the familiar rights of life, liberty, and pursuit of happiness that have become codified in our system of law. Claim rights are much more controversial. Unlike liberty rights, which require your non-interference in my affairs, claim rights require you to become involved in my affairs. If I have a right to food, clothing, shelter, education, or health care (to name a few!), then your non-involvement is not what is required, but rather your (or somebody's) involvement. The things to which I have a legitimate moral claim (a right) have to come from somewhere, they have to be produced, generated, delivered, or somehow made available to me, and that requires effort and commitment from somebody. Rather than your obligation being one of forbearance by simply letting me go about my business (as with liberty rights), claim rights instead call for your (or someone's) active engagement in my affairs. Claim rights are controversial because the moral obligations entailed by them require someone to do something for me, not merely leave me alone.

Moral rights constitute a major hurdle to anyone who proposes doing something contrary to that right. Recall from Chapter 1 how the utilitarian is concerned to maximize the greatest good in a particular situation; we also saw how this can lead to the good of the many at the expense of the individual. If I have a right to be treated with respect as an individual, and thus not to be used as an instrument for achieving overall good, then this will impose an obligation on others not to treat me as a means for the aggregate good. Such a right will limit the utilitarian, who, as we have seen, is prepared to use individuals as a means to achieve the overall good.

Do rights apply only to people? Can animals, plants, or other natural objects have rights? If nonhuman entities are capable of having rights, then, as discussed above, this means we will have obligations to those entities. (Whether the obligations are only negative or include some positive ones as well will be a separate question.) But is it possible for nonpersons to have rights? This is a difficult question, not one to be answered all at once here, since it turns on reaching a settled account of the nature of rights, something which we do not have. But if rights are construed as legitimate claims, then it seems at least possible for some nonhumans to have rights, because the idea of having a claim is not obviously limited to human beings. You don't have to be able actually to make a claim to have one. Incompetent human beings, for example, are not physically able to make claims themselves, but we still think that they have rights because they have a sake, a well-being, an interest, for which we can act. Similarly, if a case can be made for nonhumans having a legitimate claim—a sake for which we can act—then, yes, it looks as if it at least makes sense to speak of things other than people having rights.

Whether our acknowledgment of a legitimate claim is best conceived in terms of rights is another question, for it might be argued that the concept of a right is best restricted to people. Rights, one might claim, are necessarily connected to moral agency or rationality, thereby restricting rights to people. Such a restrictive account of rights will have to make a special exception for nonrational human beings. But even if we adopt a restrictive theory of rights that limits rights only to people, the question of our moral obligations to nonhumans is not answered. It is true that if something has rights, then we have moral obligations to it. This is part of what it means to have a right. But we cannot simply turn this around and think that just because something has no rights, we therefore have no obligations to it. You can have an obligation to help the needy without the needy thereby having a right to your help. So even if nonhumans cannot have rights, this tells us nothing about our obligations with respect to them.

VEGETARIANISM

Eating is essential to life. By ingesting bits of our surroundings, we are connected to all other living things. But for us, eating is no mere biological activity, like breathing. Eating is imbued with moral significance. We distinguish carefully between not only the edible and inedible—tomatoes are edible, rocks are not—but between what it is morally acceptable to eat and what is not. We make moral judgments (usually, but not always, negative) regarding the consumption of human flesh, for instance. We can also make moral judgments about eating animals. Animals are edible, but ought we to eat them? Here the moral terrain is much more controversial than it was for eating people. *Vegetarianism* as a term for someone who abstains from eating animals has been around only since 1847 when the Vegetarian Society was founded in Great Britain. Before that, abstaining from eating animals was known as the "Pythagorean diet" because the ancient Greek philosopher Pythagoras (ca 570–495 B.C.) recommended it to his followers.

In addition to giving us the formula that bears his name, Pythagoras had an enormous impact on Western thought. He postulated an eternal and perfect world beyond the senses, knowable only to the intellect. That ultimate reality might not be present to us in the everyday world of sights and sounds influenced Plato and found its way into Christianity. Pythagoras also bequeathed us the idea that souls are immortal, a view that many people accept without question. But Pythagoras also taught that souls can be reincarnated in human or animal form, a position known as metempsychosis. Pythagorean objection to the slaughter of animals and consumption of their flesh is thus ultimately anthropocentric in outlook. For if one abstains from eating animals because one fears eating a person, then the concern is over possible cannibalism irrespective of the animal itself. One wonders whether Pythagoras would have qualms about consuming animal flesh if he became convinced that metempsychosis was false.

Since the time of Pythagoras vegetarianism has been remarkably persistent, though never quite respectable. It is often associated with fringe elements of society. That may explain its current popularity among young people, artists, and celebrities. Today some 15 percent of college students report being vegetarians. Vegetarians are purported to be ethereal, compassionate, and other-worldly, an impression perhaps cultivated by its original association with the enigmatic and reclusive Pythagoreans who shunned the world to contemplate the eternal truths of mathematics. However, Adolf Hitler was a vegetarian, shattering that myth. Famous vegetarians in the history of thought include Thoreau, Benjamin Franklin (for a while), Leonardo da Vinci, Tolstoy, Voltaire, Shelly, Shaw, Plutarch, and possibly Plato. According to Daniel Dombroski in *The Philosophy of Vegetarianism,* "That the Republic [Plato's ideal state] was to be a vegetarian city is one of the best-kept secrets in the history of philosophy."

Contemporary grounds for vegetarianism are primarily these: health, environmental concerns, and ethics. Increasingly compelling evidence from multiple sources shows that animal flesh is hardly essential for good health and may even be inimical to it, at least in the quantities that Americans are used to consuming. Environmental concerns often focus on how staggeringly inefficient it is to raise animals for food. For example, to produce one pound of animal protein requires on average seven pounds of vegetable protein. The bulk of our agricultural efforts are spent growing grain that will be fed to livestock; this is food that we could consume directly rather than wasting most of it by converting it into meat. Apparently, we enjoy consuming animal flesh so much that we will tolerate such inefficiencies. And the numbers are mind-boggling. On average 130,000 cattle, 360,000 pigs, and 24 *million* chickens are slaughtered each day in the United States.

We shall focus on ethical reasons for vegetarianism. Because moral considerations normally trump other kinds of considerations (recall our discussion about the nature of moral reasons in Chapter 1), if vegetarianism can be given an ethical basis, then those considerations must be acknowledged by all moral reasoners. Unlike reasons of health or efficiency, one cannot simply dismiss ethical considerations in favor of custom or dietary preference. Imagine, by analogy, trying to assess slavery by appeal only to efficiency, environmental impact, or personal preference. The economic advantages of slavery are perversely irrelevant to the question of whether or not we ought to keep slaves. The morality of slavery is ultimately what decides the issue. Similarly, the ethical vegetarian is making a moral claim, one that allegedly applies to us all in virtue of the binding nature of moral reasons on all rational deliberators. Whether one eats meat will thus *not* be a matter of personal preference but a matter of moral assessment, if the ethical vegetarian is correct. But is the ethical vegetarian correct?

In virtue of the psychological similarity of animals to ourselves, ethical vegetarians will assert either that animal interests cannot rationally be ignored in our quest for a tasty meal or that animals have rights, among them the right to be treated with respect, which is incompatible with our rearing them for food. Different versions of ethical vegetarianism are thus possible. One might object primarily to the suffering caused animals by modern high-volume methods of factory farming, accepting, perhaps, the painless slaughter (if such a thing is possible) of free-ranging "happy" animals as morally inconsequential. Rearing animals in a humane manner would drive up the price of meat significantly, making it more of a luxury than a staple of our diets. Such a position is basically reformist, since it is not opposed to eating animals per se, but rather objects to the current manner of production, one which is insufficiently sensitive to their suffering.

Alternatively, the ethical vegetarian might argue that even if we could reform our practices so that animals do not suffer in order for us to eat them, this misses the main point. It might be held that the core moral issue in rearing animals for food turns on our willingness to view animals in wholly instrumental terms. On this version of ethical vegetarianism, animals should be seen as intrinsically valuable in the same way human beings are held to be intrinsically valuable.

If our intrinsic value is in some way a function of our mental capacities, then the ethical vegetarian will insist that animals with those same mental capacities should also have intrinsic value. What exactly those mental capacities are is a matter for debate. Here is a delicate point exploited by the ethical vegetarian: If we narrowly define the key mental attributes in virtue of which we claim intrinsic value for ourselves, such as consciousness or rationality or self-awareness, then various categories of human beings will fail to be intrinsically valuable; infants, the mentally defective, the insane, and so on. If, on the other hand, we relax our understanding of those core mental capacities, seeking instead a lowest common denominator in virtue of which all human beings have intrinsic value, then some animals will qualify for they will meet whatever minimal standards of rationality or consciousness or self-awareness we set for ourselves as a basis for our intrinsic value. In short, there does not seem to be a way, claims the ethical vegetarian, to discriminate sharply between the moral status of human beings and animals; either some animals share the moral status of human beings or some human beings share the moral status of animals.

THE READINGS

The readings for this section focus on our relationship with animals. Do we have any direct obligations to them and might this be in virtue of their having certain rights against us? The material challenges many of our preconceptions and unreflective ways of living our lives.

PETER SINGER

All Animals Are Equal

Peter Singer is one of the most well-known contemporary philosophers in the world. He is currently director of the Institute for Bioethics at Princeton University. *Animal Liberation,* his influential book from which our selection was taken, continues both to inspire and to infuriate since its publication in 1975. Singer argues that the moral principle of equal consideration applies to animals in a simple and straightforward manner. Moreover, our failure to extend equal consideration to animals constitutes a kind of discrimination he calls speciesism. According to Singer, speciesism is evident in our eating animals and in our willingness to perform experiments on them that we would never dream of doing on a human being.

CRITICAL READING QUESTIONS

1. What is the principle of equality?
2. How, according to Singer, does the principle of equality apply to other members of our species?
3. Why, according to Singer, does the principle of equality apply to other species?
4. What is *speciesism,* and why is it morally wrong, according to Singer?
5. Why does Singer think animals have interests?
6. Why does the rejection of speciesism not imply that all lives are equally valuable, according to Singer?
7. Why are animals used as subjects in experimentation? What dilemma does this pose for the researcher, according to Singer?
8. Under what circumstances does Singer think animal experimentation is morally acceptable?

Jeremy Bentham, the founder of the reforming utilitarian school of moral philosophy, incorporated the essential basis of moral equality into his system of ethics by means of the formula: "Each to count for one and none to count for more than one." In other words, the interests of every being affected by an action are to be taken into account and given the same weight as the like interests of any other being. . .

It is an implication of this principle of equality that our concern for others and our readiness to consider their interests ought not to depend on what they are like or on what abilities they may pos-

---

Peter Singer, from *Animal Liberation, 2nd* edition, New York, Random House, 1990. Reprinted by permission of Peter Singer.

sess. Precisely what our concern or consideration requires us to do may vary according to the characteristics of those affected by what we do: concern for the well-being of children growing up in America would require that we teach them to read; concern for the well-being of pigs may require no more than that we leave them with other pigs in a place where there is adequate food and room to run freely. But the basic element—the taking into account of the interests of the being, whatever those interests may be—must, according to the principle of equality, be extended to all beings, black or white, masculine or feminine, human or nonhuman. . .

It is on this basis that the case against racism and the case against sexism must both ultimately rest; and it is in accordance with this principle that the attitude that we may call "speciesism," by analogy with racism, must also be condemned. Speciesism—the word is not an attractive one but I can think of no better term—is a prejudice or attitude of bias in favor of the interests of members of one's own species and against those of members of other species. It should be obvious that the fundamental objections to racism and sexism made by Thomas Jefferson and Sojourner Truth apply equally to speciesism. If possessing a higher degree of intelligence does not entitle one human to use another for his or her own ends, how can it entitle humans to exploit nonhumans for the same purpose?

Many philosophers and other writers, have proposed the principle of equal consideration of interests, in some form or other, as a basic moral principle; but not many of them have recognized that this principle applies to members of other species as well as to our own. Jeremy Bentham was one of the few who did realize this. In a forward-looking passage written at the time when black slaves were still being treated in the way we now treat animals, Bentham wrote:

> The day may come when the rest of the animal creation may acquire those rights which never could have been withholden from them but by the hand of tyranny. The French have already discovered that the blackness of the skin is no reason why a human being should be abandoned without redress to the caprice of a tormentor. It may one day come to be recognized that the number of the legs, the villosity of the skin, or the termination of the *os sacrum* are reasons equally insufficient for abandoning a sensitive being to the same fate. What else is it that should trace the insuperable line? Is it the faculty of reason, or perhaps the faculty of discourse? But a full-grown horse or dog is beyond comparison a more rational, as well as a more conversable animal, than an infant of a day or a week or even a month, old. But suppose they were otherwise, what would it avail? The question is not, Can they *reason?* nor Can they *talk?* but, Can they *suffer?*

In this passage Bentham points to the capacity for suffering as the vital characteristic that gives a being the right to equal consideration. The capacity for suffering—or more strictly, for suffering and/or enjoyment or happiness—is not just another characteristic like the capacity for language or higher mathematics. Bentham is not saying that those who try to mark "the insuperable line" that determines whether the interests of a being should be considered happen to have chosen the wrong characteristic. By saying that we must consider the interests of all beings with the capacity for suffering or enjoyment Bentham does not arbitrarily exclude from consideration any interests at all—as those who draw the line with reference to the possession of reason or language do. The capacity for suffering and enjoyment is *a prerequisite for having interests at all,* a condition that must be satisfied before we can speak of interests in a meaningful way. It would be nonsense to say that it was not in the interests of a stone to be kicked along the road by a schoolboy. A stone does not have interests because it cannot suffer. Nothing that we can do to it could possibly make any difference to its welfare. The capacity for suffering and enjoyment is, however, not only necessary, but also sufficient for us to say that a being has interests—at an absolute minimum, an interest in not suffering. A mouse, for example, does have an interest in not being kicked along the road, because it will suffer if it is. . .

Racists violate the principle of equality by giving greater weight to the interests of members of their own race when there is a clash between their interests and the interests of those of another race. Sexists violate the principle of equality by favoring the interests of their own sex. Similarly, speciesists allow the interests of their own species to override the greater interests of members of other species. The pattern is identical in each case.

Most human beings are speciesists. . . Ordinary human beings—not a few exceptionally cruel or heartless humans, but the overwhelming majority of humans—take an active part in, acquiesce in, and allow their taxes to pay for practices that require the sacrifice of the most important interests of members of other species in order to promote the most trivial interests of our own species. . .

Do animals other than humans feel pain? How do we know? Well, how do we know if anyone, human or nonhuman, feels pain? We know that we ourselves can feel pain. We know this from the direct experience of pain that we have when, for instance, somebody presses a lighted cigarette against the back of our hand. But how do we know that anyone else feels pain? We cannot directly experience anyone else's pain, whether that "anyone" is our best friend or a stray dog. Pain is a state of consciousness, a "mental event," and as such it can never be observed. Behavior like writhing, screaming, or drawing one's hand away from the lighted cigarette is not pain itself; nor are the recordings a neurologist might make of activity within the brain observations of pain itself. Pain is something that we feel, and we can only infer that others are feeling it from various external indications.

In theory, *we could* always be mistaken when we assume that other human beings feel pain. It is conceivable that one of our close friends is really a cleverly constructed robot, controlled by a brilliant scientist so as to give all the signs of feeling pain, but really no more sensitive than any other machine. We can never know, with absolute certainty, that this is not the case. But while this might present a puzzle for philosophers, none of us has the slightest real doubt that our close friends feel pain just as we do. This is an inference, but a perfectly reasonable one, based on observations of their behavior in situations in which we would feel pain, and on the fact that we have every reason to assume that our friends are beings like us, with nervous systems like ours that can be assumed to function as ours do and to produce similar feelings in similar circumstances.

If it is justifiable to assume that other human beings feel pain as we do, is there any reason why a similar inference should be unjustifiable in the case of other animals? . . .

It may be objected that comparisons of the sufferings of different species are impossible to make and that for this reason when the interests of animals and humans clash the principle of equality gives no guidance. It is probably true that comparisons of suffering between members of different species cannot be made precisely, but precision is not essential. Even if we were to prevent the infliction of suffering on animals only when it is quite certain that the interests of humans will not be affected to anything like the extent that animals are affected, we would be forced to make radical changes in our treatment of animals that would involve our diet, the farming methods we use, experimental procedures in many fields of science, our approach to wildlife and to hunting, trapping and the wearing of furs, and areas of entertainment like circuses, rodeos, and zoos. As a result, a vast amount of suffering would be avoided. . .

Just as most human beings are speciesists in their readiness to cause pain to animals when they would not cause a similar pain to humans for the same reason, so most human beings are speciesists in their readiness to kill other animals when they would not kill human beings. . .

This does not mean that to avoid speciesism we must hold that it is as wrong to kill a dog as it is to kill a human being in full possession of his or her faculties. The only position that is irredeemably speciesist is the one that tries to make the boundary of the right to life run exactly parallel to the boundary of our own species. Those who hold the sanctity of life view do this, because while distinguishing sharply between human beings and other animals they allow no distinctions to be made within our own species, objecting to the killing of the severely retarded and the hopelessly senile as strongly as they object to the killing of normal adults.

To avoid speciesism we must allow that beings who are similar in all relevant respects have a similar right to life—and mere membership in our own biological species cannot be a morally relevant criterion for this right. Within these limits we could still hold, for instance, that it is worse to kill a normal adult human with a capacity for self-awareness and the ability to plan for the future and have meaningful relations with others, than it is to kill a mouse, which presumably does not share all of these characteristics; or we might appeal to the close family and other personal ties that humans have but mice do not have to the same degree; or we might think that it is the consequences for other humans, who will be put in fear for their own lives, that makes the crucial difference; or we might think it is some combination of these factors, or other factors altogether.

Whatever criteria we choose, however, we will have to admit that they do not follow precisely the boundary of our own species. We may legitimately hold that there are some features of certain beings that make their lives more valuable than those of other beings; but there will surely be some nonhuman animals whose lives, by any standards, are more valuable than the lives of some humans. A chimpanzee, dog, or pig, for instance, will have a higher degree of self-awareness and a greater capacity for meaningful relations with others than a severely retarded infant or someone in a state of advanced senility. So if we base the right to life on these characteristics we must grant these animals a right to life as good as, or better than, such retarded or senile humans.

This argument cuts both ways. It could be taken as showing that chimpanzees, dogs, and pigs, along with some other species, have a right to life and we commit a grave moral offense whenever we kill them, even when they are old and suffering and our intention is to put them out of their misery. Alternatively one could take the argument as showing that the severely retarded and hopelessly senile have no right to life and may be killed for quite trivial reasons, as we now kill animals. . .

What we need is some middle position that would avoid speciesim but would not make the lives of the retarded and senile as cheap as the lives of pigs and dogs now are, or make the lives of pigs and dogs so sacrosanct that we think it wrong to put them out of hopeless misery. What we must do is bring nonhuman animals within our sphere of moral concern and cease to treat their lives as expendable for whatever trivial purposes we may have. At the same time, once we realize that the fact that a being is a member of our own species is not in itself enough to make it always wrong to kill that being, we may come to reconsider our policy of preserving human lives at all costs, even when there is no prospect of a meaningful life or of existence without terrible pain.

I conclude, then, that rejection of speciesism does not imply that all lives are of equal worth. While self-awareness, the capacity to think ahead and have hopes and aspirations for the future, the capacity for meaningful relations with others and so on are not relevant to the question of inflicting pain—since pain is pain, whatever other capacities, beyond the capacity to feel pain, the being may have—these capacities are relevant to the question of taking life. It is not arbitrary to hold that the life of a self-aware being, capable of abstract thought, of planning for the future, of complex acts of communication, and so on, is more valuable than the life of a being without these capacities. . .

The practice of experimenting on nonhuman animals as it exists today throughout the world reveals the consequences of speciesism. Many experiments inflict severe pain without the remotest prospect of significant benefits for human beings or any other animals. Such experiments are not isolated instances, but part of a major industry. In the number of "scientific procedures" performed on animals, official government figures show that 3.5 million scientific procedures were performed on animals in 1988. In the United States there are no figures of comparable accuracy. . .

Among the tens of millions of experiments performed, only a few can possibly be regarded as contributing to important medical research. Huge numbers of animals are used in university departments such as forestry and psychology; many more are used for commercial purposes, to test new cosmetics, shampoos, food coloring agents, and other inessential items. All this can happen only because of our prejudice against taking seriously the suffering of a being who is not a member of our own species. Typically, defenders of experiments on animals do not deny that animals suffer. They cannot deny the animals' suffering, because they need to stress the similarities between humans and other animals in order to claim that their experiments may have some relevance for human purposes. The experimenter who forces rats to choose between starvation and electric shock to see if they develop ulcers (which they do) does so because the rat has a nervous system very similar to a human being's and presumably feels an electric shock in a similar way. . .

So the researcher's central dilemma exists in an especially acute form in psychology: either the animal is like us, in which case there is no reason for performing the experiment; or else the animal is like us, in which case we ought not to perform on the animal an experiment that would be considered outrageous if performed on one of us. . .

Once a pattern of animal experimentation becomes the accepted mode of research in a particular field, the process is self-reinforcing and difficult to break out of. Not only publications and promotions but also the awards and grants that finance research become geared to animal experiments. A proposal for a new experiment with animals is something that the administrators of research funds will be ready to support, if they have in the past supported other experiments on animals. New methods that do not make use of animals will seem less familiar and will be less likely to receive support.

All this helps to explain why it is not always easy for people outside the universities to understand the rationale for the research carried out under university auspices. Originally, perhaps, scholars and researchers just set out to solve the most important problems and did not allow themselves to be influenced by other considerations. No doubt some are still motivated by these concerns. Too often, though, academic research gets bogged down in petty and insignificant details because the big questions have been studied already and they have either been solved or proven too difficult. So the researchers turn away from the well-plowed fields in search of new territory where whatever they find will be new, although the connection with a major problem may be remote. It is not uncommon, as we have seen, for experimenters to admit that similar experiments have been done many times before, but without this or that minor variation; and the most common ending to a scientific publication is "further research is necessary". . .

When are experiments on animals justifiable? Upon learning of the nature of many of the experiments carried out, some people react by saying that all experiments on animals should be prohibited immediately. But if we make our demands as absolute as this, the experimenters have a ready reply: Would we be prepared to let thousands of humans die if they could be saved by a single experiment on a single animal?

This question is, of course, purely hypothetical. There has never been and never could be a single experiment that saved thousands of lives. The way to reply to this hypothetical question is to pose another: Would the experimenters be prepared to carry out their experiment on a human orphan under six months old if that were the only way to save thousands of lives?

If the experimenters would not be prepared to use a human infant then their readiness to use nonhuman animals reveals an unjustifiable form of discrimination on the basis of species, since adult apes, monkeys, dogs, cats, rats, and other animals are more aware of what is happening to them, more self-directing, and, so far as we can tell, at least as sensitive to pain as a human infant. (I have specified that the human infant be an orphan, to avoid the complications of the feelings of parents. Specifying the case in this way is, if anything, overgenerous to those defending the use of nonhuman animals in experiments, since mammals intended for experimental use are usually separated from their mothers at an early age, when the separation causes distress for both mother and young.)

So far as we know, human infants possess no morally relevant characteristic to a higher degree than adult nonhuman animals, unless we are to count the infants' potential as a characteristic that makes it wrong to experiment on them. Whether this characteristic should count is controversial—if we count it, we shall have to condemn abortion along with experiments on infants, since the potential of the infant and the fetus is the same. To avoid the complexities of this issue, however, we can alter our original question a little and assume that the infant is one with irreversible brain damage so severe as to rule out any mental development beyond the level of a six-month-old infant. There are, unfortunately, many such human beings, locked away in special wards throughout the country, some of them long since abandoned by their parents and other relatives, and, sadly, sometimes unloved by anyone else. Despite their mental deficiencies, the anatomy and physiology of these infants are in nearly all respects identical with those of normal humans. If, therefore, we were to force-feed them with large quantities of floor polish or drip concentrated solutions of cosmetics into their eyes, we would have a much more reliable indication of the safety of these products for humans than we now get by attempting to extrapolate the results of tests on a variety of other species. The LD50 tests, the Draize eye tests, the radiation experiments, the heatstroke experiments, and many others described earlier in this chapter could have told us more about human reactions to the experimental situation if they had been carried out on severely brain-damaged humans instead of dogs or rabbits.

So whenever experimenters claim that their experiments are important enough to justify the use of animals, we should ask them whether they would be prepared to use a brain-damaged human being at a similar mental level to the animals they are planning to use. I cannot imagine that anyone would seriously propose carrying out the experiments described in this chapter on brain-damaged human beings. Occasionally it has become known that medical experiments have been performed on human beings without their consent; one case did concern institutionalized intellectually disabled children, who were given hepatitis. When such harmful experiments on human beings become known, they usually lead to an outcry against the experimenters, and rightly so. They are, very often, a further example of the arrogance of the research worker who justifies everything on the grounds of increasing knowledge. But if the experimenter claims that the experiment is important enough to justify inflicting suffering on animals, why is it not important enough to justify inflicting suffering on humans at the same mental level? What difference is there between the two? Only that one is a member of our species and the other is not? But to appeal to that difference is to reveal a bias no more defensible than racism or any other form of arbitrary discrimination. . .

No doubt there are some fields of scientific research that will be hampered by any genuine consideration of the interests of animals used in experimentation. No doubt there have been some advances in knowledge which would not have been attained as easily without using animals. Examples of important discoveries often mentioned by those defending animal experimentation go back as far as Harvey's work on the circulation of blood. They include Baning and Best's discovery of insulin and its role in diabetes; the recognition of poliomyelitis as a virus and the development of a vaccine for it; several discoveries that served to make open heart surgery and coronary artery bypass graft surgery possible; and the understanding of our immune system and ways to overcome rejection of transplanted organs. The claim that animal experimentation was essential in making these discoveries has been denied by some opponents of experimentation. I do not intend to go into the controversy here. We have just seen that any knowledge gained from animal experimentation has made at best a very small contribution to our increased lifespan; its contribution to improving the quality of life is more difficult to estimate. In a more fundamental sense, the controversy over the benefits derived from animal experimentation is essentially unresolvable, because even if valuable discoveries were made using animals, we cannot say how successful medical research would have been if it had been compelled, from the outset, to develop alternative methods of investigation. Some discoveries would probably have been delayed, or perhaps not made at all; but many false leads would also not have been pursued, and it is possible that medicine would have developed in a very different and more efficacious direction, emphasizing healthy living rather than cure.

In any case, the ethical question of the justifiability of animal experimentation cannot be settled by pointing to its benefits for us, no matter how persuasive the evidence in favor of such benefits may be. The ethical principle of equal consideration of interests will rule out some means of obtaining knowledge. There is nothing sacred about the right to pursue knowledge. We already accept many restrictions on scientific enterprise. We do not believe that scientists have a general right to perform painful or lethal experiments on human beings without their consent, although there are many cases in which such experiments would advance knowledge far more rapidly than any other method. Now we need to broaden the scope of this existing restriction on scientific research.

Finally, it is important to realize that the major health problems of the world largely continue to exist, not because we do not know how to prevent disease and keep people healthy, but because no one is putting enough effort and money into doing what we already know how to do. The diseases that ravage Asia, Africa, Latin America, and the pockets of poverty in the industrialized West are diseases that, by and large, we know how to cure. They have been eliminated in communities that have adequate nutrition, sanitation, and health care. . .

DISCUSSION QUESTIONS

1. Is speciesism appropriately compared to racism or sexism? Why or why not?
2. Is Singer correct to claim that the principle of equality applies beyond the bounds of our own species?
3. Can we know that other people feel pain? How? What about animals?
4. Singer asserts that "mere membership in our own biological species cannot be a morally relevant criterion for [the right to life]." Is he correct?
5. Is it as morally wrong to conduct painful medical experiments on brain-damaged human infants as on chimpanzees? Why or why not? Is Singer correct to search for "some middle position that would avoid speciesism but would not make the lives of the retarded and senile as cheap as the lives of pigs and dogs now are." Why or why not?
6. Singer thinks that not all lives, including human lives, are of equal worth. Do you agree? How shall we determine which human lives are more or less worthy? Is your life worth more than a dog's life? Why? Is any human life worth more than any nonhuman life?
7. Is Singer correct to claim, "The ethical question of the justification of animal experimentation cannot be settled by pointing to its benefits for us, no matter how persuasive the evidence in favor of such benefits may be."? Is this consistent with Singer's utilitarianism? Can a utilitarian argue that animal experimentation is justified?

TOM REGAN

The Case for Animal Rights

Tom Regan is emeritus professor of philosophy at UNC-Raleigh. See his biographical sketch on page 87. This selection adumbrates his influential book *The Case for Animal Rights.* Regan argues that utilitarian and contractarian moral theories fail as adequate moral theories. Only a rights-based theory can best account for our moral intuitions. Moreover, claims Regan, once we see why people have moral rights, we will see that the same rea-

---

Tom Regan, "The Case for Animal Rights," from *In Defense of Animals,* Peter Singer, ed. Blackwell Publishers, 1985, pp. 13–26. Reprinted by permission.

sons apply to animals as well. The fundamental problem with our treatment of animals, according to Regan, is our failure to acknowledge their right to be treated with respect.

CRITICAL READING QUESTIONS

1. What does Regan regard as the fundamental wrong in our treatment of animals?
2. How does Regan distinguish between direct and indirect duty views?
3. What is contractarianism and what problems does Regan raise concerning it?
4. How does Regan criticize utilitarianism?
5. On what basis does Regan think all human beings have a right to be treated with respect?
6. How, according to Regan, does the right to be treated with respect extend to animals?
7. What does Regan mean by being an "experiencing subject of a life"?
8. What is Regan's argument against those who suggest that animals have less inherent value than human beings? What does Regan conclude about holders of inherent value?
9. What implications does Regan claim for his view regarding our treatment of animals?

I regard myself as an advocate of animal rights—as a part of the animal rights movement. That movement, as I conceive it, is committed to a number of goals, including:

1. The total abolition of the use of animals in science
2. The total dissolution of commercial animal agriculture
3. And the total elimination of commercial sport hunting and trapping.

There are, I know, people who profess to believe in animal rights who do not avow these goals. Factory farming, they say, is wrong—violates animals' rights—but traditional animal agriculture is all right. Toxicity tests of cosmetics on animals violates their rights; but not important medical research—cancer research, for example. The clubbing of baby seals is abhorrent; but not the harvesting of adult seals. I used to think I understood this reasoning. Not any more. You don't change unjust institutions by tidying them up.

What's wrong—what's fundamentally wrong—with the way animals are treated isn't the details that vary from case to case. It's the whole system. The forlornness of the veal calf is pathetic—heart wrenching; the pulsing pain of the chimp with electrodes planted deep in her brain is repulsive; the slow, torturous death of the raccoon caught in the leg hold trap, agonizing. But what is fundamentally wrong isn't the pain, isn't the suffering, isn't the deprivation. These compound what's wrong. Sometimes—often—they make it much worse. But they are not the fundamental wrong.

The fundamental wrong is the system that allows us to view animals as *our resources,* here for us—to be eaten, or surgically manipulated, or put in our crosshairs for sport or money. Once we accept this view of animals—as our resources—the rest is as predictable as it is regrettable. Why worry about their loneliness, their pain, their death? Since animals exist for us, here to benefit us in one way or another, what harms them really doesn't matter—or matters only if it starts to bother us, makes us feel a trifle uneasy when we eat our veal scampi, for example. So, yes, let us get veal calves out of solitary confinement, give them more space, a little straw, a few companions. But let us keep our veal scampi.

But a little straw, more space, and a few companions don't eliminate—don't even touch—the fundamental wrong, the wrong that attaches to our viewing and treating these animals as our resources.

A veal calf killed to be eaten after living in close confinement is viewed and treated in this way: but so, too, is another who is raised (as they say) "more humanely." To right the fundamental wrong of our treatment of farm animals requires more than making rearing methods "more human"—requires something quite different—requires the total dissolution of commercial animal agriculture.

How we do this—whether we do this, or as in the case of animals in science, whether and how we abolish their use—these are to a large extent political questions. People must change their beliefs before they change their habits. Enough people, especially those elected to public office, must believe in change—must want it—before we will have laws that protect the rights of animals. This process of change is very complicated, very demanding, very exhausting, calling for the efforts of many hands—in education, publicity, political organization and activity, down to the licking of envelopes and stamps. As a trained and practicing philosopher the sort of contribution I can make is limited, but, I like to think, important. The currency of philosophy is ideas—their meaning and rational foundation—not the nuts and bolts of the legislative process, say, or the mechanics of community organization. That's what I have been exploring over the past 10 years or so in my essays and talks and, more recently, in my book, *The Case for Animal Rights.* I believe the major conclusions I reach in that book are true because they are supported by the weight of the best arguments. I believe the idea of animal rights has reason, not just emotion, on its side.

In the space I have at my disposal here I can only sketch, in the barest outlines, some of the main features of the book. Its main themes—and we should not be surprised by this—involve asking and answering deep foundational moral questions, questions about what morality is, how it should be understood, what is the best moral theory all considered. I hope I can convey something of the shape I think this theory is. The attempt to do this will be—to use a word a friendly critic once used to describe my work—cerebral. In fact I was told by this person that my work is "too cerebral." But this is misleading. My feelings about how animals sometimes are treated are just as deep and just as strong as those of my more volatile compatriots. Philosophers do—to use the jargon of the day—have a right side to their brains. If it's the left side we contribute—or mainly should—that's because what talents we have reside there.

How to proceed? We begin by asking how the moral status of animals has been understood by thinkers who deny that animals have rights. Then we test the mettle of their ideas by seeing how well they stand up under the heat of fair criticism. If we start our thinking in this way we soon find that some people believe that we have no duties directly to animals—that we owe nothing *to them*—that we can do nothing that *wrongs them.* Rather, we can do wrong acts that involve animals, and so we have duties regarding them, though none to them. Such views may be called indirect duty views. By way of illustration:

Suppose your neighbor kicks your dog. Then your neighbor has done something wrong. But not to your dog. The wrong that has been done is a wrong to you. After all, it is wrong to upset people, and your neighbor's kicking your dog upsets you. So you are the one who is wronged, not your dog. Or again: by kicking your dog your neighbor damages your property. And since it is wrong to damage another person's property, your neighbor has done something wrong—to you, of course, not to your dog. Your neighbor no more wrongs your dog than your car would be wronged if the windshield were smashed. Your neighbor's duties involving your dog are indirect duties to you. More generally, all of our duties regarding animals are indirect duties to one another—to humanity.

How could someone try to justify such a view? One could say that your dog doesn't feel anything and so isn't hurt by your neighbor's kick, doesn't care about the pain since none is felt, is as unaware of anything as your windshield. Someone could say this but no rational person will since, among other considerations, such a view will commit one who holds it to the position that no human being feels pain either—that human beings also don't care about what happens to them. A second possibility is that though both humans and your dog are hurt when kicked, it is only human pain that matters. But, again, no rational person can believe this. Pain is pain wheresoever it occurs. If your neighbor's causing you pain is wrong because of the pain that is caused, we cannot rationally ignore or dismiss the moral relevance of the pain your dog feels.

Philosophers who hold indirect duty views—and many still do—have come to understand that they must avoid the two defects just noted—avoid, that is, both the view that animals don't feel anything as well as the idea that only human pain can be morally relevant. Among such thinkers the sort of view now favored is one or another form of what is called *contractarianism.*

Here, very crudely, is the root idea: morality consists of a set of rules that individuals voluntarily agree to abide by—as we do when we sign a contract (hence the name: contractarianism). Those who understand and accept the terms of the contract are covered directly—have rights created by, and recognized and protected in, the contract. And these contractors can also have protection spelled out for others who, though they lack the ability to understand morality and so cannot sign the contract themselves, are loved or cherished by those who can. Thus young children, for example, are unable to sign and lack rights. But they are protected by the contract nonetheless because of the sentimental interests of others, most notably their parents. So we have, then, duties involving these children, duties regarding them, but no duties to them. Our duties in their case are indirect duties to other human beings, usually their parents.

As for animals, since they cannot understand the contract, they obviously cannot sign; and since they cannot sign, they have no rights. Like children, however, some animals are the objects of the sentimental interest of others. You, for example, love your dog . . . or cat. So these animals—those enough people care about: companion animals, whales, baby seals, the American bald eagle—these animals, though they lack rights themselves, will be protected because of the sentimental interests of people. I have, then, according to contractarianism, no duty directly to your dog or any other animal, not even the duty not to cause them pain or suffering; my duty not to hurt them is a duty I have to those people who care about what happens to them. As for other animals, where no or little sentimental interest is present—farm animals, for example, or laboratory rats—what duties we have grow weaker and weaker, perhaps to the vanishing point. The pain and death they endure, though real, are not wrong if no one cares about them.

Contractarianism could be a hard view to refute when it comes to the moral status of animals if it was an adequate theoretical approach to the moral status of human beings. It is not adequate in this latter respect, however, which makes the question of its adequacy in the former—regarding animals—utterly moot. For consider: morality, according to the (crude) contractarian position before us, consists of rules people agree to abide by. What people? Well, enough to make a difference—enough, that is, so that collectively they have the power to enforce the rules that are drawn up in the contract. That is very well and good for the signatories—but not so good for anyone who is not asked to sign. And there is nothing in contractarianism of the sort we are discussing that guarantees or requires that everyone will have a chance to participate equitably in framing the rules of morality. The result is that this approach to ethics could sanction the most blatant forms of social, economic, moral, and political injustice, ranging from a repressive caste system to systematic racial or sexual discrimination. Might, on this theory, does make right. Let those who are the victims of injustice suffer as they will. It matters not so long as no one else—no contractor, or too few of them—cares about it. Such a theory takes one's moral breath away . . . as if, for example, there is nothing wrong with apartheid in South Africa if too few white South Africans are upset by it. A theory with so little to recommend it at the level of the ethics of our treatment of our fellow humans cannot have anything more to recommend it when it comes to the ethics of how we treat our fellow animals . . .

Some people think the theory we are looking for is utilitarianism. A utilitarian accepts two moral principles. The first is a principle of equality: Everyone's interests count, and similar interests must be counted as having similar weight or importance.

White or black, male or female, American or Iranian, human or animal: Everyone's pain or frustration matter and matter equally with the like pain or frustration of anyone else. The second principle a utilitarian accepts is the principle of utility: do that act that will bring about the best balance of satisfaction over frustration for everyone affected by the outcome.

As a utilitarian, then, here is how I am to approach the task of deciding what I morally ought to do: I must ask who will be affected if I choose to do one thing rather than another, how much each individual will be affected, and where the best results are most likely to lie—which option, in other words, is most likely to bring about the best results, the best balance of satisfaction over frustration. That option, whatever it may be, is the one I ought to choose. That is where my moral duty lies.

The great appeal of utilitarianism rests with its uncompromising *egalitarianism:* everyone's interests count and count equally with the like interests of everyone else. The kind of odious discrimination some forms of contractarianism can justify—discrimination based on race or sex, for example—seems disallowed in principle by utilitarianism, as is speciesism—systematic discrimination based on species membership.

The sort of equality we find in utilitarianism, however, is not the sort an advocate of animal or human rights should have in mind. Utilitarianism has no room for the equal moral rights of different individuals because it has no room for their equal inherent value or worth. What has value for the utilitarian is the satisfaction of an individual's interests, not the individual whose interests they are. A universe in which you satisfy your desire for water, food, and warmth, is, other things being equal, better than a universe in which these desires are frustrated. And the same is true in the case of an animal with similar desires. But neither you nor the animal have any value in your own right. Only your feelings do.

Here is an analogy to help make the philosophical point clearer: a cup contains different liquids—sometimes sweet, sometimes bitter, sometimes a mix of the two. What has value are the liquids: the sweeter the better, the bitter the worse. The cup—the container—has no value. It's what goes into it, not what they go into, that has value. For the utilitarian, you and I are like the cup; we have no value as individuals and thus no equal value. What has value is what goes into us, what we serve as receptacles for; our feelings of satisfaction have positive value, our feelings of frustration have negative value.

Serious problems arise for utilitarianism when we remind ourselves that it enjoins us to bring about the best consequences. What does this mean? It doesn't mean the best consequences for me alone, or for my family or friends, or any other person taken individually. No, what we must do is, roughly, as follows: we must add up—somehow!—the separate satisfactions and frustrations of everyone likely to be affected by our choice, the satisfactions in one column, the frustrations in the other. We must total each column for each of the options before us. That is what it means to say the theory is aggregative. And then we must choose that option which is most likely to bring about the best balance of totaled satisfactions over totaled frustrations. Whatever act would lead to this outcome is the one we morally ought to perform—is where our moral duty lies. And that act quite clearly might not be the same one that would bring about the best results for me personally, or my family or friends, or a lab animal. The best aggregated consequences for everyone concerned are not necessarily the best for each individual.

That utilitarianism is an aggregative theory—that different individual's satisfactions or frustrations are added, or summed, or totaled—is the key objection to this theory. My Aunt Bea is old, inactive, a cranky, sour person, though not physically ill. She prefers to go on living. She is also rather rich. I could make a fortune if I could get my hands on her money, money she intends to give me in any event, after she dies, but which she refuses to give me now. In order to avoid a huge tax bite, I plan to donate a handsome sum of my profits to a local children's hospital. Many, many children will benefit from my generosity, and much joy will be brought to their parents, relatives, and friends. If I don't get the money rather soon, all ambitions will come to naught. The once-in-a-life-time-opportunity to make a real killing will be gone. Why, then, not really kill my Aunt Bea? Oh, of course I *might* get caught. But I'm no fool and, besides, her doctor can be counted on to cooperate (he has an eye for the same investment and I happen to know a good deal about his shady past). The deed can be done . . . professionally, shall we say. There is *very* little chance of getting caught. And as for my conscience being guilt ridden, I am a resourceful sort of fellow and will take more than sufficient comfort—as I lie on the beach at Acapulco—in contemplating the joy and health I have brought to so many others.

Suppose Aunt Bea is killed and the rest of the story comes out as told. Would I have done anything wrong? Anything immoral? One would have thought that I had. But not according to utilitarianism. Since what I did brought about the best balance of totaled satisfaction over frustration for all those affected by the outcome, what I did was not wrong. Indeed, in killing Aunt Bea the physician and I did what duty required.

This same kind of argument can be repeated in all sorts of cases, illustrating, time after time, how the utilitarian's position leads to results that impartial people find morally callous. It *is* wrong to kill my Aunt Bea in the name of bringing about the best results for others. A good end does not justify an evil means. Any adequate moral theory will have to explain why this is so. Utilitarianism fails in this respect and so cannot be the theory we seek.

What to do? Where to begin anew? The place to begin, I think, is with the utilitarian's view of the value of the individual—or, rather, lack of value. In its place suppose we consider that you and I, for example, do have value as individuals—what we'll call *inherent value.* To say we have such value is to say that we are something more than, something different from, mere receptacles. Moreover, to insure that we do not pave the way for such injustices as slavery or sexual discrimination, we must believe that all who have inherent value have it equally, regardless of their sex, race, religion, birthplace, and so on. Similarly to be discarded as irrelevant are one's talents or skills, intelligence and wealth, personality or pathology, whether one is loved and admired—or despised and loathed. The genius and the retarded child, the prince and the pauper, the brain surgeon and the fruit vendor, Mother Teresa and the most unscrupulous used car salesman—all have inherent value, all possess it equally, and all have an equal right to be treated with respect, to be treated in ways that do not reduce them to the status of things, as if they exist as resources for others. My value as an individual is independent of my usefulness to you. Yours is not dependent on your usefulness to me. For either of us to treat the other in ways that fail to show respect for the other's independent value is to act immorally—is to violate the individual's rights.

Some of the rational virtues of this view—what I call the rights view—should be evident. Unlike (crude) contractarians, for example, the rights view *in principle* denies the moral tolerability of any and all forms of racial, sexual, or social discrimination, and unlike utilitarianism, this view *in principle* denies that we can justify good results by using evil means that violate an individual's rights—denies, for example, that it could be moral to kill my Aunt Bea to harvest beneficial consequences for others. That would be to sanction the disrespectful treatment of the individual in the name of the social good, something the rights view will not—categorically will not—ever allow.

The rights view—or so I believe—is rationally the most satisfactory moral theory. It surpasses all other theories in the degree to which it illuminates and explains the foundation of our duties to one another—the domain of human morality. On this score, it has the best reasons, the best arguments, on its side. Of course, if it were possible to show that only human beings are included within its scope, then a person like myself, who believes in animal rights, would be obliged to look elsewhere than to the rights view.

But attempts to limit its scope to humans only can be shown to be rationally defective. Animals, it is true, lack many of the abilities humans possess. They can't read, do higher mathematics, build a bookcase, or make *baba ghanoush.* Neither can many human beings, however, and yet we don't say—and shouldn't say—that they (these humans) therefore have less inherent value, less of a right to be treated with respect, than do others. [It is the *similarities* between those human beings who most clearly, most noncontroversially have such value—the people reading this, for example—it is our similarities, not our differences, that matter most. And the really crucial, the basic similarity is simply this; we are each of us the experiencing subject of a life, each of us a conscious creature having an individual welfare that has importance to us whatever our usefulness to others. We want and prefer things; believe and feel things; recall and expect things. And all these dimensions of our life, including our pleasure and pain, our enjoyment and suffering, our satisfaction and frustration, our continued existence or our untimely death—all make a difference to the quality of our life as lived; as experienced by us as individuals. As the same is true of those animals who concern us (those who are eaten and trapped, for example), they, too, must be viewed as the experiencing subjects of a life with inherent value of their own.

There are some who resist the idea that animals have inherent value. "Only humans have such value," they profess. How might this narrow view be defended? Shall we say that only humans have the requisite intelligence, or autonomy, or reason? But there are many, many humans who will fail to meet these standards and yet who are reasonably viewed as having value above and beyond their usefulness to others. Shall we claim that only humans belong to the right species—the species Homo sapiens? But this is blatant speciesism. Will it be said, then, that all—and only—humans have immortal souls? Then our opponents more than have their work cut out for them. I am myself not ill-disposed to there being immortal souls. Personally, I profoundly hope I have one. But I would not want to rest my position on a controversial ethical issue on the even more controversial question about who or what has an immortal soul. That is to dig one's hole deeper, not climb out. Rationally, it is better to resolve moral issues without making more controversial assumptions than are needed. The question of who has inherent value is such a question, one that is more rationally resolved without the introduction of the idea of immortal souls than by its use.

Well, perhaps some will say that animals have some inherent value, only *less* than we do. Once again, however, attempts to defend this view can be shown to lack rational justification. What could be the basis of our having more inherent value than animals? Will it be their lack of reason, or autonomy, or intellect? Only if we are willing to make the same judgement in the case of humans who are similarly deficient. But it is not true that such humans—the retarded child, for example, or the mentally deranged—have less inherent value than you or I. Neither, then, can we rationally sustain the view that animals like them in being the experiencing subjects of a life have less inherent value. All who have inherent value have it *equally*, whether they be human animals or not.

Inherent value, then, belongs equally to those who are the experiencing subjects of a life. Whether it belongs to others—to rocks and rivers, trees and glaciers, for example—we do not know. And may never know. But neither do we need to know, if we are to make the case for animal rights. We do not need to know how many people, for example, are eligible to vote in the next presidential election before we can know whether I am. Similarly, we do not need to know *how many* individuals have inherent value before we can know that some do. When it comes to the case for animal rights, then what we need to know is whether the animals who, in our culture are routinely eaten, hunted, and used in our laboratories, for example, are like us in being subjects of a life. And we *do* know this. We do *know* that many—literally, billions and billions—of these animals are the subjects of a life in the sense explained and so have inherent value if we do. And since, in order to have the best theory of our duties to one another, we must recognize our equal inherent value, as individuals, reason—not sentiment, not emotion—reason compels us to recognize the equal inherent value of these animals. And, with this, their equal right to be treated with respect.

That, *very* roughly, is the shape and feel of the case for animal rights. Most of the details of the supporting argument are missing. They are to be found in the book I alluded to earlier. Here, the details go begging and I must in closing limit myself to four final points. [Last Two Omitted. Ed.]

The first is how the theory that underlies the case for animal rights shows that the animal rights movement is a part of, not antagonistic to, the human rights movement. The theory that rationally grounds the rights of animals also grounds the rights of humans. Thus are those involved in the animal rights movement partners in the struggle to secure respect for human rights—the rights of women, for example, or minorities and workers. The animal rights movement is cut from the same moral cloth as these.

Second, having set out the broad outlines of the rights view, I can now say why its implications for farming and science, for example, are both clear and uncompromising. In the case of using animals in science, the rights view is categorically abolitionist. Lab animals are not our tasters; we are not their kings. Because these animals are treated—routinely, systematically—as if their value is reducible to their usefulness to others, they are routinely, systematically treated with a lack of respect, and thus are their rights routinely, systematically violated. This is just as true when they are used in trivial, duplicative, unnecessary or unwise research as it is when they are used in studies that hold out real promise of human benefits. We can't justify harming or killing a human being (my Aunt Bea, for example) just for these sorts of reasons. Neither can we do so even in the case of so lowly a creature as a laboratory rat. It is not just refinement or reduction that are called for, not just larger, cleaner cages, not just more generous use of anaesthetic or the elimination of multiple surgery, not just tidying up the system. It is replacement—completely. The best we can do when it comes to using animals in science is—not to use them. That is where our duty lies, according to the rights view.

As for commercial animal agriculture, the rights view takes a similar abolitionist position. The fundamental moral wrong here is not that animals are kept in stressful close confinement, or in isolation, or that they have their pain and suffering, their needs and preferences ignored or discounted. *All* these *are* wrong, of course, but they are not the fundamental wrong. They are symptoms and effects of the deeper, systematic wrong that allows these animals to be viewed and treated as lacking independent value, as resources for us—as, indeed, a renewable resource. Giving farm animals more space, more natural environments, more companions does not right the fundamental wrong, any more than giving lab animals more anaesthesia or bigger, cleaner cages would right the fundamental wrong in their case. Nothing less than the total dissolution of commercial animal agriculture will do this, just as, for similar reasons I won't develop at length here, morality requires nothing less than the total elimination of commercial sport hunting and trapping. The rights view's implications, then, as I have said, are clear—and are uncompromising.

DISCUSSION QUESTIONS

1. Could Regan's abolitionist stance be implemented? Does that matter to his moral argument? Is the right to be treated with respect incompatible with our using animals? Why or why not?
2. Are Regan's criticisms of utilitarianism and contractarian moral theories accurate? How might defenders of those moral theories reply?
3. Which animals are "experiencing subjects of a life"? How are we best to understand that expression?
4. Are all human beings experiencing subjects of a life? Why should we think that being an experiencing subject of a life is linked to inherent value?
5. Are we forced to acknowledge that "all who have inherent value have it equally"? If being an experiencing subject of a life comes in degrees, would inherent value also come in degrees?

MARY ANNE WARREN

The Rights of the Nonhuman World

Mary Anne Warren is professor of philosophy at San Francisco State University. She has written extensively on moral issues, and a number of her articles have become classics in their respective areas. Our selection is from her article "The Rights of the Nonhuman World," Warren argues that animals have certain basic moral rights, though their rights are less significant than human rights and may thus be justifiably overridden on occasion.

CRITICAL READING QUESTIONS

1. How does Warren argue that the moral status of human beings is different from that of animals?
2. On what basis does Warren conclude that animals have certain basic moral rights?
3. How does Warren compare human beings and animals with respect to the right to liberty, the right to life, and the right to happiness?
4. How does Warren respond to the claim that the capacity for autonomy is a precondition for having rights at all?
5. What reasons does Warren give for thinking brain-damaged human beings ("nonparadigm humans") still have strong moral rights?
6. How does Warren answer the objection that if animals have moral rights, then we should keep animals from violating other animals' rights.

1. WHY (SOME) ANIMALS HAVE (SOME) MORAL RIGHTS

Peter Singer is the best known contemporary proponent of animal liberation. Singer maintains that all sentient animals, human or otherwise, should be regarded as morally equal; that is, that their interests should be given equal consideration. He argues that sentience, the capacity to have conscious experiences such as pain or pleasure, is "the only defensible boundary of concern for the interests of others." In Bentham's often-quoted words, "the question is not, Can they reason? nor, Can they talk? but Can they suffer?" To suppose that the interests of animals are outside the scope of moral concern is to commit a moral fallacy analagous to sexism or racism, a fallacy which Singer calls *speciesism.* True, women and members of "minority" races are more *intelligent* than (most) animals—and almost certainly no less so than white males—but that is not the point. The point does not concern these complex capabilities at all. For, Singer says, "The claim to equality does not depend on intelligence, moral capacity, physical strength, or similar matters of fact."

As a utilitarian, Singer prefers to avoid speaking of moral *rights,* at least insofar as these are construed as claims which may sometimes override purely utilitarian considerations. There are, however, many other advocates of animal liberation who do maintain that animals have moral rights, rights which place limitations upon the use of utilitarian justifications for killing animals or causing them to suffer. Tom Regan,

Mary Anne Warren, "The Rights of the Nonhuman World," from *Environmental Philosophy: A Collection of Readings,* Robert Elliot and Aaran Gare, eds., 1983, pp.109–134. Reprinted by permission of Queensland University Press.

for example, argues that if all or most human beings have a right to life, then so do at least some animals. Regan points out that unless we hold that animals have a right to life, we may not be able to adequately support many of the conclusions that most animal liberationists think are important, for example, that it is wrong to kill animals painlessly to provide human beings with relatively trivial forms of pleasure.

This disagreement between Singer and Regan demonstrates that there is no single well-defined theory of the moral status of animals which can be identified as *the* animal liberationist position. It is clear, however, that neither philosopher is committed to the claim that the moral status of animals is completely identical to that of humans. Singer points out that his basic principle of equal *consideration* does not imply identical *treatment*. Regan holds only that animals have *some* of the same moral rights as do human beings, not that *all* of their rights are necessarily the same.

Nevertheless, none of the animal liberationists have thus far provided a clear explanation of how and why the moral status of (most) animals differs from that of (most) human beings; and this is a point which must be clarified if their position is to be made fully persuasive. That there is such a difference seems to follow from some very strong moral intuitions which most of us share. A man who shoots squirrels for sport may or may not be acting reprehensibly; but it is difficult to believe that his actions should be placed in *exactly* the same moral category as those of a man who shoots women, or black children, for sport. So too it is doubtful that the Japanese fishermen who slaughtered dolphins because the latter were thought to be depleting the local fish populations were acting quite *as* wrongly as if they had slaughtered an equal number of their human neighbors for the same reason.

Can anything persuasive be said in support of these intuitive judgments? Or are they merely evidence of unreconstructed speciesism? To answer these questions we must consider both certain similarities and certain differences between ourselves and other animals, and then decide which of these are relevant to the assignment of moral rights. To do this we must first ask just what it means to say that an entity possesses a certain moral right.

There are two elements of the concept of a moral which are crucial for our present purposes. To say that an entity, X, has a moral right to Y (some activity, benefit or satisfaction) is to imply at least the following:

1. That it would be morally wrong for any moral agent to intentionally deprive X of Y without some sufficient justification;
2. That this would be wrong, at least in part, *because of the (actual or potential) harm which it would do to the interests of X.*

On this (partial) definition of a moral right, to ask whether animals have such rights is to ask whether there are some ways of treating them which are morally objectionable because of the harm done to the animals themselves, and not merely because of some *other* undesirable results, such as damaging the environment or undermining the moral character of human beings. As Regan and other animal liberationists have pointed out, the arguments for ascribing at least some moral rights to sentient nonhuman animals are very similar to the arguments for ascribing those same rights to sentient human beings. If we argue that human beings have rights not to be tortured, starved or confined under inhumane conditions, it is usually by appealing to our knowledge that they will suffer in much the same ways that we would under like circumstances. A child must learn that other persons (and animals) can experience, for example, pain, fear or anger, on the one hand; pleasure or satisfaction, on the other, in order to even begin to comprehend why some ways of behaving towards them are morally preferable to others.

If these facts are morally significant in the case of human beings, it is attractive to suppose that they should have similar significance in the case of animals. Everything that we know about the behavior, biology and neurophysiology of, for instance, nonhuman mammals, indicates that they are capable of experiencing the same basic types of physical suffering and discomfort as we are, and it is reasonable to suppose that their pleasures are equally real and approximately as various. Doubts about the sentience of other animals are no more plausible than doubts about that of other human beings. True, most animals cannot use human language to *report* that they are in pain, but the vocalizations and "body language" through which they *express* pain, and many other psychological states, are similar enough to our own that their significance is generally clear.

But to say this is not yet to establish that animals have moral rights. We need a connecting link between the premise that certain ways of treating animals cause them to suffer, and the conclusion that such actions are *prima facie* morally wrong, that is, wrong unless proven otherwise. One way to make this connection is to hold that it is a *self-evident truth* that the unnecessary infliction of suffering upon any sentient being is wrong. Those who doubt this claim may be accused (perhaps with some justice) of lacking empathy, the ability to "feel with" other sentient beings, to comprehend the reality of their experience. It may be held that it is possible to regard the suffering of animals as morally insignificant only to the extent that one suffers from blindness to "the ontology of animal reality"; that is, from a failure to grasp the fact that they are centres of conscious experience, as we are.

This argument is inadequate, however, since there may be those who fully comprehend the fact that animals are sentient beings, but who still deny that their pains and pleasures have any direct moral significance. For them, a more persuasive consideration may be that our moral reasoning will gain in clarity and coherence if we recognize that the suffering of a nonhuman being is an evil of the same general sort as that of a human being. For if we do not recognize that suffering is an intrinsic evil, something which ought not to be inflicted deliberately without just cause, then we will not be able to fully understand why treating *human beings* in certain ways is immoral.

Toturing human beings, for example, is not wrong merely because it is illegal (where it is illegal), or merely because it violates some implicit agreement amongst human beings (though it may). Such legalistic or contractualistic reasons leave us in the dark as to why we *ought* to have, and enforce, laws and agreements against torture. The essential reason for regarding torture as wrong is that it *hurts*, and that people greatly prefer to avoid such pain—as do animals. I am not arguing, as does Kant, that cruelty to animals is wrong because it causes cruelty to human beings, a position which consequentalists often endorse. The point, rather, is that unless we view the deliberate infliction of needless pain as inherently wrong we will not be able to understand the moral objection to cruelty of *either* kind.

It seems we must conclude, therefore, that sentient nonhuman animals have certain basic moral rights, rights which they share with all beings that are psychologically organized around the pleasure/pain axis. Their capacity for pain gives them the right that pain not be intentionally and needlessly inflicted upon them. Their capacity for pleasure gives them the right not to be prevented from pursuing whatever pleasures and fulfillments are natural to creatures of their kind. Like human rights, the rights of animals may be overriden if there is a morally sufficient reason for doing so. What *counts* as a morally significant reason, however, may be different in the two cases.

2. HUMAN AND ANIMAL RIGHTS COMPARED

There are two dimensions in which we may find differences between the rights of human beings and those of animals. The first involves the *content* of those rights, while the second involves their strength; that is, the strength of the reasons which are required to override them.

Consider, for instance, the right to liberty. The *human* right to liberty precludes imprisonment without due process of law, even if the prison is spacious and the conditions of confinement cause no obvious physical suffering. But it is not so obviously wrong to imprison animals, especially when the area to which they are confined provides a fair approximation of the conditions of their natural habitat, and a reasonable opportunity to pursue the satisfactions natural to their kind. Such conditions, which often result in an increased lifespan, and which may exist in wildlife sanctuaries or even well-designed zoos need not frustrate the needs or interests of animals in any significant way, and thus do not clearly violate their rights. Similarly treated human beings, on the other hand (e.g., native peoples confined to prison-like reservations), do tend to suffer from their loss of freedom. Human dignity and the fulfillment of the sorts of plans, hopes, and desires which appear (thus far) to be uniquely human, require a more extensive freedom of movement than is the case with at least many nonhuman animals. Furthermore, there are aspects of human freedom, such as freedom of thought, freedom of speech, and freedom of political association, which simply do not apply in the case of animals.

Thus, it seems that the human right to freedom is more extensive; that is, it precludes a wider range of specific ways of treating human beings than does the corresponding right on the part of animals. The argument cuts both ways, of course. *Some* animals, for example, great whales and migratory birds, may require at least as much physical freedom as do human beings if they are to pursue the satisfactions natural to their kind, and this fact provides a moral argument against keeping such creatures imprisoned. And even chickens may suffer from the extreme and unnatural confinement to which they are subjected on modern "factory farms." Yet it seems unnecessary to claim for *most* animals a right to a freedom quite as broad as that which we claim for ourselves.

Similar points may be made with respect to the right to life. Animals, it may be argued, lack the cognitive equipment to value their lives in the way that human beings do. Ruth Cigman argues that animals have *no* right to life because death is no misfortune for them. In her view, the death of an animal is not a misfortune, because animals have no desires which are *categorical;* that is which do not "merely presuppose being alive (like the desire to eat when one is hungry), but rather answer the question whether one wants to remain alive." In other words, animals appear to lack the sorts of long-range hopes, plans, ambitions, and the like, which give human beings such a powerful interest in continued life. Animals, it seems, take life as it comes and do not specifically desire that it go on. True, squirrels store nuts for the winter and deer run from wolves; but these may be seen as instinctive or conditioned responses to present circumstances, rather than evidence that they value life as such.

These reflections probably help to explain why the death of a sparrow seems less tragic than that of a human being. Human lives, one might say, have greater intrinsic value, because they are worth more *to their possessors.* But this does not demonstrate that no nonhuman animal has *any* right to life. Premature death may be a less *severe* misfortune for sentient nonhuman animals than for human beings, but it is a misfortune nevertheless. In the first place, it is a misfortune in that it deprives them of whatever pleasures the future might have held for them, regardless of whether or not they ever *consciously anticipated* those pleasures. The fact that they are not here afterwards, to *experience* their loss, no more shows that they have not lost anything than it does in the case of humans. In the second place, it is (possibly) a misfortune in that it frustrates whatever future-oriented desires animals *may* have, unbeknownst to us. Even now, in an age in which apes have been taught to use simplified human languages and attempts have been made to communicate with dolphins and whales, we still know very little about the operation of nonhuman minds. We know much too little to assume that nonhuman animals never consciously pursue relatively distant future goals. To the extent that they do, the question of whether such desires provide them with *reasons for living* or merely *presuppose* continued life, has no satisfactory answer, since they cannot contemplate these alternatives—or, if they can, we have no way of knowing what their conclusions are. All we know is that the more intelligent and psychologically complex an animal is, the more *likely* it is that it possesses specifically future-oriented desires, which would be frustrated even by *painless* death.

For these reasons, it is premature to conclude from the apparent intellectual inferiority of nonhuman animals that they have no right to life. A more plausible conclusion is that animals do have a right to life but that it is generally somewhat weaker than that of human beings. It is, perhaps, weak enough to enable us to justify killing animals when we have no other ways of achieving such vital goals as feeding or clothing ourselves, or obtaining knowledge which is necessary to save human lives. Weakening their right to life in this way does not render meaningless the assertion that they have such a right. For the point remains that *some* serious justification for the killing of sentient nonhuman animals is always necessary; they may not be killed merely to provide amusement or minor gains in convenience.

If animals' rights to liberty and life are somewhat weaker than those of human beings, may we say the same about their right to *happiness;* that is, their right not to be made to suffer needlessly or to be deprived of the pleasures natural to their kind? If so, it is not immediately clear why. There is little reason to suppose that pain or suffering are any less unpleasant for the higher animals (at least) than they are for us. Our large brains *may* cause us to experience pain more intensely than do most animals, and *probably* cause us to suffer more from the anticipation or remembrance of pain. These facts might tend to suggest that pain is, on the whole, a worse experience for us than for them. But it may also be argued that pain may be *worse* in some respects for nonhuman animals, who are presumably less able to distract themselves from it by thinking of something else, or to comfort themselves with the knowledge that it is temporary. Brigid Brophy points out that "pain is likely to fill the sheep's whole capacity for experience in a way it seldom does in us, whose intellect and imagination can create breaks for us in the immediacy of our sensations."

The net result of such contrasting considerations is that we cannot possibly claim to know whether pain is, on the whole, worse for us than for animals, or whether their pleasures are any more or any less intense than ours. Thus, while we may justify assigning them a somewhat weaker right to life or liberty, on the grounds that they desire these goods less intensely than we do, we cannot discount their rights to freedom from needlessly inflicted pain or unnatural frustration on the same basis. There may, however, be *other* reasons for regarding all of the moral rights of animals as somewhat less stringent than the corresponding human rights.

A number of philosophers who deny that animals have moral rights point to the fact that nonhuman animals evidently lack the capacity for moral autonomy. Moral autonomy is the ability to act as a moral agent; that is, to act on the basis of an understanding of, and adherence to, moral rules or principles. H. J. McCloskey, for example, holds that "it is the capacity for moral autonomy . . . that is basic to the possibility of possessing a right." McCloskey argues that it is inappropriate to ascribe moral rights to any entity which is not a moral agent, or *potentially* a moral agent, because a right is essentially an entitlement granted to a moral agent, licensing him or her to *act* in certain ways and to *demand* that other moral agents refrain from interference. For this reason, he says, "Where there is no possibility of [morally autonomous] action, potentially or actually . . . and where the being is not a member of a kind which is normally capable of [such] action, we withhold talk of rights."

If moral autonomy—or being *potentially* autonomous, or a member of a kind which is *normally* capable of autonomy—is a necessary condition for having moral rights, then probably no nonhuman animal can qualify. For moral autonomy requires such probably uniquely human traits as "the capacity to be critically self-aware, manipulate concepts, use a sophisticated language, reflect, plan, deliberate, choose, and accept responsibility for acting."

But why, we must ask, should the capacity for autonomy be regarded as a precondition for possessing moral rights? Autonomy is clearly crucial for the *exercise* of many human moral or legal rights, such as the right to vote or to run for public office. It is less clearly relevant, however, to the more basic human rights, such as the right to life or to freedom from unnecessary suffering. The fact that animals, like many human beings, cannot *demand* their moral rights (at least not in the words of any conventional human language) seems irrelevant. For, as Joel Feinberg points out, the interests of nonmorally autonomous human beings may be defended by others, for example, in legal proceedings; and it is not clear why the interests of animals might not be represented in a similar fashion.

It is implausible, therefore, to conclude that because animals lack moral autonomy they should be accorded *no moral rights whatsoever.* Nevertheless, it may be argued that the moral autonomy of (most) human beings provides a second reason, in addition to their more extensive interests and desires, for according somewhat *stronger* moral rights to human beings. The fundamental insight behind contractualist theories of morality is that, for morally autonomous beings such as ourselves, there is enormous mutual advantage in the adoption of a moral system designed to protect each of us from the harms that might otherwise be visited upon us by others. Each of us ought to accept and promote such a system because, to the extent that others also accept it, we will all be safer from attack by our fellows, more likely to receive assistance when we need it, and freer to engage in individual as well as cooperative endeavours of all kinds.

Thus, it is the possibility of *reciprocity* which motivates moral agents to extend *full and equal* moral rights, in the first instance, only to other moral agents. I respect your rights to life, liberty, and the pursuit of happiness in part because you are a sentient being, whose interests have intrinsic moral significance. But I respect them as *fully equal to my own* because I hope and expect that you will do the same for me. Animals, insofar as they lack the degree of rationality necessary for moral autonomy, cannot agree to respect our interests as equal in moral importance to their own, and neither do they expect or demand such respect from us. Of course, domestic animals may expect to be fed, etc. But they do not, and cannot, expect to be treated as moral equals, for they do not understand that moral concept or what it implies. Consequently, it is neither pragmatically feasible nor morally obligatory to extend to them the same *full and equal* rights which we extend to human beings.

Is this a speciesist conclusion? Defenders of a more extreme animal-rights position may point out that this argument, from the lack of moral autonomy, has exactly the same form as that which has been used for thousands of years to rationalize denying equal moral rights to women and members of "inferior" races. Aristotle, for example, argued that women and slaves are naturally subordinate beings, because they lack the capacity for moral autonomy and self-direction; and contemporary versions of this argument, used to support racist or sexist conclusions, are easy to find. Are we simply repeating Aristotle's mistake, in a different context?

The reply to this objection is very simple: animals, unlike women and slaves, really *are* incapable of moral autonomy, at least to the best of our knowledge. Aristotle certainly *ought* to have known that women and slaves are capable of morally autonomous action; their capacity to use moral language alone ought to have alerted him to this likelihood. If comparable evidence exists that (some) nonhuman animals are moral agents we have not yet found it. The fact that some apes (and, possibly, some cetaceans) are capable of learning radically simplified human languages, the terms of which refer primarily to objects and events in their immediate environment, in no way demonstrates that they can understand abstract moral concepts, rules, or principles, or use this understanding to regulate their own behavior.

On the other hand, this argument implies that if we *do* discover that certain nonhuman animals are capable of moral autonomy (which is certainly not impossible), then we ought to extend full and equal moral rights to those animals. Furthermore, if we someday encounter extraterrestrial beings, or build robots, androids, or supercomputers which function as self-aware moral agents, then we must extend full and equal moral rights to these as well. Being a member of the human species is not a necessary condition for the possession of full "human" rights. Whether it is nevertheless a *sufficient* condition is the question to which we now turn.

3. THE MORAL RIGHTS OF NONPARADIGM HUMANS

If we are justified in ascribing somewhat different, and also somewhat stronger, moral rights to human beings than to sentient but nonmorally autonomous animals, then what are we to say of the rights of human beings who happen not to be capable of moral autonomy, perhaps not even potentially? Both Singer and Regan have argued that if any of the superior intellectual capacities of normal and mature human beings are used to support a distinction between the moral status of *typical*, or paradigm, human beings, and that of animals, then consistency will require us to place certain "nonparadigm" humans, such as infants, small children and the severely retarded or incurably brain damaged, in the same inferior moral category. Such a result is, of course, highly counterintuitive.

Fortunately, no such conclusion follows from the autonomy argument. There are many reasons for extending strong moral rights to nonparadigm humans; reasons which do not apply to most nonhuman animals. Infants and small children are granted strong moral rights in part because of their *potential* autonomy. But *potential* autonomy, as I have argued elsewhere, is not in itself a sufficient reason for the ascription of full moral rights; if it were, then not only human fetuses (from conception onwards) but even ununited human sperm-egg pairs would have to be regarded as entities with a right to life the equivalent of our own—thus making not only abortion, but any intentional failure to procreate, the moral equivalent of murder. Those who do not find this extreme conclusion acceptable must appeal to reasons other than the *potential* moral autonomy of infants and small children to explain the strength of the latter's moral rights.

One reason for assigning strong moral rights to infants and children is that they possess not just *potential* but *partial* autonomy, and it is not clear how much of it they have at any given moment. The fact that, unlike baby chimpanzees, they are already learning the things which will enable them to *become* morally autonomous, makes it likely that their minds have more subtleties than their speech (or the lack of it) proclaims. Another reason is simply that most of us tend to place a very high value on the lives and well-being of infants. Perhaps we are to some degree "programmed" by nature to love and protect them; perhaps our reasons are somewhat egocentric; or perhaps we value them for their potential. Whatever the explanation, the fact that we do feel this way about them is in itself a valid reason for extending to them stronger moral and legal protections than we extend to nonhuman animals, even those which may have just as well or better-developed psychological capacities. A third, and perhaps the most important, reason is that if we did *not* extend strong moral rights to infants, far too few of them would ever *become* responsible, morally autonomous adults; too many would be treated "like animals" (i.e., in ways that it is generally wrong to treat even animals), and would consequently become socially crippled, antisocial, or just very unhappy people. If any part of our moral code is to remain intact, it seems that infants and small children *must* be protected and cared for.

Analogous arguments explain why strong moral rights should also be accorded to other nonparadigm humans. The severely retarded or incurably senile, for instance, may have no potential for moral autonomy, but there are apt to be friends, relatives or other people who care what happens to them. Like children, such individuals may have more mental capacities than are readily apparent. Like children, they are more apt to achieve, or return to moral autonomy if they are valued and well cared for. Furthermore, any one of us may someday become mentally incapacitated to one degree or another, and we would all have reason to be anxious about our own futures if such incapacitation were made the basis for denying strong moral rights.

There are, then, sound reasons for assigning strong moral rights even to human beings who lack the mental capacities which justify the general distinction between human and animal rights. Their rights are based not only on the value which they themselves place upon their lives and well-being, but also on the value which other human beings place upon them.

But is this a valid basis for the assignment of moral rights? Is it consistent with the definition presented earlier, according to which X may be said to have a moral right to Y only if depriving X of Y is *prima facie* wrong *because of the harm done to the interests of X,* and not merely because of any further consequences? Regan argues that we cannot justify the ascription of stronger rights to nonparadigm humans than to nonhuman animals in the way suggested, because "what underlies the ascription of rights to any given X is that X has value independently of anyone's valuing X." After all, we do not speak of expensive paintings or gemstones as having rights, although many people value them and have good reasons for wanting them protected.

There is, however, a crucial difference between a rare painting and a severely retarded or senile human being; the latter not only has (or may have) value for other human beings but *also* has his or her own needs and interests. It may be this which leads us to say that such individuals have intrinsic value. The sentience of nonparadigm humans, like that of sentient nonhuman animals, gives them a place in the sphere of rights holders. So long as the moral rights of all sentient beings are given due recognition, there should be no objection to providing some of them with *additional* protections, on the basis of our interests as well as their own. Some philosophers speak of such additional protections, which are accorded to X on the basis of interests other than X's own, as *conferred* rights, in contrast to *natural* rights, which are entirely based upon the properties of X itself. But such "conferred" rights are not necessarily any weaker or less binding upon moral agents than are "natural" rights. Infants, and most other nonparadigm humans have the *same* basic moral rights that the rest of us do, even though the reasons for ascribing those rights are somewhat different in the two cases.

4. OTHER OBJECTIONS TO ANIMAL RIGHTS

We have already dealt with the primary objection to assigning *any* moral rights to nonhuman animals; that is, that they lack moral autonomy, and various other psychological capacities which paradigm humans possess. We have also answered the animal liberationists' primary objection to assigning somewhat *weaker*, or less-extensive rights to animals; that is, that this will force us to assign similarly inferior rights to nonparadigm humans. There are two other objections to animal rights which need to be considered. The first is that the claim that animals have a right to life, or other moral rights, has absurd consequences with respect to the natural relationship *among* animals. The second is that to accord rights to animals on the basis of their (differing degrees of) sentience will introduce intolerable difficulties and complexities into our moral reasoning.

Opponents of animal rights often accuse the animal liberationists of ignoring the realities of nature, in which many animals survive only by killing others. Callicott, for example, maintains that, whereas environmentally aware persons realize that natural predators are a vital part of the biotic community, those who believe that animals have a right to life are forced to regard all predators as "merciless, wanton, and incorrigible murderers of their fellow creatures." Similarly, Ritchie asks whether, if animals have rights, we are not morally obligated to "protect the weak among them against the strong? Must we not put to death blackbirds and thrushes because they feed on worms, or (if capital punishment offends our humanitarianism) starve them slowly by permanent captivity and vegetarian diet?"

Such a conclusion would of course be ridiculous, as well as wholly inconsistent with the environmental ethic. However, nothing of the sort follows from the claim that animals have moral rights. There are two independently sufficient reasons why it does not. In the first place, nonhuman predators are not moral agents, so it is absurd to think of them as wicked, or as *murdering* their prey. But this is not the most important point. Even if wolves and the like *were* moral agents, their predation would still be morally acceptable, given that they generally kill only to feed themselves, and generally do so without inflicting prolonged or unnecessary suffering. If we have the right to eat animals in order to avoid starvation, then why shouldn't animals have the right to eat one another for the same reason?

This conclusion is fully consistent with the lesson taught by the ecologists, that natural predation is essential to the stability of biological communities. Deer need wolves, or other predators, as much as the latter need them; without predation they become too numerous and fall victim to hunger and disease, while their overgrazing damages the entire ecosystem. Too often we have learned (or failed to learn) this lesson the hard way, as when the killing of hawks and other predators produces exploding rodent populations—which must be controlled, often in ways which cause further ecological damage. The control of natural predators may *sometimes* be necessary, for example, when human pressures upon the populations of certain species become so intense that the latter cannot endure continued *natural* predation. (The controversial case of the wolves and caribou in Alaska and Canada may or may not be one of this sort.) But even in such cases it is preferable, from a environmentalist perspective, to reduce human predation enough to leave room for natural predators as well.

Another objection to assigning moral rights to sentient nonhuman animals is that it will not only complicate our own moral system, but introduce seemingly insoluble dilemmas. As Ritchie points out, "Very difficult questions of casuistry will . . . arise because of the difference in grades of sentience." For instance, is it morally worse to kill and eat a dozen oysters (which are at most minimally sentient) or one (much more highly sentient) rabbit? Questions of this kind, considered in isolation from any of the practical circumstances in which they might arise, are virtually unanswerable. But this ought not to surprise us, since similarly abstract questions about the treatment of human beings are often equally unanswerable. (For instance, would it be worse to kill one child or to cause a hundred to suffer from severe malnutrition?)

The reason such questions are so difficult to answer is not just that we lack the skill and knowledge to make such precise comparisons of interpersonal or interspecies utility, but also that these questions are posed in entirely unrealistic terms. Real moral choices rarely depend entirely upon the comparison of two abstract quantities of pain or pleasure deprivation. In deciding whether to eat molluscs or mammals (or neither or both) a human society must consider *all* of the predictable consequences of each option, for example, their respective impacts on the ecology or the economy, and not merely the individual interests of the animals involved.

Of course, other things being equal, it would be morally preferable to refrain from killing *any* sentient animal. But other things are never equal. Questions about human diet involve not only the rights of individual animals, but also vital environmental and human concerns. On the one hand, as Singer points out, more people might be better fed if food suitable for human consumption were not fed to meat-producing animals. On the other hand, a mass conversion of humanity to vegetarianism would represent "an increase in the efficiency of the conversion of solar energy from plant to human biomass," with the likely result that the human population would continue to expand and, in the process, to cause greater environmental destruction than might occur otherwise. The issue is an enormously complex one, and cannot be solved by any simple appeal to the claim that animals have (or lack) certain moral rights.

In short, the ascription of moral rights to animals does not have the absurd or environmentally damaging consequences that some philosophers have feared. It does not require us to exterminate predatory species, or to lose ourselves in abstruse speculations about the relative degrees of sentience of different sorts of animals. It merely requires us to recognize the interests of animals as having intrinsic moral significance; as demanding some consideration, regardless of whether or not human or environmental concerns are also involved.

DISCUSSION QUESTIONS

1. Warren argues that "unless we view the deliberate infliction of needless pain as inherently wrong we will not be able to understand the moral objection to cruelty of *either* kind." By "either" she means the infliction of needless suffering on human beings as well as animals. What counts as the infliction of "needless" suffering? Does causing animals to suffer so that we can eat meat count as "needless"? What about performing experiments on animals?
2. What is cruelty? Dentists cause suffering (so do philosophy professors); are dentists cruel? See if you can detail the conditions under which you would say treatment is cruel.
3. In linking the right to liberty to a creature's capacities, is Warren unwittingly undercutting a human right to liberty as well? Do people who like to travel have a stronger right to liberty than those who do not? Is your right to liberty violated if, unknown to you, I lock you in a room in which you choose to remain?
4. Warren argues that (some) animals have a right to life that nevertheless is weaker than a human being's right to life. She concludes that "*some* serious justification for the killing of sentient nonhuman animals is always necessary." Is her support for this claim adequate? Do you agree that some serious justification is required for killing an animal? Why, why not?

5. Warren appeals to contractual reasons for thinking that human rights are morally more significant than comparable nonhuman rights. She writes, "I respect [your rights to life, liberty, and pursuit of happiness] as *fully equal to my own* because I hope and expect that you will do the same for me." Is she right?
6. If moral autonomy supplies the "extra ingredient" that makes human rights more significant than nonhuman rights, what about nonautonomous human beings? Warren argues that they should nevertheless receive the same strong human rights that autonomous human beings have. Does she supply good reasons for thinking this is so?

CARL COHEN

The Case for the Use of Animals in Biomedical Research

Carl Cohen is professor of philosophy at the University of Michigan. In this article, "The Case for the Use of Animals in Biomedical Research," which appeared in the *New England Journal of Medicine,* Cohen argues that animals have no rights because they lack the moral autonomy required for having rights. Conducting research on animals, therefore, cannot violate their rights, for they have none to violate. According to Cohen, morally correct behavior requires us to be speciesists, that is, to put human interests above animal interests, because failure to recognize the moral differences between human beings and animals will result in failure to do our duty. Moreover, according to Cohen (and contrary to Singer), a proper utilitarian analysis shows that we have a duty to increase the use of animals in medical experimentation, not reduce it.

CRITICAL READING QUESTIONS

1. How does Cohen define a right?
2. Why, according to Cohen, do human beings have rights?
3. Why, given Cohen's premises, do animals have no rights?
4. What is the relation between rights and obligations, in Cohen's view?
5. What is Cohen's response to the argument that if rights require moral autonomy, then brain-damaged human beings have no rights?
6. How does Cohen defend speciesism?
7. Why, according to Cohen, should we increase the use of animals in medical experimentation?
8. In order to be consistent, what must the critic of animal experimentation do, according to Cohen?

Carl Cohen, "The Care for the Use of Animals in Biomedical Research," *The New England Journal of Medicine,* vol 315, 1986, pp. 865–870.

Using animals as research subjects in medical investigations is widely condemned on two grounds: first, because it wrongly violates the *rights* of animals,[1] and second, because it wrongly imposes on sentient creatures much avoidable *suffering*.[2] Neither of the arguments is sound. The first relies on a mistaken understanding of rights; the second relies on a mistaken calculation of consequences. Both deserve definitive dismissal.

WHY ANIMALS HAVE NO RIGHTS

A right, properly understood is a claim, or potential claim, that one party may exercise against another. The target against whom such a claim may be registered can be a single person, a group, a community, or (perhaps) all humankind. The content of rights claims also varies greatly: repayment of loans, nondiscrimination by employers, noninterference by the state, and so on. To comprehend any genuine right fully, therefore, we must know *who* holds the right, *against whom* it is held, and *to what* it is a right.

Alternative sources of rights add complexity. Some rights are grounded in constitution and law (e.g., the right of an accused to trial by jury); some rights are moral but give no legal claims (e.g., my right to your keeping the promise you gave me); and some rights (e.g., against theft or assault) are rooted both in morals and in law.

The differing targets, contents, and sources of rights, and their inevitable conflict, together weave a tangled web. Notwithstanding all such complications, this much is clear about rights in general: they are in every case claims, or potential claims, within a community of moral agents. Rights arise, and can be intelligibly defended, only among beings who actually do, or can, make moral claims against one another. Whatever else rights may be, therefore, they are necessarily human; their possessors are persons, human beings.

The attributes of human beings from which this moral capability arises have been described variously by philosophers, both ancient and modern: the inner consciousness of a free will (Saint Augustine[3]); the grasp, by human reason, of the binding character of moral law (Saint Thomas[4]); the self-conscious participation of human beings in an objective ethical order (Hegel[5]); human membership in an organic moral community (Bradley[6]); the development of the human self through the consciousness of other moral selves (Mead[7]); and the underivative, intuitive cognition of the rightness of an action (Prichard[8]). Most influential has been Immanuel Kant's emphasis on the universal human possession of a uniquely moral will and the autonomy its use entails.[9] Humans confront choices that are purely moral; humans—but certainly not dogs or mice—lay down moral laws, for others and for themselves. Human beings are self-legislative, morally *auto-nomous*.

Animals (that is, nonhuman animals, the ordinary sense of that word) lack this capacity for free moral judgment. They are not beings of a kind capable of exercising or responding to moral claims. Animals therefore have no rights, and they can have none. This is the core of the argument about the alleged rights of animals. The holders of rights must have the capacity to comprehend rules of duty, governing all including themselves. In applying such rules, the holders of rights must recognize possible conflicts between what is in their own interest and what is just. Only in a community of beings capable of self-restricting moral judgments can the concept of a right be correctly invoked.

Humans have such moral capacities. They are in this sense self-legislative, are members of communities governed by moral rules, and do possess rights. Animals do not have such moral capacities. They are not morally self-legislative, cannot possibly be members of a truly moral community, and therefore cannot possess rights. In conducting research on animal subjects, therefore, we do not violate their rights, because they have none to violate.

To animate life, even in its simplest forms, we give a certain natural reverence. But the possession of rights presupposes a moral status not attained by the vast majority of living things. We must not infer, therefore, that a live being has, simply in being alive, a "right" to its life. The assertion that all animals, only because they are alive and have interests, also possess the "right to life"[10] is an abuse of that phrase, and wholly without warrant.

It does not follow from this, however, that we are morally free to do anything we please to animals.

Certainly not. In our dealings with animals, as in our dealings with other human beings, we have obligations that do not arise from claims against us based on rights. Rights entail obligations, but many of the things one ought to do are in no way tied to another's entitlement. Rights and obligations are not reciprocals of one another, and it is a serious mistake to suppose that they are.

Illustrations are helpful. Obligations may arise from internal commitments made: Physicians have obligations to their patients not grounded merely in their patients' rights. Teachers have such obligations to their students, shepherds to their dogs, and cowboys to their horses. Obligations may arise from differences of status: Adults owe special care when playing with young children, and children owe special care when playing with young pets. Obligations may arise from special relationships: The payment of my son's college tuition is something to which he may have no right, although it may be my obligation to bear the burden if I reasonably can; my dog has no right to daily exercise and veterinary care, but I do have the obligation to provide these things for her. Obligations may arise from particular acts or circumstances: one may be obliged to another for a special kindness done, or obliged to put an animal out of its misery in view of its condition—although neither the human benefactor nor the dying animal may have had a claim of right.

Plainly, the grounds of our obligations to humans and to animals are manifold and cannot be formulated simply. Some hold that there is a general obligation to do no gratuitous harm to sentient creatures (the principle of nonmaleficence); some hold that there is a general obligation to do good to sentient creatures when that is reasonably within one's power (the principle of beneficence). In our dealings with animals, few will deny that we are at least obliged to act humanely—that is, to treat them with the decency and concern that we owe, as sensitive human beings, to other sentient creatures. To treat animals humanely, however, is not to treat them as humans or as the holders of rights.

A common objection, which deserves a response, may be paraphrased as follows:

> If having rights requires being able to make moral claims, to grasp and apply moral laws, then many humans—the brain-damaged, the comatose, the senile—who plainly lack those capacities must be without rights. But that is absurd. This proves [the critic concludes] that rights do not depend on the presence of moral capacities.[1, 10]

This objection fails; it mistakenly treats an essential feature of humanity as though it were a screen for sorting humans. The capacity for moral judgment that distinguishes humans from animals is not a test to be administered to human beings one by one. Persons who are unable, because of some disability, to perform the full moral functions natural to human beings are certainly not for that reason ejected from the moral community. The issue is one of kind. Humans are of such a kind that they may be the subject of experiments only with their voluntary consent. The choices they make freely must be respected. Animals are of such a kind that it is impossible for them, in principle, to give or withhold voluntary consent or to make a moral choice. What humans retain when disabled, animals have never had.

A second objection, also often made, may be paraphrased as follows:

> Capacities will not succeed in distinguishing humans from the other animals. Animals also reason; animals also communicate with one another; animals also care passionately for their young; animals also exhibit desires and preferences.[11, 12] Features of moral relevance—rationality, interdependence, and love—are not exhibited uniquely by human beings. Therefore, [this critic concludes] there can be no solid moral distinction between humans and other animals.[10]

This criticism misses the central point. It is not the ability to communicate or to reason, or dependence on one another, or care for the young, or the exhibition of preference, or any such behavior that marks the critical divide. Analogies between human families and those of monkeys, or between human communities and those of wolves, and the like, are entirely beside the point. Patterns of conduct are not at issue. Animals do indeed exhibit remarkable behavior at times. Conditioning, fear, instinct, and intelligence all contribute to species survival. Membership in a community of moral agents nevertheless remains impossible for them. Actors subject to moral judgment must be capable of grasping the generality of an ethical premise in a practical syllogism. Humans act immorally often enough, but only they—never wolves or monkeys—can discern, by applying some moral rule to the facts of a case, that a given act ought or ought not to be performed. The moral restraints imposed by humans on themselves are thus highly abstract and are often in conflict with the self-interest of the agent. Communal behavior among animals, even when most intelligent and most endearing, does not approach autonomous morality in this fundamental sense.

Genuinely moral acts have an internal as well as an external dimension. Thus, in law, an act can be criminal only when the guilty deed, the actus reus, is done with a guilty mind, mens rea. No animal can ever commit a crime; bringing animals to criminal trial is the mark of primitive ignorance. The claims of moral right are similarly inapplicable to them. Does a lion have a right to eat a baby zebra? Does a baby zebra have a right not to be eaten? Such questions, mistakenly invoking the concept of right where it does not belong, do not make good sense. Those who condemn biomedical research because it violates "animal rights" commit the same blunder.

IN DEFENSE OF "SPECIESISM"

Abandoning reliance on animal rights, some critics resort instead to animal sentience—their feelings of pain and distress. We ought to desist from the imposition of pain insofar as we can. Since all or nearly all experimentation on animals does impose pain and could be readily forgone, say these critics, it should be stopped. The ends sought may be worthy, but those ends do not justify imposing agonies on humans, and by animals the agonies are felt no less. The laboratory use of animals (these critics conclude) must therefore be ended—or at least very sharply curtailed.

Argument of this variety is essentially utilitarian, often expressly so;[13] it is based on the calculation of the net product, in pains and pleasures, resulting from experiments on animals. Jeremy Bentham, comparing horses and dogs with other sentient creatures, is thus commonly quoted: "The question is not, Can they reason? nor Can they talk? but, Can they suffer?"[14]

Animals certainly can suffer and surely ought not to be made to suffer needlessly. But in inferring, from these uncontroversial premises, that biomedical research causing animals distress is largely (or wholly) wrong, the critic commits two serious errors.

The first error is the assumption, often explicitly defended, that all sentient animals have equal moral standing. Between a dog and a human being, according to this view, there is no moral difference; hence the pains suffered by dogs must be weighed no differently from the pains suffered by humans. To deny such equality, according to this critic, is to give unjust preference to one species over another; it is "speciesism." The most influential statement of this moral equality of species was made by Peter Singer:

> The racist violates the principle of equality by giving greater weight to the interests of members of his own race when there is a clash between their interests and the interests of those of another race. The sexist violates the principle of equality by favoring the interests of his own sex. Similarly the speciesist allows the interests of his own species to override the greater interests of members of other species. The pattern is identical in each case.[2]

This argument is worse than unsound; it is atrocious. It draws an offensive moral conclusion from a deliberately devised verbal parallelism that is utterly specious. Racism has no rational ground whatever. Differing degrees of respect or concern for humans for no other reason than that they are members of different races is an injustice totally without foundation in the nature of the races themselves. Racists, even if acting on the basis of mistaken factual beliefs, do grave moral wrong precisely because there is no morally relevant distinction among the races. The supposition of such differences has led to outright horror. The same is true of the sexes, neither sex being entitled by right to greater respect or concern than the other. No dispute here.

Between species of animate life, however—between (for example) humans on the one hand and cats or rats on the other—the morally relevant differences are enormous, and almost universally appreciated. Humans engage in moral reflection; humans are morally autonomous; humans are members of moral communities, recognizing just claims against their own interest. Human beings do have rights; theirs is a moral status very different from that of cats or rats.

I am a speciesist. Speciesism is not merely plausible; it is essential for right conduct, because those who will not make the morally relevant distinctions among species are almost certain, in consequence, to misapprehend their true obligations. The analogy between speciesism and racism is insidious. Every sensitive moral judgment requires that the differing natures of the beings to whom obligations are owed be considered. If all forms of animate life—or vertebrate animal life?—must be treated equally, and if therefore in evaluating a research program the pains of a rodent count equally with the pains of a human, we are forced to conclude (1) that neither humans nor rodents possess rights, or (2) that rodents possess all the rights that humans possess. Both alternatives are absurd. Yet one or the other must be swallowed if the moral equality of all species is to be defended.

Humans owe to other humans a degree of moral regard that cannot be owed to animals. Some humans take on the obligation to support and heal others, both humans and animals, as a principal duty in their lives; the fulfillment of that duty may require the sacrifice of many animals. If biomedical investigators abandon the effective pursuit of their professional objectives because they are convinced that they may not do to animals what the service of humans requires, they will fail, objectively, to do their duty. Refusing to recognize the moral differences among species is a sure path to calamity. (The largest animal rights group in the country is People for the Ethical Treatment of Animals; its codirector, Ingrid Newkirk, calls research using animal subjects, "fascism" and "supremacism." "Animal liberationists do not separate out the *human* animal," she says, so there is no rational basis for saying that a human being has special rights. A rat is a pig is a dog is a boy. They're all mammals."[15])

Those who claim to base their objection to the use of animals in biomedical research on their reckoning of the net pleasures and pains produced make a second error, equally grave. Even if it were true—as it is surely not—that the pains of all animate beings must be counted equally, a cogent utilitarian calculation requires that we weigh all the consequences of the use, and of the nonuse, of animals in laboratory research. Critics relying (however mistakenly) on animal rights may claim to ignore the beneficial results of such research, rights being trump cards to which interest and advantage must give way. But an argument that is explicitly framed in terms of interest and benefit for all over the long run must attend also to the disadvantageous consequences of not using animals in research, and to all the achievements attained and attainable *only* through their use. The sum of the benefits of their use is utterly beyond quantification. The elimination of horrible disease, the increase of longevity, the avoidance of great pain, the saving of lives, and the improvement of the quality of lives (for humans and for animals) achieved through research using animals is so incalculably great that the argument of these critics, systematically pursued, establishes not their conclusion but its reverse: to refrain from using animals in biomedical research is, on utilitarian grounds, morally wrong.

When balancing the pleasures and pains resulting from the use of animals in research, we must not fail to place on the scales the terrible pains that would have resulted, would be suffered now, and would long continue had animals not been used. Every disease eliminated, every vaccine developed, every method of pain relief devised, every surgical procedure invented, every prosthetic device implanted—indeed, virtually every modern medical therapy is due, in part or in whole, to experimentation using animals. Nor may we ignore, in the balancing process, the predictable gains in human (and animal) well-being that are probably achievable in the future but that will not be achieved if the decision is made now to desist from such research or to curtail it.

Medical investigators are seldom insensitive to the distress their work may cause animal subjects. Opponents of research using animals are frequently insensitive to the cruelty of the results of the restrictions they would impose.[2] Untold numbers of human beings—real persons, although not now identifiable—would suffer grievously as the consequence of this well-meaning but shortsighted tenderness. If the morally relevant differences between humans and animals are borne in mind, and if all relevant considerations are weighed, the calculation of long-term consequences must give overwhelming support for biomedical research using animals.

CONCLUDING REMARKS

Substitution

The humane treatment of animals requires that we desist from experimenting on them if we can accomplish the same result using alternative methods—in vitro experimentation, computer simulation, or others. Critics of some experiments using animals rightly make this point.

It would be a serious error to suppose, however, that alternative techniques could soon be used in most research now using live animal subjects. No other methods now on the horizon—or perhaps ever to be available—can fully replace the testing of a drug, a procedure, or a vaccine, in live organisms. The flood of new medical possibilities being opened by the successes of recombinant DNA technology will turn to a trickle if testing on live animals is forbidden. When initial trials entail great risks, there may be no forward movement whatever without the use of live animal subjects. In seeking knowledge that may prove critical in later clinical applications, the unavailability of animals for inquiry may spell complete stymie. In the United States, federal regulations require the testing of new drugs and other products on animals, for efficacy and safety, before human beings are exposed to them.[16, 17] We would not want it otherwise.

Every advance in medicine—every new drug, new operation, new therapy of any kind—must sooner or later be tried on a living being for the first time. That trial, controlled or uncontrolled, will be an experiment. The subject of that experiment, if it is not an animal, will be a human being. Prohibiting the use of live animals in biomedical research, therefore, or sharply restricting it, must result either in the blockage of much valuable research or in the replacement of animal subjects with human subjects. These are the consequences—unacceptable to most reasonable persons—of not using animals in research.

Reduction

Should we not at least reduce the use of animals in biomedical research? No, we should increase it, to avoid when feasible the use of humans as experimental subjects. Medical investigations putting human subjects at some risk are numerous and greatly varied. The risks run in such experiments are usually unavoidable, and (thanks to earlier experiments on animals) most such risks are minimal or moderate. But some experimental risks are substantial.

When an experimental protocol that entails substantial risk to humans comes before an institutional review board, what response is appropriate? The investigation, we may suppose, is promising and deserves support, so long as its human subjects are protected against unnecessary dangers. May not the investigators be fairly asked, Have you done all that you can to eliminate risk to humans by the extensive testing of that drug, that procedure, or that device on animals? To achieve maximal safety for humans we are right to require thorough experimentation on animal subjects before humans are involved.

Opportunities to increase human safety in this way are commonly missed; trials in which risks may be shifted from humans to animals are often not devised, sometimes not even considered. Why? For the investigator, the use of animals as subjects is often more expensive, in money and time, than the use of human subjects. Access to suitable human subjects is often quick and convenient, whereas access to appropriate animal subjects may be awkward, costly, and burdened with red tape. Physician-investigators have often had more experience working with human beings and know precisely where the needed pool of subjects is to be found and how they may be enlisted. Animals, and the procedures for their use, are often less familiar to these investigators. Moreover, the use of animals in place of humans is now more likely to be the target of zealous protests from without. The upshot is that humans are sometimes subjected to risks that animals could have borne, and should have borne, in their place. To maximize the protection of human subjects, I conclude, the wide and imaginative use of live animal subjects should be encouraged rather than discouraged. This enlargement in the use of animals is our obligation.

Consistency

Finally, inconsistency between the profession and the practice of many who oppose research using animals deserves comment. This frankly *ad hominem* observation aims chiefly to show that a coherent position rejecting the use of animals in medical research imposes costs so high as to be intolerable even to the critics themselves.

One cannot coherently object to the killing of animals in biomedical investigations while continuing to eat them. Anesthetics and thoughtful animal husbandry render the level of actual animal distress in the laboratory generally lower than that in the abattoir. So long as death and discomfort do not substantially differ in the two contexts, the consistent objector must not only refrain from all eating of animals but also protest as vehemently against others eating them as against others experimenting on them. No less vigorously must the critic object to the wearing of animal hides in coats and shoes, to employment in any industrial enterprise that uses animal parts, and to any commercial development that will cause death or distress to animals.

Killing animals to meet human needs for food, clothing, and shelter is judged entirely reasonable by most persons. The ubiquity of these uses and the virtual universality of moral support for them confront the opponent of research using animals with an inescapable difficulty. How can the many common uses of animals be judged morally worthy, while their use in scientific investigation is judged unworthy?

The number of animals used in research is but the tiniest fraction of the total used to satisfy assorted human appetites. That these appetites, often base and satisfiable in other ways, morally justify the far larger consumption of animals, whereas the quest for improved human health and understanding cannot justify the far smaller, is wholly implausible. Aside from the numbers of animals involved, the distinction in terms of worthiness of use, drawn with regard to any single animal, is not defensible. A given sheep is surely not more justifiably used to put lamb chops on the supermarket counter than to serve in testing a new contraceptive or a new prosthetic device. The needless killing of animals is wrong; if the common killing of them for our food or convenience is right, the less common but more humane uses of animals in the service of medical science are certainly not less right.

Scrupulous vegetarianism, in matters of food, clothing, shelter, commerce, and recreation, and in all other spheres, is the only fully coherent position the critic may adopt. At great human cost, the lives of fish and crustaceans must also be protected, with equal vigor, if speciesism has been forsworn. A very few consistent critics adopt this position. It is the *reductio ad absurdum* of the rejection of moral distinctions between animals and human beings.

Opposition to the use of animals in research is based on arguments of two different kinds—those relying on the alleged rights of animals and those relying on the consequences for animals. I have argued that arguments of both kinds must fail. We surely do have obligations to animals, but they have, and can have, no rights against us on which research can infringe. In calculating the consequences of animal research, we must weigh all the long-term benefits of the results achieved—to animals and to humans—and in that calculation we must not assume the moral equality of all animate species.

NOTES

1. T. Regan, *The Case for Animal Rights* (Berkeley, CA: University of California Press, 1983).
2. P. Singer, *Animal Liberation* (New York: Avon Books, 1977).
3. St. Augustine, *Confessions Book Seven. A.D. 397* (New York: Pocketbooks, 1957), pp. 104–26.

4. St. Thomas Aquinas, *Summa Theologica. A.D. 1273 Philosophic Texts* (New York: Oxford University Press, 1960), pp. 353–66.

5. G. W. F Hegel, *Philosophy of Right.* 1821 (London: Oxford University Press, 1952), pp. 105–10.

6. F. H Bradley, "Why Should I Be Moral?" 1876, in *Ethical Theories.* AI Melden, ed. (New York: Prentice-Hall, 1950) pp. 345–59.

7. G. H Mead, "The Genesis of the Self and Social Control.," 1925, in *Selected Writings,* AJ, Reck ed. (Indianapolis: Bobbs-Merrill, 1964), pp. 264–93.

8. H. A Prichard, "Does Moral Philosophy Rest on a Mistake?" 1912 In *Readings in Ethical Theory,* v. Cellars, J. Hospers, eds. (New York: Appleton-Century-Crofts, 1952) pp. 149–63.

9. I. Kant, *Fundamental Principles of the Metaphysic of Morals,* 1785. (New York: Liberal Arts Press, 1949).

10. B. E Rollin, *Animal Rights and Human Morality* (New York: Prometheus Books, 1981).

11. C. Hoff, "Immoral and Moral Uses of Animals," New England Journal of Medicine 1980; 302, pp. 115–8.

12. D. Jamieson, "Killing Persons and Other Beings," in *Ethics and Animals.* Miller H., Williams W. H., eds. (Clifton, NJ: Human Press, 1983) pp. 135–46.

13. P. Singer, "Ten Years of Animal Liberation," *New York Review of Books,* 1985: 31, pp. 46–52.

14. J. Bentham, *Introduction to the Principles of Morals and Legislation* (London: Athlone Press, 1970).

15. K. McCabe, "Who Will Live, Who Will Die?" *Washingtonian Magazine,* August 1986, p. 115.

16. U.S. Code of Federal Regulations. Title 21, Sect. 505 (1). Food, drug, and cosmetic regulations.

17. U.S. Code of Federal Regulations. Title 16, Sect. 1500.40–2. Consumer product regulations.

DISCUSSION QUESTIONS

1. Assess Cohen's claim that, "The holders of rights must have the capacity to comprehend rules of duty, governing all including themselves." Why should we think the capacity Cohen cites is a requirement for the having of rights at all?
2. Might a critic agree with Cohen about the issue of rights but still argue that we have significant obligations to animals? What might these obligations include?
3. Cohen claims, "In our dealings with animals, few will deny that we are at least obligated to act humanely." What does that mean?
4. Is Cohen's response to the argument that brain-damaged human beings do not have rights adequate? He claims it is a matter of *kind.* Do you think judgments about individuals should be made according to their biological kind or according to their individual capacities irrespective of kind?
5. What would Singer likely say about Cohen's defense of speciesism?
6. Under what circumstances is it morally acceptable to use animals in research? Under what circumstances is it morally acceptable to use human beings in research? If the conditions are different, what accounts for the difference? If they are the same, why?

JAMES RACHELS

From *Created From Animals*

James Rachels is professor of philosophy at the University of Alabama. He has written on animal ethics as well as moral issues in medicine. In this selection from his book, *Created*

From Animals, Rachels considers the relation between species membership and morality in the light of evolutionary theory, arguing that species membership in itself is not a morally relevant difference among creatures. He also considers a more plausible defense of speciesism called "qualified speciesism," ultimately rejecting it in favor of what he calls "moral individualism," that is, treating individuals according to their individual characteristics, rather than according to the characteristics of their biological kinds. He argues specifically against Cohen's claim (above) that biological kind is a morally relevant factor.

CRITICAL READING QUESTIONS

1. What is the difference between radical speciesism and mild speciesism, and qualified and unqualified speciesism?
2. What objections does Rachels raise against qualified speciesism?
3. How does Rachels answer Cohen's claim that biological kind is a morally relevant factor?
4. How, according to Rachels, is the capacity to talk a morally significant feature?
5. What is the distinction between having a moral obligation and being the beneficiary of a moral obligation? How is this relevant to Rachels' rejection of contractarian accounts of morality?
6. How does Rachels respond to the denial that animals and human beings can suffer equivalently?
7. What is the relation between morality and species, according to Rachels?

SPECIESISM

Recent writers on animal welfare have introduced the term "speciesism" to refer to systematic discrimination against nonhumans. (The term was coined by Richard Ryder, a British psychologist who quit experimenting on animals after he became convinced this was immoral, although Peter Singer's book *Animal Liberation* was responsible for popularizing the term.) Speciesism is said to be analogous to racism: It is the idea that the interests of the members of a particular species count for more than the interests of the members of other species, just as racism is the notion that the interests of the members of a particular race count for more. As Singer puts it:

> The racist violates the principle of equality by giving greater weight to the interests of members of his own race when there is a clash between their interests and the interests of those of another race. The sexist violates the principle of equality by favoring the interests of his own sex. Similarly the speciesist allows the interests of his own species to override the greater interests of members of other species. The pattern is identical in each case.

The traditional doctrine of human dignity is speciesist to the core, for it implies that the interests of humans have priority over those of all other creatures. But let me try to be a little more precise about this. Human speciesism can take two forms, one much more plausible than the other:

> *Radical speciesism:* Even the relatively trivial interests of humans take priority over the vital interests of nonhumans. Thus, if we have to choose between causing mild discomfort to a human, and causing excruciating pain to a nonhuman, we should prefer to cause pain to the nonhuman and spare the human.

This is the version of speciesism that Singer describes: One allows the interests of one's own species

---

James Rachels, 1990. Reprinted from *Created From Animals: The Moral Implications of Darwinism* by James Rachels (1990) by permission of Oxford University Press.

to override the *greater* interests of members of other species. We can, however, define a milder and more plausible version:

> *Mild speciesism:* When the choice is between a relatively trivial human interest and a more substantial interest of a nonhuman, we may choose for the nonhuman. Thus it may be better to cause a little discomfort for a human than to cause agony for an animal. However, if the interests are comparable—say, if the choice is between causing the *same* amount of pain for a human or for a nonhuman—we should give preference to the human's welfare.

Many defenders of traditional morality have embraced the radical form of speciesism. Aquinas and Kant, as we have seen, both held that the interests of nonhumans count for nothing, and therefore may be outweighed by any human interest whatever. Indeed, on their view there is no point in doing any "weighing" at all: The human always wins, no matter what. Descartes even denied that nonhumans have any interests that *could* be weighed. Contemporary readers might find their views too extreme, and yet still find mild speciesism to be an attractive doctrine.

The principle of equality, on the other hand, involves the rejection of even mild speciesism: it implies that humans and nonhumans are, in a sense, moral equals—that is, it implies that the interests of nonhumans should receive the *same* consideration as the comparable interests of humans. I suspect that, viewed in this light, the principle of equality will seem implausible to many readers. The doctrine of human dignity, at least when it is interpreted as involving only mild speciesism, might appear to be a much more plausible view. Therefore, if I am to defend the principle of equality, I need to explain why even mild speciesism should be rejected.

Unqualified Speciesism

In addition to distinguishing between radical and mild speciesism, we may distinguish between qualified and unqualified versions of the doctrine. The former distinction has to do with the extent of the view; the latter has to do with its logical basis.

Unqualified speciesism is the view that mere species alone is morally important. On this view, the bare fact that an individual is a member of a certain species, unsupplemented by any other consideration, is enough to make a difference in how that individual should be treated.

This is not a very plausible way of understanding the relation between species and morality, and generally it is not accepted even by those who defend traditional morality. To see why it is not plausible, consider the old science-fiction story "The Teacher from Mars" by Eando Binder. The main character in that story is a Martian who has come to earth to teach in a school for boys. Because he is "different"—seven feet tall, thin, with tentacles and leathery skin—he is taunted and abused by the students until he is almost driven out. Then, however, an act of heroism makes the boys realize they have been wrong, and the story ends happily with the ringleader of the bullies vowing to mend his ways.

Written in 1941, the story is a not-so-thinly-disguised morality tale about racism. But the explicit point concerns species, not race. The teacher from Mars is portrayed as being, psychologically, exactly like a human: he is equally as intelligent, and equally as sensitive, with just the same cares and interests as anyone else. The only difference is that he has a different kind of body. And surely *that* does not justify treating him with less respect. Having appreciated this point, the reader is obviously expected to draw a similar conclusion about race: the fact that there are physical differences between whites and blacks—skin color, for example—should make no moral difference either.

Although unqualified speciesism is implausible, as Binder's story shows, some philosophers have nevertheless defended it: They have argued that species alone *can* make a difference in our moral duties towards a being. Robert Nozick, for example, suggests that, in a satisfactory moral scheme,

> perhaps it will turn out that the bare species characteristic of simply being human . . . will command special respect only from other humans—this is an instance of the general principle that the members of any species may legitimately give their fellows more weight than they give members of other species (or at least

> more weight than a neutral view would grant them). Lions, too, if they were moral agents, could not then be criticized for putting other lions first.

Nozick illustrates the point with his own science-fiction example: "denizens of Alpha Centauri" would be justified in giving greater weight to the interests of other such Alpha Centaurians than they give to our interests, he says, even if we were like them in all other relevant respects. But this isn't at all obvious—in fact, it seems wrong on its face. If we substitute an Alpha Centaurian for a Martian in Binder's story, it makes no difference. Treating him less well merely because he is "different" (in this case, a member of a different species) still seems like unjustified discrimination.

What of the "general principle" Nozick suggests? It seems to be an expanded version of something that most people find plausible, namely, that one is justified in giving special weight to the interests of one's family or neighbors. If it is permissible to have special regard for family or neighbors, why not one's fellow species-members? The problem with this way of thinking is that there are lots of groups to which one naturally belongs, and these group-memberships are not always (if they are ever) morally significant. The progression from family to neighbor to species passes through other boundaries on the way—through the boundary of race, for example. Suppose it were suggested that we are justified in giving the interests of our own race greater weight than the interests of other races? Nozick's remarks might be adapted in defence of this suggestion:

> perhaps it will turn out that the bare racial characteristic of simply being white . . . will command special respect only from other whites—this is an instance of the general principle that the members of any race may legitimately give their fellows more weight than they give members of other races (or at least more weight than a neutral view would grant them). Blacks, too, could not then be criticized for putting other blacks first.

This would rightly be resisted, but the case for distinguishing by species alone is identical. As Binder's story suggests, unqualified speciesism and racism are twin doctrines.

Qualified Speciesism

But there is a more sophisticated view of the relation between morality and species, and it is this view that defenders of traditional morality have most often adopted. On this view, species alone is not regarded as morally significant. However, species-membership is correlated with *other* differences that *are* significant. The interests of humans are said to be more important, not simply because they are human, but because humans have morally relevant characteristics that other animals lack. This view might take several forms.

1. *The idea that humans are in a special moral category because they are rational, autonomous agents.* Humans, it might be said, are in a special moral category because they are rational, autonomous agents. Humans can guide their own conduct according to their own conceptions of what ought to be done. (Since Kant, this has been the most popular way of describing the difference between humans and other animals, at least among philosophers.) It is this fact, rather than the "mere" fact that they are human, that qualifies them for special consideration. This is why their interests are more important, morally speaking, than the interests of other species, although, it might be admitted, if the members of any other species were rational, autonomous agents, they would also go into the special moral category and would qualify for the favored treatment. However, defenders of traditional morality insist that as a matter of fact no other species has this characteristic. So humans alone are entitled to full moral consideration. Darwin, as we have seen, resisted the idea that humans have characteristics that are not shared by other animals. Instead he emphasized the continuities between species: If man is more rational than the apes, it is only a matter of degree, not of kind. But it may be of some interest to see what would follow *if* this were true. So let us set aside the Darwinian objection, and grant for the purpose of argument that humans are the only fully rational, autonomous agents. What would follow from this assumption?

Does the fact that someone is a rational autonomous agent make a difference in how he should be treated? Certainly it may. For such a being, the self-direction of his own life is a great good, valued not only for its instrumental worth but for its own sake. Thus paternalistic interference may be seen as an evil. To take a simple example: a woman might have a certain conception of how she wants to live her life. This conception might involve taking risks that we think are foolish. We might therefore try to change her mind; we might call attention to the risks and argue that they are not worth it. But suppose she will not heed our warnings: Are we then justified in forcibly preventing her from living her life as she chooses? It may be argued that we are not justified, for she is, after all, a rational, autonomous agent. It is different for someone who is *not* a fully rational being—a small child, for example. Then we feel justified in interfering with his conduct, to prevent him from harming himself. The fact that the child is not (yet, anyway) a fully rational agent justifies us in treating him differently from how we would treat someone who is a fully rational agent.

Of course, the same thing could be said to justify treating a human differently from a nonhuman. If we forcibly intervened to protect an animal from danger, but did not do the same for a human, we might justify this by pointing to the fact that the human is a rational autonomous agent, who knew what she was doing and who had the right to make her own choice, while this was not true of the animal.

Now notice two points about this reasoning. First, the fact that one individual is a rational autonomous agent, while another is not, sometimes justifies treating a human differently from a nonhuman, but it also justifies treating some humans differently from other humans. This consideration does not simply separate humans from animals; it separates humans from other humans as well. Thus, even if we grant (as a good Darwinian would not) that humans are the only rational, autonomous agents, we still have not identified a characteristic that separates all humans from all nonhumans.

Secondly, and more important, once we understand *why* being a rational agent makes a difference in how one may be treated, in those cases in which it does make a difference, it becomes clear that possession of this quality is not always relevant. As we have already observed, whether a difference is relevant depends on the kind of treatment that is in question. When the issue is paternalistic interference, it is relevant to note whether the individual whose behavior might be coerced is a rational agent. Suppose, however, that what is in question is not paternalistic interference, but putting chemicals in rabbits' eyes to test the safety of a new shampoo. To say that rabbits may be treated in this way, but humans may not, because human are rational agents, is comparable to saying that one law-school applicant may be accepted, and another rejected, because one has a broken arm while the other has an infection.

Therefore, the observation that humans are rational autonomous agents cannot justify the whole range of differences between our treatment of humans and our treatment of nonhumans. It can justify some differences in treatment, but not others.

There is still another problem for this form of qualified speciesism. Some unfortunate humans—perhaps because they have suffered brain damage—are not rational agents. What are we to say about them? The natural conclusion, according to the doctrine we are considering, would be that their status is that of mere animals. And perhaps we should go on to conclude that they may be used as nonhuman animals are used—perhaps as laboratory subjects, or as food?

Of course, traditional moralists do not accept any such conclusion. The interests of humans are regarded as important no matter what their "handicaps" might be. The traditional view is, apparently, that moral status is determined by what is normal for the species. Therefore, because rationality is the norm, even nonrational humans are to be treated with the respect due to the members of a rational species. Carl Cohen, a philosopher at the University of Michigan, apparently endorses this view in his defence of using animals, but not humans, in medical experiments. Cohen writes:

> Persons who are unable, because of some disability, to perform the full moral functions natural to human beings are certainly not for that reason ejected from the moral community. *The issue is one of kind.* Humans are of such a kind that they may be the subject of experiments only with their voluntary consent. The choices they make freely must be respected. Animals are of such a kind that it is impossible for them to give or withhold voluntary consent or to make a moral choice. What humans retain when disabled, animals never had.

Let us pass over the obvious point that animals do seem to be able to withhold consent from participation in experiments—their frantic efforts to escape from the research setting, particularly when they are being caused acute discomfort, suggests that very strongly. But it is the more general theoretical point that we want to consider.

This idea—that how individuals should be treated is determined by what is normal for their species—has a certain appeal, because it does seem to express our moral intuitions about mentally deficient humans. "We should not treat a person worse merely because he has been so unfortunate," we might say about someone who has suffered brain damage. But the idea will not bear close inspection. A simple thought-experiment will expose the problem. Suppose (what is probably impossible) that an unusually gifted chimpanzee learned to read and speak English. And suppose he eventually was able to converse about science, literature, and morals. Finally he expresses a desire to attend university classes. Now there might be various arguments about whether to permit this, but suppose someone argued as follows: "Only humans should be allowed to attend these classes. Humans can read, talk, and understand science. Chimps cannot." But this chimp *can* do those things. "Yes, but *normal* chimps cannot, and that is what matters." Following Cohen, it might be added that "The issue is one of kind," and not one of particular abilities accidental to particular individuals.

Is this a good argument? Regardless of what other arguments might be persuasive, this one is not. It assumes that we should determine how an individual is to be treated, not on the basis of *its* qualities, but on the basis of *other* individuals' qualities. The argument is that this chimp may be barred from doing something that requires reading, despite the fact that he can read, because other chimps cannot read. That seems not only unfair, but irrational.

2. *The idea that humans are in a special moral category because they can talk.* Traditionally, when Western thinkers characterized the differences between humans and other animals, the human capacity for language was among the first things mentioned. Descartes, as we have seen, thought that man's linguistic capacity was the clearest indication that he has a soul; and when Huxley was challenged by his working men to explain why kinship with the apes did not destroy "the nobility of manhood," he replied that "man alone possesses the marvelous endowment of intelligible and rational speech." Is the fact that humans are masters of a syntactically complicated language, vastly superior to any communication-system possessed by nonhumans, relevant to decisions about how they may be treated? In the preceding paragraphs I have already made some observations that bear on this. Clearly, it is sometimes relevant. It is relevant, for example, to the question of who will be admitted to universities. A knowledge of English is required to be a student in many universities, and humans, but not chimpanzees, meet this requirement. But not all humans qualify in this regard, and so it is reasonable to refuse admission to those humans. This means that it is the individual's particular linguistic capacity that is relevant to the admissions decision, and not the general capacities of "mankind." Moreover, there are many forms of treatment to which the question of linguistic ability is not relevant—torture, for example. (The reason why it is wrong to torture has nothing to do with the victim's ability to speak.) Therefore, the most that can be said about this "marvelous endowment" is that *most* humans have it, and that it is relevant to *some* decisions about how they should be treated. This being so, it cannot be the justification of a principled policy of always giving priority to human interests.

It might be objected that this underrates the importance of language, because the implications of language are so diffuse. It isn't *simply* that knowing English enables one to read books, to ask and answer questions, to qualify for admission to universities, and so on. In addition to such discrete achievements, we have to consider the way that having a language enriches and extends all of one's other psychological capacities as well. A being with a language can have moral and religious beliefs that would otherwise be impossible; such a being's hopes, desires, and disappointments will be more complex; its activities will be more varied; its relationships with others will be characterized by greater emotional depth; and on and on. In short, its whole life will be richer and more complex. The lives of creatures who lack such a language will be correspondingly simpler. In light of this, it will be argued, isn't it reasonable to think that human language makes human life morally special?

There is obviously something to this. I think it is true that possession of a human language enriches almost all of one's psychological capacities; that this has consequences that ramify throughout one's life; and that this is a fact that our moral outlook should accommodate. But it is not obvious exactly how this fact should figure into our moral view. What, exactly, is its significance? It does not seem right to say that, because of this, human interests should always have priority over the interests of nonhumans, for there may still be cases in which even the enriched capacities of humans are irrelevant to a particular type of treatment. I want to make a different suggestion about its significance.

Suppose the type of treatment in question is killing: say, we have to choose between causing the death of a human, and causing the death of a nonhuman animal. On what grounds may this choice be made? Although killing is a specific type of treatment, its implications are especially broad: one's death puts an end to all one's activities, projects, plans, hopes, and relationships. In short, it puts an end to one's whole life. Therefore, in making this decision it seems plausible to invoke a broadly inclusive criterion: we may say that the *kind of life* that will be destroyed is relevant to deciding which life is to be preferred. And in assessing the kind of life involved, we may refer, not just to particular facts about the creatures, but to summary judgments about what all the particular facts add up to. Humans, partly because of their linguistic capacities, have lives that are richer and more complex than the lives of other animals. For this reason, one may reasonably conclude that killing a human is worse than killing a nonhuman.

If this account is correct, it would also explain why it is worse to kill some nonhumans than others. Suppose one had to choose between killing a rhesus monkey and swatting a fly. If we compare the two, we find that the life of the monkey is far richer and more complex than that of the fly, because the monkey's psychological capacities are so much greater. The communicative abilities of the monkey, we may note, also make an important difference here. Because the monkey is able to communicate with others of its own kind—even though its communicative skills are inferior to those of humans—its relations with its peers are more complex than they would otherwise be. (This is a clear illustration of Darwin's thesis that the differences between humans and nonhumans are matters of degree, not kind.) In light of all this, we may conclude that it is better to swat the fly. This result is intuitively correct, and it lends additional plausibility to the general idea that, where killing is concerned, it is the richness and complexity of the life that is relevant to judgements about the wrongfulness of its destruction.

This is compatible with moral individualism only if we add a certain qualification, namely, that it is the richness and complexity of the *individual* life that is morally significant. Some humans, unfortunately, are not capable of having the kind of rich life that we are discussing. An infant with severe brain damage, even if it survives for many years, may never learn to speak, and its mental powers may never rise above a primitive level. In fact, its psychological capacities may be markedly inferior to those of a typical rhesus monkey. In that case, moral individualism would see no reason to prefer its life over the monkey's. This will strike many people as implausible. Certainly, the traditional doctrine of human dignity would yield a different result. Nevertheless, I think that moral individualism is correct on this point, and I will have more to say about this below.

3. *The idea that humans are in a special moral category because they alone are able to participate in the agreements on which morality depends.* A different sort of argument turns on a certain conception of the nature of morality and the sources of moral obligation. This argument is connected with the intuitively appealing idea that human beings are members of a common moral community; that morality grows out of their living together in societies and cooperating to provide for their common welfare. This creates bonds between them in which nonhumans have no part. Thus, humans have obligations to one another that are importantly different from any obligation they might have to mere animals.

Spelled out in greater detail, this argument depends crucially on the notion of *reciprocity*. It is plausible to think that moral requirements can exist only where certain conditions of reciprocity are satisfied. The basic idea is that a person is obligated to respect the interests of others, and acknowledge that they have claims against him, only if the others are willing to respect his interests and acknowledge his claims. This may be thought of as a matter of fairness: if we are to accept inconvenient restrictions on our conduct, in the interests of benefiting or at least not harming others, then it is only fair that the others should accept similar restrictions on their conduct for the sake of our interests.

The requirement of reciprocity is central to contract theories of ethics. Such a theory conceives of moral rules as rules which rational, self-interested people will agree to obey on condition that others will obey them as well. Each person can be motivated to accept such an arrangement by considering the benefits he will gain if others abide by the rules; and his own compliance with the rules is the fair price he pays to secure the compliance of others. That is the point of the "contract" which creates the moral community.

This conception helps us to understand, easily and naturally, why we have the particular moral rules we do. Why do we have a rule against killing? Because each of us has something to gain from it. It is to our advantage that others accept such a rule; for then we will be safe. Our own agreement not to harm others is the fair price we pay to secure their agreement not to harm us. Thus the rule is established. The same could be said for the rule requiring us to keep our promises, to tell the truth, and so on.

It is a natural part of such theories that nonhuman animals are not covered by the same moral rules that govern the treatment of humans, for the animals cannot participate in the mutual agreement on which the whole set-up depends. Thomas Hobbes, the first great social contract theorist, was well aware of this: "To make covenants with brute beasts," he said, "is impossible." This implication is also made explicit in the most outstanding recent contribution to contract theory, John Rawls's *A Theory of Justice*. Rawls identifies the principles of justice as those which would be accepted by rational, self-interested people in what he calls "the original position," that is, a position of ignorance with respect to particular facts about oneself and one's position in society. The question then arises as to what sorts of beings are owed the guarantees of justice, and Rawls's answer is:

> We use the characterization of the persons in the original position to single out the kinds of beings to whom the principles chosen apply. After all, the parties are thought of as adopting these criteria to regulate their common institutions and their conduct toward one another; and the description of their nature enters into the reasoning by which these principles are selected. Thus equal justice is owed to those who have the capacity to take part in and to act in accordance with the public understanding of the initial situation.

This, he says, explains why nonhuman animals do not have the "equal basic rights" possessed by humans; "they have some protection certainly but their status is not that of human beings." And of course this result is not surprising: for if rights are determined by agreements of mutual interest, and animals are not able to participate in the agreements, then how could *their* interests possibly give rise to "equal basic rights"?

The requirement of reciprocity may seem plausible, and I think that it does contain the germ of a plausible idea—I will say more about this in a moment—but nevertheless there are good reasons to reject it. To see why, we need to distinguish the conditions necessary for *having* a moral obligation from the conditions necessary for being the *beneficiary* of a moral obligation.

For example: normal adult humans have the obligation not to torture one another. What characteristics make it possible for a person to have this obligation? For one thing, he must be able to understand what torture is, and he must be capable of recognizing that it is wrong. (Linguistic capacity might be relevant here; without language one may not be able to formulate the belief that torture is wrong.) When someone—a severely retarded person, perhaps—lacks such capacities, we do not think he has such obligations and we do not hold him responsible for what he does. On the other hand, it is a very different question what characteristics qualify someone to be the beneficiary of the obligation. It is wrong to torture someone—someone is the beneficiary of our obligation not to torture—not because of his capacity for understanding what torture is, or for recognizing that it is morally wrong, but simply because of his capacity for experiencing pain. Thus a person may lack the characteristics necessary for *having* a certain obligation, and yet may still possess the characteristics necessary to qualify him as the *beneficiary* of that obligation. If there is any doubt, consider the position of severely retarded persons. A severely retarded person may not be able to understand what torture is, or see it as wrong, and yet still be able to suffer pain. So we who are not retarded have an obligation not to torture him, even though he cannot have a similar obligation not to torture us.

The requirement of reciprocity says that a person is morally obligated to accept restrictions on his conduct, in the interests of not harming others, only if the others reciprocate. The example of the retarded person shows this to be false. He is not capable of restricting his conduct in this way; nevertheless we have an obligation to restrict ours. We are in the same position with respect to nonhuman animals: like the retarded person, they may lack the characteristics necessary for having obligations; but they may nevertheless qualify as beneficiaries of our obligations. The fact that they cannot reciprocate, then, need not affect our basic obligations to them.

I said that the requirement of reciprocity, although unacceptable, does contain the germ of a plausible idea. What I have in mind is the idea that if a person *is* capable of acting considerately of our interests, and *refuses* to do so, then we are released from any similar obligations we might have had to him. This may very well be right. But whether or not this point is accepted makes no difference to our duties to nonhuman animals, since they lack the capacity to "refuse" to recognize obligations to us, just as they are not able to accept such obligations.

There is one other way that considerations of reciprocity might enter into one's decisions about what to do. Suppose that, at some time in the past, a particular person has done you a good turn. You might consider yourself to be indebted to that person, so that if you have the chance to be helpful to him in the future, you have a special obligation to do so. Thus, if you have to choose between helping him, and helping someone to whom you owe no such debt, you may legitimately choose in favor of your benefactor. (This may be a "relevant difference" between them that satisfies the demands of the principle of equality.) There is no objection to this, but at the same time it provides no particular grounds for distinguishing between one's general obligations to humans and one's general obligations to other animals. Rather it is a principle that comes into play most often in distinguishing between what one owes to different humans; and moreover, one *could* sometimes have a special obligation of this sort to a nonhuman. After all, nonhumans have on occasion performed valuable services for humans, and it would be ungrateful to think that they could never deserve any credit for this.

4. *The idea that humans are in a special moral category because they are more sensitive to harm than other creatures.* Finally, we need to consider briefly an argument that is not very impressive, but that one sometimes hears. I have said (several times in fact) that even though there are frequently important differences between humans and other animals, there may be no difference in their capacities for experiencing pain. Humans and nonhumans both suffer; and so, regardless of what other differences may exist, we have the same basic reason for objecting to tormenting an animal that we would have for objecting to tormenting a human. At this fundamental level, humans and nonhumans are surely equal.

But it might be objected that this is not so, that humans suffer more than other animals when they are caused distress. Because of their capacity of foresight, humans can anticipate painful experiences and dread them in advance. This dread can have a vivid, detailed quality: One knows, not simply that one will suffer, but that one will suffer in particular ways; and afterwards, the memory may remain to haunt one indefinitely. Animals with less extensive cognitive abilities will suffer fewer of these ancillary effects. This applies not only to physical suffering, but to psychological suffering as well. A human mother, forcibly separated from her child, may grieve the loss for the rest of her life. A female rhesus monkey whose baby is taken away might also be traumatized, but she will soon get over it. One cannot, therefore, equate the mistreatment of a human with the mistreatment of an animal, even when they appear on the surface to be similar.

There is obviously something to this; but it is important to understand what follows from it and what does not. Nothing in this line of reasoning invalidates the fundamental idea that the interests of nonhumans should receive the same consideration as the *comparable* interests of humans. All that follows is that we must be careful in assessing when their interests are really comparable. The situation may be represented schematically as follows. Suppose we must choose between causing x units of pain for a human or a nonhuman. Because of the human's superior cognitive abilities, the after-effects for him will include y additional units of suffering; thus the human's total misfortune will be $x + y$, while the nonhuman's total will be only x. Thus the human has more at stake, and the principle of equality would recommend favoring him. On the other hand, suppose we alter the example to make the nonhuman's initial pain somewhat more intense, so that it equals $x + y$. Then the total amounts of suffering would once again be comparable, and the point about the human's greater sensitivities would not provide any justification for preferential treatment.

Qualified speciesism is the view that the interests of humans are morally more important, not simply because they are human, but because humans have morally significant characteristics that other animals lack. But what are those characteristics? We have now considered several possibilities: that humans can speak; that they are rational agents; that they are moral agents, capable of having obligations; that they are capable of entering into agreements of mutual benefit with other humans, and performing services for them; and that they are more vulnerable to harm. In examining each of these, we have found no reason to abandon the approach suggested by the principle of equality: Where relevant differences between individuals exist, they may be treated differently; otherwise, the comparable interests of individuals, whether human or nonhuman, should be given comparable weight. We have found no reason to support a policy of distinguishing, in principle, between the kind of consideration that should be accorded to humans and that which should be accorded to other animals.

Where does this leave the relation between species and morality? The picture that emerges is more complex, but also more true to the facts, than traditional morality. The fact is that human beings are not simply "different" from other animals. In reality, there is a complex pattern of similarities and differences. The matching moral idea is that in so far as a human and a member of another species are similar, they should be treated similarly, while to the extent that they are different they should be treated differently. This will allow the human to assert a right to better treatment whenever there is some difference between him and the other animal that justifies treating him better. But it will not permit him to claim greater rights simply because he is human, or because humans in general have some quality that he lacks, or because he has some characteristic that is irrelevant to the particular type of treatment in question.

DISCUSSION QUESTIONS

1. Rachels rejects the idea that we may legitimately give preference to those close to us, such as our friends or family members, on the grounds that racial or gender preferences would thereby also be sanctioned. Is this so? And if not, might one then prefer the interests of one's species without thereby being committed to racism?
2. Is Rachels' response to Cohen regarding biological kinds a good one? Assess his example of the talking chimpanzee. How is this an example of moral individualism?
3. Is Rachels committed to the view that the life of a brain-damaged human being is as valuable as an animal at the same emotional and cognitive level? Does this seem plausible or implausible to you? Why or why not?
4. Rachels claims, "We have found no reason to support a policy of distinguishing, in principle, between the kind of consideration that should be accorded to humans and that which should be accorded to other animals." Review and assess the case Rachels has made for this claim. Is he right? Are there grounds he did not consider that would change matters?

You Decide!

1. SAVE THE WHALERS!

In May 1999, under permission granted by the International Whaling Commission and the Clinton administration, a group of Makah Indians slaughtered a gray whale as part of a tribal ritual. Whaling is a traditional practice of these Northwest coastal people, one they have been forbidden to exercise for 70 some years ever since the gray whale was hunted to near extinction by the whaling industry and subsequent killings were banned by the United States in 1937. Gray whales were removed from the endangered species list in 1994 and the Makah successfully sought permission to hunt them under a treaty signed with the federal government in 1855. They may kill up to 20 whales over the next four years only for "subsistence and ceremonial purposes." This means no commercial whaling.

Makah hunters stalked the 30-foot juvenile gray whale from traditional cedar canoes and used steel-tipped harpoons in their initial strike, but the whale was ultimately killed with several shots from a .50 caliber assault rifle and towed to shore by a motorized boat with triumphant hunters riding on the carcass.

For the Makah, killing the whale was a reclamation of their tribal heritage. They report a deep sense of kinship with their ancestors and the legends and songs of their culture now have new meaning. Some environmentalists protested the hunt.

Discussion Questions

1. Should the Makah be permitted to hunt gray whales for "subsistence and ceremonial purposes"?
2. Should there be limits on acceptable traditional practices of indigenous people allowed by the government? What if ritual human sacrifice was an important tribal ceremony? Suppose the tribe petitioned the government to kill ceremonially a few convicted prisoners on death row? (The killings would be done in accordance with ancient tribal laws of respect and dignity—prayers would be offered for the lives about to be taken.)
3. Is it possible to judge the moral standards of another culture?
4. Does the whale have a right not to be killed? Are the reasons for killing the whale trivial?

2. IVORY AND THE KILLING OF POACHERS

In 1989, the United Nations-sponsored Convention on International Trade in Endangered Species (CITIES) voted to put elephants on its most endangered species list, thus banning international sale of ivory and other elephant products such as hides. Before the ban on international ivory sales, some 2,000 elephants were killed each week, bringing the African elephant population from 1.3 million in the 1970s to about 600,000 in 1989. The ban on international sale of ivory put a halt to the slaughter. But in 1999, under heavy pressure from countries opposed to the CITIES ruling, most notably Zimbabwe, Botswana, and Namibia—countries that have lost many millions of dollars because of the ban on ivory sales—CITIES allowed a partial lifting of the ban. It permitted those countries to sell 60 tons of ivory to Japan, a country with a strong ivory market. Critics argued that permitting the sale will increase poaching of elephants, since the elaborate safeguards intended to permit only the sale of ivory from culled elephants and those who died natural deaths will be impossible to enforce. Apparently, the critics were right. According to reports from the Environmental Investigation Agency, an environmental advocacy group (www.eia-international.org) as well as other sources, poachers are again slaughtering elephants for their ivory.

None of this was going through Mengistu's mind as he surveyed the surrounding underbrush from his secluded spot on a hillside. A newly commissioned conservation officer in Zimbabwe's effort to curtail illegal poaching, he was aware that elephants were again being killed by poachers since CITIES lifted the total ban on ivory sales. Last year in the region under his jurisdiction, 29 elephants were killed, five times more than during the previous years when the CITIES ban on ivory sales was in place. He was also aware that his work was dangerous; the heavily armed poachers often fight those seeking to stop them. As Mengistu mulled over the sad situation that drives poor desperate villagers to poach elephants—the average monthly income in his district is $10—he noticed three young men moving carefully through the undercover. Poachers! He knew they were stalking the herd of elephants that passed through the area about an hour ago. As Mengistu fumbled for his radio to alert his reinforcements, who would surround the poachers to get them to surrender, it was hoped without a fight, he recalled the last time they tried to arrest a group of poachers. A firefight broke out and a conservation officer was killed along with several poachers. Maybe the prudent thing would be simply to sit quietly until the poachers came within range. Mengistu had a modern fully automatic weapon, so he had much more firepower than the poachers with their crude, though powerful, elephant guns. So he waited. The three poachers moved cautiously but efficiently through the brush, drawing ever closer. Mengistu raised his gun, took careful aim, waited a bit longer, and then fired three quick bursts into the poachers, killing them.

Discussion Questions

1. Was Mengistu morally justified in killing the elephant poachers?
2. Should there be capital punishment for convicted elephant poachers?
3. Does what the poachers need the money for change your assessment of what they are doing?
4. Should CITIES attempt to reinstate an absolute ban on sale of ivory? Would such a ban be a matter of imposing our moral beliefs on others? Why or why not?

3. "THOSE DAMN DEER!"

. . . shouted Richard storming into the house. "They ate all the new shrubbery we just planted—what was that, $300 wasn't it?" he asked his wife, Betty, who was busy at the table. "I can't believe it," he continued, "something has got to happen. I am just about fed up with the deer around here. Why don't they go live in the woods where they belong instead of in the middle of this community. These are the suburbs, there are cars and roads and shopping centers."

"And woods and lawns and golf courses," added Betty.

Deer had become a major headache for the entire area. The expensive landscaping and lush gardens of this upscale neighborhood offered a cornucopia of tasty things for deer to eat. The many golf courses and protected spaces, not to mention the parks and lawns—all things that made this a desirable area to live—made it desirable for the deer as well. Their numbers had been increasing dramatically. About the only thing that kept the population in check was collisions with automobiles, something that had been happening with greater frequency lately. Suburban deer are adaptable, fecund, and a source of consternation. Not only do they nibble shrubbery, cause automobile accidents (including some deaths), and harbor deer ticks, the main vector for Lyme disease, but they also provoke community controversy. People quickly become polarized on the issue: Some think the deer should be shot, while others feed them and put out salt licks.

Among the lethal means considered by the town for dealing with the problem were these: hire sharpshooters from the U.S. Department of Agriculture or permit specially certified suburban bow hunters to shoot deer quietly from portable stands in neighborhood trees. Non-lethal means involved either capturing the deer for transport elsewhere or trying an experimental contraceptive. Of the available alternatives, many community members favored suburban bow hunters. Federal sharpshooters were too expensive, and discharging firearms would be unacceptably disruptive. Capturing and transporting the deer elsewhere seemed like a good idea until people saw the cost of such a program. Moreover, many transported deer die from shock anyway. Experimental contraceptives were not a realistic solution in the short term, and it involved considerable cost as well.

A local bow hunting group had offered its services to the city for free. It certified its hunters on the model established by Bowhunt Associates, a Pennsylvania bow hunting group specializing in suburban deer hunting. Suburban bow hunters wear no camouflage since the deer are accustomed to people anyway. Hunters are not permitted to display deer taken or strap them to car hoods and they must hunt from portable stands in trees so that arrows are shot toward the ground. Permissible times to hunt are negotiated with the homeowners.

This was a tough decision for Richard. He was no animal rights activist, but he did not like the idea of killing deer with bows and arrows, since they would likely suffer a good bit. Moreover, he disliked the sport mentality of the hunters, since this just seemed like an excuse to kill deer, deer that were virtually tame. But nothing else presented itself as a plausible alternative.

Discussion Questions

1. Should Richard just modify his life and accept deer as a feature of the neighborhood?
2. Is Richard being overly sensitive in his concern for whatever suffering the deer will experience if they are hunted?
3. How should conflicts between human beings and wildlife be settled?

FURTHER READING ON POULTRY

1. *Poultry Science* (Animal Agriculture Series), M. E. Ensminger, 3rd edition, Interstate Publishers, Inc. Danville, IL, 1992.
2. *Poultry USA* (Trade Journal)
3. *Farm Animal Welfare: Social, Bioethical, and Research Issues,* Rollin, Bernard, 1995, Ames: Iowa State University Press.
4. *Chickens Under Contract: The US Broiler Industry Today,* Publication by The Humane Society of the United States, 2100 L St. NW. Washington, DC, 1998.
5. *Prisoned Chickens Poisoned Eggs,* Karon Davis, Book Publishing Co., Summertown, TN., 1996.

CHAPTER 6

Biocentrism: The Extension of Interests

MODERN TIMES: BRAVE NEW WORLD OF BIOTECHNOLOGY

You have probably heard about scientists genetically engineering bananas to produce vaccines, or monarch butterfly caterpillars reportedly dying from exposure to genetically altered pollen, or consumer protests against "Frankenfoods," prompting Frito-Lay, Gerber and other U.S. food companies publicly promise never to use genetically modified crops in their products. Genetic engineering is in the news almost daily. Pharmaceutical and agricultural corporations heavily invested in biotechnology seek to allay public concerns while various public interest groups and environmental organizations, such as Greenpeace, The Environmental Defense Fund, and the Union of Concerned Scientists take a dim view toward this burgeoning activity. (And burgeoning it is; just try an Internet search on biotechnology!) It seems as if all of a sudden we are faced with a visceral and divisive issue of global proportions.

Broadly interpreted, biotechnology is nothing new. We have been manipulating organisms for centuries to make products. Yeast for brewing beer and baking bread can be considered biotechnology. But modern biotechnology is different because it harnesses life processes at the most fundamental molecular levels to produce desired substances or functions. Enthusiastic supporters see enormous potential for improving our lives, confident that whatever problems engendered by this new technology can be solved; others are less sure, either because of moral or religious qualms about tinkering with life at such a basic level or because of a less sanguine appraisal of possible harmful consequences for the environment, other living organisms, and, of course, for ourselves. Similar reactions probably greet any new technology. This is not to suggest that we should be complacent, for modern biotechnology raises questions of extreme importance. But before we can explore those questions, we need to understand what modern biotechnology is.

Traditionally, crossbreeding was used to identify certain desirable traits in plants and animals, which would then be selected for further propagation. This can be tedious, especially for organisms that take a long time to reproduce, plus it is limited to organisms that can be crossbred. With modern biotechnology, genes from one organism can be directly inserted into a completely different species. For example, genes from cold-water fish can be put into tomatoes to make them resistant to freezing. No longer confined to crossbreeding as a way of producing useful plant and animal characteristics, the possibilities are virtually endless for mixing and matching genes from unrelated organisms. This aspect of biotechnology—called genetic engineering—holds the greatest promise and causes the most concern.

Genetically engineering plants and animals has moved from laboratory science to a multibillion-dollar industry within the past 20 years. Its commercial application is vast and promises to revolutionize all the life sciences, most notably medicine and agriculture. Because of its environmental implications, we shall focus on agricultural uses of genetically modified crops. More than 70 million acres of genetically modified crops are planted in the United State each year, and approximately 20 percent of corn grown today has been genetically modified. Without a doubt, we have entered a brave new world in our relationship with nature.

People have long noticed that different characteristics of plants and animals pass from generation to generation, supposing there was some vague mixing of features during reproduction. In 1865, the Austrian monk Gregor Mendel described laws governing the inheritance of features among peas. A trait that can be passed from generation to generation is called a gene, the basic unit of heredity. But this is a purely functional definition; What are genes? Since during cell division, DNA (deoxyribonucleic acid) makes copies of itself, which are transmitted to subsequent cells, scientists discovered that the substance within cells responsible for inheritance is DNA. So genes are segments of DNA. This remarkable realization identifies a purely theoretical concept—a gene—with something observable in cells.

Using special enzymes, scientists can cut various segments of DNA containing genes for a desired trait in one species and move that DNA segment into the DNA—the genome—of a different species, where it will be replicated along with normal cell division. If all goes according to plan, the new gene will be "expressed," that is, give rise in the plant to the trait controlled by that gene. The new gene can be introduced into the genome of the target plant in several ways. One way to produce "transgenic" plants is by piggybacking the new gene on a special bacterium that infects plants. The soil bacterium *Agrobacterium tumefaciens* attacks plant roots causing tumors to develop that contain bacterial DNA. Using viruses or chemical methods to first add a desired gene to the bacterium's DNA, subsequently infected plant tumor cells will contain bacterial DNA along with the newly introduced gene. Individual plant tumor cells can then be cultivated into plants whose seeds contain the new gene, as will succeeding generations of the plant. But not all plants are susceptible to infection by this bacterium, including important crops such as grasses and cereals. Another common method for introducing new genes into a plant's genome is by literally shooting microscopic metal particles coated with the new gene into plant cells with a gunpowder charge, lodging the particles just inside the cell wall. For reasons scientists do not understand, genes introduced in this fashion are incorporated into the cell's DNA. Individual cells are then grown into plants whose seeds form the basis of a new genetically modified crop. By inserting the genes for desirable traits from one plant species to another, crops can be engineered to tolerate certain herbicides and to resist frost, drought, insects, salinity, diseases, and other environmental pressures. Some truly bizarre combinations are possible: Inserting the firefly bioluminescence gene in tobacco plants causes them to glow.

Of the myriad possible genetic manipulations, herbicide tolerance and insect resistance are among the most widely developed. Plants have been genetically engineered to tolerate chemicals sprayed on fields to kill unwanted plants—weeds. This means farmers can apply herbicides freely without fear of damaging their crops. It sounds good in theory, but inevitably some weeds will resist the herbicides, necessitating spraying of even more herbicides as sturdier and sturdier weeds develop. Also, as noted by the authors in a standard textbook called *Plants, Genes, and Agriculture,*

> Some of the big agrichemical companies anticipate their greatest potential profits in selling farmers integrated packages of seeds, fertilizers, and pesticides. Most seed companies are owned by large agrichemical companies—a relatively recent development in the developed world—and the aim is to produce transgenic seeds that are compatible with the chemicals produced by the parent company. This strategy is likely to increase rather than decrease the reliance on agricultural chemicals. Furthermore, this trend exacerbates the evolution of the dominant agricultural system in the direction of a high-input agriculture, rather than a sustainable agriculture.
>
> —*Plants, Genes, and Agriculture*
> Chrispeers, Chrispeers & David Sadava, 1994, p. 430

Development of insect-resistant crops relies on incorporating a gene from the bacterium *Bacillus thuringiensis,* Bt for short, into the plant's genome. Bt crops produce a substance toxic to insects, initially minimizing the amount of insecticide needed to grow the crops. However, as with the overuse of herbicide-resistant plants, Bt crops subject insect pests to tremendous evolutionary pressure to develop resistance to the toxin. For Bt-engineered crops to remain effective, agricultural scientists recommend planting some non-Bt crops to maintain breeding populations of insects that will remain susceptible to the toxin. In some respects, this obviates the point of developing Bt crops since a portion of the crop will have to be grown for insects to eat anyway.

Since indiscriminate use of ordinary herbicides and insecticides will also promote the evolution of resistant strains of weeds and insects, these problems are not unique to genetically engineered crops. But these problems do show that genetically engineered crops are not a miracle breakthrough for agriculture nor does genetic engineering automatically mean having to use less agricultural chemicals, which is sometimes claimed as a distinct advantage for genetically engineered crops.

There are other worries about genetically engineered crops. What if the genetically altered plants crossbreed with wild relatives? If herbicide-tolerant or insect-resistant crops crossbreed with wild relatives, the wild plants could be very difficult to control. Other genetically engineered traits such as drought or salt resistance might similarly confer a distinct biological advantage on any wild relatives were crossbreeding to occur. The resulting "super weeds" might then upset established ecosystems by crowding out native species with effects that can ripple throughout a food web, since particular insects, birds, and other animals in an ecosystem have all evolved dependent upon a specific plant base.

Although extensive field tests of genetically engineered crops are conducted before seeds are released for commercial application, there is a huge difference between test farming and planting many millions of acres of a genetically altered crop worldwide. On the massive scale of commercial agriculture, the worries about crossbreeding of genetically modified crops with wild relatives should be taken seriously. A recent controversy exemplifies this problem. Hundreds of varieties of corn are native to Mexico. This diversity is important to agricultural scientists because it functions as a "gene bank" for developing new strains of corn. Mexico banned planting genetically modified (GM) corn in 1998 out of concern that genetic drift from GM corn might affect native varieties. But GM corn intended for consumption was evidently not covered by the ban and some was imported from the United States. Rather than consume the corn, Mexican peasants planted it instead. A huge scientific dispute broke out when, in a study published in the prestigious journal *Nature,* evidence of genetic markers from the GM corn was allegedly found in wild varieties. The authors' research methods were severely criticized by some members of the scientific community, prompting the editor to retract the article. However, according to further tests conducted by the Mexican government in early 2002, it now appears that the original article was correct (even if some of the research methods were flawed). This case promises to become infamous as exactly the sort of problem GM crops can pose. And similar cases of genetic drift from GM plants to wild relatives are bound to multiply as more and more GM crops make their way into agricultural use. Given the uncertainties involved, a conservative approach to GM crops is only prudent.

The environmental movement has taught us that tinkering with ecosystems can have unanticipated consequences, consequences that are not adequately met by yet another technological fix. In a particularly striking instance of such hubris, early concerns that insect-resistant crops would also affect "good" insects, not just the "bad" ones, attempts were made to engineer toxic resistance into the "good" insects—and so we begin a race reminiscent of the scene in Walt Disney's "The Sorcerer's Apprentice" where Mickey Mouse's effort to destroy the brooms only creates more of them.

What, then, should we make of genetically engineered crops? It is far too simplistic to be for them or against them, though that is how the public debate is sometimes cast. The issues are complex and not adequately reduced to sound bites. Moreover, public discussion presupposes a minimal understanding of the science involved, perhaps a major hurdle when a majority of our society does not know that dinosaurs existed before human beings or that continents ride on tectonic plates. Genetically engineered crops are here to stay, and they can be used to great advantage. As with any technology, we need to distinguish between proper and improper application. But what counts as proper and improper use of the technology ought not to be determined by a small circle of insiders.

Because genetic engineering is so new, regulatory authorities such as the Environmental Protection Agency, the U.S. Department of Agriculture, and the Food and Drug Administration have not coordinated their efforts very well, according to a committee of the National Research Council. Perry Adkisson, chancellor emeritus and distinguished professor emeritus at Texas A&M University, chair of the committee, wrote, "These agencies should monitor the ecological impacts of GM crops on a long-term basis in order to detect any problems that may not have been predicted from tests conducted during the registration and approval process. And the regulatory process should be more open and accessible to help the public understand the benefits and risks associated with this new technology." (*Star Tribune,* May 10, 2000). Proponents and opponents of genetically engineered crops should thus be able to agree on the need for strong independent environmentally sensitive regulations governing their use.

THE SCOPE OF MORALITY

A recurring question in environmental ethics is over the extent of the **moral community.** Which things have direct moral standing and why? Our discussion of genetically engineered plants looked at some implications of their genetic manipulation for our well-being, but might plants also have their own well-being that we should consider in our moral deliberations? As we have seen, Western moral philosophy typically draws the circle of moral standing tightly around our own species. Anthropocentrism, the view that all and only members of the class *Homo sapiens* are of direct moral significance, is hard to defend rationally, as our study of animal ethics demonstrated (Chapter 5). Whatever criterion we use to try to restrict direct moral standing to human beings will either apply to some animals or fail to cover all human beings. Unless we are willing to admit that some human beings—the brain damaged, senile, deranged, and so on—have no moral status, it seems that we must acknowledge the moral importance of comparable interests irrespective of species membership. But are we now on a slippery slope? Must we continue to expand the moral community beyond animals to include plants too?

The debate about the moral standing of animals was driven by interests shared by human beings and animals, notably, an interest in not suffering. The capacity to suffer depends upon some level of mentality; no mentality means no interest in not suffering. But many entities considered in environmental philosophy are devoid of mentality: plants, forests, species, and ecosystems, to name a few. If the scope of the moral community is defined by the capacity to suffer—"the insuperable line" as Bentham called it—then only sentient beings are possible objects of direct moral consideration. Everything else belongs in the category of "thing."

Consider a house. A house is a thing. It is important to maintain a house, repair the gutters and paint it, but only because it serves our interests when it is comfortable and secure. The condition of a house is irrelevant to the house itself. Whether it collapses tomorrow or stands for 100 years matters only to us. It is only with respect to us that a house has value and its value is exhausted by its instrumentality. What counts as good or bad for a house is defined by our interests, for it has no good of its own with respect to which events can even be classified one way or the other. Were there no people to care about the house (or other valuers for whom the house could have value), whether the roof leaked or not would be a matter of indifference. As a thing in the full sense of the word, a house lacks self-definition, a good of its own with respect to which conditions could even qualify as harms or benefits; without us it is just a pile of wood.

The question of the scope of morality can thus be recast as a question of where thinghood stops and moral patiency begins. By "moral patient" I mean something with direct moral standing. We are asking about the outer limits of direct moral consideration; what is the minimum something must be like even to get into the moral ballpark? Since morality is essentially concerned with the assessment of harms and benefits, the boundary of the moral will include all and only those entities with interests that can be affected for better or worse by our actions. As the philosopher Joel Feinberg put it, "A mere thing, however valuable to others, has no good of its own. The explanation of that fact, I suspect, consists in the fact that mere things have no conative life: no conscious wishes, desires, and hopes; or urges and impulses; or unconscious drives, aims, and goals; or latent tendencies, direction of growth, and natural fulfillments. Interests must be compounded somehow out of conations; hence mere things have no interests." And if mere things have no interests, then mere things have no sake for which we could act, nothing that could be conceived as their due or worthy of our recognition as moral agents.

Since we can distinguish between how much something counts and whether it counts at all, asking about the boundary of the moral is not the same as asking about the degree of moral significance something might have. There is no reason to think that all things that meet the minimum to count morally count morally the same. Even if rats, for example, as sentient beings have interests, your life is arguably of greater moral significance than a rat's. It will be important to keep this distinction in mind as we reflect on the very minimum necessary for something to cross the line from true thinghood to the first intimations of direct moral standing.

SENTIENCE AND MORAL STANDING

Is there any reason to think that interests must be limited to sentient beings? The extension of interests beyond anthropocentrism to include all sentient beings might be just the first step in a dramatic expansion of the moral community. We can distinguish between interests that presuppose mentality and interests that do not, since you can obviously have an interest in something that is not in your interest, smoking, for example. You might desire to smoke but smoking is not good for you. The idea of having a good that is logically independent of desire is the key move because it is then possible for something to have its own good irrespective of whether it has wants at all. Plants, for example, might have interests in the sense of conditions that are good or bad for them, even though they have no mental life.

But can we separate having a good from having states of mind? We do speak of conditions that are good for plants, meaning that those conditions contribute to their flourishing. It seems very much as if individual plants have a sake for which we can act, that they have a good of their own that we can either promote or hinder by our actions. We can even adopt their point of view. I am not suggesting that plants have a point of view, but that we can see the world from a plant's perspective by determining which conditions promote or hinder its flourishing. Sunlight is good, no water is bad. And what makes these things good or bad has nothing to do with us; their goodness or badness is defined solely with respect to the plant's own good. It seems, therefore, that plants are not mere things; they can intelligibly be ascribed interests even though they lack mentality. Since plants have a good of their own for which we can act, they apparently cross the threshold into the realm of the moral. How much moral significance we are to accord plant interests is another matter. Perhaps it is vanishingly small compared to the interests of sentient beings. But recall that we are here concerned only with the boundaries of the moral community, not the question of moral significance.

THE MACHINE OBJECTION

However, once we accord interests to living things in virtue of their having a good of their own irrespective of sentience, it becomes hard to see why we should stop there. What about machines; can they have interests too? Think of a refrigerator. It has an internal structure designed to respond to various temperatures; it seeks to maintain a constant temperature through feedback loops and internal controls, adjusting accordingly. How is the refrigerator so different from, say, a tree? And would it not be absurd to think that if plants can have interests, so can refrigerators?

If we note the obvious, namely, that the tree is alive and the refrigerator is not, then the next question is: What is it to be alive? We like to think that there is an irreducibly basic difference between living organisms and the inert physical world. **Vitalism** is the view that life cannot be explained in mechanistic or biochemical terms alone. But what else is needed to account for life besides a complete biochemical explanation is left a mystery. Appeal to a "life force," for example, is completely unhelpful since scientific explanations for phenomena must limit themselves to empirical concepts and the notion of a life force is not an empirical concept. Popular in the 19th century, vitalism has been abandoned by modern biologists in favor of mechanistic explanations for life. At root, a mechanistic explanation for life is one that refers only to complex arrangements of chemicals and their interactions. So unless we want to be vitalists, we must admit that biological life is an exceedingly complex arrangement of interlocking biochemical subsystems. And once we do that, the difference between the tree and the refrigerator is really only a matter of degree.

That the fundamental difference between machines and living organisms is just degree of complexity is an uncomfortable thought. Perhaps we can distinguish between the refrigerator and the tree by noting that the tree is made of carbon and the refrigerator is made of metal. True, but why should that difference matter to whether or not something can have interests? Is focusing on composition as a morally relevant difference a bit like focusing on species membership or, among human beings, on gender or race? Here is a thought experiment: Suppose you discovered that your best friend is made of a different substance than you. Would that matter? It would be a very interesting scientific fact, but it is hard to see why it should make a moral difference. Similarly, it is hard to see why the material out of which the tree is made should matter morally. It is true that the tree is made of carbon and the refrigerator is made of metal, but they share important functional similarities irrespective of what they are made. They are both goal-directed mechanisms that seek to maintain a certain internal state in response to external conditions. Their goal-directedness allows us to see the world from their point of view, as it were. Certain conditions are conducive to the goal, others not.

But the tree, we might say, has a good of its own, whereas the refrigerator does not. The refrigerator was designed to serve our purposes, so what even counts as its good is parasitic on our good. The tree, by contrast, has its own good independent of our good. Recall that having one's own good is the feature, cited above, that is supposed to distinguish mere things from entities with interests. Will this allow us to distinguish between the tree and the refrigerator? It is true that the tree has a good of its own whereas the refrigerator does not. What counts as good or bad for the refrigerator is linked to our good, but why is having a good of one's own rather than a parasitic good decisive for having interests? Suppose we could genetically engineer completely new forms of life to suit our purposes. Such organisms would be artifacts just like the refrigerator. Would these creatures then not have interests simply because they were wholly designed to meet our needs? Does a genetically engineered pig still have an interest in not suffering or a genetically engineered plant an interest in sunlight? Alternatively, suppose it turned out that we were created by God to serve some larger purpose, that our good is not intrinsically our own but determined by something external to us, just as the refrigerator's good is determined by our desires. Would that then mean that we do not have interests? Surely not. Our good would not be "our own," but that seems irrelevant to whether or not we have interests.

It appears that any goal-directed system can be conceived as having a good defined with respect to its goal, and thus interests with respect to achieving its good. Conditions that contribute to achieving the goal are good from its point of view. Whether the goal is intrinsic or depends on some other entity with its own good is irrelevant. All that is necessary for the ascription of interests is that the entity is "trying" to do something, as the refrigerator is trying to maintain a constant temperature by responding to the hot casserole dish you just placed in it.

Yet something has gone very wrong if we have to admit refrigerators into the moral community, even a little bit. Trees maybe, perhaps even sophisticated machines such as one sees in science fiction movies, were they to exist, but not refrigerators! Recall that we got into this situation by prying interests free from mentality. Doing so allowed for an expansion of the moral community to include, plausibly perhaps, all living things irrespective of whether they have any states of mind. This view is called '**biocentrism,**' since being alive is taken as the fundamental criterion for direct moral standing. The problem now is to figure out a way of keeping simple machines that are functionally similar to living things from acquiring moral standing as well.

THE READINGS

The readings for this chapter explore the limits of the moral community. It is thus another perspective on a question that we have been building on throughout the book, namely, what is the criterion for direct moral standing? Here we shall consider articles that propose to answer that question in terms of simply being alive, irrespective of sentience.

PAUL TAYLOR

The Ethics of Respect for Nature

Paul Taylor is emeritus professor of philosophy at Brooklyn College, City University of New York. In this article, "The Ethics of Respect for Nature," which summarizes his influential book of the same title, Taylor argues for the direct moral significance of all living things. Key to understanding his position is grasping what he means by the "biocentric outlook," which itself has four components. The biocentric outlook is a mix of scientific insights and moral norms, which, if accepted, underwrites the attitude of respect for individual living things. Crucial to the biocentric outlook is a denial of human superiority. If we try to argue that human beings are superior to other living things because we are rational, or can think,

---

Paul Taylor, "The Ethics of Respect for Nature," *Environmental Ethics,* vol 3, no. 3 (Fall 1981), pp. 197–218. Reprinted by permission.

or speak, Taylor presses the question of why that particular feature should be taken as a mark of superiority. After all, plants can photosynthesize, fish can breathe under water, and birds can fly. Why not take those properties as conferring superiority? Evidently, then, we beg the question when we assume that rationality or any other human quality is a mark of superiority. We pick self-serving criteria in an attempt to show our superiority over other life forms. Rejection of human superiority leads to species impartiality. Taylor's view can thus be called biocentric egalitarianism.

CRITICAL READING QUESTIONS

1. According to Taylor, to what do we have prima facie moral obligations?
2. As Taylor sees it, what two concepts are essential to adopting a life-centered ethic?
3. Why does Taylor not think that sentience is the boundary of the moral?
4. Why should moral agents regard wild living things as possessing inherent worth, according to Taylor?
5. What role does having a good of one's own play in Taylor's position?
6. How does Taylor distinguish his position from one centered on love of nature? In what way does this make his a genuinely moral view?
7. What are the components of the biocentric outlook and what is the relation between the biocentric outlook and the attitude of respect for nature?
8. What does Taylor mean by regarding organisms as "teleological centers of life"? Why is this important for his view?
9. How does Taylor argue that human beings cannot legitimately maintain their superiority over other living things?
10. What does Taylor's discussion of class structure, classical Greek humanism, Cartesian dualism, and the Great Chain of Being have to do with the denial of human superiority?

I. HUMAN-CENTERED AND LIFE-CENTERED SYSTEMS OF ENVIRONMENTAL ETHICS

In this paper I show how the taking of a certain ultimate moral attitude toward nature, which I call "respect for nature," has a central place in the foundations of a life-centered system of environmental ethics. I hold that a set of moral norms (both standards of character and rules of conduct) governing human treatment of the natural world is a rationally grounded set if and only if, first, commitment to those norms is a practical entailment of adopting the attitude of respect for nature as an ultimate moral attitude, and second, the adopting of that attitude on the part of all rational agents can itself be justified. When the basic characteristics of the attitude of respect for nature are made clear, it will be seen that a life-centered system of environmental ethics need not be holistic or organicist in its conception of the kinds of entities that are deemed the appropriate objects of moral concern and consideration. Nor does such a system require that the concepts of ecological homeostasis, equilibrium, and integrity provide us with normative principles from which could be derived (with the addition of factual knowledge) our obligations with regard to natural ecosystems. The "balance of nature" is not itself a moral norm, however important may be the role it plays in our general outlook on the natural world that underlies the attitude of respect for nature. I argue that finally it is the good (well-being, welfare) of individual organisms, considered as entities having inherent worth, that determines our moral relations with the Earth's wild communities of life.

In designating the theory to be set forth as life-centered, I intend to contrast it with all anthropocentric views. According to the latter, human actions affecting the natural environment and its nonhuman inhabitants are right (or wrong) by either of two criteria: They have consequences which are favorable (or unfavorable) to human well-being, or they are consistent (or inconsistent) with the system of norms that protect and implement human rights. From this human-centered standpoint it is to humans and only to humans that all duties are ultimately owed. We may have responsibilities *with regard* to the natural ecosystems and biotic communities of our planet, but these responsibilities are in every case based on the contingent fact that our treatment of those ecosystems and communities of life can further the realization of human values and/or human rights. We have no obligation to promote or protect the good of nonhuman living things, independently of this contingent fact.

A life-centered system of environmental ethics is opposed to human-centered ones precisely on this point. From the perspective of a life-centered theory, we have prima facie moral obligations that are owed to wild plants and animals themselves as members of the Earth's biotic community. We are morally bound (other things being equal) to protect or promote their good for *their* sake. Our duties to respect the integrity of natural ecosystems, to preserve endangered species, and to avoid environmental pollution stem from the fact that these are ways in which we can help make it possible for wild species populations to achieve and maintain a healthy existence in a natural state. Such obligations are due those living things out of recognition of their inherent worth. They are entirely additional to and independent of the obligations we owe to our fellow humans. Although many of the actions that fulfill one set of obligations will also fulfill the other, two different grounds of obligation are involved. Their well-being, as well as human well-being, is something to be realized *as an end in itself.*

If we were to accept a life-centered theory of environmental ethics, a profound reordering of our moral universe would take place. We would begin to look at the whole of the Earth's biosphere in a new light. Our duties with respect to the "world" of nature would be seen as making prima facie claims upon us to be balanced against our duties with respect to the "world" of human civilization. We could no longer simply take the human point of view and consider the effects of our actions exclusively from the perspective of our own good.

II. THE GOOD OF A BEING AND THE CONCEPT OF INHERENT WORTH

What would justify acceptance of a life-centered system of ethical principles? In order to answer this it is first necessary to make clear the fundamental moral attitude that underlies and makes intelligible the commitment to live by such a system. It is then necessary to examine the considerations that would justify any rational agent's adopting that moral attitude.

Two concepts are essential to the taking of a moral attitude of the sort in question. A being which does not "have" these concepts, that is, which is unable to grasp their meaning and conditions of applicability, cannot be said to have the attitude as part of its moral outlook. These concepts are, first, that of the good (well-being, welfare) of a living thing, and second, the idea of an entity possessing inherent worth. I examine each concept in turn.

1. Every organism, species population, and community of life has a good of its own which moral agents can intentionally further or damage by their actions. To say that an entity has a good of its own is simply to say that, without reference to any *other* entity, it can be benefited or harmed. One can act in its overall interest or contrary to its overall interest, and environmental conditions can be good for it (advantageous to it) or bad for it (disadvantageous to it). What is good for an entity is what "does it good" in the sense of enhancing or preserving its life and well-being. What is bad for an entity is something that is detrimental to its life and well-being.[1]

We can think of the good of an individual nohuman organism as consisting in the full development of its biological powers. Its good is realized to the extent that it is strong and healthy. It possesses whatever capacities it needs for successfully coping with its environment and so preserving its existence throughout the various stages of the normal life cycle of its species. The good of a population or community of such individuals consists in the population or community maintaining itself from generation to generation as a coherent system of genetically and ecologically related organisms whose average good is at an optimum level for the given environment. Mere *average good* means that the degree of realization of the good of *individual organisms* in the population or community is, on average, greater than would be the case under any other ecologically functioning order of interrelations among those species populations in the given ecosystem.)

The idea of a being having a good of its own, as I understand it, does not entail that the being must have interests or take an interest in what affects its life for better or for worse. We can act in a being's interest or contrary to its interest without its being interested in what we are doing to it in the sense of wanting or not wanting us to do it. It may, indeed, be wholly unaware that favorable and unfavorable events are taking place in its life. I take it that trees, for example, have no knowledge or desires or feelings. Yet it is undoubtedly the case that trees can be harmed or benefited by our actions. We can crush their roots by running a bulldozer too close to them. We can see to it that they get adequate nourishment and moisture by fertilizing and watering the soil around them. Thus we can help or hinder them in the realization of their good. It is the good of trees themselves that is thereby affected. We can similarly act so as to further the good of an entire tree population of a certain species (say, all the redwood trees in a California valley) or the good of a whole community of plant life in a given wilderness area, just as we can do harm to such a population or community.

When construed in this way, the concept of a being's good is not coextensive with sentience or the capacity for feeling pain. William Frankena has argued for a general theory of environmental ethics in which the ground of a creature's being worthy of moral consideration is its sentience. I have offered some criticisms of this view elsewhere, but the full refutation of such a position, it seems to me, finally depends on the positive reasons for accepting a life-centered theory of the kind I am defending in this essay.[2]

It should be noted further that I am leaving open the question of whether machines—in particular, those which are not only goal-directed, but also self-regulating—can properly be said to have a good of their own.[3] Since I am concerned only with human treatment of wild organisms, species populations, and communities of life as they occur in our planet's natural ecosystems, it is to those entities alone that the concept "having a good of its own" will here be applied. I am not denying that other living things, whose genetic origin and environmental conditions have been produced, controlled, and manipulated by humans for human ends, do have a good of their own in the same sense as do wild plants and animals. It is not my purpose in this essay, however, to set out or defend the principles that should guide our conduct with regard to their good. It is only insofar as their production and use by humans have good or ill effects upon natural ecosystems and their wild inhabitants that the ethics of respect for nature comes into play.

2. The second concept essential to the moral attitude of respect for nature is the idea of inherent worth. We take that attitude toward wild living things (individuals, species populations, or whole biotic communities) when and only when we regard them as entities possessing inherent worth. Indeed, it is only because they are conceived in this way that moral agents can think of themselves as having validly binding duties, obligations, and responsibilities that are *owed* to them as their *due*. I am not at this juncture arguing why they *should* be so regarded; I consider it at length below. But so regarding them is a presupposition of our taking the attitude of respect toward them and accordingly understanding ourselves as bearing certain moral relations to them. This can be shown as follows: What does it mean to regard an entity that has a good of its own as possessing inherent worth? Two general principles are involved: the principle of moral consideration and the principle of intrinsic value.

According to the principle of moral consideration, wild living things are deserving of the concern and consideration of all moral agents simply in virtue of their being members of the Earth's community of life. From the moral point of view their good must be taken into account whenever it is affected for better or worse by the conduct of rational agents. This holds no matter what species the creature belongs to. The good of each is to be accorded some value and so acknowledged as having some weight in the deliberations of all rational agents. Of course, it may be necessary for such agents to act in ways contrary to the good of this or that particular organism or group of organisms in order to further the good of others, including the good of humans. But the principle of moral consideration prescribes that, with respect to each being an entity having its own good, every individual is deserving of consideration.

The principle of intrinsic value states that, regardless of what kind of entity it is in other respects, if it is a member of the Earth's community of life, the realization of its good is something *intrinsically* valuable. This means that its good is prima facie worthy of being preserved or promoted as an end in itself and for the sake of the entity whose good it is. Insofar as we regard any organism, species population, or life community as an entity having inherent worth, we believe that it must never be treated as if it were a mere object or thing whose entire value lies in being instrumental to the good of some other entity. The well-being of each is judged to have value in and of itself.

Combining these two principles, we can now define what it means for a living thing or group of living things to possess inherent worth. To say that it possesses inherent worth is to say that its good is deserving of the concern and consideration of all moral agents, and that the realization of its good has intrinsic value, to be pursued as an end in itself and for the sake of the entity whose good it is.

The duties owed to wild organisms, species populations, and communities of life in the Earth's natural ecosystems are grounded on their inherent worth. When rational, autonomous agents regard such entities as possessing inherent worth, they place intrinsic value on the realization of their good and so hold themselves responsible for performing actions that will have this effect and for refraining from actions having the contrary effect.

III. THE ATTITUDE OF RESPECT FOR NATURE

Why should moral agents regard wild living things in the natural world as possessing inherent worth? To answer this question we must first take into account the fact that, when rational, autonomous agents subscribe to the principles of moral consideration and intrinsic value and so conceive of wild living things as having that kind of worth, such agents are *adopting a certain ultimate moral attitude toward the natural world.* This is the attitude I call "respect for nature." It parallels the attitude of respect for persons in human ethics. When we adopt the attitude of respect for persons as the proper (fitting, appropriate) attitude to take toward all persons as persons, we consider the fulfillment of the basic interests of each individual to have intrinsic value. We thereby make a moral commitment to live a certain kind of life in relation to other persons. We place ourselves under the direction of a system of standards and rules that we consider validly binding on all moral agents as such.[4]

Similarly, when we adopt the attitude of respect for nature as an ultimate moral attitude we make a commitment to live by certain normative principles. These principles constitute the rules of conduct and standards of character that are to govern our treatment of the natural world. This is, first, an *ultimate* commitment because it is not derived from any higher norm. The attitude of respect for nature is not grounded on some other, more general, or more fundamental attitude. It sets the total framework for our responsibilities toward the natural world. It can be justified, as I show below, but its justification cannot consist in referring to a more general attitude or a more basic normative principle.

Second, the commitment is a *moral* one because it is understood to be a disinterested matter of principle. It is this feature that distinguishes the attitude of respect for nature from the set of feelings and dispositions that comprise the love of nature. The latter stems from one's personal interest in and response to the natural world. Like the affectionate feelings we have toward certain individual human beings, one's love of nature is nothing more than the particular way one feels about the natural environment and its wild inhabitants. And just as our love for an individual person differs from our respect for all persons as such (whether we happen to love them or not), so love of nature differs from respect for nature. Respect for nature is an attitude we believe all moral agents ought to have simply as moral agents, regardless of whether or not they also love nature. Indeed, we have not truly taken the attitude of respect for nature ourselves unless we believe this. To put it in a Kantian way, to adopt the attitude of respect for nature is to take a stance that one wills it to be a universal law for all rational beings. It is to hold that stance categorically, as being validly applicable to every moral agent without exception, irrespective of whatever personal feelings toward nature such an agent might have or might lack.

Although the attitude of respect for nature is in this sense a disinterested and universalizable attitude, anyone who does adopt it has certain steady, more or less permanent dispositions. These dispositions, which are themselves to be considered disinterested and universalizable, comprise three interlocking sets: dispositions to seek certain ends, dispositions to carry on one's practical reasoning and deliberation in a certain way, and dispositions to have certain feelings. We may accordingly analyze the attitude of respect for nature into the following components. (a) The disposition to aim at, and to take steps to bring about, as final and disinterested ends, the promoting and protecting of the good of organisms, species populations, and life communities in natural ecosystems. (These ends are "final" in not being pursued as means to further ends. They are "disinterested" in being independent of the self-interest of the agent.) (b) The disposition to consider actions that tend to realize those ends to be prima facie obligatory *because* they have that tendency. (c) The disposition to experience positive and negative feelings toward states of affairs in the world *because* they are favorable or unfavorable to the good of organisms, species populations, and life communities in natural ecosystems.

The logical connection between the attitude of respect for nature and the duties of a life-centered system of environmental ethics can now be made clear. Insofar as one sincerely takes that attitude and so has the three sets of dispositions, one will at the same time be disposed to comply with certain rules of duty (such as nonmaleficence and noninterference) and with standards of character (such as fairness and benevolence) that determine the obligations and virtues of moral agents with regard to the Earth's wild living things. We can say that the actions one performs and the character traits one develops in fulfilling these moral requirements are the way one *expresses* or *embodies* the attitude in one's conduct and character. In his famous essay, "Justice as Fairness," John Rawls describes the rules of the duties of human morality (such as fidelity, gratitude, honesty, and justice) as "forms of conduct in which recognition of others as persons is manifested."[5] I hold that the rules of duty governing our treatment of the natural world and its inhabitants are forms of conduct in which the attitude of respect for nature is manifested.

IV. THE JUSTIFIABILITY OF THE ATTITUDE OF RESPECT FOR NATURE

I return to the question posed earlier, which has not yet been answered: why *should* moral agents regard wild living things as possessing inherent worth? I now argue that the only way we can answer this question is by showing how adopting the attitude of respect for nature is justified for all moral agents. Let us suppose that we were able to establish that there are good reasons for adopting the attitude, reasons which are intersubjectively valid for every rational agent. If there are such reasons, they would justify anyone's having the three sets of dispositions mentioned above as constituting what it means to have the attitude. Since these include the disposition to promote or protect the good of wild living things as a disinterested and ultimate end, as well as the disposition to perform actions for the reason that they tend to realize that end, we see that such dispositions commit a person to the principles of moral consideration and intrinsic value. To be disposed to further, as an end in itself, the good of any entity in nature just because it is that kind of entity, is to be disposed to give consideration to *every* such entity and to place intrinsic value on the realization of its good. Insofar as we subscribe to these two principles we regard living things as possessing inherent worth. Subscribing to the principle is what it *means* to so regard them. To justify the attitude of respect for nature, then, is to justify commitment to these principles and thereby to justify regarding wild creatures as possessing inherent worth.

We must keep in mind that inherent worth is not some mysterious sort of objective property belonging to living things that can be discovered by empirical observation or scientific investigation. To ascribe inherent worth to an entity is not to describe it by citing some feature discernible by sense perception or inferable by inductive reasoning. Nor is there a logically necessary connection between the concept of a being having a good of its own and the concept of inherent worth. We do not contradict ourselves by asserting that an entity that has a good of its own lacks inherent worth. In order to show that such an entity "has" inherent worth we must give good reasons for ascribing that kind of value to it (placing that kind of value upon it, conceiving of it to be valuable in that way). Although it is humans (persons, valuers) who must do the valuing, for the ethics of respect for nature, the value so ascribed is not a human value. That is to say, it is not a value derived from considerations regarding human well-being or human rights. It is a value that is ascribed to nonhuman animals and plants themselves, independently of their relationship to what humans judge to be conducive to their own good.

Whatever reasons, then, justify our taking the attitude of respect for nature as defined above are also reasons that show why we *should* regard the living things of the natural world as possessing inherent worth. We saw earlier that, since the attitude is an ultimate one, it cannot be derived from a more fundamental attitude nor shown to be a special case of a more general one. On what sort of grounds, then, can it be established?

The attitude we take toward living things in the natural world depends on the way we look at them, on what kind of beings we conceive them to be, and on how we understand the relations we bear to them. Underlying and supporting our attitude is a certain *belief system* that constitutes a particular worldview or outlook on nature and the place of human life in it. To give good reasons for adopting the attitude of respect for nature, then, we must first articulate the belief system which underlies and supports that attitude. If it appears that the belief system is internally coherent and well-ordered, and if, as far as we can now tell, it is consistent with all known scientific truths relevant to our knowledge of the object of the attitude (which in this case includes the whole set of the Earth's natural ecosystems and their communities of life), then there remains the task of indicating why scientifically informed and rational thinkers with a developed capacity of reality awareness can find it acceptable as a way of conceiving of the natural world and our place in it. To the extent we can do this we provide at least a reasonable argument for accepting the belief system and the ultimate moral attitude it supports.

I do not hold that such a belief system can be *proven* to be true, either inductively or deductively. As we shall see, not all of its components can be stated in the form of empirically verifiable propositions. Nor is its internal order governed by purely logical relationships. But the system as a whole, I contend, constitutes a coherent, unified, and rationally acceptable "picture" or "map" of a total world. By examining each of its main components and seeing how they fit together, we obtain a scientifically informed and well-ordered conception of nature and the place of humans in it.

This belief system underlying the attitude of respect for nature I call (for want of a better name) "the biocentric outlook on nature." Since it is not wholly analyzable into empirically confirmable assertions, it should not be thought of as simply a compendium of the biological sciences concerning our planet's ecosystems. It might best be described as a philosophical worldview, to distinguish it from a scientific theory or explanatory system. However, one of its major tenets is the great lesson we have learned from the science of ecology: the interdependence of all living things in an organically unified order whose balance and stability are necessary conditions for the realization of the good of its constituent biotic communities.

Before turning to an account of the main components of the biocentric outlook, it is convenient here to set forth the overall structure of my theory of environmental ethics as it has now emerged. The ethics of respect for nature is made up of three basic elements: a belief system, an ultimate moral attitude, and a set of rules of duty and standards of character. These elements are connected with each other in the following manner. The belief system provides a certain outlook on nature which supports and makes intelligible an autonomous agent's adopting, as an ultimate moral attitude, the attitude of respect for nature. It supports and makes intelligible the attitude in the sense that, when an autonomous agent understands its moral relations to the natural world in terms of this outlook, it recognizes the attitude of respect to be the only *suitable* or *fitting* attitude to take toward all wild forms of life in the Earth's biosphere. Living things are now viewed as *the appropriate objects of the attitude of respect* and are accordingly regarded as entities possessing inherent worth. One then places intrinsic value on the promotion and protection of their good. As a consequence of this, one makes a moral commitment to abide by a set of rules of duty and to fulfill (as far as one can by one's own efforts) certain standards of good character. Given one's adoption of the attitude of respect, one makes that moral commitment because one considers those rules and standards to be validly binding on all moral agents. They are seen as embodying forms of conduct and character structures in which the attitude of respect for nature is manifested.

This three-part complex which internally orders the ethics of respect for nature is symmetrical with a theory of human ethics grounded on respect for persons. Such a theory includes, first, a conception of oneself and others as persons, that is, as centers of autonomous choice. Second, there is the attitude of respect for persons as persons. When this is adopted as an ultimate moral attitude it involves the disposition to treat every person as having inherent worth or "human dignity." Every human being, just in virtue of her or his humanity, is understood to be worthy of moral consideration, and intrinsic value is placed on the autonomy and well-being of each. This is what Kant meant by conceiving of persons as ends in themselves. Third, there is an ethical system of duties which are acknowledged to be owed by everyone to everyone. These duties are forms of conduct in which public recognition is given to each individual's inherent worth as a person.

This structural framework for a theory of human ethics is meant to leave open the issue of consequentialism (utilitarianism) versus **nonconsequentialism** (deontology). That issue concerns the particular kind of system of rules defining the duties of moral agents toward persons. Similarly, I am leaving open in this paper the question of what particular kind of system of rules defines our duties with respect to the natural world.

V. THE BIOCENTRIC OUTLOOK ON NATURE

The biocentric outlook on nature has four main components. (1) Humans are thought of as members of the Earth's community of life, holding that membership on the same terms as apply to all the nonhuman members. (2) The Earth's natural ecosystems as a totality are seen as a complex web of interconnected elements, with the sound biological functioning of each being dependent on the sound biological functioning of the others. (This is the component referred to above as the great lesson that the science of ecology has taught us.) (3) Each individual organism is conceived of as a teleological center of life, pursuing its own good in its own way. (4) Whether we are concerned with standards of merit or with the concept of inherent worth, the claim that humans by their very nature are superior to other species is a groundless claim and, in the light of elements (1), (2), and (3) above, must be rejected as nothing more than an irrational bias in our own favor.

The conjunction of these four ideas constitutes the biocentric outlook on nature. In the remainder of this paper I give a brief account of the first three components, followed by a more detailed analysis of the fourth. I then conclude by indicating how this outlook provides a way of justifying the attitude of respect for nature.

VI. HUMANS AS MEMBERS OF THE EARTH'S COMMUNITY OF LIFE

We share with other species a common relationship to the Earth. In accepting the biocentric outlook we take the fact of our being an animal species to be a fundamental feature of our existence. We consider it an essential aspect of "the human condition." We do not deny the differences between ourselves and other species, but we keep in the forefront of our consciousness the fact that in relation to our planet's natural ecosystems we are but one species population among many. Thus we acknowledge our origin in the very same evolutionary process that gave rise to all other species and we recognize ourselves to be confronted with similar environmental challenges to those that confront them. The laws of genetics, of natural selection, and of adaptation apply equally to all of us as biological creatures. In this light we consider ourselves as one with them, not set apart from them. We, as well as they, must face certain basic conditions of existence that impose requirements on us for our survival and well-being. Each animal and plant is like us in having a good of its own. Although our human good (what is of true value in human life, including the exercise of individual autonomy in choosing our own particular value systems) is not like the good of a nonhuman animal or plant, it can no more be realized than their good can without the biological necessities for survival and physical health.

When we look at ourselves from the evolutionary point of view, we see that not only are we very recent arrivals on Earth, but that our emergence as a new species on the planet was originally an event of no particular importance to the entire scheme of things. The Earth was teeming with life long before we appeared. Putting the point metaphorically, we are relative newcomers, entering a home that has been the residence of others for hundreds of millions of years, a home that must now be shared by all of us together.

The comparative brevity of human life on Earth may be vividly depicted by imagining the geological time scale in spatial terms. Suppose we start with algae, which have been around for at least 600 million years. (The earliest protozoa actually predated this by several *billion* years.) If the time that algae have been here were represented by the length of a football field (300 feet), then the period during which sharks have been swimming in the world's oceans and spiders have been spinning their webs would occupy three quarters of the length of the field; reptiles would show up at about the center of the field; mammals would cover the last third of the field; hominids (mammals of the family *Hominidae*) the last two feet; and the species *Homo sapiens* the last six inches.

Whether this newcomer is able to survive as long as other species remains to be seen. But there is surely something presumptuous about the way humans look down on the "lower" animals, especially those that have become extinct. We consider the dinosaurs, for example, to be biological failures, though they existed on our planet for 65 million years. One writer has made the point with beautiful simplicity:

> We sometimes speak of the dinosaurs as failures; there will be time enough for that judgment when we have lasted even for one tenth as long . . .[6]

The possibility of the extinction of the human species, a possibility which starkly confronts us in the contemporary world, makes us aware of another respect in which we should not consider ourselves privileged beings in relation to other species. This is the fact that the well-being of humans is dependent upon the ecological soundness and health of many plant and animal communities, while their soundness and health does not in the least depend upon human well-being. Indeed, from their standpoint the very existence of humans is quite unnecessary. Every last man, woman, and child would disappear from the face of the Earth without any significant detrimental consequence for the good of wild animals and plants. On the contrary, many of them would be greatly benefited. The destruction of their habitats by human "developments" would cease. The poisoning and polluting of their environment would come to an end. The Earth's land, air, and water would no longer be subject to the degradation they are now undergoing as the result of large-scale technology and uncontrolled population growth. Life communities in natural ecosystems would gradually return to their former healthy state. Tropical rain forests, for example, would again be able to make their full contribution to a life-sustaining atmosphere for the whole planet. The rivers, lakes, and oceans of the world would (perhaps) eventually become clean again. Spilled oil, plastic trash, and even radioactive waste might finally, after many centuries, cease doing their terrible work. Ecosystems would return to their proper balance, suffering only the disruptions of natural events such as volcanic eruptions and glaciation. From these the community of life could recover, as it has so often done in the past. But the ecological disasters now perpetrated on it by humans—disasters from which it might never recover—these it would no longer have to endure.

If, then, the total, final, absolute extermination of our species (by our own hands?) should take place and if we should not carry all the others with us into oblivion, not only would the Earth's community of life continue to exist, but in all probability its well-being would be enhanced. Our presence, in short, is not needed. If we were to take the standpoint of the community and give voice to its true interest, the ending of our six-inch epoch would most likely be greeted with a hearty "Good riddance!"

VII. THE NATURAL WORLD AS AN ORGANIC SYSTEM

To accept the biocentric outlook and regard ourselves and our place in the world from its perspective is to see the whole natural order of the Earth's biosphere as a complex but unified web of interconnected organisms, objects, and events. The ecological relationships between any community of living things and their environment form an organic whole of functionally interdependent parts. Each ecosystem is a small universe itself in which the interactions of its various species populations comprise an intricately woven network of cause-effect relations. Such dynamic but at the same time relatively stable structures as food chains, predator-prey relations, and plant succession in a forest are self-regulating, energy-recycling mechanisms that preserve the equilibrium of the whole.

As far as the well-being of wild animals and plants is concerned, this ecological equilibrium must not be destroyed. The same holds true of the well-being of humans. When one views the realm of nature from the perspective of the biocentric outlook, one never forgets that in the long run the integrity of the entire biosphere of our planet is essential to the realization of the good of its constituent communities of life, both human and nonhuman.

Although the importance of this idea cannot be overemphasized, it is by now so familiar and so widely acknowledged that I shall not further elaborate on it here. However, I do wish to point out that this "holistic" view of the Earth's ecological systems does not itself constitute a moral norm. It is a factual aspect of biological reality, to be understood as a set of causal connections in ordinary empirical terms. Its significance for humans is the same as its significance for nonhumans, namely, in setting basic conditions for the realization of the good of living things. Its ethical implications for our treatment of the natural environment lie entirely in the fact that our *knowledge* of these causal connections is an essential *means* to fulfilling the aims we set for ourselves in adopting the attitude of respect for nature. In addition, its theoretical implications for the ethics of respect for nature lie in the fact that it (along with the other elements of the biocentric outlook) makes the adopting of that attitude a rational and intelligible thing to do.

VIII. INDIVIDUAL ORGANISMS AS TELEOLOGICAL CENTERS OF LIFE

As our knowledge of living things increases, as we come to a deeper understanding of their life cycles, their interactions with other organisms, and the manifold ways in which they adjust to the environment, we become more fully aware of how each of them is carrying out its biological functions according to the laws of its species-specific nature. But besides this, our increasing knowledge and understanding also develop in us a sharpened awareness of the uniqueness of each individual organism. Scientists who have made careful studies of particular plants and animals, whether in the field or in laboratories, have often acquired a knowledge of their subjects as identifiable individuals. Close observation over extended periods of time has led them to an appreciation of the unique "personalities" of their subjects. Sometimes a scientist may come to take a special interest in a particular animal or plant, all the while remaining strictly objective in the gathering and recording of data. Nonscientists may likewise experience this development of interest when, as amateur naturalists, they make accurate observations over sustained periods of close acquaintance with an individual organism. As one becomes more and more familiar with the organism and its behavior, one becomes fully sensitive to the particular way it is living out its life cycle. One may become fascinated by it and even experience some involvement with its good and bad fortunes (that is, with the occurrence of environmental conditions favorable or unfavorable to the realization of its good). The organism comes to mean something to one as a unique, irreplaceable individual. The final culmination of this process is the achievement of a genuine understanding of its point of view and, with that understanding, an ability to "take" that point of view. *Conceiving of it as a center of life, one is able to look at the world from its perspective.*

This development from objective knowledge to the recognition of individuality, and from the recognition of individuality to full awareness of an organism's standpoint, is a process of heightening our consciousness of what it means to be an individual living thing. We grasp the particularity of the organism as a teleological center of life, striving to preserve itself and to realize its own good in its own unique way.

It is to be noted that we need not be falsely anthropomorphizing when we conceive of individual plants and animals in this manner. Understanding them as teleological centers of life does not necessitate "reading into" them human characteristics. We need not, for example, consider them to have consciousness. Some of them may be aware of the world around them and others may not. Nor need we deny that different kinds and levels of awareness are exemplified when consciousness in some form is present. But conscious or not, all are equally teleological centers of life in the sense that each is a unified system of goal-oriented activities directed toward their preservation and well-being.

When considered from an ethical point of view, a teleological center of life is an entity whose "world" can be viewed from the perspective of *its* life. In looking at the world from that perspective we recognize objects and events occurring in its life as being beneficent, maleficent, or indifferent. The first are occurrences which increase its powers to preserve its existence and realize its good. The second decrease or destroy those powers. The third have neither of these effects on the entity. With regard to our human role as moral agents, we can conceive of a teleological center of life as a being whose standpoint we can take in making judgments about what events in the world are good or evil, desirable or undesirable. In making those judgments it is what promotes or protects the being's own good, not what benefits moral agents themselves, that sets the standard of evaluation. Such judgments can be made about anything that happens to the entity which is favorable or unfavorable in relation to its good. As we pointed out earlier, the entity itself need not have any (conscious) *interest* in what is happening to it for such judgments to be meaningful and true.

It is precisely judgments of this sort that we are disposed to make when we take the attitude of respect for nature. In adopting that attitude those judgments are given weight as reasons for action in our practical deliberation. They become morally relevant facts in the guidance of our conduct.

IX. THE DENIAL OF HUMAN SUPERIORITY

The fourth component of the biocentric outlook on nature is the single most important idea in establishing the justifiability of the attitude of respect for nature. Its central role is due to the special relationship it bears to the first three components of the outlook. This relationship will be brought out after the concept of human superiority is examined and analyzed.[7]

In what sense are humans alleged to be superior to other animals? We are different from them in having certain capacities that they lack. But why should these capacities be a mark of superiority? From what point of view are they judged to be signs of superiority and what sense of superiority is meant? After all, various nonhuman species have capacities that humans lack. There is the speed of a cheetah, the vision of an eagle, the agility of a monkey. Why should not these be taken as signs of *their* superiority over humans?

One answer that comes immediately to mind is that these capacities are not as *valuable* as the human capacities that are claimed to make us superior. Such uniquely human characteristics as rational thought, aesthetic creativity, autonomy and self-determination, and moral freedom, it might be held, have a higher value than the capacities found in other species. Yet we must ask: valuable to whom, and on what grounds?

The human characteristics mentioned are all valuable to humans. They are essential to the preservation and enrichment of our civilization and culture. Clearly it is from the human standpoint that they are being judged to be desirable and good. It is not difficult here to recognize a begging of the question. Humans are claiming human superiority from a strictly human point of view, that is, from a point of view in which the good of humans is taken as the standard of judgment. All we need to do is look at the capacities of nonhuman animals (or plants, for that matter) from the standpoint of *their* good to find a contrary judgment of superiority. The speed of the cheetah, for example, is a sign of its superiority to humans when considered from the standpoint of the good of its species. If it were as slow a runner as a human, it would not be able to survive. And so for all the other abilities of nonhumans which further their good but which are lacking in humans. In each case the claim to human superiority would be rejected from a nonhuman standpoint.

When superiority assertions are interpreted in this way, they are based on judgments of *merit*. To judge the merits of a person or an organism one must apply grading or ranking standards to it. (As I show below, this distinguishes judgments of merit from judgments of inherent worth.) Empirical investigation then determines whether it has the "good-making properties" (merits) in virtue of which it fulfills the standards being applied. In the case of humans, merits may be either moral or nonmoral. We can judge one person to be better than (superior to) another from the moral point of view by applying certain standards to their character and conduct. Similarly, we can appeal to nonmoral criteria in judging someone to be an excellent piano player, a fair cook, a poor tennis player, and so on. Different social purposes and roles are implicit in the making of such judgments, providing the frame of reference for the choice of standards by which the nonmoral merits of people are determined. Ultimately such purposes and roles stem from a society's way of life as a whole. Now a society's way of life may be thought of as the cultural form given to the realization of human values. Whether moral or nonmoral standards are being applied, then, all judgments of people's merits finally depend on human values. All are made from an exclusively human standpoint.

The question that naturally arises at this juncture is: Why should standards that are based on human values be assumed to be the only valid criteria of merit and hence the only true signs of superiority? This question is especially pressing when humans are being judged superior in merit to nonhumans. It is true that a human being may be a better mathematician than a monkey, but the monkey may be a better tree climber than a human being. If we humans value mathematics more than tree climbing, that is because our conception of civilized life makes the development of mathematical ability more desirable than the ability to climb trees. But is it not unreasonable to judge nonhumans by the values of human civilization, rather than by values connected with what it is for a member of *that* species to live a good life? If all living things have a good of their own, it at least makes sense to judge the merits of nonhumans by standards derived from *their* good. To use only standards based on human values is already to commit oneself to holding that humans are superior to nonhumans, which is the point in question.

A further logical flaw arises in connection with the widely held conviction that humans are *morally* superior beings because they possess, while others lack, the capacities of a moral agent (free will, accountability, deliberation, judgment, practical reason). This view rests on a conceptual confusion. As far as moral standards are concerned, only beings that have the capacities of a moral agent can properly be judged to be *either* moral (morally good) *or* immoral (morally deficient). Moral standards are simply not applicable to beings that lack such capacities. Animals and plants cannot therefore be said to be morally inferior in merit to humans. Since the only beings that can have moral merits *or be deficient in such merits* are moral agents, it is conceptually incoherent to judge humans as superior to nonhumans on the ground that humans have moral capacities while nonhumans don't.

Up to this point I have been interpreting the claim that humans are superior to other living things as a grading or ranking judgment regarding their comparative merits. There is, however, another way of understanding the idea of human superiority. According to this interpretation, humans are superior to nonhumans not as regards their merits but as regards their inherent worth. Thus the claim of human superiority is to be understood as asserting that all humans, simply in virtue of their humanity, have *a greater inherent worth* than other living things.

The inherent worth of an entity does not depend on its merits.[8] To consider something as possessing inherent worth, we have seen, is to place intrinsic value on the realization of its good. This is done regardless of whatever particular merits it might have or might lack, as judged by a set of grading or ranking standards. In human affairs, we are all familiar with the principle that one's worth as a person does not vary with one's merits or lack of merits. The same can hold true of animals and plants. To regard such entities as possessing inherent worth entails disregarding their merits and deficiencies, whether they are being judged from a human standpoint or from the standpoint of their own species.

The idea of one entity having more merit than another, and so being superior to it in merit, makes perfectly good sense. Merit is a grading or ranking concept, and judgments of comparative merit are based on the different degrees to which things satisfy a given standard. But what can it mean to talk about one thing being superior to another in inherent worth? In order to get at what is being asserted in such a claim it is helpful first to look at the social origin of the concept of degrees of inherent worth.

The idea that humans can possess different degrees of inherent worth originated in societies having rigid class structures. Before the rise of modern democracies with their egalitarian outlook, one's membership in a hereditary class determined one's social status. People in the upper classes were looked up to, while those in the lower classes were looked down upon. In such a society one's social superiors and social inferiors were clearly defined and easily recognized.

Two aspects of these class-structured societies are especially relevant to the idea of degrees of inherent worth. First, those born into the upper classes were deemed more worthy of respect than those born into the lower orders. Second, the superior worth of upper-class people had nothing to do with their merits nor did the inferior worth of those in the lower classes rest on their lack of merits. One's superiority or inferiority entirely derived from a social position one was born into. The modern concept of a meritocracy simply did not apply. One could not advance into a higher class by any sort of moral or nonmoral achievement. Similarly, an aristocrat held his title and all the privileges that went with it just because he was the eldest son of a titled nobleman. Unlike the bestowing of knighthood in contemporary Great Britain, one did not earn membership in the nobility by meritorious conduct.

We who live in modern democracies no longer believe in such hereditary social distinctions. Indeed, we would wholeheartedly condemn them on moral grounds as being fundamentally unjust. We have come to think of class systems as a paradigm of social injustice, it being a central principle of the democratic way of life that among humans there are no superiors and no inferiors. Thus we have rejected the whole conceptual framework in which people are judged to have different degrees of inherent worth. That idea is incompatible with our notion of human equality based on the doctrine that all humans, simply in virtue of their humanity, have the same inherent worth. (The belief in universal human rights is one form that this egalitarianism takes.)

The vast majority of people in modern democracies, however, do not maintain an egalitarian outlook when it comes to comparing human beings with other living things. Most people consider our own species to be superior to all other species and this superiority is understood to be a matter of inherent worth, not merit. There may exist thoroughly vicious and depraved humans who lack all merit. Yet because they are human they are thought to belong to a higher class of entities than any plant or animal. That one is born into the species *Homo sapiens* entitles one to have lordship over those who are one's inferiors, namely, those born into other species. The parallel with hereditary social classes is very close. Implicit in this view is a hierarchical conception of nature according to which an organism has a position of superiority or inferiority in the Earth's community of life simply on the basis of its genetic background. The "lower" orders of life are looked down upon and it is considered perfectly proper that they serve the interests of those belonging to the highest order, namely humans. The intrinsic value we place on the well-being of our fellow humans reflects our recognition of their rightful position as our equals. No such intrinsic value is to be placed on the good of other animals, unless we choose to do so out of fondness or affection for them. But their well-being imposes no moral requirement on us. In this respect there is an absolute difference in moral status between ourselves and them.

This is the structure of concepts and beliefs that people are committed to insofar as they regard humans to be superior in inherent worth to all other species. I now wish to argue that this structure of concepts and beliefs is completely groundless. If we accept the first three components of the biocentric outlook and from that perspective look at the major philosophical traditions which have supported that structure, we find it to be at bottom nothing more than the expression of an irrational bias in our own favor. The philosophical traditions themselves rest on very questionable assumptions or else simply beg the question. I briefly consider three of the main traditions to substantiate the point. These are classical Greek humanism, Cartesian dualism, and the Judeo-Christian concept of the Great Chain of Being.

The inherent superiority of humans over other species was implicit in the Greek definition of man as a rational animal. Our animal nature was identified with "brute" desires that need the order and restraint of reason to rule them (just as reason is the special virtue of those who rule in the ideal state). Rationality was then seen to be the key to our superiority over animals. It enables us to live on a higher plane and endows us with a nobility and worth that other creatures lack. This familiar way of comparing humans with other species is deeply ingrained in our Western philosophical outlook. The point to consider here is that this view does not actually provide an argument *for* human superiority but rather makes explicit the framework of thought that is implicitly used by those who think of humans as inherently superior to nonhumans. The Greeks who held that humans, in virtue of their rational capacities, have a kind of worth greater than that of any nonrational being, never looked at rationality as but one capacity of living things among many others. But when we consider rationality from the standpoint of the first three elements of the ecological outlook, we see that its value lies in its importance for *human* life. Other creatures achieve their species-specific good without the need of rationality, although they often make use of capacities that humans lack. So the humanistic outlook of classical Greek thought does not give us a neutral (nonquestion-begging) ground on which to construct a scale of degrees of inherent worth possessed by different species of living things.

The second tradition, centering on the Cartesian dualism of soul and body, also fails to justify the claim to human superiority. That superiority is supposed to derive from the fact that we have souls while animals do not. Animals are mere automata and lack the divine element that makes us spiritual beings. I won't go into the now familiar criticisms of this two-substance view. I only add the point that, even if humans are composed of an immaterial, unextended soul and a material, extended body, this in itself is not a reason to deem them of greater worth than entities that are only bodies. Why is a soul substance a thing that adds value to its possessor? Unless some theological reasoning is offered here (which many, including myself, would find unacceptable on epistemological grounds), no logical connection is evident. An immaterial something which thinks is better than a material something which does not think only if thinking itself has value, either intrinsically or instrumentally. Now it is intrinsically valuable to humans alone, who value it as an end in itself, and it is instrumentally valuable to those who benefit from it, namely humans.

For animals that neither enjoy thinking for its own sake nor need it for living the kind of life for which they are best adapted, it has no value. Even if "thinking" is broadened to include all forms of consciousness, there are still many living things that can do without it and yet live what is for their species a good life. The anthropocentricity underlying the claim to human superiority runs throughout Cartesian dualism.

A third major source of the idea of human superiority is the Judeo-Christian concept of the Great Chain of Being. Humans are superior to animals and plants because their Creator has given them a higher place on the chain. It begins with God at the top, and then moves to the angels, who are lower than God but higher than humans, then to humans, positioned between the angels and the beasts (partaking of the nature of both), and then on down to the lower levels occupied by nonhuman animals, plants, and finally inanimate objects. Humans, being "made in God's image," are inherently superior to animals and plants by virtue of their being closer (in their essential nature) to God.

The metaphysical and epistemological difficulties with this conception of a hierarchy of entities are, in my mind, insuperable. Without entering into this matter here, I only point out that if we are unwilling to accept the metaphysics of traditional Judaism and Christianity, we are again left without good reasons for holding to the claim of inherent human superiority.

The foregoing considerations (and others like them) leave us with but one ground for the assertion that a human being, regardless of merit, is a higher kind of entity than any other living thing. This is the mere fact of the genetic makeup of the species *Homo sapiens.* But this is surely irrational and arbitrary. Why should the arrangement of genes of a certain type be a mark of superior value, especially when this fact about an organism is taken by itself, unrelated to any other aspect of its life? We might just as well refer to any other genetic makeup as a ground of superior value. Clearly we are confronted here with a wholly arbitrary claim that can only be explained as an irrational bias in our own favor.

That the claim is nothing more than a deep-seated prejudice is brought home to us when we look at our relation to other species in the light of the first three elements of the biocentric outlook. Those elements taken conjointly give us a certain overall view of the natural world and of the place of humans in it. When we take this view we come to understand other living things, their environmental conditions, and their ecological relationships in such a way as to awake in us a deep sense of our kinship with them as fellow members of the Earth's community of life. Humans and nonhumans alike are viewed together as integral parts of one unified whole in which all living things are functionally interrelated. Finally, when our awareness focuses on the individual lives of plants and animals, each is seen to share with us the characteristic of being a teleological center of life striving to realize its own good in its own unique way.

As this entire belief system becomes part of the conceptual framework through which we understand and perceive the world, we come to see ourselves as bearing a certain moral relation to nonhuman forms of life. Our ethical role in nature takes on a new significance. We begin to look at other species as we look at ourselves, seeing them as beings which have a good they are striving to realize just as we have a good we are striving to realize. We accordingly develop the disposition to view the world from the standpoint of their good as well as from the standpoint of our own good. Now if the groundlessness of the claim that humans are inherently superior to other species were brought clearly before our minds, we would not remain intellectually neutral toward that claim but would reject it as being fundamentally at variance with our total world outlook. In the absence of any good reasons for holding it, the assertion of human superiority would then appear simply as the expression of an irrational and self-serving prejudice that favors one particular species over several million others.

Rejecting the notion of human superiority entails its positive counterpart: the doctrine of species impartially. One who accepts that doctrine regards all living things as possessing inherent worth—the *same* inherent worth, since no one species has been shown to be either "higher" or "lower" than any other. Now we saw earlier that, insofar as one thinks of a living thing as possessing inherent worth, one considers it to be the appropriate object of the attitude of respect and believes that attitude to be the only fitting or suitable one for all moral agents to take toward it.

Here, then, is the key to understanding how the attitude of respect is rooted in the biocentric outlook on nature. The basic connection is made through the denial of human superiority. Once we reject the claim that humans are superior either in merit or in worth to other living things, we are ready to adopt the attitude of respect. The denial of human superiority is itself the result of taking the perspective on nature built into the first three elements of the biocentric outlook.

Now the first three elements of the biocentric outlook, it seems clear, would be found acceptable to any rational and scientifically informed thinker who is fully "open" to the reality of the lives of nonhuman organisms. Without denying our distinctively human characteristics, such a thinker can acknowledge the fundamental respects in which we are members of the Earth's community of life and in which the biological conditions necessary for the realization of our human values are inextricably linked with the whole system of nature. In addition, the conception of individual living things as teleological centers of life simply articulates how a scientifically informed thinker comes to understand them as the result of increasingly careful and detailed observations. Thus, the biocentric outlook recommends itself as an acceptable system of concepts and beliefs to anyone who is clear-minded, unbiased, and factually enlightened, and who has a developed capacity of reality awareness with regard to the lives of individual organisms. This, I submit, is as good a reason for making the moral commitment involved in adopting the attitude of respect for nature as any theory of environmental ethics could possibly have.

X. MORAL RIGHTS AND THE MATTER OF COMPETING CLAIMS

I have not asserted anywhere in the foregoing account that animals or plants have moral rights. This omission was deliberate. I do not think that the reference class of the concept, bearer of moral rights, should be extended to include nonhuman living things. My reasons for taking this position, however, go beyond the scope of this paper. I believe I have been able to accomplish many of the same ends which those who ascribe rights to animals or plants wish to accomplish. There is no reason, moreover, why plants and animals, including whole species populations and life communities, cannot be accorded *legal* rights under my theory. To grant them legal protection could be interpreted as giving them legal entitlement to be protected, and this, in fact, would be a means by which a society that subscribed to the ethics of respect for nature could give public recognition to their inherent worth.

There remains the problem of competing claims, even when wild plants and animals are not thought of as bearers of moral rights. If we accept the biocentric outlook and accordingly adopt the attitude of respect for nature as our ultimate moral attitude, how do we resolve conflicts that arise from our respect for persons in the domain of human ethics and our respect for nature in the domain of environmental ethics? This is a question that cannot be adequately dealt with here. My main purpose in this paper has been to try to establish a base point from which we can start working toward a solution to the problem. I have shown why we cannot just begin with an initial presumption in favor of the interests of our own species. It is after all within our power as moral beings to place limits on human population and technology with the deliberate intention of sharing the Earth's bounty with other species. That such sharing is an ideal difficult to realize even in an approximate way does not take away its claim to our deepest moral commitment.

NOTES

1. The conceptual links between an entity *having* a good, something being good *for* it, and events doing good to it are examined by G. H. Von Wright in *The Varieties of Goodness* (New York: Humanities Press, 1963), chaps. 3 and 5.
2. See W. K. Frankena, "Ethics and the Environment," in *Ethics and Problems of the 21st Century* eds., K. E. Goodpaster and K. M. Sayre, (Notre Dame: University of Notre Dame Press, 1979), pp. 3–20. I critically examine Frankena's views in "Frankena on Environmental Ethics," *Monist,* forthcoming.
3. In the light of considerations set forth in Daniel Dennett's *Brain Storms: Philosophical Essays on Mind and Psychology* (Montgomery, VT: Bradford Books, 1978), it is advisable to leave this question unsettled at this time. When machines are developed that function in the way our brains do, we may well come to deem them proper subjects of moral consideration.
4. I have analyzed the nature of this commitment of human ethics in "On Taking the Moral Point of View," *Midwest Studies in Philosophy,* vol. 3, *Studies in Ethical Theory* (1978), pp. 35–61.
5. John Rawls, "Justice As Fairness," *Philosophical Review* 67 (1958): 183.
6. Stephen R. L. Clark, *The Moral Status of Animals* (Oxford: Clarendon Press, 1977), p. 112.
7. My criticisms of the dogma of human superiority gain independent support from a carefully reasoned essay by R. and V. Routley showing the many logical weaknesses in arguments for human-centered theories of environmental ethics. R. and V. Routley, "Against the Inevitability of Human Chauvinism," in K. E. Goodpaster and K. M. Sayre, eds., *Ethics and Problems of the 21st Century* (Notre Dame: University of Notre Dame Press, 1979), pp. 36–59.
8. For this way of distinguishing between merit and inherent worth, I am indebted to Gregory Vlastos, "Justice and Equality," in R. Brandt, ed., *Social Justice* (Englewood Cliffs, NJ: Prentice-Hall, 1962), pp. 31–72.

DISCUSSION QUESTIONS

1. Has Taylor convinced you that it is question-begging for human beings to assert their superiority over other living things? Must we follow Taylor and embrace a moral egalitarianism for all living things?
2. Why must each individual's good be accorded some value?
3. In what respects does Taylor's position about respect for nature parallel Kant's position on respect for persons?
4. Is it possible to live according to Taylor's ethics of respect for nature? Does that matter?

KENNETH GOODPASTER

On Being Morally Considerable

In his seminal article, "On Being Morally Considerable" philosophy professor Kenneth Goodpaster explores the minimal requirements for an entity to belong to the moral community. He rejects both anthropocentrism and a sentience-based criterion for moral con-

Kenneth Goodpaster, "On Being Morally Considerable," *The Journal of Philosophy* LXXV, vol 6, June 1978, pp. 308–25. Reprinted by permission.

siderability. According to Goodpaster, only a life-centered, or "biocentric," ethic can best define the limits of the moral community.

CRITICAL READING QUESTIONS

1. What does Goodpaster mean when he claims that modern moral philosophy takes egoism as its "principal foil"?
2. How does Goodpaster distinguish between rights and moral considerability?
3. What is the distinction between a criterion of moral considerability and a criterion of moral significance, according to Goodpaster?
4. Why does Goodpaster agree with Warnock in rejecting the "Kantian principle"?
5. What, according to Goodpaster, is Feinberg's argument for thinking the capacity to suffer is the criterion for moral considerability?
6. How does Goodpaster criticize Feinberg's view?
7. Consider closely Goodpaster's responses to objections 3, 4, and 6.

> A thing is right when it tends to preserve the integrity, stability and beauty of the biotic community. It is wrong when it tends otherwise.
>
> —Aldo Leopold

What follows is a preliminary inquiry into a question which needs more elaborate treatment than an essay can provide. The question can be and has been addressed in different rhetorical formats, but perhaps G. J. Warnock's formulation of it[1] is the best to start with:

> Let us consider the question to whom principles of morality apply from, so to speak, the other end—from the standpoint not of the agent, but of the "patient." What, we may ask here, is the condition of moral *relevance?* What is the condition of having a claim to be *considered,* by rational agents to whom moral principles apply?

In terminology of R. M. Hare (or even Kant), the same question might be put thus: In universalizing our putative moral maxims, what is the scope of the variable over which universalization is to range? A more legalistic idiom, employed recently by Christopher D. Stone,[2] might ask: What are the requirements for "having standing" in the moral sphere? However the question gets formulated, the thrust is in the direction of necessary and sufficient conditions on *X* in

> 1. For all *A, X* deserves moral consideration from *A* where *A* ranges over rational moral agents and moral "consideration" is construed broadly to include the most basic forms of practical respect (and so is not restricted to "possession of rights" by *X*). . . .

I

Modern moral philosophy has taken ethical egoism as its principal foil for developing what can fairly be called a *humanistic* perspective on value and obligation. That is, both Kantian and Humean approaches to ethics tend to view the philosophical challenge as that of providing an epistemological and motivational generalization of an agent's natural self-interested concern. Because of this preoccupation with moral "take-off," however, too little critical thought has been devoted to the flight and its destination. One result might be a certain feeling of impotence in the minds of many moral philosophers when faced with the sorts of issues mentioned earlier, issues that question the breadth of the moral enterprise more than its departure point. To be sure, questions of conservation, preservation of the environment, and technology assessment *can* be approached simply as application questions, e.g., "How shall we evaluate the alternatives available to us instrumentally in relation to humanistic satisfactions?" But there is something distressingly uncritical in this way of framing such issues—distressingly uncritical in the way that deciding foreign policy solely in terms of "the national interest" is uncritical. Or at least, so I think.

It seems to me that we should not only wonder about, but actually follow "the road not taken into the wood." Neither rationality nor the capacity to experience pleasure and pain seem to me necessary (even though they may be sufficient) conditions for moral considerability. And only our hedonistic and concentric forms of ethical reflection keep us from acknowledging this fact. Nothing short of the condition of *being alive* seems to me to be a plausible and nonarbitrary criterion. What is more, this criterion, if taken seriously, could admit of application to entities and systems of entities heretofore unimagined as claimants on our moral attention (such as the biosystem itself). Some may be inclined to take such implications as a *reductio* of the move "beyond humanism." I am beginning to be persuaded, however, that such implications may provide both a meaningful ethical vision and the hope of a more adequate action guide for the long-term future. Paradigms are crucial components in knowledge—but they can conceal as much as they reveal. Our paradigms of moral considerability are individual persons and their joys and sorrows. I want to venture the belief that the universe of moral consideration is more complex than these paradigms allow.

II

My strategy, now that my cards are on the table, will be to spell out a few rules of the game (in this section) and then to examine the "hands" of several respected philosophers whose arguments seem to count against casting the moral net as widely as I am inclined to . . . In the concluding section . . . , I will discuss several objections and touch on further questions needing attention.

The first . . . distinctions that must be kept clear in addressing our question [have] already been alluded to. It is that between moral *rights* and moral *considerability*. My inclination is to construe the notion of rights as more specific than that of considerability, largely to avoid what seem to be unnecessary complications over the requirements for something's being an appropriate "bearer of rights." The concept of rights is used in wider and narrower senses, of course. Some authors (indeed, one whom we shall consider later in this paper) use it as roughly synonymous with Warnock's notion of "moral relevance." Others believe that being a bearer of rights involves the satisfaction of much more demanding requirements. The sentiments of John Passmore[3] are probably typical of this narrower view:

> The idea of "rights" is simply not applicable to what is non-human . . . It is one thing to say that it is wrong to treat animals cruelly, quite another to say that animals have rights.

I doubt whether it is so clear that the class of rights-bearers is or ought to be restricted to human beings, but I propose to suspend this question entirely by framing the discussion in terms of the notion of moral considerability (following Warnock), except in contexts where there is reason to think the widest sense of "rights" is at work. Whether beings who deserve moral consideration in themselves, not simply by reason of their utility to human beings, also possess moral *rights* in some narrow sense is a question which will, therefore, remain open here—and it is a question the answer to which need not be determined in advance.

A second distinction is that between what might be called a *criterion of moral considerability* and a *criterion of moral significance*. The former represents the central quarry here, while the latter, which might easily get confused with the former, aims at governing *comparative* judgments of moral "weight" in cases of conflict. Whether a tree, say, deserves any moral consideration is a question that must be kept separate from the question of whether trees deserve more or less consideration than dogs, or dogs than human persons. We should not expect that the criterion for having "moral standing" at all will be the same as the criterion for adjudicating competing claims to priority among beings that merit that standing. . .

III

Let us begin with Warnock's own answer to the question, now that the question has been clarified somewhat. In setting out his answer, Warnock argues (in my view, persuasively) against two more restrictive candidates. The first, what might be called the *Kantian principle,* amounts to little more than a reflection of the requirements of moral *agency* onto those of moral considerability:

> 2. For *X* to deserve moral consideration from *A*, *X* must be a rational human person.

Observing that such a criterion of considerability eliminates children and mentally handicapped adults, among others, Warnock dismisses it as intolerably narrow.

The second candidate, actually a more generous variant of the first, sets the limits of moral considerability by disjoining "potentiality":

> 3. For all *A, X* deserves moral consideration from *A* if and only if *X* is a rational human person or is a potential rational human person.

Warnock's reply to this suggestion is also persuasive. Infants and imbeciles are no doubt potentially rational, but this does not appear to be the reason why we should not maltreat them. And we would not say that an imbecile reasonably judged to be incurable would thereby reasonably be taken to have no moral claims. In short, it seems arbitrary to draw the boundary of moral *considerability* around rational human beings (actual or potential), however plausible it might be to draw the boundary of moral *responsibility* there.

Warnock then settles upon his own solution. The basis of moral claims, he says, may be put as follows:

> Just as liability to be judged as a moral agent follows from one's general capability of alleviating, by moral action, the ills of the predicament, and is for that reason confined to rational beings, so the condition of being a proper "beneficiary" of moral action is the capability of *suffering* the ills of the predicament—and for that reason is not confined to rational beings, nor even to potential members of that class.

The criterion of moral considerability then, is located in the *capacity to suffer:*

> 4. For all *A, X* deserves moral consideration from *A* if and only if *X* is capable of suffering pain (or experiencing enjoyment).

And the defense involves appeal to what Warnock considers to be (analytically) the *object* of the moral enterprise: amelioration of "the predicament."

Now two issues arise immediately in the wake of this sort of appeal. The first has to do with Warnock's own over-all strategy in the context of the quoted passage. Earlier on in his book, he insists that the appropriate analysis of the concept of morality will lead us to an "object" whose pursuit provides the framework for ethics. But the "object" seems to be more restrictive:

> The general object of moral evaluation must be to contribute in some respects, by way of the actions of rational beings, to the amelioration of the human predicament—that is, of the conditions in which *these* rational beings, humans, actually find themselves (emphasis in the original).

It appears that, by the time moral considerability comes up later in the book, Warnock has changed his mind about the object of morality by enlarging the "predicament" to include nonhumans.

The second issue turns on the question of analysis itself. As I suggested earlier, it is difficult to keep conceptual and substantive questions apart in the present context. We can, of course, stipulatively *define* "morality" as both having an object and having the object of mitigating suffering. But, in the absence of more argument, such definition is itself in need of a warrant. Twentieth-century preoccupation with the naturalistic or definist fallacy should have taught us at least this much.

Neither of these two observations shows that Warnock's suggested criterion is wrong, of course. But they do, I think, put us in a rather more demanding mood. And the mood is aggravated when we look to two other writers on the subject who appear to hold similar views.

W. K. Frankena, in a recent paper,[4] joins forces:

> Like Warnock, I believe that there are right and wrong ways to treat infants, animals, imbeciles, and idiots even if or even though (as the case may be) they are not persons or human beings—just because they are capable of pleasure and suffering, and not just because their lives happen to have some value to or for those who clearly are persons or human beings.

And Peter Singer[5] writes:

> If a being is not capable of suffering, or of experiencing enjoyment or happiness, there is nothing to be taken into account. This is why the limit of sentience (using the term as a convenient, if not strictly accurate, shorthand for the capacity to suffer or experience enjoyment or happiness) is the only defensible boundary of concern for the interests of others.

I say that the mood is aggravated because, although I acknowledge and even applaud the conviction expressed by these philosophers that the capacity to suffer (or perhaps better, *sentience*) is sufficient for moral considerability, I fail to understand their reasons for thinking such a criterion necessary. To be sure, there are hints at reasons in each case. Warnock implies that nonsentient beings could not be proper "beneficiaries" of moral action. Singer seems to think that beyond sentience "there is nothing to take into account." And Frankena suggests that nonsentient beings simply do not provide us with moral reasons for respecting them unless it be potentiality for sentience.[6] Yet it is so clear that there *is* something to take into account, something that is not merely "potential sentience" and which surely does qualify beings as beneficiaries and capable of harm—namely, *life*—that the hints provided seem to me to fall short of good reasons.

Biologically, it appears that sentience is an adaptive characteristic of living organisms that provides them with a better capacity to anticipate, and so avoid, threats to life. This at least suggests, though of course it does not prove, that the capacities to suffer and to enjoy are ancillary to something more important rather than tickets to considerability in their own right. In the words of one perceptive scientific observer:

> If we view pleasure as rooted in our sensory physiology, it is not difficult to see that our neurophysiological equipment must have evolved via variation and selective retention in such a way as to record a positive signal to adaptationally satisfactory conditions and a negative signal to adaptationally unsatisfactory conditions . . . The pleasure signal is only an evolutionarily derived indicator, not the goal itself. It is the applause which signals a job well done, but not the actual completion of the job.[7]

Nor is it absurd to imagine that evolution might have resulted (indeed might still result?) in beings whose capacities to maintain, protect, and advance their lives did not depend upon mechanisms of pain and pleasure at all.

So far, then, we can see that the search for a criterion of moral considerability takes one quickly and plausibly beyond humanism. But there is a tendency, exhibited in the remarks of Warnock, Frankena, and Singer, to draw up the wagons around the notion of sentience. I have suggested that there is reason to go further and not very much in the way of argument not to. But perhaps there is a stronger and more explicit case that can be made for sentience. I think there is, in a way, and I propose to discuss it in detail in the section that follows.

IV

Joel Feinberg offers what may be the clearest and most explicit case for a restrictive criterion on moral considerability (restrictive with respect to life). . .[8]

[In] Feinberg's discussion . . . we discover the clearest line of argument in favor of something like sentience, an argument which was only hinted at in the remarks of Warnock, Frankena, and Singer.

The central thesis defended by Feinberg is that a being cannot intelligibly be said to possess moral rights (read: deserve moral consideration) unless that being satisfies the "interest principle," and that only the subclass of humans and higher animals among living beings satisfies this principle:

> The sorts of beings who can have rights are precisely those who have (or can have) interests. I

> have come to this tentative conclusion for two reasons: (1) because a right holder must be capable of being represented and it is impossible to represent a being that has no interests, and (2) because a right holder must be capable of being a beneficiary in his own person, and a being without interests is a being that is incapable of being harmed or benefited, having no good or "sake" of its own.

Implicit in this passage are the following two arguments, interpreted in terms of moral considerability:

> (A1) Only beings who can be represented can deserve moral consideration.
>
> Only beings who have (or can have) interests can be represented.
>
> Therefore, only beings who have (or can have) interests can deserve moral consideration.
>
> (A2) Only beings capable of being beneficiaries can deserve moral consideration.
>
> Only beings who have (or can have) interests are capable of being beneficiaries.
>
> Therefore, only beings who have (or can have) interests can deserve moral consideration.

I suspect that these two arguments are at work between the lines in Warnock, Frenkena, and Singer, though of course one can never be sure. In any case, I propose to consider them as the best defense of the sentience criterion in recent literature.

I am prepared to grant, with some reservations, the first premises in each of these obviously valid arguments. The second premises, though, are *both* importantly equivocal. To claim that only beings who have (or can have) interests can be represented might mean that "mere things" cannot be represented because they have nothing to represent, no "interests" as opposed to "usefulness" to defend or protect. Similarly, to claim that only beings who have (or can have) interests are capable of being beneficiaries might mean that "mere things" are incapable of being benefited or harmed—they have no "well-being" to be sought or acknowledged by rational moral agents. So construed, Feinberg seems to be right; but he also seems to be committed to allowing any *living* thing the status of moral considerability. For as he himself admits, even plants

> are not "mere things"; they are vital objects with inherited biological propensities determining their natural growth. Moreover we do say that certain conditions are "good" or "bad" for plants, thereby suggesting that plants, unlike rocks, are capable of having a "good."

But Feinberg pretty clearly wants to draw the nets tighter than this—and he does so by interpreting the notion of "interests" in the two second premises more narrowly. The contrast term he favors is not "mere things" but "mindless creatures." And he makes this move by insisting that "interests" logically presuppose *desires* or *wants* or *aims*, the equipment for which is not possessed by plants (nor, we might add, by many animals or even some humans?).

But why should we accept this shift in strength of the criterion? In doing so, we clearly abandon one sense in which living organisms like plants do have interests that can be represented. There is no absurdity in imagining the representation of the needs of a tree for sun and water in the face of a proposal to cut it down or pave its immediate radius for a parking lot. We might of course, on reflection, decide to go ahead and cut it down or do the paving, but there is hardly an intelligibility problem about representing the tree's interest in our deciding not to. In the face of their obvious tendencies to maintain and heal themselves, it is very difficult to reject the idea of interests on the part of trees (and plants generally) in remaining alive.[9]

Nor will it do to suggest, as Feinberg does, that the needs (interests) of living things like trees are not really their own but implicitly *ours:* "Plants may need things in order to discharge their functions, but their functions are assigned by human interests, not their own." As if it were human interests that assigned to trees the tasks of growth or maintenance! The interests at stake are clearly those of the living things themselves, not simply those of the owners or users or other human persons involved. Indeed, there is a suggestion in this passage that, to be capable of being represented, an organism must *matter* to human beings somehow—a suggestion whose implications for human rights (disenfranchisement) let alone the rights of animals (inconsistently for Feinberg, I think) are grim.

The truth seems to be that the "interests" that nonsentient beings share with sentient beings (over and against "mere things") are far more plausible as criteria of *considerability* than the "interests" that sentient beings share (over and against "mindless creatures"). This is not to say that interests construed in the latter way are morally irrelevant—for they may play a role as criteria of moral *significance*—but it is to say that psychological or hedonic capacities seem unnecessarily sophisticated when it comes to locating the minimal conditions for something's deserving to be valued for its own sake. Surprisingly, Feinberg's own reflections on "mere things" appear to support this very point:

> Mere things have no conative life: no conscious wishes, desires, and hopes; or urges and impulses; or unconscious drives, aims, and goals; or latent tendencies, direction of growth, and natural fulfillments. Interests must be compounded somehow out of conations; hence mere things have no interests.

Together with the acknowledgment, quoted earlier, that plants, for example, are not "mere things," such observations seem to undermine the interest principle in its more restrictive form. I conclude, with appropriate caution, that the interest principle either grows to fit what we might call a "life principle" or requires an arbitrary stipulation of psychological capacities (for desires, wants, etc.) which are neither warranted by (A1) and (A2) nor independently plausible.

V

Thus far, I have examined the views of four philosophers on the necessity of sentience or interests (narrowly conceived) as a condition on moral considerability. I have maintained that these views are not plausibly supported, when they are supported at all, because of a reluctance to acknowledge in nonsentient living beings the presence of independent needs, capacities for benefit and harm, etc. I should like, briefly, to reflect on a more general level about the roots of this reluctance before proceeding to a consideration of objections against the "life" criterion which I have been defending. In the course of this reflection, we might gain some insight into the sources of our collective hesitation in viewing environmental ethics in a "nonchauvinistic" way.

When we consider the reluctance to go beyond sentience in the context of moral consideration—and look for both explanations and justifications—two thoughts come to mind. The first is that, given the connection between beneficence (or nonmaleficence) and morality, it is natural that limits on moral considerability will come directly from limits on the range of beneficiaries (or "maleficiaries"). This is implicit in Warnock and explicit in Feinberg. The second thought is that, if one's conception of the good is *hedonistic* in character, one's conception of a beneficiary will quite naturally be restricted to beings who are capable of pleasure and pain. If pleasure or satisfaction is the only ultimate gift we have to give, morally, then it is to be expected that only those equipped to receive such a gift will enter into our moral deliberation. And if pain or dissatisfaction is the only ultimate harm we can cause, then it is to be expected that only those equipped for it will deserve our consideration. There seems, therefore, to be a noncontingent connection between a hedonistic or quasi-hedonistic theory of value and a response to the moral-considerability question which favors sentience or interest possession (narrowly conceived).

One must, of course, avoid drawing too strong a conclusion about this connection. It does not follow from the fact that hedonism leads naturally to the sentience criterion either that it entails that criterion or that one who holds that criterion must be a hedonist in his theory of value. For one might be a hedonist with respect to the good and yet think that moral consideration was, on other grounds, restricted to a subclass of the beings capable of enjoyment or pain. And one might hold to the sentience criterion for considerability while denying that pleasure, for example, was the only intrinsically good thing in the life of a human (or nonhuman) being. So hedonism about value and the sentience criterion of moral considerability are not logically equivalent. Nor does either entail the other. But there is some sense, I think, in which they mutually support each other—both in terms of "rendering plausible" and in terms of "helping to explain." As Derek Parfit is fond of putting it, "there are no entailments, but then there seldom are in moral reasoning."[10]

Let me hazard the hypothesis, then, that there is a nonaccidental affinity between a person's or a society's conception of value and its conception of moral considerability. More specifically, there is an affinity between hedonism or some variation on hedonism and a predilection for the sentience criterion of considerability or some variation on it. The implications one might draw from this are many. In the context of a quest for a richer moral framework to deal with a new awareness of the environment, one might be led to expect significant resistance from a hedonistic society unless one forced one's imperatives into an instrumental form. One might also be led to an appreciation of how technology aimed at largely hedonistic goals could gradually "harden the hearts" of a civilization to the biotic community in which it lives—at least until crisis or upheaval raised some questions.

VI

Let us now turn to several objections that might be thought to render a "life principle" of moral considerability untenable quite independently of the adequacy or inadequacy of the sentience or interest principle.

(O1) A principle of moral respect or consideration for life in all its forms is mere Schweitzerian romanticism, even if it does not involve, as it probably does, the projection of mental or psychological categories beyond their responsible boundaries into the realms of plants, insects, and microbes.

(R1) This objection misses the central thrust of my discussion, which is *not* that the sentience criterion is necessary, but applicable to all life forms—rather the point is that the possession of sentience is not necessary for moral considerability. Schweitzer himself may have held the former view—and so have been "romantic"—but this is beside the point.

(O2) To suggest seriously that moral considerability is coextensive with life is to suggest that conscious, feeling beings have no more central role in the moral life than vegetables, which is downright absurd—if not perverse.

(R2) This objection misses the central thrust of my discussion as well, for a different reason. It is consistent with acknowledging the moral considerability of all life forms to go on to point out differences of moral significance among these life forms. And as far as perversion is concerned, history will perhaps be a better judge of our civilization's treatment of animals and the living environment on that score.

(O3) Consideration of life can serve as a criterion only to the degree that life itself can be given a precise definition; and it can't.

(R3) I fail to see why a criterion of moral considerability must be strictly decidable in order to be tenable. Surely rationality, potential rationality, sentience, and the capacity for or possession of interests fare no better here. Moreover, there do seem to be empirically respectable accounts of the nature of living beings available which are not intolerably vague or open-textured:

> The typifying mark of a living system . . . appears to be its persistent state of low entropy, sustained by metabolic processes for accumulating energy, and maintained in equilibrium with its environment by homeostatic feedback processes.[11]

Granting the need for certain further qualifications, a definition such as this strikes me as not only plausible in its own right, but ethically illuminating, since it suggests that the core of moral concern lies in respect for self-sustaining organization and integration in the face of pressures toward high entropy.

(O4) If life, as understood in the previous response, is really taken as the key to moral considerability, then it is possible that larger systems besides our ordinarily understood "linear" extrapolations from human beings (e.g., animals, plants, etc.) might satisfy the conditions, such as the biosystem as a whole. This surely would be a *reductio* of the life principle.

(R4) At best, it would be a *reductio* of the life principle in this form or without qualification. But it seems to be that such (perhaps surprising) implications, if true, should be taken seriously. There is some evidence that the biosystem as a whole exhibits behavior approximating to the definition sketched above,[12] and I see no reason to deny it moral considerability on that account. Why should the universe of moral considerability map neatly onto our medium-sized framework of organisms?

(O5) There are severe epistemological problems about imputing interests, benefits, harms, etc. to non-sentient beings. What is it for a tree to have needs?

(R5) I am not convinced that the epistemological problems are more severe in this context than they would be in numerous others which the objector would probably not find problematic. Christopher Stone has put this point nicely:

> I am sure I can judge with more certainty and meaningfulness whether and when my lawn wants (needs) water than the Attorney General can judge whether and when the United States wants (needs) to take an appeal from an adverse judgment by a lower court. The lawn tells me that it wants water by a certain dryness of the blades and soil—immediately obvious to the touch—the appearance of bald spots, yellowing, and a lack of springiness after being walked on; how does "the United States" communicate to the Attorney General?[13]

We make decisions in the interests of others or on behalf of others every day—"others" whose wants are far less verifiable than those of most living creatures.

(O6) Whatever the force of the previous objections, the clearest and most decisive refutation of the principle of respect for life is that one cannot *live* according to it, nor is there any indication in nature that we were intended to. We must eat, experiment to gain knowledge, protect ourselves from predation (macroscopic and microscopic), and in general deal with the overwhelming complexities of the moral life while remaining psychologically intact. To take seriously the criterion of considerability being defended, all these things must be seen as somehow morally wrong.

(R6) This objection, if it is not met by implication in (R2), can be met, I think, by recalling the distinction made earlier between regulative and operative moral consideration. It seems to me that there clearly are limits to the operational character of respect for living things. We must eat, and usually this involves killing (though not always). We must have knowledge, and sometimes this involves experimentation with living things and killing (though not always). We must protect ourselves from predation and disease, and sometimes this involves killing (though not always). The regulative character of the moral consideration due to all living things asks, as far as I can see, for sensitivity and awareness, not for suicide (psychic or otherwise). But it is not vacuous, in that it does provide a *ceteris paribus* encouragement in the direction of nutritional, scientific, and medical practices of a genuinely life-respecting sort.

As for the implicit claim, in the objection, that since nature doesn't respect life, we needn't, there are two rejoinders. The first is that the premise is not so clearly true. Gratuitous killing in nature is rare indeed. The second, and more important, response is that the issue at hand has to do with the appropriate moral demands to be made on rational moral agents, not on beings who are not rational moral agents. Besides, this objection would tell equally against *any* criterion of moral considerability so far as I can see, if the suggestion is that nature is amoral.

NOTES

1. *The Object of Morality* (New York: Methuen, 1971).
2. Stone, *Should Trees Have Standing?* (Los Altos: William Kaufmann, 1974).
3. Passmore, *Man's Responsibility for Nature* (New York: Scribners, 1974).
4. "Ethics and the Environment" in *Ethics and Problems of the 21st Century,* eds: K. Goodpaster and K. Sayre (Notre Dame, IN: Notre Dame University Press, 1978).
5. "All Animals Are Equal," in *Animal Rights and Human Obligations,* Tom Regan and Peter Singer (Englewood Cliffs, NJ: Prentice Hall, 1976), p. 316.
6. "I can see no reason, from the moral point of view, why we should respect something that is alive but has no conscious sentiency and so can experience no pleasure or pain, joy or suffering, unless perhaps it is potentially a consciously sentient being, as in the case of a fetus. Why, if leaves and trees have no capacity to feel pleasure or to suffer, should I tear no leaf from a tree? Why should I respect its location any more than

that of a stone in my driveway, if no benefit or harm comes to any person or sentient being by my moving it?" ("Ethics and the Environment").

7. Mark W. Lipsey, "Value Science and Developing Society," paper delivered to the Society for Religion in Higher Education, Institute on Society, Technology and Values (July 15–August 4, 1973).
8. Joel Feinberg, "The Rights of Animals and Unborn Generations" in *Philosophy and Environmental Crisis.*
9. See Albert Szent-Gyorgyi, *The Living State* (New York: Academic Press, 1972), esp. ch. vi, "Vegetable Defense Systems."
10. "Later Selves and Moral Principles," in *Philosophy and Personal Relations,* ed. A. Montefiori (Boston: Routledge & Kegan Paul, 1973), p. 147.
11. K. M. Sayre, *Cybernetics and the Philosophy of Mind* (New York: Humanities, 1976), p. 91.
12. See J. Lovelock and S. Epton, "In Quest for Gaia," *The New Scientist* LXV, 935 (Feb. 6, 1975).
13. Stone, op. cit., p. 24.

DISCUSSION QUESTIONS

1. Does it seem to you that the "take-off" point for moral inquiry is, as Goodpaster puts it, a generalization of the self?
2. How does Goodpaster argue against limiting moral considerability by sentience? Do you agree that stopping at sentience is as arbitrary as stopping at the boundary of the species *Homo sapiens?*
3. What does Goodpaster mean when he claims, "Psychological or hedonic capacities seem unnecessarily sophisticated when it comes to locating the minimal conditions for something's deserving to be valued for its own sake"? Do you think he is right?
4. Consider Goodpaster's response to objection 3. Does his account also include refrigerators in the moral community?
5. Consider Goodpaster's response to objection 4. Is it true that the ecosystem as a whole is alive? (If it is, are refrigerators alive too?) What kinds of obligations might we have to the whole ecosystem if it is alive?
6. In his response to objection 6, Goodpaster denies that his life criterion for moral considerability is vacuous. What does he mean and is he right? Do Goodpaster's views have implications for genetic engineering?

GARY VARNER

Biocentric Individualism

Gary Varner is associate professor of philosophy at Texas A&M University. In his recent book, *In Nature's Interests? Interests, Animal Rights, and Environmental Ethics,* as well as in a series of articles, Varner defends biocentric individualism. Biocentric individualism is the view that living things, even nonconscious ones such as plants, have morally significant

Gary Varner, "Biocentric Individualism," from *Environmental Ethics: What Really Matters, What Really Works,* David Schmidtz and Elizabeth Willott, eds., Oxford University Press, 2002, pp. 108–120. Reprinted by permission of Oxford University Press.

interests. However, unlike Taylor (and others) who argue for egalitarianism among interests, Varner maintains that some interests are morally more significant than others, thus attempting to show that biocentric individualism is a practicable position. Varner writes, "[I]t is plausible to conclude that the lives of plants are, generally, less valuable than the lives of desiring creatures, including yours and mine. And that goes a long way toward showing that biocentric individualism is a practicable view, although most environmental philosophers have doubted that it is."

CRITICAL READING QUESTIONS

1. For Varner, how are moral standing, interests, and intrinsic value connected?
2. What is the mental state theory of individual welfare and how does Varner argue against it?
3. How does Varner adapt G. E. Moore's argument about the intrinsic value of beauty to argue for the intrinsic value of living things?
4. How does Varner propose to construct a hierarchy of interests?

INTRODUCTION

As a boy, I often wandered in the woods near my home in central Ohio. One August day, I dug up a maple seedling from the woods and planted it in one of my mother's flowerbeds beside the house. Within hours, the seedling was terribly wilted. Convinced that I had mortally wounded the plant, I felt a wave of guilt and, wishing to hasten what I believed to be its inevitable and imminent demise, I pulled it up, broke its small stalk repeatedly, and stuffed it in the trash. When my mother later explained that the plant was only in temporary shock from being transplanted into full sun, I felt an even larger wave of guilt for having dispatched it unnecessarily.

Was I just a soft-headed lad? Even then, I did not think that the plant was conscious, and since childhood, I have not again tried to "euthanize" a doomed plant. I feel no guilt about weeding the garden, mowing the lawn, or driving over the plants which inevitably crowd the four-wheel-drive paths I gravitate towards while camping. Nevertheless, I now let "weeds" grow indiscriminately in my wooded backyard, I mow around the odd wildflower that pops up amid the Bermuda grass out front, and I sometimes swerve to avoid a plant when tracking solitude in my truck. I believe that insects are not conscious, that they are in the same category, morally speaking, as plants, yet I often carry cockroaches and wasps outside rather than kill them. I'll even pause while mowing to let a grasshopper jump to safety. My relative diffidence regarding insects could just be erring on the side of caution. I believe that insects *probably* are not conscious, whereas I am *cock-sure* that plants are not; so when I do dispatch an insect, I make a point of crushing it quite thoroughly, including its head. Similarly, my current plant-regarding decisions are doubtless inspired in part by aesthetic judgments rather than concern for their nonconscious well-being. The wildflowers in my front yard are just more interesting to look at than a continuous stretch of Bermuda grass, and my unkempt backyard buffers me from my neighbors. Still, I believe it is better—*morally* better—that plants thrive rather than die, even if they do not benefit humans or other, conscious creatures. So if I was just soft-headed to feel bad about that maple seedling, then my gray matter hasn't quite firmed up yet.

But *am* I just soft-headed, or is there a rational case to be made for plants and other presumably nonconscious organisms? A few philosophers have thought so. The famous doctor and theologian, Albert Schweitzer, wrote:

> A man is truly ethical only when he obeys the compulsion to help all life which he is able to

> assist, and shrinks from injuring anything that lives. He does not ask how far this or that life deserves one's sympathy as being valuable, nor, beyond that, whether and to what degree it is capable of feeling. Life as such is sacred to him. He tears no leaf from a tree, plucks no flower, and takes care to crush no insect. If in summer he is working by lamplight, he prefers to keep the window shut and breathe a stuffy atmosphere rather than see one insect after another fall with singed wings upon his table.

If he walks on the road after a shower and sees an earthworm which has strayed on it, . . . he lifts it from the deadly stone surface, and puts it on the grass. If he comes across an insect which has fallen into a puddle, he stops a moment in order to hold out a leaf or a stalk on which it can save itself.[1]

And in the contemporary literature of environmental ethics, Paul Taylor's 1986 book, *Respect For Nature: A Theory of Environmental Ethics,* is a must-read for any serious student of the field. In it Taylor argues that extending a Kantian ethic of respect to nonconscious individuals is plausible once one understands that organisms, "conscious or not, all are equally teleological centers of life in the sense that each is a unified system of goal-oriented activities directed toward their preservation and well-being," that each has a good of its own which is "prima facie worthy of being preserved or promoted as an end in itself and for the sake of the entity whose good it is."[2]

I call views like Schweitzer's and Taylor's *biocentric individualism,* because they attribute moral standing to all living things while denying that holistic entities like species or ecosystems have moral standing. Hence they are *bio*centric—rather than, say anthropocentric or sentientist—but they are still *individualist* views—rather than versions of holism.

Schweitzer's and Taylor's views differ in important ways. Perhaps most significantly, Schweitzer talks as if we incur guilt every time we harm a living thing, even when we do so to preserve human life. He writes:

> Whenever I in any way sacrifice or injure life, I am not within the sphere of the ethical, but I become guilty, whether it be egoistically guilty for the sake of maintaining my own existence or welfare, or unegoistically guilty for the sake of maintaining a greater number of other existences or their welfare.[3]

In the '40s and '50s, Schweitzer was celebrated in the popular media for bringing modern hospital services to the heart of Africa. Yet he appears to have thought that he incurred guilt when he saved human lives by killing disease microbes, not to mention when he killed things to eat. By contrast, in his book, Taylor makes it clear that he believes we are justified in violating plants' (and some animals') most basic interests in a range of cases: certainly for the sake of surviving, but also for the sake of furthering nonbasic, but culturally important, interests of humans. He does impose on this a requirement of "minimum wrong," that is, harming as few living things as possible in the process[4] but Taylor, unlike Schweitzer, believes that we can prioritize interests in a way that justifies us in preserving our own lives and pursuing certain nonbasic interests at the expense of plants' (and some animals') most basic interests.

I will return to this question of which interests take precedence in various cases of conflict later. That is certainly an important question for any biocentric individualist. After all, if you think that even disease microbes and radishes have moral standing, then you need an explanation of how your interests can override those of millions of plants and microbes which must be doomed in the course of living a full human life. Otherwise, you are left with Schweitzer's perpetual guilt. But if I wasn't just being a soft-headed lad when I regretted killing that maple seedling—if there is a rational case to be made for plants (and other nonconscious organisms) having moral standing—then the first question is: Why think this?

WHY THINK THAT PLANTS HAVE MORAL STANDING?

I have two basic arguments for the conclusion that they do. Before discussing these arguments, however, it is important to be more clear about what, specifically, is being asked.

As I use the terms, to say that an entity has moral standing is to say that it has interests, and to say that it has interests is to say that it has needs and/or desires, and that the satisfaction of those needs and/or desires creates intrinsic value. When I say that their satisfaction creates intrinsic value, I mean that it makes the world a better place, independent of the entity's relations to other things. As the introduction to this volume emphasizes, the term "intrinsic value" is a key one in environmental ethics, but it is also a very nuanced one. There certainly is a distinction to be drawn between valuing something because it is useful, and valuing it apart from its usefulness. One way of expressing the biocentric individualist stance, then, would be to describe it as the view that moral agents ought to value plants' lives intrinsically rather than merely instrumentally. However, putting it this way suggests that plants' flourishing might not be a good thing if there were no conscious valuers around to consider it, and one of my arguments for biocentric individualism purports to show that plants' flourishing is a good thing independent of there being any conscious valuers around at all. So I define biocentric individualism in terms of plants having interests, the satisfaction of which creates intrinsic value as defined above, whether or not there are any conscious valuers around.

A second thing to be clear about is what I mean by "plants." For simplicity's sake, I will speak simply of "plants," but unless stated otherwise, what I mean by this is *all nonconscious organisms.* Later I will take up the question of which nonhuman animals lack consciousness. For now, suffice it to say that even after the taxonomic revisions of the 1970s, the animal kingdom includes a number of organisms that are poor candidates for consciousness, e.g. barnacles and sponges. Besides plants, the new taxonomy includes three whole kingdoms, the members of which are equally poor candidates. The fungi are just heterotrophic plants. Organisms in the new kingdoms monera and protista—single-celled organisms like bacteria and amoebas (respectively)—were previously classified as animals. But in this essay, "plants" is a shorthand for all of these nonconscious organisms.

In summary, I assume the following definitions of these key terms:

Moral standing: An entity has moral standing if and only if it has interests.

Interests: An entity has interests if and only if the fulfillment of its needs and/or desires creates intrinsic value.

Intrinsic value: Intrinsic value is the value something has independently of its relationships to other things. If a thing has intrinsic value, then its existence (flourishing, etc.) makes the world a better place, independently of its value to anything else or any other entity's awareness of it.

Plants: Unless stated otherwise, "plants" refers to all nonconscious organisms, including (presumably) all members of the plant kingdom, but also all members of the kingdoms fungi, monera, and protista, as well as some members of the animal kingdom (to be specified later).

So the question is: Why think that all those "plants" have interests, the satisfaction of which creates intrinsic value, independently of any conscious organism's interest in them?

My first argument for this conclusion is developed in detail in my book, *In Nature's Interests?*[5] There I argue against the dominant, mental state theory of individual welfare (for short, the mental state theory). The dominant account of individual welfare in recent Western moral philosophy has identified what is in an individual's interests with what the individual actually desires, plus what the individual would desire if he or she were both adequately informed and impartial across phases of his or her life. This dominant account then identifies what is in an individual's *best* interests with the latter, with what he or she would desire under those idealized conditions. Formally:

The mental state theory of individual welfare:
X is in an individual A's interests just in case:

1. A actually desires X, or
2. A would desire X if A were sufficiently informed and impartial across phases of his or her life; and
3. What is in A's *best* interests is defined in terms of clause (2).

Something like this theory is accepted by most contemporary moral and political philosophers.

My first argument for the moral standing of plants begins by pointing to an inadequacy of the mental state theory.

> **Argument 1:** The mental state theory seems to provide an inadequate account of the interests of conscious individuals. If that is so, and if the way to fix it involves acknowledging that intrinsic value is created by the satisfaction of nonconscious, biologically based needs of such individuals, then it makes sense to attribute interests to plants. For although plants are incapable of having desires, they have biologically based needs just as do conscious individuals.

Here is an example that brings out the problem I see in the mental state theory:

> **Example 1:** By the 19th century, British mariners were carrying citrus fruit on long sea voyages to prevent the debilitating disease of scurvy. It was not until this century that scientists discovered that we need about 10 milligrams of ascorbic acid a day, and that citrus fruits prevent scurvy because they contain large amounts of ascorbic acid.

To see how this raises a problem, consider what is meant by being "adequately informed" in the second clause of the mental state theory. Some authors limit "adequate information" to the best scientific knowledge of the day. But then it would be false that those mariners had any interest in getting 10 milligrams of ascorbic acid a day. This is because they did not in fact desire it (they did not even know it exists), and even having the best scientific knowledge of the day would not have led them to desire it because no one then knew about it. The problem is that it certainly seems wrong to say that getting 10 milligrams of ascorbic acid a day was not in their interests.

This problem is easily avoided by adding a clause about biologically based needs to our theory of individual welfare. Renamed appropriately, the theory would now be something like this:

> **The psycho-biological theory of individual welfare:** X is in an individual A's interests just in case:
>
> 1. A actually desires X,
> 2. A would desire X if A were sufficiently informed and impartial across phases of his or her life; or
> 3. X serves some biologically based need of A.

In my book,[6] I give a detailed analysis of the complex notion of a biologically based need, arguing that these can be determined by examining the evolutionary history of an organism. Here, I think it unnecessary to revisit that analysis. Ascorbic acid clearly served a biologically based need of sailors before modern scientists discovered it. So, on this psycho-biological theory, it was in those sailors' interest to get enough of it, even though no one knew anything about ascorbic acid at the time.

Note that this new theory says nothing about what is in one's *best* interests. I replaced clause (3) in the mental state theory rather than adding another clause because identifying what is in one's best interests with what one would desire under ideal motivational and informational conditions—clause (2)—faces similar problems. Other things being equal, it seems that getting enough ascorbic acid was in those mariners' best interests, even though they would still not have desired it even under the best motivational and informational conditions. So even after adding a clause about biologically based needs, it would still be a mistake to identify what is in one's best interests with clause (2).

One limitation of the 19th-century mariners example is that being "sufficiently informed" can be analyzed other than in terms of having "the best scientific knowledge of the day." We could, for instance, analyze it in terms of having all the scientific knowledge that humans will ever or could ever accumulate. I believe there are other problems with this analysis,[7] but it would solve the problem raised by the above example. However, here is another example that brings out the same kind of problem with the mental state theory, and where the alternative analysis of "sufficiently informed" doesn't help:

> **Example 2:** Like many cat owners, I grapple with the question of whether and when to allow my cat, Nanci, to go outside. Cats find the outdoors endlessly fascinating, but they also

encounter health risks outside, including exposure to feline leukemia virus (FeLV) and fleas (which Nanci happens to be allergic to).

I frankly do not know whether or not keeping Nanci indoors is in her best interests, all things considered. Nonetheless, it does seem clear that keeping her inside would serve some interests of hers, in at least some ways. For instance, it would prevent exposure to FeLV and fleas. Yet the mental state theory does not support this intuition because it is not clear that it even makes sense to talk about what an animal like Nanci would desire if she were "sufficiently informed and impartial across phases of her life." I assume that Nanci is congenitally incapable of understanding the relevant information about FeLV and fleas. So on the mental state theory, what are we to say about her going outside? It looks like we have to conclude that, whenever she in fact wants to go out, she has no interest whatsoever in staying inside, because clause (2) is irrelevant in her case. It just doesn't make sense, in the case of animals like Nanci, to talk about what they would desire were they "sufficiently informed" (let alone "impartial across phases of their lives"). What is in their interests is whatever they happen to desire at any moment in time. This is another counterintuitive implication of the mental state theory, and one which the psycho-biological theory avoids. Although the psycho-biological theory as formulated above is silent on the issue of what is in an individual's best interests, it at least supports the intuition that Nanci has some interest in staying inside (because doing so would serve her biologically based needs by preventing exposure to FeLV and fleas), even if she now desires to go outside and no sense can be made of what an animal like her would desire under ideal epistemological and motivational conditions.

The examples of Nanci and the 19th-century mariners together illustrate a general problem for the mental state theory. The theory ties all of our interests to what we desire, either actually or under ideal epistemological and motivational conditions, but not all of our interests are tied in this way to our conscious desires and beliefs. Most (maybe even all) of our desires are tied to our beliefs about the world, because as our beliefs change, our desires change. For instance, suppose that I desire to marry Melody, primarily because I believe that she is a fine fiddler. When I find out that my belief about her is false, my desire to marry her will presumably be extinguished. Similarly, if I do not desire to marry Melinda only because I believe that she is a lousy fiddler, when I find out that she is actually a virtuoso, I will presumably form a desire to marry her. My interest in marrying each woman comes and goes with my beliefs about her. However, nothing I could possibly believe about the world, whether true or false, could change the fact that I need about 10 milligrams a day of ascorbic acid to stay healthy, and no matter how strongly I might desire it, I will never be able to make it true that going without ascorbic acid is in my interest. My interest in ascorbic acid is determined by a biological need that exists wholly independent of my beliefs and desires. This is a central advantage of the psycho-biological theory over the mental state theory. Some things are only in our interests if we happen to desire them or have certain beliefs about the world, but other things are in our interests no matter what we desire or believe, or what we would desire and believe under ideal conditions. We can refer to the former as preference interests and to the latter as biological interests. The mental state theory errs by identifying all of our interests with our preference interests. The psycho-biological theory acknowledges these, but also accounts for biological interests that are wholly independent of our preference interests.

That being said, my first argument for the moral standing of plants is now complete. The above examples are intended to illustrate how the dominant, mental state theory of individual welfare is flawed, because it ties all of individuals' interests to their actual or hypothetical desires. An obvious way to fix this problem is to hold that individuals also have biological interests in the fulfillment of their various biologically based needs, whether they (like the 19th-century mariners) could only become aware of these needs under special circumstances, or they (like Nanci the cat) are congenitally incapable of desiring that those needs be fulfilled. But then, since plants too have biologically based needs, they too have interests, even though they are congenitally incapable of desiring anything at all.

I did not include my second argument for the view that plants have moral standing in my 1998 book because, frankly, I doubted that it would be persuasive to anyone not already essentially convinced. Nevertheless, I think that this second argument expresses very clearly the most basic value assumption of the biocentric individualist. It also ties in to famous thought experiments in ethical theory and environmental ethics, and so I include it here.

The argument is driven by a variant of a famous thought experiment that British philosopher G. E. Moore used to cast doubt on sentientism (the view that only sentient—that is conscious—organisms have moral standing). Moore discussed the classical utilitarians (Jeremy Bentham, John Stuart Mill, and Henry Sidgwick, who were all sentientists) at length and in particular responded to Sidgwick's claim that "No one would consider it rational to aim at the production of beauty in external nature, apart from any possible contemplation of it by human beings." Moore responded:

> Well, I may say at once, that I, for one, do consider this rational; and let us see if I cannot get any one to agree with me. Consider what this admission really means. It entitles us to put the following case. Let us imagine one world exceedingly beautiful. Imagine it as beautiful as you can; put into it whatever on this earth you most admire—mountains, rivers, the sea; trees, and sunsets, stars and moon. Imagine these all combined in the most exquisite proportions, so that no one thing jars against another, but each contributes to increase the beauty of the whole. And then imagine the ugliest world you can possibly conceive. Imagine it simply one heap of filth, containing everything that is most disgusting to us, for whatever reason, and the whole, as far as may be, without one redeeming feature. Such a pair of worlds we are entitled to compare: they fall within Prof. Sidgwick's meaning, and the comparison is highly relevant to it. The only thing we are not entitled to imagine is that any human being ever has or ever, by any possibility, *can*, live in either, can ever see and enjoy the beauty of the one or hate the foulness of the other. Well, even so, supposing them quite apart from any possible contemplation by human beings; still, is it irrational to hold that it is better that the beautiful world should exist, than the one which is ugly? Would it not be well, in any case, to do what we could to produce it rather than the other?[8]

Moore thought we would agree with him in answering yes. But then, he continued:

> If it be once admitted that the beautiful world *in itself* is better than the ugly, then it follows, that however many beings may enjoy it, and however much better their enjoyment may be than it is itself, yet its mere existence adds *something* to the goodness of the whole.[9]

That is, Moore concluded, the mere existence of beauty adds intrinsic value to the world.

I have always been unsure what to think about Moore's thought experiment, so apparently I am of two minds when it comes to saying that the mere existence of beauty adds intrinsic value to the world. However, I have always felt certain about my answer to an analogous question. Suppose that instead of choosing between creating a beautiful world and an ugly world, the choice were between creating a world devoid of life and a world brimming with living things, neither of which would ever evolve conscious life or even be visited or known about by any conscious organisms. If, like me, you believe that it matters which world is produced and that it would be better to produce the world chock-full of nonconscious life, then you seem to be committed to biocentric individualism. For you appear to believe that life—even nonconscious life—has intrinsic value. To paraphrase Moore:

> **Argument 2:** If we admit that a world of nonconscious living things is *in itself* better than a world devoid of all life, then it follows that however much better it is to be both conscious and alive, the mere existence of nonconscious life adds *something* to the goodness of the world.

Note that this contrasts with the "last man" thought experiment (where the last person on earth destroys a tree "just for fun") in two important ways. First, in my variant of Moore's thought experiment, it is stipulated that there is no person on the scene at all. This is important because an anthropocentrist might try to explain the problem with the last man in terms of his action's effects on his own character. Second, and more importantly, in the "last man" case, the tree is said to be "the last remaining Redwood," but in my variant of Moore's thought experiment, nothing is said about the plants in question being rare. If we agree that it matters which of my worlds is produced, and that it would be better to produce the plant-filled world, then we seem to agree that the lives of even the most mundane plants add intrinsic value to the world.

JUST WHAT ARE PLANTS' INTERESTS WORTH?

The next question has to be: Just *how valuable* are the interests of plants, in relation to those of humans and other animals? Moral hierarchies are unpopular in many quarters. In particular, feminist philosophers often condemn hierarchical views of beings' relative moral significance for being instruments of patriarchal oppression. But as a biocentric individualist, I feel forced to endorse one. Otherwise, how could I live with myself? I gleefully tear radishes from the garden for a snack, swatting mosquitoes all the while. I take antibiotics for a persistent sinus infection, and (at least when I'm not on antibiotics) I send countless intestinal bacteria on a deadly joyride into the city sewer system every morning. Unless I can give good reasons for thinking that my interests somehow trump those of microbes and plants (if not also animals), I am left with Albert Schweitzer's view, quoted above, that we "become guilty" whenever we "in any way sacrifice or injure life," even when fighting off disease organisms, eating, and defecating. In my book,[10] I argue that a plausible assumption about what I call "hierarchically structured interests" does the trick, when coupled with empirical observations about certain broad categories of interests.

Here is what I mean by hierarchically structured interests:

> **Hierarchically structured interests:** Two interests are hierarchically structured when the satisfaction of one requires the satisfaction of the other, but not vice versa.

Certain types of interests clearly stand in this relationship to other types of interests. For example, satisfying my desire to succeed professionally requires the satisfaction of innumerable more particular desires across decades, but not vice versa. It takes years to succeed professionally, and therefore I have to satisfy innumerable day-to-day desires to eat this or that in the course of completing that long-term project. But each particular desire to eat can be satisfied without satisfying my long-term desire to succeed professionally. So my desires to eat and to succeed professionally are hierarchically structured in the above sense.

Generally, what the contemporary American philosopher Bernard Williams calls "ground projects" and "categorical desires" stand in this relationship to day-to-day desires for particular things. Here is how Williams defines these terms:

> **Ground projects and categorical desires:** A ground project is "a nexus of projects . . . which are closely related to [one's] existence and which to a significant degree give a meaning to [one's] life," and a categorical desire is one that answers the question "Why is life worth living?"[11]

A person's ground project normally is a nexus of categorical desires, and generally, a ground project requires decades to complete. There are, of course, exceptions. It is conceivable that a person might have literally only one categorical desire, a desire which he or she could satisfy in one fell swoop. Perhaps a young gymnast aiming at a gold medal in the Olympics is a realistic approximation of this, but notice that even in the case of the gymnast: (1) satisfying the desire for a gold medal requires years of training, and (2) we would probably think it unhealthy and abnormal if the gymnast had no other ground project, if there were no other, longer-term desires that made her life worth living beyond the Olympics. So a ground project normally involves a host of very long-term desires, which bear the above kind of hierarchical relationship with the individual's day-to-day desires for this or that specific thing.

Here is a plausible assumption about interests that are clearly hierarchically structured:

> **Assumption:** Generally speaking, ensuring the satisfaction of interests from similar levels in

> similar hierarchies of different individuals creates similar amounts of value, and the dooming of interests from similar levels in similar hierarchies of different individuals creates similar levels of disvalue.

In stating the assumption in this way, I do not mean to imply that we can make very fine-tuned judgements about which interests are more valuable than others.[12] All I claim is that interests from certain very broad categories *generally* bear this relationship to interests from other very broad categories. In particular, I argue that the following two principles are reasonable in light of the assumption:

> **Principle P1 (the priority of desires principle):** Generally speaking, the death of an entity that has desires is a worse thing than the death of an entity that does not.
>
> **Principle P2′ (the priority of ground projects principle):** Generally speaking, the satisfaction of ground projects is more important than the satisfaction of noncategorical desires.

Since I introduced the above assumption by discussing human ground projects, let me begin with principle P2′.

I call it P2′, rather than just P2, because in my book I first introduce, and dismiss, this principle:

> **Principle P2 (the priority of *human* desires principle)**: The satisfaction of the desires of humans is more important than the satisfaction of the desires of animals.

Principle P2 would solve the problem under discussion in this section, but it is transparently speciesist. It says that humans' desires are more important than any other organisms' simply because they are desires of *humans*. Principle P2′ compares ground projects to noncategorical desires without asserting that humans' desires are more important than any other organisms'. If it turns out that some nonhuman animals have ground projects, then Principle P2′ applies equally to theirs. Which animals, if any, have ground projects is an empirical question, as is the question of whether all human beings do. Surely some human beings do not. For instance, anencephalic babies and the permanently comatose clearly do not, and perhaps others, like the most profoundly retarded, or those who have lost the will to live, do not. Regarding animals, my hunch is that very few if any nonhuman animals have ground projects, but maybe some do (perhaps some great apes or cetaceans). The crucial thing to note is that principle P2′ is not speciesist. It does not say that humans' interests are more important *because they are humans' interests*. Principle P2′ only says that ground projects, wherever they occur, generally have more value than noncategorical desires. P2′ leaves the question of which beings have ground projects open for empirical investigation; it does not stipulate that only humans have this especially valuable kind of interest.

So why think that ground projects are more valuable than noncategorical desires? The reason is that, as we saw above, ground projects normally stand in a hierarchical relationship to day-to-day desires for particular things; satisfying a ground project requires the satisfaction of innumerable day-to-day desires for particular things, but not vice versa. So under the above assumption (that various interests within each type generally have similar amounts of value), satisfying a ground project generally creates more value than satisfying any such day-to-day desire.

I will discuss the implications of P2′ in the next section, along with those of P1. First, however, let me discuss the justification of P1. Notice that P1 does not assert that just any desire trumps any biological need or set thereof. Some day-to-day desires for particular things are incredibly trivial and it would be implausible to say that these trivial desires trump seemingly important biological interests like one's biological interest in good cardiovascular health. But all that principle P1 states is that "Generally speaking, the death of an entity that has desires is a worse thing than the death of an entity that does not." This is plausible under the assumption stated above, given the following general fact: maintenance of the capacity to form and satisfy desires requires the ongoing satisfaction of the lion's share of one's biological needs. Certainly not every biological need of a conscious organism must be fulfilled for it to go on forming desires. In particular, the account I give in my book implies that the continued functioning of my vasa deferentia is in my biological interest,[13] but obviously I would go on desiring sex (among other things) after a vasectomy. One of the deep challenges to my position (as Vermont philosopher Bill Throop has driven home to me in conversation) is deciding how to individuate interests. Do I have just one biological interest in the continued functioning of my whole cardiovascular system? One interest in the functioning of my heart and another in the functioning of my vascular system? Or do I have myriad interests, in the functioning of my various ventricles, veins, arteries, and so on? This is a difficult issue, but however it gets sorted out, it seems plausible to say that just as satisfying a ground project requires the satisfaction of innumerable day-to-day desires for particular things, maintaining the general capacity to form and satisfy desires requires the ongoing satisfaction of the lion's share of one's biological needs. As a conscious process, maintenance of the capacity to form and satisfy desires presumably requires maintenance of myriad biological organs and subsystems, including, at the very least, the respiratory and cardiovascular systems, and most of the central nervous system. The argument for principle P1, then, is this: The only interests plants have in common with conscious organisms are biological interests. The ability to form and satisfy desires stands in a hierarchical relationship to such biological interests. But if interests of these two types generally have similar value, then conscious animals' lives have more value than plants' lives, because animals satisfy both types of interests in the course of their lives, whereas plants satisfy only one type.

The question posed in this section has not been answered precisely. My argument has not shown precisely how much the interests of plants are worth, relative to the interests of humans or other animals. For reasons given in my book,[14] I think it is impossible to give such a precise answer to this question. However, if principle P1 is indeed justified by the principle of inclusiveness (coupled with the assumption articulated above), then it is plausible to conclude that the *lives* of plants are, generally, less valuable than the *lives* of desiring creatures, including yours and mine. And that goes a long way towards showing that biocentric individualism is a practicable view, although most environmental philosophers have doubted that it is.

IS BIOCENTRIC INDIVIDUALISM PRACTICABLE?

One reason for doubt would be that before Paul Taylor, the only well-known biocentric individualist was Albert Schweitzer, and as we have seen, he said flatly that we are guilty for merely keeping ourselves alive by eating and fighting disease. However, as the foregoing section shows, a biocentric individualist can reasonably endorse a hierarchy of interests and related principles showing why it is better that we do this than let ourselves perish. We can at least say that my view implies this rough hierarchy of value:

ground projects
noncategorical desires
biological interests

Principle P2′ states that the satisfaction of a ground project is better than (creates more value than) the satisfaction of any interest of the other two kinds. Thus killing an individual with a ground project robs the world of a special kind of value. According to principle P1, the lives of many nonhuman animals have more value than the lives of plants, because these conscious organisms have both biological interests and noncategorical desires, whereas plants have only biological interests. Thus killing an animal robs the world of more value than does killing a plant.

The second part of this value hierarchy focuses attention on questions about consciousness that were alluded to earlier: which animals are conscious, which ones have desires? These questions are related, but not equivalent. I assume that all "genuine" desires are conscious, or at least potentially conscious, just as pain is. However, the evidence for desires in nonhuman animals may not overlap the evidence for pain, because I also assume that desires require relatively sophisticated cognitive capacities, whereas the bare consciousness of pain may not. A detailed treatment of this issue is beyond the scope of this essay, but here is a summary of the conclusions I reach from the more detailed treatment in my book.[15] All normal, mature mammals and birds very probably *do* have desires, and there is a somewhat weaker case for saying that "herps" (reptiles and amphibians) do too. The case for saying that fish have desires is decisively weaker. However, the available evidence makes it very likely that all vertebrates, including fish, can feel pain. This is a curious result—it sounds odd to say that fish could feel pain without desiring an end to it—and so I suspect that as more kinds of scientific studies are available than I considered in my book, the evidence for pain and for desire in the animal kingdom will converge. However, for the sake of discussion here, I assume that although mammals and birds have desires, fish and invertebrates do not.[16]

We can now spell out more specifically the implications of the principles defended in the preceding section. Principle P1 tells us that it is better to kill desireless organisms than desiring ones. This addresses Schweitzer's hyperbolic guilt, because it shows that it would be worse for a human being to kill herself than it would be for her to kill any plant or microbe for the sake of good nutrition or fighting off disease. However, in light of the above discussion of consciousness, this does not imply that vegetarian diets are better, since most invertebrates apparently lack consciousness, and even fish may lack desires. Also, since it is possible to obtain animal by-products like eggs and dairy foods from animals without killing them, a lacto-ovo diet might be perfectly respectful of animals' intrinsic value. (There are other ethical considerations, of course, as well as complicated issues in human nutrition. For an overview, see the essays in Comstock.)[17]

I also suspect that Principle P2′ can be used to make a case for the humane killing of animals who clearly have (noncategorical) desires. My reasoning is as follows. To the extent that hunting and slaughter-based animal agriculture play an important role in sustainable human communities, the value of protecting the background conditions for satisfying humans' ground projects would seem to support the necessary killing, at least if the animals live good lives and are killed humanely. Obviously, various animals, including mammals and birds, played a very large role in both paleolithic hunting-gathering societies and in the emergence of agriculture. Domesticated mammals continue to have a crucial role in sustainable agricultural systems in so-called "developing" nations, where they provide not only food but draft power and fertilizer. But at present it is still unclear to me just how much killing of animals might be necessary in utopian sustainable communities of the future.

In light of these implications of Principles P1 and P2′, the biocentric individualist stance hardly looks unlivable in the way Schweitzer's talk of perpetual guilt would suggest. There is a deeper reason that many environmental philosophers dismiss the biocentric individualist stance, however. They fear that it somehow devalues nature and thus, even if it is not literally an unlivable ethic, it is "inadequate" as an *environmental* ethic. This charge of "inadequacy" takes at least two distinct forms, and the biocentric individualist response to each must be different.

First, it is often claimed that individualist theories in general (that is, anthropocentrism and sentientism in addition to biocentric individualism) have implications that do not comport with the environmentalist agenda, which includes things like endangered species programs, the elimination of exotic species from natural areas, and the whole emphasis on preserving remaining natural areas. The heart of this claim is that because they focus on individuals, such theories get the wrong answers in a range of cases. For instance, environmentalists are keenly interested in preserving remaining natural areas, but, so this objection goes, biocentric individualism cannot justify this emphasis. For if we compare a woods and a cultivated field, or an old growth forest and a managed timber lot, they may look equally valuable from a biocentric individualist stance. Simply put, if only biological interests are at stake, then a cultivated area supporting thousands of thriving plants creates just as much value as a wild area that supports the same number of plants. Similarly, the biological interests of common plants seem no more valuable than the biological interests of rare plants.

This first version of the "inadequacy" charge misfires precisely because there *is* more at stake than the biological interests of the plants involved. Environmentalists commonly claim that in order to preserve the ecological context in which humans can live healthy, productive, and innovative lives into the indefinite future, we must stop the current trend of species extinctions and preserve most remaining wild areas. Characterizing the environmentalists' claim as a general need to safeguard background biological diversity in our environment, my response to the first version of the inadequacy charge is this. Principle P2′ attaches preeminent importance to safeguarding humans' ability to satisfy their ground projects. But if safeguarding this ability requires safeguarding background biological diversity in our environment, then doing so is of preeminent importance, at least instrumentally, in my view. That is, to the extent that environmentalists are correct that their practical agenda safeguards long-term human interests, any version of biocentric individualism which, like mine, attributes preeminent importance to certain interests of humans can probably endorse their agenda.

At this point it is important to note that two senses of the term "anthropocentric" are sometimes conflated in discussions of environmental ethics. In one sense of the term, a view is anthropocentric just in case it denies that nonhuman nature has any intrinsic value whatsoever. Obviously, biocentric individualism is not anthropocentric in this sense. But in another sense, a view is called anthropocentric if it gives pride of place to certain interests which only humans have. Schweitzer's version of biocentric individualism is not anthropocentric in this second sense, but because I doubt that any nonhuman animals have ground projects, mine is. For clarity's sake, I use the labels "valuational anthropocentrism" and "axiological anthropocentrism" to refer, respectively, to views that deny all intrinsic value to nonhumans and to views that acknowledge the intrinsic value of some nonhuman beings but insist that only humans have certain preeminently important interests.[18]

The other form of the "inadequacy" charge focuses on the fact that for the biocentric individualist, even if holistic entities like species and ecosystems have enormous value, this value is still only instrumental. Environmentalists, it is claimed, tend to think that such entities have intrinsic value rather than merely instrumental value, and thus environmentalists tend to think more like holists.

I think this version of the "inadequacy" charge misconstrues one of the central questions of environmental ethics. As environmental philosophers, we should not think of ourselves as focusing on the question: What do environmentalists *in fact* think has intrinsic value? Rather, we should be asking: What *should* we think has intrinsic value? Or, what do we *have good reasons* to think has intrinsic value? Defining an "adequate" environmental ethic as one that matches the pre-theoretic intuitions of self-professed environmentalists turns the discipline of environmental ethics into a kind of moral anthropology rather than a reasoned search for truth. In this essay, I have not developed a case against environmental holism, but the arguments of this section do show that biocentric individualism cannot be summarily dismissed as impracticable, either generally or in regard to environmental policy specifically.

CONCLUSION

My larger goal in this essay has been to show that one need not be soft-headed to think that it matters, morally speaking, how we treat plants. It would, in my judgment, be unreasonable to obsess on the microbes one's immune system is killing every day or on how one's dinner vegetables were dealt their death-blows, but it is not irrational to think that it is good to save the life of plants and nonconscious animals when one can. Good arguments can be given for thinking this, and someone who thinks this can consistently live a good human life.

And, of course, if it is reasonable to think that plants' lives have intrinsic value, then it was not irrational for me to feel at least a little bit guilty about killing that maple seedling unnecessarily.

NOTES

1. Albert Schweitzer, *The Philosophy of Civilization* (New York: Macmillan, 1955), p. 310.
2. Paul Taylor, "The Ethics of Respect for Nature," *Environmental Ethics* 3 (1981), p. 210.
3. Schweitzer, *Philosophy of Civilization,* p. 325.

4. Paul Taylor, Respect for Nature: A Theory of Environmental Ethics (Princeton: Princeton University Press, 1986), p. 289.
5. Gary E. Varner, *In Nature's Interests? Interests, Animal Rights, and Environmental Ethics* (New York: Oxford University Press, 1998) chap. 3.
6. Ibid., pp. 64–71.
7. Ibid., pp. 58–60.
8. G. E. Moore, *Principia Ethica* (London: Cambridge University Press, 1903), p. 83.
9. Ibid., pp. 83–85 (emphases in original).
10. Varner, *In Nature's Interests?* chap. 4
11. Bernard Williams, *Moral Luck* (Cambridge: Cambridge University Press, 1981), pp. 12–13, and Bernard Williams, *Problems of the Self* (Cambridge: Cambridge University Press, 1973), pp. 85–86.
12. Strictly speaking, my view is that the *satisfaction* of interests creates intrinsic value, but in this essay I speak interchangeably of "the value of various interests," "the value of various intrests, satisfaction," and "the value created by the satisfaction of various interests."
13. Varner, *In Nature's Interests?* p. 97.
14. Ibid., pp. 80–88.
15. Ibid., pp. 26–30.
16. The issue is further complicated by the phenomenon of convergent evolution—some invertebrates could have evolved coping strategies that most other invertebrates have not. In particular, cephalopods (octopus, squid, and cuttlefish) may have evolved consciousness of pain and cognitive capacities that other invertebrates lack but most or all vertebrates have.
17. Gary Comstock, "Might Morality Require Veganism?" *Journal of Agricultural and Environmental Ethics* 7, no. 1 (Special issue, 1994).
18. Varner, *In Nature's Interests?* p. 121.

DISCUSSION QUESTIONS

1. Is it mere sentimentalism to express concern for plants?
2. If nonconscious beings can have a good, are there no limits to what can have a good? Why stop, as Varner does, with living things? Does moral concern for plants commit one to having to extend moral standing to machines? How about houses or rocks?
3. Is Varner committed to thinking that some human lives are worth more than others? Is this a problem for his view?
4. Is Varner successful in answering the charge that his view is not an adequate environmental ethic because such things as species, forests, ecosystems, and mountains are not alive (and therefore do not have direct moral standing)? (Hint: Varner discusses this issue in the last section of the article.)
5. Is mentality necessary for having interests? Consider fetuses, future generations, and dead people.

MARK BERNSTEIN

Well-Being

Mark Bernstein is associate professor of philosophy at the University of Texas-San Antonio. In his recent article, "Well-Being," Bernstein undertakes to defend a sentience cri-

Mark Bernstein, "Well Being," *American Philosophical Quarterly*, vol 35, no. 1, January 1998, pp. 39–55. Reprinted by permission.

terion of moral standing. He argues that plants cannot have a well-being (read: interests) in any meaningful sense because plants are not enough like us. He writes, "For an individual to own a well-being, it must own a well-being like ours."

CRITICAL READING QUESTIONS

1. According to Bernstein, what is the relation between having a well-being and being a moral patient?
2. How does Bernstein employ the idea of "life as we know it" to illuminate the concepts of welfare, benefit, and harm?
3. What does Bernstein find unpersuasive about trying to conceive diseased roots on analogy with a diseased mouth?
4. What is Bernstein's analogy of the machine that prints numbers supposed to show ?
5. What, according to Bernstein, makes a life worth living?
6. How does Bernstein explain our propensity to think that damaging a plant's roots constitutes a harm to the plant?

Let us now turn to the second strategy proffered to throw doubt upon the sentience criterion of welfare. The suggestion is that the possession of sentience is not necessary for an individual to possess a welfare; there are nonphenomenological ways for items in the world to be made better and worse off.

This suggestion can lay some claim to be rooted in commonsense and ordinary language. We frequently talk of the insentient tree being made better off by the proper proportions of water and sunlight, and being made worse off by the recent fungus infestation. The basic idea is that the good of a tree is constituted by its mature, developed state and that events that aid in its journey toward this end are considered benefits to it (i.e., enhancements to its welfare), while states of affairs that hinder its sojourn diminish its well-being. The tree, in a nonconscious, nonphenomenological way, of course, behaves in ways to effect this species-specific journey. It does what it can to extend its roots during times of drought, and resists, as best as it is able, the onslaught of disease. Its behavior is goal-directed, although being without consciousness, there is no recognition of this fact on behalf of the tree . . .

Still, I will argue that there is no warrant for attributing welfares to trees in any sense robust enough to found moral patienthood. The sense in which it makes sense to speak of a tree's well-being is the same sense in which we can speak of a stove's or pencil's well-being. Even the most generous moral inclusionist would admit that such an attribution would be far too attenuated to bestow moral patienthood upon its subject.

We begin by reflecting upon the truism that the concepts of benefit and harm, being better and worse off, and having a welfare, are human concepts. They are the concepts they are in virtue of the sorts of beings we are. It is in virtue of the way that we think, perceive, act, and feel, that these concepts (along with all other concepts) have the use they do. Part of the use we make of these concepts of well-being is that we ascribe them to others as well as to ourselves. If another is to be credited with a well-being, with the capacities to be benefited and harmed, and these attributions are to be understood in their literal implementations, then, at the very least, the subjects of these qualities must be enough like us to sustain them. If another is said to be harmed, it must, as a minimal matter of intelligibility, be harmed in ways analogous to the ways in which we humans—the inventors, users, and authorities of these concepts—are harmed.

Conceived in the right way, this point should be uncontested. However, confusions have arisen because either this point is unrecognized or misapplied. As an instance of the first source of confusion, consider the oft-heard comment that although there may be life on Mars, it surely will not be "life as we know it." This qualification is nonsense; the only sort of life that there is—and this is a matter of intelligibility and not of biology—*is* life as we know it. Nor need we travel beyond the Earth to encounter this problem. If someone were to suggest that the piece of chalk he now holds in his hand is alive, but not in the way we happen to think of living things, the correct response is to point out that, unless the speaker is using words in a metaphorical or technical sense, he is taking back with one hand what he offers with the other. Presumably the speaker admits that the chalk neither breathes, metabolizes, expends energy, moves on its own, and so forth. The debate is not whether the chalk manifests behavior, albeit in very diminished ways, that mirrors the actions of other uncontentiously living items like humans, animals, and trees; this question *would* be one best settled by biologists. Rather, the speaker is suggesting that the chalk lives, although not in the "ordinary" manner in which familiar things live. But what could this claim amount to? The chalk, by mutual consent, paradigmatically manifests all the "behavior" of an inanimate object. Indeed, the speaker cheerfully admits that the piece of chalk is inanimate—inanimate "as we know it." Alice-in-Wonderland tactics are being employed in the cases of the extraterrestrial and chalk and nothing but superfluous confusion can result.

The conceptual point that lives just are lives as we know them places no *a priori* limits upon scientific investigation; to think otherwise is to misapply the principle. We might, for all anyone knows, confront living organisms that are not carbon-based. Whether it is a metaphysical fact about the universe that only carbon-based individuals have the capacity for life is certainly not something that can be ascertained in one's private study. If all that is meant by those who claim that we may encounter life on some distant planet but "not as we know it" is that silicon-based life might be forthcoming, then there is no quarrel. Additionally, the conceptual point should not be read as presupposing a sort of behaviorism. The truism does not rest on an assumption that life is reducible to a set of behaviors, let alone that it is reducible to a determinate and restricted set of overt manifestations.

With life, so too with the qualities of welfare, benefit, and harm. For an individual to own a well-being, it must own a well-being like ours, where the qualification is pleonastic. To maintain that an individual has a welfare, can be benefited and harmed, but just not in the ways that we recognize as such, is being not merely quixotic but inconsistent. Perhaps the point can be supported by considerations regarding translatability. Would it make sense to translate an alien word as "benefit" when we know that she occasionally feels pain on occasions of its use, grimaces and winces on these occasions, and expresses the desire to remain in this state *for its own sake*?. . .

What follows from this is that a necessary condition for another possessing a welfare is that we be able to "relate empathetically" to what the other is enduring. That is, we—the inventors, users, authorities and in this case, paradigms of our concepts—must be able to understand what it is like for this other to be made better and worse off. (Here, I make the assumption, safe, I trust, in this situation, that we know what it is for ourselves to be made better and worse off). This understanding, in turn, minimally requires that the harm or benefit of the other be analogous or comparable to our own harms and benefits. In order to attribute benefits and harms legitimately to another, we need, minimally, to recognize how something like those putative benefits and harms would be benefits and harms to us.

Admittedly this sounds jarring. There is an almost automatic impulse to object that the metaphysical fact about another being benefited and harmed surely cannot depend upon our psychological abilities. At best, so it would seem, these empathetic relationships are required for knowing or appreciating that another is undergoing enjoyment or suffering, but it seems mistaken to believe that these ontic truths about the world depend upon our mental abilities. My point, however, is about the intelligibility of these claims, what one means when she attributes welfares to individuals. My claim is that without understanding benefits and harms in a way in which we humans can relate empathetically, the notions of benefits and harms lack sense; all that remains are the homonyms of meaningful discourse.

This requirement placed upon meaningful welfare attributions does not imply that the event that we attribute legitimately to another as a harm need constitute a harm to ourselves. Failure of a math exam may cause Frank great distress and so diminish his welfare, while an equally poor showing by Sally may leave her unaffected. Slapping a cat may bring about substantial pain while a similarly powerful blow placed upon Mike Tyson's arm would go completely unnoticed. Nonetheless, Sally and Mike, as well as the rest of us, can presumably understand how such events can diminish the well-being of another despite the fact that the acts would not have the negative effects upon ourselves. The basis for this understanding is hardly enigmatic. Sally realizes that if she failed her government exam she would feel as badly as Frank feels when he failed his math test and Tyson recognizes that if the blow to his arm were struck with far more force, he, too, would be deleteriously affected. We are able to make analogies from events that do not constitute harms to ourselves to like events that do, or would, constitute harms to us. Sally can see how a math grade has significance to Frank by comparing it to the significance that a failing government grade has to her. Tyson recognizes that the degree of the force of the blow is all that separates the cat's pain from his own. And, in these regards, we are all Sallys and Mikes. If we were not, if we were unable to analogize the events perpetrated on Frank and the cat as harms to us, there would be no justification, indeed, no sense, to speak about those events as harms to Frank and the cat, respectively.

The problem with attributing benefits and harms to trees is that there is no (nontechnical, nonstipulative) way to analogize what transpires to a tree as an event that would constitute either a benefit or harm to us. But to show this we should not succumb to the temptation of thinking that the basis for an empathetic relationship must be a common subjectivity. The objectivist would agree that I can understand how a blow to the cat can be a harm to me by merely intensifying its force, or, what amounts to much the same, I can imagine myself, in the relevant ways, being a cat and so receiving the original punch as a welfare-diminishing experience. She would admit that, in virtue of the lack of subjectivity, an empathetic relationship with a tree must find a different ground. But this source, she would insist, is not difficult to find. While we cannot imagine ourselves as trees (i.e., imagine how the world would seem to us were we trees), if we base our analogy on function, this lack of empathetic imagination poses no obstacle. So, for example, as the roots of the tree act as a point of entry for water and nutrition, we should analogize the roots to a human mouth. Since there is no problem in understanding a diseased mouth as making a human worse off, so too, there is no problem in assessing diseased roots as harms to trees.

The first problem is that this analogy by function casts too wide a net. Consider a machine that we build that, in the presence of minimally favorable conditions, prints the natural numbers in order. Incorporated in the machine are both means by which it can recognize certain attempts to interfere with its manufactured purpose and means by which some of these attempts can be circumvented. Suppose that some intervention with the machine manages to bypass these safeguards and consequently it prints only the even integers sequentially. No one would think that this intervention diminished the well-being of the machine. The machine is not any worse off in virtue of this intervention, although we, its creators and users, may be negatively affected. There is no particular number-printing state that makes a number-printing machine either better or worse off, and so it is senseless to view any intervention with the machine as involving a (direct) moral component.

What we have drawn, of course, is an artificial mirror-image of the natural tree complete with development and adaptation. But it is difficult to discern why being natural should be the significant factor. Why should the possession of a welfare be dependent upon the fact that the individual is purposively created by God rather than by us, or even that it is created totally without design as a product of the Big Bang? What is essential to the existence of a well-being are the capacities inherent in the individual; the source of these capacities is inconsequential.

There is a deeper issue. A diseased human mouth constitutes (a nonphenomenological) harm in virtue of inhibiting the proper intake of nutrients for a life worth living, an individual, in other words, for whom death is a harm. For most humans, death is a harm because it eternally deprives the individual of any future enjoyable, or at least mildly pleasant, experiences. Some confirmation of this presents itself when we consider an individual whose continued life would be filled solely with pain and suffering. Without having a life worth living, there is no reason to characterize the individual's painless death as a harm. There is no particular difficulty of understanding how a fully competent, informed, rational human being acting purely from self-interested motives, would opt to end her life in the face of this disturbing prospect. In fact, the choice to continue her life under these conditions (religious reasons to the side) is the more difficult one to fathom.

This might seem to denigrate the traditional Christian religious view that homicide is a harm to the person murdered despite the fact that he will find himself with far greater pleasures in the afterlife. But my view need not judge such believers thoroughly confused. The homicide would, in most instances, still deprive the victim of pleasant experiences, albeit earthly ones, that he would have had otherwise. Moreover, even these traditional Christians tend to see the murder as less of a harm to the victim if the victim is greatly suffering and has no prospects for relief. Some might characterize the murder as a "blessing in disguise." Secondly, most Christians would, *ceteris paribus,* evaluate a greater harm accruing to a young child than to an elderly person. More likely than not, the former rather than the latter, would be considered tragic. My view provides a simple explanation for this assessment: It is most likely that the murdered young child loses far more and far more deeply felt pleasant experiences than does the murdered elderly man.

Bracketing religious considerations, my view does imply that the killing of an irreversible anhedonic is not a harm to the victim. Obviously, my view does not condone, let alone endorse, such acts, for there is little doubt that they cause great suffering to the hedonic population. Nevertheless, some find the implication morally repugnant. Although I respect this intuition, I simply do not share it. Although admittedly nothing more than an autobiographical expression of my intuition, I do not see how my life has been made worse *for me* were my life terminated from a hedonically neutral phenomenological state.

For a life to be worth living *for* an individual, for death to be a harm *to* an individual the agent needs the capacity for an "inscape." But trees (or machines), *ex hypothesi,* lack any interior life and so cannot have a life worth living or suffer death as a harm. Thus, the analogical attempt to make sense of a tree being harmed ultimately fails; the diseased roots of a tree are not relevantly similar to the diseased mouth of a typical human being.

It may be demanded that I provide an explanation why virtually all of us immediately believe both that the destruction of a tree's roots constitutes a harm, rather than a benefit for the tree, and that the cleaning of a stove aids rather than worsens the well-being of a stove. The point here is that if it really makes no sense to attribute welfares to trees and stoves, we seem impotent to provide some reason to explain why we so spontaneously and overwhelmingly think of some events as benefits to them rather than harms, and conversely. It surely defies the laws of probability that these weighted sentiments are merely randomly produced.

I believe that the answer lies in the instrumental value that trees and stoves have for us. A tree with damaged roots cannot serve its (anthropocentric) function well; it cannot accurately provide us with fruit or shade. Similarly a dirty stove retards its capacity to cook our meals. Some confirmation of this explanation is afforded if we consider a case where we ask which of two options is better for a perspectiveless individual where both options provide us with equal benefit. If we were to ask young children whether it enhances or diminishes the welfare of a piece of chalk, say, to be enclosed in a glass casing or secured in a wooden desk, my guess is that the results would be about evenly split.

The behaviors of the very young are also instructive when they unhesitatingly speak of dolls being hurt when they fall from tables or cartoon characters being harmed when they fall from cliffs. Surely they attribute modifications of welfare to these individuals which lack them because they very much physically resemble the human beings with whom the youngster is associated. Children seem never to be concerned about the well-being of the floor that was impacted by the doll's fall or the welfare of the rock that broke in two as a result of Wily Coyote's misplaced step. Young children see their dolls somewhat as they see us, as individuals with faces, arms, and legs. Presumably, most of us learn that our concerns about the welfares of the dolls and cartoon characters were misplaced (which is not to suggest that they do not serve an extremely useful purpose); we learn, again at a comparatively early age, that dolls and cartoon characters are not enough like us to sustain the attribution of welfares. Dolls neither care nor feel pain when they are dropped. Cartoon characters respond to crashes in very unhumanlike ways. Empathetic relationship, then, is not sufficient for legitimate attribution of well-being. It is a defesible criterion which can be subjected to reasoned scrutiny. It remains, however, a *sine qua non* for the intelligible attribution of welfare to another.

Can we empathetically relate to another while cognizant that there is no subjectivity lurking behind its behavior? Consider now a robot physically indistinct from other humans. We know that this is a robot, and we may suppose for the sake of discussion, that this includes the knowledge that this metallic individual has no interior mental life. I submit that our attitudes toward this individual would be profoundly different from those we would have if we lacked this knowledge. Of course, the figures of zombies and robots are window dressing. The suggestion amounts to the experientialist idea, that the possession of subjectivities are requirements for sustaining welfares. If one finds this thought-experiment compelling and recognizes that there would be this dramatic reversal of attitudes after discovering that we are confronting a robot who is "wincing" and "moaning," rather than an individual who is wincing and moaning, then one should be most skeptical about the attribution of welfares to trees and stoves. For what does the attitude shift indicate other than you no longer believe that the individual before you is, for example, ("really") feeling pain ("pain as we know it," to put it redundantly)? If this is a correct characterization of these circumstances, since the only relevant change is the acquired knowledge that the humanlike individual lacks an interior life, parallel reasoning would suggest that we ought not (and do not) consider trees and stoves—entities that we all have agreed lack subjectivities—as having the capacity to be made better and worse off.

Admittedly, there appear to be cases of empathetic relationships with individuals whom we know lack subjectivities. In grade school, students are sometimes asked what their preferences would be were they a tree, or even a clock or a stove. If my observation is correct, none of these exercises are really intelligible. Yet it seems as though we are imagining *something* when we respond to the teacher's inquiry; it is not as though we throw up our hands and complain that we find her request incomprehensible. We are imagining something. When we accede to the teacher's request, we think of ourselves as having Roman numerals surround our face, having thin metal bars for arms, and so forth, but this no more constitutes imagining ourselves clocks than does donning a Halloween costume allows us to imagine ourselves ghosts.

All and only sentient individuals have welfares. Such individuals exhaust our moral domain; they are what morally matter . . . Although moral engagement can attach only to those with subjectivities, those with subjectivities have more to consider than how they are phenomenologically faring.

DISCUSSION QUESTIONS

1. Is Bernstein right that empathetic identification is required for intelligible attribution of welfare?
2. Is Bernstein's analogy of the machine that prints numbers a "mirror-image of the natural tree," as he claims? Why or why not?
3. Bernstein claims "naturalness" as opposed to artificiality is not a relevant feature when it comes to having a well-being (read: interests). How would Varner respond? Who has the better position in your view? Why?
4. If Bernstein is right about the conditions for having a life worth living, who then has a life worth living?

5. Is Bernstein's explanation adequate for why we uncritically do believe that damage to a plant's roots constitutes a harm?
6. Can you imagine being a tree? What would that be like? What does Bernstein think about that question? Do you agree?
7. What are the logical relations between harm, damage, and well-being?

You Decide!

1. MONARCH BUTTERFLIES AND BT CORN

Bt corn is corn that has been genetically engineered to produce a substance toxic to corn borers, a major pest for corn farmers that causes more than $1 billion of damage yearly. The gene comes from the bacterium called *Bacillus thuringiensis,* hence Bt. In 1999, a scientific study suggested that monarch butterfly larva could be killed by ingesting pollen from Bt corn. This finding set off a huge and often acrimonious debate among scientists and the public about genetically engineered crops, as well it should, for this is precisely the sort of consequence that proponents and opponents of genetically modified crops fear.

After two years of studies and further review, the EPA decided in 2001 to allow farmers to continue to plant Bt corn, declaring that the crop poses no serious threat to monarch butterflies or the environment. However, farmers and seed companies must follow EPA rules designed to keep corn borers from developing resistance to Bt corn, such as planting non-Bt corn to maintain insect susceptibility to the toxin. Moreover, seed companies are required to monitor for resistance among corn borers.

The news is not all good. EPA scientists advocate further monitoring and one little-used variety of Bt corn apparently did pose a danger to monarch butterflies.

Discussion Questions

1. Should we be concerned about the possible effects of Bt corn on monarch butterflies? What if it harmed mosquitoes?
2. If you were the EPA administrator, what level of harm to monarch butterflies would you regard as sufficient to ban Bt corn? Is your answer consistent with other practices, such as farming itself or urban living?
3. Is assessing the potential risks and benefits the only way to evaluate genetically engineered crops?

2. LIFE FORCE?

What distinguishes living from nonliving things? What is it to be alive? Since biocentrism proposes to extend moral standing to all living things, we should spend time thinking about what it is to be alive. In the early 1900s, the German biologist Hans Driesch conducted several important experiments demonstrating, he maintained, that being alive is not just a mechanical process. In Driesch's view, being alive requires a special "life force," or "entelechy" as he called it. This is allegedly an autonomous, nonspatial, immaterial, fluid-like substance that infuses organisms, giving direction to their development and biological activities. It is life itself. According to Driesch, "The material systems which we call living organisms are not mechanical systems." Driesch's view, called vitalism, was widely accepted at the time. Driesch defined it as follows: "One indicates by the name of 'vitalism' the doctrine of the autonomy of vital processes, namely the doctrine according to which processes that take place in the living organisms are neither a result nor a combination of physical and chemical processes (which, in last analysis, are mechanical)." (Hans Driesch, "Le Vitalisme," *Scientia,* 1924, p. 13.)

Vitalism has become a relic of intellectual history. Almost no contemporary scientists or philosophers regard themselves as vitalists, at least in Driesch's sense, though in unguarded moments the view does seem intuitively compelling. How did Driesch come to vitalism? He showed that after the initial cell division of a fertilized sea urchin egg, if one of the two resulting cells is killed, a complete embryo will develop. According to Driesch, this shows that life process cannot be simply mechanical, because cutting a machine in half would affect its operation. Because cutting the developing sea urchin egg in half does not affect its operation, the process cannot be strictly mechanical. There must be, argued Driesch, something other than just cellular machinery which guides its development.

Discussion Questions

1. What do you make of Driesch's reasoning? Do his experiments show that life cannot be merely chemical and mechanical processes? Can you think of a way to refute Driesch's argument?
2. If we reject Driesch's claim, what are we to suppose life is?
3. Could scientists create life in a lab? Are the problems to be overcome merely technical ones or is there a metaphysical reason why this could not occur?
4. If vitalism were true, would that support biocentrism?

FURTHER READING ON AGRICULTURAL BIOTECHNOLOGY

Grace, Eric. *Biotechnology Unzipped.* Washington, DC: Joseph Henry Press, 1997.

Rissler, Jane, and Margaret Mellon. *The Ecological Risks of Engineered Crops.* Cambridge, MA: MIT Press, 1996.

Fox, Michael. *Superpigs and Wondercorn.* New York: Lyons and Burford Publishing, 1992.

Chrispeels, Maarten, and David Sadava. *Plants, Genes, and Agriculture.* Boston, MA: Jones and Bartlett Publishers, 1994.

CHAPTER 7

Ecocentric Ethics

MODERN TIMES: THE CONCEPT OF AN ECOSYSTEM

In 1935, the Oxford botanist Alfred Tansley coined the term *ecosystem* to refer, holistically, to the interactions among the living and nonliving components of the natural world. In his seminal article, "The Use and Abuse of Vegetational Concepts and Terms," which appeared in the scientific journal *Ecology,* Tansley wrote:

> But the more fundamental conception is, as it seems to me, the whole *system* (in the sense of physics), including not only the organism-complex, but also the whole complex of physical factors forming what we call the environment of the biome—the habitat factors in the widest sense.
>
> It is the systems so formed which, from the point of view of the ecologist, are the basic units of nature on the face of the earth.
>
> These *ecosystems,* as we may call them, are of the most various kinds and sizes. They form one category of the multitudinous physical systems of the universe, which range from the universe as a whole down to the atom.

As conceived by Tansley, an ecosystem is an actual thing, a kind of physical reality somewhere between, as he put it, the universe as a whole (which is the biggest thing there is) and an atom, conceived as the basic constituent of all physical systems. (Today, atoms are not viewed as the basic units of physical entities because atoms are made of even smaller components—protons, neutrons, and electrons—which are themselves composed of yet more mysterious things, such as quarks and leptons.) Ecosystems are composed of both plants and animals, but nonliving elements such as geological factors, water, sunlight, and weather comprise the system as well.

According to Tansley, ecosystems are the "basic units of nature." This is an interesting claim, for ecosystems are then the objects of study by ecology. So conceived and strictly speaking, this means that ecology is not a subfield of biology. Biology studies living organisms—plants and animals—but ecologists study something different, ecosystems, which contain plants and animals, but which are systems of a different order. Just as chemistry investigates chemical elements and psychology investigates people (people, too, are "units" along the scale from atoms to the universe as a whole), so ecology investigates ecosystems.

The disciplinary independence of ecology from biology has never really been accepted by the scientific community. This is probably due, at least in part, to the legacy of Frederic Clements, a plant ecologist from the Carnegie Institution in Washington. In the early 1900s, Clements studied plant succession, the process whereby certain plants colonize a previously disturbed area, giving way over time to different communities of plants in an apparent orderly succession to a so-called "climax-community," that is, a dynamically stable plant community beyond which there is no further development. In the northeastern United States, for example, deciduous forests are the climax community; this is the steady state toward which disturbed areas tend. Although Clements did not use the term *ecosystem* (that was coined later by Tansley), he nevertheless spoke of biotic communities undergoing a developmental process. But what is striking is that Clements and others (such as John Phillips, a South African ecologist) conceived of the biological communities they studied as high-level living things. These complex superorganisms had a life of their own and developed in accordance with internal propensities; they were regarded as holistic living entities. If ecology investigates the properties of large living organisms, then just as cetologists study whales, ecologists study ecosystems; so, in this view, ecology is a biological science after all.

Two pressing philosophical questions thus arise when we consider the history of the concept of an ecosystem:

1. Are ecosystems actual real things—the basic units of nature?
2. If they are real things, are they living things?

The first question has logical priority, for if ecosystems are not real things, then they cannot be living things. Once we have determined whether ecosystems are real things, then it will at least make sense to wonder about whether they are living superorganisms. Are ecosystems, then, real things? This may seem an odd question, but it is quite important and raises serious issues in the philosophy of science and metaphysics. For how do we tell when "something" really exists? Or to put the question in a slightly different way, when we undertake an inventory of reality, what gets included? According to Tansley, ecosystems are objectively existing things—the "basic units of nature"—in the same way atoms are objectively existing units out of which physical objects are composed or cells are objectively existing units out of which living organisms are composed.

The notion of a thing is admittedly vague. To say that something is a thing does not tell us much, and it seems that almost anything can count as a thing! Are numbers things? What about days of the week or novels? We shall limit our discussion of things in a way that is relevant to the question of whether ecosystems are things; we shall understand *thing* in the sense of being a scientific entity. We want to know whether ecosystems count as real scientific entities. Again, this may seem odd to ask; perhaps you are inclined to say that of course ecosystems are real scientific entities. But not so fast. Science sometimes makes mistakes about what exists. For many years, scientists postulated the existence of "ether" as the alleged medium through which light traveled. It turned out, however, that there is no ether. For hundreds of years, scientists "knew" that there were four elements: earth, air, fire, and water; that disease was caused by imbalance among the bodily humors; that there is an *elan vital* in living organisms; that things are hot because of the amount of "caloric fluid" they contain; and so on. The history of science is littered with "things" that do not exist. Perhaps the same holds for ecosystems; scientists in the next century might come to regard our ecologists in the same way we regard alchemists, astrologers, and phrenologists.

One thing we can say is that if something is a real scientific entity, then it will exist objectively. What does objective existence mean? According to philosopher Michael Devitt in his book *Reason and Truth* (1984), "To say that an object has objective existence . . . is to say that its existence and nature is in no way dependent on our epistemic capacities. It is not constituted by our knowledge, by the synthesizing power of the mind, nor by our imposition of concepts or theories." Consider, by way of contrast, constellations. The Big Dipper does not exist as a real thing in the sky. Its existence depends entirely on our seeing the stars (that really do exist) in a certain way. Unlike constellations, a real thing will exist independent of our perception or conceptualizing. How far our conceptualizing extends is a difficult question. It is possible to hold that our conceptualizing covers much more than we ordinarily think; perhaps nothing exists in its own right independent of our minds. However, such an extreme view is no help when it comes to ecosystems, for then ecosystems along with everything else would just be a matter of our conceptualizing reality in a way that is meaningful to us. We shall suppose instead that there are objectively existing scientific entities that constitute the natural world; we shall suppose, in other words, that there are mountains, oceans, microbes, and trees independent of our theorizing. Our concern is over the status of ecosystems: Are they more like constellations, which are utterly dependent on our perception or more like trees, which exist independent of us?

One promising approach to the question of whether ecosystems are objectively real entities, not just figments of our theorizing, is to ask whether ecosystems have their own properties. If something has properties that are not merely the properties of its parts, then the entity in question is not just an assemblage, but has instead an integrity of its own. We are now talking about a controversial subject in the philosophy of science, namely, "emergent properties," properties that emerge only at a higher level of organization. Consider the property of being a chair. Being a chair is "more than the sum of the parts." The components of the chair are not themselves chairs; it is only when various pieces of wood are arranged in a certain way that the property of being a chair *emerges*. So far, so good. The controversial aspect of emergent properties is whether all the properties that emerge at one level can be understood solely in terms of properties at a lower level. The phenomenon of heat, for example, can be understood simply in terms of molecular motion, and the chair can be understood in terms of its component parts. So while a chair, as a whole, is "more than the sum of its parts," it is so in a way that is unobjectionable, since the chair can be reduced to its component parts. An assemblage, on the other hand, is not more than the sum of its parts, it just *is* the sum of its parts.

Are ecosystems wholes in the sense that we can meaningfully speak of emergent properties? A contemporary and influential ecologist, Frank Golley, thinks so. He writes, referring to the flow of water and dissolved minerals in a mountain watershed,

> Is the export of nutrients a genuine property of an ecosystem? Yes, it is. Although each individual plant and animal on the watershed takes up and releases water and nutrients, there is in addition to these biological processes physical-chemical processes at work. Nutrients stored in the soil through chemical bonding are held in clay lattices. These nutrients are released chemically when hydrogen ions replace calcium ions on the binding sites. The outputs are not merely the sum of the component processes. The system output depends upon the interaction of the biota, the rock, the water, the atmosphere, and the soil. Thus, we can conclude

> that the water and chemical flux in the watershed ecosystem is a genuine property, and the watershed ecosystem is therefore, by definition, a whole. (*A History of the Ecosystem Concept in Ecology; More Than the Sum of the Parts,* 1993. p. 193)

The chemical fluxes described by Golley occur independently of our theorizing and form an emergent property of a whole. Were ecosystems mere assemblages, there would be no emergent properties, for each component of an assemblage retains whatever properties it had, contributing nothing toward the emergence of new properties at a higher level. So rather than being like constellations, ecosystems seem more like trees. They are not just an aspect of our theorizing; they are wholes, for they have emergent properties that result from relations among the constituent parts.

Another approach to the question of "thinghood" involves individuation—can the entities in question be counted? Can we tell when we have one or two of them and can we reidentify the same one over time; that is, can we say, yes, that is the same thing we saw yesterday? Is this tree the same one that we saw last week? We know how to answer that question, in principle at least. We could take precise measurements of the tree's location the first time we saw it or mark it with paint. But even here questions can arise; is this mighty oak the same tree as the sapling we saw 100 years ago? The current oak is composed of completely different matter than the sapling—so what makes it the same tree? With ecosystems, similar questions about identity can arise. For example, a lake ecosystem is bounded by the shore, so by reidentifying the lake we are also reidentifying the ecosystem. However, the phenomenon of plant succession may make it harder to claim that the same terrestrial ecosystem exists over time. Imagine an abandoned field going through the sort of succession described by Clements—first there are grasses, then shrubs, then trees. Is this the same ecosystem undergoing changes or do different ecosystems successively occupy the space? How could we tell?

Yet another approach to the question of thinghood (and hence to the question of whether ecosystems are things) involves the idea of causal manipulation. Genuine things have structural integrity. This means the components of a genuine thing are causally related to one another so that doing something to one part will affect some other part (notice that using the term *part* already conceptually commits us to wholes, since there cannot be parts *as such* without wholes). Pruning the tree will cause it to send out new shoots; reducing an animal's caloric intake will cause shifts in metabolic pathways. Causal manipulability is especially evident with systems, for a system just consists of interlocking causal connections and feedback loops. Consider a toilet; as water rises in the reservoir tank a float shuts off the water. This is a simple feedback mechanism that regulates water level. More complex systems will be composed of many more interlocking causal connections, such as engines and computers; natural systems are vastly more complex, but the basic idea remains the same: Interlocking causal connections permit structural integrity, which allows for causal manipulation, which increases our confidence in thinghood. So we can be confident that the lake is a thing, not just because we can see it, but because, as limnologists tell us, there are complex interlocking connections between algae growth and dissolved oxygen regulated by nutrient concentrations in the water. We can thus affect algae growth by manipulating nutrient concentrations.

It turns out that what makes something a thing (in the sense of a scientific entity) is not as easy as we thought. But an investigation of this sort is necessary if we are to tackle the question of whether ecosystems are things, for if they are things, they are not so in the usual sense in which a cat or a glacier is a thing. The idea of a thing is irremediably vague, but we have nevertheless identified some typical markers of thinghood: objective existence, emergent properties, individuation, causal manipulation. Paradigmatic things are things in virtue of these features. Once we are clear about typical things, we can then ask about atypical cases, such as ecosystems. As our discussion has revealed, it is not eccentric to regard ecosystems as objectively existing scientific entities—things. Ecosystems have emergent properties, properties that are not simply a function of our theorizing; it is often possible to count and reidentify particular ecosystems; and ecosystems are subject to causal manipulation because of the causal pathways that constitute them and integrate their components into an entity in its own right.

However, ecosystems still do not seem to be very robust things. Can there be degrees of thinghood? Is a tree more of a thing than a cloud or a hurricane? Perhaps. But even if a tree is more of a thing than a hurricane, we can still meaningfully talk about hurricanes, study them, predict their behavior, and so forth. And the fact that hurricanes can ultimately be understood in terms of the motions of the particles of air that constitute them is no threat to their existence as scientific entities. Imagine arguing that there are no trees because trees are made of cells and the emergent tree properties can all be explained by properties of the components. Such a highly reductionist approach to ordinary things seems to miss an aspect of reality. If trees can be "explained away" in this fashion, then so can anything. We are then driven to admit that the only things that *really* exist are the ultimate constituents of matter. It may be that given the sorts of creatures we are, we cannot help but see trees, even though they (and everything else, for that matter) can be reduced out of existence by analyzing all their properties into their constituent parts. The same may hold for ecosystems, though "seeing" them is not as obvious to us as seeing trees. It may take considerable training to see them (*apprehend* might be a better term). Being visible to the naked eye is hardly sufficient for thinghood and being invisible is not necessarily a mark against something's being a thing. For example, shadows and mirages are visible—meaning people see them—yet they fail many of the other tests for thinghood we have been discussing. Atoms are invisible, but that is evidently no strike against their existence. That we do not see ecosystems in the same way we see tables and chairs is thus no reason to think they do not exist. The history of science is replete with examples of our coming to see aspects of the world only after much scientific work; consider galaxies, chemical elements, microbes, atoms, distant planets, even the earth itself!

If ecosystems (barely?) make it into the category of an objectively existing scientific entity, could they possibly be living things? Recall that Clements and other early ecologists conceived ecosystems to be superorganisms. Ant and bee colonies are sometimes viewed this way; we can speak of the colony thriving, dying, acting, and so forth. Is seeing an ant colony as a single superorganism similar to seeing the Big Dipper, that is, purely a figment of our theorizing, or might a colony actually be a superorganism in its own right? The famed contemporary naturalist E. O. Wilson described a fascinating case of colonies that very much seem to be single organisms. Apparently, there are colonies of hydrozoans (jellyfish) of the order Siphonophora that look like ordinary jellyfish but actually consist of numerous individuals clinging together. There are some 300 species of such colonies; the Portuguese man-of-war is a well-known version. Individual members of the colony undertake specialized functions—some propel the colony, others catch food and distribute it among their fellows, others form protective layers, and so forth—but they act in a coordinated fashion remaining all the while discrete individuals closely united. To the untrained eye the colony appears to be a single organism. So why call it a colony? According to Wilson, each zooid (as the individual colony members are called) retains its own nervous system and behaves independently of the others. Furthermore, the evolutionary ancestors of these highly integrated colonies display a much looser association among the individual zooids; evidently, there has been an evolving integration of the colony to the point where it is now difficult to distinguish the colony from an individual living organism. So the idea of discrete individuals forming yet a larger living entity, a superorganism, is hardly absurd.

But why think an ecosystem is a superorganism? It is not at all like the colony described by Wilson, which is composed of many separate (and similar) living individuals. Ecosystems are not made up of individual living organisms—Tansley and other ecologists stress the importance of including nonliving elements in an ecosystem. If ecosystems are living entities in their own right, it will be in a very unusual sense. Here we have to think about what it means to be alive. Recall the abstract account of being alive cited by Goodpaster in the previous chapter: He spoke of homeostatic feedback mechanisms that maintain self-integrity. As we saw, such an abstract account of life allows ecosystems to be living things, but, as we also saw, it applies to machines too. Because ecosystems are not alive in any ordinary sense (they do not reproduce, they do not have DNA, they do not evolve) it is probably best to ignore claims about their status as superorganisms. One could always insist that they are living things, but to what end? Perhaps talking of ecosystems as living things is a useful way of conceptualizing them—a heuristic device. Financial analysts sometimes talk about the stock market this way too, as a single entity that decides to go up or down in response to interest rates announced by the federal government. Such talk, however, is a useful fiction; the same is likely true of talk about ecosystems being living organisms.

THE MORAL STATUS OF ECOSYSTEMS

Given that ecosystems exist, we can raise a perplexing question, one that requires a great leap of imagination even to ask. Might ecosystems fall within the scope of morality? Throughout this book, we have repeatedly considered the philosophical basis for moving beyond a narrow sort of anthropocentrism. The question has forced us to consider carefully the basis for including something within the moral. Environmental ethics is so very challenging in just this way, for we are required to articulate clearly the grounds for direct moral significance. We shall now consider whether ecosystems are properly conceived as moral patients (to use Goodpaster's apt expression).

A number of prominent environmental thinkers, beginning with the visionary forester Aldo Leopold (1887–1948), have thought that ecosystems are properly within the sphere of the moral. This means that ecosystems themselves would have direct moral standing. And this means it would be possible for an ecosystem to be the object of direct moral appraisal; we could do things that are morally right or wrong to an ecosystem itself. Usually, we think it wrong (say) to pollute a lake because it will affect people (or, more generously, sentient beings) whose well-being is dependent upon the lake. But if a genuine *ecocentric* ethic can be erected, then there will be grounds for regarding the lake itself—as an ecosystem—as the object of our moral concern. It would be wrong to pollute the lake not because various sentient creatures depend upon it (though this may be an additional wrong) but simply because the lake ecosystem is harmed.

What possible reason could there be to include ecosystems within the moral? We cannot argue that *because* ecosystems are so very important to our well-being, ecosystems *therefore* have direct moral standing. This is a tempting but mistaken approach to the question. Moral standing is not a matter of instrumental importance to us or to anything else. We could just as easily argue that oxygen molecules are directly morally significant because we need oxygen to stay alive. Asking about the moral significance of something is not the same as asking whether it is instrumentally important to us. As we have seen, the question of direct moral significance is a matter of inquiring into the grounds for moral patiency, the basis on which moral agents *ought* to recognize something as morally significant in its own right (see Chapter 4).

If ecosystems were living superorganisms, then a consistent biocentric ethic would include them within the scope of the moral, for on a biocentric ethic, merely being alive is sufficient for direct moral standing. This thought may be in the back of the minds of those who wish to claim that ecosystems are alive. We have seen, however, not only the problems facing a biocentric ethic (Chapter 6) but that ecosystems are not plausibly regarded as alive in the same sense in which an undisputed living thing, such a frog, is alive. That there can be superorganism colonies is a step in the direction of true holistic living entities, but ecosystems are not made up of separate (living) individuals in the way that a colony is made of individuals all acting together. Rather than being organisms, ecosystems, as the name implies, are systems; that is, integrated units of causal linkages among dissimilar biological and nonbiological components. Ecosystems are more like enormous complicated machines than organisms.

The philosophical hurdle for an ecocentric ethic, as distinct from a biocentric ethic, is to acknowledge that ecosystems are not alive, but that they nevertheless merit direct moral standing. Moral standing must therefore be founded somehow in the functional integrity of an ecosystem. Leopold summarized the ecocentric perspective in what has become a widely quoted and deeply controversial aphorism: “A thing is right when it tends to preserve the integrity, stability, and beauty of the biotic community. It is wrong when it tends otherwise.” This is an intriguing idea, one whose implications become all the more profound as we contemplate them further.

ETHICAL ATOMISM VERSUS ETHICAL HOLISM

Ethical **atomism** is the view that moral assessment applies only to individuals, whereas ethical **holism** maintains that collectives or wholes are subject to moral appraisal as well. Consider corporations. We can make moral assessments of corporate behavior. Suppose a tobacco company intentionally markets cigarettes to children. We hold this to be morally wrong (why?); but who or what is the object of our judgment? Is the corporation just a convenient fiction for the people running the place who made the decision? On an atomistic view, the corporation is not distinct from the aggregate of the people who work there—they are the “atoms” that comprise the organization—and our moral judgment applies only to those individuals. We can make no sense of “corporate responsibility” over and above the moral responsibility of individual employees.

Ethical holism, by contrast, is committed to the intelligibility of wholes as more than assemblages and to the idea that we can make moral judgments regarding the whole. Corporate responsibility, for an ethical holist, is not just a convenient way of talking about individual moral responsibility. Corporate responsibility is a moral assessment that can be made of the corporation as an ongoing legal entity irrespective of who the individual managers happen to be. Individual managers come and go; the corporation itself is an emergent legal object of moral appraisal. After all, the corporation is subject to legal action, not the managers (this is the rationale for a corporation in the first place; the individual people who comprise it have limited liability).

In environmental thought, ethical holism refers not to corporations but to the functional integrity of ecosystems. Ethical holism obviously regards ecosystems as wholes, but it goes further to imbue the functional integrity of the whole with moral significance. The eco-holist sees actions that interfere with the natural functioning of ecosystems as not just shortsighted or bound to backfire (since all the biological and nonbiological elements are woven together into a seamless fabric), but also as morally wrong *because* they disrupt the natural functioning of the whole system.

Why is it morally wrong to disrupt ecosystems? Again, it may be unwise to do so, and perhaps it is morally wrong to act foolishly, but even the most committed anthropocentrist agrees with this. As a distinct, indeed revolutionary, moral position, **ecocentrism** must explain why functioning ecosystems merit moral recognition in their own right. One way to defend this idea is to find intrinsic value in ecosystems. Recall our discussion of intrinsic value (Chapter 4). We concluded that value presupposes valuers; in other words, intrinsic value is ascribed, not discovered. We reached this conclusion because it was hard to envision how intrinsic value could exist objectively in the world, that is, apart from our (or some valuer's) so valuing. But even if values presuppose valuers, it does not follow that the values ascribed must all relate to the well-being of the valuer. It is possible to value something for itself, irrespective of its instrumentality even if, in the end, intrinsic value is a matter of ascription. Ecocentrism thus posits intrinsic value in the functional integrity of ecosystems.

However, this defense of ecocentrism has to explain why it is plausible to posit intrinsic value in ecosystemic integrity. Intrinsic value cannot just be ascribed indiscriminately to one thing or another. We would find it absurd to ascribe intrinsic value to cars, for example. What is so special about ecosystems? J. Baird Callicott, a prominent defender of ecocentrism, has offered the following explanation for why we attribute intrinsic value to ecosystems (see his article in this section): An ecosystem can be conceived as an extension of our community, and just as our sympathy can be triggered by evolutionarily ingrained biological mechanisms that extend our feelings of allegiance along lines of kinship and community, so we can extend sympathetic concern to the ecosystem. Callicott's explanation for the extension of concern to ecosystems (thus underwriting attribution of intrinsic value) is a psychological explanation; it is certainly not a justification for why we *should* see ecosystems as intrinsically valuable. And that is the hard question. After all, perhaps our concern is misplaced even though we are evolutionarily predisposed to evince such concern.

Callicott's account of how we might come to attribute intrinsic value to ecosystems is another example of our tendency to see ourselves in the natural world. Apparently, even very distantly perceived kinship relations and community linkages can give rise to moral sentiments, at least according to Callicott. One wonders, though, whether such attenuated connections really do give rise to those sentiments, since few people seem emotionally invested in ecosystems. But what if Callicott is right and some such causal pathway exists? We would then be naturally disposed to see ecosystems as intrinsically valuable. But is natural disposition enough for proper attribution of intrinsic value? Recall our discussion of intrinsic value from Chapter 4. We concluded that attributions of intrinsic value involve recognizing something akin to our wills at work in things around us and thus valuing them for that reason. In so far as an ecosystem can be construed as a genuine community, not a mere assemblage of components nor an impersonal mechanism, then it at least makes sense to think ecosystems are intrinsically valuable. Just as one can plausibly see an entire culture or way of life as intrinsically valuable, so too can an ecosystem be intrinsically valued. So if Callicott is right, not only are we disposed to attribute intrinsic value to ecosystems, but those attributions may be appropriate.

THE CHALLENGE OF ECOCENTRISM

I have referred to ecocentrism as revolutionary. Ecocentrism is a radical departure from ethics as usual for two reasons:

1. The importance of the well-being of people is in doubt, and, if nothing else, ethics is traditionally preoccupied with the well-being of people.
2. Morality is a matter of holistic assessment, not individual welfare.

Recall Leopold's summary statement of ecocentrism: "A thing is right when it tends to preserve the stability, integrity, and beauty of the biotic community. It is wrong when it tends otherwise." This remark is subject to much analysis, but on one natural reading of it, the well-being of ecosystems determines morality. Promoting the stability and integrity of ecosystems is what makes an action morally right. (We can leave beauty out, since that is not an objective feature of ecosystems; ecologists can assess integrity and stability—they are objective scientific properties. Is beauty an objective scientific property?)

In one respect, Leopold's account of morality is utterly traditional, for he attempts to define morality in natural terms. All so-called naturalistic ethical theories define right and wrong by appeal to natural properties. Utilitarianism, for example, appeals to pleasure and pain; other forms of ethical naturalism appeal to other natural properties to define the basic moral concepts. Ecocentrism is thus a naturalistic moral theory, but the natural property to which it appeals to define right and wrong is unprecedented in the history of ethics, for human well-being has nothing to do with morality. Morality is determined by ecosystemic well-being, not human well-being.

As already noted, ecocentric ethics affords moral standing to the ecosystem as a whole, not to the individuals who comprise it. Ethical holism is thus at odds with ethical atomism, for the well-being of individuals is subordinate to the well-being of the whole. For this reason, ecocentrism has been dubbed by its critics as "environmental fascism." Fascism is a totalitarian political structure where citizens exist for the good of the state; it is the reverse of our liberal conception of government where the government exists for the good of the citizens. Clearly, human rights cannot flourish in a fascist state because human rights presuppose something denied by fascism, namely, the worth of the individual person.

The same problem arises for ethical holism in environmental thought. If the worth of individual organisms is contingent upon their contribution to the stability and integrity of the ecosystem, then it will make little sense to talk of individual moral significance that is somehow independent of the ecosystem. The only measure of value will be contribution to ecosystemic integrity (on pure party-line ecocentrism, at least); thus, the relative moral importance of different species can be apportioned according to their contribution to the well-being of the whole. This implies, for instance, that the well-being of highly aware yet numerous sentient creatures that contribute little to the stability and integrity of the ecosystem, such as deer, is a matter of complete indifference, whereas the well-being of a critical ecological linchpin, such as a particular kind of plant or an insect that pollinates that plant, will be of much greater importance.

Perhaps the most unsettling implication of ecocentrism is that it applies to human beings too. Our burgeoning population is certainly not contributing to the stability and integrity (much less the beauty) of the ecosystem. So population increase is wrong (and wrong, remember, not because we will suffer, but because ecosystems become less stable). Plagues, famines, wars, and the like, because they drastically reduce our numbers (and hence contribute to ecological stability), are right. Rather than being special creatures in the scheme of things, we are just "ordinary citizens" of the biotic community; we merit no special consideration, according to ecocentrism. This is a shocking thought. Since the whole point of morality, at least as traditionally conceived, is to promote the well-being of people, it is hard to see how ecocentrism even qualifies as a moral theory.

We can interpret ecocentrism so that it does not have such untoward consequences for humanity. Rather than ecosystemic integrity defining all of morality, perhaps it is just a component of morality. That is, ecosystemic integrity could be morally significant even if it is not the only thing of moral significance; considerations such as the well-being of people and animals (even plants?) might be morally significant as well. While such a move may make ecocentrism more palatable, it opens a series of other questions. How much moral weight does human well-being have compared to ecosystemic disruption? Why call such a modified view ecocentrism if ecosystems are not central to morality? (Sometimes the term *eco-holism* is preferred, perhaps for this reason.) Nevertheless, even the modified version of ecocentrism (read: eco-holism) would be a revolution in moral thought, for if ecosystems are directly morally significant, albeit not the sole determinant of morally, then a hitherto completely unrecognized moral patient, and an exceedingly abstract one at that, would join the moral community.

A FURTHER QUESTION FOR ECOCENTRIC ETHICS

Ecosystems may display stability and integrity, but how do these natural facts, in themselves, create moral force? How is it that because ecosystems are a certain way, they ought to remain that way, that it would be wrong to disrupt them? David Hume (1711–1776), the great Scottish philosopher, first noticed the logical difference between a factual description of something and pronouncements concerning how it ought to be. The naturalistic fallacy, as the attempt to deduce *ought* from *is* has come to be known, is a problem for all naturalistic ethical theories (theories that define moral terms with natural terms), not just ecocentrism, since we can always intelligibly ask, concerning the natural property used to define good (or right), is that property good (or would that action be right)? The intelligibility of the question shows that the terms cannot mean the same. How?

Recall that utilitarianism defines right actions as those that maximize pleasure. Pleasure is a natural property, and whether a particular action maximizes pleasure is an objective natural fact about the world. This makes utilitarianism a naturalistic ethical theory.

But we can still intelligibly ask whether it would be right to perform an action that maximizes pleasure, suggesting that right cannot be understood simply as that which maximizes pleasure. In other words, we can agree that a particular action will maximize pleasure, but is it right to maximize pleasure? If right *means* maximize pleasure, then this question is senseless. But since it is sensible, the two terms cannot mean the same.

Ecocentrism has this problem with a vengeance, for the natural properties most often cited as good by naturalistic theories in ethics relate somehow to human (or sentient) well-being. Naturalistic ethical theories might appeal to pleasure/pain, survival of our species, the welfare of society, various states of consciousness, rational preference, the promotion of human excellence, and so on as the natural properties by which moral terms are ultimately to be understood. But ecocentrism selects a natural property—ecosystemic integrity—that is completely different from the usual sorts of properties favored by naturalistic moral theories. Ecosystems are not conscious, they do not experience pleasure or pain, they have no desires, they are not alive or rational, they are not even basic individuals but holistic entities. And then we are asked to define morality with respect to the functional integrity of something that is so different from ourselves that it is hard to grasp what morality has to do with ecosystemic integrity at all.

Ecocentrism seems arbitrary. Why latch onto the functional integrity of ecosystems as definitional of morality (or, more charitably, sufficient for direct moral standing) over any other natural property that is independent of consciousness, such as color, chemical composition, weight, or size? Suppose we claimed that big things are more morally significant than small things, that size in itself is morally important. Perhaps we could even parody Leopold's claim about ecosystems: A thing is right when it tends to augment size; wrong when it tends otherwise. It might be difficult to refute the claim that size is morally significant—we have size too—but it sure would seem odd. Why size? A persistent worry is that ecocentrism has similarly latched onto a peculiar natural property to define moral concepts.

A defender of ecocentrism might respond that the natural property in question is hardly arbitrary; it is community membership. As Leopold expressed it, ecocentrism "change[s] the role of *Homo sapiens* from conqueror of the land-community to plain member and citizen of it." As community members (part of the "biotic team"), people are required to respect the community "as such." Put this way, community membership does sound like a plausible natural property to form the basis of morality, until we stop to realize that according to ecocentrism the community in question just *is* the ecosystem. Community members thus consist of peculiar "fellow citizens," such as trees, rocks, water, carbon cycles, nutrient flows, temperature gradients, and the like, and respect for the community will be defined as that which contributes to ecosystemic integrity and stability. So the idea of community membership, upon analysis, reverts to the idea of ecosystem integrity, and our earlier worries about the peculiarity of this natural property as a ground for morality remain.

The challenge for ecocentrism is to identify something about ecosystems that plausibly grounds moral concepts so that an ecosystem itself will be the object of moral assessment. That is, ecosystems will have direct moral standing *because* of that feature. But this criterion for moral standing must be such that it does not also apply to other systems with functional integrity, such as machines, computer software, chemical reactions, or the weather, otherwise those systems will acquire moral significance as well. So ecocentrism is faced not only with the uphill challenge of establishing functional integrity as the (an?) appropriate criterion for moral standing, but also of making sure that once established the criterion does not "run away" by applying to patently absurd cases too.

THE READINGS

The readings for this section deal with the moral status of ecosystems. Ecocentrism raises fundamental questions about the scope of the moral community and represents a severe challenge not only to anthropocentrism, but also to all individualistic moral theories.

ALDO LEOPOLD

The Land Ethic

We shall begin with Aldo Leopold's immortal essay "The Land Ethic." This essay is the final chapter of his environmental classic, *A Sand County Almanac,* in which he chronicles a year spent living in a small hut in rural Wisconsin. His acute observations and reflections on nature have inspired many, and his speculation on the moral status of nature sparked a new facet of moral inquiry.

CRITICAL READING QUESTIONS

1. What point does Leopold make by referring to Odysseus (same person as Ulysses whose travels were told by the ancient poet Homer in *The Odyssey*) and his treatment of the slave-girls? How does this relate to the land ethic?
2. What does Leopold mean by "the land"?
3. What does Leopold mean by "the ethical sequence"?
4. Sketch Leopold's conception of the land (the "land pyramid"); according to Leopold, what is the fundamental relation among the components?
5. According to Leopold, what is the "key log" (and what is a key log?) that must be moved, and what will moving it accomplish?

When god-like Odysseus returned from the wars in Troy, he hanged all on one rope a dozen slave-girls of his household whom he suspected of misbehavior during his absence.

This hanging involved no question of propriety. The girls were property. The disposal of property was then, as now, a matter of expediency, not of right and wrong.

Concepts of right and wrong were not lacking from Odysseus' Greece: Witness the fidelity of his wife through the long years before at last his black-prowed galleys clove the wine-dark seas for home. The ethical structure of that day covered wives, but had not yet been extended to human chattels. During the 3000 years which have since elapsed, ethical criteria have been extended to many fields of conduct, with corresponding shrinkages in those judged by expediency only.

THE ETHICAL SEQUENCE

This extension of ethics, so far studied only by philosophers, is actually a process in ecological evolution. Its sequences may be described in ecological as well as in philosophical terms. An ethic, ecologically, is a limitation on freedom of action in the struggle for existence. An ethic, philosophically, is a differentiation of social from antisocial conduct. These are two definitions of one thing. The thing has its origin in the tendency of interdependent individuals or groups to evolve modes of cooperation. The ecologist calls these symbioses. Politics and economics are advanced symbioses in which the original free-for-all competition has been replaced, in part, by cooperative mechanisms with an ethical content.

The complexity of cooperative mechanisms has increased with population density, and with the efficiency of tools. It was simpler, for example, to define the antisocial uses of sticks and stones in the days of the mastodons than of bullets and billboards in the age of motors.

The first ethics dealt with the relation between individuals; the Mosaic Decalogue is an example. Later accretions dealt with the relation between the individual and society. The Golden Rule tries to integrate the individual to society; democracy to integrate social organization to the individual.

There is as yet no ethic dealing with man's relation to land and to the animals and plants which grow upon it. Land, like Odysseus' slave-girls, is still property. The land-relation is still strictly economic, entailing privileges but not obligations.

The extension of ethics to this third element in human environment is, if I read the evidence correctly, an evolutionary possibility and an ecological necessity. It is the third step in a sequence. The first two have already been taken. Individual thinkers since the days of Ezekiel and Isaiah have asserted that the despoliation of land is not only inexpedient but wrong. Society, however, has not yet affirmed their belief. I regard the present conservation movement as the embryo of such an affirmation.

An ethic may be regarded as a mode of guidance for meeting ecological situations so new or intricate, or involving such deferred reactions, that the path of social expediency is not discernible to the average individual. Animal instincts are modes of guidance for the individual in meeting such situations. Ethics are possibly a kind of community instinct in-the-making.

THE COMMUNITY CONCEPT

All ethics so far evolved rest upon a single premise: that the individual is a member of a community of interdependent parts. His instincts prompt him to compete for his place in the community, but his ethics prompt him also to cooperate (perhaps in order that there may be a place to compete for).

The land ethic simply enlarges the boundaries of the community to include soils, waters, plants, and animals, or collectively: the land.

This sounds simple: do we not already sing our love for and obligation to the land of the free and the home of the brave? Yes, but just what and whom do we love? Certainly not the soil, which we are sending helter-skelter downriver. Certainly not the waters, which we assume have no function except to turn turbines, float barges, and carry off sewage. Certainly not the plants, of which we exterminate whole communities without batting an eye. Certainly not the animals, of which we have already extirpated many of the largest and most beautiful species. A land ethic of course cannot prevent the alteration, management, and use of these "resources," but it does affirm their right to continued existence, and, at least in spots, their continued existence in a natural state.

In short, a land ethic changes the role of *Homo sapiens* from conqueror of the land-community to plain member and citizen of it. It implies respect for his fellow-members, and also respect for the community as such.

In human history, we have learned (I hope) that the conqueror role is eventually self-defeating. Why? Because it is implicit in such a role that the conqueror knows, *ex cathedra,* just what makes the community clock tick, and just what and who is valuable, and what and who is worthless, in community life. It always turns out that he knows neither, and this is why his conquests eventually defeat themselves.

In the biotic community, a parallel situation exists. Abraham knew exactly what the Land was for: it was to drip milk and honey into Abraham's mouth. At the present moment, the assurance with which we regard this assumption is inverse to the degree of our education.

The ordinary citizen today assumes that science knows what makes the community clock tick; the scientist is equally sure that he does not. He knows that the biotic mechanism is so complex that its workings may never be fully understood.

That man is, in fact, only a member of a biotic team is shown by an ecological interpretation of history. Many historical events, hitherto explained solely in terms of human enterprise, were actually biotic interactions between people and land. The characteristics of the land determined the facts quite as potently as the characteristics of the men who lived on it.

Consider, for example, the settlement of the Mississippi valley. In the years following the Revolution, three groups were contending for its control: the native Indian, the French and English traders, and the American settlers. Historians wonder what would have happened if the English at Detroit had thrown a little more weight into the Indian side of those tipsy scales which decided the outcome of the colonial migration into the cane-lands of Kentucky. It is time now to ponder the fact that the cane-lands, when subjected to the particular mixture of forces represented by the cow, plow, fire, and ax of the pioneer, became bluegrass. What if the plant succession inherent in this dark and bloody ground had, under the impact of these forces, given us some worthless sedge, shrub, or weed? Would Boone and Kenton have held out? Would there have been any overflow into Ohio, Indiana, Illinois, and Missouri? Any Louisiana Purchase? Any transcontinental union of new states? Any Civil War?

Kentucky was one sentence in the drama of history. We are commonly told what the human actors in this drama tried to do, but we are seldom told that their success, or the lack of it, hung in large degree on the reaction of particular soils to the impact of the particular forces exerted by their occupancy. In the case of Kentucky, we do not even know where the bluegrass came from—whether it is a native species, or a stowaway from Europe.

Contrast the cane-lands with what hindsight tells us about the Southwest, where the pioneers were equally brave, resourceful, and persevering. The impact of occupancy here brought no bluegrass, or other plant fitted to withstand the bumps and buffetings of hard use. This region, when grazed by livestock, reverted through a sense of more and more worthless grasses, shrubs, and weeds to a condition of unstable equilibrium. Each recession of plant types bred erosion; each increment to erosion bred a further recession of plants. The result today is a progressive and mutual deterioration, not only of plants and soils, but of the animal community subsisting thereon. The early settlers did not expect this: on the ciénegas of New Mexico some even cut ditches to hasten it. So subtle has been its progress that few residents of the region are aware of it. It is quite invisible to the tourist who finds this wrecked landscape colorful and charming (as indeed it is, but it bears scant resemblance to what it was in 1848).

This same landscape was "developed" once before, but with quite different results. The Pueblo Indians settled the Southwest in pre-Columbian times, but they happened *not* to be equipped with range livestock. Their civilization expired, but not because their land expired.

In India, regions devoid of any sod-forming grass have been settled, apparently without wrecking the land, by the simple expedient of carrying the grass to the cow, rather than vice versa. (Was this the result of some deep wisdom, or was it just good luck? I do not know.)

In short, the plant succession steered the course of history; the pioneer simply demonstrated, for good or ill, what successions inhered in the land. Is history taught in this spirit? It will be, once the concept of land as a community really penetrates our intellectual life.

THE ECOLOGICAL CONSCIENCE

Conservation is a state of harmony between men and land. Despite nearly a century of propaganda, conservation still proceeds at a snail's pace; progress still consists largely of letterhead pieties and convention oratory. On the back 40 we still slip two steps backward for each forward stride.

The usual answer to this dilemma is "more conservation education." No one will debate this, but is it certain that only the *volume* of education needs stepping up? Is something lacking in the *content* as well?

It is difficult to give a fair summary of its content in brief form, but, as I understand it, the content is substantially this: obey the law, vote right, join some organizations, and practice what conservation is profitable on your own land; the government will do the rest.

Is not this formula too easy to accomplish anything worthwhile? It defines no right or wrong, assigns no obligation, calls for no sacrifice, implies no change in the current philosophy of values. In respect of land-use, it urges only enlightened self-interest. Just how far will such education take us? An example will perhaps yield a partial answer.

By 1930 it had become clear to all except the ecologically blind that southwestern Wisconsin's topsoil was slipping seaward. In 1933 the farmers were told that if they would adopt certain remedial practices for five years, the public would donate CCC labor to install them, plus the necessary machinery and materials. The offer was widely accepted, but the practices were widely forgotten when the five-year contract period was up. The farmers continued only those practices that yielded an immediate and visible economic gain for themselves.

This led to the idea that maybe farmers would learn more quickly if they themselves wrote the rules. Accordingly the Wisconsin Legislature in 1937 passed the Soil Conservation District Law. This said to farmers, in effect: *We, the public, will furnish you free technical service and loan you specialized machinery, if you will write your own rules for land-use. Each county may write its own rules, and these will have the force of law.* Nearly all the counties promptly organized to accept the proffered help, but after a decade of operation, *no county has yet written a single rule.* There has been visible progress in such practices as strip-cropping, pasture renovation, and soil liming, but none in fencing woodlots against grazing, and none in excluding plow and cow from steep slopes. The farmers, in short, have selected those remedial practices which were profitable anyhow, and ignored those which were profitable to the community, but not clearly profitable to themselves.

When one asks why no rules have been written, one is told that the community is not yet ready to support them; education must precede rules. But the education actually in progress makes no mention of obligations to land over and above those dictated by self-interest. The net result is that we have more education but less soil, fewer healthy woods, and as many floods as in 1937.

The puzzling aspect of such situations is that the existence of obligations over and above self-interest is taken for granted in such rural community enterprises as the betterment of roads, schools, churches, and baseball teams. Their existence is not taken for granted, nor as yet seriously discussed, in bettering the behavior of the water that falls on the land, or in the preserving of the beauty or diversity of the farm landscape. Land-use ethics are still governed wholly by economic self-interest, just as social ethics were a century ago.

To sum up: We asked the farmer to do what he conveniently could to save his soil, and he has done just that, and only that. The farmer who clears the woods off a 75 percent slope, turns his cows into the clearing, and dumps its rainfall, rocks, and soil into the community creek, is still (if otherwise decent) a respected member of society. If he puts lime on his fields and plants his crops on contour, he is still entitled to all the privileges and emoluments of his Soil Conservation District. The District is a beautiful piece of social machinery, but it is coughing along on two cylinders because we have been too timid, and too anxious for quick success, to tell the farmer the true magnitude of his obligations. Obligations have no meaning without conscience, and the problem we face is the extension of the social conscience from people to land.

No important change in ethics was ever accomplished without an internal change in our intellectual emphasis, loyalties, affections, and convictions. The proof that conservation has not yet touched these foundations of conduct lies in the fact that philosophy and religion have not yet heard of it. In our attempt to make conservation easy, we have made it trivial.

SUBSTITUTES FOR A LAND ETHIC

When the logic of history hungers for bread and we hand out a stone, we are at pains to explain how much the stone resembles bread. I now describe some of the stones which serve in lieu of a land ethic.

One basic weakness in a conservation system based wholly on economic motives is that most members of the land community have no economic value. Wildflowers and songbirds are examples. Of the 22,000 higher plants and animals native to Wisconsin, it is doubtful whether more than 5 percent can be sold, fed, eaten, or otherwise put to economic use. Yet these creatures are members of the biotic community, and if (as I believe) its stability depends on its integrity, they are entitled to continuance.

When one of these noneconomic categories is threatened, and if we happen to love it, we invent subterfuges to give it economic importance. At the beginning of the century songbirds were supposed to be disappearing. Ornithologists jumped to the rescue with some distinctly shaky evidence to the effect that insects would eat us up if birds failed to control them. The evidence had to be economic in order to be valid.

It is painful to read these circumlocutions today. We have no land ethic yet, but we have at least drawn nearer the point of admitting that birds should continue as a matter of biotic right, regardless of the presence or absence of economic advantage to us.

A parallel situation exists in respect of predatory mammals, raptorial birds, and fish-eating birds. Time was when biologists somewhat overworked the evidence that these creatures preserve the health of game by killing weaklings, or that they control rodents for the farmer, or that they prey only on "worthless" species. Here again, the evidence had to be economic in order to be valid. It is only in recent years that we hear the more honest argument that predators are members of the community, and that no special interest has the right to exterminate them for the sake of a benefit, real or fancied, to itself. Unfortunately this enlightened view is still in the talk stage. In the field the extermination of predators goes merrily on: witness the impending erasure of the timber wolf by fiat of Congress, the Conservation Bureaus, and many state legislatures.

Some species of trees have been "read out of the party" by economics-minded foresters because they grow too slowly, or have too low a sale value to pay as timber crops: white cedar, tamarack, cypress, beech, and hemlock are examples. In Europe, where forestry is ecologically more advanced, the noncommercial tree species are recognized as members of the native forest community, to be preserved as such, within reason. Moreover some (like beech) have been found to have a valuable function in building up soil fertility. The interdependence of the forest and its constituent tree species, ground flora, and fauna is taken for granted.

Lack of economic value is sometimes a character not only of species or groups, but of entire biotic communities: marshes, bogs, dunes, and "deserts" are examples. Our formula in such cases is to relegate their conservation to government as refuges, monuments, or parks. The difficulty is that these communities are usually interspersed with more valuable private lands; the government cannot possibly own or control such scattered parcels. The net effect is that we have relegated some of them to ultimate extinction over large areas. If the private owner were ecologically minded, he would be proud to be the custodian of a reasonable proportion of such areas, which add diversity and beauty to his farm and to his community.

In some instances, the assumed lack of profit in these "waste" areas has proved to be wrong, but only after most of them had been done away with. The present scramble to reflood muskrat marshes is a case in point.

There is a clear tendency in American conservation to relegate to government all necessary jobs that private landowners fail to perform. Government ownership, operation, subsidy, or regulation is now widely prevalent in forestry, range management, soil and watershed management, park and wilderness conservation, fisheries management, and migratory bird management, with more to come. Most of this growth in governmental conservation is proper and logical, some of it is inevitable. That I imply no disapproval of it is implicit in the fact that I have spent most of my life working for it. Nevertheless the question arises: What is the ultimate magnitude of the enterprise? Will the tax base carry its eventual ramifications? At what point will governmental conservation, like the mastodon, become handicapped by its own dimensions? The answer, if there is any, seems to be in a land ethic, or some other force which assigns more obligation to the private landowner.

Industrial landowners and users, especially lumbermen and stockmen, are inclined to wail long and loudly about the extension of government ownership and regulation to land, but (with notable exceptions) they show little disposition to develop the only visible alternative: the voluntary practice of conservation on their own lands.

When the private landowner is asked to perform some unprofitable act for the good of the community, he today assents only with outstretched palm. If the act costs him cash this is fair and proper, but when it costs only forethought, open-mindedness, or time, the issue is at least debatable. The overwhelming growth of land-uses subsidies in recent years must be ascribed, in large part, to the government's own agencies for conservation education: the land bureaus, the agricultural colleges, and the extension services. As far as I can detect, no ethical obligation toward land is taught in these institutions.

To sum up: a system of conservation based solely on economic self-interest is hopelessly lopsided. It tends to ignore, and thus eventually to eliminate, many elements in the land community that lack commercial value, but that are (as far as we know) essential to its healthy functioning. It assumes, falsely, I think, that the economic parts of the biotic clock will function without the uneconomic parts. It tends to relegate to government many functions eventually too large, too complex, or too widely dispersed to be performed by government.

An ethical obligation on the part of the private owner is the only visible remedy for these situations.

THE LAND PYRAMID

An ethic to supplement and guide the economic relation to land presupposes the existence of some mental image of land as a biotic mechanism. We can be ethical only in relation to something we can see, feel, understand, love, or otherwise have faith in.

The image commonly employed in conservation education is "the balance of nature." For reasons too lengthy to detail here, this figure of speech fails to describe accurately what little we know about the land mechanism. A much truer image is the one employed in ecology: the biotic pyramid. I shall first sketch the pyramid as a symbol of land, and later develop some of its implications in terms of land-use.

Plants absorb energy from the sun. This energy flows through a circuit called the biota, which may be represented by a pyramid consisting of layers. The bottom layer is the soil. A plant layer rests on the soil, an insect layer on the plants, a bird and rodent layer on the insects, and so on up through various animal groups to the apex layer, which consists of the larger carnivores.

The species of a layer are alike not in where they came from, or in what they look like, but rather in what they eat. Each successive layer depends on those below it for food and often for other services, and each in turn furnishes food and services to those above. Proceeding upward, each successive layer decreases in numerical abundance. Thus, for every carnivore there are hundreds of his prey, thousands of their prey, millions of insects, uncountable plants. The pyramidal form of the system reflects this numerical progression from apex to base. Man shares an intermediate layer with the bears, raccoons, and squirrels which eat both meat and vegetables.

The lines of dependency for food and other services are called food chains. Thus soil-oak-deer-Indian is a chain that has now been largely converted to soil-corn-cow-farmer. Each species, including ourselves, is a link in many chains. The deer eats a hundred plants other than oak, and the cow a hundred plants other than corn. Both, then, are links in a hundred chains. The pyramid is a tangle of chains so complex as to seem disorderly, yet the stability of the system proves it to be a highly organized structure. Its functioning depends on the cooperation and competition of its diverse parts.

In the beginning, the pyramid of life was low and squat; the food chains short and simple. Evolution has added layer after layer, link after link. Man is one of thousands of accretions to the height and complexity of the pyramid. Science has given us many doubts, but it has given us at least one certainty: The trend of evolution is to elaborate and diversify the biota.

Land, then, is not merely soil; it is a fountain of energy flowing through a circuit of soils, plants, and animals. Food chains are the living channels which conduct energy upward; death and decay return it to the soil. The circuit is not closed; some energy is dissipated in decay, some is added by absorption from the air, some is stored in soils, peats, and long-lived forests; but it is a sustained circuit, like a slowly augmented revolving fund of life. There is always a net loss by downhill wash, but this is normally small and offset by the decay of rocks. It is deposited in the ocean and, in the course of geological time, raised to form new lands and new pyramids.

The velocity and character of the upward flow of energy depend on the complex structure of the plant and animal community, much as the upward flow of sap in a tree depends on its complex cellular organization. Without this complexity, normal circulation would presumably not occur. Structure means the characteristic numbers, as well as the characteristic kinds and functions, of the component species. This interdependence between the complex structure of the land and its smooth functioning as an energy unit is one of its basic attributes.

When a change occurs in one part of the circuit, many other parts must adjust themselves to it. Change does not necessarily obstruct or divert the flow of energy; evolution is a long series of self-induced changes, the net result of which has been to elaborate the flow mechanism and to lengthen the circuit. Evolutionary changes, however, are usually slow and local. Man's invention of tools has enabled him to make changes of unprecedented violence, rapidity, and scope.

One change is in the composition of floras and faunas. The larger predators are lopped off the apex of the pyramid; food chains, for the first time in history, become shorter rather than longer. Domesticated species from other lands are substituted for wild ones, and wild ones are moved to new habitats. In this worldwide pooling of faunas and floras, some species get out of bounds as pests and diseases, others are extinguished. Such effects are seldom intended or foreseen; they represent unpredicted and often untraceable readjustments in the structure. Agricultural science is largely a race between the emergence of new pests and the emergence of new techniques for their control.

Another change touches the flow of energy through plants and animals and its return to the soil. Fertility is the ability of soil to receive, store, and release energy. Agriculture, by overdrafts on the soil, or by too radical a substitution of domestic for native species in the superstructure, may derange the channels of flow or deplete storage. Soils depleted of their storage, or of the organic matter which anchors it, wash away faster than they form. This is erosion.

Waters, like soil, are part of the energy circuit. Industry, by polluting waters or obstructing them with dams, may exclude the plants and animals necessary to keep energy in circulation.

Transportation brings about another basic change: the plants or animals grown in one region are now consumed and returned to the soil in another. Transportation taps the energy stored in rocks, and in the air, and uses it elsewhere; thus we fertilize the garden with nitrogen gleaned by the guano birds from the fishes of seas on the other side of the Equator. Thus the formerly localized and self-contained circuits are pooled on a worldwide scale.

The process of altering the pyramid for human occupation releases stored energy, and this often gives rise, during the pioneering period, to a deceptive exuberance of plant and animal life, both wild and tame. These releases of biotic capital tend to becloud or postpone the penalties of violence.

This thumbnail sketch of land as an energy circuit conveys three basic ideas:

1. That land is not merely soil.
2. That the native plants and animals kept the energy circuit open; others may or may not.
3. That man-made changes are of a different order than evolutionary changes, and have effects more comprehensive than is intended or foreseen.

These ideas, collectively, raise two basic issues: Can the land adjust itself to the new order? Can the desired alterations be accomplished with less violence?

Biotas seem to differ in their capacity to sustain violent conversion. Western Europe, for example, carries a far different pyramid than Caesar found there. Some large animals are lost; swampy forests have become meadows or plowland; many new plants and animals are introduced, some of which escape as pests; the remaining natives are greatly changed in distribution and abundance. Yet the soil is still there and, with the help of imported nutrients, still fertile; and waters flow normally; the new structure seems to function and to persist. There is no visible stoppage or derangement of the circuit.

Western Europe, then, has a resistant biota. Its inner processes are tough, elastic, resistant to strain. No matter how violent the alterations, the pyramid, so far, has developed some new *modus vivendi* which preserves its habitability for man, and for most of the other natives.

Japan seems to present another instance of radical conversion without disorganization.

Most other civilized regions, and some as yet barely touched by civilization, display various stages of disorganization, varying from initial symptoms to advanced wastage. In Asia Minor and North Africa diagnosis is confused by climatic changes, which may have been either the cause or the effect of advanced wastage. In the United States the degree of disorganization varies locally; it is worst in the Southwest, the Ozarks, and parts of the South, and least in New England and the Northwest. Better land-uses may still arrest it in the less advanced regions. In parts of Mexico, South America, South Africa, and Australia a violent and accelerating wastage is in progress, but I cannot assess the prospects.

This almost worldwide display of disorganization in the land seems to be similar to disease in an animal, except that it never culminates in complete disorganization or death. The land recovers, but at some reduced level of complexity, and with a reduced carrying capacity for people, plants, and animals. Many biotas currently regarded as "lands of opportunity" are in fact already subsisting on exploitative agriculture, i.e. they have already exceeded their sustained carrying capacity. Most of South America is overpopulated in this sense.

In arid regions we attempt to offset the process of wastage by reclamation, but it is only too evident that the prospective longevity of reclamation projects is often short. In our own West, the best of them may not last a century.

The combined evidence of history and ecology seems to support one general deduction: the less violent the man-made changes, the greater the probability of successful readjustment in the pyramid. Violence, in turn, varies with human population density; a dense population requires a more violent conversion. In this respect, North America has a better chance for permanence than Europe, if she can contrive to limit her density.

This deduction runs counter to our current philosophy, which assumes that because a small increase in density enriched human life, that an indefinite increase will enrich it indefinitely. Ecology knows of no density relationship that holds for indefinitely wide limits. All gains from density are subject to a law of diminishing returns.

Whatever may be the equation for men and land, it is improbable that we as yet know all its terms. Recent discoveries in mineral and vitamin nutrition reveal unsuspected dependencies in the up-circuit: incredibly minute quantities of certain substances determine the value of soils to plants, of plants to animals. What of the down-circuit? What of the vanishing species, the preservation of which we now regard as an esthetic luxury? They helped build the soil; in what unsuspected ways may they be essential to its maintenance? Professor Weaver proposes that we use prairie flowers to reflocculate the wasting soils of the dust bowl; who knows for what purpose cranes and condors, otters and grizzlies may some day be used?

LAND HEALTH AND THE A-B CLEAVAGE

A land ethic, then, reflects the existence of an ecological conscience, and this in turn reflects a conviction of individual responsibility for the health of the land. Health is the capacity of the land for self-renewal. Conservation is our effort to understand and preserve this capacity.

Conservationists are notorious for their dissensions. Superficially these seem to add up to mere confusion, but a more careful scrutiny reveals a single plane of cleavage common to many specialized fields. In each field one group (A) regards the land as soil, and its function as commodity-production; another group (B) regards the land as a biota, and its function as something broader. How much broader is admittedly in a state of doubt and confusion.

In my own field, forestry, group A is quite content to grow trees like cabbages, with cellulose as the basic forest commodity. It feels no inhibition against violence; its ideology is agronomic. Group B, on the other hand, sees forestry as fundamentally different from agronomy because it employs natural species, and manages a natural environment rather than creating an artificial one. Group B prefers natural reproduction on principle. It worries on biotic as well as economic grounds about the loss of species like chestnut, and the threatened loss of the white pines. It worries about a whole series of secondary forest functions: wildlife, recreation, watersheds, wilderness areas. To my mind, Group B feels the stirrings of an ecological conscience.

In the wildlife field, a parallel cleavage exists. For Group A the basic commodities are sport and meat; the yardsticks of production are ciphers of take in pheasants and trout. Artificial propagation is acceptable as a permanent as well as a temporary recourse—if its unit costs permit. Group B, on the other hand, worries about a whole series of biotic side-issues. What is the cost in predators of producing a game crop? Should we have further recourse to exotics? How can management restore the shrinking species, like prairie grouse, already hopeless as shootable game? How can management restore the threatened rarities, like trumpeter swan and whooping crane? Can management principles be extended to wildflowers? Here again it is clear to me that we have the same A-B cleavage as in forestry.

In the larger field of agriculture I am less competent to speak, but there seem to be somewhat parallel cleavages. Scientific agriculture was actively developing before ecology was born, hence a slower penetration of ecological concepts might be expected. Moreover the farmer, by the very nature of his techniques, must modify the biota more radically than the forester or the wildlife manager. Nevertheless, there are many discontents in agriculture which seem to add up to a new vision of "biotic farming."

Perhaps the most important of these is the new evidence that poundage or tonnage is no measure of the food-value of farm crops; the products of fertile soil may be qualitatively as well as quantitatively superior. We can bolster poundage from depleted soils by pouring on imported fertility, but we are not necessarily bolstering food-value. The possible ultimate ramifications of this idea are so immense that I must leave their exposition to abler pens.

The discontent that labels itself "organic farming," while bearing some of the earmarks of a cult, is nevertheless biotic in its direction, particularly in its insistence on the importance of soil flora and fauna.

The ecological fundamentals of agriculture are just as poorly known to the public as in other fields of land-use. For example, few educated people realize that the marvelous advances in technique made during recent decades are improvements in the pump, rather than the well. Acre for acre, they have barely sufficed to offset the sinking level of fertility.

In all of these cleavages, we see repeated the same basic paradoxes: man the conqueror *versus* man the biotic citizen; science the sharpener of his sword *versus* science the searchlight on his universe; land the slave and servant *versus* land the collective organism. Robinson's injunction to Tristram may well be applied, at this juncture, to *Homo sapiens* as a species in geological time:

> Whether you will or not
> You are a King, Tristram, for you are one
> Of the time-tested few that leave the world,
> When they are gone, not the same place it was.
> Mark what you leave.

THE OUTLOOK

It is inconceivable to me that an ethical relation to land can exist without love, respect, and admiration for land, and a high regard for its value. By value, I of course mean something far broader than mere economic value; I mean value in the philosophical sense.

Perhaps the most serious obstacle impeding the evolution of a land ethic is the fact that our educational and economic system is headed away from, rather than toward, an intense consciousness of land. Your true modern is separated from the land by many middlemen, and by innumerable physical gadgets. He has no vital relation to it; to him it is the space between cities on which crops grow. Turn him loose for a day on the land, and if the spot does not happen to be a golf links or a "scenic" area, he is bored stiff. If crops could be raised by hydroponics instead of farming, it would suit him very well. Synthetic substitutes for wood, leather, wool, and other natural land products suit him better than the originals. In short, land is something he has "outgrown."

Almost equally serious as an obstacle to a land ethic is the attitude of the farmer for whom the land is still an adversary, or a taskmaster that keeps him in slavery. Theoretically, the mechanization of farming ought to cut the farmer's chains, but whether it really does is debatable.

One of the requisites for an ecological comprehension of land is an understanding of ecology, and this is by no means co-extensive with "education"; in fact, much higher education seems deliberately to avoid ecological concepts. An understanding of ecology does not necessarily originate in courses bearing ecological labels; it is quite as likely to be labeled geography, botany, agronomy, history, or economics. This is as it should be, but whatever the label, ecological training is scarce.

The case for a land ethic would appear hopeless but for the minority which is in obvious revolt against these "modern" trends.

The "key-log" which must be moved to release the evolutionary process for an ethic is simply this: Quit thinking about decent land-use as solely an economic problem. Examine each question in terms of what is ethically and esthetically right, as well as what is economically expedient. A thing is right when it tends to preserve the integrity, stability, and beauty of the biotic community. It is wrong when it tends otherwise.

It of course goes without saying that economic feasibility limits the tether of what can or cannot be done for land. It always has and it always will. The fallacy the economic determinists have tied around our collective neck, and which we now need to cast off, is the belief that economics determines *all* land-use. This is simply not true. An innumerable host of actions and attitudes, comprising perhaps the bulk of all land relations, is determined by the land-users' tastes and predilections, rather than by his purse. The bulk of all land relations hinges on investments of time, forethought, skill, and faith rather than on investments of cash. As a land-user thinketh, so is he.

I have purposely presented the land ethic as a product of social evolution because nothing so important as an ethic is ever "written." Only the most superficial student of history supposes that Moses "wrote" the Decalogue; it evolved in the minds of a thinking community, and Moses wrote a tentative summary of it for a "seminar." I say tentative because evolution never stops.

The evolution of a land ethic is an intellectual as well as emotional process. Conservation is paved with good intentions which prove to be futile, or even dangerous, because they are devoid of critical understanding either of the land, or of economic land-use. I think it is a truism that as the ethical frontier advances from the individual to the community, its intellectual content increases.

The mechanism of operation is the same for any ethic: social approbation for right actions, social disapproval for wrong actions.

By and large, our present problem is one of attitudes and implements. We are remodeling the Alhambra with a steamshovel, and we are proud of our yardage. We shall hardly relinquish the shovel, which after all has many good points, but we are in need of gentler and more objective criteria for its successful use.

DISCUSSION QUESTIONS

1. Do you think ethics can be extended to the land? How? According to Leopold, "The land ethic simply enlarges to boundaries of the community to include soils, waters, plants, and animals, or collectively: the land." Consider Leopold's proposal.
2. What are some of the implications of changing the "role of *Homo sapiens* from conqueror of the land-community to plain member and citizen of it"? Is this a role we should adopt? Why?
3. Assess Leopold's most memorable quote, "A thing is right when it tends to preserve the integrity, stability, and beauty of the biotic community. It is wrong when it tends otherwise." Consider each of the elements—integrity, stability, and beauty.

J. BAIRD CALLICOTT

The Conceptual Foundations of the Land Ethic

J. Baird Callicott has done more than any other contemporary thinker to explain Leopold's ideas to the philosophical community. He is one of the undisputed founders of environmental philosophy and his work is widely read and deeply influential. In our selection, "The Conceptual Foundations of the Land Ethic," Callicott seeks to show how Leopold's land ethic is grounded in a Darwinian theory of moral sentiments. Further, he argues that Leopold's land ethic, though revolutionary, is not committed to sacrificing human needs to the environment.

CRITICAL READING QUESTIONS

1. What does Callicott see as central to a biological account of ethics?
2. According to Callicott, what role does community play in ethics? (Consider here his quote from Darwin on "savage" morality.)
3. What does Callicott mean when he writes, "The simplest reason, to paraphrase Darwin, should, therefore, tell each individual that he or she ought to extend his or her social instincts and sympathies to all members of the biotic community though different from him or her in appearance or habits."
4. Sketch the Humean account of ethics employed by Leopold, according to Callicott. How is a Humean moral philosophy different from ones we have considered so far?
5. According to Callicott, how do the traditional moral theories of Kant and Bentham actually function? (Hint: This is part of his discussion on Goodpaster's analysis of moral theory.)

---

6. What does Callicott mean when he writes, "Hume and Darwin, furthermore, recognize inborn moral sentiments which have society as such as their natural object"?
7. What does Callicott mean when he says that moral communities develop more like the rings of a tree than a balloon, which expands without leaving a trace of where it was before?

The two great cultural advances of the past century were the Darwinian theory and the development of geology . . . Just as important, however, as the origin of plants, animals, and soil is the question of how they operate as a community. That task has fallen to the new science of ecology, which is daily uncovering a web of interdependencies so intricate as to amaze—were he here—even Darwin himself, who, of all men, should have least cause to tremble before the veil.

Aldo Leopold, fragment 6B16, no. 36, Leopold Papers, University of Wisconsin–Madison Archives

I

As Wallace Stegner observes, *A Sand County Almanac* is considered "almost a holy book in conservation circles," and Aldo Leopold a prophet, "an American Isaiah." And as Curt Meine points out, "The Land Ethic" is the climactic essay of *Sand County*, "the upshot of 'The Upshot.' " One might, therefore, fairly say that the recommendation and justification of moral obligations on the part of people to nature is what the prophetic *A Sand County Almanac* is all about.

But, with few exceptions, "The Land Ethic" has not been favorably received by contemporary academic philosophers. Most have ignored it. Of those who have not, most have been either nonplussed or hostile. Distinguished Australian philosopher John Passmore dismissed it out of hand, in the first book-length academic discussion of the new philosophical subdiscipline called "environmental ethics." In a more recent and more deliberate discussion, the equally distinguished Australian philosopher H. J. McCloskey patronized Aldo Leopold and saddled "The Land Ethic" with various far-fetched "interpretations." He concludes that "there is a real problem in attributing a coherent meaning to Leopold's statements, one that exhibits his land ethic as representing a major advance in ethics rather than a retrogression to a morality of a kind held by various primitive peoples." Echoing McCloskey, English philosopher Robin Attfield went out of his way to impugn the philosophical respectability of "The Land Ethic." And Canadian philosopher L. W. Sumner has called it "dangerous nonsense." Among those philosophers more favorably disposed, "The Land Ethic" has usually been simply quoted, as if it were little more than a noble, but naive, moral plea, altogether lacking a supporting theoretical framework—that is, foundational principles and premises which lead, by compelling argument, to ethical precepts.

The professional neglect, confusion, and (in some cases) contempt for "The Land Ethic" may, in my judgment, be attributed to three things: (1) Leopold's extremely condensed prose style in which an entire conceptual complex may be conveyed in a few sentences, or even in a phrase or two; (2) his departure from the assumptions and paradigms of contemporary philosophical ethics; and (3) the unsettling practical implications to which a land ethic appears to lead. "The Land Ethic," in short, is, from a philosophical point of view, abbreviated, unfamiliar, and radical.

Here I first examine and elaborate the compactly expressed abstract elements of the land ethic and expose the "logic" which binds them into a proper, but revolutionary, moral theory. I then discuss the controversial features of the land ethic and defend them against actual and potential criticism. I hope to show that the land ethic cannot be ignored as merely the groundless emotive exhortations of a moonstruck conservationist or dismissed as entailing wildly untoward practical consequences. It poses, rather, a serious intellectual challenge to business-as-usual moral philosophy.

II

"The Land Ethic" opens with a charming and poetic evocation of Homer's Greece, the point of which is to suggest that today land is just as routinely and remorselessly enslaved as human beings then were. A panoramic glance backward to our most distant cultural origins, Leopold suggests, reveals a slow but steady moral development over three millennia. More of our relationships and activities ("fields of conduct") have fallen under the aegis of moral principles ("ethical criteria") as civilization has grown and matured. If moral growth and development continue, as not only a synoptic review of history, but recent past experience suggest that it will, future generations will censure today's casual and universal environmental bondage as today we censure the casual and universal human bondage of three thousand years ago.

A cynically inclined critic might scoff at Leopold's sanguine portrayal of human history. Slavery survived as an institution in the "civilized" West, more particularly in the morally self-congratulatory United States, until a mere generation before Leopold's own birth. And Western history from imperial Athens and Rome to the Spanish Inquisition and the Third Reich has been a disgraceful series of wars, persecutions, tyrannies, pogroms, and other atrocities.

The history of moral practice, however, is not identical with the history of moral consciousness. Morality is not descriptive; it is prescriptive or normative. In light of this distinction, it is clear that today, despite rising rates of violent crime in the United States and institutional abuses of human rights in Iran, Chile, Ethiopia, Guatemala, South Africa, and many other places, and despite persistent organized social injustice and oppression in still others, moral consciousness is expanding more rapidly now than ever before. Civil rights, human rights, women's liberation, children's liberation, animal liberation, and so forth, all indicate, as expressions of newly emergent moral ideals, that ethical consciousness (as distinct from practice) has if anything recently accelerated—thus confirming Leopold's historical observation.

III

Leopold next points out that "this extension of ethics, so far studied only by philosophers"—and therefore, the implication is clear, not very satisfactorily studied "is actually a process in ecological evolution" (p. 202). What Leopold is saying here, simply, is that we may understand the history of ethics, fancifully alluded to by means of the Odysseus vignette, in biological as well as philosophical terms. From a biological point of view, an ethic is "a limitation on freedom of action in the struggle for existence" (p. 202) . . .

Let me put the problem in perspective. How, . . . did ethics originate and, once in existence, grow in scope and complexity?

The oldest answer in living human memory is theological. God (or the gods) imposes morality on people. And God (or the gods) sanctions it. A most vivid and graphic example of this kind of account occurs in the Bible when Moses goes up on Mount Sinai to receive the Ten Commandments directly from God. That text also clearly illustrates the divine sanctions (plagues, pestilences, droughts, military defeats, and so forth) for moral disobedience. Ongoing revelation of the divine will, of course, as handily and as simply explains subsequent moral growth and development.

Western philosophy, on the other hand, is almost unanimous in the opinion that the origin of ethics in human experience has somehow to do with human reason. Reason figures centrally and pivotally in the "social contract theory" of the origin and nature of morals in all its ancient, modern, and contemporary expressions from Protagoras, to Hobbes, to Rawls. Reason is the well-spring of virtue, according to both Plato and Aristotle, and of categorical imperatives, according to Kant. In short, the weight of Western philosophy inclines to the view that we are moral beings because we are rational beings. The ongoing sophistication of reason and the progressive illumination it sheds upon the good and the right explain "the ethical sequence," the historical growth and development of morality, noticed by Leopold.

An evolutionary natural historian, however, cannot be satisfied with either of these general accounts of the origin and development of ethics. The idea that God gave morals to man is ruled out in principle—as any supernatural explanation of a natural phenomenon is ruled out in principle in natural science. And while morality might *in principle* be a function of human reason (as, say, mathematical calculation clearly is), to suppose that it is so *in fact* would be to put the cart before the horse. Reason appears to be a delicate, variable, and recently emerged faculty. It cannot, under any circumstances, be supposed to have evolved in the absence of complex linguistic capabilities which depend, in turn, for their evolution upon a highly developed social matrix. But we cannot have become social beings unless we assumed limitations on freedom of action in the struggle for existence. Hence we must have become ethical before we became rational.

Darwin, probably in consequence of reflections somewhat like these, turned to a minority tradition of modern philosophy for a moral psychology consistent with and useful to a general evolutionary account of ethical phenomena. A century earlier, Scottish philosophers David Hume and Adam Smith had argued that ethics rest upon feelings or "sentiments"—which, to be sure, may be both amplified and informed by reason. And since in the animal kingdom feelings or sentiments are arguably far more common or widespread than reason, they would be a far more likely starting point for an evolutionary account of the origin and growth of ethics.

Darwin's account, to which Leopold unmistakably (if elliptically) alludes in "The Land Ethic," begins with the parental and filial affections common, perhaps, to all mammals. Bonds of affection and sympathy between parents and offspring permitted the formation of small, closely knit social groups, Darwin argued. Should the parental and familial affections bonding family members chance to extend to less closely related individuals, that would permit an enlargement of the family group. And should the newly extended community more successfully defend itself and/or more efficiently provision itself, the inclusive fitness of its members severally would be increased, Darwin reasoned. Thus the more diffuse familial affections, which Darwin (echoing Hume and Smith) calls the "social sentiments" would be spread throughout a population.

Morality, properly speaking—that is, morality as opposed to mere altruistic instinct—requires, in Darwin's terms, "intellectual powers" sufficient to recall the past and imagine the future, "the power of language" sufficient to express "common opinion," and "habituation" to patterns of behavior deemed, by common opinion, to be socially acceptable and beneficial. Even so, ethics proper, in Darwin's account, remains firmly rooted in moral feelings or social sentiments which were—no less than physical faculties, he expressly avers—naturally selected, by the advantages for survival and especially for successful reproduction, afforded by society.

The protosociobiological perspective on ethical phenomena, to which Leopold as a natural historian was heir, leads him to a generalization which is remarkably explicit in his condensed and often merely resonant rendering of Darwin's more deliberate and extended paradigm: Since "the thing [ethics] has its origin in the tendency of interdependent individuals or groups to evolve modes of co-operation, . . . all ethics so far evolved rest upon a single premise: that the individual is a member of a community of interdependent parts" (pp. 202–3).

Hence, we may expect to find that the scope and specific content of ethics will reflect both the perceived boundaries and actual structure or organization of a cooperative community or society. *Ethics and society or community are correlative.* This single, simple principle constitutes a powerful tool for the analysis of moral natural history, for the anticipation of future moral development (including, ultimately, the land ethic), and for systematically deriving the specific precepts, the prescriptions and proscriptions, of an emergent and culturally unprecedented ethic like a land or environmental ethic.

IV

Anthropological studies of ethics reveal that in fact the boundaries of the moral community are generally coextensive with the perceived boundaries of society. And the peculiar (and, from the urbane point of view, sometimes inverted) representation of virtue and vice in tribal society—the virtue, for example, of sharing to the point of personal destitution and the vice of privacy and private property—reflects and fosters the life way of tribal peoples. Darwin, in his leisurely, anecdotal discussion, paints a vivid picture of the intensity, peculiarity, and sharp circumscription of "savage" mores: "A savage will risk his life to save that of a member of the same community, but will be wholly indifferent about a stranger." As Darwin portrays them, tribespeople are at once paragons of virtue "within the limits of the same tribe" and enthusiastic thieves, manslaughterers, and torturers without.

For purposes of more effective defense against common enemies, or because of increased population density, or in response to innovations in subsistence methods and technologies, or for some mix of these or other forces, human societies have grown in extent or scope and changed in form or structure. Nations—like the Iroquois nation or the Sioux nation—came into being upon the merger of previously separate and mutually hostile tribes. Animals and plants were domesticated and erstwhile hunter-gatherers became herders and farmers. Permanent habitations were established. Trade, craft, and (later) industry flourished. With each change in society came corresponding and correlative changes in ethics. The moral community expanded to become co-extensive with the newly drawn boundaries of societies and the representation of virtue and vice, right and wrong, good and evil, changed to accommodate, foster, and preserve the economic and institutional organization of emergent social orders.

Today we are witnessing the painful birth of a human supercommunity, global in scope. Modern transportation and communication technologies, international economic interdependencies, international economic entities, and nuclear arms have brought into being a "global village." It has not yet become fully formed and it is at tension—a very dangerous tension—with its predecessor, the nation-state. Its eventual institutional structure, a global federalism or whatever it may turn out to be, is at this point completely unpredictable. Interestingly, however, a corresponding global human ethic—the "human rights" ethic, as it is popularly called—has been more definitely articulated.

Most educated people today pay lip service at least to the ethical precept that all members of the human species, regardless of race, creed, or national origin, are endowed with certain fundamental rights which it is wrong not to respect. According to the evolutionary scenario set out by Darwin, the contemporary moral ideal of human rights is a response to a perception—however vague and indefinite—that mankind worldwide is united into one society, one community, however indeterminate or yet institutionally unorganized. As Darwin presciently wrote:

> As man advances in civilization, and small tribes are united into larger communities, the simplest reason would tell each individual that he ought to extend his social instincts and sympathies to all the members of the same nation, though personally unknown to him. This point being once reached, there is only an artificial barrier to prevent his sympathies extending to the men of all nations and races. If, indeed, such men are separated from him by great differences of appearance or habits, experience unfortunately shows us how long it is, before we look at them as our fellow-creatures.

According to Leopold, the next step in this sequence beyond the still incomplete ethic of universal humanity, a step that is clearly discernible on the horizon, is the land ethic. The "community concept" has, so far, propelled the development of ethics from the savage clan to the family of man. "The land ethic simply enlarges the boundary of the community to include soils, water, plants, and animals, or collectively: the land" (p. 204).

As the foreword to *Sand County* makes plain, the overarching thematic principle of the book is the inculcation of the idea—through narrative description, discursive exposition, abstractive generalization, and occasional preachment—"that land is a community" (viii). The community concept is "the basic concept of ecology" (viii). Once land is popularly perceived as a biotic community—as it is professionally perceived in ecology—a correlative land ethic will emerge in the collective cultural consciousness.

V

Although anticipated as far back as the mid-18th century—in the notion of an "economy of nature"—the concept of the biotic community was more fully and deliberately developed as a working model or paradigm for ecology by Charles Elton in the 1920s. The natural world is organized as an intricate corporate society in which plants and animals occupy "niches," or as Elton alternatively called them, "roles" or "professions," in the economy of nature. As in a feudal community, little or no socioeconomic mobility (upward or otherwise) exists in the biotic community. One is born to one's trade.

Human society, Leopold argues, is founded, in large part, upon mutual security and economic interdependency and preserved only by limitations on freedom of action in the struggle for existence—that is, by ethical constraints. Since the biotic community exhibits, as modern ecology reveals, an analogous structure, it too can be preserved, given the newly amplified impact of "mechanized man," only by analogous limitations on freedom of action—that is, by a land ethic (viii). A land ethic, furthermore, is not only "an ecological necessity," but an "evolutionary possibility" because a moral response to the natural environment—Darwin's social sympathies, sentiments, and instincts translated and codified into a body of principles and precepts—would be automatically triggered in human beings by ecology's social representation of nature (p. 203).

Therefore, the key to the emergence of a land ethic is, simply, universal ecological literacy.

VI

The land ethic rests upon three scientific cornerstones: (1) evolutionary and (2) ecological biology set in a background of (3) Copernican astronomy. Evolutionary theory provides the conceptual link between ethics and social organization and development. It provides a sense of "kinship with fellow-creatures" as well, "fellow-voyagers" with us in the "odyssey of evolution" (p. 109). It establishes a diachronic link between people and nonhuman nature.

Ecological theory provides a synchronic link—the community concept—a sense of social integration of human and nonhuman nature. Human beings, plants, animals, soils, and waters are "all interlocked in one humming community of cooperations and competitions, one biota." The simplest reason, to paraphrase Darwin, should, therefore, tell each individual that he or she ought to extend his or her social instincts and sympathies to all the members of the biotic community though different from him or her in appearance or habits.

And although Leopold never directly mentions it in *A Sand County Almanac,* the Copernican perspective, the perception of the earth as "a small planet" in an immense and utterly hostile universe beyond, contributes, perhaps subconsciously, but nevertheless very powerfully, to our sense of kinship, community, and interdependence with fellow denizens of the earth household. It scales the earth down to something like a cozy island paradise in a desert ocean.

Here in outline, then, are the conceptual and logical foundations of the land ethic: Its conceptual elements are a Copernican cosmology, a Darwinian protosociobiological natural history of ethics, Darwinian ties of kinship among all forms of life on earth, and an Eltonian model of the structure of biocenoses all overlaid on a Humean-Smithian moral psychology. Its logic is that natural selection has endowed human beings with an affective moral response to perceived bonds of kinship and community membership and identity; that today the natural environment, the land, is represented as a community, the biotic community; and that, therefore, an environmental or land ethic is both possible—the biopsychological and cognitive conditions are in place—and necessary, since human beings collectively have acquired the power to destroy the integrity, diversity, and stability of the environing and supporting economy of nature. In the remainder of this essay I discuss special features and problems of the land ethic germane to moral philosophy.

The most salient feature of Leopold's land ethic is its provision of what Kenneth Goodpaster has carefully called "moral considerability" for the biotic community per se, not just or fellow members of the biotic community.

> In short, a land ethic changes the role of *Homo sapiens* from conqueror of the land-community to plain member and citizen of it. It implies respect for his fellow-members, *and also respect for the community as such.* (p. 204, emphasis added)

The land ethic, thus, has a holistic as well as an individualistic cast.

Indeed, as "The Land Ethic" develops, the focus of moral concern shifts gradually away from plants, animals, soils, and waters severally to the biotic community collectively. Toward the middle, in the subsection called "Substitutes for a Land Ethic," Leopold invokes the "biotic rights" of *species*—as the context indicates—of wildflowers, songbirds, and predators. In "The Outlook," the climactic section of "The Land Ethic," nonhuman natural entities, first appearing as fellow members, then considered in profile as species, are not so much as mentioned in what might be called the "summary moral maxim" of the land ethic: "A thing is right when it tends to preserve the integrity, stability, and beauty of the biotic community. It is wrong when it tends otherwise" (pp. 224–25).

By this measure of right and wrong, not only would it be wrong for a farmer, in the interest of higher profits, to clear the woods off a 75 percent slope, turn his cows into the clearing and dump its rainfall, rocks, and soil into the community creek, it would also be wrong for the federal fish and wildlife agency, in the interest of individual animal welfare, to permit populations of deer, rabbits, feral burros, or whatever to increase unchecked and thus to threaten the integrity, stability, and beauty of the biotic communities of which they are members. The land ethic not only provides moral considerability for the biotic community per se, but ethical consideration of its individual members is preempted by concern for the preservation of the integrity, stability, and beauty of the biotic community. The land ethic, thus, not only has a holistic aspect; it is holistic with a vengeance.

The holism of the land ethic, more than any other feature, sets it apart from the predominant paradigm of modern moral philosophy. It is, therefore, the feature of the land ethic which requires the most patient theoretical analysis and the most sensitive practical interpretation.

VII

As Kenneth Goodpaster pointed out, mainstream modern ethical philosophy has taken egoism as its point of departure and reached a wider circle of moral entitlement by a process of generalization: I am sure that *I*, the enveloped ego, am intrinsically or inherently valuable and thus that *my* interests ought to be considered, taken into account, by "others" when their actions may substantively affect *me*. My own claim to moral consideration, according to the conventional wisdom, ultimately rests upon a psychological capacity—rationality or sentiency were the classical candidates of Kant and Bentham, respectively—which is arguably valuable in itself and which thus qualifies *me* for moral standing. However, then I am forced grudgingly to grant the same moral consideration I demand from others, on this basis, to those others who can also claim to possess the same general psychological characteristic.

A criterion of moral value and consideration is thus identified. Goodpaster convincingly argues that mainstream moral theory is based, when all the learned dust has settled, on this simple paradigm of ethical justification and logic exemplified by the Benthamic and Kantian prototypes. If the criterion of moral values and consideration is pitched low enough—as it is in Bentham's criterion of sentiency—a wide variety of animals are admitted to moral entitlement. If the criterion of moral value and consideration is pushed lower still—as it is in Albert Schweitzer's reverence-for-life ethic—all minimally conative things (plants as well as animals) would be extended moral considerability. The contemporary animal liberation/rights, and reverence-for-life/life-principle ethics are, at bottom, simply direct applications of the modern classical paradigm of moral argument. But this standard modern model of ethical theory provides no possibility whatever for the moral consideration of wholes—of threatened population of animals and plants, or of endemic, rare, or endangered species, or of biotic communities, or most expansively, of the biosphere in its totality—since wholes per se have no psychological experience of any kind. Because mainstream modern moral theory has been "psychocentric," it has been radically and intractably individualistic or "atomistic" in its fundamental theoretical orientation.

Hume, Smith, and Darwin diverged from the prevailing theoretical model by recognizing that altruism is as fundamental and autochthonous in human nature as is egoism. According to their analysis, moral value is not identified with a natural quality objectively present in morally considerable beings—as reason and/or sentiency is objectively present in people and/or animals—it is, as it were, projected by valuing subjects.

Hume and Darwin, furthermore, recognize inborn moral sentiments which have society as such as their natural object. Hume insists that "we must renounce the theory which accounts for every moral sentiment by the principle of self-love. We must adopt a more *publick affection* and allow that the *interests of society* are not, *even on their own account,* entirely indifferent to us." And Darwin, somewhat ironically (since "Darwinian evolution" very often means natural selection operating exclusively with respect to individuals), sometimes writes as if morality had no other object than the commonweal, the welfare of the community as a corporate entity:

> We have now seen that actions are regarded by savages, and were probably so regarded by primeval man, as good or bad, solely as they obviously affect the welfare of the tribe,—not that of the species, nor that of the individual member of the tribe. This conclusion agrees well with the belief that the so called moral sense is aboriginally derived from social instincts, for both relate at first exclusively to the community.

Theoretically then, the biotic community owns what Leopold, in the lead paragraph of "The Outlook," calls "value in the philosophical sense"—that is, direct moral considerability—because it is a newly discovered proper object of a specially evolved "publick affection" or "moral sense" which all psychologically normal human beings have inherited from a long line of ancestral social primates (p. 223).

VIII

In the land ethic, as in all earlier stages of social–ethical evolution, there exists a tension between the good of the community as a whole and the "rights" of its individual members considered severally . . .

In any case, the conceptual foundations of the land ethic provide a well-informed, self-consistent theoretical basis for including both fellow members of the biotic community and the biotic community itself (considered as a corporate entity) within the purview of morals. The preemptive emphasis, however, on the welfare of the community as a whole, in Leopold's articulation of the land ethic, while certainly consistent with its Humean–Darwinian theoretical foundations, is not determined by them alone. The overriding holism of the land ethic results, rather, more from the way our moral sensibilities are informed by ecology.

IX

Ecological thought, historically, has tended to be holistic in outlook. Ecology is the study of the relationships of organisms to one another and to the elemental environment. These relationships bind the *relata*—plants, animals, soils, and waters—into a seamless fabric. The ontological primacy of objects and the ontological subordination of relationships characteristic of classical Western science is, in fact, reversed in ecology. Ecological relationships determine the nature of organisms rather than the other way around. A species is what it is because it has adapted to a niche in the ecosystem. The whole, the system itself, thus, literally and quite straightforwardly shapes and forms its component species.

Antedating Charles Elton's community model of ecology was F. E. Clements and S. A. Forbes's organism model. Plants and animals, soils and waters, according to this paradigm, are integrated into one superorganism. Species are, as it were, its organs; specimens its cells. Although Elton's community paradigm (later modified, as we shall see, by Arthur Tansley's ecosystem idea) is the principal and morally fertile ecological concept of "The Land Ethic," the more radically holistic superorganism paradigm of Clements and Forbes resonates in "The Land Ethic" as an audible overtone. In the peroration of "Land Health and the A–B Cleavage," for example, which immediately precedes "The Outlook," Leopold insists that

> in all these cleavages, we see repeated the same basic paradoxes: man the conqueror *versus* man the biotic citizen; science the sharpener of his sword *versus* science the searchlight on his universe; land the slave and servant *versus* land the collective organism. (p. 223)

And on more than one occasion Leopold, in the latter quarter of "The Land Ethic," talks about the "health" and "disease" of the land—terms which are at once descriptive and normative and which, taken literally, characterize only organisms proper.

In an early essay, "Some Fundamentals of Conservation in the Southwest," Leopold speculatively flirted with the intensely holistic superorganism model of the environment as a paradigm pregnant with moral implications . . .

Had Leopold retained this overall theoretical approach in "The Land Ethic," the land ethic would doubtless have enjoyed more critical attention from philosophers. The moral foundations of a land or, as he might then have called it, "earth" ethic would rest upon the hypothesis that the Earth is alive and ensouled—possessing inherent psychological characteristics, logically parallel to reason and sentiency. This notion of a conative whole earth could plausibly have served as a general criterion of intrinsic worth and moral considerability, in the familiar format of mainstream moral thought.

Part of the reason, therefore, that "The Land Ethic" emphasizes more and more the integrity, stability, and beauty of the environment as a whole, and less and less the biotic right of individual plants and animals to life, liberty, and the pursuit of happiness, is that the superorganism ecological paradigm invites one, much more than does the community paradigm, to hypostatize, to reify the whole, and to subordinate its individual members.

In any case, as we see, rereading "The Land Ethic" in light of "Some Fundamentals," the whole Earth organism image of nature is vestigially present in Leopold's later thinking. Leopold may have abandoned the "earth ethic" because ecology had abandoned the organism analogy in favor of the community analogy as a working theoretical paradigm. And the community model was more suitably given moral implications by the social/sentimental ethical natural history of Hume and Darwin.

Meanwhile, the biotic community, ecological paradigm itself had acquired, by the late 30s and 40s, a more holistic cast of its own. In 1935 British ecologist Arthur Tansley pointed out that from the perspective of physics the "currency" of the "economy of nature" is energy. Tansley suggested that Elton's qualitative and descriptive food chains, food webs, trophic niches, and biosocial professions could be quantitatively expressed by means of a thermodynamic flow model. It is Tansley's state-of-the-art thermodynamic paradigm of the environment that Leopold explicitly sets out as a "mental image of land" in relation to which "we can be ethical" (p. 214). And it is the ecosystemic model of land which informs the cardinal practical precepts of the land ethic.

"The Land Pyramid" is the pivotal section of "The Land Ethic"—the section which effects a complete transition from concern for "fellow-members" to the "community as such." It is also its longest and most technical section. A description of the "ecosystem" (Tansley's deliberately nonmetaphorical term) begins with the sun. Solar energy "flows through a circuit called the biota" (p. 215). It enters the biota through the leaves of green plants and courses through plant-eating animals, and then on to omnivores and carnivores. At last the tiny fraction of solar energy converted to biomass by green plants remaining in the corpse of a predator, animal feces, plant detritus, or other dead organic material is garnered by decomposers—worms, fungi, and bacteria. They recycle the participating elements and degrade into entropic equilibrium any remaining energy. According to this paradigm

> land, then, is not merely soil; it is a fountain of energy flowing through a circuit of soils, plants, and animals. Food chains are the living channels which conduct energy upward; death and decay return it to the soil. The circuit is not closed; . . . but it is a sustained circuit, like a slowly augmented revolving fund of life. (p. 216)

In this exceedingly abstract (albeit poetically expressed) model of nature, process precedes substance and energy is more fundamental than matter. Individual plants and animals become less autonomous beings than ephemeral structures in a patterned flux of energy. According to Yale biophysicist Harold Morowitz,

> viewed from the point of view of modern [ecology], each living thing . . . is a dissipative structure, that is it does not endure in and of itself but only as a result of the continual flow of energy in the system. An example might be instructive. Consider a vortex in a stream of flowing water. The vortex is a structure made of an ever-changing group of water molecules. It does not exist as an entity in the classical Western sense; it exists only because of the flow of water through the stream. In the same sense, the structures out of which biological entities are made are transient, unstable entities with constantly changing molecules, dependent on a constant flow of energy from food in order to maintain form and structure . . . From this point of view the reality of individuals is problematic because they do not exist per se but only as local perturbations in this universal flow.

Though less bluntly stated and made more palatable by the unfailing charm of his prose, Leopold's proffered mental image of land is just as expansive, systemic, and distanced as Morowitz's. The maintenance of "the complex structure of the land and its smooth functioning as an energy unit" emerges in "The Land Pyramid" as the *summum bonum* of the land ethic (p. 216).

X

From this good Leopold derives several practical principles slightly less general, and therefore more substantive, than the summary moral maxim of the land ethic distilled in "The Outlook." "The trend of evolution [not its "goal," since evolution is ateleological] is to elaborate and diversify the biota" (p. 216). Hence, among our cardinal duties is the duty to preserve what species we can, especially those at the apex of the pyramid—the top carnivores. "In the beginning, the pyramid of life was low and squat; the food chains short and simple. Evolution has added layer after layer, link after link" (pp. 215–16). Human activities today, especially those like systematic deforestation in the tropics, resulting in abrupt massive extinctions of species, are in effect "devolutionary"; they flatten the biotic pyramid; they choke off some of the channels and gorge others (those which terminate in our own species).

The land ethic does not enshrine the ecological status quo and devalue the dynamic dimension of nature. Leopold explains that "evolution is a long series of self-induced changes, the net result of which has been to elaborate the flow mechanism and to lengthen the circuit. Evolutionary changes, however, are usually slow and local. Man's invention of tools has enabled him to make changes of unprecedented violence, rapidity, and scope" (pp. 216–17). "Natural" species extinction, that is, species extinction in the normal course of evolution, occurs when a species is replaced by competitive exclusion or evolves into another form. Normally speciation outpaces extinction. Mankind inherited a richer, more diverse world than had ever existed before in the 3.5 billion-year odyssey of life on Earth. What is wrong with anthropogenic species extirpation and extinction is the *rate* at which it is occurring and the *result:* biological impoverishment instead of enrichment.

Leopold goes on here to condemn, in terms of its impact on the eco-system, "the worldwide pooling of faunas and floras," that is, the indiscriminate introduction of exotic and domestic species and the dislocation of native and endemic species, mining the soil for its stored biotic energy, leading ultimately to diminished fertility and to erosion; and polluting and damming water courses (p. 217).

According to the land ethic, therefore: Thou shalt not extirpate or render species extinct; thou shalt exercise great caution in introducing exotic and domestic species into local ecosystems, in extracting energy from the soil and releasing it into the biota, and in damming or polluting water courses; and thou shalt be especially solicitous of predatory birds and mammals. Here in brief are the express moral precepts of the land ethic. They are all explicitly informed—not to say derived—from the energy circuit model of the environment.

XI

The living channels—food chains—through which energy courses are composed of individual plants and animals. A central, stark fact lies at the heart of ecological processes: Energy, the currency of the economy nature, passes from one organism to another, not from hand to hand, like coined money, but, so to speak, from stomach to stomach. Eating *and being eaten,* living *and dying* are what make the biotic community hum.

The precepts of the land ethic, like those of all previous accretions, reflect and reinforce the structure of the community to which it is correlative. Trophic asymmetries constitute the kernel of the biotic community. It seems unjust, unfair. But that is how the economy of nature is organized (and has been for thousands of millions of years). The land ethic, thus, affirms as good, and strives to preserve, the very inequities in nature whose social counterparts in human communities are condemned as bad and would be eradicated by familiar social ethics, especially by the more recent Christian and secular egalitarian exemplars. A "right to life" for individual members is not consistent with the structure of the biotic community and hence is not mandated by the land ethic. This disparity between the land ethic and its more familiar social precedents contributes to the apparent devaluation of individual members of the biotic community and augments and reinforces the tendency of the land ethic, driven by the systemic vision of ecology, toward a more holistic or community-per-se orientation.

Of the few moral philosophers who have given the land ethic a moment's serious thought, most have regarded it with horror because of its emphasis on the good of the community and its deemphasis on the welfare of individual members of the community. Not only are other sentient creatures members of the biotic community and subordinate to its integrity, beauty, and stability; so are *we.* Thus, if it is not only morally permissible, from the point of view of the land ethic, but morally required, that members of certain species be abandoned to predation and other vicissitudes of wild life or even deliberately culled (as in the case of alert and sentient whitetail deer) for the sake of the integrity, stability, and beauty of the biotic community, how can we consistently exempt ourselves from a similar draconian regime? We too are only "plain members and citizens" of the biotic community. And our global population is growing unchecked. According to William Aiken, from the point of view of the land ethic, therefore, "massive human diebacks would be good. It is our duty to cause them. It is our species' duty, relative to the whole, to eliminate 90 percent of our numbers." Thus, according to Tom Regan, the land ethic is a clear case of "environmental fascism."

Of course Leopold never intended the land ethic to have either inhumane or antihumanitarian implications or consequences. But whether he intended them or not, a logically consistent deduction from the theoretical premises of the land ethic might force such untoward conclusions. And given their magnitude and monstrosity, these derivations would constitute a *reductio ad absurdum* of the whole land ethic enterprise and entrench and reinforce our current human chauvinism and moral alienation from nature. If this is what membership in the biotic community entails, then all but the most radical misanthropes would surely want to opt out.

XII

The land ethic, happily, implies neither inhumane nor inhuman consequences. That some philosophers think it must follows more from their own theoretical presuppositions than from the theoretical elements of the land ethic itself. Conventional modern ethical theory rests moral entitlement, as I earlier pointed out, on a criterion or qualification. If a candidate meets the criterion—rationality or sentiency are the most commonly posited—he, she, or it is entitled to equal moral standing with others who possess the same qualification in equal degree. Hence, reasoning in this philosophically orthodox way, and forcing Leopold's theory to conform: If human beings are, with other animals, plants, soils, and waters, equally members of the biotic community, and if community membership is the criterion of equal moral consideration, then not only do animals, plants, soils, and waters have equal (highly attenuated) "rights," but human beings are equally subject to the same subordination of individual welfare and rights in respect to the good of the community as a whole.

But the land ethic, as I have been at pains to point out, is heir to a line of moral analysis different from that institutionalized in contemporary moral philosophy. From the biosocial evolutionary analysis of ethics upon which Leopold builds the land ethic, it (the land ethic) neither replaces nor overrides previous accretions. Prior moral sensibilities and obligations attendant upon and correlative to prior strata of social involvement remain operative and preemptive.

Being citizens of the United States, or the United Kingdom, or the Soviet Union, or Venezuela, or some other nation-state, and therefore having national obligations and patriotic duties, does not mean that we are not also members of smaller communities or social groups—cities or townships, neighborhoods, and families—or that we are relieved of the peculiar moral responsibilities attendant upon and correlative to these memberships as well. Similarly, our recognition of the biotic community and our immersion in it does not imply that we do not also remain members of the human community—the "family of man" or "global village"—or that we are relieved of the attendant and correlative moral responsibilities of that membership, among them to respect universal human rights and uphold the principles of individual human worth and dignity. The biosocial development of morality does not grow in extent like an expanding balloon, leaving no trace of its previous boundaries, so much like the circumference of a tree. Each emergent, and larger, social unit is layered over the more primitive, and intimate, ones.

Moreover, as a general rule, the duties correlative to the inner social circles to which we belong eclipse those correlative to the rings farther from the heartwood when conflicts arise. Consider our moral revulsion when zealous ideological nationalists encourage children to turn their parents in to the authorities if their parents dissent from the political or economic doctrines of the ruling party. A zealous environmentalist who advocated visiting war, famine, or pestilence on human populations (those existing somewhere else, of course) in the name of the integrity, beauty, and stability of the biotic community would be similarly perverse. Family obligations in general come before nationalistic duties and humanitarian obligations in general come before environmental duties. The land ethic, therefore, is not draconian or fascist. It does not cancel human morality. The land ethic may, however, as with any new accretion, demand choices which affect, in turn, the demands of the more interior social-ethical circles. Taxes and the military draft may conflict with family-level obligations. While the land ethic, certainly, does not cancel human morality, neither does it leave it unaffected.

Nor is the land ethic inhumane. Nonhuman fellow members of the biotic community have no "human rights," because they are not, by definition, members of the human community. As fellow members of the biotic community, however, they deserve respect.

How exactly to express or manifest respect, while at the same time abandoning our fellow members of the biotic community to their several fates or even actively consuming them for our own needs (and wants), or deliberately making them casualties of wildlife management for ecological integrity, is a difficult and delicate question.

Fortunately, American Indian and other traditional patterns of human–nature interaction provide rich and detailed models. Algonkian woodland peoples, for instance, represented animals, plants, birds, waters, and minerals as other-than-human persons engaged in reciprocal, mutually beneficial socioeconomic intercourse with human beings. Tokens of payment, together with expressions of apology, were routinely offered to the beings whom it was necessary for these Indians to exploit. Care not to waste the usable parts and care in the disposal of unusable animal and plant remains were also an aspect of the respectful, albeit necessarily consumptive, Algonquian relationship with fellow members of the land community. As I have more fully argued elsewhere, the Algonquian portrayal of human–nature relationships is, indeed, although certainly different in specifics, identical in abstract form to that recommended by Leopold in the land ethic . . . Is the land ethic prudential or deontological? Is the land ethic, in other words, a matter of enlightened (collective, human) self-interest, or does it genuinely admit nonhuman natural entities and nature as a whole to true moral standing?

The conceptual foundations of the land ethic, as I have here set them out, and much of Leopold's hortatory rhetoric, would certainly indicate that the land ethic is deontological (or duty oriented) rather than prudential. In the section significantly titled "The Ecological Conscience," Leopold complains that the then-current conservation philosophy is inadequate because "it defines no right or wrong, assigns no obligation, calls for no sacrifice, implies no change in the current philosophy of values. In respect of land-use, it urges *only* enlightened self-interest" (pp. 207–8, emphasis added). Clearly, Leopold himself thinks that the land ethic goes beyond prudence. In this section he disparages mere "self-interest" two more times, and concludes that "obligations have no meaning without conscience, and the problem we face is the extension of the social conscience from people to land" (p. 209).

In the next section, "Substitutes for a Land Ethic," he mentions rights twice—the "biotic right" of birds to continuance and the absence of a right on the part of human special interest to exterminate predators.

Finally, the first sentences of "The Outlook" read: "It is inconceivable to me that an ethical relation to land can exist without love, respect, and admiration for land, and a high regard for its value. By value, I of course mean something far broader than mere economic value; I mean value in the philosophical sense" (p. 223). By "value in the philosophical sense," Leopold can only mean what philosophers more technically call "intrinsic value" or "inherent worth." Something that has intrinsic value or inherent worth is valuable in and of itself, not because of what it can do for us. "Obligation," "sacrifice," "a conscience," "respect," the ascription of rights, and intrinsic value—all of these are consistently opposed to self-interest and seem to indicate decisively that the land ethic is of the deontological type.

Some philosophers, however, have seen it differently. Scott Lehmann, for example, writes,

> Although Leopold claims for communities of plants and animals a "right to continued existence," his argument is homocentric, appealing to the human stake in preservation. Basically it is an argument from enlightened self-interest, where the self in question is not an individual human being but humanity—present and future—as a whole.

Lehmann's claim has some merits, even though it flies in the face of Leopold's express commitments. Leopold does frequently lapse into the language of (collective, long-range, human) self-interest. Early on, for example, he remarks, "in human history, we have learned (I hope) that the conqueror role is eventually *self*-defeating" (p. 204, emphasis added). And later, of the 95 percent of Wisconsin species which cannot be "sold, fed, eaten, or otherwise put to economic use," Leopold reminds us that "these creatures are members of the biotic community, and if (as I believe) its stability depends on its integrity, they are entitled to continuance" (p. 210). The implication is clear: the economic 5 percent cannot survive if a significant portion of the uneconomic 95 percent are extirpated; nor may *we,* it goes without saying, survive without these "resources."

Leopold, in fact, seems to be consciously aware of this moral paradox. Consistent with the biosocial foundations of his theory, he expresses it in sociobiological terms:

> An ethic may be regarded as a mode of guidance for meeting ecological situations so new or intricate, or involving such deferred reactions, that the path of social expediency is not discernible to the average individual. Animal instincts are modes of guidance for the individual in meeting such situations. Ethics are possibly a kind of community instinct in-the-making. (p. 203)

From an objective, descriptive sociobiological point of view, ethics evolve because they contribute to the inclusive fitness of their carriers (or, more reductively still, to the multiplication of their carriers' genes); they are expedient. However, the path to self-interest (or to the self-interest of the selfish gene) is not discernible to the participating individuals (nor, certainly, to their genes). Hence, ethics are grounded in instinctive feeling—love, sympathy, respect—not in self-conscious calculating intelligence. Somewhat like the paradox of hedonism—the notion that one cannot achieve happiness if one directly pursues happiness per se and not other things—one can only secure self-interest by putting the interests of others on a par with one's own (in this case long-range collective human self-interest and the interest of other forms of life and of the biotic community per se).

So, is the land ethic deontological or prudential, after all? It is both—self-consistently both—depending upon one's point of view. From the inside, from the lived, felt point of view of the community member with evolved moral sensibilities, it is deontological. It involves an affective–cognitive posture of genuine love, respect, admiration, obligation, self-sacrifice, conscience, duty, and the ascription of intrinsic value and biotic rights. From the outside, from the objective and analytic scientific point of view, it is prudential. "There is no other way for land to survive the impact of mechanized man," nor, therefore, for mechanized man to survive his own impact upon the land (p. viii).

DISCUSSION QUESTIONS

1. Consider Callicott's account of how the land ethic is supposed to evolve out of a more limited ethical position. Does this seem plausible to you? Why or why not?
2. What strengths and what weaknesses do you see with a sentiment-based moral theory?
3. Is Callicott's defense of the land ethic against the charge of fascism adequate? He claims ecocentrism "does not cancel human morality." What changes does it make, if Callicott is right?

LAWRENCE JOHNSON

From *A Morally Deep World*

Lawrence Johnson is a prominent environmental philosopher from Australia. Reprinted here are selections from his book, *A Morally Deep World.* Johnson argues for morally significant interests throughout the nonhuman world (that's what makes it "morally deep"). In his view, anything with a well-being has interests and thus merits our moral attention; this includes not only individuals, living or not, but also holistic entities, such as species and ecosystems.

CRITICAL READING QUESTIONS

1. How does fire show that ecosystems have interests, according to Johnson?
2. How did Leopold justify hunting? How is Leopold's view on hunting relevant to what Johnson is discussing?

Lawrence Johnson, from *A Morally Deep World: An Essay on Moral Significance and Environmental Ethics,* by Lawrence Johnson, Cambridge University Press, 1991. Reprinted with the permission of Cambridge University Press.

3. How does Johnson propose to reconcile atomistic and holistic ethical views?
4. The usual tension between atomistic and holistic ethics involves subordinating individual interests to the whole; what does Johnson think of this tension?
5. Does Leopold's view commit us to not doing anything that will affect ecosystems, in Johnson's view?
6. Under what conditions do we not "sin against the biosphere," according to Johnson?

ECO-INTERESTS—AND FOREST FIRES

A piece of proverbial wisdom that is actually somewhat true is that there is such a thing as the balance of nature—though we must not take that to mean anything exact or unchanging. Ecosystems display quite a high level of homeostasis. That they do so is virtually a truism, in that they maintain themselves through time in the midst of quite a lot happening. Nor is it a matter of different things remaining more or less stable in parallel. Barry Commoner's "first law of ecology," that "everything is connected to everything else," is particularly true of ecosystems. Not only do they maintain themselves, they do so with a very high degree of interconnection. Just as we may think of an individual organism as an ongoing life process, manifested in a continually changing combination of material elements, and a species as an ongoing process progressively embodied in different individuals, so may we think of an ecosystem as an ongoing process taking place through a complex system of interrelationships between organisms, and between organisms and their nonliving environment. The organisms change, and the interrelationships may vary somewhat, but there is a continuity to the ecosystem, and a center of homeostasis around which the states of the ecosystem fluctuate, which defines its self-identity. Normally, an ecosystem maintains its stability through an intricately complex feedback system. One example of that is the forage–deer–mountain lion balance, which remains roughly constant through continuous oscillation. However, an ecosystem can suffer stress and be impaired. It can be degraded to lower levels of stability and interconnected complexity. It can have its self-identity ruptured. In short, an ecosystem has well being interests—and therefore has moral significance.

No more than in the case of species or individual organisms are the interests of an ecosystem the aggregated interests of its components, and, as in those cases, the various interests might sometimes be in conflict. It may even be in the interests of an ecosystem for a particular species (or sometimes for particular individuals) to die off, allowing the ecosystem to develop in accordance with its inherent nature. It is often the case that a particular species is a useful component of a given ecosystem only during certain stages of the ecosystem's life cycle. In such a case, the interests of the ecosystem are still the interests of a whole life process that integrally incorporates the problematic component. In some of the valleys of California's Sierra Nevada, for instance, ecosystems often contain a high proportion of junipers, which, in the natural progression, eventually make way for the more slowly growing oaks.[1] Junipers grow rapidly and, being full of sap, are very combustible. Under natural conditions, fires caused by lightening periodically burn out the juniper, preventing it from crowding out the oaks and other plants. After a fire, not only the oaks but the smaller plants and grasses have the opportunity to flourish, and there is an attendant increase in the populations of animals, birds, and insects. If the fires do not come, the juniper, together with a few other species, largely takes over, leading to an ecosystem of reduced diversity and stability. The integrity of the complex whole and its diverse living unity is compromised in favor of an impoverished uniformity.

This is not to say that the juniper is only a weed, one that ought to be exterminated. The juniper has its role in the life of an ecosystem. There should always be a few around so that they may (re)establish themselves in that or a neighboring ecosystem if the conditions should ever become appropriate. When, for instance, there is a total burnout, completely devastating an area, the rapidly growing junipers are very useful in restoring the biotic community and maintaining it until the more slowly growing trees and the other beings of the mature ecosystem again hold sway. Most fires, though, do not devastate an area. They are generally benign. They burn through quickly, removing such things as juniper, and providing growing room for the annuals and other rapidly growing small plants. On the larger scale, they clear the way for the more slowly growing fire-resistant trees. Such trees usually sustain relatively little damage. Minor fires do not burn deeply enough to kill the living soil. When minor fires do not occur from time to time, there is a buildup of undergrowth and debris, and an overgrowth of highly flammable trees such as juniper. Then any fire will be a major one, killing everything including the soil. At certain stages, then, the juniper is helpful to the ecosystem and at others harmful to it. The ecosystem, it would be fair to say, is a life process having a self-identity distinct from that of its component entities, and which may call for juniper at some times and not at others, just as the life process of an oak calls for acorns at some times and not at others . . .

HOLISTIC ETHICS AND ATOMISTIC ETHICS

There are clear divergences between the *prima facie* demands of a humane ethic and those of a land ethic. We have noted that Regan, and others who concentrate on the welfare of individuals, would in extremus, countenance the destruction of species in preference to an injury to sentient beings that, on the individual level, would be a greater evil. In contrast, a land ethic would put the premium on the preservation of species, as conducive to the well-being of the biotic community, even at the expense of individual beings. Indeed, advocates of land ethics often seem to disregard the moral status of individual animals, even when the well-being of the biotic community is not at all at stake. This has seemed quite shockingly wrong to many who put the moral focus on the welfare of individuals. Not only did Leopold, for instance, partake of a carnivorous diet, he waxed quite lyrical about the joys of hunting, even while expounding our moral duties to the land community as a whole.

Leopold offered no moral justification for the killing of animals as such, and certainly he felt no moral anomaly in hunting. I doubt that it would have occurred to him that it needed to be justified. He no more than the wolf required an excuse for killing and eating deer. The moral question was whether the hunting was pursued in a manner consistent with the well-being of the biotic community. Indeed, Leopold saw considerable value in hunting and other activities that bring us into contact with wild things, one important benefit being that such experiences remind us of our dependency on and membership in the biotic community. (Accordingly, he castigated methods of hunting that separate hunter from nature through the interposition of gadgetry and artificial contrivance.) Moreover, hunting can be of value in developing a sense of sportsmanship and responsibility toward the biotic community (though it does not always have that effect). In several passages Leopold wrote beautifully of the hunting experience, conveying to me the impression that he took part in the activity as an expression of loving membership in the land community. Certainly there was loving appreciation of that which he hunted. Consider his description of the sky dance of the woodcock:

> He flies in low from some neighboring thicket, alights on the bare moss, and at once begins the overture: a series of queer throaty *peents* spaced about two seconds apart . . . Suddenly the peenting ceases and the bird flutters skyward in a series of wide spirals, emitting a musical twitter. Up and up he goes, the spirals steeper and smaller, the twittering louder and louder, until the performer is only a speck in the sky. Then, without warning, he tumbles like a crippled plane, giving voice in a soft liquid warble that a March bluebird might envy. At a few feet from the ground he levels off and returns to his peenting ground, usually to the exact spot where the performance began, and there resumes his peenting.
>
> The woodcock is a living refutation of the theory that the utility of a game bird is to serve as a target, or to pose gracefully on a slice of toast. No one would rather hunt woodcock in October

> than I, but since learning of the sky dance, I find myself calling one or two birds enough. I must be sure that, come April, there will be no dearth of dancers in the sunset sky.

Whether or not such love ought to be compatible with hunting, it is manifest that Leopold loved the woodcock.

Extending moral consideration beyond human concerns, then, does not automatically entail a disapproval of killing nonhumans, nor would everyone be shocked by the juxta-position of approval of hunting with concern for the biotic community. Callicott remarks that the land ethic is not just an extrapolation from humanistic and humane ethics, but represents a difference in kind:

> The land ethic is not part of this linear series of steps [from humanistic ethics to humane ethics to . . .] and hence may be represented as a point off the scale. The principle difference . . . is that the land ethic is collective or "holistic" while the others are distributive or "atomistic." Another relevant difference is that . . . the land ethic . . . abandons the "higher"/"lower" ontological and axiological schema, in favor of a functional system of value. The land ethic, in other words, is inclined to establish value distinctions not on the basis of higher and lower orders of being, but on the basis of the importance of organisms, minerals, and so on to the biotic community. Some bacteria, for example, may be of greater value to the health or economy of nature than dogs, and thus command more respect.

Here indeed, we have a gap that truly does seem to be unbridgeable. On the one side are humane and humanistic ethics, atomistic in nature, while on the other side is the holistic land ethic, unitarian in ontology and axiology. The biotic community is the one being with which the land ethic is concerned, and its welfare is the one value. I maintain that we can span the problematic chasm.

We are not forced to make a narrow choice between the interests of sentient beings on the one hand and the effective functioning of the biosphere on the other hand, with no body of coherent ethical theory between the two hands. The unifying moral principle is that of due respect for the well-being interests of every entity that has well-being interests. Neither are we restricted to morally considering the interests of only one class of entity—unless the relevant class is simply that of interest haver. Individuals have interests and ecosystems have interests, and there is no need to absorb the former into the latter, or to reduce the latter to the former. There is no forced choice between atomism and holism, parts and wholes. Everything that has well-being interests counts morally.

We must not let our ethics get bogged down by an ontological tunnel vision that sees only part of what there is. Consider: An animal is made up of a very large number of cells (plus various other stuff not properly described as cells, which I shall ignore). The animal is not just the collection of those individual cells, but it is not anything other than those cells. In saying this I am *not* buying into the formula, "the whole is greater than the sum of its parts." I do not even know what it means, since I do not know what "greater than" and "sum of" mean in such a context. I can accept that some wholes are *different* from the collection of their parts. How the parts are arranged and what they have to do with one another is critical. To again use the wave analogy, a wave is not just a certain amount of water, nor is it even that water arranged into a certain shape. There is nothing, or at least no thing, there in addition to the water, but if we just mention the water and not the wave we omit features of importance. If we think only of parts and not of wholes, we omit giving consideration to many well-being interests, and that leaves a hole in our morality.

We might think of an animal's life as a life process, going through different bits of matter, different cells, at different times. If we think only of the cells, we leave out important features, including the morally important feature of having well-being interests. In fact, if we took that approach to animals, or to ourselves, we would leave out just about everything which matters—including ourselves. If we take an extreme reductivist approach to the living world around us, seeing only individual living beings, we lose track of a lot of important things. The ongoing life processes of species and ecosystems form entities that are materially important to us and which have morally significant interests in their own right. Again, by losing sight of the part and seeing *only* the whole, we lose track of important things. Individuals undoubtedly are real and count morally. Losing sight of either the holistic side of things or the individual side of things is just as shortsighted morally as it is materially. Atomism or holism on its own, either one without the other, is not only incomplete, it is incoherent. We can understand neither the tree without the leaf, nor the leaf without the tree. The same goes for photosynthesis and leaf, for tree and ecosystem. Neither can we morally understand things in isolation. The well-being needs of an individual are a matter of its nature, and the nature and needs of a being cannot be understood except in context. We are what we are as individuals, but we also are what we are with respect to our social group, our species, and the biosphere, and this affects moral issues. Morally and ontologically, then, we must recognize different aspects of reality.

In all honesty, it must be admitted that a measure of responsibility for the perceived problem in reconciling the moral claims of holism and atomism must rest with none other than Aldo Leopold. When he writes that "a thing is right when it tends to preserve the integrity, stability and beauty of the biotic community. It is wrong when it tends otherwise," he seems to be suggesting that the welfare of the biotic community is the one and only criterion of right and wrong. According to Regan: "The implications of this view include the clear prospect that the individual may be sacrificed for the greater biotic good, in the name of 'the integrity, stability and beauty of the biotic community.' " This is the view Regan went on to characterize and castigate as "environmental fascism." Indeed, if the welfare of the biotic community is the *sole* standard of right and wrong, then if I beat my wife, cheat on my income tax, torture kittens, ax-murder my neighbor, and burn down the local schoolhouse, my actions are morally neutral so long as I do not allow the sparks to start a bushfire. That is obviously ridiculous. In fairness to Leopold, it should be pointed out that the context indicates that he was talking about the morality of our dealings with the land community. I, not idiosyncratically, interpret Leopold as saying that *when it comes to dealing with the land community,* here is the way to tell right from wrong. We need not interpret Leopold as claiming that the land community is the one and only thing that has moral significance. It is unnecessary, and I think uncharitable, to attribute to Leopold that latter, less reasonable, position. In any case, *we* certainly need not adopt such a position.[2]

It may very well be that, as Regan fears, the interests of the biotic community will morally take priority over those of an individual in some particular cases. That prospect does not, of itself, horrify me. It is merely a consequence of the biotic community having moral standing. A consequence of recognizing that others have moral standing is that we must, in some circumstances, defer to their interests. Even if we do not accord them full moral standing, according them any moral standing at all entails that there must be some conceivable cases wherein we ought to defer. It is quite absurd to imagine that a being could have moral standing without it being possible that this might some time morally require us to give way. Because (to take an extreme example) I believe that even amoebas have morally significant interests, I am committed to the view that it is conceivable that some interest of an amoeba (or some number of amoebas) might morally take priority over some very minimal interest of mine—although nearly anything would tip the scales against the amoeba. I doubt that such a case would ever arise in practice, but I find no absurdity in thinking it theoretically possible. Much less do I think it absurd that the interests of the biotic community might morally take priority over even a major interest of an individual. Perhaps sometimes interests of the biotic community will outweigh interests of the individual, and sometimes the shoe will be on the other foot, as both the biotic community and the individual have moral standing. That the biotic community has moral standing does not mean that it must invariably take precedence. Although dumping soapy dishwater into a clear mountain stream stresses the biotic community, and is therefore wrong, it is not so important that I ought to commit murder to prevent some oaf from doing so . . .

RESPECTING THE BIOSPHERE

As Leopold points out, the trend of evolution has been to "elaborate and diversify the biota." This, rather than any particular trend in the direction of producing *Homo sapiens,* has been the overall direction of evolution. Evolutionary processes seem to have gone pretty far in that direction, having produced an inconceivably intricate complex of interconnected, interacting, and overlapping life processes. Those life processes have—in a sense, *are*—an equally intricate complex of interconnected, interacting, overlapping interests. To be sure, the fabric of the biosphere is more richly woven in some places than in others, but everywhere it is rich enough for the interests to be morally significant. Of course we cannot just conclude, merely on the basis of evolutionary tendency, that encouraging elaborateness and diversity is the moral thing to do, for we have no reason to conclude that the trend of evolution is in a morally good direction. Still, these factors, together with organic unity, contribute to the moral importance of an interest. How, then, are we to act morally toward such a tangle of entities with tangled, overlapping, conflicting interests? Is it possible to do so at all? If we build a house, operate a farm, or just gather nuts and berries in the wild, any way we have of living will have an impact on the biosphere (though in modern economies, much of the impact will often be caused by others on our behalf). Everything we do, even if it is only to wash our hands, injures some interests. Can we look for guidance to Leopold's ethic, calling for us to "preserve the integrity, stability, and beauty of the biotic community"? I certainly think we can find guidance there, at least with respect to holistic entities, though I do believe that his recommendations must be interpreted in terms of interest satisfaction. In interpreting them, we would do well to bear in mind the ideal of acting without acting.

Let us start with beauty, which is perhaps the most problematic part of Leopold's recommendation. Prizing beauty can easily be to take a human-centered point of view, valuing natural things for their instrumental value in producing pleasing aesthetic experiences. As Mark Sagoff points out, valuing nature for its beauty, like valuing a woman for her beauty, tends to trivialize the object, valuing it not for what it is in itself but for how it pleases us. I think we might largely avoid that result by analyzing beauty in terms of harmony, balance, complex unity, and other things being in the interests of the biosphere. Certainly there is beauty in the workings of the biosphere. Yet some natural things that are ecologically important—such as maggots or lice (or the snail darter?)—hardly seem beautiful. Still, if we acted to preserve those features of the biosphere that are (generally agreed to be) beautiful, taking those steps that were causally useful to preserve that beauty, we would be going a considerable way toward protecting the essential functions of the biosphere. Even so, we have to go further than that.

The stability criterion has a great deal to recommend it. Maintaining the overall stability of its life processes is clearly very important for the well-being of ecosystems and the biosphere, and too often we have sinned against them by disrupting their vital functions. Yet stability in itself cannot be the ultimate good. Apart from the extreme and obvious counterexample that the extermination of life on earth would lead to a condition of much greater stability, there is the fact that degraded ecosystems are sometimes more stable than they were in their richer but more precariously balanced original condition. But mere stability for the sake of stability is not at all what Leopold was advocating. What is important is maintaining the viability of the life processes within the biosphere, in all of their richness and diversity. That is the stability that is morally important, being a matter of the protection of vital interests. Diversity, a factor commonly mentioned in connection with stability, is very important and must be interpreted in much the same way. No more than stability is diversity an end in its own right. Otherwise, packing ecosystems with alien species would be the thing to do, so long as introductions outnumbered extinctions. But to do that to an ecosystem would be to undermine its coherence and self-identity. Rather, the thing to do is to respect that characteristic integrated diversity so essential to the well-being of the biosphere and its ecosystems, species, and so on. This interpretation would certainly be consistent with Leopold's writings.

Integrity, the other factor mentioned by Leopold, is the one of critical importance. We cannot avoid affecting the world around us, but the important thing is to avoid *injuring* it. That is, we ought to avoid violations of the vital interests of the land community, or the erosion of its self-identity.

This, I suggest, would be a viable interpretation and elaboration of Leopold's views. What it comes to is that the morally right way to treat the biosphere is to protect the essential life processes of the biosphere in all of their richness and integrated coherent diversity. In so doing, we would thereby be respecting the well-being interests of the biosphere and of those holistic entities within the biosphere that have enough self-identity to have well-being interests. Ecosystems would be protected from degradation and species from extinction, and so on, but these are not things with which we ought to try to deal one item at a time. Our primary moral concern is not with artificially isolated entities, but with life processes that are often not discrete and often have overlapping interests. When it comes to the biosphere, our primary concern is with the whole flow of its ongoing life processes.

At this point, I think we can start to see the outline of some answers to our questions about whether we can farm, mine, build houses, and so forth without acting wrongly. It would seem to be *reductio ad absurdum* if we could act no other way than wrongly, but I do think it is possible for us to live and yet act rightly toward the things of the biosphere. Indeed, by living in balance with nature—and with ourselves—we would live better lives in our own right. Like the old man in the mountain stream, we must act without acting. Let us suppose that we were considering engaging in some activity that affected the biosphere. Perhaps we contemplate clearing some land for farming—an example that may serve for general purposes. To clear the land would be at least to reduce the native ecosystem in size, and would destroy it if we cleared totally. This, as we all know, has often happened. Even if it were not destroyed totally, an ecosystem may be qualitatively altered if it is reduced below a certain critical size, as certain species and other life processes require large ranges in order to continue. Moreover, if an ecosystem becomes too restricted, even species that survive may lose a significant portion of their genetic variability. That erodes the richness of the self-identity of both species and ecosystem. We must also bear in mind that ecosystems overlap and are related in intricate ways to other ecosystems. We might merely reduce one ecosystem in size and thereby, quite unknowingly, completely upset a related ecosystem, as when we fill mangrove swamps and so upset marine food chains. The mangrove ecosystem seems the same, only smaller, with the dramatic differences showing up offshore. All that being acknowledged, though, I think we can still avoid the conclusion that we ought never to affect an ecosystem. To avoid that totally would not be possible for us, and it would not be required if it were.

We do not sin against the biosphere if we allow its life processes to carry on, healthily and unendangered by our interference. It is possible to farm, chop trees, build houses, dig mines, and so forth without upsetting the life processes of the ecosystems affected, though we might well reduce the extent of the territory in which certain processes are carried out. The interests of the environmental holistic entities involved are threatened only when there is danger that a life process might be terminated, or that its self-identity might be eroded due to qualitative changes springing from a severe change of scale. We must take care that the impact of our actions be not too massive or of the wrong sort. So long as the life processes are not threatened, reduction in scale is not of itself injurious. Chopping some trees is one thing, then, but destroying a forest is something else. In our dealings with the world, we should always stop short of entirely destroying or irreparably degrading any ecosystem, species, or other such holistic entity. Our farms, cities, factories, mines, and resorts ought always to coexist with, rather than disrupt or displace, the morally significant entities of the biosphere. If we maintain species, if we preserve viable remnants of ecosystems of all types, and if, as good husbanders, we respect the integrity of even those living systems that we have modified for our own benefit, we shall have done well. This is moral advice. As a general policy, following this advice also has considerable practical value. Although we can often get away with acting to the contrary, we have too often found to our cost that disrupting the biosphere can rebound against us in unexpected ways. In Tao the only motion is returning.

We can never be absolutely certain that our actions will not have catastrophic consequences, a point that applies with respect to the effects of our actions on other humans as well as on the biosphere; however, we can often be reasonably certain that they will not. The moral to draw is not that we should give up acting, but that we should monitor the effects of our actions closely, and that we should be particularly wary of things that are novel in the type or scale of their effects. There is much to be done. In doing, we should take good care to act in accordance with the flow of nature.

A MATTER OF DEGREE

We must recognize that it is not always possible to respect the interests of all holistic entities such as ecosystems. Trivially, one drop of water in the hollow of a leaf is an ecosystem in its own right, as is the decaying body of a dead mouse. We destroy thriving ecosystems whenever we lop a rotten tree branch or scrub the bathroom floor. We cannot avoid destroying such ecosystems from time to time, and there seems no plausible reason to think it a tragedy that this is so. These are only small components of more encompassing systems. Yet that goes for every living system, as nothing short of the biosphere is absolutely discrete. So, do even these very minor ecosystems count as having some slight degree of moral significance? A possible reason why they do not may be that none of their life processes are unique. The bacterial growth in the dead mouse and the life processes of the molds on the bathroom tiles are not separate processes unique in those mini-ecosystems, but are merely local manifestations of processes found many other places. Unlike material objects, processes do not have to be all in the same place. There is nothing going on in the dead mouse that is not going on many other places, and nothing that would be lost were that tiny ecosystem disrupted. This is in contrast to, let us say, a rain forest, where there is a very great deal to be lost. Even if, quite contrary to actual fact, the species and other life processes found there were all to be found elsewhere, the forest would still have its own separate self-identity in the coherent integrated unity of those life processes in their unique manifestation there. On the other hand, although the species and other life processes involved in the dead mouse have moral significance in their own right, their combination in the dead mouse has no very significant self-identity about which to be concerned.

I find this way of looking at things largely satisfactory, but only largely. Even in the tiny dead-mouse ecosystem, or in a drop of stagnant water, there is still *some* self-identity to have moral significance. Although the web of life covers the whole earth, every portion of the web has at least some self-identity with some degree of coherent integrated unity, giving that portion its own significance. Not only would each rotifer in the drop of water have some very minimal degree of moral significance, the whole drop-of-water ecosystem would have some minuscule moral significance, even though it is very like countless other stagnant drops. Once again we come to what is a matter of degree, with the bottom end of the scale being virtually negligible. At the lower end of the scale, instances of ecosystems degenerate into such relatively trivial cases as drops of water or rotting stumps, species into insignificant variations in genetic detail, and individual organisms into the simplest of microorganisms. Their moral significance is also a matter of degree, ranging to very much from not quite nothing.

The thing for us to do is to find our way in the world, while giving due respect to the widely disparate interests of other beings. This is not essentially different from what we ought to do concerning other humans. Other humans also have widely divergent interests, ranging from the insignificant to the monumental, and it is for us to make appropriate moral responses. In morally dealing with others, human or nonhuman, we must estimate the importance of various interests of various entities (including ourselves). In so doing it would be appropriate to consider how highly developed an entity and its interests are, how vital an interest is to it, and what the alternatives are. Whether we are dealing with individual or holistic entities, it remains a matter of assessing interests and interest packages, which remains a matter of trying to estimate such things as level of complex unity and the role within it of a given interest. From there we must go on to work out the moral priorities.

There is no unambiguously right way to assign moral priorities, nor, with the best will in the world, is there any way at all in which we can avoid affecting and sometimes injuring the interests of other beings, individual or holistic. Yet we cannot take the lack of certitude and the inevitability of injury as an excuse for shedding a guilt-relieving tear and proceeding to do whatever suits our own inclinations. We can no more use that excuse with reference to nonhuman entities than we can with reference to humans. Everything we do, even if it is only eating and taking up space affects other humans, but that does not make it a matter of moral indifference how we treat others. Neither is it a matter of indifference how we treat the biosphere and the nonhuman entities within it.

NOTES

1. This material is based on public presentations at Yosemite National Park, California, and on my discussions with the staff there.
2. Even were we unable to reconcile properly environmentalism with humanistic or humane ethics, that, it should be obvious, is no reason why we ought to neglect one or another area of moral application. Although Callicott says that "environmental ethics locates ultimate value in the 'biotic community' and assigns differential moral values to the constitutive individuals relative to that standard," we must not conclude that environmental ethics requires this to be the *only* standard relative to which individuals have moral value.

DISCUSSION QUESTIONS

1. Do you think Johnson has reconciled atomistic and holistic ethics? Was there a genuine difference between these approaches to ethical questions to begin with?
2. How far do you think the idea of well-being interests can be extended? If species and ecosystems have well-being interests, can cars and houses also have them? Why or why not? What are the implications of your answer to this question for Johnson's view?
3. Consider Johnson's modest proposal for respecting ecosystems; apparently, in his view, it is OK for us to carry on so long as we do not upset an ecosystem's "life processes." Does this go far enough, in your view? Might an anthropocentrist also agree? Sketch the basis for such agreement; on what point(s) would there be fundamental disagreement between Johnson and an anthropocentrist?

HARLEY CAHEN

Against the Moral Considerability of Ecosystems

Harley Cahen is a recent graduate of the Department of Natural Resources, Cornell University. He argues that ecosystems are not likely candidates for moral considerability because they do not have interests; and they do not have interests because they do not have genuine goals. What may appear to be systemic goals might just be by-products instead.

CRITICAL READING QUESTIONS

1. What is the goal/by-product distinction?
2. What is the connection between goals and interests, in Cahen's view?

3. Why is Cahen willing to concede that plants have interests?
4. Why is goal-directedness not sufficient for moral considerability, according to Cahen?
5. What role does goal-directedness have in defining the moral community?
6. What is Wright's analysis of goal-directed behavior? Can you see how Cahen applies it to car rust?
7. What do the observations of the Martian biologist show?
8. On what grounds does Cahen deny that ecosystems have genuine goals?

I

If natural areas had no value at all for human beings, would we still have a duty to preserve them? Some preservationists think that we would. Aldo Leopold, for instance, argues brilliantly for the cultural and psychological value of wilderness; yet he insists that even "enlightened" self-interest is not enough. According to Leopold, an "ecological conscience" recognizes "obligations to land." The ecological conscience sees that preservation is a good thing in itself—something we have a prima facie duty to promote—apart from any contribution it makes to human welfare. For convenience, let us call this conviction the *preservationist intuition.*

I share this intuition. Can we justify it? I see at least four plausible strategies. We might, first, appeal to the intrinsic value of natural ecosystems. A second strategy relies on the interests of the individual creatures that are inevitably harmed when we disturb an ecosystem. A third possibility is a virtue-based approach. Perhaps what offends us—as preservationists—is that anyone who would damage an ecosystem for inadequate reasons falls short of our "ideals of human excellence." Each of these three strategies has something to recommend it. But none captures the element of the preservationist intuition that involves a feeling of obligation *to* "land." This suggests a fourth strategy, the appeal to what Kenneth Goodpaster calls *moral considerability.* This strategy represents an ecosystem as something that has interests of its own, and thus can directly be victimized or benefited by our actions. If ecosystems do have interests of their own, perhaps we owe it to them to consider those interests in our moral deliberations. This fourth strategy is the one that I wish to call into question.

There is a fifth strategy—an appeal to the moral right of a natural ecosystem to be left alone. This strategy is similar to the fourth one but may be distinct. Rights, some would say, automatically "trump" other kinds of moral claim. If so, an appeal to ecosystem rights would be much stronger than an appeal to moral considerability. (Too strong, I suspect: I find it best to regard talk of the rights of nonhumans as an enthusiastic way of asserting moral considerability.) We can leave this question open, though, for if they are trumps, moral rights have at least this much in common with moral considerability: they both presuppose interests.

I contend that ecosystems cannot be morally considerable *because* they do not have interests—not even in the broad sense in which we commonly say that plants and other nonsentient organisms "have interests." The best we can do on behalf of plant interests, I believe, is the argument from *goal-directedness.* Nonsentient organisms—those not capable of consciously taking an interest in anything—have interests (and thus are candidates for moral considerability) in achieving their biological goals. Should ecosystems, too, turn out to be goal directed, they would be candidates for moral considerability.

Harley Cahen, "Against the Moral Considerability of Ecosystems," *Environmental Ethics,* vol. 10, no. 3 (Fall 1988), pp. 195–216. Reprinted by permission.

Although the argument from goal-directedness fails, we should not dismiss the argument too hastily. Some ecosystems are strikingly stable and resilient. They definitely have a goal-directed look. Yet there are reasons to doubt whether this apparent goal-directedness is genuine. The key is to distinguish the goals of a system's behavior from other outcomes that are merely behavioral *by-products.* Armed with this distinction, we can see that the conditions for genuine goal-directedness are tougher than environmental ethicists typically realize. Ecosystems seem unlikely to qualify.

In sections two and three of this paper I define *moral considerability* and distinguish it from other ways that something can matter morally. In section four I establish that goal-directedness plays a key role in arguments for the considerability of plants and other nonsentient organisms. In sections five and six I argue that this appeal to goal-directedness is plausible as long as we keep the goal/by-product distinction in mind. In sections seven through nine, I argue that ecology and evolutionary biology cast serious doubt on the possibility that ecosystems are genuinely goal-directed.

II

The literature of environmental ethics is full of appeals to the interests of ecosystems. Consider Aldo Leopold's famous remark: "A thing is right when it tends to preserve the integrity, stability, and beauty of the biotic community. It is wrong when it tends otherwise." Is Leopold suggesting that the biotic community has an interest in its own integrity and stability? Some commentators interpret his remark this way. James Heffernan, for instance, defends Leopold by insisting that "even ecosystems . . . are *things* that have interests and hence, may be benefited or harmed." Holmes Rolston, III, likewise would found an "ecological ethic" upon the obligation to promote "ecosystemic interests."

More often the appeal to ecosystem interests is implicit. Consider John Rodman, criticizing animal liberationists such as Peter Singer for drawing the moral considerability boundary to include only sentient beings. Rodman complains: "The moral atomism that focuses on individual animals . . . does not seem well adapted to coping with ecological systems." Why is "atomism" inadequate? Because, Rodman explains, an ecological community as a whole has a good of its own, a "welfare":

> I need only to stand in the midst of clear-cut forest, a strip-mined hillside, a defoliated jungle, or a dammed canyon to feel uneasy with assumptions that could yield the conclusion that no human action can make any difference to the welfare of anything but sentient animals.

Of course, Rodman believes that individual plants and nonsentient animals are morally considerable, too. That is reason enough for him to feel uneasy with Singer's assumptions. It cannot be his only reason, however, for it would leave him as guilty of moral atomism as Singer. Whose *welfare* could Rodman have in mind? The welfare, I take it, of the communities themselves.

III

Moral considerability is a potentially confusing term. Let me clarify and defend my use of it. I take moral considerability to be the moral status *x* has if, and only if (a) *x* has interests (a good of its own), (b) it would be prima facie wrong to frustrate *x*'s interests (to harm *x*), and (c) the wrongness of frustrating *x*'s interests is direct—that is, does not depend on how the interests of any other being are affected. It is the concern with interests that distinguishes moral considerability from the other varieties of moral status upon which the preservationist intuition might possibly be based.

Goodpaster plainly means to restrict moral considerability to beings with *interests.* In his first paper on moral considerability he explains that life is the "key" to moral considerability because living things have interests; this, he points out, is what makes them "capable of being beneficiaries." Goodpaster makes a point of agreeing with Joel Feinberg about what Feinberg calls "mere things." "Mere things," Goodpaster says, are not candidates for moral considerability because they are "incapable of being benefited or harmed—they have no 'well-being' to be sought or acknowledged." That is why he insists that "*x*'s being a living being" is not only sufficient for moral considerability but is also *necessary*.

In Goodpaster's subsequent work, he characterizes the entire biosphere as a "bearer of value." Yet he does not appear to have changed his understanding of the requirements for moral considerability. "The biosystem as a whole" is considerable, he says. Why? Because it is, in effect, an "organism"—"an integrated, self-sustaining unity which puts solar energy to work in the service of growth and maintenance." Goodpaster's focus remains on interests and he expresses his confidence that the "biosystem as a whole" has them.

Some philosophers speak of moral considerability but do not associate it with interests at all. Andrew Brennan, for instance, asserts that natural objects such as ecosystems, mountains, deserts, the air, rocky crests, and rivers may have this moral status though they have no interests and thus can be harmed only metaphorically. This is no longer moral considerability as I understand it.

Other philosophers equate moral considerability with intrinsic value, holding that both equally presuppose interests. Robin Attfield, for instance, writes, "I follow Goodpaster in holding that things which lack a good of their own cannot be morally considerable . . . or have intrinsic value." J. Baird Callicott attributes to Goodpaster the view that because "life is intrinsically valuable . . . all living beings should be granted moral considerability." As Callicott sums up his own view:

> If the self is intrinsically valuable, then nature is intrinsically valuable. If it is rational for me to act in my own best interest, and I and nature are one, then it is rational for me to act in the best interests of nature.

The association of intrinsic value with interests seems odd to me. Many readers will suppose that "mere things"—things which have no interests, no good of their own—might conceivably be intrinsically valuable. As Eric Katz puts it, "many natural entities worth preserving [i.e., valuable in their own right] are not clearly the possessors of interests."

Is this just a quibble about words? I think not. We have more than one paradigm of moral relevance, and it makes a difference which one we adopt as the model for our ethical thinking about ecosystems. If we aim to justify preservation by appeal to the intrinsic value of natural ecosystems, our arguments must build on the way ecosystems resemble other things that we preserve for their intrinsic *value*. Moral considerability is another matter. To ground the preservationist intuition upon the *interests* of ecosystems, we have to look for an analogy between ecosystems and beings that clearly have interests. Given that ecosystems are not sentient, the most promising models are plants and other nonsentient organisms.

IV

Some ethicists would object that we cannot even get this argument for ecosystems off the ground—it is absurd, they would say, to think that plants could be morally considerable. Such a dismissal of plants, however, is too quick, for it ignores goal-directedness. Peter Singer, for instance, regards *rocks* as representative of all nonsentient beings. "A stone," he says, "does not have interests because it cannot suffer. Nothing that we can do to it could possibly make any difference to its welfare." He therefore boldly concludes: "If a being is not capable of suffering, or of experiencing enjoyment or happiness, there is nothing to be taken into account."

Although sentience may turn out, after all, to be necessary for moral considerability, this just cannot be as obvious as Singer assumes. There is a world of difference between plants and rocks. Surely there might be something to "take into account" even in the absence of sentience. All we need, as Bryan Norton observes, is something appropriately analogous to sentience. Norton rejects the possibility of ecosystem "rights" because "collectives such as mountain ranges, species, and ecosystems have no significant analogues to human sentience on which to base assignments of interests." Since collectives lack any analogue to sentience, he reasons, "the whole enterprise of assigning interests [to them] becomes virtually arbitrary." Norton reaches this conclusion too quickly, as I argue below, but he makes two crucial points. First, we can plausibly attribute moral considerability to *x* only when we have a nonarbitrary way of identifying *x*'s interests. Second, this project does not require actual sentience. It is plain enough that plants, for instance, have interests in a straightforward sense, though they feel nothing. Paul Taylor puts it this way:

> Trees have no knowledge or feelings. Yet it is undoubtedly the case that trees can be harmed or benefited by our actions. We can crush their roots by running a bulldozer too close to them. We can see to it that they get adequate nourishment and moisture . . . It is the good of trees themselves that is thereby affected.

In general, Taylor explains, "the good of an individual nonhuman organism [consists in] the full development of its biological powers." Every organism is "a being whose standpoint we can take in making judgments about what events in the world are good or evil."

Let us grant, in spite of Singer and his allies, that there is something about trees that we might intelligibly "take into account" for moral purposes. Can we be more specific? What is it that plants have and rocks do not? The obvious, but unilluminating answer is "life." Just what is it about being alive that makes plants candidates for moral considerability?

Goal-directedness is the key. Taylor, for instance, describes organisms as "teleological centers of life." Goodpaster points to plants' "tendencies [to] maintain and heal themselves" and locates the "core of moral concern" in "respect for self-sustaining organization and integration." Attfield writes of a tree's "latent tendencies, direction of growth and natural fulfillment." Jay Kantor bases his defense of plant interests on their "self-regulating and homeostatic functions." Rodman condemns actions that impose our will upon "natural entities that have their own internal structures, needs, and potentialities," potentialities that are actively "striving to actualize themselves." Finally, James K. Mish'alani points to each living thing's *self-ameliorative competence:* "that is, a power for coordinated movement towards favorable states, a capacity to adjust to its circumstances in a manner to enhance its survival and natural growth."

The goal-directedness of living things gives us a plausible and nonarbitrary standard upon which to "base assignments of interests." If ecosystems, though not sentient, are goal-directed, then we may (without absurdity) attribute interests to them, too. Goodpaster is right: there is no *a priori* reason to think that "the universe of moral considerability [must] map neatly onto our medium-sized framework of organisms." Of course, we must not get carried away with this line of thinking. Goal-directedness is certainly not sufficient for moral considerability. One problem is that some machines are goal-directed—e.g., guided missiles, thermostatic heating systems, chess-playing computers, and "The Terminator." The defender of moral considerability for plants must distinguish plants, morally, from goal-directed but inanimate objects. *Still, the possession of goals is what makes the notion of a plant's "standpoint" intelligible.* Can we locate an ecosystem's standpoint by understanding its goals? Not if it doesn't have any goals.

V

We often know goal-directedness when we see it. The analysis of goal-directedness is, however, a terribly unsettled subject in the philosophy of science. In light of this unsettledness, one must be cautious. Here are three claims. First, the attribution of goal-directedness to organisms can be scientifically and philosophically respectable—even when the organisms in question are nonsentient. Teleology talk need not be vitalistic, anthropomorphic, or rooted in obsolete Aristotelian biology or physics. It does not imply "backward causation." Nor need it run afoul of the "missing goal-object" problem.

Second, some of these respectable accounts of goal-directedness are useful for the environmental ethicist. They enable us to resist crude versions of the common slippery-slope argument against the moral considerability of plants and other nonsentient living things. Once we admit nonsentient beings into the moral considerability club, how can we bar the door to ordinary inanimate objects? Porches, paintings, automobiles, garbage dumps, buildings, and other ordinary objects are allegedly lurking just outside, waiting for us to admit plants. Goal-directedness can keep them out.

Third, we ought to recognize a distinction between goals and behavioral by-products. A defensible conception of goal-directedness must distinguish true goals from outcomes that a system achieves incidentally. Ecosystem resilience and stability look like goals, but this appearance may deceive us. An ecosystem property such as stability might turn out to be just a by-product, the incidental result of individual activities aimed exclusively at the individuals' own goals.

I shall discuss two of the main approaches to understanding goal-directedness. The approaches differ in important ways. I favor the second, but either will do for my purposes. The first approach is propounded by Ernest Nagel (among many others). Nagel holds that a system is goal-directed when it can reach (or remain in) some particular state by means of behavior that is sufficiently *persistent and plastic.* Persistence refers to the system's ability to "compensate" for interfering factors that would otherwise take the system away from its goal. Plasticity refers to the system's ability to reach the same outcome in a variety of ways.

Nagel assumes that this approach will count all living things as goal-directed. It seems to. There are problems, to be sure. Chief among these is the danger that it will include some behavior that plainly is not goal-directed—the movement of a pendulum, for instance, or the behavior of a buffered chemical solution. Nagel, however, shows that with some plausible tinkering—mainly, by adding a third condition that he calls "orthogonality"—we can deal with these counterexamples.

The second approach, pioneered by Charles Taylor, insists that goal-directed behavior "[really does] occur 'for the sake of' the state of affairs which follows." Subsequent philosophers have developed this basic insight in various ways.

An especially influential exponent of Taylor's approach is Larry Wright. Taylor's considered formulation of his insight requires that the behavior in question be both necessary and sufficient for the goal. Wright finds this unsatisfactory—too generous in some ways and too strict in others. He suggests what he calls an "etiological" account, one that focuses on the causal background of the behavior in question. A system is goal-directed, Wright contends, *only* if it behaves as it does just because that is the type of behavior that tends to bring about that type of goal. Formally, behavior *B* occurs for the sake of goal-state *G* if "(i) *B* tends to bring about *G*," and "(ii) *B* occurs because (i.e. is brought about by the fact that) it tends to bring about *G*." The key condition is (ii). Some machines, say guided missiles, meet it, for a machine may *B* because it is designed to *B*, and it may be designed to *B*, in turn, because *B* tends to bring about some *G* desired by the designer. Organisms meet it, too, because of the way that natural selection operates. The fitness of an organism usually depends on how appropriate its behavior is—that is, the extent to which it does the sort of thing (say, *B*) that tends to help that kind of organism survive and reproduce. If the disposition to *B* is heritable, organisms whose tendency to *B* helps make them fit will leave descendants that tend to *B*. Those descendants are disposed to *B*, then, in part because *B* is an appropriate type of behavior.

Some people emphatically do not find Wright's approach respectable. He has, for example, recently been accused of "misrepresenting" natural selection as a teleological process in the old-fashioned (and discredited) sense according to which nature selects with certain outcomes in mind. This charge, however, misses the mark, for there is nothing wrong with Wright's understanding of natural selection. In addition, Wright has also dealt effectively with other, better-founded criticisms that need not be discussed here.

Wright's development of Taylor's insight is the best approach for my purposes because alternative versions of Taylor's approach are not as good for sustaining attributions of goal-directedness to plants and lower animals. With regard specifically to the slippery slope and the alleged "needs" of paintings and porches, Nagel's approach seems good enough, for these objects do not act persistently or plastically toward any result that we could seriously be tempted to call a goal. With Wright's criteria, however, we sidestep questions of degree that can plague Nagel. Consider my car, which responds to the upstate New York environment by rusting. The car rusts in spite of my efforts to stop it, and it would rust even if I tried much harder.

Eventually it will fall apart. Does this unpleasantly persistent behavior count as goal-directed? A dedicated slippery-sloper might suggest that the car has the goal of rusting, a "need" to rust. Both Nagel and Wright can resist this suggestion, but Nagel would have a tougher time due to the vagueness of his persistence and plasticity conditions. Wright would simply check the behavior's etiology. My car, we may safely say, does not rust *because* rusting tends to cause cars to fall apart. It rusts because rust is just what happens when steel meets moisture and road salt. The car's behavior fails Wright's condition (ii).

We can imagine an etiology that would make my car's rusting genuinely goal-directed. Assume that car designers know how to make sturdy rust-free cars. Suppose, however, that they greedily conspire to build cars that are susceptible to rust in order to force people to buy new cars more frequently. We would then be unable fully to understand my car's rusting as a purely chemical process, for—on the conspiracy theory of rust—my car would be rusting (in part) because rusting tends to cause cars to fall apart.

Now, what about ecosystems? I concede that the heralded stability and resilience of some ecological systems make them prima facie goal-directed. When such an ecosystem is perturbed in any one of various ways, it bounces back. The members of the ecosystem do just what is necessary (within limits) to restore the system to equilibrium. But are they cooperating in order to restore equilibrium? That is surely imaginable. On the other hand, each creature might instead be "doing its own thing," with the fortunate but incidental result that the ecosystem remains stable. *If this is correct, then we are dealing with a behavioral by-product, not a systemic goal.*

The goal/by-product distinction is well entrenched in the literature on natural selection and biological adaptation. Let me illustrate this distinction with an example from George Williams. Williams asks us to consider the behavior of a panic-stricken crowd rushing from a burning theater. A biologist newly arrived from Mars, he suggests, might be impressed by

> [the group's] rapid 'response' to the stimulus of fire. It went rapidly from a widely dispersed distribution to the formation of dense aggregates that very effectively sealed off the exits.

If the crowd clogs the exits in spite of strenuous crowd-control efforts, would our Martian be entitled to report that he had observed a crowd that was goal-directed toward self-destruction via the sealing off of the exits? Of course not. We know that the clogging of the exits is just incidental. The people are trying to get out. The crowd clogs the exits in spite of the dreadful consequences.

Any theory of goal-directedness ought to be able to avoid the Martian's conclusion. Wright's theory does that easily via condition (ii): *G* can be a goal of behavior *B* only if *B* occurs *because* it tends to bring about *G*. If *G* plays no explanatory role it cannot be a genuine goal.

Nagel's account also permits us to distinguish goal from by-product. The persistence condition does the work here. There is no reason to think that the theater crowd's behavior is truly persistent toward clogging the exits. If there were more exits, or larger exits, the people would have escaped smoothly. We may be sure that the crowd would not compensate for greater ease of exit by modifying its behavior in order to achieve clogging.

VI

If the idea that organisms have morally considerable "interests" seems plausible, it must, I think, be because *organisms are genuinely goal-directed.* When Taylor, for instance, characterizes a tree's good as "the full realization of its biological powers," we know what he means. We naturally assume that *powers* does not refer to everything that can happen to a tree—disease, say, or stunting from lack of nutrients. The tree's powers are the capabilities that the tree exercises in the service of its goals of growth, survival, and reproduction. We certify that those are the tree's goals, in turn, by employing criteria such as Wright's or Nagel's.

Should we find moral significance in an organism's goals? Perhaps not. We may coherently admit that plants have goals, yet deny that we have duties to them. Still, there is a tempting analogy between the goal-directed behavior of organisms and the intentional behavior of humans. Recall the rhetorical role that the notion of natural "striving" plays in

Paul Taylor's argument for an ethic of respect for nature. Recall Katz's choice of the term *autonomy* to characterize an organism's capacity for independent pursuit of its own interests. Indeed the word *interests* itself conveys the flavor of intention. This flavor lends persuasiveness to arguments such as Taylor's.

Let us, in any event, grant that to have *natural* goals is to have morally considerable interests. Where does this leave behavioral by-products? It leaves them where they were—morally irrelevant. We need a nonarbitrary standard for deciding which states of affairs are good ones from the organism's own "standpoint." Sentience gives us such a standard by way of the organism's own preferences (which we are capable of discovering in various ways). By analogy, a nonsentient organism's biological goal—its "preferred" states—can do the same thing. But is there any reason at all for supposing that either mere natural tendencies or behavioral by-products give rise to interests? I think not. Why, from a given system's "standpoint," should it matter whether some natural tendency, unconnected (except incidentally) to the system's goals, plays itself out?

Consider John Rodman's account of why it is wrong to dam a wild river. Rodman emphasizes that the river "struggles" against the dam "like an instinct struggles against inhibition." One might be tempted to say that this way of talking is unnecessary, that every natural tendency is morally privileged. Such a claim, however, is implausible. What leads Rodman to talk of instinct and struggle is, I take it, the notion that the river actually has goals and would be frustrated, by the dam, in its pursuit of them.

I do not expect this example to be convincing. To see clearly that mere tendencies are in themselves morally irrelevant, we should consider something really drastic—like *death*. Usually, death is something that just happens—by accident, by disease, or simply when the body wears out. Organisms tend to die, but they do not ordinarily aim to die. As Jonathan Bennett puts it: "Every animal is tremendously plastic in respect of becoming dead: throw up what obstacles you may, and death will still be achieved. Yet animals seldom have their deaths as a goal."

Consider a salmon of a species whose members routinely die after spawning. Even here death seems unlikely to be the organism's goal. The salmon dies because the arduous upstream journey has worn it out. If it could spawn without dying, it would do so. Once in a while that actually happens. When it does, do we say (without further evidence) that the salmon has been frustrated in its efforts to die after spawning? No. We would say that the salmon has managed to spawn without having had the misfortune to die.

Behavioral by-products, like mere tendencies, seem not to generate anything we can comfortably call "interests." The salmon example illustrates this, if we interpret the death of the adult as a by-product of its spawning. Williams' theater example illustrates it, too. It would be truly bizarre to suggest that the panicky crowd has an interest in being trapped and incinerated.

Although there is much more that needs to be said about whether the argument from goal-directedness can establish the moral considerability of plants, let us go ahead and accept plant moral considerability. But does ecosystem moral considerability follow? No, an obstacle remains: *the goal/by-product distinction.* We still need to determine whether stability (or any other property) of an ecosystem is a genuine goal of the whole system rather than merely a by-product of self-serving individual behavior . . .

X

Earlier I mentioned several distinct strategies for justifying what I call the "preservationist intuition"—intrinsic value, the good of individual plants and animals, and ideals of human excellence. Any of these might be enough. Still, we may find ourselves tempted to believe that whole ecosystems have interests and are therefore morally considerable. This avenue, however, is not promising. Genuine goal-directedness is a step—an essential step—toward moral considerability. It makes sense (as I have argued) to claim that plants and other nonsentient organisms are morally considerable—but only because those beings' own biological goals provide a nonarbitrary standard for our judgments about their welfare. Were ecosystems genuinely goal-directed, we could try for the next step.

Some ecosystems do indeed appear to have goals—stability, for example. There is a complication, however. Mere behavioral by-products, which are outcomes of no moral significance, can look deceptively like goals. Moreover, on what I take to be our best current ecological and evolutionary understanding, the goal-directed appearance of ecosystems is in fact deceptive. Stability and other ecosystem properties are by-products, not goals. Ecosystem interests are, I conclude, a shaky foundation for the preservationist intuition.

DISCUSSION QUESTIONS

1. How can you tell whether something is goal-directed?
2. Is it plausible, in your view, to link goal-directedness and moral considerability?
3. What are we to make of goal-directed machines? How does Cahen deal with this issue?
4. Consider carefully the idea that *G* can be a goal of behavior *B* only if *B* occurs *because* it tends to bring about *G*. Explain this principle. Does it seem correct to you? How does it apply to ecosystems (if it applies)?

ELLIOTT SOBER

Philosophical Problems for Environmentalism

Elliott Sober is a well-known philosopher of science at the University of Wisconsin-Madison. In this essay, Sober argues that the theoretical basis for environmentalism, conceived as the attempt to found noninstrumental value in nature, faces serious conceptual difficulties.

CRITICAL READING QUESTIONS

1. What is the basic theoretical difficulty facing environmentalism, according to Sober?
2. Why does the instrumental value of nature present no special conceptual difficulties?
3. What is the argument from ignorance and how do environmentalists use it, according to Sober?
4. How does Sober's example of risking an airplane crash when you fly apply to environmental matters?
5. According to Sober, slippery slope reasoning compels environmentalists to regard each species as important. What approach to species extirpation does Sober recommend?
6. What problems do appeals to needs and interests create for environmentalists, according to Sober?
7. On what basis does Sober criticize ecocentrism?
8. What is the "demarcation problem"?

I. INTRODUCTION

A number of philosophers have recognized that the environmental movement, whatever its practical political effectiveness, faces considerable theoretical difficulties in justification.[1] It has been recognized that traditional moral theories do not provide natural underpinnings for policy objectives and this has led some to skepticism about the claims of environmentalists, and others to the view that a revolutionary reassessment of ethical norms is needed. In this chapter, I will try to summarize the difficulties that confront a philosophical defense of environmentalism. I also will suggest a way of making sense of some environmental concerns that does not require the wholesale jettisoning of certain familiar moral judgments.

Preserving an endangered species or ecosystem poses no special conceptual problem when the instrumental value of that species or ecosystem is known. When we have reason to think that some natural object represents a resource to us, we obviously ought to take that fact into account in deciding what to do. A variety of potential uses may be under discussion, including food supply, medical applications, recreational use, and so on. As with any complex decision, it may be difficult even to agree on how to compare the competing values that may be involved. Willingness to pay in dollars is a familiar least common denominator, although it poses a number of problems. But here we have nothing that is specifically a problem for environmentalism.

The problem for environmentalism stems from the idea that species and ecosystems ought to be preserved for reasons additional to their known value as resources for human use. The feeling is that even when we cannot say what nutritional, medicinal, or recreational benefit the preservation provides, there still is a value in preservation. It is the search for a rationale for this feeling that constitutes the main conceptual problem for environmentalism.

The problem is especially difficult in view of the holistic (as opposed to individualistic) character of the things being assigned value. Put simply, what is special about environmentalism is that it values the preservation of species, communities, or ecosystems, rather than the individual organisms of which they are composed. "Animal liberationists" have urged that we should take the suffering of sentient animals into account in ethical deliberation.[2] Such beasts are not mere things to be used as cruelly as we like no matter how trivial the benefit we derive. But in "widening the ethical circle," we are simply including in the community more individual organisms whose costs and benefits we compare. Animal liberationists are extending an old and familiar ethical doctrine—namely, utilitarianism—to take account of the welfare of other individuals. Although the practical consequences of this point of view may be revolutionary, the theoretical perspective is not at all novel. If suffering is bad, then it is bad for any individual who suffers.[3] Animal liberationists merely remind us of the consequences of familiar principles.[4]

But trees, mountains, and salt-marshes do not suffer. They do not experience pleasure and pain, because, evidently, they do not have experiences at all. The same is true of species. Granted, individual organisms may have mental states: but the species—taken to be a population of organisms connected by certain sorts of interactions (preeminently, that of exchanging genetic material in reproduction)—does not. Or put more carefully, we might say that the only sense in which species have experiences is that their member organisms do: the attribution at the population level, if true, is true simply in virtue of its being true at the individual level. Here is a case where reductionism is correct.

So perhaps it is true in this reductive sense that some species experience pain. But the values that environmentalists attach to preserving species do not reduce to any value of preserving organisms. It is in this sense that environmentalists espouse a holistic value system. Environmentalists care about entities that by no stretch of the imagination have experiences (e.g., mountains). What is more, their position does not force them to care if individual organisms suffer pain, so long as the species is preserved. Steel traps may outrage an animal liberationist because of the suffering they inflict, but an environmentalist aiming just at the preservation of a balanced ecosystem might see here no cause for complaint. Similarly, environmentalists think that the distinction between wild and domesticated organisms is important, in that it is the preservation of "natural" (i.e., not created by the "artificial interference" of human beings) objects that matters, whereas animal liberationists see the main problem in terms of the suffering of any organism—domesticated or not.[5] And finally, environmentalists and animal liberationists diverge on what might be called the $n + m$ question. If two species—say blue and sperm whales—have roughly comparable capacities for experiencing pain, an animal liberationist might tend to think of the preservation of a sperm whale as wholly on an ethical par with the preservation of a blue whale. The fact that one organism is part of an endangered species while the other is not does not make the rare individual more intrinsically important. But for an environmentalist, this holistic property—membership in an endangered species—makes all the difference in the world: a world with n sperm and m blue whales is far better than a world with $n + m$ sperm and 0 blue whales. Here we have a stark contrast between an ethic in which it is the life situation of individuals that matters, and an ethic in which the stability and diversity of populations of individuals are what matter.[6]

Both animal liberationists and environmentalists wish to broaden our ethical horizons—to make us realize that it is not just human welfare that counts. But they do this in very different, often conflicting, ways. It is no accident that at the level of practical politics the two points of view increasingly find themselves at loggerheads.[7] This practical conflict is the expression of a deep theoretical divide.

II. THE IGNORANCE ARGUMENT

"Although we might not now know what use a particular endangered species might be to us, allowing it to go extinct forever closes off the possibility of discovering and exploiting a future use." According to this point of view, our ignorance of value is turned into a reason for action. The scenario envisaged in this environmentalist argument is not without precedent; who could have guessed that penicillin would be good for something other than turning out cheese? But there is a fatal defect in such arguments, which we might summarize with the phrase *out of nothing, nothing comes:* rational decisions require assumptions about what is true and what is valuable (in decision-theoretic jargon, the inputs must be probabilities and utilities). If you are completely ignorant of values, then you are incapable of making a rational decision, either for or against preserving some species. The fact that you do not know the value of a species, by itself, cannot count as a reason for wanting one thing rather than another to happen to it.

And there are so many species. How many geese that lay golden eggs are there apt to be in that number? It is hard to assign probabilities and utilities precisely here, but an analogy will perhaps reveal the problem confronting this environmentalist argument. Most of us willingly fly on airplanes, when safer (but less convenient) alternative forms of transportation are available. Is this rational? Suppose it were argued that there is a small probability that the next flight you take will crash. This would be very bad for you. Is it not crazy for you to risk this, given that the only gain to you is that you can reduce your travel time by a few hours (by not going by train, say)? Those of us who not only fly, but congratulate ourselves for being rational in doing so, reject this argument. We are prepared to accept a small chance of a great disaster in return for the high probability of a rather modest benefit. If this is rational, no wonder that we might consistently be willing to allow a species to go extinct in order to build a hydroelectric plant.

That the argument from ignorance is no argument at all can be seen from another angle. If we literally do not know what consequences the extinction of this or that species may bring, then we should take seriously the possibility that the extinction may be beneficial as well as the possibility that it may be deleterious. It may sound deep to insist that we preserve endangered species precisely because we do not know why they are valuable. But ignorance on a scale like this cannot provide the basis for any rational action.

Rather than invoke some unspecified future benefit, an environmentalist may argue that the species in question plays a crucial role in stabilizing the ecosystem of which it is a part. This will undoubtedly be true for carefully chosen species and ecosystems, but one should not generalize this argument into a global claim to the effect that *every* species is crucial to a balanced ecosystem. Although ecologists used to agree that the complexity of an ecosystem stabilizes it, this hypothesis has been subject to a number of criticisms and qualifications, both from a theoretical and an empirical perspective.[8] And for certain kinds of species (those which occupy a rather small area and whose normal population is small) we can argue that extinction would probably not disrupt the community. However fragile the biosphere may be, the extreme view that everything is crucial is almost certainly not true.

But, of course, environmentalists are often concerned by the fact that extinctions are occurring now at a rate much higher than in earlier times. It is mass extinction that threatens the biosphere, they say, and this claim avoids the spurious assertion that communities are so fragile that even one extinction will cause a crash. However, if the point is to avoid a mass extinction of species, how does this provide a rationale for preserving a species of the kind just described, of which we rationally believe that its passing will not destabilize the ecosystem? And, more generally, if mass extinction is known to be a danger to us, how does this translate into a value for preserving any particular species? Notice that we have now passed beyond the confines of the argument from ignorance; we are taking as a premise the idea that mass extinction would be a catastrophe (since it would destroy the ecosystem on which we depend). But how should that premise affect our valuing the California condor, the blue whale, or the snail darter?

III. THE SLIPPERY SLOPE ARGUMENT

Environmentalists sometimes find themselves asked to explain why each species matters so much to them, when there are, after all, so many. We may know of special reasons for valuing particular species, but how can we justify thinking that each and every species is important? "Each extinction impoverishes the biosphere" is often the answer given, but it really fails to resolve the issue. Granted, each extinction impoverishes, but it only impoverishes a little bit. So if it is the *wholesale* impoverishment of the biosphere that matters, one would apparently have to concede that each extinction matters a little, but only a little. But environmentalists may be loathe to concede this, for if they concede that each species matters only a little, they seem to be inviting the wholesale impoverishment that would be an unambiguous disaster.[9] So they dig in their heels and insist that each species matters a lot. But to take this line, one must find some other rationale than the idea that mass extinction would be a great harm. Some of these alternative rationales we will examine later. For now, let us take a closer look at the train of thought involved here.

Slippery slopes are curious things: if you take even one step on to them, you inevitably slide all the way to the bottom. So if you want to avoid finding yourself at the bottom, you must avoid stepping on to them at all. To mix metaphors, stepping on to a slippery slope is to invite being nickel and dimed to death.

Slippery slope arguments have played a powerful role in a number of recent ethical debates. One often hears people defend the legitimacy of abortions by arguing that since it is permissible to abort a single-celled fertilized egg, it must be permissible to abort a fetus of any age, since there is no place to draw the line from 0 to 9 months. Antiabortionists, on the other hand, sometimes argue in the other direction: since infanticide of newborns is not permissible, abortion at any earlier time is also not allowed, since there is no place to draw the line. Although these two arguments reach opposite conclusions about the permissibility of abortions, they agree on the following idea: since there is no principled place to draw the line on the continuum from newly fertilized egg to fetus gone to term, one must treat all these cases in the same way. Either abortion is always permitted or it never is, since there is no place to draw the line. Both sides run their favorite slippery slope arguments, but try to precipitate slides in opposite directions.

Starting with 10 million extant species, and valuing overall diversity, the environmentalist does not want to grant that each species matters only a little. For having granted this, commercial expansion and other causes will reduce the tally to 9,999,999. And then the argument is repeated, with each species valued only a little, and diversity declines another notch. And so we are well on our way to a considerably impoverished biosphere, a little at a time. Better to reject the starting premise—namely, that each species matters only a little—so that the slippery slope can be avoided.

Slippery slopes should hold no terror for environmentalists, because it is often a mistake to demand that a line be drawn. Let me illustrate by an example. What is the difference between being bald and not? Presumably, the difference concerns the number of hairs you have on your head. But what is the precise number of hairs marking the boundary between baldness and not being bald? There is no such number. Yet, it would be a fallacy to conclude that there is no difference between baldness and hairiness. The fact that you cannot draw a line does not force you to say that the two alleged categories collapse into one. In the abortion case, this means that even if there is no precise point in fetal development that involves some discontinuous, qualitative change, one is still not obliged to think of newly fertilized eggs and fetuses gone to term as morally on a par. Since the biological differences are ones of degree, not kind, one may want to adopt the position that the moral differences are likewise matters of degree. This may lead to the view that a woman should have a better reason for having an abortion, the more developed her fetus is. Of course, this position does not logically follow from the idea that there is no place to draw the line; my point is just that differences in degree do not demolish the possibility of there being real moral differences.

In the environmental case, if one places a value on diversity, then each species becomes more valuable as the overall diversity declines. If we begin with 10 million species, each may matter little, but as extinctions continue, the remaining ones matter more and more. According to this outlook, a better and better reason would be demanded for allowing yet another species to go extinct. Perhaps certain sorts of economic development would justify the extinction of a species at one time. But granting this does not oblige one to conclude that the same sort of decision would have to be made further down the road. This means that one can value diversity without being obliged to take the somewhat exaggerated position that each species, no matter how many there are, is terribly precious in virtue of its contribution to that diversity.

Yet, one can understand that environmentalists might be reluctant to concede this point. They may fear that if one now allows that most species contribute only a little to overall diversity, one will set in motion a political process that cannot correct itself later. The worry is that even when the overall diversity has been drastically reduced, our ecological sensitivities will have been so coarsened that we will no longer be in a position to realize (or to implement policies fostering) the preciousness of what is left. This fear may be quite justified, but it is important to realize that it does not conflict with what was argued above. The political utility of making an argument should not be confused with the argument's soundness.

The fact that you are on a slippery slope, by itself, does not tell you whether you are near the beginning, in the middle, or at the end. If species diversity is a matter of degree, where do we currently find ourselves—on the verge of catastrophe, well on our way in that direction, or at some distance from a global crash? Environmentalists often urge that we are fast approaching a precipice; if we are, then the reduction in diversity that every succeeding extinction engenders should be all we need to justify species preservation.[10]

Sometimes, however, environmentalists advance a kind of argument not predicated on the idea of fast approaching doom. The goal is to show that there is something wrong with allowing a species to go extinct (or with causing it to go extinct), even if overall diversity is not affected much. I now turn to one argument of this kind.

IV. APPEALS TO WHAT IS NATURAL

I noted earlier that environmentalists and animal liberationists disagree over the significance of the distinction between wild and domesticated animals. Since both types of organisms can experience pain, animal liberationists will think of each as meriting ethical consideration. But environmentalists will typically not put wild and domesticated organisms on a par.[11] Environmentalists typically are interested in preserving what is natural, be it a species living in the wild or a wilderness ecosystem. If a kind of domesticated chicken were threatened with extinction, I doubt that environmental groups would be up in arms. And if certain unique types of human environments—say urban slums in the United States—were "endangered," it is similarly unlikely that environmentalists would view this process as a deplorable impoverishment of the biosphere.

The environmentalist's lack of concern for humanly created organisms and environments may be practical rather than principled. It may be that, at the level of values, no such bifurcation is legitimate, but that, from the point of view of practical political action, it makes sense to put one's energies into saving items that exist in the wild. This subject has not been discussed much in the literature, so it is hard to tell. But I sense that the distinction between wild and domesticated has a certain theoretical importance to many environmentalists. They perhaps think that the difference is that we created domesticated organisms which would otherwise not exist, and so are entitled to use them solely for our own interests. But we did not create wild organisms and environments, so it is the height of presumption to expropriate them for our benefit. A more fitting posture would be one of "stewardship": We have come on the scene and found a treasure not of our making. Given this, we ought to preserve this treasure in its natural state.

I do not wish to contest the appropriateness of "stewardship." It is the dichotomy between artificial (domesticated) and natural (wild) that strikes me as wrong-headed. I want to suggest that to the degree that "natural" means anything biologically, it means very little ethically. And, conversely, to the degree that "natural" is understood as a normative concept, it has very little to do with biology.

Environmentalists often express regret that we human beings find it so hard to remember that we are part of nature—one species among many others—rather than something standing outside of nature. I will not consider here whether this attitude is cause for complaint; the important point is that seeing us as part of nature rules out the environmentalist's use of the distinction between artificial–domesticated and natural–wild described above. *If we are part of nature, then everything we do is part of nature, and is natural in that primary sense.*[12] When we domesticate organisms and bring them into a state of dependence on us, this is simply an example of one species exerting a selection pressure on another. If one calls this "unnatural," one might just as well say the same of parasitism or symbiosis (compare human domestication of animals and plants and "slave-making" in the social insects).

The concept of naturalness is subject to the same abuses as the concept of normalcy. *Normal* can mean *usual* or it can mean *desirable.* Although only the total pessimist will think that the two concepts are mutually exclusive, it is generally recognized that the mere fact that something is common does not by itself count as a reason for thinking that it is desirable. This distinction is quite familiar now in popular discussions of mental health, for example. Yet, when it comes to environmental issues, the concept of naturalness continues to live a double life. The destruction of wilderness areas by increased industrialization is bad because it is unnatural. And it is unnatural because it involves transforming a natural into an artificial habitat. Or one might hear that although extinction is a natural process, the kind of mass extinction currently being precipitated by our species is unprecedented, and so is unnatural. Environmentalists should look elsewhere for a defense of their policies, lest conservation simply become a variant of uncritical conservatism in which the axiom "Whatever is, is right" is modified to read "Whatever is (before human beings come on the scene), is right."

This conflation of the biological with the normative sense of "natural" sometimes comes to the fore when environmentalists attack animal liberationists for naïve do-goodism. Callicott writes:

> The value commitments of the humane movement seem at bottom to betray a world-denying or rather a life-loathing philosophy. The natural world as actually constituted is one in which one being lives at the expense of others. Each organism, in Darwin's metaphor, struggles to

> maintain its own organic integrity . . . To live *is* to be anxious about life, to feel pain and pleasure in a fitting mixture, and sooner or later to die. That is the way the system works. *If nature as a whole is good, then pain and death are also good.* Environmental ethics in general require people to play fair in the natural system. The neo-Benthamites have in a sense taken the uncourageous approach. People have attempted to exempt themselves from the life/death reciprocities of natural processes and from ecological limitations in the name of a prophylactic ethic of maximizing rewards (pleasure) and minimizing unwelcome information (pain). To be fair, the humane moralists seem to suggest that we should attempt to project the same values into the non-human animal world and to widen the charmed circle—no matter that it would be biologically unrealistic to do so or biologically ruinous if, per impossible, such an environmental ethic were implemented.
>
> There is another approach. Rather than imposing our alienation from nature and natural processes and cycles of life on other animals, we human beings could reaffirm our participation in nature by accepting life as it is given without a sugar coating.[13]

In n. 45 Callicott quotes with approval Shepard's remark that "the humanitarian's projection onto nature of illegal murder and the rights of civilized people to safety not only misses the point but is exactly contrary to fundamental ecological reality: the structure of nature is a sequence of killings."[14]

Thinking that what is found in nature is beyond ethical defect has not always been popular, Darwin wrote:

> That there is much suffering in the world no one disputes. Some have attempted to explain this in reference to man by imagining that it serves for his moral improvement. But the number of men in the world is as nothing compared with that of all other sentient beings, and these often suffer greatly without any moral improvement. A being so powerful and so full of knowledge as a God who could create the universe, is to our finite minds omnipotent and omniscient, and it revolts our understanding to suppose that his benevolence is not unbounded, for what advantage can there be in the sufferings of millions of the lower animals throughout almost endless time? This very old argument from the existence of suffering against the existence of an intelligent first cause seems to me a strong one; whereas, as just remarked, the presence of much suffering agrees well with the view that all organic beings have been developed through variation and natural selection.[15]

Darwin apparently viewed the quantity of pain found in nature as a melancholy and sobering consequence of the struggle for existence. But once we adopt the Panglossian attitude that this is the best of all possible worlds ("there is just the right amount of pain," etc.), a failure to identify what is natural with what is good can only seem "world-denying," "life-loathing," "in a sense uncourageous," and "contrary to fundamental ecological reality."[16]

Earlier in his essay, Callicott expresses distress that animal liberationists fail to draw a sharp distinction "between the very different plights (and rights) of wild and domestic animals."[17] Domestic animals are creations of man, he says. "They are living artifacts, but artifacts nevertheless . . . There is thus something profoundly incoherent (and insensitive as well) in the complaint of some animal liberationists that the "natural behavior" of chickens and bobby calves is cruelly frustrated on factory farms. It would make almost as much sense to speak of the natural behavior of tables and chairs."[18] Here again we see teleology playing a decisive role: Wild organisms do not have the natural function of serving human ends, but domesticated animals do. Cheetahs in zoos are crimes against what is natural; veal calves in boxes are not.

The idea of "natural tendency" played a decisive role in pre-Darwinian biological thinking. Aristotle's entire science—both his physics and his biology—is articulated in terms of specifying the natural tendencies of kinds of objects and the interfering forces that can prevent an object from achieving its intended state.[19] Heavy objects in the sublunar sphere have location at the center of the earth as their natural state; each tends to go there, but is prevented from doing so.[20] Organisms likewise are conceptualized in terms of this natural state model: "[for] any living thing that has reached its normal development and which is unmutilated, and whose mode of generation is not spontaneous, the most natural act is the production of another like itself, an animal producing an animal, a plant a plant"[21]

But many interfering forces are possible, and in fact the occurrence of "monsters" is anything but uncommon. According to Aristotle, mules (sterile hybrids) count as deviations from the natural state. In fact, females are monsters as well, since the natural tendency of sexual reproduction is for the offspring to perfectly resemble the father, who, according to Aristotle, provides the "genetic instructions" (to put the idea anachronistically) while the female provides only the matter.[22]

What has happened to the natural state model in modern science? In physics, the idea of describing what a class of objects will do in the absence of "interference" lives on: Newton specified this "zero-force state" as rest or uniform motion, and, in general relativity, this state is understood in terms of motion along geodesics. But one of the most profound achievements of Darwinian biology has been the jettisoning of this kind of model.[23] It isn't just that Aristotle was wrong in his detailed claims about mules and women; the whole structure of the natural state model has been discarded. Population biology is not conceptualized in terms of positing some characteristic that all members of a species would have in common, were interfering forces absent. Variation is not thought of as a deflection from the natural state of uniformity. Rather, variation is taken to be a fundamental property in its own right. Nor, at the level of individual biology, does the natural state model find an application. Developmental theory is not articulated by specifying a natural tendency and a set of interfering forces. The main conceptual tool for describing the various developmental pathways open to a genotype is the norm of reaction.[24] The norm of reaction of a genotype within a range of environments will describe what phenotype the genotype will produce in a given environment. Thus, the norm of reaction for a corn plant genotype might describe how its height is influenced by the amount of moisture in the soil. The norm of reaction is entirely silent on which phenotype is the "natural" one. The idea that a corn plant might have some "natural height," which can be augmented or diminished by "interfering forces" is entirely alien to post-Darwinian biology.

The fact that the concepts of natural state and interfering force have lapsed from biological thought does not prevent environmentalists from inventing them anew. Perhaps these concepts can be provided with some sort of normative content; after all, the normative idea of "human rights" may make sense even if it is not a theoretical underpinning of any empirical science. But environmentalists should not assume that they can rely on some previously articulated scientific conception of "natural."

V. APPEALS TO NEEDS AND INTERESTS

The version of utilitarianism considered earlier (according to which something merits ethical consideration if it can experience pleasure and/or pain) leaves the environmentalist in the lurch. But there is an alternative to Bentham's hedonistic utilitarianism that has been thought by some to be a foundation for environmentalism. Preference utilitarianism says that an object's having interests, needs, or preferences gives it ethical status. This doctrine is at the core of Stone's affirmative answer to the title question of his book *Should Trees Have Standing?*[25] "Natural objects *can* communicate their wants (needs) to us, and in ways that are not terribly ambiguous . . . The lawn tells me that it wants water by a certain dryness of the blades and soil—immediately obvious to the touch—the appearance of bald spots, yellowing, and a lack of springiness after being walked on." And if plants can do this, presumably so can mountain ranges, and endangered species. Preference utilitarianism may thereby seem to grant intrinsic ethical importance to precisely the sorts of objects about which environmentalists have expressed concern.

The problems with this perspective have been detailed by Sagoff.[26] If one does not require of an object that it have a mind for it to have wants or needs, what *is* required for the possession of these ethically relevant properties? Suppose one says that an object needs something if the object will cease to exist if it does not get it. Then species, plants, and mountain ranges have needs, but only in the sense that automobiles, garbage dumps, and buildings do too. If everything has needs, the advice to take needs into account in ethical deliberation is empty, unless it is supplemented by some technique for weighting and comparing the needs of different objects. A corporation will go bankrupt unless a highway is built. But the swamp will cease to exist if the highway is built. Perhaps one should take into account all relevant needs, but the question is how to do this in the event that needs conflict.

Although the concept of need can be provided with a permissive, all-inclusive definition, it is less easy to see how to do this with the concept of want. Why think that a mountain range "wants" to retain its unspoiled appearance, rather than house a new amusement park?[27] Needs are not at issue here, since in either case, the mountain continues to exist. One might be tempted to think that natural objects like mountains and species have "natural tendencies," and that the concept of want should be liberalized so as to mean that natural objects "want" to persist in their natural states. This Aristotelian view, as I argued in the previous section, simply makes no sense.[28] Granted, a commercially undeveloped mountain will persist in this state, unless it is commercially developed. But it is equally true that a commercially untouched hill will become commercially developed, unless something causes this not to happen. I see no hope for extending the concept of wants to the full range of objects valued by environmentalists.

The same problems emerge when we try to apply the concepts of needs and wants to species. A species may need various resources, in the sense that these are necessary for its continued existence. But what do species want? Do they want to remain stable in numbers, neither growing nor shrinking? Or since most species have gone extinct, perhaps what species really want is to go extinct, and it is human meddlesomeness that frustrates this natural tendency? Preference utilitarianism is no more likely than hedonistic utilitarianism to secure autonomous ethical status for endangered species.

Ehrenfeld describes a related distortion that has been inflicted on the diversity–stability hypothesis in theoretical ecology.[29] If it were true that increasing the diversity of an ecosystem causes it to be more stable, this might encourage the Aristotelian idea that ecosystems have a natural tendency to increase their diversity. The full realization of this tendency—the natural state that is the goal of ecosystems—is the "climax" or "mature" community. Extinction diminishes diversity, so it frustrates ecosystems from attaining their goal. Since the hypothesis that diversity causes stability is now considered controversial (to say the least), this line of thinking will not be very tempting. But even if the diversity–stability hypothesis were true, it would not permit the environmentalist to conclude that ecosystems have an interest in retaining their diversity.

Darwinism has not banished the idea that parts of the natural world are goal-directed systems, but has furnished this idea with a natural mechanism. We properly conceive of organisms (or genes, sometimes) as being in the business of maximizing their chances of survival and reproduction. We describe characteristics as adaptations—as devices that exist for the furtherance of these ends. Natural selection makes this perspective intelligible. But Darwinism is a profoundly individualistic doctrine.[30] Darwinism rejects the idea that species, communities, and ecosystems have adaptations that exist for their own benefit. These higher-level entities are not conceptualized as goal-directed systems; what properties of organization they possess are viewed as artifacts of processes operating at lower levels of organization. An environmentalism based on the idea that the ecosystem is directed toward stability and diversity must find its foundation elsewhere.

VI. GRANTING WHOLES AUTONOMOUS VALUE

A number of environmentalists have asserted that environmental values cannot be grounded in values based on regard for individual welfare. Aldo Leopold wrote in *A Sand County Almanac* that "a thing is right when it tends to preserve the integrity, stability, and beauty of the biotic community. It is wrong when it tends otherwise."[31] Callicott develops this idea at some length, and ascribes to ethical environmentalism the view that "the preciousness of individual deer, *as of any other specimen,* is inversely proportional to the population of the species."[32] In his *Desert Solitaire,* Edward Abbey notes that he would sooner shoot a man than a snake.[33] And Garrett Hardin asserts that human beings injured in wilderness areas ought not to be rescued: making great and spectacular efforts to save the life of an individual "makes sense only when there is a shortage of people. I have not lately heard that there is a shortage of people."[34] The point of view suggested by these quotations is quite clear. It isn't that preserving the integrity of ecosystems has autonomous value, to be taken into account just as the quite distinct value of individual human welfare is. Rather, the idea is that the only value is the holistic one of maintaining ecological balance and diversity. Here we have a view that is just as monolithic as the most single-minded individualism; the difference is that the unit of value is thought to exist at a higher level of organization.

It is hard to know what to say to someone who would save a mosquito, just because it is rare, rather than a human being, if there were a choice. In ethics, as in any other subject, rationally persuading another person requires the existence of shared assumptions. If this monolithic environmentalist view is based on the notion that ecosystems have needs and interests, and that these take total precedence over the rights and interests of individual human beings, then the discussion of the previous sections is relevant. And even supposing that these higher-level entities have needs and wants, what reason is there to suppose that these matter and that the wants and needs of individuals matter not at all? But if this source of defense is jettisoned, and it is merely asserted that only ecosystems have value, with no substantive defense being offered, one must begin by requesting an argument: *why* is ecosystem stability and diversity the only value?

Some environmentalists have seen the individualist bias of utilitarianism as being harmful in ways additional to its impact on our perception of ecological values. Thus, Callicott writes:

> On the level of social organization, the interests of society may not always coincide with the sum of the interests of its parts. Discipline, sacrifice, and individual restraint are often necessary in the social sphere to maintain social integrity as within the bodily organism. A society, indeed, is particularly vulnerable to disintegration when its members become preoccupied totally with their own particular interest, and ignore those distinct and independent interests of the community as a whole. One example, unfortunately our own society, is altogether too close at hand to be examined with strict academic detachment. The United States seems to pursue uncritically a social policy of reductive utilitarianism, aimed at promoting the happiness of all its members severally. Each special interest accordingly clamors more loudly to be satisfied while the community as a whole becomes noticeably more and more infirm economically, environmentally, and politically.[35]

Callicott apparently sees the emergence of individualism and alienation from nature as two aspects of the same process. He values "the symbiotic relationship of Stone Age man to the natural environment" and regrets that "civilization has insulated and alienated us from the rigors and challenges of the natural environment. The hidden agenda of the humane ethic," he says, "is the imposition of the anti-natural prophylactic ethos of comfort and soft pleasure on an ever wider scale. The land ethic, on the other hand, requires a shrinkage, if at all possible, of the domestic sphere; it rejoices in a recrudescence of the wilderness and a renaissance of tribal cultural experience."[36]

Callicott is right that "strict academic detachment" is difficult here. The reader will have to decide whether the United States currently suffers from too much or too little regard "for the happiness of all its members severally" and whether we should feel nostalgia or pity in contemplating what the Stone Age experience of nature was like.

VII. THE DEMARCATION PROBLEM

Perhaps the most fundamental theoretical problem confronting an environmentalist who wishes to claim that species and ecosystems have autonomous value is what I will call the *problem of demarcation.*

Every ethical theory must provide principles that describe which objects matter for their own sakes and which do not. Besides marking the boundary between these two classes by enumerating a set of ethically relevant properties, an ethical theory must say why the properties named, rather than others, are the ones that count. Thus, for example, hedonistic utilitarianism cites the capacity to experience pleasure and/or pain as the decisive criterion; preference utilitarianism cites the having of preferences (or wants, or interests) as the decisive property. And a Kantian ethical theory will include an individual in the ethical community only if it is capable of rational reflection and autonomy.[37] Not that justifying these various proposed solutions to the demarcation problem is easy; indeed, since this issue is so fundamental, it will be very difficult to justify one proposal as opposed to another. Still, a substantive ethical theory is obliged to try.

Environmentalists, wishing to avoid the allegedly distorting perspective of individualism, frequently want to claim autonomous value for wholes. This may take the form of a monolithic doctrine according to which the only thing that matters is the stability of the ecosystem. Or it may embody a pluralistic outlook according to which ecosystem stability and species preservation have an importance additional to the welfare of individual organisms. But an environmentalist theory shares with all ethical theories an interest in not saying that everything has autonomous value. The reason this position is proscribed is that it makes the adjudication of ethical conflict very difficult indeed. (In addition, it is radically implausible, but we can set that objection to one side.)

Environmentalists, as we have seen, may think of natural objects, like mountains, species, and ecosystems, as mattering for their own sake, but of artificial objects, like highway systems and domesticated animals, as having only instrumental value. If a mountain and a highway are both made of rock, it seems unlikely that the difference between them arises from the fact that mountains have wants, interests, and preferences, but highway systems do not. But perhaps the place to look for the relevant difference is not in their present physical composition, but in the historical fact of how each came into existence. Mountains were created by natural processes, whereas highways are humanly constructed. But once we realize that organisms construct their environments in nature, this contrast begins to cloud.[38] Organisms do not passively reside in an environment whose properties are independently determined. Organisms transform their environments by physically interacting with them. An ant-hill is an artifact just as a highway is. Granted, a difference obtains at the level of whether conscious deliberation played a role, but can one take seriously the view that artifacts produced by conscious planning are thereby *less* valuable than ones that arise without the intervention of mentality?[39] As we have noted before, although environmentalists often accuse their critics of failing to think in a biologically realistic way, their use of the distinction between "natural" and "artificial" is just the sort of idea that stands in need of a more realistic biological perspective.

My suspicion is that the distinction between natural and artificial is not the crucial one. On the contrary, certain features of environmental concerns imply that natural objects are exactly on a par with certain artificial ones. Here the intended comparison is not between mountains and highways, but between mountains and works of art. My goal in what follows is not to sketch a substantive conception of what determines the value of objects in these two domains, but to motivate an analogy.

For both natural objects and works of art, our values extend beyond the concerns we have for experiencing pleasure. Most of us value seeing an original painting more than we value seeing a copy, even when we could not tell the difference. When we experience works of art, often what we value is not just the kinds of experiences we have, but, in addition, the connections we usually have with certain real objects. Routley and Routley have made an analogous point about valuing the wilderness experience: a "wilderness experience machine" that caused certain sorts of hallucinations would be no substitute for actually going into the wild.[40] Nor is this fact about our valuation limited to such aesthetic and environmentalist contexts. We love various people in our lives. If a molecule-for-molecule replica of a beloved person were created, you would not love that individual, but would continue to love the individual to whom you actually were historically related.[41] Here again, our attachments are to objects and people as they really are, and not just to the experiences that they facilitate.

Another parallel between environmentalist concerns and aesthetic values concerns the issue of context. Although environmentalists often stress the importance of preserving endangered species, they would not be completely satisfied if an endangered species were preserved by putting a number of specimens in a zoo or in a humanly constructed preserve. What is taken to be important is preserving the species in its natural habitat. This leads to the more holistic position that preserving ecosystems, and not simply preserving certain member species, is of primary importance. Aesthetic concerns often lead in the same direction. It was not merely saving a fresco or an altarpiece that motivated art historians after the most recent flood in Florence. Rather, they wanted to save these works of art in their original ("natural") settings. Not just the painting, but the church that housed it; not just the church, but the city itself. The idea of objects residing in a "fitting" environment plays a powerful role in both domains.

Environmentalism and aesthetics both see value in rarity. Of two whales, why should one be more worthy of aid than another, just because one belongs to an endangered species? Here we have the $n + m$ question mentioned in Section I. As an ethical concern, rarity is difficult to understand. Perhaps this is because our ethical ideas concerning justice and equity (note the word) are saturated with individualism. But in the context of aesthetics, the concept of rarity is far from alien. A work of art may have enhanced value simply because there are very few other works by the same artist, or from the same historical period, or in the same style. It isn't that the price of the item may go up with rarity; I am talking about aesthetic value, not monetary worth. Viewed as valuable aesthetic objects, rare organisms may be valuable because they are rare.

A disanalogy may suggest itself. It may be objected that works of art are of instrumental value only, but that species and ecosystems have intrinsic value. Perhaps it is true, as claimed before, that our attachment to works of art, to nature, and to our loved ones extends beyond the experiences they allow us to have. But it may be argued that what is valuable in the aesthetic case is always the relation of a valuer to a valued object.[42] When we experience a work of art, the value is not simply in the experience, but in the composite fact that we and the work of art are related in certain ways. This immediately suggests that if there were no valuers in the world, nothing would have value, since such relational facts could no longer obtain. So, to adapt Routley and Routley's "last man argument," it would seem that if an ecological crisis precipitated a collapse of the world system, the last human being (whom we may assume for the purposes of this example to be the last valuer) could set about destroying all works of art, and there would be nothing wrong in this.[43] That is, if aesthetic objects are valuable only in so far as valuers can stand in certain relations to them, then when valuers disappear, so does the possibility of aesthetic value. This would deny, in one sense, that aesthetic objects are intrinsically valuable: it isn't they, in themselves, but rather the relational facts that they are part of, that are valuable.

In contrast, it has been claimed that the "last man" would be wrong to destroy natural objects such as mountains, salt-marshes, and species.[44] (So as to avoid confusing the issue by bringing in the welfare of individual organisms. Routley and Routley imagine that destruction and mass extinctions can be caused painlessly, so that there would be nothing wrong about this undertaking from the point of view of the nonhuman organisms involved.) If the last man ought to preserve these natural objects, then these objects appear to have a kind of autonomous value; their value would extend beyond their possible relations to valuers. If all this were true, we would have here a contrast between aesthetic and natural objects, one that implies that natural objects are more valuable than works of art.

Routley and Routley advance the last man argument as if it were decisive in showing that environmental objects such as mountains and salt-marshes have autonomous value. I find the example more puzzling than decisive. But, in the present context, we do not have to decide whether Routley and Routley are right. We only have to decide whether this imagined situation brings out any relevant difference between aesthetic and environmental values. Were the last man to look up on a certain hillside, he would see a striking rock formation next to the ruins of a Greek temple. Long ago the temple was built from some of the very rocks that still stud the slope. Both promontory and temple have a history, and both have been transformed by the biotic and the abiotic environments. I myself find it impossible to advise the last man that the peak matters more than the temple. I do not see a relevant difference. Environmentalists, if they hold that the solution to the problem of demarcation is to be found in the distinction between natural and artificial, will have to find such a distinction. But if environmental values are aesthetic, no difference need be discovered.

Environmentalists may be reluctant to classify their concern as aesthetic. Perhaps they will feel that aesthetic concerns are frivolous. Perhaps they will feel that the aesthetic regard for artifacts that has been made possible by culture is antithetical to a proper regard for wilderness. But such contrasts are illusory. Concern for environmental values does not require a stripping away of the perspective afforded by civilization; to value the wild, one does not have to "become wild" oneself (whatever that may mean). Rather, it is the material comforts of civilization that make possible a serious concern for both aesthetic and environmental values. These are concerns that can become pressing in developed nations in part because the populations of those countries now enjoy a certain substantial level of prosperity. It would be the height of condescension to expect a nation experiencing hunger and chronic disease to be inordinately concerned with the autonomous value of ecosystems or with creating and preserving works of art. Such values are not frivolous, but they can become important to us only after certain fundamental human needs are satisfied. Instead of radically jettisoning individualist ethics, environmentalists may find a more hospitable home for their values in a category of value that has existed all along.[45]

NOTES

1. Mark Sagoff. "On Preserving the Natural Environment." *Yale Law Review* 84 (1974): 205–67; J. Baird Callicott in Essay II of this volume; and Bryan Norton, "Environmental Ethics and Nonhuman Rights," *Environmental Ethics*, 4 (1982): 17–36.
2. Peter Singer, *Animal Liberation* (New York: Random House, 1975), has elaborated a position of this sort.
3. Occasionally, it has been argued that utilitarianism is not just *insufficient* to justify the principles of environmentalism, but is actually mistaken in holding that pain is intrinsically bad. Callicott writes: "I herewith declare in all soberness that I see nothing wrong with pain. It is a marvellous method, honed by the evolutionary process, of conveying important organic information. I think it was the late Alan Watts who somewhere remarks that upon being asked if he did not think there was too much pain in the world replied, "No, I think there's just enough" (Essay II). Setting to one side the remark attributed to Watts, I should point out that pain can be intrinsically bad and still have some good consequences. The point of calling pain intrinsically bad is to say that one essential aspect of experiencing it is negative.
4. See Sagoff "Natural Environment"; Callicott Essay II; and Norton, "Ethics and Nonhuman Rights."
5. See Essay II.
6. A parallel with a quite different moral problem will perhaps make it clearer how the environmentalist's holism conflicts with some fundamental ethical ideas. When we consider the rights of individuals to receive compensation for harm, we generally expect that the individuals compensated must be one and the same as the individuals harmed. This expectation runs counter to the way an affirmative action program might be set up, if individuals were to receive compensation simply for being members of groups that have suffered certain kinds of discrimination, whether or not they themselves were victims of discrimination. I do not raise this example to suggest that a holistic conception according to which groups have entitlements is beyond consideration. Rather, my point is to exhibit a case in which a rather common ethical idea is individualistic rather than holistic.

7. Peter Steinhart, "The Advance of the Ethic," *Audubon,* 82 (January 1980): 126–7.
8. David Ehrenfeld, "The Conservation of Non-Resources," *American Scientist,* 64 (1976): 648–56. For a theoretical discussion see Robert M. May, *Stability and Complexity in Model Ecosystems* (Princeton: Princeton University Press, 1973).
9. See Thomas E. Lovejoy, "Species Leave the Ark One by One," in *The Preservation of Species,* ed. B. Norton (Princeton: Princeton University Press, 1986), pp. 13–27.
10. See Bryan G. Norton, "On the Inherent Danger of Undervaluing Species," in Norton, *The Preservation of Species,* pp. 110–37.
11. See Essay II.
12. Elliott Sober, "Evolution, Population Thinking, and Essentialism," *Philosophy of Science* 47 (1980): 350–83; and John McCloskey, "Ecological Ethics and Its Justification: A Critical Appraisal," in *Environmental Philosophy,* Monograph Series 2 D. S. Mannison, M. A. McRobbie, and R. Routley, ed. (Philosophy Department, Australian National University, 1980), pp. 65–87.
13. See Essay II (my emphasis).
14. Paul Shepard, "Animal Rights and Human Rites," *North American Review,* Winter 1974, pp. 35–41.
15. Charles Darwin, *The Autobiography of Charles Darwin* (London: Collins, 1876, 1958), p. 90.
16. The idea that the natural world is perfect, besides being suspect as an ethical principle, is also controversial as biology. In spite of Callicott's confidence that the amount of pain found in nature is biologically optimal (see n. 3), this adaptationist outlook is now much debated. See e.g. Richard Lewontin and Stephen Jay Gould, "The Spandrels of San Marco and the Panglossian Paradigm: A Critique of the Adaptationist Programme," *Proceedings of the Royal Society of London,* 205 (1979): 581–98; and John Maynard Smith, "Optimization Theory in Evolution," *Annual Review of Ecology and Systematics* 9 (1978): 31–56. Both are reprinted in E. Sober, ed., *Conceptual Issues in Evolutionary Biology* (Cambridge, MA: MIT Press, 1984).
17. See Essay II.
18. Ibid.
19. Sober, "Evolution, Population Thinking, and Essentialism," pp. 360–5.
20. G. E. R. Lloyd, *Aristotle: The Growth and Structure of His Thought* (Cambridge: Cambridge University Press, 1968), p. 162.
21. Aristotle, *De Anima,* pp. 415–26.
22. See Sober, "Evolution, Population Thinking, and Essentialism," pp. 360–5. See also Elliott Sober, *The Nature of Selection* (Cambridge, MA: MIT Press, 1984) for further discussion.
23. Ernst Mayr, "Typological versus Population Thinking," in *Evolution and Diversity of Life,* Ernst Mayr, ed., (Cambridge, MA: Harvard University Press, 1976), pp. 26–9, reprinted in Sober, ed., *Conceptual Issues in Evolutionary Biology;* Richard Lewontin, "Biological Determinism as a Social Weapon," in *Ann Arbor Science for the People Editorial Collection: Biology as a Social Weapon* (Minneapolis: Burgess Publishing Company, 1977), pp. 6–20; Sober, "Evolution, Population Thinking, and Essentialism," pp. 372–9; and Elliott Sober, "Darwin's Evolutionary Concepts: A Philosophical Perspective," in *The Darwinian Heritage,* David Kohn, ed. (Princeton: Princeton University Press, 1986).
24. Lewontin, "Biological Determinism," p. 10.
25. Christopher Stone, *Should Trees Have Standing?* (Los Altos, CA: William Kaufmann, 1972), p. 24.
26. Sagoff, "Natural Environment," pp. 220–4.
27. The example is Sagoff's, ibid.
28. I argue this view in more detail in "Evolution, Population Thinking, and Essentialism," pp. 360–79.
29. Ehrenfeld, "The Conservation of Non-Resources," pp. 651–2.
30. George C. Williams, *Adaptation and Natural Selection* (Princeton: Princeton University Press, 1966); and Sober, *The Nature of Selection.*
31. Aldo Leopold, *A Sand County Almanac* (New York: Oxford University Press, 1949), pp. 224–5.
32. Essay II (emphasis mine).
33. Edward Abbey, *Desert Solitaire* (New York: Ballantine Books, 1968), p. 20.
34. Garrett Hardin, "The Economics of Wilderness," *Natural History,* 78 (1969): 176.
35. Essay II.
36. Ibid.
37. John Rawls, *A Theory of Justice* (Cambridge, MA: Harvard University Press, 1971).

38. Richard Levins and Richard Lewontin, "Dialectic and Reductionism in Ecology," *Synthése* 43 (1980): 47–78.
39. Here we would have an inversion, not just a rejection, of a familiar Marxian doctrine—the labor theory of value.
40. Essay VI.
41. Mark Sagoff, "On Restoring and Reproducing Art," *Journal of Philosophy* 75 (1978): 453–70.
42. Donald H. Regan, "Duties of Preservation," in *The Preservation of Species*, pp. 195–222.
43. Essay VI.
44. Ibid.
45. I am grateful to Donald Crawford, Jon Moline, Bryan Norton, Robert Stauffer, and Daniel Wikler for useful discussion. I also wish to thank the National Science Foundation and the Graduate School of the University of Wisconsin-Madison for financial support.

DISCUSSION QUESTIONS

1. Has Sober raised fair philosophical criticisms of environmentalism (and what does Sober mean by *environmentalism*)?
2. Are the theoretical problems raised by Sober worse for environmentalism than whatever theoretical problems one could raise for anthropocentrism? Explain.
3. How might Johnson answer Sober's argument about ecosystems and other natural objects not having interests?
4. Is Sober right about the "demarcation problem," and how serious a problem is it? Sober thinks it is "the most fundamental theoretical problem confronting an environmentalist who wishes to claim that species and ecosystems have autonomous value." Is he right? How might an environmentalist answer Sober?

You Decide!

1. ECO-TERRORISM

The FBI defines terrorism as, "the unlawful use of force or violence against persons or property to intimidate or coerce a government, the civilian population, or any segment thereof, in furtherance of political or social objectives." The FBI has established a special unit on domestic terrorism to investigate terrorist acts that originate within the United States and are aimed at domestic interests. In addition to anarchist, antiabortion, and white supremacy activities, the FBI unit on domestic terrorism also investigates terrorist actions performed for the sake of nature, so-called "eco-terrorism."

The two leading organizations for eco-terrorism are the Animal Liberation Front (ALF) and the Earth Liberation Front. ALF is responsible for some of the crimes committed on behalf of animal welfare with its "Operation Bite Back," a campaign that targeted mink farms, laboratories, and other facilities which exploit animals (such as corrals holding wild horses).

ELF, as its name implies, is focused on terrorist acts for the sake of the environment, not just animal welfare. ELF recently split off from the radical environmental organization Earth First! ("!" is part of its name) because, in part, Earth First! is slowly evolving into a legitimate environmental protection organization. Even though Earth First! will never become the sort of mainline voice for conservation that one hears from, say, the Sierra Club, it is apparently becoming too conservative for some members, who subsequently formed ELF. Earth First! officially neither condones nor condemns acts of environmental terrorism.

As of early 2001, ELF claimed a running total of about $37 million in damage to machinery and facilities for the sake of protecting nature. The organization's biggest strike so far was to burn a $12 million ski resort in Vail, Colorado, in 1998, an act of eco-terrorism that received national attention.

Though primarily a phenomenon of the Pacific Northwest, ELF activities are spreading east. Recently, ELF claimed credit for arson attacks on ritzy subdivision homes being built in Long Island, ostensibly in protest to urban sprawl.

Discussion Questions

1. Contemplate the name *Earth First!* Assess its philosophical presuppositions.
2. Do you accept the FBI's definition of terrorism? Is terrorism ever justified? Under what conditions? Could eco-terrorism be justified? Is there a distinction to be made between the effectiveness of terrorism and its justification? Explain. Is terrorism the proper description of the actions undertaken by ELF?
3. Craig Rosebraugh, publicist for but nonmember of ELF, claims that ELF is committed to nonviolence. "In the history of ELF, both in the United States and abroad, there have been no injuries to human life. The people take precautions so that no one gets hurt and their actions speak for themselves." What do you think? Why should it matter whether or not people get hurt? Does Rosebraugh's statement have a theoretical basis or is it simply political rhetoric (or perhaps strategy)?
4. It is illegal for environmental activists to destroy a bulldozer owned by a timber company; yet it is legal for the timber company to destroy a particular ecosystem by, for example, clear-cutting a forest. Are the two cases parallel? If they are what does this say about how we as a society view the values that are at stake? What values are at stake—on both sides. If the cases are not parallel, why not?

2. INDUSTRIAL ECOLOGY

The term *industrial ecology* can be found from time to time in newspapers and other mass media. It sounds oxymoronic, like *dehydrated water,* or *atheist minister.* However, *industrial ecology* refers to an emerging conception of industrial processes that are designed to mimic ecosystems. In the natural world, there is no waste. Whatever one organism casts off is used by another. Ecosystems consist of complex dependencies among different organisms, each kind playing a functional role in maintaining the whole. Some organisms are primary producers; others are consumers (of both the primary producers and the consumers themselves—some animals eat plants and other animals eat those animals). Other organisms are decomposers, making the components of living organisms available for other uses within the system. Solar energy drives the system, but the system is pretty much self-contained. The movement of material tends to be cyclical, not linear. The environmental movement has taught us that what goes around comes around.

Industrial engineers have begun thinking about ways to make manufacturing processes virtually self-contained as well. The key idea of industrial ecology is to arrange industries and manufacturing processes so that the "waste" of one industry becomes a resource for another. For example, the excess steam from an electrical power plant can be used by a chemical manufacturer. Multiple industrial dependencies can be built, forming an "industrial ecosystem," or an "eco-industrial park." Rather than acting in isolation from one another, integrating industrial processes in a single location makes both good business and ecological sense.

Industrial ecology is nothing new. People have long tried to sustain one business venture off the waste from another. It was common, for example, for pigs to be raised near breweries so they could be fed the spent grain. But industrial ecology takes that simple insight and applies it to modern manufacturing techniques. A cement plant might be located near a power plant to use the ash as a component of cement; a sulphuric acid company might be located near an oil refinery to use the sulphur removed from crude oil. Industrial engineers are coming up with increasingly complex ways in which manufacturing processes can be integrated with one another, using the waste from one component as the starting point for the next. Eco-industrial parks are a good example of an economic advantage being derived from something that makes good environmental sense, given, of course, that we have those industrial processes in the first place. The industries that "feed" off one another are no more altruistic than the organisms that feed off one another in nature. Their close integration is driven by economic considerations alone, and apparently the economic advantages of sensibly linked industries are considerable.

The textbook case of a highly developed industrial ecosystem is in Kalundborg, a small city in Denmark. Four main industries feed on each other's waste: a coal-fired power plant, a refinery, a pharmaceutical and enzyme manufacturer, and a plasterboard company. Other smaller businesses are involved as well. The industrial system works as follows: The power company supplies residual steam to the gas refinery, and the refinery supplies gas that used to be vented to the power company to produce electricity and steam. Excess steam also drives some pharmaceutical processes. Sludge from the pharmaceutical company is used on the fields of local farms. Ash from the power company's coal furnaces is used by the cement plant and the plasterboard manufacturer, and a sulphuric acid producer derives sulphur from the refinery and from the power plant (oil and coal contain sulphur). A fish farm is also run off excess heat. The power company is the primary producer—the equivalent of plants capturing solar energy in an ecosystem—and it drives a host of other industrial consumers from the energy (ultimately solar!) stored in coal. The Kalundborg experiment began in the 1970s and evolved slowly to the highly efficient integrated system of today.

Discussion Questions

1. Kalundborg was not the result of industrial planning, but rather something that took shape on its own as a result of businesses seeking economic advantage. Should eco-industrial parks be planned in advance, or is it better just to let "market forces" work on their own?
2. What happens when one of the industries gets in financial trouble? For example, if there is a big drop in the construction industry, then the plasterboard company at Kalundborg will not need as much ash from the power company. Integration seems great when everything works, but it also means the fates of the different companies are now linked. If you

were the CEO of a company contemplating joining an eco-industrial park (and you have millions of dollars at risk), what sorts of considerations would come to mind?

3. Imagine a highly evolved eco-industrial system. Is it conceivable that the eco-industrial system itself could have moral standing? Why or why not?

3. GOATS VERSUS ECOSYSTEMS

In the days of sailing ships, getting enough food during extended voyages was a constant problem. It became fairly common for ships to put goats on islands to afford a supply of fresh meat. Goats are hardy and adaptable; they eat almost anything and being very fecund, even a few individuals can quickly generate sizable herds. With no predators to keep their numbers in check, goat populations on islands flourished. The problem is that introducing goats onto islands causes extensive damage to fragile ecosystems. Goats strip the vegetation. In fact, goats are under consideration as a way of clearing the accumulated forest undergrowth in the mainland United States. Ecologists now realize that a low-intensity fire is cleansing and good for the ecosystem, but because so much undergrowth has built up from a wrong-headed policy of fire suppression (remember Smokey the Bear?), fires now tend to be raging infernos that incinerate everything. Goats offer one solution to the undergrowth problem. But on islands, goats are a destructive force.

On Santa Catalina (off the coast of California), the Catalina mahogany tree, a type of mahogany tree found nowhere else, is threatened by feral goats. On the Galapagos Islands (visited by Darwin who subsequently developed the theory of evolution as a result of his studies of the many unique species of those islands) giant tortoises are endangered by goats; the tortoises feed exclusively on specific types of plants that the goats eat too. According to one report, on Isabela (an island in the Galapagos) there were 10 goats in 1982; by 1995 there were 10,000.

Most ecologists agree that the goats must be eliminated if we are to save fragile island ecosystems, but how to eliminate the goats? The most effective method is to shoot them, often from helicopters. The terrified goats can be corralled into mountain canyons where they are killed by sharpshooters. Poison bait is too risky to other forms of wildlife (for example, on the Galapagos it was feared the tortoises would eat it too), and trapping is expensive and, though the evidence is in dispute, many captured animals apparently die from shock anyway. Putting up fences to protect portions of the islands will starve the goats once they denude the areas to which they have access, a fate presumably worse than being shot. Among the techniques used by hunters is to put radio transmitters on females so they can be followed; as males are attracted, they are shot.

Discussion Questions

1. Is it morally acceptable to shoot the goats to protect endangered island ecosystems?
2. Should goats be eliminated from islands even where they are not currently threatening the ecosystem but are likely to do so in the future?
3. Should predators be introduced to control the goat population?
4. On the Galapagos, for example, in addition to the goats, tourists are a major threat to the ecosystem. If we eliminate goats to protect the ecosystem, should people also be prohibited from visiting the islands (what about strict limits on their numbers and activities)?

5. An official for the Santa Catalina Island Conservancy, an environmental group working to preserve the island ecosystem, said, "The goats are not part of the ecosystem on Catalina. Unfortunately, we have to undo what was done in error before." Assess this judgment.

FOR FURTHER READING ON ECOSYSTEMS

Golley, Frank, B., *A History of the Ecosystem Concept in Ecology,* New Haven: Yale University Press, 1993.

Kormondy, Edward, *Concepts of Ecology,* Englewood Cliffs, NJ: Prentice Hall, 1969.

Pomeroy, Lawrence, *Concepts of Ecosystem Ecology: A Comparative View,* New York: Springer-Verlag, 1988.

CHAPTER 8

A New Anthropocentrism?

MODERN TIMES: HEAT WAVE; GLOBAL WARMING AND THE FUTURE OF HUMANITY

Ah, *Homo sapiens,* literally "wise man." Now we'll see how wise we are. Perhaps we can be forgiven for not realizing that our activities could alter the atmosphere; after all, the atmosphere is huge. (A few forward-thinking souls did guess; the French scientist Jean-Baptiste-Joseph Fourier first described the mechanism by which the earth retains warmth from the sun in 1820, the greenhouse effect.) But now that the facts of global warming are slowly dawning on us, we can no longer plead ignorance.

What are the facts? We have become accustomed to science telling us the facts, and we get impatient when those who are supposed to know use measured, cautious, jargon-laden language. But a consensus is definitely emerging among atmospheric scientists regarding not only the fact of global warming but also its cause. Increasingly, it looks as if we are the major cause. A handful of maverick scientists continue to deny that human activity is the major cause of global warming, but just as the link between smoking and cancer became increasingly hard for reputable scientists to deny, so the link between human activity—specifically, burning fossil fuels—and global warming is also becoming increasingly difficult to deny. Most of the uncertainty now centers not on whether we are contributing to global warming but on what its effects are likely to be. In some sense this is progress; when Charles Callendar first proposed in 1938 that industrial activity affects global temperature, his thesis was widely regarded as preposterous.

A prestigious international body of some 2,500 of the world's atmospheric scientists called the Intergovernmental Panel on Climate Change (IPCC) is perhaps the most authoritative organization reporting on global warming. The IPCC is affiliated with the United Nations and the World Meteorological Society. So far the IPCC has issued three major reports, most recently in February 2001. Its findings are sobering. Apparently, previous estimates of global warming for the new century were mistaken; instead of the average global temperature rising by a maximum of 3.5 degrees Celsius by 2100 (6.3 degrees Fahrenheit), more accurate models put the maximum rise at approximately 5.8 degrees C (10.4 F). This is almost twice as high as predicted in the early 1990s. When it is all averaged out worldwide, the temperatures could rise anywhere from 1.5 degrees C (2.7 F) under the best conditions to 5.8 degrees C (10.4 F) under the worst-case scenario. These predictions are hardly infallible, but as measurements are refined and better and more powerful models are developed, confidence in their accuracy increases as well.

According to the IPCC, an increase in average global temperature will not come about smoothly. We can expect violent extremes of weather as the atmosphere warms. Very high highs and very low lows will be coupled with an increase in major disturbances, such as hurricanes, droughts, shifting weather patterns, and severe storms. The likelihood of an increase in such major disturbances caused by global warming is, according to the IPCC, either "very likely" (defined in their report to mean "90 to 99 percent chance") or "likely" (defined to mean "66 to 90 percent chance") depending on the phenomenon in question and the part of the world. For example, because hurricanes are fueled by warm ocean water, a greater expanse of warm ocean water—a result of global warming—can sustain more frequent and larger hurricanes beyond their current range.

Data presented by the respected Worldwatch Institute's report, *The State of the World 2001,* shows that the 1990s had the largest number of natural catastrophes of any decade in the 20th century, and many of those natural disasters were weather-related, such as major killer hurricanes, floods, and mud slides (due to too much rain). In 1991, for example, a cyclone and storm surge hit Bangladesh, killing some 200,000 people. This documented increase in violent weather is thoroughly consistent with predictions in the IPCC report. The worry is that we are now in the early stages of major weather disturbances caused by global warming. No single event can be attributed to global warming, but when we stand back and consider trends over decades, more and more experts are becoming concerned.

The best-case and worst-case scenarios (and everything in between) presented in the latest IPCC report depend on different models for how our patterns of production and consumption will develop. Will we continue to rely on fossil fuels? Will populations stabilize or continue to grow? Will we develop significant nonfossil fuel energy sources? What kinds of feedback loops will emerge? (For example, if it gets hot, people will use more air-conditioning, which will use more electricity, the generation of which will produce more carbon dioxide, which will further accelerate global warming.) Basically, different future scenarios are based on the interplay between population, economic development, and energy production.

In one sense, the details of global warming are well understood. Concentrations of carbon dioxide, methane, and nitrous oxide, along with "aerosols"—suspended particles in the atmosphere—have been carefully charted over time, showing an unmistakable coincidence between their increase and a commensurate increase in global temperature. This much is clear. That global warming nicely follows a documented increase in greenhouse gas concentrations does not establish a causal connection between the two, since there have been fluctuations in mean global temperature for millennia. Global warming skeptics and apologists for industries that contribute significant quantities of greenhouse gases never fail to seize on this point, and it would indeed be a fallacy (*post hoc;* see Chapter 2) to claim that just because one event follows another that the first is the cause of the second.

Even if the earth is entering a warm spell, we are in all probability exacerbating that trend. The problem is separating anthropogenic (human-caused) warming from what may be a concurrent natural rise in global temperature. According to the 2001 IPCC report, we are now experiencing no ordinary warming spell: "[T]he increase in temperature in the 20th century is likely to have been the largest of any century during the past 1,000 years." ("likely" = 66 to 90 percent chance). The report goes on to claim (and support with data), "There is new and stronger evidence that most of the warming observed over the last 50 years is attributable to human activities." This is a much more definitive statement than the 1995 IPCC report which said only, "The balance of evidence suggests that there is a discernible human influence on global climate." Thus, natural variability in global temperature is the least likely explanation for the current increase, an increase whose rate "is very likely to be without precedent during at least the last 10,000 years" ("very likely" = 90 to 99 percent chance). Moreover, "most of the warming occurred during the 20th century, during two periods, 1910 to 1945 and 1976 to 2000." These two periods correspond to times of vigorous industrial activity.

Critics of global warming are right to insist that no definitive causal connection has been established between industrial activity and global warming, just as no definitive causal connection has been established between smoking and lung cancer. But just as the evidence is compelling for the smoking–lung cancer link, so there is compelling evidence for linking global warming with human activity. Not only does the rise in temperature closely follow industrial activity, but also the rate of temperature increase is unprecedented. Moreover, and most critically, the mechanisms by which greenhouse gases trap heat are understood; in other words, scientists can explain the phenomenon of global warming as a consequence of the physical properties of the gases involved. In this respect, anthropogenic global warming is at least as well understood as the link between smoking and lung cancer, since exactly how tobacco toxins operate on the molecular level to cause cancer remains somewhat speculative. But this does not matter: It is one thing to know that *A* causes *B*, and another to know *how A* causes *B*. Given what is at stake with global warming, prudence would counsel not holding out until the last shred of evidence makes a causal connection between industrial activity and dangerous levels of global warming undeniable. (Though that is pretty much the case now, according to evidence made available in the IPCC report; what further evidence could convince skeptics?)

What happens next? This is the hard question. There are numerous scenarios, mostly speculative and mostly unappealing. For example, as temperatures lurch upward the oceans may release huge quantities of dissolved CO_2, like warmed soda, further exacerbating global warming. Higher temperatures will mean more evaporation, which will put more water vapor in the atmosphere (which also functions as a greenhouse gas). More water vapor means more clouds, and more clouds might reflect more light, which could cool the earth, offsetting global warming. Or perhaps more clouds will blanket the earth, driving temperatures even higher, turning the atmosphere into a giant sauna. Nobody knows. More water vapor in the atmosphere means more rain, a lot more rain in some locations, but in the northern latitudes if the increased moisture falls as snow and if the snow pack somehow accumulates faster than it melts, more light will be reflected, cooling the earth, possibly triggering another ice age! Then again, maybe not. More atmospheric CO_2 and higher temperatures could produce more plant growth, which would temporarily sequester CO_2, but higher temperatures will speed up all biological systems, including decay, which will release CO_2. Also, higher temperatures will likely yield more insects and diseases. Ocean levels, which are rising, are expected to continue to do so as the earth warms (projected between .09 to .88 meters by 2100; 1 meter = 39.37 inches). But a higher ocean level is not just a result of ice melt (already Arctic ice is reported to be thinning), but also because hot water expands more than hot land. Rising sea levels will have enormous consequences for coastal cities and islands, some of which may disappear, such as the Maldives. Global warming is also expected to thaw vast stretches of the now-frozen tundra, releasing huge amounts of methane, another potent greenhouse gas. Apparently, too, ocean currents that regulate so much of the weather are themselves threatened by global warming.

There are hundreds of scenarios for what can happen as temperatures rise and as scientists direct their attention toward the implications of global warming, more potentially disastrous scenarios come to light. Not all the scenarios are disastrous, however. Milder weather might mean longer growing seasons in some parts of the world and more CO_2 in the atmosphere might produce more luxurious plant growth. We are definitely moving into uncharted territory—a vast experiment of global proportions. The truly disturbing thing is that temperatures *are* rising and there is very little that we can do about it now. Even if we radically altered our ways immediately, atmospheric processes already in motion will take many decades, if not centuries, to abate. By the time the magnitude of the problem becomes readily apparent to all, there will be little we can do except to "ride it out" and hope for the best. Reading the IPCC report gives one an eerie sense of unreality; the unemotional flat scientific prose portrays the very real prospect of a worldwide catastrophe just ahead. Our repeated attempts to cobble together a few ineffectual international treaties to control greenhouse gas emissions seem laughably inadequate given the enormity of the problem.

One aspect of global warming that receives little attention is its threat to democracy. At first glance, global warming and democracy seem unrelated, but a moment's reflection makes clear just how fragile the environmental underpinnings of democracy are. The United States has strong democratic traditions, so shifting weather patterns and increases in freak storms, droughts, and floods can likely be accommodated, though at considerable cost. But even in our own country, we can imagine threats to our democratic traditions from a string of weather-related emergencies—emergencies that seem to keep happening, one after another. Imagine a big hurricane hitting Florida during a period of protracted drought in California while at the same time the aquifers run dry in the Midwest corn belt, sending food prices sky high, as the Northeast struggles to recover from several winters of record snowfalls. Many insurance companies could go bankrupt, the federal government's ability to deal with all these crises simultaneously would be stretched and the National Guard could be called out to maintain order. It's not an appealing scenario, but not that far-fetched either.

Shifting weather patterns, storms, droughts, floods, and rising seas all introduce additional stresses in fragile democratic regimes in other parts of the world, especially if, as is currently projected, increasing demand for food runs up against our diminishing ability to grow it. The United Nations projects a world population of 9.8 billion by 2050 (probably within your lifetime; it is about 6 billion today), yet our capacity to coax more and more food out of the land is not keeping up. Feeding a hungry world has always been a grim race between agricultural techniques and demand, but some experts think crop yields worldwide have plateaued. There is hardly any new land to farm and plants have been pushed close to their physiological limits by agricultural science, according to some agricultural experts. As the *State of the World 2001* notes, worldwide grain productivity is slowing markedly. "From 1950 until 1990, world grain yield per hectare rose 2.1 percent a year. Between 1990 and 2000, however, the annual gain was only 1.2 percent. Most of the rise in crop land productivity since agriculture began was compressed into the four-decade span between 1950 and 1990, when average yield per hectare climbed from 1.1 to 2.5 tons per hectare." This means that population growth will soon outpace the world's ability to feed everyone, if it has not already done so. Famine will become a reality for many hundreds of millions of people.

We often hear that famine is a political problem, not a production problem, that there really is enough food to go around if we would distribute it wisely. Perhaps that has been the case, but it will become increasingly a matter of production, not distribution, especially when one factors in agricultural disruptions caused by global warming. According to Oxford University's Norman Myers, who writes extensively on environmental issues, global-warming-induced droughts are likely to affect the midsection of the United States, southern Canada, southern Europe, and Australia, all areas that produce much of the food that sustains more than 100 developing countries. If grain production in these areas falters due to drought—as happened in 1988 and is predicted to occur at least three times a decade under plausible global warming scenarios—then massive famines could cause the starvation deaths of anywhere from 50 million to 400 million people, according to some calculations. In *Environmental Exodus,* published by the Climate Institute in 1995, Myers writes, "Mega-scale famines are held at bay today in part through food shipments from the great grain belt of North America among other food-exporting regions. In a greenhouse-affected world, this grain belt could become unbuckled to an extent that there would be fewer such shipments as Americans find it harder to feed themselves, let alone other communities."

Long before ecosystems simply collapse biologically, a more insidious problem will emerge: environmental refugees, that is, people who can no longer live in their traditional homelands because of environmental degradation. As life becomes increasingly difficult because of repeated droughts, storms, floods, and rising oceans (which contaminate wells and poison farmland with salt water), people will start migrating. Where will they go? Already huge and largely ungovernable cities containing more than 10 million people attract those displaced from their homelands. Cities such as Shanghai, Bombay, Mexico City, Buenos Aires, Sao Paulo, New York, Calcutta, Rio de Janiero, and others are expected to swell as millions of dislocated people gravitate toward them because they have nowhere else to go. According to the United Nations Population Fund, between 1991 and 2010, more than one *billion* rural people are expected to migrate to these and other "megacities," making this shift from rural to urban living one of the most dramatic in the history of civilization. Of the world's 26 largest cities, 21 are in developing countries. Slums and urban decay will spread as authorities find it increasingly difficult to meet even the basic needs for tolerable urban life, such energy, housing, water, sewage disposal, and transportation. Such concentrations of desperate people will surely be a source of political instability. Political instability, famine, drought, shifting weather patterns—these all threaten democracy, which requires certain background conditions of material comfort and security. For example, military ventures are not democratically undertaken; a general does not call for a vote among the troops whether they should attack or retreat. Captains of ships and airplanes are not democratic leaders among their crews. Under some conditions, democracy seems either dangerous or foolish.

John Rawls, the most influential contemporary political philosopher in the world, considers the conditions of life necessary for democracy in his major work, *A Theory of Justice.* Among the required physical conditions for democracy, he notes, "Natural and other resources are not so abundant that schemes of cooperation become superfluous, nor are conditions so harsh that fruitful ventures must inevitably break down." In other words, democracy requires conditions of moderate scarcity—cooperative efforts can result in mutual benefit, otherwise they are pointless. Democracy is unnecessary in a world of superabundance, since cooperative undertakings are not necessary for us to thrive. Democracy would be pointless in the Garden of Eden, for example. With more than enough food, property, and resources to go around, we would not have to worry about fair distribution. Obviously, concern is not over superabundance but "conditions so harsh that fruitful ventures must inevitably break down." Democracy cannot function under conditions where no matter what we do our lives remain miserable. For the bulk of humanity in a globally warmed world, conditions may simply be too harsh for the kind of government that we take for granted today. The stresses of global warming may make U.S. foreign policy to cultivate democracies worldwide even more difficult than it is currently.

ENLIGHTENED ANTHROPOCENTRISM

Global warming presents a stark vision for the future of humanity and for the future of democracy. These are, admittedly, anthropocentric concerns. But even so, they are still very important to us. Anthropocentrism—the view that only human beings have direct moral standing—has been under attack throughout most of our discussion. The idea that humanity is the center of the moral universe is rejected by proponents of animal rights, biocentrism, and ecocentrism. It may seem, in fact, that a proper understanding of our relation to the nonhuman world requires rejecting anthropocentrism and that much of environmental philosophy is engaged in a project of reconstituting the moral community.

This is not an altogether inaccurate assessment of environmental philosophy. However, the philosophical problems involved in widening the moral community are considerable. In his celebrated essay, "The Land Ethic" (see Chapter 7), Aldo Leopold says, "The land ethic *simply* enlarges the boundaries of the community to include soils, waters, plants, and animals, or collectively: the land" (emphasis added). How the boundary of the moral community can be expanded is hardly simple, since we need first to articulate a criterion of moral significance and, as we have seen, that takes us deep into moral philosophy. Also, any intelligible expansion of the moral community seemingly involves locating person-like properties beyond the realm of humanity, so for the nonhuman world (or just aspects of it) to fall within the scope of morality, it must be rather like us, and isn't this anthropocentrism?

It is time to take another look at anthropocentrism. Though often criticized as the root of our environmental problems, anthropocentrism can take various forms, some more plausible than others. The crudest version of anthropocentrism would have us pursue short-term human interests at the expense of the natural world. Cut down the forests, dam the rivers, burn the oil—exploit nature to the fullest extent possible to generate a robust and thriving, though short-lived, economy. However, nothing in anthropocentrism says we have to be so stupid in pursuit of our well-being. Human well-being is intimately connected with clean air, clean water, and healthy ecosystems. Our interests are surely not advanced by taking a ruthlessly exploitative attitude toward nature because an orgy of consumption will only lead to huge problems later. Being self-interested does not imply being shortsighted, and anthropocentrism can be quite enlightened and so does not portend the destruction of nature, as is sometimes feared.

As a theory about moral standing, enlightened anthropocentrism has distinct philosophical advantages. It is reasonably simple and straightforward, capturing our initial moral intuitions regarding the scope of the moral community. We do not have to look for intrinsic value or morally significant interests beyond the realm of humanity, nor do we have to engage in the questionable undertaking of looking for vestiges of persons in nature to support an expansion of the moral community. In this view, there are no loci of intrinsic value outside of humanity for us to take into account—the moral universe consists of just us, the human persons. Perplexing questions about intrinsic value outside the human realm simply vanish because all questions of nonanthropocentric value are transformed into questions of instrumental value. How can we use nature to best serve our needs? And our needs are not only physical ones, but emotional and spiritual as well. As an environmental theory, anthropocentrism is undeniably attractive—but is it true?

One might be attracted to anthropocentrism because in some sense it appears to be a "natural" ethical position. By focusing exclusively on our own well-being, one might argue, we would be acting just as any other species. Other species pursue their own good, so why shouldn't we pursue ours? This is simply how the natural world works. We are sometimes admonished by environmentalists to function more "in tune" with nature (rather than against it), so setting out to pursue human interests exclusively would reassert our position as just one species among others that are each pursuing their own good. Moreover, if each species pursues its own interests exclusively, then the best total outcome for all is achieved, namely, a healthy ecosystem. In this view, the natural world is rather like a pure capitalist economy where individuals each pursue their own interests and the "invisible hand of the marketplace" ensures a maximal benefit for all. We might be tempted to conclude enlightened anthropocentrism is the best view because it is "natural." By focusing on pursuit of our own well-being, we would be functioning just like any other form of life and, through competition, achieve what is best for all. Or so it might be argued.

Is this "argument from nature" in favor of anthropocentrism a good one? No. Just because other species inevitably pursue their own interests is not a reason to think we should too. This is a classic case of moving from *is* to *ought* (see Chapter 2, naturalistic fallacy). As a moral position, anthropocentrism has to hold not merely that people *do* what is in their best interest exclusively, but that is what they *ought* to do. Anthropocentrism is prescriptive, not merely descriptive. It is true that other species do pursue their own interests—they have little choice in the matter—but is that a reason for us to do the same? We do have a choice; this is what makes us moral agents.

To determine whether we (that is, humanity) ought to pursue our own interests exclusively, we need to determine whether there are other interests—albeit nonhuman—that ought to be considered in addition to our own. In other words, we are back to asking questions about the extent of the moral community. In the end, for anthropocentrism to be a justified moral position, it must be shown that no interests other than human interests are morally significant. If there are morally significant non-human interests, then we would not be justified in pursuing our own interests to the exclusion of those other interests, no more than I would be justified in pursuing my own interests to the exclusion of yours (see Chapter 4 on egoism).

Furthermore, the argument that if humanity just looked after human interests then all of nature would benefit is not really an argument for anthropocentrism. Rather than being a moral theory about what is intrinsically valuable, anthropocentrism would then just be a means to an end, the stability of nature. This might be a fine rule for developing environmental policy, since we can regard ourselves as something of a "marker species." In other words, what is good for us is good for nature. Though it seems utterly disingenuous to argue that pursuit of human interests exclusively is done in service of the larger goal, the well-being of nature. Despite the initial attractions of anthropocentrism, fundamental questions about the composition of the moral community are unavoidable, difficult though they may be.

CHARACTER AND THE ENVIRONMENT

Resolving questions about the extent of the moral community does not resolve all the moral questions we could ask about our relation to the natural world. We have to consider not just the moral status of various entities but also what we should be like as people. *Even if* humanity and humanity alone constitutes the moral community, as maintained by anthropocentrism, we can still raise moral questions concerning what we should be like as people. Consider someone who buys plastic dolls at the toy store only to take them home to club them to pieces or someone who laughs upon reading about a terrible airplane crash that killed many people. There is nothing morally wrong in breaking plastic toys—they have no independent moral status—nor is there anything wrong in laughing at something one reads in the paper, but someone who did these things would nevertheless display a warped character. The best explanation for why this behavior is problematic is not that it might lead to harming persons, for even if it did not, we still think these are serious character defects. We can ask important questions about our character even if we are not dealing with entities that have any moral status or if our actions are not directly wrong.

In Chapter 1, we looked briefly at virtue ethics. We will now consider more closely how character is relevant to the environment. The crucial theoretical point is that certain aspects of character will be good to have even if the natural world is without direct moral significance. If direct moral significance extends beyond humanity, then appropriately cultivated characters ought to recognize that fact, but the failure of nonanthropocentric theories of value still need not result in our adopting an exploitative approach to the natural world. How we act toward nature says much about the sort of people we are, which raises questions about what sort of people we ought to be.

If you could wave a magic wand and make people, what would you want them to be like? We were created, but not all at once. Our parents had wishes for how we would turn out; what sorts of things we would be sensitive to; how we would react to different situations, people, and the ups and downs of life. And those of us who rear children have hopes for how they will emerge from our care as fully autonomous well-adjusted individuals. So we can reflect meaningfully on the traits of character we want people to have. Not that we want everyone to be the same, but there are character traits that are good to have no matter what the details of one's life. These traits constitute what it is for us to flourish as human beings. Among the character traits it is good for someone to have is a proper appreciation for nature. Nature has long been seen as teacher—the Boy Scout virtues of self-reliance and preparedness are allegedly cultivated by spending time in the woods. Children are sent off to summer camp with the thought that being in the wild is not mere recreation, but deeply instructive.

To appreciate the connection between character and nature, let us consider what we shall say about someone who is indifferent to the natural world. Suppose this person is utterly bored by beautiful fossils, colorful insects, majestic vistas, and all the diversity and intricacy found in nature. How sad, we say. We suspect this person lacks an aesthetic sense, for he or she is incapable of appreciating what for many of us is an inexhaustible source of aesthetic fascination. A whole dimension of enjoyment is inaccessible to this unfortunate individual, and we would likely pity this person for his or her inability to experience what ordinarily brings so much delight to the rest of us.

We might suspect someone who is indifferent to nature as having an arrogance or inability to see themselves with the proper perspective. Think of the loud American tourist who is indifferent to foreign cultures and norms of behavior, eats only at McDonald's overseas, and expects people to speak to him in English. We would rightly hold our boorish tourist in contempt for being so arrogant and uncomprehending of his position in a foreign culture. Someone who is indifferent to nature might be similarly incapable of appreciating her position in the natural world; such a person lacks a kind of perspective on life.

It is easy to lose perspective on our lives, living as many of us do surrounded by affluence, comfort, gadgets and material plenty. We are cut off from much interaction with nature. Gardening or golf or something similarly tame is how many of us experience the natural world. Yet standing alone on a beach or mountaintop can bring our humanity and our vulnerability home in a powerful, sometimes scary, manner. Our concerns seem so insignificant when we step back and try to comprehend our lives from the broader perspective exposure to nature seems to force on us. Such an experience can be an important corrective to human arrogance.

We want people to be aesthetically sensitive, comprehending their lives as natural beings, and properly humble toward the mysteries of existence. Someone who is indifferent to nature is likely incapable of these things and therefore not the sort of person we wish ourselves or our loved ones to be.

THE READINGS

The readings for this chapter either assume or argue for a mild form of anthropocentrism.

STEPHEN JAY GOULD

The Golden Rule—A Proper Scale for Our Environmental Crisis

Harvard University's Stephen Jay Gould (1941–2002) was one of the world's foremost popular writers on natural history; he was also a respected paleontologist, specializing in ancient snails. In this selection from "The Golden Rule—A Proper Scale for Our Environmental

---

Crisis," Gould argues that in our folly we may well bring destruction upon ourselves, but it is mere hubris to think we can destroy life on the planet. Paleontology shows us the vastness of the time scales that govern life on earth. Gould recommends that we focus not on the planet but on ourselves, and extend the golden rule to our relationship with nature. Deliberately anthropomorphizing the planet Gould writes, "If we treat her nicely, she will keep us going for a while. If we scratch her, she will bleed, kick us out, bandage up, and go about her business at her planetary scale."

CRITICAL READING QUESTIONS

1. What does Gould see as a flawed basis for an environmental ethic?
2. According to Gould, what is the relevance of proper time scales to our environmental concerns?
3. What is the Golden Rule? How does Gould apply it?

This decade, a prelude to the millennium, is widely and correctly viewed as a turning point that will lead either to environmental perdition or stabilization. We have fouled local nests before and driven regional faunas to extinction, but we have never been able to unleash planetary effects before our current concern with ozone holes and putative global warming. In this context, we are searching for proper themes and language to express our environmental worries.

I don't know that paleontology has a great deal to offer, but I would advance one geological insight to combat a well-meaning, but seriously flawed (and all too common), position and to focus attention on the right issue at the proper scale. Two linked arguments are often promoted as a basis for an environmental ethic:

1. That we live on a fragile planet now subject to permanent derailment and disruption by human intervention;
2. That humans must learn to act as stewards for this threatened world.

Such views, however well intentioned, are rooted in the old sin of pride and exaggerated self-importance. We are one among millions of species, stewards of nothing. By what argument could we, arising just a geological microsecond ago, become responsible for the affairs of a world 4.5 billion years old, teeming with life that has been evolving and diversifying for at least three-quarters of that immense span? Nature does not exist for us, had no idea we were coming, and doesn't give a damn about us. Omar Khayyám was right in all but his crimped view of the earth as battered when he made his brilliant comparison of our world to an eastern hotel:

> Think, in this battered Caravanserai
> Whose Portals are alternate
> Night and Day,
> How Sultan after Sultan with his Pomp
> Abode his destined Hour, and
> went his way.

This assertion of ultimate impotence could be countered if we, despite our late arrival, now held power over the planet's future (argument number one above). But we don't, despite popular misperception of our might. We are virtually powerless over the earth at our planet's own geological time scale. All the megatonnage in our nuclear arsenals yield but one ten-thousandth the power of the asteroid that might have triggered the Cretaceous mass extinction. Yet the earth survived that larger shock and, in wiping out dinosaurs, paved the road for the evolution of large mammals, including humans. We fear global warming, yet even the most radical model yields an earth far cooler than many happy and prosperous times of a prehuman past. We can surely destroy ourselves, and take many other species with us, but we can barely dent bacterial diversity and will surely not remove many million species of insects and mites. On geological scales, our planet will take good care of itself and let time clear the impact of any human malfeasance. The earth need never seek a henchman to wreak Henry's vengeance upon Thomas á Becket: "Who will free me from this turbulent priest?" Our planet simply waits.

People who do not appreciate the fundamental principle of appropriate scales often misread such an argument as a claim that we may therefore cease to worry about environmental deterioration . . . But I raise the same counterargument. We cannot threaten at geological scales, but such vastness is entirely inappropriate. We have a legitimately parochial interest in our own lives, the happiness and prosperity of our children, the suffering of our fellows. The planet will recover from nuclear holocaust, but we will be killed and maimed by the billions, and our cultures will perish. The earth will prosper if polar icecaps melt under a global greenhouse, but most of our major cities, built at sea level as ports and harbors, will founder, and changing agricultural patterns will uproot our populations.

We must squarely face an unpleasant historical fact. The conservation movement was born, in large part, as an elitist attempt by wealthy social leaders to preserve wilderness as a domain for patrician leisure and contemplation (against the image, so to speak, of poor immigrants traipsing in hordes through the woods with their Sunday picnic baskets). We have never entirely shaken this legacy of environmentalism as something opposed to immediate human needs, particularly of the impoverished and unfortunate. But the Third World expands and contains most of the pristine habitat that we yearn to preserve. Environmental movements cannot prevail until they convince people that clean air and water, solar power, recycling, and reforestation are best solutions (as they are) for human needs at human scales—and not for impossibly distant planetary futures.

I have a decidedly unradical suggestion to make about an appropriate environmental ethic—one rooted in the issue of appropriate human scale versus the majesty, but irrelevance, of geological time. I have never been much attracted to the Kantian categorical imperative in searching for an ethic—to moral laws that are absolute and unconditional and do not involve any ulterior motive or end. The world is too complex and sloppy for such uncompromising attitudes (and God help us if we embrace the wrong principle, and then fight wars, kill, and maim in our absolute certainty). I prefer the messier "hypothetical imperatives" that involve desire, negotiation, and reciprocity. Of these "lesser," but altogether wiser and deeper, principles, one has stood out for its independent derivation, with different words but to the same effect, in culture after culture. I imagine that our various societies grope toward this principle because structural stability, and basic decency necessary for any tolerable life, demand such a maxim. Christians call this principle the "golden rule"; Plato, Hillel, and Confucius knew the same maxim by other names. I cannot think of a better principle based on enlightened self-interest. If we all treated others as we wish to be treated ourselves, then decency and stability would have to prevail.

I suggest that we execute such a pact with our planet. She holds all the cards and has immense power over us—so such a compact, which we desperately need but she does not at her own time scale, would be a blessing for us, and an indulgence for her. We had better sign the papers while she is still willing to make a deal. If we treat her nicely, she will keep us going for a while. If we scratch her, she will bleed, kick us out, bandage up, and go about her business at her planetary scale. Poor Richard told us that "necessity never made a good bargain," but the earth is kinder than human agents in the "art of the deal." She will uphold her end; we must now go and do likewise.

DISCUSSION QUESTIONS

1. Who are the "others" in the Golden Rule?
2. Can the Golden Rule be applied to the earth? How?
3. Is the Golden Rule a genuine moral principle or just a rule of enlightened self-interest? What is the difference?
4. Is Gould's position an ethical one? Why or why not?

BRYAN G. NORTON

Environmental Ethics and Weak Anthropocentrism

Bryan Norton is a professor in the school of Public Policy at the Georgia Institute of Technology and a frequent contributor to discussions in environmental philosophy. He has been a long-standing defender of what he calls "weak" anthropocentrism, the view that morally relevant interests consist of the considered preferences of human beings only. Weak anthropocentrism is contrasted with strong anthropocentrism, where all interests are reducible to the felt preferences of human beings. The difference between considered and felt preferences is that considered preferences can be rationally assessed, since one might have felt preferences that, upon consideration, one realizes one ought not to have. According to Norton, "One need not make the questionable ontological commitments involved in attributing intrinsic value to nature, since weak anthropocentrism provides a framework adequate to criticize current destructive practices . . . and to account for the distinctive nature of environmental ethics."

CRITICAL READING QUESTIONS

1. How does Norton characterize an "adequate" ethic? In what way does he think weak anthropocentrism is an adequate ethic?
2. How, on weak anthropocentrism, is nature a "teacher" of values?
3. In what way does Norton think environmental ethics is distinctive?
4. What is "Parfit's paradox," and why, according to Norton, must appreciation of the paradox drive environmental ethics to focus on wholes, not individuals? What is the whole at issue in Norton's discussion?
5. What is the trust fund analogy supposed to show?
6. What are the two levels of environmental ethic, according to Norton?

I. INTRODUCTION

[I]n the present paper . . . I address the question of whether there must be a distinctively environmental ethic.

Discussions of this question in the literature have equated a negative answer with the belief that the standard categories of rights, interests, and duties of individual human beings are adequate to furnish ethical guidance in environmental decision making. A positive answer is equated with the suggestion that nature has, in some sense, intrinsic value. In other words, the question of whether environmental ethics is distinctive is taken as equivalent to the question of whether an environmental ethic must reject anthropocentrism, the view that only humans are loci of fundamental value.[1] Environmental ethics is seen as distinctive vis-à-vis standard ethics if and only if environmental ethics can be founded upon principles which assert or presup-

Bryan Norton, "Environmental Ethics and Weak Anthropocentrism," from *Environmental Ethics,* vol. 6, no. 2 (Summer 1984). Reprinted by permission.

pose that nonhuman natural entities have value independent of human value.

I argue that this equivalence is mistaken by showing that the anthropocentrism/nonanthropocentrism debate is far less important than is usually assumed. Once an ambiguity is noted in its central terms, it becomes clear that nonanthropocentrism is not the only adequate basis for a truly environmental ethic.[2] I then argue that another dichotomy, that of individualism versus nonindividualism, should be seen as crucial to the distinctiveness of environmental ethics and that a successful environmental ethic cannot be individualistic in the way that standard contemporary ethical systems are. Finally, I examine the consequences of these conclusions for the nature and shape of an environmental ethic.

Before beginning these arguments, I need to clarify how I propose to test an adequate environmental ethic. I begin by assuming that all environmentally sensitive individuals believe that there is a set of human behaviors which do or would damage the environment. Further, I assume that there is considerable agreement among such individuals about what behaviors are included in that set. Most would decry, for example, careless storage of toxic wastes, grossly overpopulating the world with humans, wanton destruction of other species, air and water pollution, and so forth. There are other behaviors which would be more controversial, but I take the initial task of constructing an adequate environmental ethic to be the statement of some set of principles from which rules can be derived proscribing the behaviors included in the set which virtually all environmentally sensitive individuals agree are environmentally destructive. The further task of refining an environmental ethic then involves moving back and forth between the basic principles and the more or less controversial behaviors, adjusting principles and/or rejecting intuitions until the best possible fit between principles and sets of proscribed behaviors is obtained for the whole environmental community. In the present paper I address the prior question of basic principles. I am here only seeking to clarify which principles do (and which do not) support the large set of relatively uncontroversial cases of behaviors damaging to the environment. An ethic will be adequate, on this approach, if its principles are sufficient to entail rules proscribing the behaviors involved in the noncontroversial set. My arguments, then, are not directed at determining which principles are *true,* but which are *adequate* to uphold certain shared intuitions. Questions concerning the truth of such principles must be left for another occasion.

II. ANTHROPOCENTRISM AND NONANTHROPOCENTRISM

I suggest that the distinction between anthropocentrism and nonanthropocentrism has been given more importance in discussions of the foundations of environmental ethics than it warrants because a crucial ambiguity in the term *anthropocentrism* has gone unnoticed.[3] Writers on both sides of the controversy apply this term to positions which treat humans as the only loci of intrinsic value.[4] Anthropocentrists are therefore taken to believe that every instance of value originates in a contribution to human values and that all elements of nature can, at most, have value instrumental to the satisfaction of human interests.[5] Note that anthropocentrism is defined by reference to the position taken on *loci* of value. Some nonanthropocentrists say that human beings are the *source* of all values, but that they can designate nonhuman objects as loci of fundamental value.[6]

It has also become common to explain and test views on this point by reference to "last man examples" which are formulated as follows.[7] Assume that a human being, *S,* is the last living member of *Homo sapiens* and that *S* faces imminent death. Would *S* do wrong to wantonly destroy some object *X?* A positive answer to this question with regard to any nonhuman *X* is taken to entail nonanthropocentrism. If the variable *X* refers to some natural object, a species, an ecosystem, a geological formation, etc., then it is thought that positions on such questions determine whether a person is an anthropocentrist or not, because the action in question cannot conceivably harm any human individual. If it is wrong to destroy *X,* the wrongness must derive from harm to *X* or to some other natural object. But one can harm something only if it is a good in its own right in the sense of being a locus of fundamental value.

Or so the story goes. I am unconvinced because not nearly enough has been said about what counts as a human interest. In order to explore this difficult area, I introduce two useful definitions. A *felt preference* is any desire or need of a human individual that can at least temporarily be sated by some specifiable experience of that individual. A *considered preference* is any desire or need that a human individual would express after careful deliberation, including a judgment that the desire or need is consistent with a rationally adopted world view—a world view which includes fully supported scientific theories and a metaphysical framework interpreting those theories, as well as a set of rationally supported aesthetic and moral ideals.

When interests are assumed to be constructed merely from felt preferences, they are thereby insulated from any criticism or objection. Economic approaches to decision making often adopt this approach because it eschews "value judgments"—decision makers need only ask people what they want, perhaps correct these preferences for intensity, compute the preferences satisfied by the various possible courses of action, and let the resulting ordinal ranking imply a decision.

A considered preference, on the other hand, is an idealization in the sense that it can only be adopted after a person has rationally accepted an entire world view and, further, has succeeded in altering his felt preferences so that they are consonant with that world view. Since this is a process no one has ever completed, references to considered preferences are hypothetical—they refer to preferences the individual would have if certain contrary-to-fact conditions were fulfilled. Nonetheless, references to considered preferences remain useful because it is possible to distinguish felt preferences from considered preferences when there are convincing arguments that felt preferences are not consistent with some element of a world view that appears worthy of rational support.

It is now possible to define two forms of anthropocentrism. A value theory is *strongly anthropocentric* if all value countenanced by it is explained by reference to satisfactions of felt preferences of human individuals. A value theory is *weakly anthropocentric* if all value countenanced by it is explained by reference to satisfaction of some felt preference of a human individual or by reference to its bearing upon the ideals which exist as elements in a world view essential to determinations of considered preferences.

Strong anthropocentrism, as here defined, takes unquestioned felt preferences of human individuals as determining value. Consequently, if humans have a strongly consumptive value system, then their "interests" (which are taken merely to be their felt preferences) dictate that nature will be used in an exploitative manner. Since there is no check upon the felt preferences of individuals in the value system of strong anthropocentrism, there exists no means to criticize the behavior of individuals who use nature merely as a storehouse of raw materials to be extracted and used for products serving human preferences.

Weak anthropocentrism, on the other hand, recognizes that felt preferences can be either rational or not (in the sense that they can be judged not consonant with a rational world view). Hence, weak anthropocentrism provides a basis for criticism of value systems which are purely exploitative of nature. In this way, weak anthropocentrism makes available two ethical resources of crucial importance to environmentalists. First, to the extent that environmental ethicists can make a case for a world view that emphasizes the close relationship between the human species and other living species, they can also make a case for ideals of human behavior extolling harmony with nature. These ideals are then available as a basis for criticizing preferences that merely exploit nature.

Second, weak anthropocentrism as here defined also places value on human experiences that provide the basis for value formation. Because weak anthropocentrism places value not only on felt preferences, but also on the process of value formation embodied in the criticism and replacement of felt preferences with more rational ones, it makes possible appeals to the value of experiences of natural objects and undisturbed places in human value formation. To the extent that environmentalists can show that values are formed and informed by contact with nature, nature takes on value as a teacher of human values. Nature need no longer be seen as a mere satisfier of fixed and often consumptive values—it also becomes an important source of inspiration in value formation.[8]

In the final section of this paper I develop these two sources of value in nature more fully. Even there my goal is not to defend these two bases for environmental protection as embodying true claims about the value of nature—that, as I said at the outset is a larger and later task. My point is only that, within the limits set by weak anthropocentrism as here defined, there exists a framework for developing powerful reasons for protecting nature. Further, these reasons do not resemble the extractive and exploitative reasons normally associated with strong anthropocentrism.

And they do not differ from strongly anthropocentric reasons in merely theoretical ways. Weakly anthropocentric reasoning can affect behavior as can be seen by applying it to last man situations. Suppose that human beings choose, for rational or religious reasons, to live according to an ideal of maximum harmony with nature. Suppose also that this ideal is taken seriously and that anyone who impairs that harmony (by destroying another species, by polluting air and water, etc.) would be judged harshly. But such an ideal need not attribute intrinsic value to natural objects, nor need the prohibitions implied by it be justified with nonanthropocentric reasoning attributing intrinsic value to nonhuman natural objects. Rather, they can be justified as being implied by the ideal of harmony with nature. This ideal, in turn, can be justified either on religious grounds referring to human spiritual development or as being a fitting part of a rationally defensible world view.

Indeed, there exist examples of well developed world views that exhibit these characteristics. The Hindus and Jains, in proscribing the killing of insects, etc., show concern for their own spiritual development rather than for the actual lives of those insects. Likewise, Henry David Thoreau is careful not to attribute independent, intrinsic value to nature. Rather he believes that nature expresses a deeper spiritual reality and that humans can learn spiritual values from it.[9] Nor should it be inferred that only spiritually oriented positions can uphold weakly anthropocentric reasons. In a post-Darwinian world, one could give rational and scientific support for a world view that includes ideals of living in harmony with nature, but which involve no attributions of intrinsic value to nature.

Views such as those just described are weakly anthropocentric because they refer only to human values, but they are not strongly so because human behavior is limited by concerns other than those derivable from prohibitions against interfering with the satisfaction of human felt preferences. And practically speaking, the difference in behavior between strong anthropocentrists and weak anthropocentrists of the sort just described and exemplified is very great. In particular, the reaction of these weak anthropocentrists to last man situations is undoubtedly more similar to that of nonanthropocentrists than to that of strong anthropocentrists. Ideals such as that of living in harmony with nature imply rules proscribing the wanton destruction of other species or ecosystems even if the human species faces imminent extinction . . .

Nor need weak anthropocentrism collapse into strong anthropocentrism. It would do so if the dichotomy between preferences and ideals were indefensible. If all values can, ultimately, be interpreted as satisfactions of preferences, then ideals are simply human preferences. The controversy here is reminiscent of that discussed by early utilitarians. John Stuart Mill, for example, argued that because higher pleasures ultimately can be seen to provide greater satisfactions, there is thus only a single scale of values—preference satisfaction.[10] It is true that weak anthropocentrists must deny that preference satisfaction is the only measure of human value. They must take human ideals seriously enough so that they can be set against preference satisfactions as a limit upon them. It is therefore no surprise that weak anthropocentrists reject the reductionistic position popular among utilitarians. Indeed, it is precisely the rejection of that reductionism that allows them to steer their way between strong anthropocentrism and nonanthropocentrism. The rejection of this reduction is, of course, a commitment that weak anthropocentrists share with nonanthropocentrists. Both believe there are values distinct from human preference satisfaction, rejecting the reduction of ideals to preferences.

They differ not on this point, but on whether the justification of those ideals must appeal to the intrinsic value of nonhuman objects.

Weak anthropocentrism is, therefore, an attractive position for environmentalists. It requires no radical, difficult-to-justify claims about the intrinsic value of nonhuman objects and, at the same time, it provides a framework for stating obligations that goes beyond concern for satisfying human preferences. It, rather, allows the development of arguments to the effect that current, largely consumptive attitudes toward nature are indefensible, because they do not fit into a world view that is rationally defensible in terms not implying intrinsic value for nonhumans. It can also emphasize the value of nature in forming, rather than in satisfying human preferences, as preferences can be modified in the process of striving toward a consistent and rationally defensible world view.

III. INDIVIDUALISM AND NONINDIVIDUALISM

The distinctions and arguments presented above convince me that, while the development of a nonanthropocentric axiology committed to intrinsic value for nonhuman natural entities remains an interesting philosophical enterprise, the dichotomy on which it is based has less importance for the nature of environmental ethics than is usually thought. In particular, I see no reason to think that, if environmental ethics is distinctive, its distinctiveness derives from the necessity of appeals to the intrinsic value of nonhuman natural objects. Once two forms of anthropocentrism are distinguished, it appears that from one, weak anthropocentrism, an adequate environmental ethic can be derived. If that is true, authors who equate the question of the distinctiveness of an adequate environmental ethic with the claim that nature or natural objects have intrinsic value are mistaken.

There is, nevertheless, reason to believe that an adequate environmental ethic is distinctive. In this section, I argue that no successful environmental ethic can be derived from an individualistic basis, whether the individuals in question are human or nonhuman. Since most contemporary ethical systems are essentially individualistic, an adequate environmental ethic is distinctive, not by being necessarily nonanthropocentric as many environmental ethicists have argued or assumed, but, rather, by being nonindividualistic.

Standard contemporary ethical theories, at least in the United States and Western Europe are essentially individualistic. By this I mean that the behavioral prohibitions embodied in them derive from the principle that actions ought not to harm other individuals unjustifiably. Utilitarians derive ethical rules from the general principle that all actions should promote the greatest possible happiness for the greatest possible number of individuals. This means that actions (or rules) are judged to be legitimate or not according to whether more good (and less harm) for individuals will result from the action than from any alternative. On this view, the satisfaction of each individual interest is afforded an initial prima facie value. Some such interests are not to be satisfied because the information available indicates that if they are, some greater interest or sets of interests of some individuals cannot be satisfied concurrently with them. The utilitarian principle, supplemented by empirical predictions about the consequences of actions for individuals, filters happiness-maximizing actions from others that do not maximize happiness. For present purposes, the important point is that the satisfaction of individual interests are the basic unit of value for utilitarians, and in this sense, utilitarianism (either of the act or rule variety) is essentially individualistic.[11]

Contemporary deontologists derive ethical prohibitions from individual rights and obligations to protect those rights.[12] Individuals make claims, and when these claims conflict with claims made by other individuals, they are judged to be legitimate or illegitimate according to a set of ethical rules designed to make such decisions. Although these rules, in essence, are the embodiment of a system of justice and fairness, the rules adjudicate between claims of individuals, and consequently modern deontology is essentially individualistic.[13] Therefore, both utilitarianism and modern deontology are essentially individualistic in the sense that the basic units of ethical concern are interests or claims of individuals.

It is characteristic of the rules of environmental ethics that they must prohibit current behaviors that have effects upon the long-range future as well as the present. For example, storage of radioactive wastes with a half-life of thousands of years in containers that will deteriorate in a few centuries must be prohibited by an adequate environmental ethic, even if such actions, on the whole, provide the most benefits and no harms to currently living individuals. Likewise, human demographic growth, if subsequent generations continue that policy, will create severe overpopulation, a behavior negatively affecting the future of the environment, and hence human reproductive behavior must be governed by an adequate environmental ethic. An adequate environmental ethic must therefore prohibit current activities generally agreed to have negative effects on the environment of the future.

I have argued at length elsewhere that a paradox, due to Derek Parfit, effectively precludes systems of ethics which are individualistic in the sense defined above from governing current decisions by reference to their effects on future individuals.[14] To summarize that argument briefly, it exploits the insight that no system of ethics built exclusively upon adjudications of interests of present and future individuals can govern current decisions and their effects on future individuals because current environmental decisions determine what individuals will exist in the future. Parfit's argument notes that current decisions regarding consumption determine how many individuals and which individuals will be born in the future. On a policy of fast demographic growth and high consumption, different individuals will exist a century from now than would exist if the current generation adopts a policy of low growth and moderate consumption. Assume, as most environmentalists do, that a policy of high growth and immoderate consumption will leave the future with a lower quality of life than more moderate growth policies would. The individuals who are, in fact, born as a result of the immoderate growth policies cannot complain that they would have been better off had the policies been different—for they would not even have existed had moderate policies been adopted. That is, Parfit's paradox shows that current policy cannot be governed by reference to harms to the interests of future individuals, because those policies determine who those individuals will be and what interests they will have. Attempts to govern behaviors affecting the distant future cannot, therefore, be governed by appeal to individual interests of future persons, since the very existence of such individuals hangs in the balance until all relevant decisions are made.

Since the ethical intuitions shared by all environmentally sensitive individuals include prohibitions against behaviors which may have negative effects only in the long-term future (and not in the present), the rules of environmental ethics cannot be derived from the usual, individualistic systems of ethics currently in vogue. Note, also, that my argument concerning individualism makes no assumption that only human individuals make claims or have interests and rights. Future nonhuman individuals are, likewise, affected by human policies regarding consumption and reproduction. Consequently, expansion of the loss of individual rights holders, or preference havers to include nonhumans in no way affects the argument. No ethical system which is essentially individualistic, regardless of how broadly the reference category of individuals is construed, can offer ethical guidance concerning current environmental policy in all cases.

IV. A PROPOSAL FOR AN ADEQUATE ANTHROPOCENTRIC ENVIRONMENTAL ETHIC

The arguments of the last section are surprisingly simple and general, but if they are sound, they explain the fairly general intuition that environmental ethics must be distinctive in some sense, although not in the sense usually assumed. So far my conclusions have all been negative—I have argued that an adequate environmental ethic *need not* be nonanthropocentric and that an adequate environmental ethic *must not* be limited to considerations of individual interests. From these conclusions a new direction for environmental ethics emerges which is weakly anthropocentric—it finds all value in human loci—and which is also nonindividualistic in the sense that value is not restricted to satisfactions of felt preferences of human individuals. In other words, the arguments of the first two sections of the paper (1) positively define a space by establishing the possibility of a weakly, but not strongly, anthropocentric environmental ethic and (2) negatively constrain that ethic by eliminating the possibility that it be purely individualistic.

My purpose now is not to demonstrate that the ethical principles I have set out are definitely correct or that they are the only adequate principles available. My goal, rather, is to present a valid alternative for environmental ethics that is adequate in a manner that no purely individualistic, strongly anthropocentric ethic can be, while avoiding difficult-to-defend references to the intrinsic value of nonhuman natural objects.

I begin my explication with an analogy. Suppose an extremely wealthy individual, through a will, sets up a very large trust fund "to be managed for the economic well-being of my descendants." Over the years, descendants will be born and die, and the class of beneficiaries will change through time. Suppose, also, that the family drifts apart emotionally and becomes highly contentious. I suggest that two sorts of controversies, each with its own distinctive logic, could arise concerning the fund. First, there may be issues about the *fair distribution* of proceeds of the trust. Some descendants might claim that other descendants are not entitled to full shares, because they are, or are descended from, an illegitimate offspring of a member of the family. Or it might be disputed whether adopted children of descendants are included in the terms of the will.

Second, there may well be disputes about the *management* of the trust. Here, there may be questions concerning what sorts of investments are "good investments." Should all investments be safe ones, thereby insuring a continued, although smaller income? Might the principle of the trust be invaded in years where the income from investments is unusually low? Might one generation simply spend the principle, dividing it fairly among themselves, showing no concern for future descendants?

To apply this analogy in obvious ways, ethical questions about the environment can be divided into ones concerning distributional fairness within generations and others concerning longer-term, cross-generational issues. If the arguments in the third section are correct, then the latter are not reducible to the former; nor do they have the same logic. It can be assumed that many environmental concerns, as well as nonenvironmental ones, can be resolved as issues of distributional fairness. If a property owner pollutes a stream running through his property, this action raises a question of fairness between him and his downstream neighbor.[15] These moral issues are, presumably, as amenable resolution using the categories and rules of standard, individualistic ethics as are nonenvironmental ones.

But there are also many questions in environmental ethics that are analogous to questions of management of a trust across time. Soil, water, forests, coal, oil, etc. are analogous to the principle of the trust. If they are used up, destroyed, or degraded, they no longer provide benefits. The income from the trust provides an analogy for renewable resources. As long as the productive resource (analogous to the principle of the trust) is intact, one can expect a steady flow of benefits.

One feature that makes environmental ethics distinctive is concern for protection of the resource base through indefinite time. Parfit's paradox shows that these concerns cannot be accounted for by reference to concerns for individuals and to the obligation not to harm other individuals unjustifiably. The obligations are analogous to those accepted by an individual who is appointed executor of the trust fund. Although decisions made by the executor affect individuals and their well-being, the obligation is to the integrity of the trust, not to those individuals. While one might be tempted to say that the obligation of the executor is to future individuals who will be born, but who are at this time unknown, this conceptualization also involves a failure to perceive the profundity of Parfit's paradox. Suppose all of the members of a given generation of the family in question sign an agreement not to have offspring and thereby convince the executor to disburse the principle of the trust equally among current beneficiaries. Perhaps this is consistent with the terms of the trust, but it shows that the current choices of the executor cannot be guided by abstract conceptions of "future individuals." When current decisions about management are interlocked with not-yet-decided questions affecting the future existence of individuals, it is impossible to refer to those individuals as the basis of guidance in making current management decisions.

Suppose a generation of the entire human species freely decided to sterilize itself, thereby freeing itself to consume without fear of harming future individuals. Would they do wrong? Yes.[16] The perpetuation of the human species is a good thing because a universe containing human consciousness is preferable to one without it.[17] This value claim implies that current generations must show concern for future generations. They must take steps to avoid the extinction of the species and they must provide a reasonably stable resource base so that future generations will not suffer great deprivation. These are the bases of rules of management analogous to the rules for administering a trust fund. They do not have individuals or individual interests as their reference point, but they do govern behavior that will affect future individuals.

It is now possible to outline a weakly anthropocentric, nonindividualistic environmental ethic. Such an ethic has two levels. The distributional level has as its principle that one ought not to harm other human individuals unjustifiably. This principle rests upon the assumption that felt preferences, desires that occur within individual human consciousness, have equal prima facie value. Rules for the fair treatment of individuals are derived from the principle of no harm and prescribe fair treatment of individuals, whether regarding benefits derived from the environment or from other sources. Since there is nothing distinctive about the environmental prescriptions and proscriptions that occur on this level—they do not differ in nature from other issues of individual fairness—I do not discuss them further.

Decisions on the second level of environmental ethics, which I call the level of "allocation," cannot, however, be based upon individual considerations. The central value placed on human consciousness is not a result of aggregating the value of individual consciousnesses, because the value of ongoing consciousness cannot be derived from the value of individual consciousnesses—they cannot be identified or counted prior to the making of decisions on resource allocation.[18] Therefore, obligations on this level are owed to no individual and can be called "generalized obligations." They are obligations of the current generation to maintain a stable flow of resources into the indefinite future and, consequently, they are stated vis-à-vis resources necessary for ongoing human life, not vis-à-vis individual requirements. Resources represent the means for supporting life looked at from a nonindividual perspective. The individual perspective determines needs and wants and then seeks means to fulfill them. Concern for the continued flow of resources insures that sources of goods and services such as ecosystems, soil, forests, etc. remain "healthy" and are not deteriorating. In this way, options are held open and reasonable needs of individuals for whatever goods and services can be fulfilled with reasonable labor, technology, and ingenuity. The emphasis of this concern, however, is not individualistic since it is not focused on the fulfillment of specifiable needs, but rather on the integrity and health of ongoing ecosystems as holistic entities.

While the long-term nature of the concern implies that the stability of the resource base must be protected, this stability is not the same thing as ecological stability. It is an open (and controversial) question as to what the stability of ecosystems means. Further, there are controversies concerning the extent to which there are scientifically supportable generalizations about what is necessary to protect ecological stability. For example, it is highly controversial whether diversity, in general, promotes and/or is necessary for ecological stability.[19] These controversies are too complex to enter into here, but they are relevant. To the extent that scientists know what is necessary to protect the resource base, there is an obligation to act upon it. Even if there are few sweeping generalizations such as those concerning diversity and stability, there are a wide variety of less general rules that are well supported and are being systematically ignored in environmental policy. Ecologists and resource managers know that clear-cutting tropical forests on steep slopes causes disastrous erosion, that intensely tilling monocultures causes loss of top-soil, and that overexploitation of fisheries can cause new and far less productive species compositions. Further, there is an obligation, where knowledge is lacking, to seek that knowledge in order to avoid unintentional destruction.

An ethic of resource allocation should apply to nonrenewable resources as well as to renewable ones and should also imply a population policy. The general injunction to maintain the stability of the resource base across generations follows from the value of human consciousness. It implies that, with respect to renewable, or interest-bearing resources, present generations should not harvest more than the maximum sustainable yield of the resource. But what does stability imply with respect to nonrenewable resources? Although at first glance it would seem to suggest that a stable supply can only be sustained if no utilization takes place, this reasoning is based on a confusion—it is not the case that there is an obligation to have a certain, fixed amount of goods in supply, but rather there is an obligation to maintain a stable level of goods *available for use.* The ethical principle, in other words, is directed at maintaining the possibility of human consciousness which requires resource use. What is required, then, is a constant supply of resources available for utilization by succeeding generations. Once the problem is framed in this manner, human technology and the phenomenon of substitutability of products become relevant. Present humans may use up nonrenewable resources, provided they take steps to provide suitable substitutes. If, for example, the present generation uses up a major portion of the accumulated fossil fuels available, they will have done nothing wrong if they leave the next generation with a technology capable of deriving energy from renewable sources such as the sun, wind, or ocean current.[20] There are significant trade-offs available back and forth between renewable and nonrenewable resources.

Note also that this system implies a population principle—the level of population in any given generation should be determined by the requirements for the stability of the resource flow. Such a determination would be based on an assessment of (a) how many people are consistent with the maximal sustainable yield of renewable resources and (b) how many people are consistent with a level of use for nonrenewable resources which does not outstrip the ability of the existing technology to produce suitable substitutes. A population principle follows, in turn, from this stability principle. One need not identify future individuals or worry about utilities of possible individuals on this approach. The obligation is to maintain maximum sustainable yield consistent with the stability of the resource flow. The population principle sets a population policy for a generation as a whole based on the carrying capacity of the environment. Questions about who, in a given generation, should have children and how many each individual can have, may be treated as questions of interpersonal equity among the existing individuals of any given generation.

The ethical obligations constituting an ethic of allocation are quite simple as they derive from a single value—that of ongoing human consciousness. In general form, however, they do not state specifically what to do; they only require actions necessary to retain a stable resource base through indefinite time. Scientific knowledge can, in principle, nevertheless, indicate specific actions necessary in order to fulfill that obligation. Scientific evidence is sufficient to imply that many currently widespread practices violate those obligations either directly or cumulatively and are, in terms of this system, immoral. There are also areas where scientific knowledge is insufficient to decide whether and how certain practices are destructive. Here, the obligation is to be cautious and to proceed to obtain the information necessary.

While science plays a crucial role in this system, the system is not naturalistic. It does not derive moral obligations from purely scientific statements. Central to all obligations of present individuals to the future is an obligation to perpetuate the value of human consciousness. Science elucidates and makes concrete the specific obligations flowing from that central obligation but does not support it.

V. RELATING THE TWO LEVELS

The ethic proposed has two levels—one has the prima facie equality of felt preferences of individual humans as its central value principle; the other has the value of ongoing human life and consciousness as its central value principle. Rules and behaviors justified on these two levels can, of course, conflict. If felt preferences are overly consumptive, then the future of human life may be threatened. Conversely, one can imagine situations where concern for the future of the human species might lead to draconian measures threatening the life or livelihood of current individuals by limiting the satisfaction of felt preferences. Weak anthropocentrism, nevertheless, because it recognizes the important difference between felt and considered preferences, can adjudicate these disputes.

The most common conflict, the one many environmentalists fear we now face, exists when overly consumptive felt preferences cause serious overexploitation of nature and thereby threaten the resource base necessary for continued human life. This conflict can be resolved by taking human ideals into consideration. If, for example, one's total world view contains as an ideal the continuation of human life and consciousness, then the felt preferences in question are irrational—they are inconsistent with an important ethical ideal. Similarly, if a rational world view recognizing that the human species evolved from other life forms includes an ideal calling for harmony with nature, this ideal, likewise, can function to criticize and alter felt preferences. By building ecological principles and ideals regarding the proper human treatment of nature into a rationally supported world view, weak anthropocentrists can develop vast resources for criticizing felt preferences of human individuals which threaten environmental stability and harmony.

It can be argued that experiences of nature are essential in constructing a rational world view. Likewise, scientific understanding of nature seems essential for the construction of such a world view. Nor would it be very surprising if it turned out that analogies, symbols, and metaphors drawn from nature provided an essential source of guidance in choosing ethical and aesthetic ideals as well.[21] Other species and unspoiled places would thereby have great value to humans not only for the way in which they satisfy human felt preferences but also for the way they serve to enlighten those preferences. Once one recognizes the distinction between felt preferences and considered preferences, nature assumes a crucial role in informing values by contributing to the formation of a rational world view, the criterion by which felt preferences are criticized.

VI. ENVIRONMENTAL ETHICS AND INTRINSIC VALUE

The conflicts that exist between the levels of distributive fairness and allocation require thoughtful discussion and debate, but that discussion and debate can take place without appeal to the intrinsic value of nonhuman natural objects. The value of ongoing human consciousness and the rules it implies for resource allocation can serve as a basis for criticism of consumptive and exploitative felt preferences. Further, ideas such as that of human harmony with nature and the human species' evolutionary affinity to other species, can serve to strengthen and add flesh to the world view available for the critique of current environmentally destructive behaviors.

When I refer to an environmental ethic, then, I refer, first of all, to the rules of distributive fairness guiding behaviors affecting other human beings' use of the environment. Second, I refer to the rules of allocation affecting the long-term health of the biosphere as a functioning, organic unit. An environmental ethic, nevertheless, is more than these rules: it also encompasses the ideals, values, and principles that constitute a rational world view regarding the human species' relationship to nature. In these sources are bases for evaluating the rules of right action and for criticizing currently felt preferences. Aesthetic experience of nature is an essential part of the process of forming and applying these ideals and, hence, is also a central part of the environmental ethic here described.

Some nonanthropocentrists, such as J. Baird Callicott, have developed in more detail such ideas as the human affinity to other species and have concluded that it is rational for humans to "attribute" intrinsic value to other species on the basis of affective feelings toward them,[22] but if as I have argued, a sense of harmony with nature can, once it becomes an entrenched part of our world view, serve to correct felt preferences, then it can also serve to bring felt preferences more in line with the requirements of resource allocation without any talk about intrinsic value. Of course, since human beings, as highly evolved animals, share many needs for clean air, clean water, ecosystem services, etc., in the long term with other species it would not be surprising that *speaking as if* nature has intrinsic value could provide useful guidance in adjusting human felt preferences. And since these preferences are now far too exploitative and too consumptive for the good of our own species, showing concern for other species that share our long-term needs for survival might be one useful tool in a very large kit.

The point of this essay, however, has been to show that one need not make the questionable ontological commitments involved in attributing intrinsic value to nature, since weak anthropocentrism provides a framework adequate to criticize current destructive practices to incorporate concepts of human affinity to nature, and to account for the distinctive nature of environmental ethics. All of these are essential elements in an ethic that recognizes the distinction between felt and considered preferences and includes important aesthetic and ethical ideals. These ideals, which can be derived from spiritual sources or from a rationally constructed world view, can be based on and find their locus in human values. And yet they are sufficient to provide the basis of criticism of currently over-consumptive felt preferences. As such they adjudicate between ethical concerns for distributional fairness in the present and concerns of allocation which have reference to the long-term future. Essential to this adjudication is the development of principles of conduct that respect the ongoing integrity of functioning ecosystems seen as *wholes*. In this way they transcend concern for individualistically expressed felt preferences and focus attention on the stable functioning of ongoing systems. If all of this is true, Occam's razor surely provides a basis for favoring weak anthropocentrism over nonanthropocentrism.

NOTES

1. See, for example, Richard Routley, "Is There a Need for a New, an Environmental Ethic?" *Proceedings of the XV World Congress of Philosophy*, vol. 1 (1973), pp. 205–10; Holmes Rolston, III, "Is There an Ecological Ethic?" *Ethics* 85 (1975): 93–109; Tom Regan, "The Nature and Possibility of an Environmental Ethic," *Environmental Ethics* 3 (1981): 19–34; and Evelyn B. Pluhar, "The Justification of an Environmental Ethic," *Environmental Ethics* 4 (1982): 319–37.
2. See Regan, "The Nature and Possibility of an Environmental Ethic," who distinguishes "an ethic of the environment" from "an ethic for the use of the environment" (p. 20), where the former, but not the latter, recognizes the intrinsic (inherent) value of nonhuman elements of nature. If the arguments of this paper are persuasive, Regan's distinction will lose interest.
3. My thoughts on this subject have been deeply affected by discussions of the work of Donald Regan and J. Baird Callicott. See, Donald Regan, "Duties of Preservation," and J. Baird Callicott, "On the Intrinsic Value of Nonhuman Species," in *The Preservation of Species,* ed. Bryan G. Norton (in preparation).
4. I borrow this phrase from Donald Scherer, "Anthropocentrism, Atomism, and Environmental Ethics," *Environmental Ethics* 4 (1982): 115–23.
5. I take anthropocentrism to be interchangeable with homocentrism. See R. and V. Routley, "Against the Inevitability of Human Chauvinism," in *Ethics and Problems of the 21st Century,* ed. K. E. Goodpaster and K. M. Sayre (Notre Dame, IN: University of Notre Dame Press, 1979), pp. 56–7. Routley and Routley show that "human chauvinism" (anthropocentrism, homocentrism) are equivalent to the thesis of man's "dominion," which they describe as "the view that the earth and all its nonhuman contents exist or are available for man's benefit and to serve his interests."
6. See J. Baird Callicott, "On the Intrinsic Value of Nonhuman Species," in Norton, *The Preservation of Species* (in preparation), and Pluhar, "The Justification of an Environmental Ethic."
7. See, for example, Richard Routley, "Is There a Need for a New, an Environmental, Ethic?" p. 207; Routley and Routley, "Human Chauvinism and Environmental Ethics," in *Environmental Philosophy,* ed. D. S. Mannison, M. A. McRobbie, and R. Routley (Canberra: Australian National University, Department of Philosophy, 1980), p. 121; and Donald Regan, "Duties of Preservation," in Norton, *The Preservation of Species.*
8. For fuller discussions of this point, see Mark Sagoil, "On Preserving the Natural Environ-

ment," *Yale Law Journal* 84 (1974): 205–67; Holmes Rolston, III, "Can and Ought We to Follow Nature?" *Environmental Ethics* 1 (1979): 7–21; and Bryan G. Norton, *The Spice of Life* (in preparation).

9. See Henry David Thoreau, *Walden* (New York: Harper and Row, 1958). Note page 64, for example, where Thoreau writes: "One value of even the smallest well is, that when you look into it you see that earth is not continent but insular. This is as important as that it keeps butter cool."
10. John Stuart Mill, *Utilitarianism,* chap. 2.
11. I do not intend to imply here that utilitarians are limited to treating human interests as felt preferences. Utilitarians adopt varied interpretations of interests in relation to happiness. My point is only that human individual interests, however determined, are the basis of their moral calculus.
12. I qualify the position here discussed as "contemporary" deontology because there is a strain of thought in Kant which emphasizes that the imperatives are abstract principles. Modern neo-Kantians such as Rawls, however, emphasize the more individualistic strains in Kant, placing him more in the contractarian tradition. Contractarian deontologists—those that fit clearly into the liberal tradition—are my concern here. (I am indebted to Douglas Berggren for clarifying this point.)
13. For a clear explanation of how rights function to adjudicate individual claims, see Joel Feinberg, "The Nature and Value of Rights," *Journal of Value Inquiry* 4 (1970): 243–57. While not all writers agree that rights originate in claims, the disputes are immaterial here. For example, McCloskey's linkage of rights to "entitlements" is not inconsistent with my point. H. J. McCloskey, "Rights," *Philosophical Quarterly* 15 (1965): 115–27.
14. See, "Energy and the Further Future," in *Energy and the Future,* ed. Douglas MacLean and Peter G. Brown (Totowa, NJ: Rowman and Littlefield, 1983). I apply Parfit's "paradox" to environmental ethics in "Environmental Ethics and the Rights of Future Generations," *Environmental Ethics* 4 (1982): 321. See that essay for a more detailed discussion.
15. This is not to suggest, of course, that such action could not also have more long-term effects raising issues of the second sort as well.
16. This answer implies a disanalogy with the trust fund situation, provided one accepts the judgment that no wrong would be committed if a generation of the family chose not to reproduce. I think there is a disanalogy here, as different reproductive obligations would arise if the future of the human species were at stake. Suppose one answers this question negatively regarding the future of human kind and then considers the possibility that the last human individual might wantonly destroy other species, natural places, etc. I would still reject such wanton acts as inconsistent with good human behavior, relying upon weakly anthropocentric arguments as described above.
17. I willingly accept the implication of this value claim that, in a situation of severely contracting human population, some or all individuals would have an obligation to reproduce, but I will not defend this central claim here. Although I believe it can be defended, I am more interested in integrating it into a coherent ethical system than in defending it.
18. On a closely related point, see Brian Barry, "Circumstances of Justice and Future Generations," in *Obligations to Future Generations,* ed. Sikara and Barry (Philadelphia: Temple University Press, 1978).
19. See Norton, *The Spice of Life.*
20. I am, for the sake of the example, ignoring other long-term effects of the use of fossil fuels. Problems due to the greenhouse effect would, of course, also have to be solved.
21. See references in note 8 above.
22. Callicott, "On the Intrinsic Value of Nonhuman Species." Also see Pluhar, "The Justification of an Environmental Ethic" for a somewhat different approach to attribution of intrinsic value.

DISCUSSION QUESTIONS

1. Do you think felt and considered preferences can be separated? What is the difference? Might considered preferences collapse into felt preferences? What would this imply for Norton?

2. Is environmental ethics distinctive in any way? Do you think Norton has adequately accounted for its distinctiveness (if it is distinctive)?
3. Consider Parfit's paradox. Is Norton's approach to that paradox the only way to deal with it?
4. Norton writes, "Suppose a generation of the entire human species freely decided to sterilize itself, thereby freeing itself to consume without fear of harming future individuals. Would they do wrong? Yes." Why would it be wrong? Does Norton give an adequate defense of his answer?
5. Are the "ontological commitments" of positing intrinsic value in nature any worse than regarding human beings as intrinsically valuable? Does Norton unwittingly accept a certain account of intrinsic value? (See Chapter 4.)

THOMAS E. HILL, JR.

Ideals of Human Excellence and Preserving the Natural Environment

Thomas Hill is professor of philosophy at the University of North Carolina at Chapel Hill. In this piece, Hill sidesteps vexing questions of intrinsic value in nature, considering instead the relation between character and nature. He begins by asking a simple question, one that you have probably asked yourself when you encounter a soda can tossed along a trail in the woods: What kind of a person would do that?

CRITICAL READING QUESTIONS

1. Why does Hill attempt to shift discussion away from the composition of the moral community to questions about the character of people?
2. What, according to Hill, is indifference to nature likely to signal about a person's character?
3. What does Hill mean when he writes, "What leads a child to care about what happens to a lost hamster or a stray dog he will not see again is likely also to generate concern for a lost toy or a favorite tree where he used to live"?
4. What, according to Hill, is the link between self-acceptance and concern for the environment?

Thomas E. Hill, Jr., "Ideals of Human Excellence and Preserving the Natural Environment," from *Eviromental Ethics,* vol 5 (Fall 1983), pp. 98–110. Reprinted by permission.

I

A wealthy eccentric bought a house in a neighborhood I know. The house was surrounded by a beautiful display of grass, plants, and flowers, and it was shaded by a huge old avocado tree. But the grass required cutting, the flowers needed tending, and the man wanted more sun. So he cut the whole lot down and covered the yard with asphalt. After all it was his property and he was not fond of plants.

It was a small operation, but it reminded me of the strip mining of large sections of the Appalachians. In both cases, of course, there were reasons for the destruction, and property rights could be cited as justification. But I could not help but wonder, "What sort of person would do a thing like that?"

Many Californians had a similar reaction when a recent governor defended the leveling of ancient redwood groves, reportedly saying, "If you have seen one redwood, you have seen them all."

Incidents like these arouse the indignation of ardent environmentalists and leave even apolitical observers with some degree of moral discomfort. The reasons for these reactions are mostly obvious. Uprooting the natural environment robs both present and future generations of much potential use and enjoyment. Animals too depend on the environment; and even if one does not value animals for their own sakes, their potential utility for us is incalculable. Plants are needed, of course, to replenish the atmosphere quite aside from their aesthetic value. These reasons for hesitating to destroy forests and gardens are not only the most obvious ones, but also the most persuasive for practical purposes. But, one wonders, is there nothing more behind our discomfort? Are we concerned solely about the potential use and enjoyment of the forests, etc., for ourselves, later generations, and perhaps animals? Is there not something else which disturbs us when we witness the destruction or even listen to those who would defend it in terms of cost/benefit analysis?

Imagine that in each of our examples those who would destroy the environment argue elaborately that, even considering future generations of human beings and animals, there are benefits in "replacing" the natural environment which outweigh the negative utilities which environmentalists cite.[1] No doubt we could press the argument on the facts, trying to show that the destruction is shortsighted and that its defenders have underestimated its potential harm or ignored some pertinent rights or interests. But is this all we could say? Suppose we grant, for a moment, that the utility of destroying the redwoods, forests, and gardens is equal to their potential for use and enjoyment by nature lovers and animals. Suppose, further, that we even grant that the pertinent human rights and animal rights, if any, are evenly divided for and against destruction. Imagine that we also concede, for argument's sake, that the forests contain no potentially useful endangered species of animals and plants. Must we then conclude that there is no further cause for moral concern? Should we then feel morally indifferent when we see the natural environment uprooted?

II

Suppose we feel that the answer to these questions should be negative. Suppose, in other words, we feel that our moral discomfort when we confront the destroyers of nature is not fully explained by our belief that they have miscalculated the best use of natural resources or violated rights in exploiting them. Suppose, in particular, we sense that part of the problem is that the natural environment is being viewed exclusively as a natural *resource.* What could be the ground of such a feeling? That is, what is there in our system of normative principles and values that could account for our remaining moral dissatisfaction?

Some may be tempted to seek an explanation by appeal to the interests, or even the rights, of plants. After all, they may argue, we only gradually came to acknowledge the moral importance of all human beings, and it is even more recently that consciences have been aroused to give full weight to the welfare (and rights?) of animals. The next logical step, it may be argued, is to acknowledge a moral requirement to take into account the interests (and rights?) of plants. The problem with the strip miners, redwood cutters, and the like, on this view, is not just that they ignore the welfare and rights of people and animals; they also fail to give due weight to the survival and health of the plants themselves.

The temptation to make such a reply is understandable if one assumes that all moral questions are exclusively concerned with whether *acts* are right or wrong and that this, in turn, is determined by how the acts impinge on the rights and interests of those directly affected. On this assumption, if there is cause for moral concern, some right or interest has been neglected; and if the rights and interests of human beings and animals have already been taken into account, then there must be some other pertinent interests, for example, those of plants. A little reflection will show that the assumption is mistaken; but, in any case, the conclusion that plants have rights or morally relevant interests is surely untenable. We do speak of what is "good for" plants, and they can "thrive" and also be "killed." But this does not imply that they have "interests" in any morally relevant sense. Some people apparently believe that plants grow better if we talk to them, but the idea that the plants suffer and enjoy, desire and dislike, etc., is clearly outside the range of both common sense and scientific belief. The notion that the forests should be preserved to avoid *hurting* the trees or because they have a *right* to life is not part of a widely shared moral consciousness, and for good reason.[2]

Another way of trying to explain our moral discomfort is to appeal to certain religious beliefs. If one believes that all living things were created by a God who cares for them and entrusted us with the use of plants and animals only for limited purposes, then one has a reason to avoid careless destruction of the forests, etc., quite aside from their future utility. Again, if one believes that a divine force is immanent in all nature, then too one might have reason to care for more than sentient things. But such arguments require strong and controversial premises, and, I suspect, they will always have a restricted audience.

Early in this century, due largely to the influence of G. E. Moore, another point of view developed which some may find promising.[3] Moore introduced, or at least made popular, the idea that certain states of affairs are intrinsically valuable—not just valued, but valuable, and not necessarily because of their effects on sentient beings. Admittedly Moore came to believe that in fact the only intrinsically valuable things were conscious experiences of various sorts,[4] but this restriction was not inherent in the idea of intrinsic value. The intrinsic goodness of something, he thought, was an objective, nonrelational property of the thing, like its texture or color, but not a property perceivable by sense perception or detectable by scientific instruments. In theory at least, a single tree thriving alone in a universe without sentient beings, and even without God, could be intrinsically valuable. Since, according to Moore, our duty is to maximize intrinsic value, his theory could obviously be used to argue that we have reason not to destroy natural environments independently of how they affect human beings and animals. The survival of a forest might have worth beyond its worth *to* sentient beings.

This approach, like the religious one, may appeal to some but is infested with problems. There are, first, the familiar objections to intuitionism, on which the theory depends. Metaphysical and epistemological doubts about nonnatural, intuited properties are hard to suppress, and many have argued that the theory rests on a misunderstanding of the words *good, valuable,* and the like. Second, even if we try to set aside these objections and think in Moore's terms, it is far from obvious that everyone would agree that the existence of forests, etc., is intrinsically valuable. The test, says Moore, is what we would say when we imagine a universe with just the thing in question, without any effects or accompaniments, and then we ask, "Would its existence be better than its nonexistence?" Be careful, Moore would remind us, not to construe this question as, "Would you *prefer* the existence of that universe to its nonexistence?" The question is, "Would its existence have the objective, nonrelational property, intrinsic goodness?"

Now even among those who have no worries about whether this really makes sense, we might well get a diversity of answers. Those prone to destroy natural environments will doubtless give one answer, and nature lovers will likely give another. When an issue is as controversial as the one at hand, intuition is a poor arbiter.

The problem, then, is this. We want to understand what underlies our moral uneasiness at the destruction of the redwoods, forests, etc., even apart from the loss of these as resources for human beings and animals. But I find no adequate answer by pursuing the questions, "Are rights or interests of plants neglected,?" "What is God's will on the matter?" and "What is the intrinsic value of the existence of a tree or forest?" My suggestion, which is in fact the main point of this paper, is that we look at the problem from a different perspective. That is, let us turn for a while from the effort to find reasons why certain *acts* destructive of natural environments are morally wrong to the ancient task of articulating our ideals of human excellence. Rather than argue directly with destroyers of the environment who say, "Show me why what I am doing is *immoral,*" I want to ask, "What sort of person would want to do what they propose?" The point is not to skirt the issue with an ad hominem, but to raise a different moral question, for even if there is no convincing way to show that the destructive acts are wrong (independently of human and animal use and enjoyment), we may find that the willingness to indulge in them reflects the absence of human traits that we admire and regard morally important.

This strategy of shifting questions may seem more promising if one reflects on certain analogous situations. Consider, for example, the Nazi who asks, in all seriousness. "Why is it wrong for me to make lampshades out of human skin—provided, of course, I did not myself kill the victims to get the skins?" We would react more with shock and disgust than with indignation, I suspect, because it is even more evident that the question reveals a defect in the questioner than that the proposed act is itself immoral. Sometimes we may not regard an act wrong at all though we see it as reflecting something objectionable about the person who does it. Imagine, for example, one who laughs spontaneously to himself when he reads a newspaper account of a plane crash that kills hundreds. Or, again, consider an obsequious grandson who, having waited for his grandmother's inheritance with mock devotion, then secretly spits on her grave when at last she dies. Spitting on the grave may have no adverse consequences and perhaps it violates no rights. The moral uneasiness which it arouses is explained more by our view of the agent than by any conviction that what he did was immoral. Had he hesitated and asked, "Why shouldn't I spit on her grave?" it seems more fitting to ask him to reflect on the sort of person he is than to try to offer reasons why he should refrain from spitting.

III

What sort of person, then, would cover his garden with asphalt, strip mine a wooded mountain, or level an irreplaceable redwood grove? Two sorts of answers, though initially appealing, must be ruled out. The first is that persons who would destroy the environment in these ways are either shortsighted, underestimating the harm they do, or else are too little concerned for the well-being of other people. Perhaps too they have insufficient regard for animal life. But these considerations have been set aside in order to refine the controversy. Another tempting response might be that we count it a moral virtue, or at least a human ideal, to love nature. Those who value the environment only for its utility must not really love nature and so in this way fall short of an ideal. But such an answer is hardly satisfying in the present context, for what is at issue is *why* we feel moral discomfort at the activities of those who admittedly value nature only for its utility. That it is ideal to care for nonsentient nature beyond its possible use is really just another way of expressing the general point which is under controversy.

What is needed is some way of showing that this ideal is connected with other virtues, or human excellences, not in question. To do so is difficult and my suggestions, accordingly, will be tentative and subject to qualification.

The main idea is that, though indifference to nonsentient nature does not *necessarily* reflect the absence of virtues, it often signals the absence of certain traits which we want to encourage because they are, in most cases, a natural basis for the development of certain virtues. It is often thought, for example, that those who would destroy the natural environment must lack a proper appreciation of their place in the natural order, and so must either be ignorant or have too little humility. Though I would argue that this is not necessarily so, I suggest that, given certain plausible empirical assumptions, their attitude may well be rooted in ignorance, a narrow perspective, inability to see things as important apart from themselves and the limited groups they associate with, or reluctance to accept themselves as natural beings. Overcoming these deficiencies will not guarantee a proper moral humility, but for most of us it is probably an important psychological preliminary. Later I suggest, more briefly, that indifference to nonsentient nature typically reveals absence of either aesthetic sensibility or a disposition to cherish what has enriched one's life and that these, though not themselves moral virtues, are a natural basis for appreciation of the good in others and gratitude.

Consider first the suggestion that destroyers of the environment lack an appreciation of their place in the universe. Their attention, it seems, must be focused on parochial matters, on what is, relatively speaking, close in space and time. They seem not to understand that we are a speck on the cosmic scene, a brief stage in the evolutionary process, only one among millions of species on Earth, and an episode in the course of human history. Of course, they know that there are stars, fossils, insects, and ancient ruins; but do they have any idea of the complexity of the processes that led to the natural world as we find it? Are they aware how much the forces at work within their own bodies are like those which govern all living things and even how much they have in common with inanimate bodies? Admittedly scientific knowledge is limited and no one can master it all; but could one who had a broad and deep understanding of his place in nature really be indifferent to the destruction of the natural environment?

This first suggestion, however, may well provoke a protest from a sophisticated anti-environmentalist. "Perhaps *some* may be indifferent to nature from ignorance," the critic may object, "but *I* have studied astronomy, geology, biology, and biochemistry, and I still unashamedly regard the nonsentient environment as simply a resource for our use. It should not be wasted, of course, but what should be preserved is decidable by weighing long-term costs and benefits." "Besides," our critic may continue, "as philosophers you should know the old Humean formula, 'You cannot derive an *ought* from an *is*.' All the facts of biology, biochemistry, etc., do not entail that I ought to love nature or want to preserve it. What one understands is one thing; what one values is something else. Just as nature lovers are not necessarily scientists, those indifferent to nature are not necessarily ignorant."

Although the environmentalist may concede the critic's logical point, he may well argue that, as a matter of fact, increased understanding of nature tends to heighten people's concern for its preservation. If so, despite the objection, the suspicion that the destroyers of the environment lack deep understanding of nature is not, in most cases, unwarranted, but the argument need not rest here.

The environmentalist might amplify his original idea as follows: "When I said that the destroyers of nature do not appreciate their place in the universe, I was not speaking of intellectual understanding alone, for, after all, a person can *know* a catalog of facts without ever putting them together and seeing vividly the whole picture which they form. To see oneself as just one part of nature is to look at oneself and the world from a certain perspective which is quite different from being able to recite detailed information from the natural sciences. What the destroyers of nature lack is this perspective, not particular information."

Again our critic may object, though only after making some concessions: "All right," he may say, "*some* who are indifferent to nature may lack the cosmic perspective of which you speak, but again there is no *necessary* connection between this failing, if it is one, and any particular evaluative attitude toward nature. In fact, different people respond quite differently when they move to a wider perspective. When *I* try to picture myself vividly as a brief, transitory episode in the course of nature, I simply get depressed. Far from inspiring me with a love of nature, the exercise makes me sad and hostile. You romantics think only of poets like Wordsworth and artists like Turner, but you should consider how differently Omar Khayyám responded when he took your wider perspective. His reaction, when looking at his life from a cosmic viewpoint, was 'Drink up, for tomorrow we die.' Others respond in an almost opposite manner with a joyless Stoic resignation, exemplified by the poet who pictures the wise man, at the height of personal triumph, being served a magnificent banquet, and then consummating his marriage to his beloved, all the while reminding himself, 'Even this shall pass away.' "[5] In sum, the critic may object, "Even if one should try to see oneself as one small transitory part of nature, doing so does not dictate any particular normative attitude. Some may come to love nature, but others are moved to live for the moment; some sink into sad resignation; others get depressed or angry. So indifference to nature is not necessarily a sign that a person fails to look at himself from the larger perspective."

The environmentalist might respond to this objection in several ways. He might, for example, argue that even though some people who see themselves as part of the natural order remain indifferent to nonsentient nature, this is not a common reaction. Typically, it may be argued, as we become more and more aware that we are parts of the larger whole we come to value the whole independently of its effect on ourselves. Thus, despite the possibilities the critic raises, indifference to nonsentient nature is still in most cases a sign that a person fails to see himself as part of the natural order.

If someone challenges the empirical assumption here, the environmentalist might develop the argument along a quite different line. The initial idea, he may remind us, was that those who would destroy the natural environment fail to *appreciate* their place in the natural order. "Appreciating one's place" is not simply an intellectual appreciation. It is also an attitude, reflecting what one values as well as what one knows. When we say, for example, that both the servile and the arrogant person fail to *appreciate* their place in a society of equals, we do not mean simply that they are ignorant of certain empirical facts, but rather that they have certain objectionable attitudes about their importance relative to other people. Similarly, to fail to appreciate one's place in nature is not merely to lack knowledge or breadth of perspective, but to take a certain attitude about what matters. A person who *understands* his place in nature but still views nonsentient nature merely as a resource takes the attitude that nothing is *important* but human beings and animals. Despite first appearances, he is not so much like the pre-Copernican astronomers who made the intellectual error of treating the Earth as the "center of the universe" when they made their calculations. He is more like the racist who, though well aware of other races, treats all races but his own as insignificant.

So construed, the argument appeals to the common idea that awareness of nature typically has, and should have, a humbling effect. The Alps, a storm at sea, the Grand Canyon, towering redwoods, and "the starry heavens above" move many a person to remark on the comparative insignificance of our daily concerns and even of our species, and this is generally taken to be a quite fitting response.[6] What seems to be missing, then, in those who understand nature but remain unmoved is a proper humility.[7] Absence of proper humility is not the same as selfishness or egoism, for one can be devoted to self-interest while still viewing one's own pleasures and projects as trivial and unimportant. And one can have an exaggerated view of one's own importance while grandly sacrificing for those one views as inferior. Nor is the lack of humility identical with belief that one has power and influence, for a person can be quite puffed up about himself while believing that the foolish world will never acknowledge him. The humility we miss seems not so much a belief about one's relative effectiveness and recognition as an attitude which measures the importance of things independently of their relation to oneself or to some narrow group with which one identifies. A paradigm of a person who lacks humility is the self-important emperor who grants status to his family because it is *his*, to his subordinates because *he* appointed them, and to his country because *he* chooses to glorify it. Less extreme but still lacking proper humility is the elitist who counts events significant solely in proportion to how they affect his class. The suspicion about those who would destroy the environment, then, is that what they count important is too narrowly confined insofar as it encompasses only what affects beings who, like us, are capable of feeling.

This idea that proper humility requires recognition of the importance of nonsentient nature is similar to the thought of those who charge meat eaters with "speciesism." In both cases it is felt that people too narrowly confine their concerns to the sorts of beings that are most like them. But, however intuitively appealing, the idea will surely arouse objections from our nonenvironmentalist critic. "Why," he will ask, "do you suppose that the sort of humility I *should* have requires me to acknowledge the importance of nonsentient nature aside from its utility? You cannot, by your own admission, argue that nonsentient nature *is* important, appealing to religious or intuitionist grounds. And simply to assert, without further argument, that an ideal humility requires us to view nonsentient nature as important for its own sake begs the question at issue. If proper humility is acknowledging the relative importance of things as one should, then to show that I must lack this you must first establish that one *should* acknowledge the importance of nonsentient nature."

Though some may wish to accept this challenge, there are other ways to pursue the connection between humility and response to nonsentient nature. For example, suppose we grant that proper humility requires only acknowledging a due status to sentient beings. We must admit, then, that it is logically possible for a person to be properly humble even though he viewed all nonsentient nature simply as a resource. But this logical possibility may be a psychological rarity.

It may be that, given the sort of beings we are, we would never learn humility before persons without developing the general capacity to cherish, and regard important, many things for their own sakes. The major obstacle to humility before persons is self-importance, a tendency to measure the significance of everything by its relation to oneself and those with whom one identifies. The processes by which we overcome self-importance are doubtless many and complex, but it seems unlikely that they are exclusively concerned with how we relate to other people and animals. Learning humility requires learning to feel that something matters besides what will affect oneself and one's circle of associates. What leads a child to care about what happens to a lost hamster or a stray dog he will not see again is likely also to generate concern for a lost toy or a favorite tree where he used to live. Learning to value things for their own sake, and to count what affects them important aside from their utility, is not the same as judging them to have some intuited objective property, but it is necessary to the development of humility and it seems likely to take place in experiences with nonsentient nature as well as with people and animals. If a person views all nonsentient nature merely as a resource, then it seems unlikely that he has developed the capacity needed to overcome self-importance.

IV

This last argument, unfortunately, has its limits. It presupposes an empirical connection between experiencing nature and overcoming self-importance, and this may be challenged. Even if experiencing nature promotes humility before others, there may be other ways people can develop such humility in a world of concrete, glass, and plastic. If not, perhaps all that is needed is limited experience of nature in one's early, developing years; mature adults, having overcome youthful self-importance, may live well enough in artificial surroundings. More importantly, the argument does not fully capture the spirit of the intuition that an ideal person stands humbly before nature. That idea is not simply that experiencing nature tends to foster proper humility before other people; it is, in part, that natural surroundings encourage and are appropriate to an ideal sense of oneself as part of the natural world. Standing alone in the forest, after months in the city, is not merely good as a means of curbing one's arrogance before others; it reinforces and fittingly expresses one's acceptance of oneself as a natural being.

Previously we considered only one aspect of proper humility, namely, a sense of one's relative importance with respect to other human beings. Another aspect, I think, is a kind of *self-acceptance*. This involves acknowledging, in more than a merely intellectual way, that we are the sort of creatures that we are. Whether one is self-accepting is not so much a matter of how one attributes *importance* comparatively to oneself, other people, animals, plants, and other things as it is a matter of understanding, facing squarely, and responding appropriately to who and what one is, e.g., one's powers and limits, one's affinities with other beings and differences from them, one's unalterable nature and one's freedom to change. Self-acceptance is not merely intellectual awareness, for one can be intellectually aware that one is growing old and will eventually die while nevertheless behaving in a thousand foolish ways that reflect a refusal to acknowledge these facts. On the other hand, self-acceptance is not passive resignation, for refusal to pursue what one truly wants within one's limits is a failure to accept the freedom and power one has. Particular behaviors, like dying one's gray hair and dressing like those 20 years younger, do not *necessarily* imply lack of self-acceptance, for there could be reasons for acting in these ways other than the wish to hide from oneself what one really is. One fails to accept oneself when the patterns of behavior and emotion are rooted in a desire to disown and deny features of oneself, to pretend to oneself that they are not there. This is not to say that a self-accepting person makes no value judgments about himself, that he likes all facts about himself, wants equally to develop and display them; he can, and should feel remorse for his past misdeeds and strive to change his current vices. The point is that he does not disown them, pretend that they do not exist or are facts about something other than himself. Such pretense is incompatible with proper humility because it is seeing oneself as better than one is.

Self-acceptance of this sort has long been considered a human excellence, under various names, but what has it to do with preserving nature? There is, I think, the following connection. As human beings we are part of nature, living, growing, declining, and dying by natural laws similar to those governing other living beings; despite our awesomely distinctive human powers, we share many of the needs, limits, and liabilities of animals and plants. These facts are neither good nor bad in themselves, aside from personal preference and varying conventional values. To say this is to utter a truism which few will deny, but to accept these facts, as facts about oneself, is not so easy—or so common. Much of what naturalists deplore about our increasingly artificial world reflects, and encourages, a denial of these facts, an unwillingness to avow them with equanimity.

Like the Victorian lady who refuses to look at her own nude body, some would like to create a world of less transitory stuff, reminding us only of our intellectual and social nature, never calling to mind our affinities with "lower" living creatures. The "denial of death," to which psychiatrists call attention, reveals an attitude incompatible with the sort of self-acceptance which philosophers, from the ancients to Spinoza and on, have admired as a human excellence. My suggestion is not merely that experiencing nature causally promotes such self-acceptance, but also that those who fully accept themselves as part of the natural world lack the common drive to disassociate themselves from nature by replacing natural environments with artificial ones. A storm in the wilds helps us to appreciate our animal vulnerability, but, equally important, the reluctance to experience it may *reflect* an unwillingness to accept this aspect of ourselves. The person who is too ready to destroy the ancient redwoods may lack humility, not so much in the sense that he exaggerates his importance relative to others, but rather in the sense that he tries to avoid seeing himself as one among many natural creatures.

V

My suggestion so far has been that, though indifference to nonsentient nature is not itself a moral vice, it is likely to reflect either ignorance, a self-importance, or a lack of self-acceptance which we must overcome to have proper humility. A similar idea might be developed connecting attitudes toward nonsentient nature with other human excellences. For example, one might argue that indifference to nature reveals a lack of either an aesthetic sense or some of the natural roots of gratitude.

When we see a hillside that has been gutted by strip miners or the garden replaced by asphalt, our first reaction is probably, "How ugly!" The scenes assault our aesthetic sensibilities. We suspect that no one with a keen sense of beauty could have left such a sight. Admittedly not everything in nature strikes us as beautiful, or even aesthetically interesting, and sometimes a natural scene is replaced with a more impressive architectural masterpiece. But this is not usually the situation in the problem cases which environmentalists are most concerned about. More often beauty is replaced with ugliness.

At this point our critic may well object that, even if he does lack a sense of beauty, this is no moral vice. His cost/benefit calculations take into account the pleasure others may derive from seeing the forests, etc., and so why should he be faulted?

Some might reply that, despite contrary philosophical traditions, aesthetics and morality are not so distinct as commonly supposed. Appreciation of beauty, they may argue, is a human excellence which morally ideal persons should try to develop. But, setting aside this controversial position, there still may be cause for moral concern about those who have no aesthetic response to nature. Even if aesthetic sensibility is not itself a moral virtue, many of the capacities of mind and heart which it presupposes may be ones which are also needed for an appreciation of other people. Consider, for example, curiosity, a mind open to novelty, the ability to look at things from unfamiliar perspectives, empathetic imagination, interest in details, variety, and order, and emotional freedom from the immediate and the practical. All these, and more, seem necessary to aesthetic sensibility, but they are also traits which a person needs to be fully sensitive to people of all sorts. The point is not that a moral person must be able to distinguish beautiful from ugly people; the point is rather that unresponsiveness to what is beautiful, awesome, dainty, dumpy, and otherwise aesthetically interesting in nature probably reflects a lack of the awareness of mind and spirit necessary to appreciate the best in human beings.

The anti-environmentalist, however, may refuse to accept the charge that he lacks aesthetic sensibility. If he claims to appreciate 17th-century miniature portraits, but to abhor natural wildernesses, he will hardly be convincing. Tastes vary, but aesthetic sense is not *that* selective. He may, instead, insist that he *does* appreciate natural beauty. He spends his vacations, let us suppose, hiking in the Sierras, photographing wildflowers, and so on. He might press his argument as follows: "I enjoy natural beauty as much as anyone, but I fail to see what this has to do with preserving the environment independently of human enjoyment and use. Nonsentient nature is a resource, but one of its best uses is to give us pleasure. I take this into account when I calculate the costs and benefits of preserving a park, planting a garden, and so on. But the problem you raised explicitly set aside to preserve nature as a means to enjoyment. I say, let us enjoy nature fully while we can, but if all sentient beings were to die tomorrow, we might as well blow up all plant life as well. A redwood grove that no one can use or enjoy is utterly worthless."

The attitude expressed here, I suspect, is not a common one, but it represents a philosophical challenge. The beginnings of a reply may be found in the following. When a person takes joy in something, it is a common (and perhaps natural) response to come to cherish it. To cherish something is not simply to be happy with it at the moment, but to care for it for its own sake. This is not to say that one necessarily sees it as having feelings and so wants it to feel good; nor does it imply that one judges the thing to have Moore's intrinsic value. One simply wants the thing to survive and (when appropriate) to thrive, and not simply for its utility. We see this attitude repeatedly regarding mementos. They are not simply valued as a means to remind us of happy occasions; they come to be valued for their own sake. Thus, if someone really took joy in the natural environment, but was prepared to blow it up as soon as sentient life ended, he would lack this common human tendency to cherish what enriches our lives. While this response is not itself a moral virtue, it may be a natural basis of the virtue we call "gratitude." People who have no tendency to cherish things that give them pleasure may be poorly disposed to respond gratefully to persons who are good to them. Again the connection is not one of logical necessity, but it may nevertheless be important. A nonreligious person unable to "thank" anyone for the beauties of nature may nevertheless feel "grateful" in a sense; and I suspect that the person who feels no such "gratitude" toward nature is unlikely to show proper gratitude toward people.

Suppose these conjectures prove to be true. One may wonder what is the point of considering them. Is it to disparage all those who view nature merely as a resource? To do so, it seems, would be unfair, for, even if this attitude typically stems from deficiencies which affect one's attitudes toward sentient beings, there may be exceptions and we have not shown that their view of nonsentient nature is itself blameworthy. But when we set aside questions of blame and inquire what sorts of human traits we want to encourage, our reflections become relevant in a more positive way. The point is not to insinuate that all anti-environmentalists are defective, but to see that those who value such traits as humility, gratitude, and sensitivity to others have reason to promote the love of nature.

NOTES

I thank Gregory Kavka, Catherine Harlow, the participants at a colloquium at the University of Utah, and the referees for *Environmental Ethics,* Dale Jamieson and Donald Scherer, for helpful comments on earlier drafts of this paper.

1. When I use the expression "the natural environment," I have in mind the sort of examples with which I began. There is also a broad sense, as Hume and Mill noted, in which all that occurs, miracles aside, is "natural." As will be evident, I shall use "natural" in a narrower, more familiar sense.
2. I assume here that having a right presupposes having interests in a sense which in turn presupposes a capacity to desire, suffer, etc. Since my main concern lies in another direction, I do not argue the point, but merely note that some regard it as debatable.
3. G. E. Moore, *Principia Ethica* (Cambridge: Cambridge University Press, 1903), and *Ethics* (London: Holt, 1912).
4. G. E. Moore, "Is Goodness a Quality?" in *Philosophical Papers* (London: George Allen & Unwin, 1959), pp. 95–97.
5. T. Tildon, "Even This Shall Pass Away," in *The Best Loved Poems of the American People,* ed. Hazel Felleman (Garden City, New York: Doubleday, 1936).
6. An exception, apparently, was Kant, who thought "the starry heavens" sublime and compared them with "the moral law within," but did not for all that see our species as comparatively insignificant.
7. By "proper humility" I mean that sort and degree of humility that is a morally admirable character trait. How precisely to define this is, of course, a controversial matter; but the point for present purposes is just to set aside obsequiousness, false modesty, underestimation of one's abilities, and the like.

DISCUSSION QUESTIONS

1. Do you think Hill is successful in arguing that moral uneasiness about the destruction of nature cannot be adequately dealt with except by looking at the character of persons? Explain.
2. What is a proper humility of persons before the natural world? Is it possible to be too humble, that is servile, with respect to nature?
3. Assess the role of self-acceptance in Hill's discussion. What is self-acceptance and is it a good thing? Why?
4. Think of someone you know who knows a lot about the natural world. What aspects of his or her character do you admire and is it connected to that person's knowledge of nature?

You Decide!

1. URBAN ECOLOGY

Just as the term *industrial ecology* causes one to look twice (see You Decide!, Chapter 7), *urban ecology* sounds similarly odd; it combines into a single thought two seemingly incompatible notions: cities and nature. But we have a lot to learn from nature in the construction of our cities. Today's megacities, defined as cities containing more than 10 million people, are the largest structures human beings have created on the planet, though "created" might not be the correct term, since that implies planning. Mostly, cities have just grown haphazardly. And grown they have. We are now basically an urban species—*Homo urbanus*—since approximately half the world's population now lives in urban areas. By 2020, two-thirds of humanity will live in cities. The urbanization of humanity is one of the most dramatic events in our history, rivaling perhaps our ability to control fire. Thus, the conditions of urban living have vast implication for the well-being of humanity.

The great cities of antiquity, such as Ur, Damascus, and Babylon, drew material support from their immediate surroundings, and when the local environment was depleted the cities declined. Because transportation was limited in ancient times, it would simply have been too difficult to haul from great distances all the goods, water, fuel, building material, and food necessary to keep a high concentration of people alive once resources in the immediate vicinity were used up. Ur, for example, rediscovered in the late 1800s after being buried by desert sands for centuries in what is now Iraq, is thought to be some 4,000 years old, one of the world's first cities. When excavated, a thick layer of mud was found throughout, the apparent result of run-off from deforestation of the surrounding countryside to supply the city with wood.

Today cities are no less vulnerable to the condition of their surroundings. The major difference between modern cities and ancient cities is that modern cities draw their resources—water, food, energy, material—from a huge geographical region, not just the immediate surroundings. Thanks to our ability to move vast quantities of things around (largely because of internal combustion engines) modern cities have lifelines that tether them to the rest of the world. But they are still subject to the same basic environmental limitations that governed ancient urban centers.

A city can be conceived as an organism or an ecosystem (see Chapter 7), with input and outflow, and even a sort of metabolism. How much fuel, food, water, building material, and resources of all sorts come in and how much garbage, hot air, polluted water, CO_2, and waste go out? Quantifying these dimensions of urban living will establish what is known as the "ecological footprint" of a city.

Discussion Questions

1. How might you define a "sustainable city"? Is it a worthy goal? Why?
2. Can you think of ways to improve a city's "metabolism"? (Urban agriculture?)
3. Why do people live in cities?
4. Do you think the urbanization of humanity is good or bad for the environment? How about for us?

2. DDT

Dichlor-diphenyl-trichloroethane, or as we commonly know it, DDT, is part of our collective environmental consciousness. It represents the shortsighted and misguided attempts of humanity to operate with arrogant disregard for the workings of nature. This is the message in Rachel Carson's *Silent Spring.* Published in 1962, this eloquently written account of the harmful effects of DDT is often cited as the beginning of the environmental movement. Carson claims,

> Along with the possibility of the extinction of mankind by nuclear war, the central problem of our age has therefore become the contamination of man's total environment with such substances of incredible potential for harm—substances that accumulate in the tissues of plants and animals and even penetrate the germ cells to shatter or alter the very material of heredity upon which the shape of the future depends.

She is referring to DDT, now banned in the United States and much of the world. Were it not for Carson, we very likely would have silent springs, springs where no birds sing because they had been killed by DDT.

Though we tend to see DDT as a categorical evil, it is responsible for saving more human lives than any other manufactured substance, including penicillin. Malaria, an ancient scourge of humanity, routinely killed millions of people worldwide. DDT kills the mosquito that transmits malaria. In large portions of the world, malaria has been either eliminated or its incidence very dramatically reduced, thanks to DDT. In India, for example, malaria used to kill some 800,000 people a year; by the 1960s fatalities had dropped to almost zero. Paul Muller, the scientist who first synthesized DDT, received a Nobel Prize in 1948.

Typically, a solution of DDT is sprayed on the inside walls of a house. After a mosquito feeds on someone, it lights on the wall to digest its meal, absorbing traces of DDT through its feet, which subsequently kill it. To break the cycle of the disease, the mosquito population must be vigorously suppressed for several years for the malaria virus to die for lack of hosts (the virus lives in human beings as well as other animals; mosquitoes are the "vector" for the virus). Because DDT exerts tremendous selective pressure on the mosquito population, however, a new resistant strain of mosquito will inevitably develop, requiring even more DDT to kill it. But between the initial spraying of DDT and the emergence of a resistant strain of mosquito, enough time elapses for the malaria virus to die. Mosquito populations can then return to normal without consequence, for there are no infected people upon which they can feed; the people have either died or gotten better.

Malaria still kills approximately 2.5 million people a year, and DDT remains the most cost-effective way of controlling the disease. Worldwide, the incidence of malaria is on the rise. A number of factors are responsible, including, some surmise, global warming, which affords the species of mosquito most responsible for the transmission of malaria a wider range within which to operate.

Discussion Questions

1. Is there an important distinction to be made between agricultural uses of DDT and malaria control? What might it be?
2. Should DDT be completely banned?

FOR FURTHER READING ON GLOBAL WARMING AND THE STATE OF THE WORLD

State of the World: Series published by Worldwatch Institute; W. W. Norton & Co New York.

Creating Sustainable Cities, 1999 by Herbert Girardet, for The Schumacher Society J. W. Arrowsmith Ltd., Bristol, UK.

"The Mosquito Killer; Millions of people owe their lives to Fred Soper. Why isn't he a hero?" By Malcolm Gladwell, *The New Yorker,* July 2, 2001.

Visit the Intergovernmental Panel on Climate Change (IPCC) website: www.ipcc.ch

CHAPTER 9

Environmental Economics and Policy

MODERN TIMES: YOUR GOVERNMENT AT WORK—EPA

The Environmental Protection Agency was created in 1970 by an executive order from President Nixon. Concerned that Democrats might use a still new but amazingly widespread (and therefore politically significant) environmental awareness to their advantage in the upcoming election, Nixon sought to demonstrate that the Republican Party cared about the environment too. Though created largely for political ends at a time when government found itself playing catch-up to public sentiment, Nixon's executive order placed under one administrative structure a variety of programs concerning the environment. Other departments of the federal government, such as Interior, Agriculture, and Energy retain some regulatory authority in environmental matters, but the EPA has primary responsibility to oversee regulations concerning air and water quality, hazardous waste disposal (including radioactive waste), chemicals, and toxic substances. It is now the largest federal regulatory agency.

The EPA is responsible for implementing 10 major pieces of environmental legislation passed by Congress. Congress has the easy part. As elected representatives, the members of Congress respond to public concern by drafting bills. But the lofty language of legislation has to be transformed into the nitty-gritty details of regulatory standards, and this is the job of the EPA. To do so requires vast technical and scientific expertise, as well as political and legal sophistication, since implementing environmental legislation invariably has economic consequences. The regulatory standards proposed by the EPA are routinely challenged by industries affected, thus guaranteeing years of litigation, compromise, missed deadlines, and selective enforcement.

The EPA implements and administers the Clean Air Act, which mandates automobile exhaust emission standards as well as air quality standards; the Clean Water Act, which concerns standards for all discharges into U.S. waters; the Safe Drinking Water Act; and the Toxic Substances Control Act, which requires the EPA to test chemicals and regulate their use. The EPA also has oversight of the Comprehensive Environmental Response, Compensation, and Liability Act, known as "Superfund," which is a $ 1.6 billion trust to pay to clean up hazardous sites.

The impact on our way of life of these and other pieces of legislation administered by the EPA is huge. Consider, for example, what is at stake in establishing automobile emission standards, as required by the Clean Air Act. The EPA has to deal with the automobile industry as well as the oil industry—two giants that virtually define contemporary American life. Because every EPA proposal to increase engine efficiency or to tinker with gasoline additives to reduce toxic emissions (see introductory discussion about gasoline in Chapter 5) will have enormous economic consequences, and be legally enforceable, how the EPA functions, whether it has sufficient funds to operate effectively, who administers it, and how its regulations are drafted and enforced are all important matters. Will the agency have the regulatory independence required to carry out its mandate, which is really our mandate since we impose these regulations on ourselves through our elected officials, or will the agency be mired in litigation and staffed by people "too close" to the industries they are called upon to regulate? The history of the EPA is mixed.

When he created the EPA, President Nixon appointed William Ruckelhaus, a young attorney from the U.S. Justice Department, its first administrator. Ruckelhaus moved quickly and aggressively against some of the worst violators. In the early 1970s, there were plenty to choose from, so even though politics undoubtedly played a role in who the EPA targeted (democratic mayoral administrations in Atlanta, Detroit, and Cleveland for sewage discharge were early targets, for example), still, by making a public spectacle of major polluters the EPA established itself as a tough regulatory agency, not to be pushed around by industry or special interests.

Things changed dramatically in 1981 with the election of Ronald Reagan as president, who ran on a promise of less government. He appointed Anne Burford to administer the EPA. She sought to ease enforcement of environmental laws and placed more emphasis on industry's voluntary compliance to EPA-mandated standards. Moreover, she oversaw a 29 percent decrease in the EPA's operating budget and an incredible 45 percent reduction in its enforcement budget, as well as a staff reduction of 3,000. Perhaps most damaging was that under Burford many EPA appointments came directly from the industries regulated and were apparently made largely on ideological grounds. The chief EPA lawyer was formerly a lawyer with Exxon; the assistant administrator in charge of air quality was a former lobbyist for a paper and pulp manufacturer; and Burford's chief of staff came from the building material industry. As a result, the agency became highly politicized, ineffective, and demoralized. A series of scandals forced Burford to resign, and William Ruckelhaus took over for a second time in 1983, quickly replacing Burford's ideologically appointed subordinates with people who had relevant regulatory experience. There have been four chief administrators since then, and although the EPA has recovered some of its luster, worries remain about its ability to function effectively because it has an enormous administrative burden spread out among many aspects of environmental management.

One source of concern is the structure of the agency, divided into separate departments that each deal with a particular "medium" for environmental protection: water, air, radioactive waste, chemicals, pesticides and toxic substances, Superfund, and so on. But environmental problems do not come neatly packaged so that they can be farmed out to the appropriate subdivision; they often involve several media simultaneously. Acid rain, for example is not just a water problem. Without some coordinating oversight among the different subdivisions, when a problem is addressed by one department it might shift matters to another department. The danger exists of simply moving a problem around rather than dealing with it effectively. Consider, for example, the task of regulating hazardous wastes from thousands of electroplating companies. If the companies were permitted to flush untreated wastewater into municipal water systems, residual metals would kill bacteria necessary for sewage treatment. So EPA water discharge regulations prohibit that. But removing the metal creates a toxic sludge that, according to different EPA regulations, cannot be buried in landfills. A similar problem occurs when a toxic river bottom is dredged, leaving toxic mud to deal with on land. Another example: acid rain apparently leaches metals from the soil, creating a hazard for drinking water. But acid rain concerns are addressed by the air quality department, while drinking water is regulated by a different EPA department. An environmental issue that cuts across several media—air, water, land—can fall under separate, sometimes incompatible, EPA regulations.

Not only is the EPA internally fragmented, but also regulatory authority for environmental matters as a whole is divided among other departments of the federal government, such as Interior, Agriculture, and Energy. This virtually assures bureaucratic confusion as different departments struggle to coordinate their regulations, as well as engage in the inevitable maneuvering over turf, authority, funding, and personnel. In the early 1980s, for example, the EPA, the Montana Department of Agriculture, and the U.S. Fish and Wildlife Service (an agency within the Department of Interior) all issued conflicting regulations concerning the consumption of wild ducks exposed to a particular pesticide.

Is the EPA meeting its stated mission, which is "to protect human health and to safeguard the natural environment—air, water, and land—upon which life depends"? As with most questions of this sort, it depends upon how one defines *success*. The costs of EPA-administered policies almost always seem larger than the benefits, since the costs tend to be immediate and are easier to calculate, while the benefits are more diffuse and long term. Higher prices at the gas pump now, for example, may lead to improved air quality, discernible only after years of policy enforcement and perhaps just to scientists measuring pollutants in parts per million. Forgoing immediate returns for anticipated benefits is never easy. Critics of EPA policies routinely complain about the uncertainty of the benefits because scientific studies upon which the regulations depend are frequently incomplete or, given the nature and scope of environmental problems, uncertain. As an exasperated administrator once said, "Our scientists told me that we can defend any standard between 150 and 250 parts per million. So pick a number."

In some respects, the EPA is meeting its mission. Experts claim that nationwide air quality regulations are having an effect, that lead, sulfur dioxide, carbon monoxide, particulate matter, ozone, and other smog-causing pollutants are significantly lower today than they were when the Clean Air Act was enacted in 1970. But according to some analysts, water quality nationwide has not improved significantly and Superfund cleanup of hazardous waste sites is haphazard. Analysts differ among themselves regarding the effectiveness of EPA policies. But this much can be said: Without the EPA, things would likely be much worse. That enforcement of EPA regulations has generated environmental improvement does not mean that things are fine now, since we may have gone from very bad to just bad (at least rivers do not catch on fire now, as the Cayahoga River in Cleveland did in 1969). It was easy to address the worst problems, but now our commitment to environmental regulation will be tested as the problems become less visible. It is one thing to stop polluters from turning a river into a stinking cesspool, but what costs will we impose on ourselves to reduce the emission of invisible gases measured in parts per million? Furthermore, it becomes increasingly difficult (read: expensive) to control proportionally more of a pollutant, so rather than rid the environment of, say, lead, we have to decide what level of lead we are willing to live with, and this requires risk assessment. What level of risk is acceptable and who decides?

Many critics of the EPA attribute its mixed success to early reliance on a regulatory approach that was virtually bound to fail. Under a so-called command-and-control model, what the EPA commands, we do, under pain of penalty (fines). Such strong-arm tactics irritate regulated industries, which then seek to influence Congress to amend what they regard as stifling regulations. Under command-and-control regulation, regulated industries have no incentive to comply quickly and efficiently and regulations are routinely challenged in courts (which can take years to settle), and penalties, if they are paid at all, can be delayed in all sorts of ways and, in the end, might just become a cost of doing business. Because command-and-control regulation causes so much resistance (without being all that effective), the EPA is becoming more sensitive to market mechanisms as a way of managing its programs. There is still a strong element of command and control, since industries are regulated, but economic incentives are increasingly used to motivate industry to meet mandated pollution goals. The basic idea is to make pollution prevention and reduction economically attractive. For example, a factory might be imagined to exist in regulatory "bubble" and thus permitted to increase emission of a toxic substance in one place if it reduces it in another, so there is no net increase.

Another initiative allows for "pollution credits" as a way to reach mandated standards. It works like this: Imagine that, according to EPA standards, 100 units of a hypothetical pollutant are allowed. The EPA will then issue 100 pollution permits for the relevant manufacturers to purchase on the open market. Each permit will allow the manufacturer to produce one unit of the pollutant. The more permits one has, the more one may legally pollute—but at an increasing cost. It will now make economic sense for manufacturers to reduce their emissions and so reduce their production costs. What was once an "externality," that is, a cost not born by the producer, is forced to become a production cost. "Good" manufacturers that figure out ways to reduce emissions (thus saving money because they do not have to buy so many permits) can sell their unused pollution allowances to "bad" companies that either cannot comply so readily or choose not to, thus driving up their production costs and ultimately making them nonviable economically.

Though seemingly straightforward in theory, the verdict is still out on the effectiveness of such programs. Problems need to be addressed. For example, how are the pollution permits to be distributed initially? Are they to be auctioned off to the highest bidders? What if a certain manufacturer buys them all (or a disproportionate share), thus effectively controlling the market because nobody else can legally release that pollutant into the environment? Are the permits to be initially distributed equally among the relevant polluters? That would not seem fair, since not all of them are the same size or pollute to the same extent. And distributing them based on past pollution records will require very detailed knowledge of just how much pollution a manufacturer produces and, it would seem, reward those who pollute a lot, since they would presumably get more permits. These problems are not insurmountable but indicate the complexity of a pollution permit scheme.

Environmentalists sometimes complain that any pollution credit program amounts to a right to pollute, denying that there ought to be such a right. But this complaint seems overstated because some level of pollution is an inescapable part of production, or at least production that makes affordable products. We *could* in theory make products with zero spillover into the environment, but they would be very expensive. The environment can absorb some level of pollution, so why impose those costs on ourselves if we do not have to? If we are going to have a modern industrial society—and that is not an idle question to raise—the trick is to minimize pollution, consistent with other goals and values of a modern society. Apparently, though, we want our cake and to eat it too; we want a consumer-driven economy with cheap prices and a pristine environment. That would be ideal, perhaps, but it is not achievable. But we can aim in that direction. Minimally, pollution credits are a way of trying to make manufacturers more responsible for the costs of their activities while at the same time rewarding those who can function most efficiently. While the *true* production costs to the environment are not addressed, such an absolute reckoning seems unnecessary. Perhaps a counterargument to this view would insist on the intrinsic values in nature affected by our economic activities, but even so it is not clear why there cannot be trade-offs. If on occasion we allow people (who are intrinsically valuable) to be negatively affected for the good of others, why not permit the same sort of thing to occur between our economy and nature? Environmentalist opposition to pollution permits thus may display an absolutist valuation of nature, one that admits of no compromise or balancing with other values.

So will the EPA live up to its mission to protect human health and to safeguard the natural environment? We have been so terribly abusive of the environment that we cannot expect miracles overnight. The amelioration of environmental problems bears a structural similarity to the problems themselves—they are mostly incremental, often hard to notice, but cumulative; over time lots of small steps begin to add up to something significant. Let us hope that through the EPA we are taking lots of small steps in the right direction.

PHILOSOPHICAL ASPECTS OF ENVIRONMENTAL REGULATION

The job of the EPA and other governmental regulatory agencies is to transform legislation into enforceable regulation, or specific rules governing behavior. But how is this supposed to occur? To answer this question will take us into questions about the basis of regulation, the proper role of government in our lives, and what it means to be a citizen. We shall see that though the issues are complex, environmental philosophy has a crucial and legitimate role in environmental regulation, for in the end we are dealing with competing visions of human nature and the good life.

For many people involved with issues of public policy, the justification for all government regulation is that it is needed to correct market failures. A market failure is a deviation from what in economic theory is taken to be an ideal market. In an ideal (hence nonexistent) market, people are purely rational (that is, self-interested), completely informed, and able to engage in voluntary exchanges for mutual benefit with other similarly abstract perfected individuals. Economists say a market where voluntary exchanges among individuals can increase their mutual satisfaction is an "inefficient" one, the term *efficient* being used in an unusual technical sense. For example, if you are willing to pay to have your lawn mowed and I am willing to mow it, then an inefficiency exists; we will each be better off (read: more satisfied) if I mow your lawn and you pay me. An existing market inefficiency has been exploited by our transaction, thus raising our level of satisfaction; I get money and you get your lawn mowed. In a maximally efficient market, by definition, no such further exchanges are possible. We are each as satisfied as possible under the circumstances; hence any exchanges in a maximally efficient market must be either involuntary or result from irrationality or ignorance. (Note: A maximally efficient market is thus not the same as a market where everyone is satisfied, for it seems possible that the conditions under which no further exchanges could increase satisfaction might remain rather grim. A prison camp might be a maximally efficient market.)

The laissez-faire (literally, to allow to do) marketplace, the darling of so much economic theory, was articulated by the father of free market capitalism, Adam Smith, in his great work, *Inquiry into the Nature and Causes of the Wealth of Nations,* published in 1776. In Smith's memorable phrase, each of us, though motivated only by self-interest, is nevertheless led by "an invisible hand" of the marketplace to maximize the satisfaction of all. The person who sells you shoes in all likelihood does not care about you as a person; he or she is doing it just to make money. But the transaction benefits both—you get shoes and the merchant gets money. Theoretically, now you are both better off than before, provided you acted freely, rationally, and with perfect knowledge of the shoes you were buying. Now you can appreciate several ways in which an actual market deviates from an ideal one, for you might not have acted rationally (why do you want yet *another* pair of shoes?) and your knowledge of the shoe industry is surely less than perfect (are these the very best ones you could buy for the money you spent?). You might also contemplate the conditions under which a market decision of yours is voluntary; is being moved by the latest fashion, for example, a voluntary decision?

Markets can fail in other ways. The game Monopoly gives us significant insight into the workings of a pure free market. As the game proceeds, somebody begins to accumulate more and more wealth; that person has Boardwalk and Park Place and all the railroads, and gets more and more, while the rest of the players descend into poverty. That is nearly how things were before government regulations made monopolies illegal. Similarly, government steps into the marketplace to regulate wages, working conditions, health and safety standards, professional certification, interstate commerce, food labeling and purity, and on and on. Were it up to the market alone, let the buyer beware—and let the buyer be omniscient. We often like to think that ours is a free market, but it is not; ours is a heavily regulated market. Government regulations are intended to make up for the discrepancy between our actual market, where there are routine failures of rationality, freedom, and knowledge, and an ideal market, where no such imperfections exist. So while our economic ideology is free market capitalism, government regulation is needed to correct real-world imperfections that result largely from limitations on our part. Most of us would be very unhappy in a pure free market.

Environmental regulation, as distinct from other sorts of regulation, is often justified by yet another kind of market failure, namely, the failure of a producer to bear the entire cost of production. The technical term for this is an *externality.* If I can dump my polluted effluent into a nearby river instead of paying to treat it, then I get to dispose of my waste for free. For polluters, the prices charged for what they produce do not really reflect what we as a society have to give up to have their products. In this instance the invisible hand of the marketplace will not increase our collective satisfaction but, rather, the satisfaction of only a few, such as the factory owners, while the rest of us suffer with polluted land, air, and water.

As a society, we might make a calculated trade-off between environmental quality and the prices of goods and services. We might decide that we like low prices better than a clean environment, in which case we would tolerate polluted rivers aware of the trade-off we are making. But increasingly that is not the case; it hardly seems rational considering that our well-being depends upon a clean environment. We realize that pollution is a cost, which means that it is something we have to pay for to get the goods and services we want. And once we recognize pollution as a cost, it must be accounted for when we determine the true costs of production. Manufacturers pass their increased production costs through to us, the consumers, but this, presumably, is how we want it. Would you want more environmental destruction just so you could have low prices? Even today the prices of many things do not reflect the environmental damage required to produce them.

SOME PROBLEMS WITH A MARKET-BASED APPROACH TO ENVIRONMENTAL REGULATION

A market approach to environmental regulation makes a number of huge assumptions. First and most obviously, markets are oriented to satisfying human preferences. Their whole point is to satisfy our consumer desires. This is straightforward anthropocentrism, a view that we have seen to be fraught with difficulties. We cannot simply assume that human beings (persons?) are the only entities with preferences; moreover, if some nonhumans have preferences too, on what grounds are their preferences irrelevant to market decisions made by human beings? Animals cannot function in the marketplace—they do not buy things, comparison shop, seek to further their economic well-being, and all that—but not all human beings can function in the marketplace either. So exactly who or what is covered by a market approach to environmental regulation, and why? (See Chapter 5 for an extended discussion of anthropocentrism.)

In addition to operating uncritically from an anthropocentric perspective, a market approach to environmental regulation holds that our willingness to pay for something is a measure of its value. Edward Mishan, a leading economist who wrote the definitive work on cost–benefit analysis (*Cost Benefit Analysis,* 1976; see below) claims, "In economics . . . the worth or value of a thing to a person is determined simply by what a person is willing to pay for it." Is it true that the value of something to a person can be exhaustively understood in terms of willingness to pay? Let's explore the conception of people assumed by an economic conception of valuation.

Recall how an inefficient market is defined as one where exchanges among perfected hypothetical consumers result in their increased satisfaction (thanks to the "invisible hand"). But can people be usefully conceived just by their wants, desires, preferences, or inclinations, which markets undertake to satisfy? The problem is not so much that actual consumers inevitably fall short of a theoretical ideal, in the way, for instance, any actual circle drawn on paper will fall short of being a perfect circle. The problem is with the ideal itself, for it presupposes a one-dimensional person, namely, someone comprised wholly by their desires such that the satisfaction of those desires is the only source of valuation.

Markets are good at measuring the intensity of preferences—that is another way of talking about consumer willingness to pay—but not all values can be plausibly construed as preferences. Moral matters, for example, are not usefully regarded as preferences to be gauged by willingness to pay. We would hardly think public policy regarding abortion should be determined by how much right-to-lifers are willing to pay to prevent abortions or pro-choicers are willing to pay to allow them. Similarly, the morality of capital punishment does not turn on our willingness to bear the expenses involved, though one does sometimes hear that capital punishment saves money, with the predictable response about how expensive capital trials are, as if the most cost-effective way determines whether or not we are justified in using capital punishment.

Questions that involve justice, truth, and morality have an objective component that cannot be translated into consumer preference. Earth remains the third planet from the sun and $7 + 5 = 12$ no matter how much someone is willing to pay for them to be otherwise. These are objective matters and the subjectivity of personal preference is irrelevant to their being so. Similarly, abortion or capital punishment remain either morally justifiable or unjustifiable, independent of the market or personal preferences, and those practices must, therefore, be evaluated in their own terms, not in terms of the intensity of feelings. Because moral judgments are subject to rational analysis—the assessment of reasons—and what makes something a good or a bad reason is an objective matter, mere personal preferences are irrelevant to morality. No matter how much people may prefer or abhor slavery, the morality of slavery is not decided by assessing the intensity of those feelings. The morality of slavery is to be determined on objective, not subjective, grounds, and it is morally acceptable or unacceptable apart from how we happen to feel.

What does the distinction between reasons and preferences have to do with environmental policy? Since the market is capable of handling only matters that can be translated into personal preferences (willingness to pay), and not all questions of public policy can be plausibly understood as willingness to pay, not all questions of public policy can be assessed by the market alone. Because environmental policy involves moral questions about the environment (that is what this book is about!), environmental policy therefore cannot be reasonably understood in market terms alone. Markets measure only consumer preferences; so if environmental issues involve more than consumer preferences, then environmental issues cannot be handled just by the market. Though seemingly obvious, this conclusion is at odds with the justification for environmental regulation favored by many policy analysts, politicians, economists, and others who see market mechanisms as the only proper way to address environmental problems.

The 18th century political philosopher Jean-Jacques Rousseau drew a sharp distinction between a person concerned just with his or her private affairs and the citizen who is concerned with what is best for the state. The person concerned about his own well-being is irremediably partial, whereas the citizen adopts an impartial perspective in asking not what is good for oneself, but what is good for the state. This distinction between our economic selves and our citizen selves is present in each one of us: We deplore cheap gasoline as we shop around to fill our cars as inexpensively as possible. Markets cater to the consumer, but the citizen responds to something different. The consumer is out to satisfy preferences and will favor policies that allow that to happen easily, whereas the citizen thinks that environmental policy should be based on grand ideas like the intrinsic value of nature, the moral standing of natural objects, the extent to which nature is like us, or the aesthetic or religious values at stake; in other words, on what is worthy or right, true, just, beautiful, correct. The consumer is moved by intensity of feeling, whereas the citizen is moved by rational argumentation; the consumer makes no claims about truth, whereas the citizen claims to know what is worthy or right. Environmental policy that considers our willingness to pay as the sole source of valuation not only denies our personhood by making us feelers rather than thinkers, but it also makes the further mistake of conflating preferences and reasons. Consumer preference as the sole basis for environmental policy is thus deeply destructive to the state as a democratic institution, for it seeks to substitute the consumer for the citizen.

Proponents of a market approach to environmental regulation might appeal to utilitarianism as the underlying moral justification for their view. Recall from Chapter 1 that utilitarians seek to maximize the happiness for all concerned. Markets, someone might claim, seek to do that by satisfying consumer preferences. We are all happier by having our preferences met, or so it is claimed. But is preference satisfaction the same as happiness? On only the crudest views will they be identical, since it seems plausible to hold that the satisfaction of some preferences will not contribute to happiness. The drug addict, for example, strongly desires to take drugs, but will taking drugs lead to happiness? The very intelligibility of this question shows that happiness and preference satisfaction are not identical. We can distinguish between what someone prefers (wants, desires, etc.) and what is in their interest, understood as their good. Not all preference satisfaction contributes to their good; and if happiness is connected to realizing one's good, rather than simply having one's desires met, then happiness will involve more than mere preference satisfaction. Happiness and preference satisfaction may significantly overlap, but the ideas remain distinct. So it seems that a proponent of a market approach to environmental policy who appeals to utilitarianism as an ultimate moral justification is making an unwarranted assumption by conflating preference satisfaction and happiness. Human happiness is likely more a matter of rational autonomy, rather than simply satisfaction of desires. We should, therefore, be skeptical of a market-approach to environmental policy and of whether markets alone can make us happy.

COST–BENEFIT ANALYSIS

A cost–benefit analysis seeks to assess the costs relative to the benefits of a proposed action. It appears to be the model of rational planning because it undertakes to compare what we have to give up to get what we want. Clearly, if we have to give up more than we get, it is not worth doing. You engage in an intuitive sort of cost–benefit analysis every time you contemplate the price of something; is the movie ticket worth $10 to you? However, intuition is not a good guide for large projects costing many millions (or billions) of dollars, affecting the lives of many, and possibly causing social change. This requires a more formal approach to the question of costs and benefits. Cost–benefit analyses for major undertakings are themselves major undertakings (might this lead to an infinite regress of cost–benefit analyses?).

The costs and the benefits must be expressed in similar terms, otherwise we are comparing apples and oranges. That the costs and benefits be commensurable is both the strength and weakness of cost–benefit analyses. If they can be sized up in equivalent terms, then comparing them should tell us what we want to know; and if they cannot, then such an analysis will not tell us what we want to know. Costs and benefits are almost invariably expressed economically—money. Clearly, then, one major question over the use of cost–benefit analysis is whether the costs and benefits can be expressed in monetary terms. This question is particularly salient in environmental matters, since a dollar value must be put on things such as a lower concentration of a pollutant, a clear vista, and the like. In the end, it all comes down to what we are willing to pay to achieve those things. A house with a pleasing view costs more than a similar one without a view, so we can get a broad sense of what people are willing to pay for aspects of environmental quality, according to proponents of this approach. However, as discussed above, even if willingness to pay can somehow be determined, the identification of all value with preference appears fundamentally misguided.

In addition to theoretical worries about the appropriateness of cost–benefit analysis for certain issues, there are pressing practical problems in its use. Since costs are frequently easier to determine than benefits, which may be diffuse and long range, especially for environmental matters, cost–benefit analyses tend to favor the status quo, since it will seem that we are spending good money now for uncertain benefits in the future. Do we really need to spend all that money to reduce the emission from 200 parts per million to 100 parts per million? What if we did not do that? Would more people die? Cost–benefit analyses thus raise questions of risk assessment, which gets into the uncomfortable area of the dollar value of a human life. We could, for example, rid the environment of anthropogenic lead or sulfur dioxide, thus sparing health problems for many people, but the cost of such an undertaking would be staggering. The entire productive capacity of the economy and all our efforts would have to be myopically and bizarrely focused on this one project, which would become the single organizing principle of our lives. If this strikes you as absurd, then you have decided that ridding the environment of those pollutants is not worth the effort. The benefits are not worth the cost.

In 1981, President Reagan issued an executive order mandating cost–benefit analyses for all major pieces of regulation. According to the executive order, "Regulatory action shall not be undertaken unless the potential benefits to society from regulation outweigh the potential costs to society." While a seemingly sensible requirement in the abstract—we just want to make sure society is getting its money's worth—the routine use of cost–benefit analyses had the predictable effect of confounding governmental regulatory agencies. This was part of Reagan's avowed policy of smaller and less obtrusive government by reducing the "regulatory burden" on individuals and the economy. Also, who figures the pluses and minuses matters a great deal. Conscious or not, partisans can exaggerate or minimize. Even proponents of cost–benefit analysis caution against relying on it mechanically, routinely, and uncritically.

Even though cost–benefit analyses can be cynically constructed and manipulated, and even though they are incapable of assessing all that is at stake in a proposed piece of environmental regulation, they still have an important use in social policy formation. Rather than being an initial screen to weed out proposals, they can be used to decide among alternative ways of reaching a goal that has already been decided on other grounds. We might, for example, decide to preserve a section of old-growth forest, not because the recreational benefits outweigh what we can get by selling the lumber, but because we think it is right to do so or because the forest is part of our national heritage; or we might decide to ban killing whales, not because whale watchers are willing to pay more than the whale meat is worth, but because we think it wrong to kill such majestic creatures. Once the decisions have been made for reasons having to do with what is right, just, beautiful, or wise, we can then use cost–benefit analysis to figure out how to get there most effectively.

THE READINGS

The readings for this chapter are organized around questions of policy and environmental regulation.

WILLIAM BAXTER

The Case for Optimal Pollution

William Baxter, who died in 1998, was a widely respected law professor at Stanford University. As assistant attorney general during the Reagan administration, he was the architect of several important government antitrust measures, such as the breakup of AT&T in the early 1980s. Baxter takes a no-nonsense approach to environmental regulation. He is unapologetically anthropocentric, largely because, as he says, no other approach "corresponds to reality."

CRITICAL READING QUESTIONS

1. Why, according to Baxter, should we stop using DDT?
2. How does Baxter defend his anthropocentrism? (What are his six reasons?)
3. On what grounds does Baxter argue that "nature" has no normative connotations? (By "normative connotations" Baxter means "moral." So Baxter is arguing that nature is without moral significance; how does he purport to show this?)
4. What, according to Baxter, follows from abandoning a normative definition of "the natural state"?
5. What is the optimal state of pollution, according to Baxter?
6. How are pollution costs best expressed, according to Baxter?

I start with the modest proposition that, in dealing with pollution, or indeed with any problem, it is helpful to know what one is attempting to accomplish. Agreement on how and whether to pursue a particular objective, such as pollution control, is not possible unless some more general objective has been identified and stated with reasonable precision. We talk loosely of having clean air and clean water, of preserving our wilderness areas, and so forth. But none of these is a sufficiently general objective: Each is more accurately viewed as a means rather than as an end.

With regard to clean air, for example, one may ask, "how clean?" and "what does clean mean?" It is even reasonable to ask, "why have clean air?" Each of these questions is an implicit demand that a more general community goal be stated—a goal sufficiently general in its scope and enjoying sufficiently general assent among the community of actors that such "why" questions no longer seem admissible with respect to that goal.

If, for example, one states as a goal the proposition that "every person should be free to do whatever he wishes in contexts where his actions do not interfere with the interests of other human beings," the speaker is unlikely to be met with a response of "why." The goal may be criticized as uncertain in its implications or difficult to implement, but it is so basic a tenet of our civilization—it reflects a cultural value so broadly shared, at least in the abstract—that the question "why" is seen as impertinent or imponderable or both.

I do not mean to suggest that everyone would agree with the "spheres of freedom" objective just stated. Still less do I mean to suggest that a society could subscribe to four or five such general objectives that would be adequate in their coverage to

---

From *People or Penguins: The Case for Optimal Pollution,* 1974, Columbia University Press, New York. Reprinted with permission of the publisher.

serve as testing criteria by which all other disagreements might be measured. One difficulty in the attempt to construct such a list is that each new goal added will conflict, in certain applications, with each prior goal listed; and thus each goal serves as a limited qualification on prior goals.

Without any expectation of obtaining unanimous consent to them, let me set forth four goals that I generally use as ultimate testing criteria in attempting to frame solutions to problems of human organization. My position regarding pollution stems from these four criteria. If the criteria appeal to you and any part of what appears hereafter does not, our disagreement will have a helpful focus: which of us is correct, analytically, in supposing that his position on pollution would better serve these general goals. If the criteria do not seem acceptable to you, then it is to be expected that our more particular judgments will differ, and the task will then be yours to identify the basic set of criteria upon which your particular judgments rest.

My criteria are as follows:

1. The spheres of freedom criterion stated above.
2. Waste is a bad thing. The dominant feature of human existence is scarcity—our available resources, our aggregate labors, and our skill in employing both have always been, and will continue for some time to be, inadequate to yield to every man all the tangible and intangible satisfactions he would like to have. Hence, none of those resources, or labors, or skills, should be wasted—that is, employed so as to yield less than they might yield in human satisfactions.
3. Every human being should be regarded as an end rather than as a means to be used for the betterment of another. Each should be afforded dignity and regarded as having an absolute claim to an evenhanded application of such rules as the community may adopt for its governance.
4. Both the incentive and the opportunity to improve his share of satisfactions should be preserved to every individual. Preservation of incentive is dictated by the "no-waste" criterion and enjoins against the continuous, totally egalitarian redistribution of satisfactions, or wealth; but subject to that constraint, everyone should receive, by continuous redistribution if necessary, some minimal share of aggregate wealth so as to avoid a level of privation from which the opportunity to improve his situation becomes illusory.

The relationship of these highly general goals to the more specific environmental issues at hand may not be readily apparent, and I am not yet ready to demonstrate their pervasive implications. But let me give one indication of their implications. Recently scientists have informed us that use of DDT in food production is causing damage to the penguin population. For the present purposes let us accept that assertion as an indisputable scientific fact. The scientific fact is often asserted as if the correct implication—that we must stop agricultural use of DDT—followed from the mere statement of the fact of penguin damage. But plainly it does not follow if my criteria are employed.

My criteria are oriented to people, not penguins. Damage to penguins, or sugar pines, or geological marvels is, without more, simply irrelevant. One must go further, by my criteria, and say: Penguins are important because people enjoy seeing them walk about rocks; and furthermore, the well-being of people would be less impaired by halting use of DDT than by giving up penguins. In short, my observations about environmental problems will be people-oriented, as are my criteria. I have no interest in preserving penguins for their own sake.

It may be said by way of objection to this position, that it is very selfish of people to act as if each person represented one unit of importance and nothing else was of any importance. It is undeniably selfish. Nevertheless I think it is the only tenable starting place for analysis for several reasons. First, no other position corresponds to the way most people really think and act—i.e., corresponds to reality.

Second, this attitude does not portend any massive destruction of nonhuman flora and fauna, for people depend on them in many obvious ways, and they will be preserved because and to the degree that humans do depend on them.

Third, what is good for humans is, in many respects, good for penguins and pine trees—clean air for example. So that humans are, in these respects, surrogates for plant and animal life.

Fourth, I do not know how we could administer any other system. Our decisions are either private or collective. Insofar as Mr. Jones is free to act privately, he may give such preferences as he wishes to other forms of life: He may feed birds in winter and do with less himself, and he may even decline to resist an advancing polar bear on the ground that the bear's appetite is more important than those portions of himself that the bear may choose to eat. In short my basic premise does not rule out private altruism to competing life-forms. It does rule out, however, Mr. Jones' inclination to feed Mr. Smith to the bear, however hungry the bear, however despicable Mr. Smith.

Insofar as we act collectively on the other hand, only humans can be afforded an opportunity to participate in the collective decisions. Penguins cannot vote now and are unlikely subjects for the franchise—pine trees more unlikely still. Again each individual is free to cast his vote so as to benefit sugar pines if that is his inclination. But many of the more extreme assertions that one hears from some conservationists amount to tacit assertions that they are specially appointed representatives of sugar pines, and hence that their preferences should be weighted more heavily than the preferences of other humans who do not enjoy equal rapport with "nature." The simplistic assertion that agricultural use of DDT must stop at once because it is harmful to penguins is of that type.

Fifth, if polar bears or pine trees or penguins, like men, are to be regarded as ends rather than means, if they are to count in our calculus of social organization, someone must tell me how much each one counts, and someone must tell me how these life-forms are to be permitted to express their preferences, for I do not know either answer. If the answer is that certain people are to hold their proxies, then I want to know how those proxy-holders are to be selected: self-appointment does not seem workable to me.

Sixth, and by way of summary of all the foregoing, let me point out that the set of environmental issues under discussion—although they raise very complex technical questions of how to achieve any objective—ultimately raise a normative question: what *ought* we to do? Questions of *ought* are unique to the human mind and world—they are meaningless as applied to a nonhuman situation.

I reject the proposition that we *ought* to respect the "balance of nature" or to "preserve the environment" unless the reason for doing so, express or implied, is the benefit of man.

I reject the idea that there is a "right" or "morally correct" state of nature to which we should return. The word "nature" has no normative connotation. Was it "right" or "wrong" for the earth's crust to heave in contortion and create mountains and seas? Was it "right" for the first amphibian to crawl up out of the primordial ooze? Was it "wrong" for plants to reproduce themselves and alter the atmospheric composition in favor of oxygen? For animals to alter the atmosphere in favor of carbon dioxide both by breathing oxygen and eating plants? No answers can be given to these questions because they are meaningless questions.

All this may seem obvious to the point of being tedious, but much of the present controversy over environment and pollution rests on tacit normative assumptions about just such nonnormative phenomena: that it is "wrong" to impair penguins with DDT, but not to slaughter cattle for prime rib roasts. That it is wrong to kill stands of sugar pines with industrial fumes, but not to cut sugar pines and build housing for the poor. Every man is entitled to his own preferred definition of Walden Pond, but there is no definition that has any moral superiority over another, except by reference to the selfish needs of the human race.

From the fact that there is no normative definition of the natural state, it follows that there is no normative definition of clean air or pure water—hence no definition of polluted air—or of pollution—except by reference to the needs of man. The "right" composition of the atmosphere is one which has some dust in it and some lead in it and some hydrogen sulfide in it—just those amounts that attend a sensibly organized society thoughtfully and knowledgeably pursuing the greatest possible satisfaction for its human members.

The first and most fundamental step toward solution of our environmental problems is a clear recognition that our objective is not pure air or water but rather some optimal state of pollution. That step immediately suggests the question: How do we define and attain the level of pollution that will yield the maximum possible amount of human satisfaction?

Low levels of pollution contribute to human satisfaction but so do food and shelter and education and music. To attain ever lower levels of pollution, we must pay the cost of having less of these other things. I contrast that view of the cost of pollution control with the more popular statement that pollution control will "cost" very large numbers of dollars. The popular statement is true in some senses, false in others; sorting out the true and false senses is of some importance. The first step in that sorting process is to achieve a clear understanding of the difference between dollars and resources. Resources are the wealth of our nation; dollars are merely claim checks upon those resources. Resources are of vital importance; dollars are comparatively trivial.

Four categories of resources are sufficient for our purposes: At any given time a nation, or a planet if you prefer, has a stock of labor, of technological skill, of capital goods, and of natural resources (such as mineral deposits, timber, water, land, etc.). These resources can be used in various combinations to yield goods and services of all kinds—in some limited quantity. The quantity will be larger if they are combined efficiently, smaller if combined inefficiently. But in either event the resource stock is limited, the goods and services that they can be made to yield are limited; even the most efficient use of them will yield less than our population, in the aggregate, would like to have.

If one considers building a new dam, it is appropriate to say that it will be costly in the sense that it will require x hours of labor, y tons of steel and concrete, and z amount of capital goods. If these resources are devoted to the dam, then they cannot be used to build hospitals, fishing rods, schools, or electric can openers. That is the meaningful sense in which the dam is costly.

Quite apart from the very important question of how wisely we can combine our resources to produce goods and services is the very different question of how they get distributed—who gets how many goods? Dollars constitute the claim checks which are distributed among people and which control their share of national output. Dollars are nearly valueless pieces of paper except to the extent that they do represent claim checks to some fraction of the output of goods and services. Viewed as claim checks, all the dollars outstanding during any period of time are worth, in the aggregate, the goods and services that are available to be claimed with them during that period—neither more nor less.

It is far easier to increase the supply of dollars than to increase the production of goods and services—printing dollars is easy. But printing more dollars doesn't help because each dollar then simply becomes a claim to fewer goods, i.e., becomes worth less.

The point is this: Many people fall into error upon hearing the statement that the decision to build a dam, or to clean up a river, will cost $\$X$ million. It is regrettably easy to say: "It's only money. This is a wealthy country, and we have lots of money." But you cannot build a dam or clean a river with $\$X$ million—unless you also have a match, you can't even make a fire. One builds a dam or cleans a river by diverting labor and steel and trucks and factories from making one kind of goods to making another. The cost in dollars is merely a shorthand way of describing the extent of the diversion necessary. If we build a dam for $\$X$ million, then we must recognize that we will have $\$X$ million less housing and food and medical care and electric can openers as a result.

Similarly, the costs of controlling pollution are best expressed in terms of the other goods we will have to give up to do the job. This is not to say the job should not be done. Badly as we need more housing, more medical care, and more can openers, and more symphony orchestras, we could do with somewhat less of them, in my judgment at least, in exchange for somewhat cleaner air and rivers. But that is the nature of the trade-off, and analysis of the problem is advanced if that unpleasant reality is kept in mind. Once the trade-off relationship is clearly perceived, it is possible to state in a very general way what the optimal level of pollution is. I would state it as follows:

People enjoy watching penguins. They enjoy relatively clean air and smog-free vistas. Their health is improved by relatively clean water and air. Each of these benefits is a type of good or service. As a society we would be well advised to give up one washing machine if the resources that would have gone into that washing machine can yield greater human satisfaction when diverted into pollution control. We should give up one hospital if the resources hereby freed would yield more human satisfaction when devoted to elimination of noise in our cities. And so on, trade-off by trade-off, we should divert our productive capacities from the production of existing goods and services to the production of a cleaner, quieter, more pastoral nation up to—and no further than—the point at which we value more highly the next washing machine or hospital that we would have to do without than we value the next unit of environmental improvement that the diverted resources would create.

Now this proposition seems to me unassailable but so general and abstract as to be unhelpful—at least unadministerable in the form stated. It assumes we can measure in some way the incremental units of human satisfaction yielded by very different types of goods. The proposition must remain a pious abstraction until I can explain how this measurement process can occur . . .

But I insist that the proposition stated describes the result for which we should be striving—and again, that it is always useful to know what your target is even if your weapons are too crude to score a bull's-eye.

DISCUSSION QUESTIONS

1. Assess the six reasons Baxter presents for his anthropocentrism; which ones seem weakest; which ones strongest? Why? Is he successful in making the case for anthropocentrism?
2. Is there a moral difference between human beings polluting the atmosphere with (say) sulfur dioxide and a similar amount being released into the atmosphere by volcanic eruptions? What is Baxter's view of the matter?
3. What is pollution?
4. Assess Baxter's argument that the natural world is devoid of moral significance. Do you agree? Why or why not?
5. In what respect might Baxter's position be construed as enlightened anthropocentrism?

MARK SAGOFF

At the Monument to General Meade, or On the Difference Between Beliefs and Benefits

Mark Sagoff is senior research scholar at the Center for Philosophy and Public Policy at the University of Maryland. He has made numerous significant contributions to environmental philosophy and environmental policy. Our selection is taken from his recent article "At the Monument to General Meade, or On the Difference Between Beliefs and Benefits," which continues the discussion of his earlier well-known article "At the Shrine of Our Lady of Fatima; or, Why Political Questions Are Not All Economic." In both articles, Sagoff ar-

Arizona Law Review, Vol 42, No. 2 Summer 2000, pp. 433–462. (Notes deleted) Reprinted by permission.

gues that environmental values cannot be captured by willingness to pay. In "Monument to General Meade" he writes, "A person who believes that society ought to protect a species of butterfly may have no expectation at all that he or she will benefit as a result."

CRITICAL READING QUESTIONS

1. What did Sagoff propose to the seminar he conducted at Gettysburg College?
2. What problem does Sagoff have with economic arguments that oppose private development of places with intrinsic value?
3. Does Sagoff think that existence value is a kind of economic value?
4. According to Sagoff, what do respondents express on CV surveys (and what is CV)?
5. How does Sagoff argue that beliefs are not benefits?

When you visit Gettysburg National Military Park, you can take a tour that follows the course of the three-day battle. The route ends at the National Cemetery, where, four months after the fighting, Abraham Lincoln gave the 270-word speech that marked the emergence of the United States as one nation. The tour will not cover all of the battlefield, however, because much of it lies outside the park. Various retail outlets and restaurants, including a Hardee's and a Howard Johnson's, stand where General Pickett, at 2 o'clock on a July afternoon in 1863, marched 15,000 Confederate soldiers to their deaths. The Peach Orchard and Wheatfield, where General Longstreet attacked, is now the site of a Stuckey's family restaurant. The Cavalry Heights Trailer Park graces fields where General George Custer turned back the final charge of the Confederate cavalry. Over his restaurant, Colonel Sanders, purveyor of fried chicken, smiles with neon jowls upon the monument to George Meade, the victorious Union general. Above this historic servicescape looms a 310-foot commercial observation tower many Civil War buffs consider to be "a wicked blight on the battlefield vista."

One spring day, on my way to give a seminar on "economics and the environment" at Gettysburg College, I drove quickly past the battlefield where 23,000 Union and 28,000 Confederate soldiers fell in three days. I felt guilty speeding by the somber fields, but I had to teach at 2 o'clock. I checked my watch. I did not want to be late. How do you keep your appointments and still find time to pay homage to history?

My ruminations were soon relieved by a strip of tawdry motels, restaurants, amusement arcades, and gift shops touting plastic soldiers and "original bullets! $6.95 each." At the battlefield entrance, I caught sight of the famous golden arches of the battlefield McDonald's where, on a previous occasion, my then 8-year-old son enjoyed a Happy Meal combo called the "burger and cannon." Nearby, a sign for General Pickett's All-You-Can-Eat Buffet beckoned me to a restaurant that marks the spot where rifle and artillery fire had torn apart Pickett's underfed troops. If you have young children, you understand the deep and abiding significance of fast food and convenient restrooms in historic and scenic areas. You may ask yourself, though, how you can have comfort, convenience, and commerce and at the same time respect "hallowed ground."

I. ARE BATTLEFIELDS SCARCE RESOURCES?

I began the seminar at Gettysburg College by describing a Park Service plan, then under discussion, to build new facilities to absorb the tide of visitors—an increase of 400,000 to 1.7 million annually—that welled up in response to "Gettysburg," a 1993 movie based on Michael Shaara's blockbuster novel, *The Killer Angels*. Working with a private developer, the Park Service proposed to construct a new $40 million visitor center, including a 500-seat family food court, a 450-seat theater, and a 150-seat "upscale casual" restaurant with "white tablecloth" service, gift shops, parking lots, and a bus terminal not far from the place where Lincoln delivered the Gettysburg Address. Several senators, including Senate Majority Leader Trent Lott (R-Miss.), objected that the project "commercializes the very ground and principle we strive to preserve."

It is one thing to commercialize the *ground;* it is another to commercialize the *principle* we strive to preserve. Tour buses, fast food, and trinket shops, although they commercialize the ground, express a local entrepreneurial spirit consistent with the freedom, vitality, and mystery of the place. The soldiers probably would have liked such haunts as the National Wax Museum, the Colt Firearms Museum, and the Hall of Presidents. They certainly would have appreciated General Lee's Family Restaurant, which serves great hamburgers practically at the site of Lee's headquarters. Homespun businesses try to tell the story and perpetuate the glory of Gettysburg—and even when they succeed only absurdly, they do so with an innocence and ineptitude that does not intrude on the dignity and drama of the park.

In contrast, the upscale tourist mall envisioned by the initial Park Service plan seemed, at least to Senator Lott, to elevate commercialism into a principle for managing Gettysburg. Rather than stand by the principle of commercialism or consumer sovereignty, however, the Park Service scaled back its plan. In its defense, the Service pointed out that Ziegler's Grove, where its Visitor Center and Cyclorama now stand, overlooks the main battle lines. The revised proposal, which received Interior Department approval in November 1999, calls for razing these facilities and for returning Ziegler's Grove to its 1863 appearance, in order, as one official said, "to honor the valor and sacrifices of those men who fought and died on that ground for their beliefs."

Since the seminar took place in midafternoon—siesta time in civilized societies—I had to engage the students. I did so by proposing a thesis so outrageous and appalling that the students would attack me and it. I told the class that the value of any environment—or of any of its uses—depends on what people now and in the future are willing to pay for it. Accordingly, the Park Service should have stuck with its original plan or, even better, it should have auctioned the battlefield to the highest bidder, for example, to Disney Enterprises.

I asked the students to bear with me long enough to consider my proposal in relation to the subject of the seminar, the theory of environmental economics. This theory defends consumer sovereignty as a principle for environmental policy. More specifically, this theory asserts that the goal of environmental policy is to maximize social welfare at least when equity issues—matters involving the distribution of benefits among individuals—are not pressing. Welfare, in turn, is defined and measured by consumer willingness to pay ("WTP") for goods and services. According to this theory, environmental policy should allocate goods and services efficiently, that is, to those willing to pay the most for them and who, in that sense, will benefit from their enjoyment, possession, or use.

In the United States, unlike Europe, I explained, battlefields are scarce resources which, like any scarce environmental asset, should be allocated efficiently. To be sure, the Park Service tries to accommodate tourists. The problem, though, is that the Park Service does not exploit heritage values as efficiently as a competitive market would. At present, Gettysburg is woefully underutilized, or so I argued. Even Dollywood, Dolly Parton's theme park in rural east Tennessee, attracts more visitors every year. The Park Service does not even try to allocate the resources efficiently. It pursues goals that are not economic but ethical; it seeks to educate the public and honor "the valor and sacrifices of those men who fought and died on that ground for their beliefs."

A young lady in the class blurted out, "But that's what the Park Service should do." She acknowledged that the Park Service has to provide visitor services. It should do so, she said, only to the extent that it will not "detract from what they did here," to paraphrase President Lincoln. This young lady thought that the history of the place, rather than what people are willing to pay for alternative uses of it, determined its value. She understood the significance of "what they did here" in moral and historical, rather than in economic, terms. The value of hallowed ground or of any object with intrinsic value has nothing to do with market behavior or with WTP, she said.

I explicated her concern the following way. A private developer, I explained, might not realize in gate receipts at Gettysburg the WTP of those individuals, like herself, who wished to protect an area for ethical or aesthetic reasons. I promised to describe to the class the contingent valuation ("CV") method economists have developed to determine how much individuals are willing to pay for policies consistent with their disinterested moral beliefs. Using this method, the Park Service could take her preference and therefore her welfare into account. It could then identify the policy that maximizes benefits over costs for all concerned, whether that concern is based on consumer desire or on ethical commitment.

This reply, I am afraid, did little more than taunt the student. In stating her opinion, she said, she implied nothing about her own well-being. She described what she thought society ought to do, not what would make her better off. The student did not see how scientific management, by measuring costs and benefits, served democracy. The Park Service, she added, had no responsibility, legal or moral, to maximize "satisfactions," including hers. Rather, it had an obligation to keep faith with those who died on that ground for their beliefs. No CV survey, no amount of WTP, she said, could add to or detract from the value of Gettysburg. No action we take could alter, though it may honor or dishonor, what the soldiers did there; no cost–benefit study, however scientific, could change our obligation to those who gave their lives that this nation might live.

II. CONSERVATION REVISITED

To prepare for the seminar, I had asked the students to read *Conservation Reconsidered,* an essay economist John V. Krutilla published in 1967 in response to neoclassical economists, who studied the effects of technological advance on economic growth. Neoclassical macroeconomists like James Tobin, Robert Solow, and William Nordhaus argued that technological progress would always make more abundant materials do the work of less abundant ones—for example, the way kerosene substituted for whale oil in providing household illumination. Solow, a Nobel laureate in economics, wrote that "[h]igher and rising prices of exhaustible resources lead competing producers to substitute other materials that are more plentiful and therefore cheaper." These economists adopted a model of economic growth that contained two factors: capital (including technology) and the labor to apply it. This model differed from that of classical economists, such as Ricardo and Malthus, because "resources, the third member of the classical triad, have generally been dropped."

In his essay, Krutilla cited studies to show that advancing technology has "compensated quite adequately for the depletion of the higher quality natural resource stocks." He observed that "the traditional concerns of conservation economics—the husbanding of natural resource stocks for the use of future generations—may now be outmoded by advances in technology." Krutilla, along with other environmental economists in the 1970s, rejected the view that the resource base imposes limits on growth. Had they accepted the Malthusian position, they would have risked losing credibility both with their mainstream colleagues and with foundations and institutions, such as the World Bank, that supported their work . . .

III. MORAL COMMITMENT AS MARKET DEMAND

At about the time neoclassical economics removed resource scarcity as a cause for concern, citizens across the country swelled the rolls of organizations such as the Sierra Club, which sought to preserve pristine places, endangered species, wild rivers, and other natural objects. These environmentalists, Krutilla pointed out, contributed to organizations such as the World Wildlife Fund "in an effort to save exotic species in remote areas of the world which few subscribers to the Fund ever hope to see." Krutilla noted that people "place a value on the mere existence" of resources, such as species, even though they do not intend to consume or own them, as they would ordinary resources.

Krutilla argued that if people value natural objects because they are natural, then technological advance cannot provide substitutes for them. Among the permanently scarce phenomena of nature, Krutilla cited familiar examples including "the Grand Canyon, a threatened species, or an entire ecosystem or biotic community essential to the survival of the threatened species." On this basis, Krutilla and many colleagues reinvented environmental economics as a "new conservation" that addresses the failure of markets to respond to the "existence" or "nonuse" value of natural objects people want to preserve but may not intend to experience, much less use or consume.

Krutilla was correct, of course, in observing that people often are willing to pay to preserve natural objects such as endangered species. Among them, for example, is Tom Finger, a Mennonite, who said, "We're eliminating God's creatures. All these nonhuman creatures . . . have a certain intrinsic worth because they are part of God's creation." People who believe species have an intrinsic worth may be willing to pay to protect them. Does this suggest that endangered species are scarce resources? Do those who believe extinction is wrong suffer a loss, a kind of social cost, when species vanish? Does endangered species habitat have an economic value that market prices fail to reflect?

Krutilla thought so. He reasoned that those who wished to protect natural objects or environments find it difficult to communicate their WTP to those who own those resources. Given this practical difficulty, "the private resource owner would not be able to appropriate in gate receipts the entire social value of the resources when used in a manner compatible with preserving the natural state." Accordingly, Krutilla proposed that the analysis Pigou had offered to justify the regulation of pollution might also serve to justify governmental action to protect species, wilderness, and other natural objects. He wrote, "Private and social returns . . . are likely to diverge significantly."

Krutilla's analysis suggests an argument to show that a private firm should manage Dollywood but not Gettysburg, even if the principle of consumer sovereignty applies equally to both. At Dollywood, the owners can capture in gate and table receipts total WTP for the goods and services the resort provides. Owners who respond to market signals supply just those goods and services the public most wants to buy. The managers of Dollywood, moreover, cover all the costs in labor, materials, etc., of their business. The prices they charge, then, will reflect the full social costs involved in producing what they sell.

At Gettysburg, it is different. Patriotic Americans, many of whom may never visit the area, may be willing to pay to restore the battlefield or to save it from commercial exploitation. Private, for-profit owners of Gettysburg would have no incentive to take this WTP into account, however, because they cannot capture it in gate and table receipts. The prices managers charge for attractions, then, will not reflect the full social costs of providing them—particularly the costs to patriotic Americans who would suffer if the battlefield is desecrated. Because price signals distort true WTP for preservation, the government, rather than a for-profit firm, should manage or at least regulate Gettysburg. Thus, a Pigouvian argument may provide an economic and, in that sense, scientific rationale for the belief that society should restore Gettysburg to its 1863 condition rather than sell the area to Disney Enterprises to run as a theme park.

This kind of economic argument may appeal to environmentalists because it opposes the privatization of places, such as Gettysburg, that possess intrinsic value. This argument seems especially appealing because it rejects privatization for economic reasons—the very sorts of reasons that might be thought to justify it. Since this Pigouvian analysis leads to comfortable conclusions, environmentalists might embrace it. Why not agree with economic theory that the goal of social policy is to maximize net benefits with respect to all environmental assets, whether in places like Dollywood or in places like Gettysburg? After all, the cost–benefit analysis, once it factors in the WTP of environmentalists, surely will come out in favor of protecting the environment.

The problem is this: to buy into this argument, one must accept the idea that the same goal or principle—net benefits maximization—applies to both Dollywood and Gettysburg. Critics of economic theory may contend, however, that the approach to valuation appropriate at Daydream Ridge in Dollywood is not appropriate at Cemetery Ridge in Gettysburg. At Daydream Ridge, the goal is to satisfy consumer demand. At Cemetery Ridge, the goal is to pay homage to those who died that this nation might live.

To say that the nation has a duty to pay homage to those from whom it received the last full measure of devotion is to state a moral fact. You can find other moral facts stated, for example, in the Ten Commandments. The imperative "Thou shalt not murder" should not be understood as a policy preference for which Moses and other like-minded reformers were willing to pay. Rather, like every statement of moral fact, it presents a hypothesis about what we stand for—what we maintain as true and expect others to believe—insofar as we identify ourselves as a moral and rational community.

Our Constitution puts certain questions, for example, religious belief, beyond the reach of democracy. Other moral questions, over military intervention in conflicts abroad, for example, invite reasoned deliberation in appropriate legislative councils. Environmental controversies, once the issues of resource scarcity are removed from the agenda, turn on the discovery and acceptance of moral and aesthetic judgments as facts. The belief that society should respect the sanctity of Cemetery Ridge states a moral fact so uncontroversial nobody would doubt it. This tells us nothing, however, about a scarcity of battlefields, an inelasticity of hallowed ground, market failure, or the divergence of social and private costs. It suggests only that the principle of consumer sovereignty that economists apply to evaluate management decisions at Dollywood do not apply at Gettysburg or, indeed, wherever the intrinsic value of an environment is at stake.

IV. ARE BELIEFS BENEFITS?

By construing intrinsic or existence value as a kind of demand that market prices fail to reflect, Krutilla and other environmental economists envisioned a brilliant strategy to respond to the quandary in which neoclassical economic theory had placed them. They kept their credentials as mainstream economists by accepting the neoclassical macroeconomic model with respect to resources the economy uses. Yet they also "greened" their science by attributing a general scarcity to "nonuse" resources such as wilderness, species, scenic rivers, historical landmarks, and so on, that people believe society has a duty to preserve. Indeed, by applying the divergence-of-private-and-social-cost argument not just to pollution but also to every plant, animal, or place that anyone may care about for ethical or cultural reasons, economic theory performed a great service to environmentalists. Environmentalists now could represent their moral, religious, or cultural beliefs that WTP market prices failed to reflect. At last, they could claim that economic science was on their side.

By transforming moral or cultural judgments about the environment into preferences for which people are willing to pay, Krutilla and his colleagues in the early 1970s achieved a great deal. First, they created a complex research agenda centering on the measurement of benefits associated with nonuse or existence value. Since 1970, indeed, research in environmental economics, both theoretical and empirical, has been preoccupied with measuring the economic benefits people are supposed to enjoy as a result of environmental policies consistent with their moral and religious beliefs.

Second, Krutilla and his colleagues created a division of labor between policy scientists and policy consumers. As policy scientists, economists lay down the goals and principles of environmental policy—indeed of all social policy—on the basis of their own theory and without any political deliberation, consultation, or process. Economists Edith Stokey and Richard Zeckhauser, for example, assert that "public policy should promote the welfare of society." A. Myrick Freeman III explains, "The basic premises of welfare economics are that the purpose of economic activity is to increase the well-being of the individuals who make up the society." In a widely used textbook, Eban Goodstein states, "Economic analysts are concerned with human welfare or well-being. From the economic perspective, the environment should be protected for the material benefit of humanity and not for strictly moral or ethical reasons."

As policy consumers, citizens make judgments about what is good for them. Economists reiterate that "each individual is the best judge of how well off he or she is in a given situation." Henry Ford is reputed to have said that people could have automobiles "in any color so long as it's black." From the standpoint of economic theory, individuals can make any social judgment they wish, as long as it concerns the extent to which policy outcomes harm or benefit them.

Economists may offer a ceremonial bow in the direction of markets, but this is quickly followed by a story of market failure followed by a call for centralized management based on cost–benefit analysis. Experts, i.e., economists themselves, must teach society how to allocate resources scientifically, since markets cannot cope with environmental public goods. In markets, individuals make choices and thus function as agents of change. In microeconomic theory, in contrast, individuals function not as agents but primarily as sites or locations where WTP may be found.

Third, as the methodology for benefits estimation developed, it typically assigned very high shadow prices to existence values, and this appealed to environmentalists. An endangered butterfly, for example, may be worth millions if every American is willing to pay a dime for its survival. Public interest groups, who associated economists with the enemy, now saw that economic science could be their friend. Environmentalists, who might have complained that industry groups had "numbers," could now come up with numbers, too. And since WTP adds up quickly when aggregated over all members of society, environmentalists could be sure that the numbers would come out "right."

V. IS EXISTENCE VALUE A KIND OF ECONOMIC VALUE?

To establish a connection between existence value and economic value, economists have to explain in what sense people benefit from the existence of goods they may neither experience nor use. To be sure, individuals are willing to pay to protect endangered species, rain forests, and other wonders of nature they may never expect to see. That they are willing to pay for them, however, does not show that they expect to benefit from them. Generally speaking, just because a person's preferences are all his own, it does not follow that the satisfaction of all or any of those preferences necessarily improves his welfare or well-being. The students in my class were quite willing to contribute to a fund to protect hallowed ground at Gettysburg. They did so, however, largely from a sense of moral obligation and not in any way or manner because they thought they would be better off personally if the battlefield were preserved.

I wrote the following syllogism on the blackboard.

> *Major premise:* The terms "economic value" and "welfare change" are equivalent.
>
> *Minor premise:* Existence value has no clear relation to welfare change.
>
> *Conclusion:* Therefore, existence value has no clear relation to economic value.

I defended the major premise by quoting leading environmental economists. According to Freeman, "[T]he terms 'economic value' and 'welfare change' can be used interchangeably." He adds that "[s]ociety should make changes in environmental and resource allocations only if the results are worth more in terms of individuals' welfare than what is given up by diverting resources and inputs from other uses." Economists Robert D. Rowe and Lauraine G. Chestnut observe that "[e]conomists define value as the well-being, or utility, derived from the consumption of a good or service."

The major premise, which equates economic value with welfare, explains the sense in which economic value is *valuable.* Unless "economic value" referred to some intrinsic good, such as felt happiness or satisfaction, one would be hard-pressed to explain the sense in which environmental economics can be a normative science.

To establish the minor premise, I argued that the statement "society ought to do *x* and I will contribute to its cost" does not entail "I shall benefit from *x*." When behavior is motivated by ethical concerns rather than by self-interest, it lacks a meaningful connection with well-being or welfare. Accordingly, economist Paul Milgrom concedes that for existence value to be considered a kind of economic value, "it would be necessary for people's individual existence values to reflect only their own personal economic motives and not altruistic motives, or sense of duty, or moral obligation."

To escape the conclusion that existence value has no relation to economic value, an economist may challenge either the major or minor premise. The major premise seems to be indispensable, however, if economics is to rest on a consequentialist moral theory such as utilitarianism. The reference to welfare explains why the benefits with which economists are concerned are *benefits*. The minor premise may be more vulnerable. This premise would be falsified if individuals made choices only in response to their beliefs about what will benefit them. Why not suppose, then, that people (other than economists) judge policy outcomes only on the basis of personal self interest? This assumption would connect preference with well-being for the ordinary citizen.

The students pointed out to me that Krutilla adopts this very position. In the essay the class read, he proposed that individuals who wish to protect the wonders of nature do so for self-seeking reasons, for example, to increase their own psychological satisfaction. Krutilla wrote that

> These would be the spiritual descendants of John Muir, the present members of the Sierra Club, the Wilderness Society, National Wildlife Federation, Audubon Society and others to whom the loss of a species or the disfigurement of a scenic area causes acute distress and a sense of genuine relative impoverishment.

The reference to "distress and a sense of genuine relative impoverishment" is crucial, of course, because these factors link existence value with economic value by connecting them with expected changes in welfare. Krutilla continued, "There are many persons who obtain satisfaction from mere knowledge that part of wilderness North America remains even though they would be appalled by the prospect of being exposed to it." The reference to "satisfaction" connects the "is" of WTP to the "ought" of economic value and valuation.

VI. CONTINGENT VALUATION

During the past 30 years, economists have worked hard to develop a method, known as contingent valuation ("CV"), to assess the "existence" or "nonuse" values of natural phenomena. The CV method, as one authority writes, "is based on asking an individual to state his or her willingness to pay to bring about an environmental improvement, such as improved visibility from lessened air pollution, the protection of an endangered species, or the preservation of a wilderness area." The authors of a textbook write that the CV method "asks people what they are willing to pay for an environmental benefit." They see this method as "uniquely suited to address nonuse values."

Contrary to what this textbook asserts, the CV questionnaire never asks people what they are willing to pay for an environmental *benefit.* It asks respondents to state their WTP for a particular policy outcome, for example, the protection of a rare butterfly. Economists interpret the stated WTP for the environmental improvement as if it were WTP for a personal benefit the respondent expects it to afford her or him. Yet a person who believes that society ought to protect a species of butterfly may have no expectation at all that he or she will benefit as a result. Indeed, as Tom Tietenberg observes, people who do not expect to benefit in any way from an environmental good may still be committed to its preservation. He notes that "people reveal strong support for environmental resources even when those resources provide no direct or even indirect benefit."

Empirical research shows that responses to CV questionnaires reflect moral commitments rather than concerns about personal welfare. In one example, a careful study showed that ethical considerations dominate economic ones in responses to CV surveys. "Our results provide an assessment of the frequency and seriousness of these considerations in our sample: they are frequent and they are significant determinants of WTP responses." In another study, researchers found that existence value "is almost entirely driven by ethical considerations precisely because it is disinterested value."

Some observers acknowledge that "existence value has been argued to involve a moral 'commitment' which is not in any way at all self-interested." They explain that: "Commitment can be defined in terms of a person choosing an act that he believes will yield a lower level of personal welfare to him than an alternative that is also available to him." If the satisfaction of "existence" value lowers welfare, then on which side of the cost–benefit equation should it be entered? The individual does not want less welfare per se, but "adherence to one's moral commitments will be as important as personal economic welfare maximization and may conflict with it."

Respondents to CV questions express disinterested views about policy rather than judgments about what will benefit them. Reviewing several CV protocols, economists concluded that "responses to CV questions concerning environmental preservation are dominated by citizen judgments concerning desirable social goals rather than by consumer preferences." Two commentators noted that the CV method asks people to "comment, without very much opportunity for thought, on a hard issue of public policy. In short, they most likely are exhibiting offhand opinions on the same policy issue to which the cost–benefit analyst purports to give his own answer, not private preferences that might be reflected in their own market transactions."

We should not confuse WTP to protect a battlefield, species, or wilderness with WTP for some sort of benefit. Battlefields and benefits constitute different goods which can be provided and should be measured separately. If economists cared to measure the economic value, i.e., the benefits, of alternative outcomes, the CV questionnaire should ask respondents to state their WTP for the welfare change they associate with an environmental policy. Here is an imaginary protocol I suggested to the class:

> Many people believe society should respect the "hallowed ground" at Gettysburg for moral, cultural, or other disinterested reasons. This questionnaire asks you to set aside all such disinterested values; it asks you not to consider what is right or wrong or good or bad from a social point of view. In responding to this survey, consider only the benefit you believe you will experience, i.e., the personal satisfaction, if the battlefield is preserved. Please state your WTP simply for the welfare change you expect, not your WTP for the protection of the battlefield itself.

Since CV questionnaires in fact ask nothing about benefits, responses to them tell us nothing relevant to economic valuation. Yet CV methodology, which economists have been developing for decades, has become the principal technique policymakers use to measure "nonmarket benefits based primarily on existence value" of assets such as old growth forests and endangered species.

As philosopher Ronald Dworkin points out, many of us recognize an obligation to places and objects that reflects a moral judgment about what society should do, not a subjective expectation about what may benefit us. He writes that many of us seek to protect objects or events—which could include endangered species, for example—for reasons that have nothing to do with our well-being. Many of us "think we should admire and protect them because they are important in themselves, and not just if or because we or others want or enjoy them." The idea of intrinsic worth depends on deeply held moral convictions and religious beliefs that underlie social policies for the environment, education, public health, and so on. Dworkin observes:

> Much of what we think about knowledge, experience, art, and nature, for example, presupposes that in different ways these are valuable in themselves and not just for their utility or for the pleasure or satisfaction they bring us. The idea of intrinsic value is commonplace, and it has a central place in our shared scheme of values and opinions.

Beliefs are not benefits. If economists believe that society should allocate resources to maximize welfare, they do not necessarily think this because they will be better off as a result. They are not simply trying to increase demand for their services. Similarly, as the evidence cited above suggests, people who believe that society should protect endangered species, old-growth forests, and other places with intrinsic value do not necessarily think that this will improve their well-being. A person who wants the Park Service to respect hallowed ground may consider that policy justified by the historical qualities of the battlefield and not by the welfare consequences for her. It is hard to understand, then, how CV measures the nonmarket benefits of environmental goods. If responses to CV surveys are based on moral beliefs or commitments, there would seem to be no relevant benefits to measure . . .

IX. DESIGNING FOR DILEMMAS

The students who attended the seminar cared about the environment. One student opined that society has an obligation to save old-growth forests, which he thought intrinsically valuable. Another mentioned pollution in the Grand Canyon. She said we have a responsibility to keep the area pristine no matter who benefits from it. Another argued that even if a species had no economic use, it is wrong to cause its extinction. Another student proposed that the government should promote prosperity and try to give everyone an opportunity to share in a booming economy. She understood the importance of macroeconomic goals but saw no reason to apply microeconomic theory to social policy.

I framed this thought for the students in the following way. If an environmental agency tries to pursue an ethical goal, for example, to minimize pollution as a moral trespass, it may have to design for a particular kind of dilemma. It must pursue its moral mission only in ways that allow the economy to prosper. The agency would have to accommodate macroeconomic indicators of economic growth such as levels of employment. Full employment, unlike the microeconomic efficiencies about which environmental economists theorize, does affect human welfare and happiness.

How might an agency balance its zeal to control pollution with its need to accommodate economic activity? To suggest an answer, I drew a graph in which the x-axis represented incremental pollution reduction and the y-axis represented the "misery index," i.e., the sum of the current unemployment and inflation rates. One may argue that statutes like the Clean Air Act mandate pollution control to the "knee of the curve." This is the area where the curve begins to go asymptotic because further reductions in pollution cause rapidly increasing gains in unemployment and inflation.

The authors of the Clean Air Act may have hoped that technological innovation would continually push the "knee of the curve" farther out along the pollution-control axis. On this reading, the statute requires the EPA to minimize pollution (as a form of coercion), rather than to optimize it (as an external cost). The EPA may adopt the "knee of the curve" as a moral principle to balance two intrinsically valuable but competing goals. One is to make the environment cleaner; the other is to allow the economy to expand.

Environmental agencies can pursue their moral missions without invoking the tautologies of welfare economics. The Park Service, for example, did not commission a cost–benefit analysis to plan for Gettysburg. It assumed it had a duty to design the Visitor Center in a way that respects hallowed ground; within that mandate, it also has to provide for the education and basic needs of visitors. Similarly, the Fish and Wildlife Service has to collaborate with landowners to design Habitat Conservation Plans that protect species while allowing economic development to take place. Sometimes, a collaborative group can find an inexpensive technical "fix," for example, by relocating the endangered creature to another habitat where it can live in peace. A deliberative body representing "stakeholders" can often deal with a particular problem better than a governmental agency located in Washington. The Clinton administration has called for initiatives to "reinvent regulation" by devolving decision making to such groups.

Environmental agencies may find it difficult, however, to embrace an approach to regulation that relies on collaboration and deliberation rather than centralized science-based decision making. The statutes under which these agencies operate, such as the Clean Air Act, tend to be so vague, so aspirational, and so precatory that they offer little or no guidance to an agency that has to answer the hard questions, such as how safe or clean or natural is enough. The agency, in the absence of a meaningful political mandate, has to find some way to give its decisions legitimacy. It therefore cloaks its ethical determinations in the language of science. Environmental professionals, in their eagerness to speak truth to power, may encourage this reliance on their disciplines.

The problem, however, is that science has no moral truth to speak; it cannot say how safe, clean, or natural is safe, clean, or natural enough. Nevertheless, agencies defend moral and political decisions with arguments to the effect that, "The science made me do it." Environmental agencies, though they must adopt regulations that are ethical at some level, rarely, if ever, offer a moral argument or principle for Congress to review and citizens to consider and debate. Instead, agencies tend to use the best available science to answer moral and political questions the science cannot possibly answer. And the environmental sciences—strained in this way well beyond their limits—lose credibility as a result.

X. RETREAT FROM GETTYSBURG

After the seminar, I chose a route out of Gettysburg that avoided the battlefield and, with it, the ghosts of the past. But my path was full of portents of the future. At a 110-acre site southeast of the battleground, which had served as a staging area for Union troops, I saw equipment gathered to construct the massive mall the Park Service decided not to build. The developer, the Boyle Group of Malvern, Pennsylvania, according to its promotional literature, promises to erect an "authentic village" containing 70 outlet stores, an 80-room country inn, and a large restaurant. According to the flyer, visitors to Gettysburg will find the village a refuge from the drudgery of touring the battlefield and learning its history. "History is about the only thing these millions of tourists take home," the promo states. "That's because there is no serious shopping in Gettysburg."

Society can count on firms such as the Boyle Group to provide shopping as serious as anyone could want at Gettysburg and everywhere else. The nation does not have to elevate shopping and, with it, the allocation of goods and services to those willing to pay the most for them, to the status of legislation. Environmental laws state general moral principles or set overall goals that reflect choices we have made together. These principles and goals do not include the empty and futile redundancy of environmental economics—the rule that society should allocate resources to those willing to pay the most for them because they are willing to pay the most for those resources.

An agency, such as the Park Service, may engage in public deliberation to determine which rule to apply in the circumstances. The principle economists tout, net benefits maximization, is rarely if ever relevant or appropriate. At Gettysburg, the principle speaks for itself. "What gives meaning to the place is the land on which the battle was fought and the men who died there," as longtime Gettysburg preservationist Robert Moore has said. "Keeping the place the same holy place, that's what's important."

DISCUSSION QUESTIONS

1. How would Sagoff likely handle questions of pollution?
2. Is Sagoff correct to argue (as in the title of the essay) that beliefs are not benefits? What does he mean by this claim?
3. What role, if any, should cost play in environmental policy? What would Sagoff likely say? Can you think of nonenvironmental contexts where cost should not be a factor, or is cost always a relevant consideration?
4. What weakness, if any, do you see in Sagoff's argument? Is his argument practical, that is, can it actually generate public policy about environmental matters?

You Decide!

1. ARSENIC AND DRINKING WATER

Shortly before he left office, President Clinton approved an EPA reassessment for allowable levels of arsenic in drinking water. Since 1942, a 50 parts per billion (ppb) standard had been used. However, a 1999 study by the National Academy of Sciences found that 50 ppb of arsenic in drinking water poses a risk of cancer, a risk that is apparently much higher than for other allowable concentrations of contaminants in drinking water. The new standard would be 10 ppb, one adopted by the European Union and the World Health Organization.

Upon assuming office, President Bush froze the previous administration's plan to reduce the allowable arsenic levels in drinking water. The new EPA administrator, Christine Whitman, said she wanted to make sure the conclusions about arsenic are supported by the "best available science." A cost–benefit analysis was ordered.

Trying to comply with the 10 ppb standard by 2006, as initially proposed, would cost a lot. In California alone, compliance costs are estimated to be $500 million. Some 13 million people served by more than 3,000 water systems nationwide have drinking water that contains more than 10 ppb of arsenic. As this is being written, the issue has yet to be resolved. Arsenic occurs naturally in some groundwater, especially in western states, but runoff from industries that use arsenic, such as wood treatment plants and mining, contribute to the contamination of water supplies. Approximately 36 million pounds of arsenic are released into the environment each year.

Discussion Questions

1. If you were in charge, how would you determine the allowable levels of contaminants for drinking water? Should there be federal standards for drinking water?
2. Should water companies be required to inform consumers about the contaminants in their water? Can you think of any reasons they should not be required to do so?
3. Is a cost–benefit analysis appropriate for resolving this issue?

2. SNOWMOBILES IN YELLOWSTONE

Some 60,000 people visit Yellowstone National Park each year on snowmobiles. Snowmobiles' popularity is soaring, and nearby businesses that rent snowmobiles are growing by leaps and bounds, particularly at the park's western edge where a trip to Old Faithful is a favorite. The town of West Yellowstone, Montana, just outside the park, bills itself as the "Snowmobile Capital of the World."

But snowmobiles are noisy and pollute a lot because they are typically powered by two-stroke engines. Two-stroke engines are lighter, simpler, and more powerful for their weight than four-stroke engines (see introduction to Chapter 4 for a discussion of four-stroke engines) largely because there are no intake or exhaust valves. Two-stroke engines have only a compression and power stroke (rather than intake, compression, power, and exhaust, as in four-stroke engines). Exhaust and intake ports are simply holes in the cylinder wall and as the piston moves up and down it exposes or occludes the holes. On the power stroke, as the piston is forced down the cylinder after the spark plug detonates the gas/air mixture, it exposes the exhaust hole, and hot exhaust gases escape; as the piston goes further down it exposes the intake hole, and gas/air flow in. However, now both exhaust and intake ports in the cylinder wall are exposed and some of the incoming gas/air mixture flows out with exhaust before the piston occludes the exhaust hole on its way back up for the compression stroke. Up to 30 percent of the fuel is wasted through the exhaust, making two-stroke engines remarkably inefficient and very polluting. Also, because there is no internal lubricating system, oil must be added to the gasoline, which makes noxious blue smoke as it is burned along with fuel in the cylinder.

Park rangers at the entrance points in Yellowstone routinely face traffic jams of noisy, stinking, polluting snowmobiles. Fresh air has to be piped into ticket booths, and rangers sometimes wear gas masks. According to a Department of the Interior study, 95 percent of the time a visitor at Old Faithful in winter will hear snowmobiles. Because the number of snowmobiles buzzing around is threatening the type of experience most people expect in their national parks, the National Park Service planned to phase out snowmobile access to Yellowstone by the winter of 2003–2004.

Snowmobile manufacturers oppose the ban, claiming that a new generation of snowmobiles is quieter and less polluting. Cleaner four-stroke engines are replacing noxious two-stroke engines and better mufflers reduce noise. The International Snowmobile Manufacturers Association filed a lawsuit prompting a review of the proposed ban by the Park Service. Rather than go forward with the snowmobile ban, proposed during the Clinton administration, the Bush administration is revisiting the issue. Several options are under consideration: delay the ban, limit the number of snowmobiles admitted to the park and tighten engine-emission and noise standards, provide motorized access with multi-passenger "snow coaches" operated by the park service. Interestingly, the EPA supports the initial Clinton-era ban, arguing that air quality standards cannot be met. According to opponents of the ban, air quality can be assured by newer snowmobile technology.

Discussion Questions

1. Which alternative should be adopted? Why?
2. Although a Park Service study does not concede that newer four-stroke snowmobiles are a vast improvement over the older two-stroke models, as the industry claims, what if they are? Would that make a difference to whether or not individual snowmobiles should be allowed rather than the coaches, which are capable of holding many more people?
3. What principles should govern use of the national parks?

FOR FURTHER READING ON THE ENVIRONMENTAL PROTECTION AGENCY

Environmental Politics and Policy, 2nd edition, Walter Rosenbaum, CQ Press, Washington, DC, 1991.

The Environmental Policy Paradox, 3rd edition, Zachary Smith, Prentice Hall, 2000.

Public Policies for Environmental Protection, Paul Portney & Robert Stauins, Eds. (Resources for the Future) RFF Press Book, Washington, DC, 2000.

CHAPTER 10

Broader Concerns: Thoreau, Deep Ecology, and Ecofeminism

MODERN TIMES: EVER MORE PRESSING—THOREAU AND ENVIRONMENTAL THOUGHT

Most of us can reasonably expect to live at least some version of the American dream—a life of convenience, relative affluence, and comfort. Our standard of living is the envy of people around the world. However, our prosperity comes at a cost: We are often driven to succeed, squeezed by competing demands at a seemingly ever-increasing pace. As we go about our daily affairs, driving to and from work, buying consumer items at the malls, seeking a better paying job, or just sitting at home watching television, it occasionally strikes us that we could abandon it all for a much simpler way of life. A common adolescent fantasy is to escape to a cabin in the woods, grow one's own food, and live close to nature. Few of us will actually ever act on that romantic thought, but we may harbor the agreeable illusion of radically altering our lives to something less hectic and more contemplative.

Henry David Thoreau (1817–1862), America's folk hero of pastoralism, antiauthoritarianism, and counterculture, actually did what so many of us only entertain as an idle daydream, and he did it well before "dropping out" became an identifiable response to contemporary life. Thoreau is unquestionably America's first environmental saint. His work is evocative and remains a fresh source of inspiration for generations of readers largely because he has so perspicaciously articulated the misgivings many people have about modernity.

Thoreau's widely read *Walden* is his account of living for two years in a small hut he built in the woods. Why did Thoreau do that? He tells us, "I went to the woods because I wished to live deliberately, to front only the essential facts of life, and see if I could not learn what it had to teach, and not, when I came to die, discover that I had not lived." Thoreau has a remarkable ability to reflect beautifully and sensitively on his surroundings, discerning profound messages in nature, voicing thoughts that have since become clichés, such as, "The mass of men lead lives of quiet desperation" and "If a man does not keep pace with his companions, perhaps it is because he hears a different drummer."

Much of Thoreau's charm comes from his exceptional prose and uncompromising independence of mind. He was utterly indifferent to the sorts of things that motivate most of us: money, fame, security, comfort, approval, possessions, social expectations, and the like. (At least that is the impression he gives.) By deliberately reducing his material wants, he found that he could live on very little and thereby devote the bulk of his time striving to comprehend what nature has to teach. *Teach* is the right word. Thoreau views nature as a source of wisdom, if only we can decipher its messages. And decipher it Thoreau did: He mused deeply about the most prosaic aspects of nature, showing us hidden meaning and rich metaphor. Under Thoreau's spell, many of our usual activities seem pointless. He comes off something like a mildly disapproving and slightly puritanical uncle who admonishes us about our ways, appealing continually to our better selves and telling us what we already dimly discern on our own but lack the fortitude to express.

Thoreau is sometimes faulted for being a hypocrite because he built his hut, not far off in the wilderness, but on Walden Pond just outside his hometown of Concord, Massachusetts. The property he occupied belonged to his friend and mentor Ralph Waldo Emerson, and he had dinner from time to time at Emerson's house. Thoreau was regarded by the townspeople as a crank and loafer because he occupied himself primarily with long walks through the countryside. What kind of a survivalist is that, you might ask? But Thoreau was not a survivalist. Rather than turning his back on society, Thoreau was seeking to define a way of life that does not compromise one's integrity. Among the many things Thoreau has to teach us, this is surely among the most significant. How much of ourselves shall be under cultivation, that is, a product of culture, and how much shall remain uncultivated, that is, wild?

One of Thoreau's most quotable quotes (and Thoreau is quoted a lot) is from his nature essay titled "Walking" where he famously claims, "In wildness is the preservation of the world." What does he mean? For Thoreau, walking—his chief occupation—is no simple matter. He tells us, "If you are ready to leave father and mother, and brother and sister, and wife and child and friends, and never see them again,—if you have paid your debts, and made your will, and settled all your affairs, and are a free man, then you are ready for a walk." Some walk! As Thoreau freely speculates, the word *saunter* is derived from Sainte-Terrer, a traveler to the holy lands. And the holy lands to which we saunter under Thoreau's influence is the wild. "Life consists with wildness. The most alive is the wildest," hence the most cultivated is the least alive, the least vivacious. Thoreau proclaims, "All good things are wild and free."

Ever the master of communicating on several levels at once, Thoreau delights in vestiges of wildness that can still be discerned in domesticated animals or neglected plants that have reverted to hardier versions of their former selves. His essay titled "Wild Apples" praises, with characteristic Thoreauian fervor, the virtues of sour, small, hard, uncultivated apples. And so it is with us, both as individuals and as a culture. Our vitality and well-being require a reservoir of something beyond our manufacture and control. "Every tree sends its fibers forth in search of the Wild. The cities import it at any price. Men plough and sail for it. From the forests and wilderness come the tonics and barks which brace mankind . . . The story of Romulus and Remus being suckled by a wolf is not a meaningless fable. The founders of every state which has risen to eminence have drawn their nourishment and vigor from a similar wild source."

Thoreau's concept of the wild helps us to understand better his (and perhaps our) uneasy relation to modern living. In exchange for the conveniences and security and comfort, modern life demands a lot from us. A mass consumer-driven society threatens to extinguish our individuality, for we too must become domesticated, regimented, orderly, and standardized. As mentioned earlier, it is a mistake to think that Thoreau simply wants to abandon society and have us all return to a preindustrial primitive world; rather, he is seeking a way of civilized life that does not compromise the individual but will instead allow the individual to flourish. Maintaining contact with wildness is his solution to what we can call the "problem of modernity," that is, how to live in a contemporary context without becoming enervated by it. Thoreau writes, "For my part, I feel that with regard to Nature I live a sort of border life, on the confines of a world into which I make occasional and transient forays only." Nature (note Thoreau's capitalization) is synonymous with wildness; Thoreau straddles both realms, drawing spiritual sustenance from Nature while continuing to function in society. Further, "I would not have every man nor every part of a man cultivated, any more than I would have every acre of earth cultivated: part will be tillage, but the greater part will be meadow and forest . . ."

This "border life" allowed Thoreau to live in a hut on the border of Concord, eat occasional meals in town with friends, and become deeply involved in civil matters (his acclaimed essay "Civil Disobedience" influenced both Martin Luther King and Gandhi) yet preserve his dignity, perspective, and independence. He could participate in modern life on *his* terms and develop in accordance with *his* predilections and insights, rather than having to submit to the norms and expectations of others. And so it is for us. Reading Thoreau often brings about an inner transformation that makes it impossible to participate fully in our market-driven, consumer-oriented society in quite the same way as before. We can continue to function within it, but henceforth at some critical distance; Thoreau has made us aware of a cherished refuge, an aspect of the psyche that we ignore at our peril. Commenting on his bean field (in *Walden*), Thoreau observes, "Mine was, as it were, the connecting link between wild and cultivated fields; as some states are civilized, and others half-civilized, and others savage or barbarous, so my field was, though not in a bad sense, a half-cultivated field. They were beans cheerfully returning to their wild and primitive state."

As we have seen, the concept of wildness is central to understanding Thoreau. But it is difficult to pin down what he means by that term since Thoreau speaks metaphorically and indirectly. We feel as if we know what he means—his language is familiar, intimate, and easy to relate to—but we search in vain for a straightforward account in Thoreau of this central concept. By "wildness" he does not mean (merely) the savage, though he often compares the hardiness of indigenous people to the insipidness of urban dwellers who are incapable of withstanding discomfort or adversity. Moreover, although Thoreau maintains that our well-being depends upon contact with wildness, he is not recommending it just for its instrumental value. The wild is evidently more significant than that. What does Thoreau mean by wildness?

We can gain some insight into Thoreau's concept of the wild if we remind ourselves that Thoreau looked to nature for instruction. How can nature teach us anything? As he says in another nature essay, "Autumnal Tints," "Verily these maples are cheap preachers, permanently settled, which preach their half-century, and century, aye, and century-and-a-half sermons, with constantly increasing unction and influence, ministering to many generations of men . . ." For Thoreau, nature preaches to us; it is infused with the divine; that is why we should study it closely and come to see what it has to say. No mere projection on our part, Thoreau thinks that the natural world really is infused with meaning, rather than just a mirror for our own thoughts. This is hardly new. People have long seen the hand of God in nature, but much traditional religious thinking puts God apart from nature; it is his creation. For Thoreau, by contrast, nature becomes divine itself, rather than being merely a medium for God to communicate with us. But nature is not God in any recognizable theological sense—it has none of the traditional divine attributes. For Thoreau, nature embodies "higher" or transcendental truths; it is thus divine in a very amorphous sense. Thoreau is best seen as a kind of nature mystic: nature is a fuzzy god, just beyond the grasp of our intellects, but whose instruction is accessible to those who will take the time to listen.

The divinity of nature is undoubtedly an aspect of its wildness, that is, a separate realm of existence, not under human control, completely "other," undomesticated and free to function in accordance with its own internal propensities. As Thoreau announced in the opening line of "Walking": "I wish to speak a word for Nature, for absolute freedom and wildness, as contrasted with a freedom and culture merely civil . . ." It is common for religions to hold, in some form or other, that there is an aspect of holiness or divinity "in" each of us, a "divine spark" that connects us to God, the universe at large, or to an ineffable something that transcends human creation. Thoreau is evidently making a similar sort of claim, though very abstractly and poetically. If we may simplify Thoreau's thoughts without doing too much of an injustice (and in *Walden* he urged us to "simplify, simplify"), he seems to affirm: Divinity = Nature = Wild = Life. Keeping in touch with wildness, by contact with the natural world, is thus to preserve that portion of the universe— that which is other, wild, and free—within us. By so doing, we integrate our lives with our surroundings in a straightforward sense and we come to see ourselves as not only beings *in* the world, but *of* it as well. To live wholly within the realm of human civilization is to shut ourselves off from nature, which, for Thoreau, is equivalent to shutting ourselves off from the divine.

Thoreau spent two years in his hut, explaining when his "experiment" was over, "I left the woods for as good a reason as I went there. Perhaps it seemed to me that I had several more lives to live and could not spare any more time for that one." Let us recall why Thoreau went to the woods initially: It was to "live deliberately," to "front only the essential facts of life," and to "learn what it had to teach." So what did he learn? Thoreau came to see that the essential fact of life is wildness; for him that *is* life. He can thus leave the woods—function in modernity—secure in the knowledge that he has discovered what will nurture and sustain us even as we pursue "several more lives."

THE DEATH OF NATURE

In *The Gay Science,* Nietzsche's madman startled the world by proclaiming the death of God and even more startlingly that, "We have killed him—you and I! We are all his murderers!" For Thoreau, the thought that God is dead is tantamount to the death of nature, and correspondingly, to our own deaths since Thoreau identifies nature (read: wildness) with life. That we might have done this awful thing makes it not just murder, but suicide. Are we capable of such a thing? The worry is that we have already done it.

In *The End of Nature,* the contemporary nature writer Bill McKibben argues that because no part of the natural world is now untouched by human activity—global warming, ozone depletion, and acid rain are global phenomena—nature, understood as that which is irremediably apart from us, no longer exists. This realization prompts a profound conceptual reorientation, for we now have our fingerprints all over what was previously "other," the vast context of nature in which we formally lived our lives. McKibben writes, "We are in charge now, like it or not. As a species we are as gods—our reach is global."

One might object to McKibben's thesis on the grounds that if nature is dead because it—all of it—bears the mark of humanity, it is long dead, for human beings have been altering the surface of the planet for a very long time. Much of the world's grasslands, for example, are believed to be the result of fires routinely set by ancient indigenous peoples to herd game, early sailors in the Pacific were thought to have assisted in the spread of coconut palms among tropical islands, and the extinction of certain large mammals in North America and Europe is thought by some anthropologists to have been caused by overhunting. So, one could argue, nature as something pristine and totally apart from human influence has not existed for thousands of years.

However, while it is likely true that human beings have affected nature all along, the effects have been piecemeal and local. Perhaps a lot of little disturbances add up, but the scale of our current effects on the earth is entirely different than ever before. We are altering fundamental aspects of atmospheric chemistry, affecting ecosystems across the globe, even raising the levels of oceans; new compounds dispersed throughout air, water, and land become incorporated into food webs and ultimately the tissues of every living organism; the worldwide loss of biodiversity at our hands rivals the great periods of extinction in geologic history, as, for example, the massive die-off in the Cretaceous era brought about (it appears) by a meteor striking the earth. It is our global reach that is new and disturbing. As a result, the earth now seems rather small and fragile rather than vast and impassive. So even if, technically speaking, nature has been "dead" for a lot longer than McKibben thinks, it is the magnitude of our current ways of affecting nature that gives pause. Differences in degree do become differences in kind.

Nature has long been dead in a different sense than our leaving physical traces everywhere. Our attitude toward the natural world vacillates uncomfortably between reifying it as a big mysterious entity, inscrutable, and having its own animating will, and conceiving it as inert, mechanical, and operating in accordance with the impersonal laws of science. The ascendancy of the scientific view purges nature of meaning and intentionality; it has no will of its own; it becomes a context, a pure thing—a vast collection of atoms that causally interact. Despite Thoreau, the scientific outlook contends that there is nothing to read *in* nature; it contains no messages or truths other than what we, in our naivete and intellectual and emotional weakness, project upon it—nature as a mirror of our thoughts rather than a sage with a message. The death of nature can thus be seen as the shift, in the modern mind, from a spiritual to a scientific understanding of the world.

But this death we need not lament for it would be a greater appreciation of our condition. In his famous essay, "The Future of an Illusion," Sigmund Freud speculates that religion develops out of our fear of nature; earthquakes, disease, storms, floods, droughts, and other calamities have long tormented humanity. But if nature is fundamentally like us, then we can at least hope to control it, by prayer, entreaty, or reason. Freud writes,

> Impersonal forces and destinies cannot be approached; they remain eternally remote. But if the elements have passions that rage as they do in our own souls, if death itself is not something spontaneous but the violent act of an evil Will, if everywhere in nature there are Beings around us of a kind that we know in our own society, then we can breathe freely, can feel at home in the uncanny and can deal by psychical means without senseless anxiety. We are still defenseless, perhaps, but we are no longer helplessly paralyzed; we can at least react. Perhaps, indeed, we are not even defenseless. We can apply the same methods against these violent supermen outside that we employ in our own society; we can try to adjure them, to appease them, to bribe them, and, by so influencing them, we may rob them of a part of their power.

When Freud refers to religion as an "illusion" he does not mean merely a false belief, but rather a belief that is motivated by wish-fulfillment (thus, even true beliefs can be illusions if they would be held no matter what the evidence to the contrary). The personification of nature is, according to Freud, an infantile stage in human development. A mature apprehension of our situation, that is, a rational one based on reason and evidence, faces the world directly.

How, then, are we to understand Thoreau? He seems to view nature as something we can converse with and relate to in personal terms. Is this not precisely the personification of nature that Freud decries? Yet surely it is preposterous to think that Thoreau is infantile; his reflections are among the most mature and insightful produced by anyone. Perhaps the issue is best resolved not simply by rejecting either Freud or Thoreau, but by accepting the profundity of Thoreau while remaining skeptical of his metaphysics. The natural world can be, as it were, a springboard for reflection, and personifying it may deepen those reflections, but we do not have literally to think that nature is personlike, at least not without argument. Ironically, Freud's work can be seen in exactly the same way. We can usefully talk about the id, ego, and superego without having literally to think that these terms refer to actual entities. So the death of nature, meaning rejection of the view that nature is actually personlike, is compatible with finding meaning and insight in a personalized natural world. Myths can be deeply meaningful without being thought literally true.

DEEP ECOLOGY

The **deep ecology** movement takes its inspiration from many sources, Thoreau prominent among them. One of the movement's guiding aphorisms, "simple in means, rich in ends," has a distinctly Thoreauian flavor, since it recommends a way of life characterized by low consumption but high quality. Deep ecology is not a readily definable philosophical position, at least not in the usual academic sense of the term *philosophy*. Supporters of deep ecology come from all over the intellectual map; some are philosophers and other academics, but others are social activists, essayists, artists, theologians, and ordinary citizens. They are united by their desire to articulate and implement a comprehensive philosophy of life, one that is respectful of the natural world and mindful of our place in it.

Norwegian philosopher Arnee Naess, founder of the movement, first expressed the distinction between "deep" and "shallow" ecology in his 1973 paper, "The Shallow and the Deep, Long-Range Ecology Movement." Shallow environmentalism focuses on technical solutions to environmental problems, such as recycling, new energy sources, increased efficiency, and the like. No fundamental shift in values is necessary; the guiding principle of shallow environmentalism is human well-being. Shallow environmentalism is really just another term for anthropocentrism. Deep ecology, by contrast, is committed to the intrinsic value of all life and hence the rejection of anthropocentrism as a guiding principle.

Because of the confusion surrounding what deep ecology means and who is a deep ecologist and who is not (after all, nobody wants to be a "shallow" anything—the terms have an unfortunate judgmental tone), Naess and fellow deep ecologist George Sessions in 1984 set out a platform of eight principles definitive of the movement. The platform is as much a political statement as a philosophical one, for it sidesteps questions about foundations, focusing instead on areas of common agreement that can be reached from different ultimate norms concerning human nature and our position in the world. Just as republicans, democrats, libertarians, and independents can all accept the U.S. Constitution even though they may have widely divergent views about what ultimately justifies it, so the deep ecology platform is intended as a set of principles acceptable to many environmentalists irrespective of their personal justificatory frameworks, or *ecosophies,* as Naess terms the different belief systems that can be used to derive the platform. Thus, thinkers starting from different intellectual traditions and assumptions—Christian, Buddhist, atheist, nature mystic, consequentialist, Spinozist, animist, Thoreauian—can all unite under the platform as a plan for social action. That is the hope. But social movements are one thing, philosophy is another. A persistent worry is that to achieve a broad following, intellectual focus will suffer.

Consider the first two points of the platform formulated by Naess and Sessions:

1. The well-being and flourishing of human and nonhuman life on earth have value in themselves (synonyms: intrinsic value, inherent worth). These values are independent of the usefulness of the nonhuman world for human purposes.
2. Richness and diversity of life forms contribute to the realization of these values and are also values in themselves.

The first point articulates a common theme in environmental philosophy: the denial of anthropocentrism. But the first point does not distinguish between equal intrinsic value among all who have it and degrees of intrinsic value. The platform statement certainly unites all who think that intrinsic value is not limited to human beings, but it says nothing about its distribution. Naess himself adopts a "biospherical egalitarianism," as do other prominent deep ecologists, but the platform point as stated hardly rules out the thought that the well-being and flourishing of some entities is more intrinsically valuable than others. This is perhaps a very picky point, but as stated the first point does not even specify that the flourishing of *all* human and nonhuman life forms is intrinsically valuable, hence it is possible that some life forms are not intrinsically valuable at all. So the first point is multiply ambiguous, perhaps intentionally so for political reasons.

The distribution of intrinsic value is important because as a social movement deep ecologists will inevitably have to make practical decisions, trade-offs, and compromises.

Such compromises and trade-offs will be possible only if we can make sense of varying degrees of intrinsic value; if, on the other hand, all natural objects have equal intrinsic value (or their well-being and flourishing is equally intrinsically valuable), how can trade-offs be contemplated? Furthermore, if the flourishing of all life forms—human and nonhuman—is equally intrinsically value, then whether you flourish—person that you are—is not more important than if a bug flourishes.

By affirming the intrinsic value of human and nonhuman life forms, the first platform point initially appears to be a statement of biocentrism (see Chapter 6). But Naess and Sessions are very clear that by *life* they do not mean just biological organisms. "The term *life*," they write, "is used here in a comprehensive nontechnical way to refer also to things biologists may classify as nonliving: rivers (watersheds), landscapes, cultures, ecosystems, 'the living earth.' " So not only organisms, but also rivers, ecosystems, even human cultures, are alive, and thus have intrinsic value. This not only conflates biocentrism with ecocentrism (see Chapter 7), it is such an expansive account of "life," one wonders what would not count as alive. If human cultures as life forms have intrinsic value too, what about our culture of consumption and exploitation of nature? If diversity is itself a value, as affirmed in point 2, then human cultures would be far less diverse if we all became deep ecologists.

Notice also that point 2 makes two claims, one evaluative and the other descriptive. The evaluative claim is that richness and diversity of life forms are values in themselves. The descriptive one is that these values contribute to the flourishing of human and nonhuman life. Start with the descriptive claim. Is it true that richness (what is that?) and diversity of life forms contribute to the flourishing of human and nonhuman life on earth? Unless the terms are defined in a question-begging manner ("diversity" *means* "contributes to flourishing"), it is not implausible to think that human beings would flourish better with less diverse life forms, for instance, if there were no AIDS or other deadly viruses, or that nonhuman life forms would flourish better if there were no human beings! The flourishing of some life forms is inimical to the flourishing of other life forms. And once we remind ourselves that "life" here includes much more than biological organisms—it seems to include just about everything—the claim that diversity contributes to flourishing becomes even harder to understand. How does diversity among, say, human cultures, contribute to the flourishing of "the living earth"?

Finally, consider the evaluative claim in point 2 of the platform: Diversity of life forms is a value in itself ("richness" is too imprecise to analyze; how is one life form richer than another?). It is hard to see how diversity can be a value "in itself." In what sense are more diverse assemblages (situations, contexts, etc.), simply by virtue of their being more diverse, better than less diverse ones? If diversity were "in itself" a value, we would have to conclude that they were, though how this could be so is scarcely intelligible. Is a room with more diverse objects in it better than one without the diversity? Suppose we dump raw sewage in a stream and thereby increase the diversity of microorganisms, is this better than before? Are rain forests better than deserts merely because they contain more diverse life forms?

Whatever its faults, the platform articulates a certain vision of an appropriate way of life, one that distinguishes sharply between quality of life and standard of living, for a high standard of living hardly translates into a high quality of life. This is certainly the kind of point Thoreau would make. (For a full statement of the platform, see Naess, "The Deep Ecological Movement: Some Philosophical Aspects," reprinted in this section). To their credit, deep ecologists have sought to express what many people intuitively sense concerning the direction taken by modern industrial societies, namely a way of life characterized by consumption and short-term means-end thinking about the natural world.

As mentioned, the platform sets out eight points constitutive of deep ecology without offering justifications for them—that is the job of specific "ecosophies." Because divergent and incompatible positions can all claim allegiance to the platform, discussion of deep ecology can be difficult. Consideration of one ecosophy will ignore another; objections leveled against one will be irrelevant to a third, and so on. Since Naess, the undisputed founder of deep ecology, has a well-developed ecosophy, his particular version of deep ecology shall be the focus of our discussion. He calls his system Ecosophy T, "T" because of his beloved mountain hut "Tvergastein," where Naess feels most at home. Thus, one's ecosophy is where one feels intellectually most at home.

Ecosophy T has one ultimate norm, that is, a moral imperative from which the rest of Naess' system is derived, including the platform. That norm is "Self-realization!" The ! indicates that it is a normative claim (not a descriptive one), and "Self" is distinct from "self." Moral maturity, for Naess, consists of an ever-expanding identification of the self until it encompasses all life (and recall that *life* is much broader than biological organisms). The maximal expansion of the self is the Self, something coextensive with, presumably, all of nature. Self-realization is perhaps the most distinctive feature of Naess's ecosophy, and it is an idea picked up and developed by other deep ecologists, such as George Sessions and Warwick Fox.

In *Ecology, Community and Lifestyle,* Naess writes,

> The ecophilosophical outlook is developed through an identification so deep that ones *own self* is no longer adequately delimited by the personal ego or the organism. One experiences oneself to be a genuine part of all life . . . The greater our comprehension of our togetherness with other beings, the greater the identification, and the greater care we will take. The road is also opened thereby for delight in the well-being of others and sorrow when harm befalls them. We seek what is best for ourselves, but through the extension of the self, our "own" best is also that of others. The own/not-own distinction survives only in grammar, not in feeling. [emphasis original]

Envisioning the self merged with its surroundings produces an oceanic feeling. How could I be my surroundings, you might ask? We must remember that in the history of philosophy, the nature of the self is a vexed and perennial topic. What is it to be you? We are used to conceiving of ourselves as in the world but still distinct from it, with a sharp boundary between "me" and "not me." Naess and other deep ecologists call this into question, accepting instead a "relational" conception of organisms "as knots in the field of intrinsic relations." This means that the natural world is not just an assemblage of self-subsisting atomic and interchangeable units that happen to exist together, as a chair, desk, and lamp might be together in a room. The chair remains a chair if it is removed, and the desk remains a desk without the lamp. One lesson of ecology is that organisms are tightly bound to one another by complex interdependencies; they are shaped by their circumstances, rather than simply coexisting. Naess is claiming that the ecological relations among organisms are "intrinsic," meaning that individual natural objects can be properly understood only with respect to their surroundings. The mouse and the tree are thus *defined* with respect to the particular landscape they help constitute (and the landscape with respect to them), much as the pieces of a chess set—rook, knight, pawn—are defined only with respect to the game that gives them meaning. Otherwise, they are just curiously shaped objects.

Mature self-awareness, according to Naess and other deep ecologists, consists in coming to appreciate this wider identification of the self with its surroundings; going from self to Self. Moral concern for the environment is thus a manifestation of Self-concern. Naess and other deep ecologists would be quick to deny that they are recommending egoism as a reigning environmental philosophy—preoccupation with self (lowercase s) has been the problem all along, they would say. But how is Self-concern different from self-concern? And like so many other philosophical views, the more they are explained and developed, the more questions they generate. Naess' deep ecology is no exception. For example, are you and I somehow both aspects of a larger Self? In identifying myself with my surroundings, do I incorporate you as well?

ECOFEMINISM

Throughout history and across cultures, for the most part, women have been dominated, oppressed, discriminated against, and, in general, treated as less worthy beings than men. Aristotle notoriously put women in the same category as slaves, children, and animals, that is, inferior creatures. Numerous theories purport to explain this widespread attitude, but that it exists is beyond doubt. Attitudes about the inferior status of women are so deeply embedded in our assumptions and habitual ways of thought and action that we scarcely recognize them any more since they can assume diverse and subtle forms. Much feminist thought seeks to expose the male-centeredness, or "androcentrism," of our cultural practices, patterns of thought, and habits of mind.

That our cultural attitude toward women might be related to our attitude toward nature is a rich and promising avenue for investigation. A moment's reflection generates many suggestive links and intuitive associations. The very word *nature,* for example, comes from Latin *natus,* meaning birth, definitely something female; and when it come to describing our actions in nature, we almost intuitively reach for sexual metaphors. Rape of wilderness is the environmentalist's outrage; hurricanes used to be given women's names because they were violent and unpredictable; and we all know Mother Nature. The systematic consideration of the ways in which the domination of women and nature are related is a new development of both environmental philosophy and feminism called **ecofeminism.** According to Karen Warren, a leading ecological feminist, "Ecofeminism is the position that there are important connections—historical, experiential, symbolic, theoretical—between the domination of women and the domination of nature, an understanding of which is crucial to both feminism and environmental ethics."

The most important connection, in the eyes of many ecofeminists, is a theoretical one. Only at a theoretical level can we see how deeply entwined the domination of women and the domination of nature are, how they both are manifestations of even more fundamental conceptual features of oppression. And the shared conceptual features of both forms of oppression are "value dualisms" and the "logic of domination." Unquestioned assumptions and seemingly straightforward patterns of thought, according to ecofeminists, can mask an insidious androcentrism (sometimes also called phallocentrism). But what do ecofeminists mean by value dualism and the logic of domination?

According to ecofeminist philosopher Val Plumwood in her book, *Feminism and the Mastery of Nature,* "Dualism is the process by which contrasting concepts (for example, masculine and feminine gender identities) are formed by domination and subordination and constructed as oppositional and exclusive." *Dualism* is thus a technical term for ecofeminists; it refers to a particular kind of opposition or dichotomy, one that arises from domination and subordination. And because domination and subordination are (uncritically) taken by ecofeminists to be necessarily wrong (or bad), dualism is necessarily bad.

The term no doubt takes its inspiration from Descartes' famous dualism between mind and body (see Chapter 3), but for ecofeminists the idea is much broader. It includes any contrast where one side is deemed positive or valuable and the other taken as negative, less worthy, and defined in opposition to the more worthy category. So Descartes' dualism between mind and body would be condemned by ecofeminists because the mental—the essential self for Descartes—is valued over the physical, which is inert and unconscious. You can probably detect a connection between Descartes' dualism (where mind is valuable, body is less valuable) and human–nature dualism, where people are more valuable, nature less so. But how is this androcentric rather than just anthropocentric? According to ecofeminists mind–body dualism is only the start, for it involves an interlocking network of other powerful dualisms, dualisms with a clear gender bias. Mind is rational, which is male; body is passion, which is female; mind is master (male), body is slave (female); mind is active (male), body is passive (female); mind is culture (male), body is nature (female). And so on. For ecofeminists, male–female dualisms are woven together with human–nature dualisms and exposing the one will reveal the other. "A main project of ecofeminism," writes Warren, "is to make visible these 'women–nature connections' and, where harmful to women and nature, to dismantle them."

Dualism sets up a gendered conceptual contrast, but then via the logic of domination (sometimes also called colonization) these gender dualisms become culturally institutionalized to legitimize subordination and domination. As the reasoning goes, because one category is superior (better, more worthy) it may "legitimately" control the other; because of their superiority, men may legitimately control women, and people may legitimately control nature. Ecofeminists (and others) obviously deny the legitimacy of the original contrast, so any control exerted by one side over the other is illegitimate, hence the morally evaluative terms *oppression, subordination,* and *domination.*

Suppose we agree; then what? If we free ourselves from dualistic thinking, then we can relate to one another on the basis of respect and mutuality, not control. According to ecofeminist Val Plumwood, "Overcoming the dualistic dynamic requires recognition of both continuity and difference; this means acknowledging the other as neither alien to and discontinuous from self nor assimilated to or an extension of self." Ecofeminists thus try to steer a path between regarding nature as something completely distinct from oneself and expanding the self to include nature, as recommended by deep ecologists. Nature is different, yes, but we are to respect the differences, not try to construct and impose polarizing patterns of thought that accentuate those differences. Also, we should learn to appreciate the ways in which nature is like us—a theme we have seen other environmental thinkers discuss—because then our emotions can be engaged; we care about it. Plumwood explains,

> Cartesian thought has stripped nature of the intentional and mindlike qualities which make an ethical response to it possible. Once nature is reconceived as capable of agency and intentionality, and human identity is reconceived in less

> polarized and disembodied ways, the great gulf which Cartesian thought established between the conscious, mindful human sphere and the mindless, clockwork natural one disappears.

Suppose we manage the reconceptualization of nature and see it as rather similar to ourselves. How are we supposed to deal with it? Many feminists—not just ecofeminists—are suspicious of traditional moral theories. The worry is that the emphasis on reason and impartiality in traditional moral theory is part of a larger gender bias in ethics that favors principles and rationality (male concerns) over compassion, personal relationships, and care as female concerns. Recall from Chapter 1 how Gilligan argued that women are characteristically oriented toward aspects of a moral issue that emphasize continuity rather than difference, care rather than right. Think of how inappropriate talk of rights, duty, and impartiality is in an intimate relationship. In a family context, for instance, one acts out of love and concern, not duty. The parent who loves the child only because it is the parent's duty to love the child is a poor parent. In her influential article, "Nature, Self, and Gender," Plumwood writes,

> A more promising approach for an ethics of nature, and also one much more in line with the current directions in feminism, would be to remove rights from the center of the moral stage and pay more attention to some other, less dualistic, moral concepts such as respect, sympathy, care, concern, compassion, gratitude, friendship, and responsibility.

So an ethics of care could serve as a moral outlook for ecofeminism, once we have purged ourselves of dualism and are ready to view others warmly, be they human or not.

CRITICAL REACTION TO ECOFEMINISM

Because ecofeminism is opposed to *all* "oppressive conceptual frameworks" (read: dualism), it loses any distinctive connection to feminism. As Warren explicitly claims, "It is by clarifying this conceptual connection between systems of oppression that a movement to end sexist oppression—traditionally the special turf of feminist theory and practice—leads to a reconceiving of feminism as *a movement to end all forms of oppression*" (emphasis original). Feminism is thus merely one way into the issue of dualism, but once the theoretical connections are made between domination of women and all other forms of domination, then the fact that women are oppressed has no more significance than any other form of oppression. One could presumably arrive at the liberation of nature by beginning instead with oppression based on class, race, ability, age, sexual orientation, species membership, or any other conceivable form of domination or oppression, rather than considering the domination of women. This is because they all employ dualism and the logic of domination. That one form of domination (sexism) involves women instead of animals, gays, elderly people, or nature is irrelevant to the true target of ecofeminists, namely, dualism. Ecofeminism is thus a misleading name, since the liberation of just women and nature is not the aim, but rather the liberation of anything that can conceivably be oppressed.

What *can* be dominated or oppressed? Ecofeminists obviously assume that "nature" can be dominated and hence liberated—this thought is core to the entire project. Ecofeminists refer to the domination of nature as "naturism," as a form of oppression just like other forms of oppression, such as sexism or racism. But can nature be oppressed? Domination or oppression in its most abstract formulation presupposes in the oppressed latent tendencies or inherent directions of development. Were it not for the oppression, forces internal to the entity in question would determine its constitution or future. It would be "free" in the sense of "unconstrained." Artifacts, for example, cannot be dominated because they have no drives or propensities for us to thwart or to pervert to our ends. Presumably, then, only things that have ends of their own can be dominated. Thus, it is an open question whether "nature" can be dominated because it is highly questionable whether nature as a whole has ends of its own. We can dominate aspects of nature, perhaps plants or animals, but for nature as a whole to be dominated requires its reification and animation. Some ecofeminists seem ready to do just that (see quote above from Plumwood calling for a reconceptualization of nature), but this highly romantic notion is at odds with a scientific understanding of the world.

Is domination necessarily bad or wrong? Again, ecofeminists seem to assume so. One sense of domination has no evaluative implications, as when, say, a mountain range dominates a landscape or a particular flavor dominates a meal. This is not what concerns ecofeminists. Their concern is on the suppression or channeling of internal propensities. If so, then for domination to be necessarily wrong, it must necessarily be wrong to suppress or pervert or deflect for one's own ends the internal propensities of something. But this hardly seems correct. Our existence requires that we dominate living things in that sense: We dominate plants to grow food; we dominate criminals, in so far as we prevent them from operating in accordance with their internal drives and desires.

Perhaps this last point is unfair. Ecofeminists might reply that the only forms of domination they oppose are ones that employ pernicious value dualisms. If pernicious value dualisms are the ones that are built on bias (gender or otherwise), then ecofeminism becomes a program for identifying and eliminating discrimination in its many forms, a worthy undertaking. If nothing else, we must thank ecofeminists for bringing to our attention the subtle and pervasive forms of discrimination.

Recall that care ethics seems to fit the bill as a moral outlook for ecofeminism, since it is respectful of differences, free from dualism, and is appropriate for intimate contexts. Although much work remains to be done, there are likely conceptual limitations on the entities about which one can care. "Nature," like "humanity," is just too abstract to be a proper object of care, even if one is a saint. Care ethics requires small-scale interpersonal closeness. It also requires reciprocity. Nel Noddings, in her well-known book on feminist ethics, *Caring: A Feminine Approach to Ethics and Moral Education,* argues that caring can exist only if the "cared-for" can interact with the "one-caring." She writes, "A caring relation requires the engrossment and motivational displacement of the one-caring, and it requires the recognition and spontaneous response of the cared-for." Acknowledgement and responsiveness in the cared-for is, according to Noddings, a condition for an ethical relation of care. Noddings, therefore, is skeptical that care ethics can be easily used to express an ethical relation to nature. She observes, by way of summary, "We then considered the plant world and found that, while caring occurs in the elliptical sense given by the 'I care,' there is no true ethical relation between humans and plants because the relation is logically one-sided and there is no other consciousness to receive the caring." So Noddings' care ethics will not serve ecofeminists as an ethics of nature in the straightforward way they had initially hoped. For care ethics to underwrite a caring attitude toward nature, the problem of 'one-sidedness' must be addressed.

THE READINGS

The readings in this chapter deal with questions about our entire way of life. Should our lives be "simple in means, rich in ends," as put forward by deep ecologists? What would such a way of life look like? Why should we even contemplate such a way of life? Is there a moral imperative to do so? Further, to what extent might our ordinary patterns of behavior and thought be subject to subtle (and not so subtle) sexual bias?

JEROME SEGAL

From *Graceful Simplicity*

Our first reading is by author and political activist Jerome Segal. It is taken from his recent book, *Graceful Simplicity: Toward a Philosophy and Politics of Simple Living,* in which Segal examines our current obsession with consumption and seeks to define an alternative way of life, one that exemplifies some of the ideals of Thoreau and deep ecology. For Segal, environmental issues are subsumed under an even larger question about the elements of "a good life."

CRITICAL READING QUESTIONS

1. What are the two versions of the "good life" sketched by Segal and how have they been manifested historically in American life?
2. What is Aristotle's challenge?
3. What is "marginal utility" and how is it relevant to consumption?
4. How is Aristotle's thought relevant to the "Alternative American Dream"?
5. In Segal's view, what is the difference between simple living and poverty?

In popular imagery, especially when seen from afar, America is often portrayed as singing a single song, as if there were only one meaning to the American Dream. This is not so. The ambivalent response that many in the world have toward American life is mirrored in an ambivalence that many Americans have toward their own life, and this is an essential part of the American tradition, even when people are "making it" in America. There is always that nagging question, "Is this really the way to live?"

Long before there was an America, there were two American Dreams, and they reflect two ways of thinking about money. In Western thought, from the very beginning to the present day, people had doubts about the real value of riches and the things money can buy. There has always been a conflict between the view that "more is better" and the view that "just enough is plenty."

This divide is reflected in two very different visions of the good life. It is the underlying thesis of this book that the Alternative Dream, the dream that rests upon the attainment of a simple life, is the sounder vision.

From *Graceful Simplicity: Toward a Philosophy and Politics of Simple Living,* Chapter 1, University of California Press, 2002. Reprinted with permission of University of California Press.

ARISTOTLE'S CHALLENGE TO OUR WAY OF LIFE

This book is about contemporary life, but I want to start with Aristotle for two reasons, First, because his challenge to a money-oriented form of life remains as powerful today as it was 2,300 years ago. Second, because, for all his wisdom, Aristotle never had to wrestle with the problems we face. So many of the contemporary problems that prevent people in the middle class from enjoying the good life emerge from three forms of genuine moral and social progress that Aristotle never envisioned: the elimination of slavery, the liberation of women, and the affirmation of the right of ordinary working people to self-fulfillment. Seeing both the strengths and weaknesses in Aristotle gives us a clearer perspective on our own situation.

Aristotle's *Politics* is surprising in that it opens with a discussion of the household. But this is exactly the right touchstone for both politics and economics. The household is a central ground of the good life, and all economic arrangements must be judged by whether they enable the household to perform its function as locus and support for the human good. This is one of the central messages of this book: We must put the proper functioning of the household at the center of the way we think about economic life.

The core issue, as Aristotle puts it, is property and "the art of acquisition"—that is, how people make a living. He starts with the observation that there are a variety of different modes of subsistence, and that this gives rise to a variety of different ways of life. This is as true among animals as it is of humans. Some animals live in herds, and others live in isolation. Some eat plants and others meat. Among human beings, Aristotle identifies five "natural" ways of life: pastoral, farming, fishing, hunting, and, interestingly, piracy. What he calls "true wealth" is acquired through these activities and consists of the amount of household property that suffices for the good life. This he regards as a limited amount. We can call this the perspective that "just enough is plenty."

In distinction to these modes of acquisition that supply the household with its needs, there is a second form of the art of acquisition, which Aristotle believes to be "unnatural":

> The other form is a matter only of retail trade, and it is concerned only with getting a fund of money, and that only by the method of conducting the exchange of commodities.
>
> The acquisition of wealth by the art of household management [as contrasted with the art of acquisition in its retail form] has a limit; and the object of that art is not an unlimited amount of wealth.

The difference is between an approach to acquisition that views it as functional to the life of the household and one in which it takes on a life of its own, such that it reproduces unchecked without regard to the larger life of the organism, and ultimately undermines that life—the very description of what we now understand as cancer.

What Aristotle presents in these lines isn't just an academic distinction, but a clash between two different ways of life, each captured by a way of thinking about money. In the first, money and the things one can buy with it play an important but limited role. Life is not about money. It is not about getting rich. It is about something higher, whether it is philosophy, or art, or the pursuit of knowledge, or participation with one's fellow citizens in the ever-absorbing process of governing the democratic polis. Every person lives within a household, and the household has its economic needs—but the point is to attain only what is sufficient to enable one to turn away from money-getting and undertake the real activities of life.

In this first vision of life, only some ways of making a living are viewed by Aristotle as acceptable. His list of farmer, hunter, fisherman, herdsman, or pirate has an arbitrary quality to it. What is important is what these choices are intended to rule out. The one thing you cannot do is spend your life grubbing for money. You do not become a businessman, a retail trader, a man of commerce. These all represent a kind of slavishness to money. Nor (one would hope) do you find yourself so destitute that you must work for someone else, for that, too, is a form of slavery. The good life requires some degree of good fortune. Ideally for Aristotle, you are born financially independent.

But how do people manage to go so wrong about money? How does it gain such control over their lives? Aristotle suggests that this emerges from a deep misconception about the nature of human happiness; it is this that leads to the focus on the pursuit of higher and higher levels of consumption and of the higher income necessary to sustain them.

Aristotle identifies what he terms "external goods"; these externals include wealth, property, power, and reputation. These are the elements that make up the standard vision of success both then and now. To these, Aristotle contrasts elements of character, what he terms the "goods of the soul," fortitude, temperance, justice, and wisdom. This is a familiar distinction, between inner and outer, between matters of worldliness and matters of virtue. We continue to make these distinctions when we are reflective, not so much about our own lives, but when we think about what we want for our children—are we more concerned that our children be rich and successful or that they develop into good human beings? We tell them that these "externals" are not what is really important in life, and we hope that they will listen.

Aristotle tells us that happiness "belongs more to those who have cultivated their character and mind to the uttermost, and kept acquisition of external goods within moderate limits." Those who lose in life are those "who have managed to acquire more external goods than they can possibly use, and are lacking in the goods of the soul." (For "soul" we might substitute "character" or "mental health.")

Of course, one might say, "Why the either/or? Why not have both?" But Aristotle, and many others, have thought that we really do have to choose. In explaining the relationship between externals and the good life, Aristotle tells us: "External goods, like all other instruments, have a necessary limit of size . . . any excessive amount of such things must either cause its possessor some injury, or at any rate, bring him no benefit."

This passage, which has been overlooked by many historians of economics, implicitly is the first statement of the principle of diminishing marginal utility. We might remember from introductory economics that marginal utility is the extra utility (or happiness, satisfaction, pleasure, fulfillment) that someone gets from each successive unit of something. Marginal utility generally declines; the pleasure from the first ice-cream cone is greater than from the second, and most of us can hardly eat a third.

Aristotle is saying that with all external goods, we find that the more we have, the less utility we receive from each additional amount, and that at some point "any excessive amount" does us no good and may even harm us.

Actually, Aristotle's view of what 19th-century economists would identify as the "utility curve" is quite radical. As we acquire more and more things, not only does the total utility (i.e., happiness, satisfaction) level fail to rise beyond an upper bound (as in classical presentations of the diminishing character of marginal utility), but the total utility level may actually diminish, implying that the marginal benefit attached to excessive amounts of external goods diminishes beyond the zero level and actually becomes harmful. Translated into a thesis about money, Aristotle's formulation tells us that beyond a given level, additional increments of money are not only useless, but negative in their effect. Translated into a thesis about the society at large, he suggests that economic growth beyond a given point is actually harmful to human happiness. It is a straightforward rejection of the idea that "more is better."

Aristotle goes further in his account. The problem is not merely of the sort that John Kenneth Galbraith described (23 centuries later) in *The Affluent Society,* where economic life is compared to life on a squirrel wheel, each of us fruitlessly expending time and resources but not getting anywhere as the wheel just spins faster and faster. For Galbraith the indictment is that we are wasting our time and energy, and thus wasting our lives.

For Aristotle the issue is even more serious than a life of wasted pursuit. The pursuit of higher and higher levels of income results in a distortion of the personality, such that we never come to be the persons that we most truly are; we are divorced from our truest selves. Instead people are "led to occupy themselves wholly in the making of money . . . using each and every capacity in a way not consonant with its nature."

When Aristotle says "the lower form of the art of acquisition has come into vogue," he is quietly telling us that he sees his own civilization threatened by a new and troubling vision of the place of money in the good life. He is giving voice to concerns that, centuries later, in religious form and in America, will be repeated in the form of fiery jeremiads issued from the pulpit.

Though he might have, Aristotle doesn't use phrases such as "we have lost our souls"—instead he speaks of a distortion of human capacities. He offers an example:

> The proper function of courage, for example, is not to produce money but to give confidence. The same is true of military and medical ability: neither has the function of producing money: the one has the function of producing victory, and the other that of producing health. But those of whom we are speaking turn all such capacities into forms of the art of acquisition, as though to make money were the one aim and everything else must contribute to that aim.

Consider this comment about "medical ability"—Aristotle is talking about what it is to be a doctor. What we once expected to encounter when we went to the doctor was someone whose motivation centered around the inherent value of medicine—the health of the patient. What we did not expect, and once would have been repelled by, was to have encountered a businessman in a white coat or an entrepreneur with aides who are specialists in billing practices. When this happens across the board, when everything is about money, a civilization is cracking apart.

It should be clear that Aristotle's critique is not merely about certain specific economic activities (e.g., retail sales as opposed to production). It is an indictment of a general outlook and form of life. When these become dominant in society, the object of criticism is then the entire form of social life or civilization.

Such a civilization, and I believe Aristotle would include much of the modern world in this category, is to be condemned as representing a distortion of human nature and a general thwarting of the possibility of human fulfillment.

When every human capacity gets placed at the service of obtaining money, *we ourselves are transformed and distorted.* That's why you can't have it all—why there is conflict between the two American Dreams—who "you" are changes through the choices you (and your household) make toward matters of acquisition, careers, "success." Within the Aristotelian framework, to say that our capacities, that is, our selves, are separated from their proper function, is to say that we are thus denied self-actualization or human fulfillment. It is also to say that we are thus denied the possibility of living well; for to live well for Aristotle is to express one's richest potentials at high levels of excellence.

It is easy to miss the full significance of this, as the Aristotelian vocabulary is not our own. But we can shift the language a bit. Perhaps we would speak of a life so absorbed in moment-to-moment gain and careerism that one loses or never deeply develops a sense of oneself and never lives the life he or she intended to. In the end, one is left with a sense of emptiness and waste. It's captured in the bumper sticker that reads: "No one ever died wishing they had spent more time at the office."

These matters largely fall by the wayside in contemporary thinking about the economic realm. Instead we hear a very different story, one in which we come to the economic realm as well-formed consumers. We have multiple wants and desires. There are limited resources. Producers compete for our spending money by creating the products that best satisfy our desires. In an efficient system, the companies that serve people's desires most adequately and efficiently make profits; the others disappear. The result is more and more consumer satisfaction. As consumers we are said to be sovereign. But to participate in the process, we must sell our labor services to those who can make best use of them. Thus, we take jobs that pay more, and we are enabled to buy more. When the system is working well, some of what is earned is reinvested, and the economy grows, gaining greater capacity to produce. Incomes rise and the level of consumption rises within, making us even better off than we were before.

In contrast we can identify an approach that might be termed Aristotelian:

- There is no distinct economic realm.
- Economic institutions and policy must be judged in terms of how they affect the good life and the healthy personality.

- The central institution to be supported by economic life is the household (which in turn supports worthwhile activity in the larger world).
- The good life is not one of consumption, but of the flourishing of our deepest selves.
- Absorption in a life of acquisitiveness distorts the personality out of all recognition.
- What we need for our well-being is only a moderate supply of material goods. As we acquire more, material possessions are of diminishing value.

Ultimately the additional contribution to the good life of having more money reaches zero, and even becomes negative.

Aristotle, in his analysis of the limited place of money in the good life, and in his emphasis on how absorption in acquisition undermines both the healthy personality and the good life, can be seen as the intellectual father of a philosophy of simple living.

But before leaving Aristotle, we must recognize the other side of the picture. Aristotle was not a believer in the general equality of all men and women. Though he did not hold a racial theory, he believed that there were some people who were "natural slaves" in that they lacked the capability of governing themselves. Of course, at some point in life—when we are children—we all lack this capability. But Aristotle believed that a significant class of adult males, and women generally, lacked the capability to govern themselves.

These views about the naturalness of slavery and the subservience of women turn out to have an intimate relationship to the question of simple living, and to graceful living in particular. Later in the book I will consider the question "What is real wealth?" Ultimately I want to argue that most wealth resides in the ability to draw on the services of other people, and this is especially true of that wealth which contributes to graceful living. We normally think of such wealth as residing in financial assets (e.g., money, stocks, bonds, real estate), but it can equally reside in relationships (e.g., friendship, parent–child relationships, marriage). It can also reside in institutionalized relations of unequal power such as slavery, rigid class distinctions, and the domination of women. When one has access to the services of others through such institutional structures, it is indeed easier to live well, even gracefully, with less money; one has found nonmonetized ways of accessing valued services. The great challenge is to find a way to live simply, gracefully, and well, not only without excessive dependence upon money, but without reliance on unjust social institutions.

For Aristotle, this never really clicked into place. While he recognized that not all who were in fact slaves were of a "slavish nature," he did not challenge slavery itself. It is similar when he considers the situation of artisans; that is, skilled craftsmen employed in making the artifacts of everyday life. He speaks of the mechanical type of artisan as being subject to a "limited servitude," by which he means that the artisan is in parts of his life subject to the will of his master. But then, in contrast to the situation with slaves, Aristotle tells us that while "the slave belongs to the class of those who are naturally what they are; . . . no shoemaker or any other artisan, belongs to that class."

Here Aristotle makes two points of great importance. First, artisans—and, we can say, most working people—are subject to a limited servitude; their lives bear some significant resemblance to slavery. (Twenty-three centuries later people would speak of "wage slavery.") Second, Aristotle says that no artisan is "naturally" what he is. That is, such limited slavery is unnatural.

Aristotle should have concluded from this that there is something unnatural, or at least inadequate, about the polis, understood as the sum of the socioeconomic processes and structures within which Greek life occurred. He fails to do so. In his discussion of the limited slavery of workers, there is no proposal for an alternative social arrangement, despite the fact that he sees the way the institution is incompatible with the fulfillment of the deeper potentials of those who labor within it. This, I believe, emerged from an unexamined assumption that such must necessarily be the case if we are to have a social order in which there are at least some people who are fully developed and living a free and flourishing existence.

There is a passage in Aristotle in which he considers the possibility of a world in which it would not be necessary for people to work in partial or full enslavement. But he offers this speculation not as a future that might someday be, but as a fantasy that cannot be. Thus, it shows why things must be as they are:

> There is only one condition in which we can imagine managers not needing subordinates, and masters not needing slaves. This condition would be that each (inanimate) instrument could do its own work, at the word of command or by intelligent anticipation . . . as a shuttle should weave of itself and a plectrum should do its own harp playing.

It is revealing that he speaks here of the "needs" of managers and masters, rather than of the needs of slaves and people who work for a living. In part this merely shows the partial blindness of even the greatest minds, but it also reflects his inability to foresee the actual occurrence of major sustained technological progress. It is too much to expect that he could have truly foreseen full automation—where the machines operate on their own. But he might have had a vision of the continued increase in the productivity of labor.

Given that Aristotle was clear about the limited value of acquiring more and more, he would have been led to the alternative use of productivity increases: not to have more and more, but to allow the ordinary person to work less and less in order to produce that limited output that is required for the good and free life. In short, through productivity growth there is a potential that can be put in the service of self-actualization for the ordinary person. It is such productivity growth that allowed us to go from the 12-hour day to the 8-hour day, and opens the possibility of the 6-hour day, or the three-day weekend. For a hundred years this was part of how we used productivity growth; we stopped doing this 60 years ago. Had he seen the deeper potentials of all people, Aristotle would have seen the polis of his day not as a model for humankind, but as modeling only in the life of its free male citizens, a life that someday might be available to all, provided that we used that productivity growth, not for ever-increasing amounts of unnecessary goods, but for the elimination of slavish forms of activity.

Put in other terms, for Aristotle the existence of mass poverty does not emerge as a problem. With his acceptance of the naturalness of slavery and the subservience of women, and his acquiescence to the limited servitude of workers, the socioeconomic framework of the polis fits neatly into a theory of human development. The polis is the environment with which human fulfillment occurs. The situation of the vast majority of persons simply falls by the wayside, as not raising any pressing problems. Having limited potential, they reach their full development within subservient roles. Indeed, it is really not until the 18th century that the equality of ordinary people in their entitlement and potential for achieving the highest levels of human development are embedded within the structures of political ideology and action. And it is not until the 20th century that equality begins to be substantially extended to women.

What Aristotle did do, however, remains of enormous importance. He challenged the idea that acquiring more and more things was good for the individual. He set his critique of commercial and acquisitive forms of life within a theory of human development that stressed the exercise and perfection of distinctly human capacities, capacities that are distorted and stunted if we allow economic pursuits to dominate our lives.

Appreciating the virtues of Aristotle along with his limitations is particularly important for a balanced appreciation of the problem inherent in our own way of life. We live in a society that, as a result of both economic growth and social struggle, is substantially along the way to overcoming historic legacies of slavery, mass poverty, and the subjugation of women. Yet many of the problems that we face, problems that make it more difficult to achieve simple living, emerge because of these legacies and transitions. But they also endure because we have lost sight of much that Aristotle has to teach us with respect to the place of the economic within the good life: *The point of an economy, even a dynamic economy, is not to have more and more; it is to liberate us from the economic—to provide a material platform from which we may go forth to build the good life. That's the Alternative American Dream.*

SIMPLE LIVING AND AMERICAN DREAMS

We entirely mistake our own history if we think of simple living as some recent fad. The idea of simple living has always been part of the American psyche—sometimes central, sometimes only a minor theme, but always present. From the earliest days of the American experience, advocates of simple living have challenged consumerism and materialism.

Simple living, especially in America, has meant many things. For Christians the central inspiration for a life of simplicity has been the life of Jesus. In the hands of the Puritans, this emerged as a life of religious devotion, a lack of ostentation, and plenty of hard work. It was certainly not a leisure expansion movement as it is today. Nor was simple living a matter of individual choice; sumptuary laws invoked the power of the state to restrict consumption display, and economic life was regulated to limit the role of greed in human affairs.

In the hands of the Quakers, the concept of the simple life underwent an evolution. For the Puritans, at least part of the motivation for sumptuary laws was to prevent those in the lower classes from putting on the manners of those above them; among Quakers, the restrictions on display and consumption became more widely applicable. Most important, the pursuit of luxurious consumption was linked to a broad range of injustices and social problems, including alcoholism, poverty, slavery, and ill treatment of the Indians. Here, perhaps, are the origins of a radical politics of plain living—the belief that if people adopted the simple life, all of society would be transformed.

The key Quaker theorist of the simple life was John Woolman. Central to Woolman's thought was the recognition that people could be "necessitated to labour too hard." He focused on the plight of those who did not own their own land but rented it from large estates. If the rent was too high, the amount of labor required of the poor would oppress them and draw them away from the proper affairs of life. But rent was an intermediate concern; what was really at issue was the extent to which one person would be required to labor so that another might have superfluous luxuries. Woolman wrote, "Were all superfluities, and the desires of outward greatness laid aside," then "moderate labour with the blessing of Heaven would answer all good purposes . . . and a sufficient number have time to attend on the proper affairs of civil society." Thus, he maintained that "every degree of luxury of what kind soever and every demand for money inconsistent with divine order hath some connexion with unnecessary labour." Woolman called on his listeners to follow the example of Jesus in simple food and dress. He saw their desire for luxurious consumption as the core motive that resulted in the practice "of fetching men to help to labour from distant parts of the world, to spend the remainder of their lives in the uncomfortable conditions of slaves." He also identified selfishness as the cause of past wars, telling us to "look upon our treasures, and the furniture of our houses, and the garment in which we array ourselves, and try whether the seeds of war have nourishment in these our possessions, or not." Were Woolman alive today, it is likely that he would extend his critique, arguing that excessive consumption, and the desire for it, is at the root of both the drug and environmental problems we face. Indeed, Woolman would probably have been receptive to the idea that the harsh poverty of many Third World countries emerges from the excessive consumption of the rich nations.

In the mid-1700s, in the years prior to the Revolution, the ideas of simple living and democratic government were intertwined. For many of the leaders of the Revolution, however, the ideal was not the simple life of Jesus, but the simple life of the self-governing citizens of ancient Greece and Rome. Key figures in the revolutionary period, in particular Samuel Adams, were deeply concerned about the relationship between our political health and the individual pursuit of luxury. The rebirth of democracy in the world brought with it an interest in the ancient Greek and Roman experiments, and why they disappeared. There was a concern (as there is today) with the virtue of officeholders. Genuine democracy seemed incompatible with too great an absorption in getting rich. There was great fear of the corrupting influences of unbridled commercialism. When the colonists boycotted British goods, it was not just a tactic of the independence movement; Britain was viewed as the Great Satan, exporting the corruptions of capitalism.

In their correspondence, John Adams and Thomas Jefferson assessed the prospects for building a nonmaterialist society. Jefferson emphasized civic virtue, and looked to public policy, in particular state-supported schools and values education, as the foundation of such a society. Adams viewed this as unrealistically "undertaking to build a new universe." He himself feared economic growth, however, and argued for preventing both extreme poverty and extravagant riches. Both men feared rather than celebrated boundless economic opportunity.

Benjamin Franklin's views on these questions are also worth noting; they, too, have a contemporary echo. In Franklin we have an unusual mixture: the espousal of frugality, hard work, and restrained consumption as the vehicles for getting ahead, the central patterns of behavior that will lead to wealth. Thus, in the preface to *Poor Richard's Almanac,* which was reprinted in 14 languages under the title *The Way to Wealth,* Franklin writes, "But dost thou love Life, then do not squander Time; for that's the stuff Life is made of." And "If Time be of all Things the most precious, wasting Time must be, as Poor Richard says, the greatest Prodigality." Franklin was concerned with how the average person might remain free in his own life, his own master. "Employ thy Time well, if thou meanest to gain Leisure." He warns of the perils of spending and in particular of borrowing. The great thing is to save. "We must add Frugality, if we would make our Industry more certainly successful. A Man may, if he knows not how to save as he gets, keep his Nose all his Life, to the Grindstone, and die not worth a Groat at last . . . If you would be wealthy . . . think of Saving as well as Getting." Note that here Franklin is advocating simple living as a means to future wealth, quite a different reason than those that animated Woolman.

Franklin warned that the dangers of excessive consumption are easily missed. And he was quite demanding in what he viewed as "excessive." He wrote, "You may think perhaps, that a little Tea, or a little Punch now and then, Diet a little more costly, Clothes a little finer, and a little Entertainment now and then, may be no great Matter; but remember what Poor Richard says, Many a Little makes a Mickle . . . A small Leak will sink a great Ship."

He continued, "The artificial Wants of Mankind thus become more numerous than the Natural . . . When you have bought one fine Thing, you must buy ten more, that your Appearance may be all of a Piece . . . 'Tis easier to suppress the first Desire, than to satisfy all that follows it . . . What Use is this Pride of Appearance, for which so much is risked, so much is suffered? It cannot promote Health, or ease Pain; it makes no Increase of Merit in the Person, it creates Envy, it hastens Misfortune."

Franklin rails against going into debt. Credit cards would have seemed to him the instruments of our undoing. "What Madness must it be to run in Debt for these Superfluities! . . . think what you do when you turn in Debt; you give to another Power over your Liberty . . . Preserve your Freedom; and maintain your Independency: Be Industrious and free; be frugal and free."

While Franklin spoke to the individual, in American history, the mode of response to the dominant commercial culture has often been communal. Americans have been utopian, not in the sense of speculation on utopia, but in the actual establishment of a community wherein this dominance by the economic is overcome. Utopian thought has a long and rich history, much of it European. But it was in America, both before and after the founding of the United States, that the impulse to go ahead and just create that better world was the strongest.

Though the formation of these communities was not unique to the American experience, the abundance and constancy of utopian communities does appear to be distinctly American. Indeed there has not been a single year in the history of the United

States without communes. One recent study of American communes concluded:

> The extent and continuity of the communal phenomenon had no equal outside the United States . . . In modern times the United States is the only place where voluntary communes have existed continuously for 250 years.

Two features of these utopian communities are particularly noteworthy. First, with few exceptions, they were communes. Property was typically held in-common, and sometimes income was pooled. And second, they were typically not merely residential sites, but work sites as well. The community collectively owned land and capital, and the community both provided for itself and collectively produced for the outside world. Thus, virtually all of these communities challenge the boundaries between household and workplace that had begun to emerge in the 17th century. In doing so as a community, through the holding of the common property of the unified home/work site, they were reestablishing the extended establishment-family. In a sense, these communities could be seen as large establishment-households.

The uninterrupted history of utopian communes throughout American history speaks of an ongoing practical discourse that seeks through actual life experiments to break the boundaries between home and economy, and to replace the harsh marketplace relations of worker/master, of owner/employer, with a simpler life within a "circle of affection." In the mid-1800s such communes flourished. In some ways this period prefigured the communes, vegetarianism, nudism, and animal rights efforts of the 1960s.

Filled with a sense of adventure and experiment, but of a more individualist bent, was Henry David Thoreau. In *Walden* he looked about him and saw mostly foolishness—people not knowing how to grab hold of the gift of life. He reveled in the energy of youth and in its ability to find out what older generations had never seen.

> Practically, the old have no very important advice to give the young, their own experience has been so partial, and their lives have been such miserable failures . . . Here is life, an experiment to a great extent untried by me . . . If I have any experience which I think valuable, I am sure to reflect that this my Mentors, said nothing about.

With words that had echoes of Aristotle, he told Americans that our necessities are few, yet we subject ourselves to endless labor. He described a world that had taken the wrong turn. "The 12 labors of Hercules were trifling in comparison with those which my neighbors have undertaken; for they were only 12 and had an end." Wealth itself is a curse because it enslaves us. "I see young men, my townsmen, whose misfortune it is to have inherited farms, houses, barns, cattle and farming tools; for these are more easily acquired than got rid of." Of most men Thoreau says, "they begin digging their graves as soon as they are born . . . Men labor under a mistake. The better part of the man is soon ploughed into the soil for compost." We must take better care of ourselves, of our potentials. "The finest qualities of our nature, like the bloom on fruits, can be preserved only by the most delicate handling. Yet we do not treat ourselves nor one another thus tenderly." We miss that which is best in life. "Most men, even in this comparatively free country, through mere ignorance and mistake, are so occupied with the factitious cares and superfluously coarse labors of life that its finer fruits cannot be plucked by them."

Yes, the necessities must be met, "for not till we have secured these are we prepared to entertain the true problems of life with freedom and a prospect of success." But "most of the luxuries, and many of the so called comforts of life are not only not indispensable, but positive hindrances to the elevation of mankind. With respect to luxuries and comforts, the wisest have ever lived a more simple and meager life than the poor." He tells us that "none can be an impartial or wise observer of human life but from the vantage ground of what we should call voluntary poverty." The dictates of wisdom call for "a life of simplicity, independence, magnanimity and trust."

For Thoreau it is not necessity that enslaves us. Rather we have become the "slave-drivers" of ourselves, "the slave and prisoner of [our] own opinion of [ourselves]." Once we have satisfied our necessities, rather than laboring for superfluities, it is time to "adventure on life." But few undertake this adventure. Instead, "the mass of men lead lives of quiet desperation." It is from a disease of the spirit that Thoreau recoils, one that people may not even be aware of. "A stereotyped but unconscious despair is concealed even under what are called the games and amusements of mankind. There is no play in them . . ."

Thus Thoreau called Americans away from their overabsorption with economic life, from their self-subjugation to a life of toil. Unlike earlier advocates of simple living, he was not calling people to religion or to civic engagement; rather he was calling us as individuals to find our own nature, to define ourselves at a higher level of experience. He called for simple living in order to enable the life of the mind, of art, literature, poetry, philosophy, and an almost reverential engagement with nature.

Interest in simple living was harder to find in the post-Civil War period, but it reemerged powerfully toward the turn of the century. There was a reaction against materialism and the hectic pace of urban life. In those days it was *The Ladies' Home Journal* (of all things) that led the charge against the dominant materialist ethos. Under a crusading editor, Edward Bok, it served as a guide for those in the middle class seeking simplicity. By 1910, the *Journal* had a circulation of close to 2 million, making it the largest-selling magazine in the world. This period also witnessed a movement of aesthetic simplicity. It was influenced by the English thinkers John Ruskin and William Morris, and recognized that only in a world which appreciated fine crafts would there be jobs for fine craftsmen. It is from this mileau that we have the "mission" furniture, much sought by antique dealers today.

"One dimension of the renewed interest in simple living was a "country life" movement that sought to use modern technology to improve country life for the small farmer and to keep young people on the farm. Later, in 1933, the Department of the Interior created a Division of Subsistence Homesteads to resettle the urban and rural poor in planned communities based on "handicrafts, community activities, closer relationships, and cooperative enterprises." About 100 such communities were established, most of them failing in their grand design to replace individualism with mutualism."

After World War II, as after World War I, the Civil War, and the American Revolution, there was a surge in consumption, and simple living receded into the background. But again in the 1960s there was a critique of the affluent lifestyle and a renewed interest in plain living. In the 1970s, with the energy crisis, this merged with a broad environmentalism. Many saw the energy crisis not as an economic or political problem to be overcome, but as an occasion for a spiritual renewal that would turn us away from the rampant materialism of modern life. One of these was President Jimmy Carter.

"We worship self-indulgence and consumption," Carter declared, taking his place in a great American tradition of social criticism. "Human identity is no longer defined by what one does but by what one owns." And, like earlier critics, Carter lamented the emptiness of such an existence. "We've discovered that owning things and consuming things does not satisfy our longing for meaning."

Carter saw the problem as residing in what he termed "a mistaken idea of freedom"—one in which we advocate "the right to grasp for ourselves some advantage over others." He called on Americans to unite together in a crusade of energy conservation:

> We often think of conservation only in terms of sacrifice . . . solutions to our energy crisis can also help us to conquer the crisis of spirit in our country. It can rekindle a sense of unity, our confidence in the future, and give our nation and all of us individually a new sense of purpose.

This was his so-called "malaise" speech, and while it failed as an effort to transform the national spirit, and certainly failed Carter politically, it did capture well the link between environmental concerns and simple living that many Americans continue to feel today. Carter was followed by the Reagan and Bush administrations, during which no similar critique was heard. But now, at the turn of the millennium, there is renewed interest in simple living, if not in the White House, then at least in the heartland.

This quick historical survey reveals that "simple living" has meant many things. There is an anticonsumptionist core in much American thinking on this subject, but great diversity with respect to the human good and the place of work, religion, civic engagement, nature, literature, and the arts. Concern with simple living has been largely apolitical at some times, and at others the heart of a general political and social vision.

Today, when there is once again a great interest in simple living in America, it is mainly an apolitical enthusiasm. Most, though not all, of the literature is of a "how to" variety, offering advice on how to live more rewardingly with less money. The attainment of a simpler, more meaningful life is seen as an individual project, not as a matter of collective politics. In the chapters that follow I will explore the limitations of this individualistic approach and argue for a "politics of simplicity."

SIMPLE LIVING AND POVERTY

The question sometimes arises, "What is the difference between simple living and poverty?" Several responses are possible. One calls attention to the difference between voluntarily choosing to live in a certain way and having to. This is certainly of great importance. Often enough, people who adopt simple living have the ability to earn more income if they choose. Thus, there is an actual and psychological freedom that attends their life. This freedom is not part of the life experience of those trapped in poverty. It is true that not all of the poor are "trapped"; some people do manage to escape from poverty. On the other hand, a person is not truly poor if the exit is readily available.

Yet this emphasis on freedom can go only so far. First, there are situations in which the choice to live a simple life is not reversible, situations in which an exit to higher levels of consumption may not be readily at hand. Second, the core of the distinction cannot rest on whether the condition is chosen. We can imagine situations in which for one reason or another (e.g., as a penance) someone chooses to live in irreversible poverty. Alternatively, there are people who have been born into a community or culture based on a tradition of simple living. Simple living is consistent with there being no choice, no awareness of alternatives, and, under some conditions, with no opportunity for opulent living.

The essential matter is not how people come to simple living as opposed to poverty, but a difference that resides in the life itself. Even with no knowledge of how someone got there, it should be possible to distinguish poverty from simple living, just by examining the life people do live.

One approach might be to say that it is a matter of degree, that simple living occupies a place between poverty and middle-class life. Thus, as government agencies sometimes do, we can define poverty arbitrarily in terms of a certain level of income (e.g., the poverty line for a family can be set at 60 percent of median family income). And proceeding in this way, we can also define simple living in terms of income, as a tier that exists between poverty and middle-class status.

While this has the virtue of clarity and precision, it offers little insight. Moreover, there are many variants of simple living, and while some operate above the income levels used to define poverty, others may be below.

Let me offer a different answer. The touchstone here is to ask, "What is it for a life itself to be impoverished?" As soon as the issue is put in this way, one must ask, "Impoverished in what dimensions?" The human good is too diverse to try to capture either its richness or its poverty in a single dimension. For instance, we can identify five forms of impoverishment:

- *Material impoverishment,* meaning inadequacies of goods and services such that the individual experiences (or is exposed to) disease, hunger, starvation. This could be caused by inadequacies of monetary income, inadequacies of public investment, inadequacies of human support systems, or even simply by bad luck.
- *Intellectual impoverishment,* meaning an inadequacy of education and/or absence of interactions with others so that the individual does not partake in a life of the mind. This can be

brought about through lack of schooling leading to illiteracy, or more commonly a culture of intellectual isolation.

- *Spiritual impoverishment,* meaning the absence of any transcendent meaning in the experiences or activities of the individual. This might include, but certainly should not be limited to or defined in terms of, religious experience.
- *Aesthetic impoverishment,* meaning the absence of beauty within the person's life, whether it be the beauty of material possessions, the natural environment, the urban world, or the absence of ceremony.
- *Social impoverishment,* meaning an absence of central relationships, of friends and loved ones.

Who are "the poor"? There is no single answer. The term covers a wide diversity of people and circumstances. In material terms, it may refer to the average person in a poor African country. There the central facts may be a persistent inadequacy of food and clean water, yet at the same time there may be a vibrant communal, family, and religious life. Alternatively, we may be speaking about the poor in the United States; yet this, too, may refer to highly varied circumstances. There is a great difference between hardworking sharecropper families in Mississippi, with limited income and education, on the one hand, and young inner-city street hustlers, without fathers, in a drug culture, amid gangs and prostitution. Both may face low levels of life expectancy, the sharecropping family from malnutrition, the inner-city drug users from a high probability of either getting shot or acquiring AIDS from shared needles.

When simple living is advocated, it is generally implicit that material needs are met. Today's popular simple living literature focuses strongly on how we can meet our material needs with limited financial means. This, however, must be thought of as a precondition for simple living—by achieving relative independence from material need, one is freed to create a life that is rich in some nonmaterial sense. The central distinction is not between simple living and material poverty (indeed, these can overlap) but between simple living and a life that is impoverished in one or more of its multiple nonmaterial dimensions.

Thus understood, the richness of simple living rests upon the material and nonmaterial wealth we both possess and successfully actualize, wealth that may be public or private, cultural or natural, aesthetic, religious, intellectual, interpersonal, or psychological. It may reside in the capabilities of our families and communities, in our relationships with others, or more narrowly within ourselves, as our human capital, psychological and physical.

From this it follows that simple living is not merely a matter of downsizing, of living on less, or of working less. It's possible to do that, and have the result be nothing more than a general impoverishment. Simple living is not the residue that emerges when one consumes less; it is an achievement. It is what can emerge when as a result of subjecting the material dimension to a larger vision, one succeeds in creating a life that is rich and exciting in its aesthetic, intellectual, spiritual, and social dimensions.

DISCUSSION QUESTIONS

1. Is the "simple life" a relative notion? To whom does the notion apply?
2. Do you agree with Segal (following Aristotle) that not only is there decreasing marginal utility in increasing material possessions, but that it is actually harmful? Explain.
3. Are you convinced by Segal's explanation of the difference between poverty and simplicity?
4. What moral force, if any, does Segal's position have?

ARNE NAESS

The Deep Ecological Movement: Some Philosophical Aspects

Arne Naess is professor emeritus at the University of Oslo, Norway. Born in 1913, he was appointed professor of philosophy at age 27, the youngest in Norway's history. After some 30 years of work on semantics, philosophy of science, Spinoza, and eastern philosophy, he resigned in 1969 to devote himself to environmental matters. In 1972, he coined the phrase *deep ecology,* to distinguish a moral relation to the natural world from simply an instrumental one. In addition to writing many articles about environmental philosophy, in *Ecology, Community and Lifestyle,* Naess sets out his "Ecosophy T," or the philosophical basis for what became codified, with deep ecologist George Sessions in 1984, as the deep ecology platform.

CRITICAL READING QUESTIONS

1. Why does Naess use the adjective *deep* to describe his view about the proper position of people in the natural world?
2. How does Naess' "deep" approach contrast with "shallow" environmentalism on pollution, resources, population, cultural diversity, and appropriate technology, land use, and education?
3. What does Naess mean when he says that deep ecology is a "derivational system"?
4. What does Naess mean by "Ecosophy T"?

1. DEEP ECOLOGY ON THE DEFENSIVE

Increasing pressures for continued growth and development have placed the vast majority of environmental professionals on the defensive. By way of illustration:

The field-ecologist Ivar Mysterud, who both professionally and vigorously advocated deep ecological principles in the late 1960s, encountered considerable resistance. Colleagues at his university said he should keep to his science and not meddle in philosophical and political matters. He should resist the temptation to become a prominent "popularizer" through mass media exposure. Nevertheless, he persisted and influenced thousands of people (including myself).

Mysterud became a well-known professional "expert" at assessing the damage done when bears killed or maimed sheep and other domestic animals in Norway. According to the law, their owners are paid damages. And licensed hunters receive permission to shoot bears if their misdeeds become considerable.[1] Continued growth and development required that the sheep industry consolidate and sheepowners became fewer, richer, and tended to live in cities. As a result of wage increases, they could not afford to hire shepherds to watch the flocks, so the sheep were left on their own even more than before. Continued growth also required moving sheep to what was traditionally considered "bear territory." In spite of this invasion, bear populations grew and troubles multiplied.

This essay originally appreared in *Philosophical Inquiry* 8, 1–2 (1986). Reprinted with permission.

How did Mysterud react to these new problems? Did he set limits to the amount of human/sheep encroachment on bear territory? Did he attempt a direct application of his deep ecological perspective to these issues? Quite the contrary. He adopted what appeared to be a shallow wildlife management perspective, and defended the sheepowners: more money to compensate for losses, quicker compensation, and the immediate hiring of hunters who killed mostly "juvenile delinquent" bears accused of killing many sheep.

Protectors of big carnivores noted with concern the change of Mysterud's public "image"; had he really abandoned his former value priorities? Privately he insisted that he hadn't. But in public he tended to remain silent.

The reason for M.'s unexpected actions was not difficult to find: The force of economic growth was so strong that the laws protecting bears would be changed in a highly unfavorable direction if the sheepowners were not soon pacified by accepting some of their not unreasonable demands. After all, it did cost a lot of money to hire and equip people to locate a flock of sheep which had been harassed by a bear and, further, to prove the bear's guilt. And the bureaucratic procedures involved were time-consuming. M. had not changed his basic value priorities at all. Rather, he had adopted a purely defensive compromise. He stopped promoting his deep ecology philosophy publicly in order to retain credibility and standing among opponents of his principles and to retain his friendships with sheepowners.

And what is true of Mysterud is also true of thousands of other professional ecologists and environmentalists. These people often hold responsible positions in society where they might strengthen responsible environmental policy, but, given the exponential forces of growth, their publications, if any, are limited to narrowly professional and specialized concerns. Their writings are surely competent, but lack a deeper and more comprehensive perspective (although I admit that there are some brilliant exceptions to this).

If professional ecologists persist in voicing their value priorities, their jobs are often in danger, or they tend to lose influence and status among those who are in charge of overall policies.[2] Privately, they admit the necessity for deep and far-ranging changes, but they no longer speak out in public. As a result, people deeply concerned about ecology and the environment feel abandoned and even betrayed by the "experts" who work within the "establishment."

In ecological debates, many participants know a lot about particular conservation policies in particular places, and many others have strong views concerning fundamental philosophical questions of environmental ethics, but only a few have both qualities. When these people are silent, the loss is formidable.

For example, the complicated question concerning how industrial societies can increase energy production with the least undesirable consequences is largely a waste of time if this increase is pointless in relation to ultimate human ends. Thousands of experts hired by the government and other big institutions devote their time to this complicated problem, yet it is difficult for the public to find out or realize that many of these same experts consider the problem to be pointless and irrelevant. What these experts consider relevant are the problems of how to stabilize and eventually decrease consumption without losing genuine quality of life for humans. But they continue to work on the irrelevant problems assigned to them while, at the same time, failing to speak out, because the ultimate power is not in their hands.

2. A CALL TO SPEAK OUT

What I am arguing for is this: Even those who completely subsume ecological policies under the narrow ends of human health and well-being cannot attain their modest aims, at least not fully, without being joined by the supporters of deep ecology. They need what these people have to contribute, and this will work in their favor more often than it will work against them. Those in charge of environmental policies, even if they are resource-oriented (and growth tolerating?) decision makers, will increasingly welcome, if only for tactical and not fundamental reasons, what deep ecology supporters have to say. Even though the more radical ethic may seem nonsensical or untenable to them, they know that its advocates are, in practice, doing conservation work that sooner or later must be done. They concur with the practice even though they operate from diverging theories. The time is ripe for professional ecologists to break their silence and express their deepest concerns more freely. A bolder advocacy of deep ecological concerns by those working within the shallow, resource-oriented environmental sphere is the best strategy for regaining some of the strength of this movement among the general public, thereby contributing, however modestly, to a turning of the tide.

What do I mean by saying that even the more modest aims of shallow environmentalism have a need for deep ecology? We can see this by considering the World Conservation Strategy—prepared by the International Union for the Conservation of Nature and Natural Resources (IUCN) in cooperation with the United Nations Environmental Programme (UNEP) and the World Wildlife Fund (WWF). The argument in this important document is thoroughly anthropocentric in the sense that all its recommendations are justified exclusively in terms of their effects upon human health and basic well-being.[3]

A more ecocentric environmental ethic is also recommended apparently for tactical reasons: "A new ethic, embracing plants and animals as well as people, is required for human societies to live in harmony with the natural world on which they depend for survival and well-being." But such an ethic would surely be more effective if it were acted upon by people who believe in its validity, rather than merely its usefulness. This, I think, will come to be understood more and more by those in charge of educational policies. Quite simply, it is indecent for a teacher to proclaim an ethic for tactical reasons only.

Furthermore, this point applies to all aspects of a world conservation strategy. Conservation strategies are more eagerly implemented by people who love what they are conserving, and who are convinced that what they love is intrinsically lovable. Such lovers will not want to hide their attitudes and values, rather they will increasingly give voice to them in public. They possess a genuine ethics of conservation, not merely a tactically useful instrument for human survival.

In short, environmental education campaigns can fortunately combine human-centered arguments with a practical environmental ethic based on either a deeper and more fundamental philosophic or religious perspective, and on a set of norms resting on intrinsic values. But the inherent strength of this overall position will be lost if those who work professionally on environmental problems do not freely give testimony to fundamental norms.

The above is hortatory in the positive etymological sense of that word. I seek "to urge, incite, instigate, encourage, cheer" (Latin: *hortari*). This may seem unacademic but I consider it justifiable because of an intimate relationship between hortatory sentences and basic philosophical views which I formulate in section 8. To trace what follows from fundamental norms and hypotheses is eminently philosophical.

3. WHAT IS DEEP ECOLOGY?

The phrase "deep ecology movement" has been used up to this point without trying to define it. One should not expect too much from definitions of movements; think, for example, of terms like "conservatism," "liberalism," or the "feminist movement." And there is no reason why supporters of movements should adhere exactly to the same definition, or to any definition, for that matter. It is the same with characterizations, criteria, or a set of proposed necessary conditions for application of the term or phrase. In what follows, a platform or key terms and phrases, agreed upon by George Sessions and myself, are tentatively proposed as basic to deep ecology.[4] More accurately, the sentences have a double function. They are meant to express important points which the great majority of supporters accept, implicitly or explicitly, at a high level of generality. Furthermore, they express a proposal to the effect that those who solidly reject one or more of these points should not be viewed as supporters of deep ecology. This might result because they are supporters of a shallow (or reform) environmental movement or rather they may simply dislike one or more of the eight points for semantical or other reapt a different set of ly the same meaning, m supporters of the t add that they *think* Skolimowski is an ex- ıt points are:

urishing of human earth have value in intrinsic value, e values are inde- ness of the non-human poses.

of life forms ization of these values themselves.

t to reduce this richness o satisfy vital needs.

man life and cultures is ostantially smaller human rishing of nonhuman life an population.

rference with the excessive, and the worsening.

fore be changed. These economic, technolog- al structures. The ffairs will be deeply present.

ange will be mainly that of uality (dwelling in situa- value) rather than adhering higher standard of living. ofound awareness of the en bigness and greatness.

ribe to the foregoing points on directly or indirectly to t the necessary changes.

ght Points

ion refers to the biosphere, or to the ecosphere as a whole to as "ecocentrism"). This includes individuals, species, populations, habitat, as well as human and nonhuman cultures. Given our current knowledge of all-pervasive intimate relationships, this implies a fundamental concern and respect.

The term "life" is used here in a more comprehensive nontechnical way also to refer to what biologists classify as "nonliving": rivers (watersheds), landscapes, ecosystems. For supporters of deep ecology, slogans such as "let the river live" illustrate this broader usage so common in many cultures.

Inherent value, as used in (1), is common in deep ecology literature (e.g., "The presence of inherent value in a natural object is independent of any awareness, interest, or appreciation of it by any conscious being").[5]

RE (2): The so-called simple, lower, or primitive species of plants and animals contribute essentially to the richness and diversity of life. They have value in themselves and are not merely steps toward the so-called higher or rational life forms. The second principle presupposes that life itself, as a process over evolutionary time, implies an increase of diversity and richness.

Complexity, as referred to here, is different from complication. For example, urban life may be more complicated than life in a natural setting without being more complex in the sense of multifaceted quality.

RE (3): The term "vital need" is deliberately left vague to allow for considerable latitude in judgment. Differences in climate and related factors, together with differences in the structures of societies as they now exist, need to be taken into consideration.

RE (4): People in the materially richest countries cannot be expected to reduce their excessive interference with the nonhuman world overnight. The stabilization and reduction of the human population will take time. Hundreds of years! Interim strategies need to be developed. But in no way does this excuse the present complacency. The extreme seriousness of our current situation must first be realized. And the longer we wait to make the necessary changes, the more drastic will be the measures needed. Until deep changes are made, substantial decreases in richness and diversity are liable to occur: the rate of extinction of species will be ten to one hundred or more times greater than in any other short period of earth history.

RE (5): This formulation is mild. For a realistic assessment, see the annual reports of the Worldwatch Institute in Washington, D.C.

The slogan of "noninterference" does not imply that humans should not modify some ecosystems, as do other species. Humans have modified the earth over their entire history and will probably continue to do so. At issue is the *nature and extent* of such interference. The per capita destruction of wild (ancient) forests and other wild ecosystems has been excessive in rich countries; it is essential that the poor do not imitate the rich in this regard.

The fight to preserve and extend areas of wilderness and near-wilderness ("free Nature") should continue. The rationale for such preservation should focus mainly on the ecological functions of these areas (one such function: large wilderness areas are required in the biosphere for the continued evolutionary speciation of plants and animals). Most of the present designated wilderness areas and game reserves are not large enough to allow for such speciation.

RE (6): Economic growth as it is conceived of and implemented today by the industrial states is incompatible with points (1) through (5). There is only a faint resemblance between ideal sustainable forms of economic growth and the present policies of industrial societies.

Present ideology tends to value things because they are scarce and because they have a commodity value. There is prestige in vast consumption and waste (to mention only several relevant factors).

Whereas "self-determination," "local community," and "think globally, act locally," will remain key terms in the ecology of human societies, nevertheless the implementation of deep changes requires increasingly global action: Action across borders.

Governments in Third World countries are mostly uninterested in deep ecological issues. When institutions in the industrial societies try to promote ecological measures through Third World governments, practically nothing is accomplished (e.g., with problems of desertification). Given this situation, support for global action through non-governmental international organizations becomes increasingly important. Many of these organizations are able to act globally "from grassroots to grassroots" thus avoiding negative governmental interference.

Cultural diversity today requires advanced technology, that is, techniques that advance the basic goals of each culture. So-called soft, intermediate, and alternative technologies are steps in this direction.

RE (7): Some economists criticize the term "quality of life" because it is supposedly vague. But, on closer inspection, what they consider to be vague is actually the nonquantifiable nature of the term. One cannot quantify adequately what is important for the quality of life as discussed here, and there is no need to do so.

RE (8): There is ample room for different opinions about priorities: what should be done first; what next? What is the most urgent? What is clearly necessary to be done, as opposed to what is highly desirable but not absolutely pressing? The frontier of the environmental crisis is long and varied, and there is a place for everyone.

The above formulations of the eight points may be useful to many supporters of the deep ecology movement. But some will certainly feel that they are imperfect, even misleading. If they need to formulate in a few words what is basic to deep ecology, then they will propose an alternative set of sentences. I shall of course be glad to refer to them as alternatives. There ought to be a measure of diversity in what is considered basic and common.

Why should we call the movement "the deep ecological movement"?[6] There are at least six other designations which cover most of the same issues: "Ecological Resistance," used by John Rodman in important discussions; "The New Natural Philosophy" coined by Joseph Meeker; "Eco-philosophy," used by Sigmund Kvaloy and others to emphasize (1) a highly critical assessment of the industrial growth societies from a general ecological point of view, and (2) the ecology of the human species; "Green Philosophy and Politics" (while the term "green" is often used in Europe, in the United States "green" has a misleading association with the rather "blue" Green agricultural revolution); "Sustainable Earth Ethics," as used by G. Tyler Miller;

and "Ecosophy" (ecowisdom), which is my own favorite term. Others could be mentioned as well.

And so, why use the adjective "deep"? This question will be easier to answer after the contrast is made between shallow and deep ecological concerns. "Deep ecology" is not a philosophy in any proper academic sense, nor is it institutionalized as a religion or an ideology. Rather, what happens is that various persons come together in campaigns and direct actions. They form a circle of friends supporting the same kind of lifestyle which others may think to be "simple," but which they themselves see as rich and many-sided. They agree on a vast array of political issues, although they may otherwise support different political parties. As in all social movements, slogans and rhetoric are indispensable for in-group coherence. They react together against the same threats in a predominantly nonviolent way. Perhaps the most influential participants are artists and writers who do not articulate their insights in terms of professional philosophy, expressing themselves rather in art or poetry. For these reasons, I use the term "movement" rather than "philosophy." But it is essential that fundamental attitudes and beliefs are involved as part of the motivation for action.

4. DEEP VERSUS SHALLOW ECOLOGY

A number of key terms and slogans from the environmental debate will clarify the contrast between the shallow and the deep ecology movements.[7]

A. Pollution

Shallow Approach: Technology seeks to purify the air and water and to spread pollution more evenly. Laws limit permissible pollution. Polluting industries are preferably exported to developing countries.

Deep Approach: Pollution is evaluated from a biospheric point of view, not focusing exclusively on its effects on human health, but rather on life as a whole, including the life conditions of every species and system. The shallow reaction to acid rain, for example, is to tend to avoid action by demanding more research, and the attempt to find species of trees which will tolerate high acidity, etc. The deep approach concentrates on what is going on in the total ecosystem and calls for a high priority fight against the economic conditions and the technology responsible for producing the acid rain. The long-range concerns are 100 years, at least.

The priority is to fight the deep causes of pollution, not merely the superficial, short-range effects. The Third and Fourth World countries cannot afford to pay the total costs of the war against pollution in their regions; consequently they require the assistance of the First and Second World countries. Exporting pollution is not only a crime against humanity, it is a crime against life in general.

B. Resources

Shallow Approach: The emphasis is upon resources for humans, especially for the present generation in affluent societies. In this view, the resources of the earth belong to those who have the technology to exploit them. There is confidence that resources will not be depleted because, as they get rarer, a high market price will conserve them, and substitutes will be found through technological progress. Further, plants, animals, and natural objects are valuable only as resources for humans. If no human use is known, or seems likely ever to be found, it does not matter if they are destroyed.

Deep Approach: The concern here is with resources and habitats for all life-forms for their own sake. No natural object is conceived of solely as a resource. This leads, then, to a critical evaluation of human modes of production and consumption. The question arises: to what extent does an increase in production and consumption foster ultimate human values? To what extent does it satisfy vital needs, locally or globally? How can economic, legal, and educational institutions be changed to counteract destructive increases? How can resource use serve the quality of life rather than the economic standard of living as generally promoted by consumerism? From a deep perspective, there is an emphasis upon an ecosystem approach rather than the consideration merely of isolated life-forms or local situations. There is a long-range maximal perspective of time and place.

C. Population

Shallow Approach: The threat of (human) "over-population" is seen mainly as a problem for developing countries. One condones or even applauds population increases in one's own country for shortsighted economic, military, or other reasons; an increase in the number of humans is considered as valuable in itself or as economically profitable. The issue of an "optimum population" for humans is discussed without reference to the question of an "optimum population" for other life-forms. The destruction of wild habitats caused by increasing human population is accepted as in inevitable evil, and drastic decreases of wildlife forms tend to be accepted insofar as species are not driven to extinction. Further, the social relations of animals are ignored. A long-term substantial reduction of the global human population is not seen to be a desirable goal. In addition, the right is claimed to defend one's borders against "illegal aliens," regardless of what the population pressures are elsewhere.

Deep Approach: It is recognized that excessive pressures on planetary life stem from the human population explosion. The pressure stemming from the industrial societies is a major factor, and population reduction must have the highest priority in those societies.

D. Cultural Diversity and Appropriate Technology

Shallow Approach: Industrialization of the Western industrial type is held to be the goal of developing countries. The universal adoption of Western technology is held to be compatible with cultural diversity, together with the conservation of the positive elements (from a Western perspective) of present nonindustrial societies. There is a low estimate of deep cultural differences in nonindustrial societies which deviate significantly from contemporary Western standards.

Deep Approach: Protection of nonindustrial cultures from invasion by industrial societies. The goals of the former should not be seen as promoting lifestyles similar to those in the rich countries. Deep cultural diversity is an analogue on the human level to the biological richness and diversity of life-forms. A high priority should be given to cultural anthropology in general education programs in industrial societies.

There should be limits on the impact of Western technology upon present existing nonindustrial countries and the Fourth World should be defended against foreign domination. Political and economic policies should favor subcultures within industrial societies. Local, soft technologies should allow for a basic cultural assessment of any technical innovations, together with freely expressed criticism of so-called advanced technology when this has the potential to be culturally destructive.

E. Land and Sea Ethics

Shallow Approach: Landscapes, ecosystems, rivers, and other whole entities of nature are conceptually cut into fragments, thus disregarding larger units and comprehensive gestalts. These fragments are regarded as the properties and resources of individuals, organizations or states. Conservation is argued in terms of "multiple use" and "cost/benefit analysis." The social costs and long-term global ecological costs of resource extraction and use are usually not considered. Wildlife management is conceived of as conserving nature for "future generations of humans." Soil erosion or the deterioration of ground water quality, for example, is noted as a human loss, but a strong belief in future technological progress makes deep changes seem unnecessary.

Deep Approach: The earth does not belong to humans. For example, the Norwegian landscapes, rivers, flora and fauna, and the neighboring sea are not the property of Norwegians. Similarly, the oil under the North Sea or anywhere else does not belong to any state or to humanity. And the "free nature" surrounding a local community does not belong to the local community.

Humans only inhabit the lands, using resources to satisfy vital needs. And if their nonvital needs come in conflict with the vital needs of nonhumans, then humans should defer to the latter. The ecological destruction now going on will not be cured by a technological fix. Current arrogant notions in industrial (and other) societies must be resisted.

F. Education and the Scientific Enterprise

Shallow Approach: The degradation of the environment and resource depletion requires the training of more and more "experts" who can provide advice concerning how to continue combining economic growth with maintaining a healthy environment. We are likely to need an increasingly more dominating and manipulative technology to "manage the planet" when global economic growth makes further environmental degradation inevitable. The scientific enterprise must continue giving priority to the "hard sciences" (physics and chemistry). High educational standards with intense competition in the relevant "tough" areas of learning will be required.

Deep Approach: If sane ecological policies are adopted, then education should concentrate on an increased sensitivity to nonconsumptive goods, and on such consumables where there is enough for all. Education should therefore counteract the excessive emphasis upon things with a price tag. There should be a shift in concentration from the "hard" to the "soft" sciences which stress the importance of the local and global cultures. The educational objective of the World Conservation Strategy ("building support for conservation") should be given a high priority, but within the deeper framework of respect for the biosphere.

In the future, there will be no shallow environmental movement if deep policies are increasingly adopted by governments, and thus no need for a special deep ecological social movement.

5. BUT WHY A "DEEP" ECOLOGY?

The decisive difference between a shallow and a deep ecology, in practice, concerns the willingness to question, and an appreciation of the importance of questioning, every economic and political policy in public. This questioning is both "deep" and public. It asks "why" insistently and consistently, taking nothing for granted!

Deep ecology can readily admit to the practical effectiveness of homocentric arguments:

> It is essential for conservation to be seen as central to human interests and aspirations. At the same time, people—from heads of state to the members of rural communities—will most readily be brought to demand conservation if they themselves recognize the contribution of conservation to the achievement of their needs as perceived by them, and the solution of their problems, as perceived by them.[8]

There are several dangers in arguing solely from the point of view of narrow human interests. Some policies based upon successful homocentric arguments turn out to violate or unduly compromise the objectives of deeper argumentation. Further, homocentric arguments tend to weaken the motivation to fight for necessary social change, together with the willingness to serve a great cause. In addition, the complicated arguments in human-centered conservation documents such as the World Conservation Strategy go beyond the time and ability of many people to assimilate and understand. They also tend to provoke interminable technical disagreements among experts. Special interest groups with narrow short-term exploitive objectives, which run counter to saner ecological policies, often exploit these disagreements and thereby stall the debate and steps toward effective action.

When arguing from deep ecological premises, most of the complicated proposed technological fixes need not be discussed at all. The relative merits of alternative technological proposals are pointless if our vital needs have already been met. A focus on vital issues activates mental energy and strengthens motivation. On the other hand, the shallow environmental approach, by focusing almost exclusively on the technical aspects of environmental problems, tends to make the public more passive and disinterested in the more crucial nontechnical, lifestyle-related, environmental issues.

Writers within the deep ecology movement try to articulate the fundamental presuppositions underlying the dominant economic approach in terms of value priorities, philosophy, and religion. In the shallow movement, questioning and argumentation comes to a halt long before this. The deep ecology movement is therefore "the ecology movement which questions deeper." A realization of the deep changes which are required, as outlined in the deep ecology eight point platform (discussed in #3 above) makes us realize the necessity of "questioning everything."

The terms "egalitarianism," "homocentrism," "anthropocentrism," and "human chauvinism" are often used to characterize points of view on the shallow-deep spectrum. But these terms usually function as slogans which are often open to misinterpretation. They can properly imply that man is in some respects only a "plain citizen" (Aldo Leopold) of the planet on a par with all other species, but they are sometimes interpreted as denying that humans have any "extraordinary" traits, or that, in situations involving vital interests, humans have no overriding obligations towards their own kind. But this would be a mistake: They have!

In any social movement, rhetoric has an essential function in keeping members fighting together under the same banner. Rhetorical formulations also serve to provoke interest among outsiders. Of the many excellent slogans, one might mention "nature knows best," "small is beautiful," and "all things hang together." But sometimes one may safely say that nature does not always know best, that small is sometimes dreadful, and that fortunately things hang together sometimes only loosely, or not at all.

Only a minority of deep ecology supporters are academic philosophers, such as myself. And while deep ecology cannot be a finished philosophical system, this does not mean that its philosophers should not try to be as clear as possible. So a discussion of deep ecology as a derivational system may be of value to clarify the many important premise/conclusion relations.

6. DEEP ECOLOGY ILLUSTRATED AS A DERIVATIONAL SYSTEM

Underlying the eight tenets or principles presented in section 3, there are even more basic positions and norms which reside in philosophical systems and in various world religions. Schematically we may represent the total views logically implied in the deep ecology movement by streams of derivations from the most fundamental norms and descriptive assumptions (level 1) to the particular decisions in actual life situations (level 4).

The pyramidal model has some features in common with hypotheticodeductive systems. The main difference, however, is that some sentences at the top (= deepest) level are normative, and preferably are expressed by imperatives. This makes it possible to arrive at imperatives at the lowest derivational level: the crucial level in terms of decisions. Thus, there are "oughts" in our premises as well as in our conclusions. We never move from an "is" to an "ought," or vice versa. From a logical standpoint, this is decisive!

The above premise/conclusion structure (or diagram) of a total view must not be taken too seriously. It is not meant in any restrictive way to characterize creative thinking within the deep ecology movement. Creative thinking moves freely in any direction. But many of us with a professional background in science and analytical philosophy find such a diagram helpful.

As we dig deeper into the premises of our thinking, we eventually stop. Those premises we stop at are our ultimates. When we philosophize, we all stop at different places. But we all use premises which, for us, are ultimate. They belong to level 1 in the diagram. Some will use a sentence like "Every life form has intrinsic value" as an ultimate premise, and therefore place it at level 1. Others try, as I do, to conceive of it as a conclusion based on a set of premises. For these people, this sentence does not belong to level 1. There will be different ecosophies corresponding to such differences.

Obviously, point 6 of the 8 point deep ecology tenets (see section 3) cannot belong to level 1 of the diagram. The statement "there must be new policies affecting basic economic structures" needs to be justified. If no logical justification is forthcoming, why not just assert instead that ecologically destructive "business as usual" economic policies should continue? In the diagram I have had ecosophies as ultimate premises in mind at level 1. None of the 8 points of the deep ecology principles belong at the ultimate level; they are derived as conclusions from premises at level 1.

Different supporters of the deep ecology movement may have different ultimates (level 1), but will nevertheless agree about level 2 (the 8 points), Level 4 will comprise concrete decisions in concrete situa-

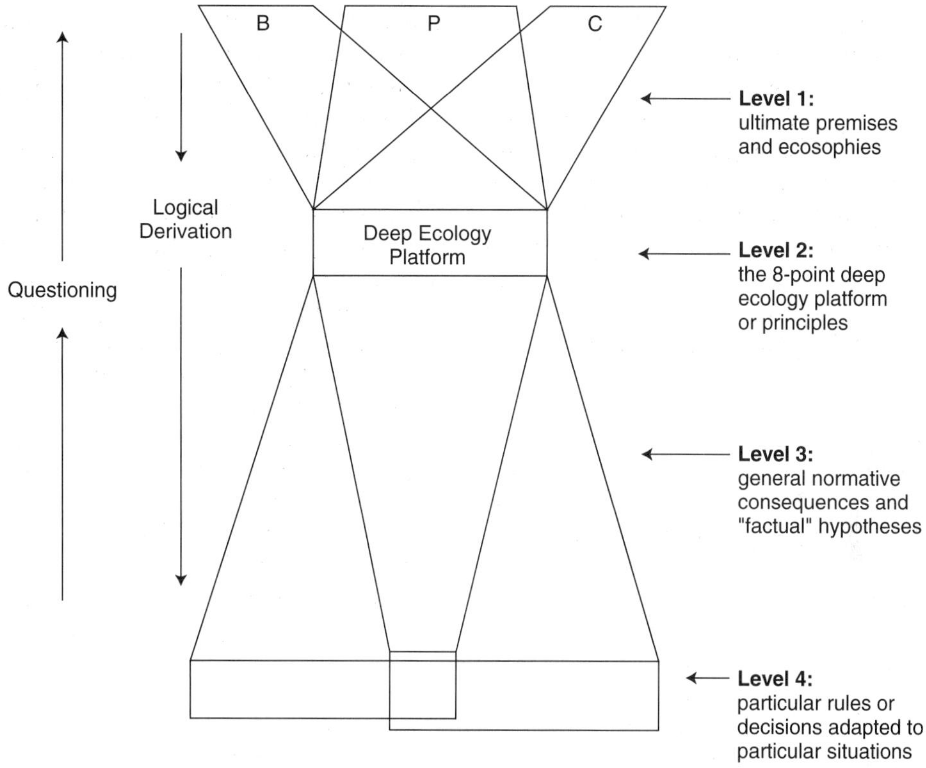

Examples of kinds of fundamental premises:

B = Buddhist
C = Christian
P = Philosophical (e.g., Spinozist or Whiteheadian)

tions which appear as conclusions from deliberations involving premises at levels 1 to 3. An important point: supporters of the deep ecology movement act from deep premises. They are motivated, in part, from a philosophical or religious position.

7. MULTIPLE ROOTS OF THE DEEP ECOLOGY PLATFORM

The deep ecology movement seriously questions the presuppositions of shallow argumentation. Even what counts as a rational decision is challenged, because what is "rational" is always defined in relation to specific aims and goals. If a decision is rational in relation to the lower level aims and goals of our pyramid, but not in relation to the highest level, then this decision should not be judged to be rational. This is an important point! If an environmentally oriented policy decision is not linked to intrinsic values or ultimates, then its rationality has yet to be determined. The deep ecology movement connects rationality with a set of philosophical or religious foundations. But one cannot expect the ultimate premises to constitute rational conclusions. There are no "deeper" premises available.

Deep ecological questioning thus reveals the fundamental normative orientations of differing positions. Shallow argumentation stops before reaching fundamentals, or it jumps from the ultimate to the particular; that is, from level 1 to level 4.

But it is not only normative claims that are at issue. Most (perhaps all) norms presuppose ideas about how the world functions. Typically the vast majority of assertions needed in normative systems are descriptive (or factual). This holds at all the levels.

As mentioned before, it does not follow that supporters of deep ecology must have identical beliefs about ultimate issues. They do have common attitudes about intrinsic values in nature, but these can, in turn (at a still deeper level), be derived from different, mutually incompatible sets of ultimate beliefs.

Thus, while a specific decision may be judged as rational from within the derivational system (if there is such) of shallow ecology, it might be judged as irrational from within the derivational system of deep ecology. Again, it should be emphasized that what is rational from within the deep ecology derivational pyramid does not require unanimity in ontology and fundamental ethics. Deep ecology as a conviction, with its subsequently derived practical recommendations, can follow from a number of more comprehensive world views, from differing ecosophies.

Those engaged in the deep ecology movement have so far revealed their philosophical or religious homes to be mainly in Christianity, Buddhism, Taoism, Baha'i, or in various philosophies. The top level of the derivational pyramid can, in such cases, be made up of normative and descriptive principles which belong to these religions and philosophies.

Since the late 1970s, numerous Christians in Europe and America, including some theologians, have actively taken part in the deep ecology movement. Their interpretations of the Bible, and their theological positions in general, have been reformed from what was, until recently, a crude dominating anthropocentric emphasis.

There is an intimate relationship between some forms of Buddhism and the deep ecology movement. The history of Buddhist thought and practice, especially the principles of nonviolence, noninjury, and reverence for life, sometimes makes it easier for Buddhists to understand and appreciate deep ecology than it is for Christians, despite a (sometimes overlooked) blessedness which Jesus recommended in peace-making. I mention Taoism chiefly because there is some basis for calling John Muir a Taoist, for instance, and Baha'i because of Lawrence Arturo.

Ecosophies are not religions in the classical sense. They are better characterized as *general* philosophies, in the sense of total views, inspired in part by the science of ecology. At level 1, a traditional religion may enter the derivational pyramid through a set of normative and descriptive assumptions which would be characteristic of contemporary interpretations (hermeneutical efforts) of that religion.

Supporters of the deep ecology movement act in contemporary conflicts on the basis of their fundamental beliefs and attitudes. This gives them a particular strength and a joyful expectation or hope for a greener future. But, naturally, few of them are actively engaged in a systematic verbal articulation of where they stand.

8. ECOSOPHY T AS AN EXAMPLE OF A DEEP ECOLOGICAL DERIVATIONAL SYSTEM

I call the ecosophy I feel at home with "Ecosophy T." My main purpose in announcing that I feel at home with Ecosophy T is didactic and dialectic. I hope to get others to announce their philosophy. If they say they have none, I maintain that they have, but perhaps don't know their own views, or are too modest or inhibited to proclaim what they believe. Following Socrates, I want to provoke questioning until others know where they stand on basic matters of life and death. This is done using ecological issues, and also by using Ecosophy T as a foil. But Socrates pretended in debate that he knew nothing. My posture seems to be the opposite. I may seem to know everything and to derive it magically from a small set of hypotheses about the world. But both interpretations are misleading! Socrates did not consistently claim to know nothing, nor do I in my Ecosophy T pretend to have comprehensive knowledge. Socrates claimed to know, for instance, about the fallibility of human claims to have knowledge.

Ecosophy T has only one ultimate norm: "Self-realization!" I do not use this expression in any narrow, individualistic sense. I want to give it an expanded meaning based on the distinction between a large comprehensive Self and narrow egoistic self as conceived of in certain Eastern traditions of *atman*.[9] This large comprehensive Self (with a capital "S") embraces all the life forms on the planet (and elsewhere?) together with their individual selves (jivas). If I were to express this ultimate norm in a few words, I would say: "Maximize (long-range, universal) Self-realization!" Another more colloquial way to express this ultimate norm would be to say "Live and let live!" (referring to all of the life forms and natural processes on the planet). If I had to give up the term fearing its inevitable misunderstanding, I would use the term "universal symbiosis." "Maximize Self-realization!" could, of course, be misinterpreted in the direction of colossal ego trips. But "Maximize symbiosis!" could be misinterpreted in the opposite direction of eliminating individuality in favor of collectivity.

Viewed systematically, not individually, maximum Self-realization implies maximizing the manifestations of all life. So next I derive the second term, "Maximize (long-range, universal) diversity!" A corollary is that the higher the levels of Self-realization attained by any person, the more any further increase depends upon the Self-realization of others. Increased self-identity involves increased identification with others. "Altruism" is a natural consequence of this identification.

This leads to a hypothesis concerning an inescapable increase of identification with other beings when one's own self-realization increases. As a result, we increasingly see ourselves in other beings, and others see themselves in us. In this way, the self is extended and deepened as a natural process of the realization of its potentialities in others.

By universalizing the above, we can derive the norm, "Self-realization for every being!" From the norm, "Maximize diversity!" and a hypothesis that maximum diversity implies a maximum of symbiosis, we can derive the norm "Maximize symbiosis!" Further, we work for life conditions such that there is a minimum of coercion in the lives of others. And so on![10] The eight points of the deep ecology platform are derived in a fairly simple way.

A philosophy as a world view inevitably has implications for practical situations. Like other ecosophies, Ecosophy T therefore moves on, without apologies, to the concrete questions of lifestyles. These will obviously show great variation because of differences in hypotheses about the world in which each of us lives, and in the "factual" statements about the concrete situations in which we make decisions.

I shall limit myself to a discussion of a couple of areas in which my "style" of thinking and behaving seem somewhat strange to friends and others who know a little about my philosophy.

First, I have a somewhat extreme appreciation of diversity; a positive appreciation of the existence of styles and behavior which I personally detest or find nonsensical (but which are not clearly incompatible with symbiosis); an enthusiasm for the "mere" diversity of species, or varieties within a genus of plants or animals; I support, as the head of a philosophy department, doctrinal theses completely at odds with my own inclinations, with the requirement only that the authors are able to understand fairly adequately some basic features of the kind of philosophy I myself feel at home with; an appreciation of combinations of *seemingly* incompatible interests and behaviors, which makes for an increase of subcultures within industrial states and which might to some extent help future cultural diversity. So much for "diversity!"

Second, I have a somewhat extreme appreciation of what Kant calls "beautiful actions" (good actions based on inclination), in contrast with actions which are performed out of a sense of duty or obligation. The choice of the formulation "Self-realization!" is in part motivated by the belief that maturity in humans can be measured along a scale from selfishness to an increased realization of Self, that is, by broadening and deepening the self, rather than being measured by degrees of dutiful altruism. I see joyful sharing and caring as a natural process of growth in humans.

Third, I believe that multifaceted high-level Self-realization is more easily reached through a lifestyle which is "simple in means but rich in ends" rather

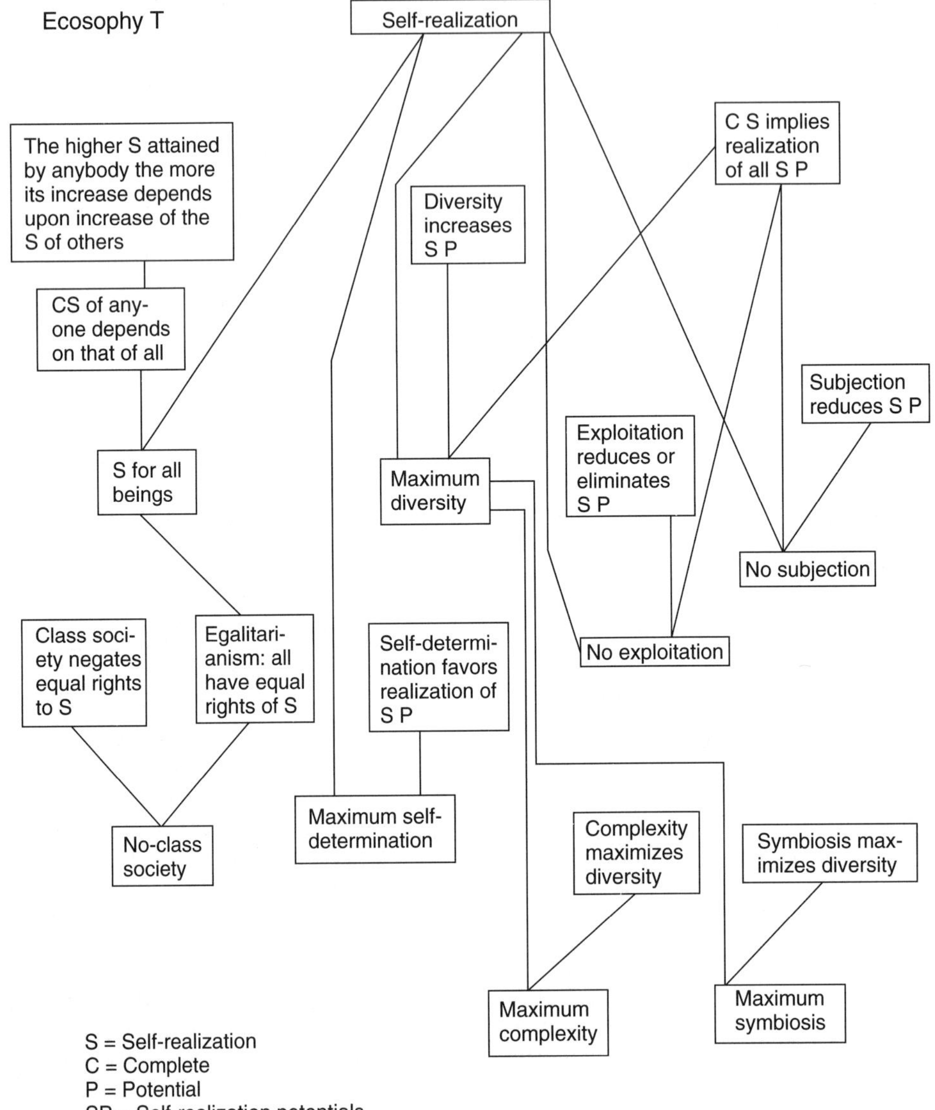

than through the material standard of living of the average citizens of industrial states.

The simple formulations of the deep ecology platform and Ecosophy T are not meant primarily to be used among philosophers, but also in dialogues with the "experts." When I wrote to the "experts" and environmental professionals personally, asking whether they accept the eight points of the platform, many answered positively in relation to most or all of the points. And this includes top people in the ministries of oil and energy! Nearly all were willing to let their written answers be widely published. It is an open question, however, as to what extent they will try to influence their colleagues who use only shallow argumentation. But the main conclusion to be drawn is moderately encouraging: there are views of the human/nature relationship, widely accepted among established experts responsible for environmental decisions, which require a pervasive, substantial change of present policies in favor of our "living" planet, and these views are held not only on the basis of short-sighted human interests.

NOTES

1. For more about interspecific community relationships, *see* Arne Naess, "Self-realization in Mixed Communities of Humans, Bears, Sheep, and Wolves," *Inquiry* 22 (1979): 321–41; Naess and Ivar Mysterud, "Philosophy of Wolf Policies I: General Principles and Preliminary Exploration of Selected Norms," *Conservation Biology* 1, 1 (1987): 22–34.
2. These problems are discussed further in Naess's keynote address to the second international Conference Conservation on Biology held at the University of Michigan in May 1985; published as "Intrinsic Value: Will the Defenders of Nature Please Rise?" *Conservation Biology* (1986): 504–15.
3. IUCN, *World Conservation Strategy: Living Resource Conservation for Sustainable Development* (Gland, Switzerland, 1980), section 13 ("Building Support for Conservation").
4. The deep ecology principles (or platform) were agreed upon during a camping trip in Death Valley, California (April 1984) and first published in George Sessions (ed.), *Ecophilosophy VI* newsletter (May 1984). They have subsequently appeared in a number of publications.
5. Tom Regan, "The Nature and Possibility of an Environmental Ethics," *Environmental Ethics* 3 (1981): 19–34, citation on p. 30.
6. I proposed the name "Deep, Long-Range Ecology Movement" in a lecture at the Third World Future Research conference in Bucharest in September 1972. A summary of that lecture ("The Shallow and the Deep, Long-Range Ecology Movement") was published in *Inquiry* 16 (1973): 95–100. Within the deep ecology movement it is fairly common to use the term "deep ecologist," whereas "shallow ecologist," I am glad to say, is rather uncommon. Both terms may be considered arrogant and slightly misleading. I prefer to use the awkward, but more egalitarian expression "supporter of the deep (or shallow) ecology movement," avoiding personification. Also, it is common to call deep ecology consistently anti-anthropocentric. This has led to misconceptions: see my "A Defense of the Deep Ecology Movement," *Environmental Ethics* 5 (1983).
7. The "shallow/deep" dichotomy is rough. Richard Sylvan has proposed a much more subtle classification; see his "A Critique of Deep Ecology," *Discussion Papers in Environmental Philosophy*. RSSS, Australian National University, No. 12 (1985).
8. *World Conservation Strategy,* section 13 (concluding paragraph).
9. The term *atman* is not taken in its absolutistic senses (not as a permanent indestructible "soul"). This makes it consistent with those Buddhist denials (the *avatman doctrine*) that the *atman* is to be taken in absolutist senses. Within the Christian tradition some theologians distinguish "ego" and "true self" in ways similar to these distinctions in Eastern religions. See the ecophilosophical interpretation of the gospel of Luke in Stephen Verney's *Onto the New Age* (Glasgow: Collins, 1976), pp. 33–41.
10. Many authors take some steps toward derivational structures, offering mild systematizations. The chapter "Environmental Ethics and Hope" (in G. Tyler Miller, *Living in the Environment,* 3rd ed. [Belmont: Wadsworth, 1983]) is a valuable start, but the derivational relations are unclear. The logic and semantics of simple models of normative systems are briefly discussed in my "Notes on the Methodology of Normative Systems," *Methodology and Science* 10 (1977): 64–79. For a defense of the thesis that as soon as people assert anything at all, they assume a total view, implicitly involving an ontology, methodology, epistemology, and ethics, see my "Reflections about Total Views," *Philosophy and Phenomenological Research* 25 (1964–65): 16–29. The best and wittiest warning against taking systematizations too seriously is to be found in Søren Kierkegaard, *Concluding Unscientific Postscript.*

    For criticism and defense of my fundamental norm ("Self-realization"), together with my answer, see *In Sceptical Wonder: Essays in Honor of Arne Naess* (Oslo: University Press, 1982). My main exposition of Ecosophy T was originally offered in the Norwegian work, *Okologi, samfunn og livsstil* (Oslo: University Press, 5th ed., 1976). Even there, the exposition is sketchy. (Editor's note: Naess's Norwegian book has been revised and reissued as Arne Naess (translated and edited by David Rothenberg), *Ecology, Community and Lifestyle* [Cambridge: Cambridge University Press, 1989].)

DISCUSSION QUESTIONS

1. Is it possible to live according to the deep ecology platform?
2. Can you derive the platform from Naess' fundamental norm Self-realization?
3. Is Self-realization possible? Is it good? Why?
4. As a social and political movement, which seems "best," deep or shallow environmentalism?

KAREN J. WARREN

The Power and the Promise of Ecological Feminism

Karen Warren's now classic article, "The Power and Promise of Ecological Feminism," sets out the ecofeminist agenda and philosophical framework. Warren and fellow ecophilosopher Val Plumwood have been instrumental in developing ecofeminism as a contribution to both feminism and environmental philosophy. In 1991, under Warren's editorship, the academic journal *Hypatia: A Journal of Feminist Philosophy* devoted an entire issue to ecofeminism. Warren has subsequently edited several books and written other important articles developing the fundamental insights articulated in "The Power and the Promise of Ecological Feminism." As she notes, "There are important connections between feminism and environmentalism, an appreciation of which is essential for the success of the women's and ecological movements."

CRITICAL READING QUESTIONS

1. What does Warren mean by a "feminist issue"?
2. What does Warren mean by patriarchy and oppressive conceptual frameworks, and what is their relation?
3. Why, according to Warren, must all feminists oppose the logic of domination?
4. According to Warren, what justifies including "naturism" among the forms of domination that feminism opposes?
5. What does the narrative about rock climbing show, according to Warren?

INTRODUCTION

Ecological feminism (ecofeminism) has begun to receive a fair amount of attention lately as an alternative feminism and environmental ethic.[1] Since Françoise d'Eaubonne introduced the term *ecoféminisme* in 1974 to bring attention to women's potential for bringing about an ecological revolution,[2] the term has been used in a variety of ways. As I use the term in this paper, ecological feminism is the position that there are important connections—historical, experiential, symbolic, theoretical—between the

---

This essay originally appreared in *Environmental Ethics* 12, 3 (Summer 1990): 125–46. Reprinted with permission.

domination of women and the domination of nature, an understanding of which is crucial to both feminism and environmental ethics. I argue that the promise and power of ecological feminism is that *it provides a distinctive framework both for reconceiving feminism and for developing an environmental ethic which takes seriously connections between the domination of women and the domination of nature.* I do so by discussing the nature of a feminist ethic and the ways in which ecofeminism provides a feminist and environmental ethic. I conclude that any feminist theory *and* any environmental ethic which fails to take seriously the twin and interconnected dominations of women and nature is at best incomplete and at worst simply inadequate.

FEMINISM, ECOLOGICAL FEMINISM, AND CONCEPTUAL FRAMEWORKS

Whatever else it is, feminism is at least the movement to end sexist oppression. It involves the elimination of any and all factors that contribute to the continued and systematic domination or subordination of women. While feminists disagree about the nature of and solutions to the subordination of women, all feminists agree that sexist oppression exists, is wrong, and must be abolished.

A "feminist issue" is any issue that contributes in some way to understanding the oppression of women. Equal rights, comparable pay for comparable work, and food production are feminist issues wherever and whenever an understanding of them contributes to an understanding of the continued exploitation or subjugation of women. Carrying water and searching for firewood are feminist issues wherever and whenever women's primary responsibility for these tasks contributes to their lack of full participation in decision making, income producing, or high status positions engaged in by men. What counts as a feminist issue, then, depends largely on context, particularly the historical and material conditions of women's lives.

Environmental degradation and exploitation are feminist issues because an understanding of them contributes to an understanding of the oppression of women. In India, for example, both deforestation and reforestation through the introduction of a monoculture species tree (e.g., eucalyptus) intended for commercial production are feminist issues because the loss of indigenous forests and multiple species of trees has drastically affected rural Indian women's ability to maintain a subsistence household. Indigenous forests provide a variety of trees for food, fuel, fodder, household utensils, dyes, medicines, and income-generating uses, while monoculture-species forests do not.[3] Although I do not argue for this claim here, a look at the global impact of environmental degradation on women's lives suggests important respects in which environmental degradation is a feminist issue.

Feminist philosophers claim that some of the most important feminist issues are *conceptual* ones: these issues concern how one conceptualizes such mainstay philosophical notions as reason and rationality, ethics, and what it is to be human. Ecofeminists extend this feminist philosophical concern to nature. They argue that, ultimately, some of the most important connections between the domination of women and the domination of nature are conceptual. To see this, consider the nature of conceptual frameworks.

A *conceptual framework* is a set of *basic* beliefs, values, attitudes, and assumptions which shape and reflect how one views oneself and one's world. It is a socially constructed lens through which we perceive ourselves and others. It is affected by such factors as gender, race, class, age, affectional orientation, nationality, and religious background.

Some conceptual frameworks are oppressive. An *oppressive conceptual framework* is one that explains, justifies, and maintains relationships of domination and subordination. When an oppressive conceptual framework is *patriarchal*, it explains, justifies, and maintains the subordination of women by men.

I have argued elsewhere that there are three significant features of oppressive conceptual frameworks: (1) value-hierarchical thinking, i.e., "up-down" thinking which places higher value, status, or prestige on what is "up" rather than on what is "down"; (2) value dualisms, i.e., disjunctive pairs in which the disjuncts are seen as oppositional (rather than as complementary) and exclusive (rather than as inclusive), *and* which place higher value (status, prestige) on one disjunct rather than the other (e.g., dualisms which give higher value or status to that which has historically been identified as "body," "emotion," and "female"); and (3) logic of domination, i.e., a structure of argumentation which leads to a justification of subordination.[4]

The third feature of oppressive conceptual frameworks is the most significant. A logic of domination is not *just* a logical structure. It also involves a substantive value system, since an ethical premise is needed to permit or sanction the "just" subordination of that which is subordinate. This justification typically is given on grounds of some alleged characteristic (e.g., rationality) which the dominant (e.g., men) have and the subordinate (e.g., women) lack.

Contrary to what many feminists and ecofeminists have said or suggested, there may be nothing *inherently* problematic about "hierarchical thinking" or even "value-hierarchical thinking" in contexts other than contexts of oppression. Hierarchical thinking is important in daily living for classifying data, comparing information, and organizing material. Taxonomies (e.g., plant taxonomies) and biological nomenclature seem to require *some* form of "hierarchical thinking." Even "value-hierarchical thinking" may be quite acceptable in certain contexts. (The same may be said of "value dualisms" in nonoppressive contexts.) For example, suppose it is true that what is unique about humans is our conscious capacity to radically reshape our social environments (or "societies"), as Murray Bookchin suggests.[5] Then one could truthfully say that humans are better equipped to radically reshape their environments than are rocks or plants—a "value-hierarchical" way of speaking.

The problem is not simply *that* value-hierarchial thinking and value dualisms are used, but *the way* in which each has been used in *oppressive conceptual frameworks* to establish inferiority and to justify subordination.[6] It is the logic of domination, *coupled with* value-hierarchical thinking and value dualisms, which "justifies" subordination. What is explanatorily basic, then, about the nature of oppressive conceptual frameworks is the logic of domination.

For ecofeminism, that a logic of domination is explanatorily basic is important for at least three reasons. First, without a logic of domination, a description of similarities and differences would be just that—a description of similarities and differences. Consider the claim, "Humans are different from plants and rocks in that humans can (and plants and rocks cannot) consciously and radically reshape the communities in which they live; humans are similar to plants and rocks in that they are both members of an ecological community." Even if humans are "better" than plants and rocks with respect to the conscious ability of humans to radically transform communities, one does not *thereby* get any *morally* relevant distinction between humans and nonhumans, or an argument for the domination of plants and rocks by humans. To get *those* conclusions one needs to add at least two powerful assumptions, viz., (A2) and (A4) in argument A below:

(A1) Humans do, and plants and rocks do not, have the capacity to consciously and radically change the community in which they live.

(A2) Whatever has the capacity to consciously and radically change the community in which it lives is morally superior to whatever lacks this capacity.

(A3) Thus, humans are morally superior to plants and rocks.

(A4) For any X and Y, if X is morally superior to Y, then X is morally justified in subordinating Y.

(A5) Thus, humans are morally justified in subordinating plants and rocks.

Without the two assumptions that *humans are morally superior* to (at least some) nonhumans, (A2), and that *superiority justifies subordination,* (A4), all one has is some difference between humans and some nonhumans. This is true *even if* that difference is given in terms of superiority. Thus, it is the logic of domination, (A4), which is the bottom line in ecofeminist discussions of oppression.

Second, ecofeminists argue that, at least in Western societies, the oppressive conceptual framework which sanctions the twin dominations of women and nature is a patriarchal one characterized by all three features of an oppressive conceptual framework. Many ecofeminists claim that, historically, within at least the dominant Western culture, a patriarchal conceptual framework has sanctioned the following argument B:

(B1) Women are identified with nature and the realm of the physical; men are identified with the "human" and the realm of the mental.

(B2) Whatever is identified with nature and the realm of the physical is inferior to ("below") whatever is identified with the "human" and the realm of the mental; or, conversely, the latter is superior to ("above") the former.

(B3) Thus, women are inferior to ("below") men; or, conversely, men are superior to ("above") women.

(B4) For any X and Y, if X is superior to Y, then X is justified in subordinating Y.

(B5) Thus, men are justified in subordinating women.

If sound, argument B establishes *patriarchy,* i.e., the conclusion given at (B5) that the systematic domination of women by men is justified. But according to ecofeminists, (B5) is justified by just those three features of an oppressive conceptual framework identified earlier: value-hierarchical thinking, the assumption at (B2); value dualisms, the assumed dualism of the mental and the physical at (B1) and the assumed inferiority of the physical vis-à-vis the mental at (B2); and a logic of domination, the assumption at (B4), the same as the previous premise (A4). Hence, according to ecofeminists, insofar as an oppressive patriarchal conceptual framework has functioned historically (within at least dominant Western culture) to sanction the twin dominations of women and nature (argument B), both argument B and the patriarchal conceptual framework, from whence it comes, ought to be rejected.

Of course, the preceding does not identify which premises of B are false. What is the status of premises (B1) and (B2)? Most, if not all, feminists claim that (B1), and many ecofeminists claim that (B2), have been assumed or asserted within the dominant Western philosophical and intellectual tradition.[7] As such, these feminists assert, as a matter of historical fact, that the dominant Western philosophical tradition has assumed the truth of (B1) and (B2). Ecofeminists, however, either deny (B2) or do not affirm (B2). Furthermore, because some ecofeminists are anxious to deny any ahistorical identification of women with nature, some ecofeminists deny (B1) when (B1) is used to support anything other than a strictly historical claim about what has been asserted or assumed to be true within patriarchal culture—e.g., when (B1) is used to assert that women properly are identified with the realm of nature and the physical.[8] Thus, from an ecofeminist perspective, (B1) and (B2) are properly viewed as problematic though historically sanctioned claims: they are problematic precisely because of the way they have functioned historically in a patriarchal conceptual framework and culture to sanction the dominations of women and nature.

What *all* ecofeminists agree about, then, is the way in which *the logic of domination* has functioned historically within patriarchy to sustain and justify the twin dominations of women and nature.[9] Since *all* feminists (and not just ecofeminists) oppose patriarchy, the conclusion given at (B5), all feminists (including ecofeminists) must oppose at least the logic of domination, premise (B4), on which argument B rests—whatever the truth-value status of (B1) and (B2) *outside of* a patriarchal context.

That *all* feminists must oppose the logic of domination shows the breadth and depth of the ecofeminist critique of B: it is a critique not only of the three assumptions on which this argument for the domination of women and nature rest, viz., the assumptions at (B1), (B2), and (B4); it is also a critique of patriarchal conceptual frameworks generally, i.e., of those oppressive conceptual frameworks which put men "up" and women "down," allege some way in which women are morally inferior to men, and use that alleged difference to justify the subordination of women by men. Therefore, ecofeminism is necessary to *any* feminist critique of patriarchy, and, hence, necessary to feminism (a point I discuss again later).

Third, ecofeminism clarifies why the logic of domination, and any conceptual framework which gives rise to it, must be abolished in order both to make possible a meaningful notion of difference which does not breed domination and to prevent feminism from becoming a "support" movement based primarily on shared experiences. In contemporary society, there is no one "woman's voice," no *woman* (or *human*) *simpliciter:* every woman (or human) is a woman (or human) of some race, class, age, affectional orientation, marital status, regional or national background, and so forth. Because there are no "monolithic experiences" that all women share, feminism must be a "solidarity movement" based on shared beliefs and interests rather than a "unity in sameness" movement based on shared experiences and shared victimization.[10] In the words of Maria Lugones, "Unity—not to be confused with solidarity—is understood as conceptually tied to domination."[11]

Ecofeminists insist that the sort of logic of domination used to justify the domination of humans by gender, racial or ethnic, or class status is also used to justify the domination of nature. Because eliminating a logic of domination is part of a feminist critique—whether a critique of patriarchy, white supremacist culture, or imperialism—ecofeminists insist that *naturism* is properly viewed as an integral part of any feminist solidarity movement to end sexist oppression and the logic of domination which conceptually grounds it.

ECOFEMINISM RECONCEIVES FEMINISM

The discussion so far has focused on some of the oppressive conceptual features of patriarchy. As I use the phrase, the "logic of traditional feminism" refers to the location of the conceptual roots of sexist oppression, at least in Western societies, in an oppressive patriarchal conceptual framework characterized by a logic of domination. Insofar as other systems of oppression (e.g., racism, classism, ageism, heterosexism) are also conceptually maintained by a logic of domination, appeal to the logic of traditional feminism ultimately locates the basic conceptual interconnections among *all* systems of oppression in the logic of domination. It thereby explains at a *conceptual* level why the eradication of sexist oppression requires the eradication of the other forms of oppression.[12] It is by clarifying this conceptual connection between systems of oppression that a movement to end sexist oppression—traditionally the special turf of feminist theory and practice—leads to a reconceiving of feminism as *a movement to end all forms of oppression.*

Suppose one agrees that the logic of traditional feminism requires the expansion of feminism to include other social systems of domination (e.g., racism and classism). What warrants the inclusion of nature in these "social systems of domination"? Why must the logic of traditional feminism include the abolition of "naturism" (i.e., the domination or oppression of nonhuman nature) among the "isms" feminism must confront? The conceptual justification for expanding feminism to include ecofeminism is twofold. One basis has already been suggested: By showing that the conceptual connections between the dual dominations of women and nature are located in an oppressive and, at least in Western societies, patriarchal conceptual framework characterized by a logic of domination, ecofeminism explains how and why feminism, conceived as a movement to end sexist oppression, must be expanded and reconceived as also a movement to end naturism. This is made explicit by the following argument C:

(C1) Feminism is a movement to end sexism.

(C2) But Sexism is conceptually linked with naturism (through an oppressive conceptual framework characterized by a logic of domination).

(C3) Thus, Feminism is (also) a movement to end naturism.

Because, ultimately, these connections between sexism and naturism are conceptual—embedded in an oppressive conceptual framework—the logic of traditional feminism leads to the embracement of ecological feminism.[13]

The other justification for reconceiving feminism to include ecofeminism has to do with the concepts of gender and nature. Just as conceptions of gender are socially constructed, so are conceptions of nature. Of course, the claim that women and nature are social constructions does not require anyone to deny that there are actual humans and actual trees, rivers, and plants. It simply implies that *how* women and nature are conceived is a matter of historical and social reality. These conceptions vary cross-culturally and by historical time period. As a result, any discussion of the "oppression or domination of nature" involves reference to historically specific forms of social domination of nonhuman nature by humans, just as discussion of the "domination of women" refers to historically specific forms of social domination of women by men. Although I do not argue for it here, an ecofeminist defense of the historical connections between the dominations of women and of nature, claims (B1) and (B2) in argument B, involves showing that within patriarchy the feminization of nature and the naturalization of women have been crucial to the historically successful subordinations of both.[14]

If ecofeminism promises to reconceive traditional feminism in ways which include naturism as a legitimate feminist issue, does ecofeminism also promise to reconceive environmental ethics in ways which are feminist? I think so. This is the subject of the remainder of the paper.

CLIMBING FROM ECOFEMINISM TO ENVIRONMENTAL ETHICS

Many feminists and some environmental ethicists have begun to explore the use of first-person narrative as a way of raising philosophically germane issues in ethics often lost or underplayed in mainstream philosophical ethics. Why is this so? What is it about narrative which makes it a significant resource for theory and practice in feminism and environmental ethics? Even if appeal to first-person narrative is a helpful literary device for describing ineffable experience or a legitimate social science methodology for documenting personal and social history, how is first-person narrative a valuable vehicle of argumentation for ethical decision making and theory building? One fruitful way to begin answering these questions is to ask them of a particular first-person narrative. Consider the following first-person narrative about rock climbing:

> For my very first rock climbing experience, I chose a somewhat private spot, away from other climbers and on-lookers. After studying "the chimney," I focused all my energy on making it to the top. I climbed with intense determination, using whatever strength and skills I had to accomplish this challenging feat. By midway I was exhausted and anxious. I couldn't see what to do next—where to put my hands or feet. Growing increasingly more weary as I clung somewhat desperately to the rock, I made a move. It didn't work. I fell. There I was, dangling midair above the rocky ground below, frightened but terribly relieved that the belay rope had held me. I knew I was safe. I took a look up at the climb that remained. I was determined to make it to the top. With renewed confidence and concentration, I finished the climb to the top.
>
> On my second day of climbing, I rappelled down about 200 feet from the top of the Palisades at Lake Superior to just a few feet above the water level. I could see no one—not my belayer, not the other climbers, no one. I unhooked slowly from the rappel rope and took a deep cleansing breath. I looked all around me—really looked—and listened. I heard a cacophony of voices—birds, trickles of water on the rock before me, waves lapping against the rocks below. I closed my eyes and began to feel the rock with my hands—the cracks and crannies, the raised lichen and mosses, the almost imperceptible nubs that might provide a resting place for my fingers and toes when I began to climb. At that moment I was bathed in serenity. I began to talk to the rock in an almost inaudible, child-like way, as if the rock were my friend. I felt an overwhelming sense of gratitude for what it offered me—a chance to know myself and the rock differently, to appreciate unforeseen miracles like the tiny flowers growing in the even tinier cracks in the rock's surface, and to come to know a sense of *being in relationship* with the natural environment. It felt as if the rock and I were silent conversational partners in a longstanding friendship. I realized then that I had come to care about this cliff which was so different from me, so unmovable and invincible, independent and seemingly indifferent to my presence. I wanted to be with the rock as I climbed. Gone was the determination to conquer the rock, to forcefully impose my will on it; I wanted simply to work respectfully with the rock as I climbed. And as I climbed, that is what I felt. I felt myself *caring* for this rock and feeling thankful that climbing provided the opportunity for me to know it and myself in this new way.

There are at least four reasons why use of such a first-person narrative is important to feminism and environmental ethics. First, such a narrative gives voice to a felt sensitivity often lacking in traditional analytical ethical discourse, viz., a sensitivity to conceiving of oneself as fundamentally "in relationship with" others, including the nonhuman environment. It is a modality which *takes relationships themselves seriously.* It thereby stands in contrast to a strictly reductionist modality that takes relationships seriously only or primarily because of the nature of the *relators* or parties to those relationships (e.g., relators conceived as moral agents, right holders, interest carriers, or sentient beings). In the rock-climbing narrative above, it is the climber's relationship with the rock she climbs which takes on special significance—which is itself a locus of value—in addition to whatever moral status or moral considerability she or the rock or any other parties to the relationship may also have.[15]

Second, such a first-person narrative gives expression to a variety of ethical attitudes and behaviors often overlooked or underplayed in mainstream Western ethics, e.g., the difference in attitudes and behaviors toward a rock when one is "making it to the top" and when one thinks of oneself as "friends with" or "caring about" the rock one climbs.[16] These different attitudes and behaviors suggest an ethically germane contrast between two different types of relationship humans or climbers may have toward a rock: An imposed conqueror-type relationship, and an emergent caring-type relationship. This contrast grows out of, and is faithful to, felt, lived experience.

The difference between conquering and caring attitudes and behaviors in relation to the natural environment provides a third reason why the use of first-person narrative is important to feminism and environmental ethics: it provides a way of conceiving of ethics and ethical meaning as *emerging out of* particular situations moral agents find themselves in, rather than as being *imposed on* those situations (e.g., as a derivation or instantiation of some predetermined abstract principle or rule). This emergent feature of narrative centralizes the importance of *voice.* When a multiplicity of cross-cultural *voices* are centralized, narrative is able to give expression to a range of attitudes, values, beliefs, and behaviors which may be overlooked or silenced by imposed ethical meaning and theory. As a reflection on a felt, lived experience, the use of narrative in ethics provides a stance from which ethical discourse can be held accountable to the historical, material, and social realities in which moral subjects find themselves.

Lastly, and for our purposes perhaps most importantly, the use of narrative has argumentative significance. Jim Cheney calls attention to this feature of narrative when he claims, "To contextualize ethical deliberation is, in some sense, to provide a narrative or story, from which the solution to the ethical dilemma emerges as the fitting conclusion."[17] Narrative has argumentative force by suggesting *what counts* as an appropriate conclusion to an ethical situation. One ethical conclusion suggested by the climbing narrative is that what counts as a proper ethical attitude toward mountains and rocks is an attitude of respect and care (whatever that turns out to be or involve), not one of domination and conquest.

In an essay entitled "In and Out of Harm's Way: Arrogance and Love," feminist philosopher Marilyn Frye distinguishes between "arrogant" and "loving" perception as one way of getting at this difference in the ethical attitudes of care and conquest.[18] Frye writes:

> The loving eye is a contrary of the arrogant eye.
>
> The loving eye knows the independence of the other. It is the eye of a seer who knows that nature is indifferent. It is the eye of one who knows that to know the seen, one must consult something other than one's own will and interests and fears and imagination. One must look at the thing. One must look and listen and check and question.
>
> The loving eye is one that pays a certain sort of attention. This attention can require a discipline but *not* a self-denial. The discipline is one of self-knowledge, knowledge of the scope and boundary of the self . . . In particular, it is a matter of being able to tell one's own interests from those of others and of knowing where one's self leaves off and another begins . . .
>
> The loving eye does not make the object of perception into something edible, does not try to assimilate it, does not reduce it to the size of the

> seer's desire, fear and imagination, and hence does not have to simplify. It knows the complexity of the other as something which will forever present new things to be known. The science of the loving eye would favor The Complexity Theory of Truth [in contrast to The Simplicity Theory of Truth] and presuppose The Endless Interestingness of the Universe.[19]

According to Frye, the loving eye is not an invasive, coercive eye which annexes others to itself, but one which "knows the complexity of the other as something which will forever present new things to be known."

When one climbs a rock as a conqueror, one climbs with an arrogant eye. When one climbs with a loving eye, one constantly "must look and listen and check and question." One recognizes the rock as something very different, something perhaps totally indifferent to one's own presence, and finds in that difference joyous occasion for celebration. One knows "the boundary of the self," where the self—the "I," the climber—leaves off and the rock begins. There is no fusion of two into one, but a complement of two entities *acknowledged* as separate, different, independent, yet *in relationship;* they are in relationship *if only* because the loving eye is perceiving it, responding to it, noticing it, attending to it.

An ecofeminist perspective about both women and nature involves this shift in attitude from "arrogant perception" to "loving perception" of the nonhuman world. Arrogant perception of nonhumans by humans presupposes and maintains *sameness* in such a way that it expands the moral community to those beings who are thought to resemble (be like, similar to, or the same as) humans in some morally significant way. Any environmental movement or ethic based on arrogant perception builds a moral hierarchy of beings and assumes some common denominator of moral considerability in virtue of which like beings deserve similar treatment or moral consideration and unlike beings do not. Such environmental ethics are or generate a "unity in sameness." In contrast, "loving perception" presupposes and maintains *difference*—a distinction between the self and other, between human and at least some nonhumans—in such a way that perception of the other as other *is* an expression of love for one who/which is recognized at the outset as independent, dissimilar, different. As Maria Lugones says, in loving perception, "Love is seen not as fusion and erasure of difference but as incompatible with them."[20] "Unity in sameness" alone is an *erasure of difference.*

"Loving perception" of the nonhuman natural world is an attempt to understand what it means *for humans* to care about the nonhuman world, a world *acknowledged* as being independent, different, perhaps even indifferent to humans. Humans *are* different from rocks in important ways, even if they are also both members of some ecological community. A moral community based on loving perception of oneself *in relationship with* a rock, or with the natural environment as a whole, is one which acknowledges and respects difference, whatever "sameness" also exists.[21] The limits of loving perception are determined only by the limits of one's (e.g., a person's, a community's) ability to respond lovingly (or with appropriate care, trust, or friendship)—whether it is to other humans or to the nonhuman world and elements of it.[22]

If what I have said so far is correct, then there are very different ways to climb a mountain and *how* one climbs it and *how* one narrates the experience of climbing it matter ethically. If one climbs with "arrogant perception," with an attitude of "conquer and control," one keeps intact the very sorts of thinking that characterize a logic of domination and an oppressive conceptual framework. Since the oppressive conceptual framework which sanctions the domination of nature is a patriarchal one, one also thereby keeps intact, even if unwittingly, a patriarchal conceptual framework. Because the dismantling of patriarchal conceptual frameworks is a feminist issue, *how* one climbs a mountain and *how* one narrates—or tells the story—about the experience of climbing also are *feminist issues.* In this way, ecofeminism makes visible why, at a conceptual level, environmental ethics is a feminist issue. I turn now to a consideration of ecofeminism as a distinctively feminist and environmental ethic.

ECOFEMINISM AS A FEMINIST AND ENVIRONMENTAL ETHIC

A feminist ethic involves a twofold commitment to critique male bias in ethics wherever it occurs, and to develop ethics which are not male-biased. Sometimes this involves articulation of values (e.g., values of care, appropriate trust, kinship, friendship) often lost or underplayed in mainstream ethics.[23] Sometimes it involves engaging in theory building by pioneering in new directions or by revamping old theories in gender sensitive ways. What makes the critiques of old theories or conceptualizations of new ones "feminist" is that they emerge out of sex-gender analyses and reflect whatever those analyses reveal about gendered experience and gendered social reality.

As I conceive feminist ethics in the prefeminist present, it rejects attempts to conceive of ethical theory in terms of necessary and sufficient conditions, because it assumes that there is no essence (in the sense of some transhistorical, universal, absolute abstraction) of feminist ethics. While attempts to formulate joint necessary and sufficient conditions of a feminist ethic are unfruitful, nonetheless, there are some necessary conditions, what I prefer to call "boundary conditions," of a feminist ethic. These boundary conditions clarify some of the minimal conditions of a feminist ethic without suggesting that feminist ethics has some ahistorical essence. They are like the boundaries of a quilt or collage. They delimit the territory of the piece without dictating what the interior, the design, the actual pattern of the piece looks like. Because the actual design of the quilt emerges from the multiplicity of voices of women in a crosscultural context, the design will change over time. It is not something static.

What are some of the boundary conditions of a feminist ethic? First, nothing can become part of a feminist ethic—can be part of the quilt—that promotes sexism, racism, classism, or any other "isms" of social domination. Of course, people may disagree about what counts as a sexist act, racist attitude, classist behavior. What counts as sexism, racism, or classism may vary cross-culturally. Still, because a feminist ethic aims at eliminating sexism and sexist bias, and (as I have already shown) sexism is intimately connected in conceptualization and in practice to racism, classism, and naturism, a feminist ethic must be anti-sexist, anti-racist, anti-classist, anti-naturist and opposed to any "ism" which presupposes or advances a logic of domination.

Second, a feminist ethic is a *contextualist* ethic. A contextualist ethic is one which sees ethical discourse and practice as emerging from the voices of people located in different historical circumstances. A contextualist ethic is properly viewed as a *collage* or *mosaic,* a *tapestry* of voices that emerges out of felt experiences. Like any collage or mosaic, the point is not to have *one picture* based on a unity of voices, but a *pattern* which emerges out of the very different voices of people located in different circumstances. When a contextualist ethic is *feminist,* it gives central place to the voices of women.

Third, since a feminist ethic gives central significance to the diversity of women's voices, a feminist ethic must be structurally pluralistic rather than unitary or reductionistic. It rejects the assumption that there is "one voice" in terms of which ethical values, beliefs, attitudes, and conduct can be assessed.

Fourth, a feminist ethic reconceives ethical theory as theory in process which will change over time. Like all theory, a feminist ethic is based on some generalizations.[24] Nevertheless, the generalizations associated with it are themselves a pattern of voices within which the different voices emerging out of concrete and alternative descriptions of ethical situations have meaning. The coherence of a feminist theory so conceived is given within a historical and conceptual context, i.e., within a set of historical, socioeconomic circumstances (including circumstances of race, class, age, and affectional orientation) and within a set of basic beliefs, values, attitudes, and assumptions about the world.

Fifth, because a feminist ethic is contextualist, structurally pluralistic, and "in-process," one way to evaluate the claims of a feminist ethic is in terms of their *inclusiveness:* those claims (voices, patterns of voices) are morally and epistemologically favored (preferred, better, less partial, less biased) which are more inclusive of the felt experiences and perspectives of oppressed persons. The condition of inclusiveness requires and ensures that the diverse voices of women (as oppressed persons) will be given legitimacy in ethical theory building. It thereby helps to minimize empirical bias, e.g., bias rising from faulty or false generalizations based on stereotyping, too small a sample size, or a skewed sample. It does so by ensuring that any generalizations which are made about ethics and ethical decision making include—indeed cohere with—the patterned voices of women.[25]

Sixth, a feminist ethic makes no attempt to provide an "objective" point of view, since it assumes that in contemporary culture there really is no such point of view. As such, it does not claim to be "unbiased" in the sense of "value-neutral" or "objective." However, it does assume that whatever bias it has as an ethic centralizing the voices of oppressed persons is a *better bias*—"better"—because it is more inclusive and therefore less partial—than those which exclude those voices.[26]

Seventh, a feminist ethic provides a central place for values typically unnoticed, underplayed, or misrepresented in traditional ethics, e.g., values of care, love, friendship, and appropriate trust.[27] Again, it need not do this at the exclusion of considerations of rights, rules, or utility. There may be many contexts in which talk of rights or of utility is useful or appropriate. For instance, in contracts or property relationships, talk of rights may be useful and appropriate. In deciding what is cost-effective or advantageous to the most people, talk of utility may be useful and appropriate. In a feminist *qua* contextualist ethic, whether or not such talk is useful or appropriate depends on the context; *other values* (e.g., values of care, trust, friendship) are *not* viewed as reducible to or captured solely in terms of such talk.[28]

Eighth, a feminist ethic also involves a reconception of what it is to be human and what it is for humans to engage in ethical decision making, since it rejects as either meaningless or currently untenable any gender-free or gender-neutral description of humans, ethics, and ethical decision making. It thereby rejects what Alison Jaggar calls "abstract individualism," i.e., the position that it is possible to identify a human essence or human nature that exists independently of any particular historical context.[29] Humans and human moral conduct are properly understood essentially (and not merely accidentally) in terms of networks or webs of historical and concrete relationships.

All the props are now in place for seeing how ecofeminism provides the framework for a distinctively feminist and environmental ethic. It is a feminism that critiques male bias wherever it occurs in ethics (including environmental ethics) and aims at providing an ethic (including an environmental ethic) which is not male biased—and it does so in a way that satisfies the preliminary boundary conditions of a feminist ethic.

First, ecofeminism is quintessentially anti-naturist. Its anti-naturism consists in the rejection of any way of thinking about or acting toward nonhuman nature that reflects a logic, values, or attitude of domination. Its anti-naturist, anti-sexist, anti-racist, anti-classist (and so forth, for all other "isms" of social domination) stance forms the outer boundary of the quilt: nothing gets on the quilt which is naturist, sexist, racist, classist, and so forth.

Second, ecofeminism is a contextualist ethic. It involves a shift *from* a conception of ethics as primarily a matter of rights, rules, or principles predetermined and applied in specific cases to entities viewed as competitors in the contest of moral standing, *to* a conception of ethics as growing out of what Jim Cheney calls "defining relationships," i.e., relationships conceived in some sense as defining who one is.[30] As a contextualist ethic, it is not that rights, or rules, or principles are *not* relevant or important. Clearly they are in certain contexts and for certain purposes.[31] It is just that what *makes* them relevant or important is that those to whom they apply are entities *in relationship with* others.

Ecofeminism also involves an ethical shift *from* granting moral consideration to nonhumans *exclusively* on the grounds of some similarity they share with humans (e.g., rationality, interests, moral agency, sentiency, right-holder status) *to* "a highly contextual account to see clearly what a human being is and what the nonhuman world might be, morally speaking, *for* human beings."[32] For an ecofeminist, *how* a moral agent is in relationship to another becomes of central significance, not simply *that* a moral agent is a moral agent or is bound by rights, duties, virtue, or utility to act in a certain way.

Third, ecofeminism is structurally pluralistic in that it presupposes and maintains difference—difference among humans as well as between humans and at least some elements of nonhuman nature. Thus, while ecofeminism denies the "nature/culture" split, it affirms that humans are both members of an ecological community (in some respects) and different from it (in other respects). Ecofeminism's attention to relationships and community is not, therefore, an erasure of difference but a respectful acknowledgement of it.

Fourth, ecofeminism reconceives theory as theory in process. It focuses on patterns of meaning which emerge, for instance, from the storytelling and first-person narratives of women (and others) who deplore the twin dominations of women and nature. The use of narrative is one way to ensure that the content of the ethic—the pattern of the quilt—may/will change over time, as the historical and material realities of women's lives change and as more is learned about women-nature connections and the destruction of the nonhuman world.[33]

Fifth, ecofeminism is inclusivist. It emerges from the voices of women who experience the harmful domination of nature and the way that domination is tied to their domination as women. It emerges from listening to the voices of indigenous peoples such as Native Americans who have been dislocated from their land and have witnessed the attendant undermining of such values as appropriate reciprocity, sharing, and kinship that characterize traditional Indian culture. It emerges from listening to voices of those who, like Nathan Hare, critique traditional approaches to environmental ethics as white and bourgeois, and as failing to address issues of "black ecology" and the "ecology" of the inner city and urban spaces.[34] It also emerges out of the voices of Chipko women who see the destruction of "earth, soil, and water" as intimately connected with their own inability to survive economically.[35] With its emphasis on inclusivity and difference, ecofeminism provides a framework for recognizing that what counts as ecology and what counts as appropriate conduct toward both human and nonhuman environments is largely a matter of context.

Sixth, as a feminism, ecofeminism makes no attempt to provide an "objective" point of view. It is a social ecology. It recognizes the twin dominations of women and nature as social problems rooted both in very concrete, historical socioeconomic circumstances and in oppressive patriarchal conceptual frameworks which maintain and sanction these circumstances.

Seventh, ecofeminism makes a central place for values of care, love, friendship, trust, and appropriate reciprocity—values that presuppose that our relationships to others are central to our understanding of who we are.[36] It thereby gives voice to the sensitivity that in climbing a mountain, one is doing something in relationship with an "other," an "other" whom one can come to care about and treat respectfully.

Lastly, an ecofeminist ethic involves a reconception of what it means to be human, and in what human ethical behavior consists. Ecofeminism denies abstract individualism. Humans are who we are *in large part* by virtue of the historical and social contexts and the relationships we are in, including our relationships with nonhuman nature. Relationships are not something extrinsic to who we are, not an "add on" feature of human nature; they play an essential role in shaping what it is to be human. Relationships of humans to the nonhuman environment are, in part, constitutive of what it is to be a human.

By making visible the interconnections among the dominations of women and nature, ecofeminism shows that both are feminist issues and that explicit acknowledgement of both is vital to any responsible environmental ethic. Feminism *must* embrace ecological feminism if it is to end the domination of women because the domination of women is tied conceptually and historically to the domination of nature.

A responsible environmental ethic also *must* embrace feminism. Otherwise, even the seemingly most revolutionary, liberational, and holistic ecological ethic will fail to take seriously the interconnected dominations of nature and women that are so much a part of the historical legacy and conceptual framework that sanctions the exploitation of nonhuman nature. Failure to make visible these interconnected, twin dominations results in an inaccurate account of how it is that nature has been and continues to be dominated and exploited and produces an environmental ethic that lacks the depth necessary to be truly *inclusive* of the realities of persons who at least in dominant Western culture have been intimately tied with that exploitation, viz., women. Whatever else can be said in favor of such holistic ethics, a failure to make visible ecofeminist insights into the common denominators of the twin oppressions of women and nature is to perpetuate, rather than overcome, the source of that oppression.

This last point deserves further attention. It may be objected that as long as the end result is "the same"—the development of an environmental ethic which does not emerge out of or reinforce an oppressive conceptual framework—it does not matter whether that ethic (or the ethic endorsed in getting there) is feminist or not. Hence, it simply is *not* the case that any adequate environmental ethic must be feminist. My argument, in contrast, has been that it *does* matter, and for three important reasons. First, there is the scholarly issue of accurately representing historical reality, and that, ecofeminists claim, requires acknowledging the historical feminization of nature and naturalization of women as part of the exploitation of nature. Second, I have shown that the conceptual connections between the domination of women and the domination of nature are located in an oppressive and, at least in Western societies, patriarchal conceptual framework characterized by a logic of domination. Thus, I have shown that failure to notice the nature of this connection leaves at best an incomplete, inaccurate, and partial account of what is required of a conceptually adequate environmental ethic. An ethic which *does not* acknowledge this is simply *not* the same as one that does, whatever else the similarities between them. Third, the claim that, in contemporary culture, one can have an adequate environmental ethic which is *not* feminist assumes that, in contemporary culture, the label *feminist* does not add anything crucial to the nature or description of environmental ethics. I have shown that at least in contemporary culture this is false, for the word *feminist* currently helps to clarify just *how* the domination of nature is conceptually linked to patriarchy and, hence, how the liberation of nature, is conceptually linked to the termination of patriarchy. Thus, because the word 'feminist' has critical bite in contemporary culture, it serves as an important reminder that in contemporary sex-gendered, raced, classed, and naturist culture, an unlabeled position functions as a privileged and "unmarked" position. That is, without the addition of the word *feminist,* one presents environmental ethics as if it has no bias, including male-gender bias, which is just what ecofeminists deny: failure to notice the connections between the twin oppressions of women and nature *is* male-gender bias.

One of the goals of feminism is the eradication of all oppressive sex-gender (and related race, class, age, affectional preference) categories and the creation of a world in which *difference does not breed domination*—say, the world of 4001. If in 4001 an "adequate environmental ethic" is a "feminist environmental ethic," the word *feminist* may then be redundant and unnecessary. However, this is *not* 4001, and in terms of the current historical and conceptual reality the dominations of nature and of women are intimately connected. Failure to notice or make visible that connection in 1990 perpetuates the mistaken (and privileged) view that "environmental ethics" is *not* a feminist issue, and that *feminist* adds nothing to environmental ethics.[37]

CONCLUSION

I have argued in this paper that ecofeminism provides a framework for a distinctively feminist and environmental ethic. Ecofeminism grows out of the felt and theorized about connections between the domination of women and the domination of nature. As a contextualist ethic, ecofeminism refocuses environmental ethics on what nature might mean, morally speaking, *for* humans, and on how the relational attitudes of humans to others—humans as well as nonhumans—sculpt both what it is to be human and the nature and ground of human responsibilities to the nonhuman environment. Part of what this refocusing does is to take seriously the voices of women and other oppressed persons in the construction of that ethic.

A Sioux elder once told me a story about his son. He sent his seven-year-old son to live with the child's grandparents on a Sioux reservation so that he could "learn the Indian ways." Part of what the grandparents taught the son was how to hunt the four leggeds of the forest. As I heard the story, the boy was taught, "to shoot your four-legged brother in his hind area, slowing it down but not killing it. Then, take the four-legged's head in your hands, and look into his eyes. The eyes are where all the suffering is. Look into your brother's eyes and feel his pain. Then, take your knife and cut the four-legged under his chin, here, on his neck, so that he dies quickly. And as you do, ask your brother, the four-legged, for forgiveness for what you do. Offer also a prayer of thanks to your four-legged kin for offering his body to you just now, when you need food to eat and clothing to wear. And promise the four-legged that you will put yourself back into the earth when you die, to become nourishment of the earth, and for the sister flowers, and for the brother deer. It is appropriate that you should offer this blessing for the four-legged and, in due time, reciprocate in turn with your body in this way, as the four-legged gives life to you for your survival." As I reflect upon that story, I am struck by the power of the environmental ethic that grows out of and takes seriously narrative, context, and such values and relational attitudes as care, loving perception, and appropriate reciprocity, and doing what is appropriate in a given situation—however that notion of appropriateness eventually gets filled out. I am also struck by what one is able to see, once one begins to explore some of the historical and conceptual connections between the dominations of women and of nature. A *re-conceiving* and *re-visioning* of both feminism and environmental ethics, is, I think, the power and promise of ecofeminism.

NOTES

1. Explicit ecological feminist literature includes works from a variety of scholarly perspectives and sources. Some of these works are Jim Cheney, "Eco-Feminism and Deep Ecology," *Environmental Ethics* 9 (1987): 115–45; Katherine Davies, "Historical Associations: Women and the Natural World," *Women & Environments* 9, no. 2 (Spring 1987): 4–6; Sharon Doubiago, "Deeper than Deep Ecology: Men Must Become Feminists," in *The New Catalyst Quarterly,* no. 10 (Winter 1987/88): 10–11; Brian Easlea, *Science and Sexual Oppression: Patriarchy's Confrontation with Women and Nature* (London: Weidenfeld & Nicholson, 1981); Ynestra King, "Feminism and the Revolt of Nature," in *Heresies #13: Feminism and Ecology* 4, no. 1 (1981): Greater King: 12–16, and "What Is Ecofeminism?" *The Nation,* 12 December 1987; Abby Peterson and Carolyn Merchant, "Peace with the Earth: Women and the Environmental Movement in Sweden," *Women's Studies International Forum* 9, no. 5–6. (1986): 465–79; Judith Plant, ed., *Healing Our Wounds: The Power of Ecological Feminisn* (Boston: New Society Publishers, 1989); Kirkpatrick Sale, "Ecofeminism—A New Perspective," *The Nation,* 26 (September 1987): 302–05; Ariel Kay Salleh, "Deeper than Deep Ecology: The Eco-Feminist Connection," *Environmental Ethics* 6 (1984): 339–45, and "Epistemology and the Metaphors of Production: An Eco-Feminist Reading of Critical Theory," in *Studies in the Humanities* 15 (1988): 130–39; Karen J. Warren, "Feminism and Ecology: Making Connections," *Environmental Ethics* 9 (1987): 3–21; Miriam Wyman, "Explorations of Eco-Feminism," *Women & Environments* (Spring 1987): 6–7; Iris Young, " 'Feminism and Ecology' and 'Women and Life on Earth: Eco-Feminism in the 80's,' " *Environmental Ethics* 5 (1983): 173–80.
2. Françoise d'Eaubonne. *Le Féminisme ou la Mort* (Paris: Pierre Horay, 1974), pp. 213–52.
3. I discuss this in my paper "Toward an Ecofeminist Ethic."
4. The account offered here is a revision of the account given earlier in my paper "Feminism and Ecology: Making Connections." I have changed the account to be about "oppressive" rather than strictly "partriarchal" conceptual frameworks in order to leave open the possibility that there may be some patriarchal conceptual frameworks (e.g., in non-Western cultures) which are *not* properly characterized as based on value dualisms.
5. Murray Bookchin, "Social Ecology versus 'Deep Ecology,' " in *Green Perspectives: Newsletter of the Green Program Project,* no. 4–5 (Summer 1987): 9.
6. It may be that in contemporary Western society, which is so thoroughly structured by categories of gender, race, class, age, and affectional orientation, that there simply is no meaningful notion of "value-hierarchical thinking" which does not

function in an oppressive context. For purposes of this paper, I leave that question open.

7. Many feminists who argue for the historical point that claims (B1) and (B2) have been asserted or assumed to be true within the dominant Western philosophical tradition do so by discussion of that tradition's conceptions of reason, rationality, and science. For a sampling of the sorts of claims made within that context, see "Reason, Rationality, and Gender," ed. Nancy Tuana and Karen J. Warren, a special issue of the American Philosophical Association's *Newsletter on Feminism and Philosophy* 88, no. 2 (March 1989): 17–71. Ecofeminists who claim that (B2) has been assumed to be true within the dominant Western philosophical tradition include: Gray, *Green Paradise Lost,* Griffin, *Woman and Nature,* Merchant, *The Death of Nature,* Ruether, *New Woman/New Earth.* For a discussion of some of these ecofeminist historical acounts, see Plumwood, "Ecofeminism." While I agree that the historical connections between the domination of women and the domination of nature is a crucial one, I do not argue for that claim here.

8. Ecofeminists who deny (B1) when (B1) is offered as anything other than a true, descriptive, historical claim about patriarchal culture often do so on grounds that an objectionable sort of biological determinism, or at least harmful female sex-gender stereotypes, underlie (B1). For a discussion of this "split" among those ecofeminists ("nature feminists") who assert and those ecofeminists ("social feminists") who deny (B1) as anything other than a true historical claim about how women are described in patriarchal culture, see Griscom, "On Healing the Nature/History Split."

9. I make no attempt here to defend the historically sanctioned truth of these premises.

10. See, e.g., Bell Hooks, *Feminist Theory: From Margin to Center* (Boston: South End Press, 1984), pp. 51–52.

11. Maria Lugones, "Playfulness, 'World-Travelling,' and Loving Perception," *Hypatia* 2, no. 2 (Summer 1987): 3.

12. At an *experiential* level, some women are "women of color," poor, old, lesbian, Jewish, and physically challenged. Thus, if feminism is going to liberate these women, it also needs to end the racism, classism, heterosexism, anti-Semitism, and discrimination against the handicapped that is constitutive of their oppression as black, or Latina, or poor, or older, or lesbian, or Jewish, or physically challenged women.

13. This same sort of reasoning shows that feminism is also a movement to end racism, classism, age-ism, heterosexism and other "isms," which are based in oppressive conceptual frameworks characterized by a logic of domination. However, there is an important caveat: ecofeminism is *not* compatible with all feminisms and all environmentalisms. For a discussion of this point, see my article "Feminism and Ecology: Making Connections." What it *is* compatible with is the minimal condition characterization of feminism as a movement to end sexism that is accepted by all contemporary feminisms (Liberal, Traditional, Marxist, radical, socialist, Blacks and non-Western).

14. See, e.g., Gray, *Green Paradise Lost;* Griffin, *Women and Nature;* Merchant, *The Death of Nature;* and Ruether, *New Woman/New Earth.*

15. Suppose, as I think is the case, that a necessary condition for the existence of a moral relationship is that at least one party to the relationship is a moral being (leaving open for our purposes what counts as a "moral being"). If this is so, then the Mona Lisa cannot properly be said to have or stand in a moral relationship with the wall on which she hangs, and a wolf cannot have or properly be said to have or stand in a moral relationship with a moose. Such a necessary-condition account leaves open the question whether *both* parties to the relationship must be moral beings. My point here is simply that however one resolves *that* question, recognition of the relationships themselves as a locus of value is a recognition of a source of value that is different from and not reducible to the values of the "moral beings" in those relationships.

16. It is interesting to note that the image of being friends with the Earth is one which cytogeneticist Barbara McClintock uses when she describes the importance of having "a feeling for the organism," "listening to the material [in this case the corn plant]," in one's work as a scientist. See Evelyn Fox Keller, "Women, Science, and Popular Mythology," in *Machina Ex Dea: Feminist Perspectives on Technology,* ed. Joan Rothschild (New York: Pergamon Press, 1983), and Evelyn Fox Keller. *A Feeling for the Organism: The Life and Work*

of Barbara McClintock (San Francisco: W. H. Freeman, 1983).

17. Cheney, "Eco-Feminism and Deep Ecology," p. 144.
18. Marilyn Frye, "In and Out of Harm's Way: Arrogance and Love," *The Politics of Reality* (Trumansburg, New York: The Crossing Press, 1983), pp. 66–72.
19. Ibid., pp. 75–76.
20. Maria Lugones, "Playfulness," p. 3.
21. Cheney makes a similar point in "Eco-Feminism and Deep Ecology," p. 140.
22. Ibid., p. 138.
23. This account of a feminist ethic draws on my paper "Toward an Ecofeminist Ethic."
24. Marilyn Frye makes this point in her illuminating paper. "The Possibility of Feminist Theory," read at the American Philosophical Association Central Division Meetings in Chicago, 29 April–1 May 1986. My discussion of feminist theory is inspired largely by that paper and by Kathryn Addelson's paper "Moral Revolution," in *Women and Values: Reading in Recent Feminist Philosophy,* ed. Marilyn Pearsall (Belmont, CA: Wadsworth Publishing Co., 1986), pp. 291–309.
25. Notice that the standard of inclusiveness does not exclude the voices of men. It is just that those voices must cohere with the voices of women.
26. For a more in-depth discussion of the notions of impartiality and bias, see my paper, "Critical Thinking and Feminism," *Informal Logic* 10, no. 1 (Winter 1988): 31–44.
27. The burgeoning literature on these values is noteworthy. See, e.g., Carol Gilligan, *In a Different Voice: Psychological Theories and Women's Development* (Cambridge: Harvard University Press, 1982); *Mapping the Moral Domain: A Contribution of Women's Thinking to Psychological Theory and Education,* ed. Carol Gilligan, Janie Victoria Ward, and Jill McLean Taylor, with Betty Bardige (Cambridge: Harvard University Press, 1988); Nel Nodings, *Caring: A Feminine Approach to Ethics and Moral Education* (Berkeley: University of California Press, 1984); Maria Lugones and Elizabeth V. Spelman, "Have We Got a Theory for You! Feminist Theory, Cultural Imperialism, and the Women's Voice," *Women's Studies International Forum* 6 (1983): 573–81; Maria Lugones, "Playfulness"; Annette C. Baier, "What Do Women Want in a Moral Theory?" *Nous* 19 (1985): 53–63.
28. Jim Cheney would claim that our fundamental relationships to one another as moral agents are not as moral agents to rights holders, and that whatever rights a person properly may be said to have are relationally defined rights, not rights possessed by atomistic individuals conceived as Robinson Crusoes who do not exist essentially in relation to others. On this view, even rights talk itself is properly conceived as growing out of a relational ethic, not vice versa.
29. Alison Jaggar, *Feminist Politics and Human Nature* (Totowa, NJ: Rowman and Allanheld, 1980), pp. 42–44.
30. Henry West has pointed out that the expression "defining relations" is ambiguous. According to West, "the defining" as Cheney uses it is an adjective, not a principle—it is not that ethics defines relationships; it is that ethics grows out of conceiving of the relationships that one is in as defining what the individual is.
31. For example, in relationships involving contracts or promises, those relationships might be correctly described as that of moral agent to rights holders. In relationships involving mere property, those relationships might be correctly described as that of moral agent to objects having only instrumental value, "relationships of instrumentality." In comments on an earlier draft of this paper, West suggested that possessive individualism, for instance, might be recast in such a way that an individual is defined by his or her property relationships.
32. Cheney, "Eco-Feminism and Deep Ecology," p. 144.
33. One might object that such permission for change opens the door for environmental exploitation. This is not the case. An ecofeminist ethic is anti-naturist. Hence, the unjust domination and exploitation of nature is a "boundary condition" of the ethic; no such actions are sanctioned or justified on ecofeminist grounds. What it *does* leave open is some leeway about what counts as domination and exploitation. This, I think, is a strength of the ethic, not a weakness, since it acknowledges that *that* issue cannot be resolved in any practical way in the abstract, independent of a historical and social context.

34. Nathan Hare, "Black Ecology," in *Environmental Ethics,* ed. K. S. Shrader-Frechette (Pacific Grove, CA: Boxwood Press, 1981), pp. 229–36.

35. For an ecofeminist discussion of the Chipko movement, see my "Toward an Ecofeminist Ethic," and Shiva's *Staying Alive.*

36. See Cheney, "Eco-Feminism and Deep Ecology," p. 122.

37. I offer the same sort of reply to critics of ecofeminism such as Warwick Fox who suggest that for the sort of ecofeminism I defend, the word *feminist* does not add anything significant to environmental ethics and, consequently, that an ecofeminist like myself might as well call herself a deep ecologist. He asks: "Why doesn't she just call it [i.e., Warren's vision of a transformative feminism] deep ecology? Why specifically attach the label *feminist* to it . . . ?" (Warwick Fox, "The Deep Ecology-Ecofeminism Debate and Its Parallels," *Environmental Ethics* 11, no. 1 [1989]: 14, n. 22). Whatever the important similarities between deep ecology and ecofeminism (or, specifically, my version of ecofeminism)—and, indeed, there are many—it is precisely my point here that the word *feminist* does add something significant to the conception of environmental ethics, and that any environmental ethic (including deep ecology) that fails to make explicit the different kinds of interconnections among the domination of nature and the domination of women will be, from a feminist (and ecofeminist) perspective such as mine, inadequate.

DISCUSSION QUESTIONS

1. Consider some of the "women-nature" connections. Is Warren correct to argue that the oppression of one is conceptually connected to the oppression of the other?
2. Can nature be dominated?
3. Assess the logic of domination. Are subordination, suppression, domination, and control necessarily bad? Can you come up with counterexamples to (B4), the logic of domination? (Warren states the principle as: "For any *X* and *Y*, if *X* is superior to *Y*, then *X* is justified in subordinating *Y*.")
4. Does the rock-climbing narrative show what Warren takes it to show? Explain. Why is narrative important for ecofeminism?

You Decide!

1. CONSUMPTION AND COLLECTIVE DECISIONS

In a series of articles in the 1980s, Garrett Hardin popularized the phrase "tragedy of the commons," referring to the inevitable destruction of an unregulated public resource by those who use it. A commons was originally a pasture for grazing flocks open to all, and its ruination is inevitable because behavior that is individually rational leads to collective catastrophe. It is foolish for me not to add sheep to my herd because you will add to your herd, using the grass that I might otherwise have saved for future use. Being rational, you reach the same conclusion, and so there is nothing to restrain either of us from adding more and more sheep to our herds, ultimately ruining the pasture by overgrazing. Why should I forgo an economic advantage (by not adding sheep to my herd) if grass conserved by me will be eaten by your sheep? The logic is relentless: use it or lose it. And the bind is a classic one between decisions that are individually rational but collectively self-defeating. The situation is thus tragic in the sense that the remorseless working of things condemns us to self-destruction.

Many environmental issues can be seen as aspects of commons-thinking. If I am a manufacturer, why should I impose expensive pollution control costs on myself if you will pollute anyway? You reach the same conclusion about me and so the effluents from our manufacturing plants befoul the environment. If we are in the fishery business, why should I not catch just as many fish as I can, because you will get any left. You think the same thing, and so we deplete the oceans of fish.

An obvious way out of the trap of commons-thinking is government regulation, for it forces us to do something we cannot achieve individually, restrain ourselves for the common good. If you and I both must have pollution control devices on our cars, then you do not have to worry that the expense you impose on yourself is not also borne by me or that whatever measures you take to keep the air clean are undone by me.

The gap between behavior that is smart for one but dumb for all can give us an insight into modern American life. Cornell University economist Robert Frank argues in *Luxury Fever* that our obsession with high-end consumer items is not making us happy. He shows that once a certain level of consumption is reached, higher consumption levels do not increase satisfaction with life. In fact, it causes harm: debt and bankruptcy are up, saving is down; people work long stressful hours, taking time away from friends, family, and recreational and cultural pursuits. Our lives become cramped and one-dimensional. Yet we continue to buy and consume ever more expensive items at an ever-increasing pace. Why? According to Frank, we do it because other people do it, that not to do so would be to impose a social disadvantage on oneself. Economically we drive ourselves way beyond what is rational or necessary; it is very much like a contagious disease. Who needs a $10,000 watch or a $200,000 car?

One might dismiss Frank's analysis, saying that if people want to do what is necessary to achieve their vision of the good life, then so be it. It is up to each individual to decide how to live. Not so, according to Frank. My consumption decisions affect you because to maintain your social standing you must now struggle to meet the level of consumption I establish. Herd animals that we are, we are naturally exquisitely sensitive to the consumption habits of those around us. And so our national pattern of consumption becomes a widespread version of "keeping up with the Joneses."

What is the solution? As in other instances, where there is a gap between individual rationality and collective stupidity, government regulation makes sense. Frank proposes changing from an income tax, which we currently have, to a "consumption tax," that is, a tax on the total amount of money spent on what we consume. People who buy more will have to pay more tax. The theory is that this will restrict consumption, especially for luxury items, thus increasing saving and making time and money available for other more worthwhile uses.

Discussion Questions

1. What is a luxury item?
2. Is there a distinction between "needs" and "wants"? Should we purchase only what we need? (Need for what?)
3. Is it wrong to buy luxury items?
4. Consider a suggestive passage from *Luxury Fever*,

> Yet ordinary consumption spending is often *precisely* analogous to activities that generate pollution. When some job seekers buy custom-tailored interview suits, they harm other

> job seekers in the same way that motorists harm others when they disconnect the catalytic converters on their cars. Yet in each case, the rational individual response to market incentives is to take these harmful actions. And we have no reason to believe that the stresses people experience in trying to keep up with escalating community consumption standards are any less damaging to their health and longevity than the soot and ozone in the air they breathe. (emphasis original)

Is Frank right to claim that consumption is just like pollution in that it harms others?

2. SPECIESISM AND SEXISM

"Well, I really think that ecofeminists have a point," said Donna. "Oh, I'm not so sure about the domination of nature and all of that, but surely they are right when it comes to the treatment of animals in agriculture."

"What do you mean?" asked Bill, looking up from his book.

"What I mean," continued Donna, "is that if you think about it, female animals are the most oppressed of all."

"Aw, come on," began Bill. But before he could say anything else Donna developed her thought.

"Sure," she said. "Look at the 'feminization of protein.' Who lays the eggs, huh? Female chickens, and they are among the most dominated of all domesticated animals. Thousands upon thousands kept in cages, virtually force-fed and pumping out eggs until production drops; then they become pot-pies. And what about the dairy industry? Do you know anything about that? To keep cows lactating they are artificially impregnated once a year. The calves are taken away so they do not get any of the precious milk, and most become veal."

Bill thought this absurd. "Look, "he said, "this doesn't have anything to do with women. I mean, we have to milk cows, not bulls, and we can't get eggs from roosters. It is purely accidental that these foods are linked to females. We don't care about the gender of beef cattle, and female crabs are supposed to be thrown back so they can lay eggs; only the males are harvested. I think your sample is selective," huffed Bill as he returned to his book.

Discussion Questions

1. Is the use of animals gender biased?
2. Can nonhumans be oppressed? Explain.
3. How might Donna respond to Bill? Who is right, in your opinion? Explain.
4. Might domesticated animals, especially farm animals, be like artifacts? (What is an artifact?) What implications would that have, if any, for their domination?

FOR FURTHER READING

Thoreau

The Environmental Imagination: Thoreau, Nature Writing, and the Formation of American Culture, Lawrence Buell, Cambridge MA: Harvard University Press, 1995

The Annotaded Walden: Walden, Or, Life in the Woods Crown Publishers, New York, 1970

Deep Ecology

Deep Ecology for the Twenty-first Century, George Sessions, Ed., Shambhala, Boston, 1995.

Ecology, Community, and Lifestyle: Outline of an Ecosophy, Arne Naess, Cambridge University Press, 1989.

Ecofeminism

Ecological Feminist Philosophies, Karen Warren, Ed., Indiana University Press, 1996.

Feminism and Ecology, Mary Mellor, New York University Press, 1997.

Glossary

Animism: the belief that natural objects, such as mountains or rivers, as well as organisms, are alive or ensouled; *anima* is Latin for "soul" or "air," p. 41, 45, 47–48, 65, 435

Anthropocentrism: the view that humanity is the center of the universe, either as the final and best product of evolution or morally; anthropocentrism is often an unquestioned assumption, p. 320–323

Anthropomorphize: to attribute human qualities to something nonhuman; literally to make in the form of man, p. 435

Argument: statements linked such that the truth of one statement is purported to have a bearing on the truth of another statement. An argument consists of at least one premise and one conclusion. The premise, if true, either guarantees the truth of the conclusion (for deductively valid arguments) or makes the conclusion more likely than not (for cogent inductive arguments), p. 234–235

Biocentrism: the view that the minimum condition for direct moral standing is being alive, p. 435

Care ethics: a moral theory that emphasizes the virtue of care rather than rights, duties, or consequences of actions, p. 19, 20, 435

Consequentialism: any moral theory that conceives of right and wrong solely according to the consequences of actions. Utilitarianism is a form of consequentialism, p. 208, 435

Deep ecology: this term often refers to the eight-point platform articulated by Norwegian philosopher Arne Naess and ecophilosopher George Sessions. "Ecosophy T" is Naess' unique version of deep ecology. At a minimum, deep ecology is nonanthropocentric; some versions question the distinction between self and environment. Since the contrast of "deep ecology" is "shallow ecology," a judgmental factor is apparently introduced by the term itself, p. 383, 404–405, 435

Direct/indirect duties: direct duties (or obligations) are duties *to* something; indirect duties are duties *regarding* it. Ordinarily Jones has a direct duty not to kick Smith and an indirect duty not to kick Smith's car. In each case, Smith is the object of the duty, but in the second Smith's car is a morally inconsequential intermediary linking Jones and Smith. Jones' duty not to kick Smith's car is *to* Smith, not the car; whereas the duty not to kick Smith is to Smith directly, rather than to something else. Environmental ethics raises questions about the range of entities to which we can have direct duties, p. 435

Dualism: Descartes' bifurcation of reality into two distinct and nonreducible categories, mind and matter. Sometimes applied more generally, especially by ecofeminists, (disparagingly) to any oppositional bifurcation, p. 39, 50, 435

Ecocentrism: the view that ecosystems have moral standing and are thus the objects of direct moral obligations. On this view, destroying an ecosystem can be wrong, not because doing so will affect human beings or other sentient beings or nonsentient beings, but simply because it affects the ecosystem. This position is associated with Aldo Leopold, who famously claimed, "A thing is right when it tends to preserve the integrity, stability, and beauty of the biotic community [read: ecosystem]. It is wrong when it tends otherwise," p. 253, 255, 256, 435

Ecofeminism: the view that there are important connections between the domination of women and the domination of nature, p. 416–417, 435

Egoism: the view that one's own interests are morally more significant than any competing interests, p. 82, 273, 435–436

Extensionism: the view that ordinary moral principles and concepts of anthropocentrism can be extended to cover nonhumans as well. According to extensionists, a "new" ethic is not necessary for environmental issues, but rather a more rigorous application of the percepts of ordinary morality, p. 83, 436

Holism/atomism: in holism, certain wholes or collectives—such as corporations, societies, or ecosystems—can have direct moral standing; in atomism, only the constituent parts—such as individual people or specific organisms—can have direct moral standing, p. 252–254, 273, 436

Interests: general term for a good or well-being and thus a fundamental category of moral assessment. What something must be like to have interests is a major question in environmental philosophy. If something has interests, then its good or well-being ought not to be conceived in instrumental terms alone, for it would have a sake that merits recognition by moral agents, p. 229, 436

Intrinsic/instrumental value: fundamental distinction between kinds of value. Instrumental (or extrinsic) value is value exhausted by usefulness; the value of money, for example, is wholly instrumental. Intrinsic (or inherent) value is the value that something has independent of its usefulness; valuable "in itself," as it is sometimes put, p. 229, 436

Is/ought: it is one thing to describe a purely factual situation and another to make an evaluation of it; thus and so is the case, but is it good or ought it to be? The natural world may be a certain way, but ought we to behave similarly? It is fallacious immediately to infer that because something is, it therefore ought to be, p. 436

Kantianism: moral philosophy of Immanuel Kant; emphasis on acts of will in accordance with duty and respect for persons, p. 11, 436

Moral agent: a being that can deliberate about what it ought and ought not to do and then act for a moral reason. In Kant's moral philosophy, persons are moral agents by definition, p. 171, 430n28, 436

Moral community: the beings to which (whom?) we have direct obligations. The composition of the moral community is the central question of environmental ethics. Do we have direct obligations only to fellow human beings? p. 198, 322–323, 436

Moral point of view: consideration of moral reasons for action; rights, interests, duties, well-being, justice, etc., are moral reasons. Moral reasons (typically) trump nonmoral reasons, such as expediency, cost, aesthetics, or self-interest, when there is a conflict between moral and nonmoral reasons. Why the moral point of view should trump the nonmoral is a deeply conflicted question in the history of ethics, p. 7–8, 436

Moral relativism: the view that morality is relative to either an individual or society, thus no moral perspective has legitimacy over any other, p. 6–7, 436

Moral rights: legitimate claims grounded in moral theory. Talk of rights is yet another way to construe moral standing or direct obligations. Which things are capable of having moral rights is controversial, p. 146, 219, 221

Moral standing: another way of talking about that to which we have direct obligations. If something has moral standing, then its good, well-being, or interests ought to figure into the deliberations of a moral agent, p. 436

Natural law ethics: moral theory that there are objective fundamental moral principles found in human nature and binding on all. These fundamental principles are in principle knowable by rational beings who can conform their behavior to them. Natural law ethics is most closely associated with St. Thomas Aquinas who held that God is the source of natural law, p. 15–17, 20, 24, 436

Nonconsequentialism: general term referring to any moral theory that does not construe right and wrong with respect to consequences of actions. Kant's moral philosophy is nonconsequentialist because it focuses on intrinsic features of action, such as intention, not on the act's consequences, p. 208, 436

Person/thing: fundamental division in Kant's moral philosophy. Persons are autonomous beings, capable of acting for the sake of a principle and thus intrinsically valuable. Because, for Kant, persons are intrinsically valuable (by definition), they ought not to be treated as if they were merely instrumentally valuable. Things, by contrast, are not autonomous or self-legislating and are moved by causes, since they have no will; thus there is nothing about things to respect. For Kant, even conscious organisms, such as dogs, are things, along with all other natural objects, p. 12–15, 436–437

Respect for persons: Kant's way of acknowledging the intrinsic value of persons. See above definition of *person/thing*, p. 13, 437

Sentience: ability to feel pleasure or pain, p. 64, 164–166, 171, 172, 437

Teleology: goal or end oriented. Organisms are teleological in so far as they seek to maintain themselves, p. 44, 302, 437

Utilitarianism: consequentialist moral theory that defines right as "greatest good for the greatest number," 'Good' is often taken as 'Pleasure' p. 437

Vitalism: largely discredited view in philosophy of biology that life is not merely a complex biochemical process. The essence of life is held to be a mysterious soul-like nonphysical entity. In biology, vitalism is comparable to Descartes' dualism regarding humanity, p. 200, 437

Virtue ethics: moral theory that focuses on character rather than actions, p. 17–20, 24, 437

Index